TEACHER'S EDITION

MOSAIK 3

German Language and Culture

VISTA®
HIGHER LEARNING

Boston, Massachusetts

On the cover: Traditional frame houses, Freudenberg, Germany

Publisher: José A. Blanco

Professional Development Director: Norah Lulich Jones

Editorial Development: Brian Contreras, Sharla Zwirek

Project Management: Sally Giangrande

Rights Management: Ashley Dos Santos, Annie Pickert Fuller

Technology Production: Fabián Montoya, Paola Ríos Schaaf, Erica Solari

Design: Radoslav Mateev, Gabriel Noreña, Andrés Vanegas

Production: Manuela Arango, Oscar Díez, Adriana Jaramillo Ch.

Student Text ISBN: 978-1-68005-135-3

Teacher's Edition ISBN: 978-1-68005-155-1

Library of Congress Control Number: 2016947899

1 2 3 4 5 6 7 8 9   WC   21 20 19 18 17 16

AP and Advanced Placement Program are registered trademarks of the College Board, which was not involved in the production of, and does not endorse, this product.

Contents

	KONTEXT	FOTOROMAN	KULTUR	STRUKTUREN	WEITER GEHT'S
KAPITEL 1	**LEKTION 1A Hallo! Wie geht's?**				
	Kontext: Wie geht's? **Aussprache und Rechtschreibung:** The German alphabet	**Folge 1:** Willkommen in Berlin!	**Im Fokus:** Hallo, Deutschland! **Porträt:** Das Brandenburger Tor	**1A.1** Gender, articles, and nouns **1A.2** Plurals **1A.3** Subject pronouns, **sein**, and the nominative case **Wiederholung** **Zapping:** *Deutsche Bahn*	**Panorama:** Die deutschsprachige Welt **Lesen:** Adressbuch **Hören** **Schreiben** **Wortschatz**
	LEKTION 1B				
	Kontext: In der Schule **Aussprache und Rechtschreibung:** The vowels **a**, **e**, **i**, **o**, and **u**	**Folge 2:** Oh, George!	**Im Fokus:** Die Schulzeit **Porträt:** Der Schultag	**1B.1 Haben** and the accusative case **1B.2** Word order **1B.3** Numbers **Wiederholung**	
KAPITEL 2	**LEKTION 2A Schule und Studium**				
	Kontext: An der Universität **Aussprache und Rechtschreibung:** Consonant sounds	**Folge 3:** Checkpoint Charlie	**Im Fokus:** Uni-Zeit, Büffel-Zeit **Porträt:** Uni Basel	**2A.1** Regular verbs **2A.2** Interrogative words **2A.3** Talking about time and dates **Wiederholung** **Zapping:** *TU Berlin*	**Panorama:** Berlin **Lesen:** Karlswald-Universität **Hören** **Schreiben** **Wortschatz**
	LEKTION 2B				
	Kontext: Sport und Freizeit **Aussprache und Rechtschreibung:** Diphthongs: **au**, **ei/ai**, and **eu/äu**	**Folge 4:** Ein Picknick im Park	**Im Fokus:** Skifahren im Blut **Porträt:** Mesut Özil	**2B.1** Stem-changing verbs **2B.2** Present tense used as future **2B.3** Negation **Wiederholung**	
KAPITEL 3	**LEKTION 3A Familie und Freunde**				
	Kontext: Johanna Schmidts Familie **Aussprache und Rechtschreibung:** Final consonants	**Folge 5:** Ein Abend mit der Familie	**Im Fokus:** Eine deutsche Familie **Porträt:** Angela Merkel	**3A.1** Possessive adjectives **3A.2** Descriptive adjectives and adjective agreement **Wiederholung** **Zapping:** *Bauer Joghurt*	**Panorama:** Die Vereinigten Staaten und Kanada **Lesen:** Hunde und Katzen **Hören** **Schreiben** **Wortschatz**
	LEKTION 3B				
	Kontext: Wie sind sie? **Aussprache und Rechtschreibung:** Consonant clusters	**Folge 6:** Unsere Mitbewohner	**Im Fokus:** Auf unsere Freunde! **Porträt:** Tokio Hotel	**3B.1** Modals **3B.2** Prepositions with the accusative **3B.3** The imperative **Wiederholung**	
KAPITEL 4	**LEKTION 4A Essen**				
	Kontext: Lebensmittel **Aussprache und Rechtschreibung:** The German **s**, **z**, and **c**	**Folge 7:** Börek für alle	**Im Fokus:** Der Wiener Naschmarkt **Porträt:** Wolfgang Puck	**4A.1** Adverbs **4A.2** The modal **mögen** **4A.3** Separable and inseparable prefix verbs **Wiederholung** **Zapping:** *Yello Strom*	**Panorama:** Österreich **Lesen:** Die ersten Monate in Graz **Hören** **Schreiben** **Wortschatz**
	LEKTION 4B				
	Kontext: Im Restaurant **Aussprache und Rechtschreibung:** The German **s** in combination with other letters	**Folge 8:** Die Rechnung, bitte!	**Im Fokus:** Wiener Kaffeehäuser **Porträt:** Figlmüller	**4B.1** The dative **4B.2** Prepositions with the dative **Wiederholung**	

	KONTEXT	FOTOROMAN	KULTUR	STRUKTUREN	WEITER GEHT'S
ÜBERBLICK Reviews material from MOSAIK 1					
KAPITEL 1 — **LEKTION 1A** Feiern	**Kontext:** Feste feiern **Aussprache und Rechtschreibung:** The consonantal **r**	**Folge 1:** Frohes neues Jahr!	**Im Fokus:** Das Oktoberfest **Porträt:** Die Sternsinger	1A.1 The **Perfekt** (Part 1) 1A.2 Accusative pronouns 1A.3 Dative pronouns Wiederholung Zapping: *Penny*	**Panorama:** Bayern **Lesen:** Deutschland heute **Hören** **Schreiben** **Wortschatz**
LEKTION 1B	**Kontext:** Kleidung **Aussprache und Rechtschreibung:** The letter combination **ch** (Part 1)	**Folge 2:** Sehr attraktiv, George!	**Im Fokus:** Deutsche Modewelt **Porträt:** Rudolf Moshammer	1B.1 The **Perfekt** (Part 2) 1B.2 **Wissen** and **kennen** 1B.3 Two-way prepositions Wiederholung	
KAPITEL 2 — **LEKTION 2A** Trautes Heim	**Kontext:** Zu Hause **Aussprache und Rechtschreibung:** The letter combination **ch** (Part 2)	**Folge 3:** Besuch von Max	**Im Fokus:** Fribourg **Porträt:** César Ritz	2A.1 The **Präteritum** 2A.2 Da-, wo-, hin-, and her- compounds 2A.3 Coordinating conjunctions Wiederholung Zapping: *Hausarbeit*	**Panorama:** Die Schweiz und Liechtenstein **Lesen:** Schweizer Immobilien **Hören** **Schreiben** **Wortschatz**
LEKTION 2B	**Kontext:** Hausarbeit **Aussprache und Rechtschreibung:** The German **k** sound	**Folge 4:** Ich putze gern!	**Im Fokus:** Haushaltsgeräte **Porträt:** Johanna Spyri	2B.1 **Perfekt** versus **Präteritum** 2B.2 Separable and inseparable prefix verbs in the **Perfekt** Wiederholung	
KAPITEL 3 — **LEKTION 3A** Urlaub und Ferien	**Kontext:** Jahreszeiten **Aussprache und Rechtschreibung:** Long and short vowels	**Folge 5:** Berlin von oben	**Im Fokus:** Windenergie **Porträt:** Klima in Deutschland	3A.1 Separable and inseparable prefix verbs (**Präteritum**) 3A.2 Prepositions of location; Prepositions in set phrases Wiederholung Zapping: *Urlaub im grünen Binnenland*	**Panorama:** Schleswig-Holstein, Hamburg und Bremen **Lesen:** Die Nordseeküste Schleswig-Holsteins in 6 Tagen **Hören** **Schreiben** **Wortschatz**
LEKTION 3B	**Kontext:** Reisen **Aussprache und Rechtschreibung:** Pure vowels versus diphthongs	**Folge 6:** Ein Sommer in der Türkei?	**Im Fokus:** Flughafen Frankfurt **Porträt:** Der ICE	3B.1 Infinitive expressions and clauses 3B.2 Time expressions 3B.3 Indefinite pronouns Wiederholung	
KAPITEL 4 — **LEKTION 4A** Verkehrsmittel und Technologie	**Kontext:** Auto und Rad fahren **Aussprache und Rechtschreibung:** Long and short vowels with an **Umlaut**	**Folge 7:** Ein Ende mit Schrecken	**Im Fokus:** Die deutsche Autobahn **Porträt:** Clärenore Stinnes	4A.1 Das Plusquamperfekt 4A.2 Comparatives and superlatives Wiederholung Zapping: *Mercedes Benz*	**Panorama:** Hessen und Thüringen **Lesen:** Vierfarbdrucker Installationsanleitung **Hören** **Schreiben** **Wortschatz**
LEKTION 4B	**Kontext:** Technik und Medien **Aussprache und Rechtschreibung:** The German **l**	**Folge 8:** Ein Spaziergang durch Spandau	**Im Fokus:** Max-Planck-Gesellschaft **Porträt:** Darmstadt	4B.1 The genitive case 4B.2 Demonstratives Wiederholung	

KONTEXT	FOTOROMAN	KULTUR	STRUKTUREN	WEITER GEHT'S
ÜBERBLICK Reviews material from MOSAIK 2				

KAPITEL 1

LEKTION 1A Gesundheit

KONTEXT	FOTOROMAN	KULTUR	STRUKTUREN	WEITER GEHT'S
Kontext: Die Alltagsroutine **Aussprache und Rechtschreibung:** Vocalic r	**Folge 1:** Guten Morgen, Herr Professor!	**Im Fokus:** Die Kur **Porträt:** Nivea	**1A.1** Reflexive verbs with accusative reflexive pronouns **1A.2** Reflexive verbs with dative reflexive pronouns **1A.3** Reciprocal verbs and reflexives used with prepositions **Wiederholung** **Zapping:** *Central Krankenversicherung*	**Panorama:** Mecklenburg-Vorpommern und Brandenburg **Lesen:** Andis Blog / Fit in 10 Minuten! **Hören** **Schreiben** **Wortschatz**

LEKTION 1B

KONTEXT	FOTOROMAN	KULTUR	STRUKTUREN	WEITER GEHT'S
Kontext: Beim Arzt **Aussprache und Rechtschreibung:** Syllabic stress	**Folge 2:** Im Krankenhaus	**Im Fokus:** Apotheken **Porträt:** Röntgen	**1B.1 Der Konjunktiv II** **1B.2 Würden** with the infinitive **Wiederholung**	

KAPITEL 2

LEKTION 2A Stadtleben

KONTEXT	FOTOROMAN	KULTUR	STRUKTUREN	WEITER GEHT'S
Kontext: Besorgungen **Aussprache und Rechtschreibung:** The glottal stop	**Folge 3:** Gute Neuigkeiten	**Im Fokus:** Fußgängerzonen **Porträt:** Die Deutsche Post	**2A.1** Subordinating conjunctions **2A.2** Adjectives used as nouns **2A.3 Das Futur I** **Kurzfilm:** *Fanny*	**Panorama:** Niedersachsen und Nordrhein-Westfalen **Lesen:** Hermann Hesse, *Allein*; Paul Celan, *Todesfuge* **Hören** **Schreiben** **Wortschatz**

LEKTION 2B

KONTEXT	FOTOROMAN	KULTUR	STRUKTUREN	WEITER GEHT'S
Kontext: In der Stadt **Aussprache und Rechtschreibung:** Loan words (Part 1)	**Folge 4:** Sabites Nacht	**Im Fokus:** Kabarett **Porträt:** Pina Bausch	**2B.1** Prepositions of direction **2B.2** Talking about nationality **Wiederholung**	

KAPITEL 3

LEKTION 3A Beruf und Karriere

KONTEXT	FOTOROMAN	KULTUR	STRUKTUREN	WEITER GEHT'S
Kontext: Im Büro **Aussprache und Rechtschreibung:** Loan words (Part 2)	**Folge 5:** Sag niemals nie	**Im Fokus:** Familienunternehmen **Porträt:** Robert Bosch	**3A.1** Relative pronouns **3A.2** The past tenses (review) **Wiederholung** **Kurzfilm:** *Die Berliner Mauer*	**Panorama:** Baden-Württemberg, das Saarland und Rheinland-Pfalz **Lesen:** Peter Bichsel, *Der Erfinder* **Hören** **Schreiben** **Wortschatz**

LEKTION 3B

KONTEXT	FOTOROMAN	KULTUR	STRUKTUREN	WEITER GEHT'S
Kontext: Berufe **Aussprache und Rechtschreibung:** Recognizing near-cognates	**Folge 6:** Schlechte Nachrichten	**Im Fokus:** Sozialversicherungen **Porträt:** Der Marshallplan	**3B.1 Das Futur II** **3B.2** Adjective endings (review) **Wiederholung**	

KAPITEL 4

LEKTION 4A Natur

KONTEXT	FOTOROMAN	KULTUR	STRUKTUREN	WEITER GEHT'S
Kontext: In der Natur **Aussprache und Rechtschreibung:** Intonation	**Folge 7:** In der Kunstgalerie	**Im Fokus:** Landschaften Deutschlands **Porträt:** Alexander von Humboldt	**4A.1 Der Konjunktiv der Vergangenheit** **4A.2 Das Partizip Präsens** **Wiederholung** **Kurzfilm:** *Bienenstich ist aus*	**Panorama:** Sachsen-Anhalt und Sachsen **Lesen:** Rose Ausländer, *Meine Nachtigall*; Rainer Maria Rilke, *Der Panther* **Hören** **Schreiben** **Wortschatz**

LEKTION 4B

KONTEXT	FOTOROMAN	KULTUR	STRUKTUREN	WEITER GEHT'S
Kontext: Die Umwelt **Aussprache und Rechtschreibung:** Tongue twisters	**Folge 8:** Auf Wiedersehen, Berlin!	**Im Fokus:** Grüne Berufe in Sachsen **Porträt:** Michael Braungart	**4B.1 Der Konjunktiv I** and indirect speech **4B.2** The passive voice **Wiederholung**	

There's more to **Mosaik** than meets the page

The **Mosaik** Supersite provides a learning environment designed especially for world language instruction. Password-protected and program-specific, this website provides seamless textbook-technology integration that helps build students' love for language learning.

For students:

- engaging media
- motivating user experience
- superior performance
- helpful resources
- plenty of practice

For educators:

- proven instructional design
- powerful course management
- time-saving tools
- enhanced support

Integrated content means a more powerful student experience

- Streaming videos—episodic dramatic series, authentic TV clips, and authentic short films
- All program audio in downloadable MP3 format
- Textbook activities and additional online-only practice—most with automatic feedback
- Video Chat and Partner Chat activities for conversational skills practice
- My Vocabulary for personalized language study
- Audio-sync readings for all **Lesen** selections
- Cultural readings in all levels and literary selections in **Mosaik 3**
- Online Student Activities Manual fully integrated with the Supersite gradebook

Specialized resources ensure a successful implementation

- Online assessments and Testing Program files in an editable format
- Audioscripts and videoscripts with English translations
- Grammar presentation slides
- Editable block and standard lesson plans
- IPAs with grading rubrics
- Digital Image Bank
- Answer keys
- "I Can" worksheets

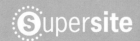

Educator tools facilitate instruction and save time

Virtual Chat

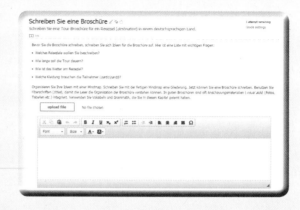

In-line editing

Easy course management

A powerful setup wizard lets you customize your class settings, copy previous courses to save time, and create your all-in-one gradebook. Grades for teacher-created assignments (e.g., pop quizzes, class participation) can be incorporated for a true, up-to-date cumulative grade.

Customized content

Tailor the Supersite to fit your needs. Create your own open-ended or video Partner Chat activities, add video or outside resources, and modify existing content with your own personalized notes.

Grading tools

Grade efficiently via spot-checking, student-by-student, and question-by-question options. Use in-line editing tools to give targeted feedback and voice comments—it's the perfect tool for busy language educators!

Assessment solutions

Administer online quizzes and tests. Use any pre-built assessment "as is" or customize them to meet your specific needs, including: adding or removing questions from a section, reordering sections or questions, and changing point values for questions.

Plus!

- A communication center for announcements, notifications, and student help requests
- Voiceboards for oral assignments, group discussions, homework, and more
- Reporting tools for summarizing student data

- Single sign-on for easy integration with your school's Learning Management System*
- Live Chat for video chat, audio chat, and instant messaging with students

* available for select LMSs

Content and tools delivered your way

Learning doesn't just happen in the classroom. With **Mosaik**, we provide you with a number of digital format options.

vText (Online)

- Browser-based electronic text for online viewing
- Links to all mouse-icon textbook activities*, audio, and video
- Access to all Supersite resources
- Highlighting and note taking
- Easy navigation with searchable table of contents
- iPad®-friendly*
- Single- and double-page view and zooming
- Automatically adds auto-graded activities to the gradebook

Available on any PC or device that has Internet connectivity.

eBook (Downloadable)

- Downloadable electronic text for offline viewing
- Embedded audio for anytime listening
- Easy navigation with searchable table of contents
- Highlighting and note taking
- Single-page view and zooming

When student is connected online:

- Links to all mouse-icon textbook activities*, audio, and video
- Access to all Supersite resources
- Automatically adds auto-graded activities in teacher gradebook

Available for a maximum of 2 computers and 2 mobile devices.

 Visit **vistahigherlearning.com/interactive-texts** to learn more.

*Students must use a computer for audio-recording.

For the **Teacher**: Plan

COMPONENT TITLE	WHAT IS IT?	📖	Ⓢ	💿
Teacher's Edition	Teacher support for core instruction	•	•	
Audioscripts	Scripts for all audio selections: • Textbook audioscripts • Testing audioscripts • Lab audioscripts • Virtual Chat audioscripts		•	•
Essential Questions	Chapter-level Essential Questions to guide instruction		•	•
Index of AP® Themes & Contexts	Listing of where the German AP® Themes and Contexts are addressed in each chapter	•	•	•
Lesson Plans	Editable block and standard schedules for every lesson		•	•
Pacing Guides	Guidelines for how to cover the instructional material for a variety of scenarios (standard and block schedules)	•	•	•
Scope & Sequence	Suggested sequence of study broken out by chapters and sections	•	•	•
Videoscripts and Translations	Scripts and translations for all videos: • *Fotoroman* • *Zapping* • *Kurzfilm*		•	•

For the **Teacher**: Teach

COMPONENT TITLE	WHAT IS IT?	📖	Ⓢ	💿
Digital Image Bank	Images and maps from the text to use for presentation in class, plus a bank of illustrations to use with teacher-generated content		•	•
Grammar Presentation Slides	Textbook grammar presentation in an editable PowerPoint format		•	•
Info Gap Activities with Answer Key	Info Gap activity worksheets and answer key		•	•
Program Audio	• Textbook Audio • Lab Program Audio		•	•
Student Activities Manual Answer Key	Answers to all activities in the Student Activities Manual (Workbook/Lab Manual/Video Manual)		•	•
Textbook Activity Worksheets	Supplemental spoken and written activities in an editable format		•	•
Video Collection	Program video, including: • *Fotoroman* • *Zapping* • *Kurzfilm*		• • •	• • •

For the **Teacher**: Assess

COMPONENT TITLE	WHAT IS IT?	📖	Ⓢ	💿
"I Can" Worksheets	Lesson objectives broken down by chapter section and written in a student-friendly "I Can" statement format		•	•
Integrated Performance Assessments	IPA tasks with grading rubrics		•	•
Testing Program with Answer Key	Lesson quizzes, chapter tests, and cumulative exam		•	•
Testing Program Audio	Audio to accompany all assessments		•	•

For the **Student**

COMPONENT TITLE	WHAT IS IT?	▮	Ⓢ	💿
Student Edition	Core instruction for students	•	•	
Audio-synced Readings	Audio to accompany all *Lesen* sections		•	
Dictionary	Easy digital access to a dictionary		•	
eBook	Downloadable Student Edition		•	
End-of-lesson Vocabulary Lists	Core vocabulary for each lesson, with linked audio online		•	
Flashcards	Provide an easy way to study vocabulary (available as part of My Vocabulary)		•	
Fotoroman Video	Engaging storyline video		•	•
Kurzfilm Video	Authentic short films from Germany		•	•
Lab Manual Activities Audio	Audio to accompany the Lab Manual portion of the Student Activities Manual		•	•
My Vocabulary	A variety of tools to practice vocabulary		•	
Partner Chats	Work with a partner online to record a conversation via video or audio and submit for grading		•	
Student Activities Manual	Combined Workbook/Lab Manual/Video Manual aligned to each lesson	•	•	
Textbook Audio	Audio to accompany all textbook listening activities		•	
Textbook Mouse Activities	Textbook activities that can also be completed digitally; many provide immediate feedback		•	
Virtual Chats	Record and submit a simulated video or audio conversation with a native speaker for online grading		•	
Vocabulary Hot Spots	Vocabulary presentations with embedded audio		•	
Voiceboards	Collaborative spaces for oral assignments, group discussions, homework, and projects		•	
vText	Virtual interactive textbook for browser-based exploration • Links to all mouse-icon activities, audio, and video • Note-taking capabilities		•	
WebSAM	Online version of the Student Activities Manual, embedded in the online gradebook, with many auto-graded options		•	
Web-only Activities	Additional online practice for students		•	
Zapping Video	Authentic TV clips from across the German-speaking world		•	

▮ Print   Ⓢ Supersite   💿 Teacher's DVD Set

Beginning with the
student in mind

Natur

KAPITEL
4

LEKTION 4A	LEKTION 4B	WEITER GEHT'S
Kontext Seite 152–155 • In der Natur • Intonation	**Kontext** Seite 170–173 • Die Umwelt • Tongue Twisters	Seite 186–192 **Panorama:** Sachsen-Anhalt und Sachsen **Lesen:** *Meine Nachtigall*, von Rose Ausländer; *Der Panther*, von Rainer Maria Rilke
Fotoroman Seite 156–157 • In der Kunstgalerie	**Fotoroman** Seite 174–175 • Auf Wiedersehen, Berlin!	**Hören:** Listen to a speech against nuclear power plants.
Kultur Seite 158–159 • Landschaften Deutschlands	**Kultur** Seite 176–177 • Grüne Berufe in Sachsen	**Schreiben:** Write about an environmental problem.
Strukturen Seite 160–169 • 4A.1 Der Konjunktiv der Vergangenheit • 4A.2 Das Partizip Präsens • Wiederholung • Kurzfilm	**Strukturen** Seite 178–185 • 4B.1 Der Konjunktiv I and indirect speech • 4B.2 The passive voice • Wiederholung	**Kapitel 4 Wortschatz**

Chapter opener photos highlight scenes from the **Fotoroman** that illustrate the chapter theme. They are snapshots of the characters that students will come to know throughout the program.

Content lists break down each chapter into its two lessons and one **Weiter Geht's** section, giving an at-a-glance summary of the vocabulary, grammar, cultural topics, and language skills covered.

Supersite

Supersite resources are available for every section of each chapter at **vhlcentral.com**. Icons show you which textbook activities are also available online, and where additional practice activities are available. The description next to the (S) icon indicates what additional resources are available for each section: videos, audio recordings, readings, presentations, and more!

Setting the stage
for communication

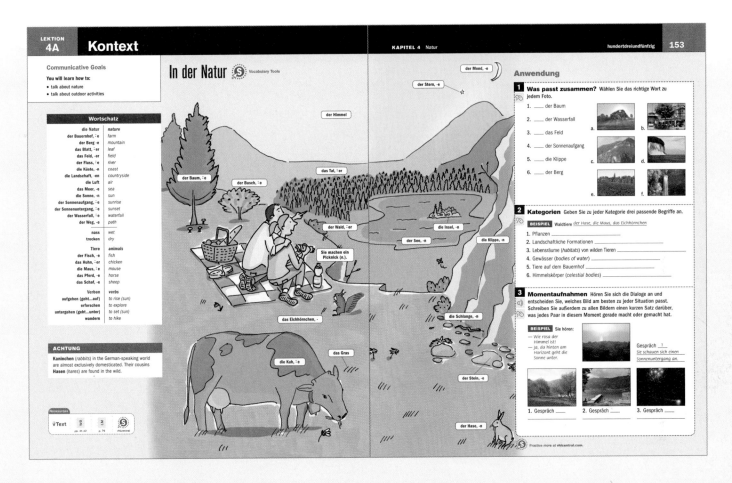

Communicative goals highlight the real-life tasks students will be able to carry out in German by the end of each lesson.

Illustrations introduce high-frequency vocabulary through expansive, full-color images.

Wortschatz sidebars call out important theme-related vocabulary in easy-to-reference German-English lists.

Ressourcen boxes indicate what print and technology ancillaries reinforce and expand on every section of every lesson.

Achtung boxes provide additional information about how and when to use certain vocabulary words or grammar structures.

Kontext always contains an audio activity that accompanies either the **Anwendung** or the **Kommunikation** practice activities. **Anwendung** follows a pedagogical sequence that starts with simpler, shorter, discrete recognition activities and builds toward longer, more complex production activities.

Supersite

- Audio recordings of all vocabulary items
- Audio for **Kontext** listening activity
- Image-based vocabulary activity with audio
- Textbook activities
- Additional online-only practice activities

Engaging students in
active communication

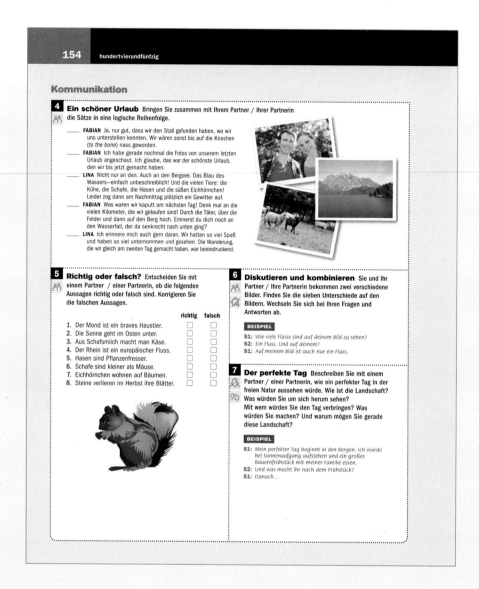

Kommunikation activities make use of discourse-level prompts, encouraging the creative use of vocabulary in interactions with a partner, a small group, or the entire class.

Pair and group icons indicate communicative activities—such as role play, games, personal questions, interviews, and surveys—for interpersonal and presentational practice.

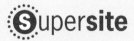

•   Chat activities for conversational skill-building and oral practice

Authenticity
in pronunciation and spelling

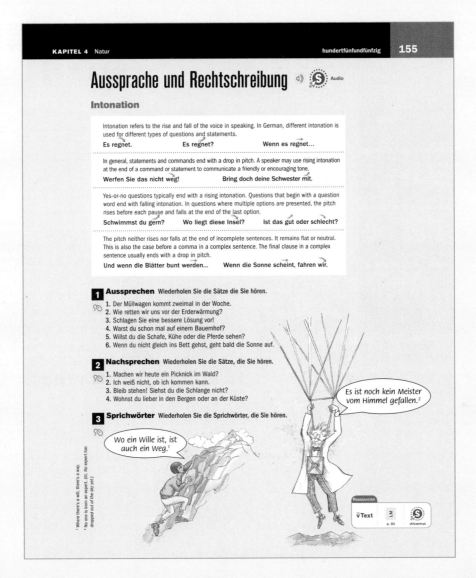

Explanations of German pronunciation and spelling are presented clearly, with abundant model words and phrases. The red highlighting feature focuses students' attention on the target structure.

Practice pronunciation and spelling at the word- and sentence-levels. The final activity features illustrated sayings and proverbs that present the target structures in an entertaining cultural context.

The audio icon at the top of the page indicates that the explanation and activities are recorded for convenient use in or outside of class.

ⓢupersite

- Audio recording of the **Aussprache und Rechtschreibung** presentation
- Record-and-compare activities

Fotoroman
bridges language and culture

Fotoroman is a versatile episodic video that can be assigned as homework, presented in class, or used as review.

Conversations reinforce vocabulary from **Kontext**. They also preview structures from the upcoming **Strukturen** section in context.

Personen features the cast of recurring **Fotoroman** characters, including four students living in Berlin: George, Sabite, Meline, and Hans.

Nützliche Ausdrücke calls out the most important words and expressions from the **Fotoroman** episode that have not been formally presented. This vocabulary is not tested. The blue numbers refer to the grammar structures presented in the lesson.

Übungen activities include comprehension questions, a communicative task, and a research-based task.

Supersite

- Streaming video for all episodes of the **Fotoroman**
- End-of-video **Zusammenfassung** section where key vocabulary and grammar from the episode are called out
- Textbook activities

Culture
presented in context

Im Fokus presents an in-depth reading about the lesson's cultural theme. Full-color photos bring to life important aspects of the topic, while charts support the main text with statistics and additional information.

Tipp boxes provide helpful tips for reading and understanding German.

Porträt spotlights notable people, places, events, and products from the German-speaking world. This article is thematically linked to the lesson.

Deutsch im Alltag presents additional vocabulary related to the lesson theme, showcasing words and phrases used in everyday spoken German. This vocabulary is not tested.

Die deutschsprachige Welt focuses on the people, places, dialects, and traditions in regions where German is spoken. This short article is thematically linked to the lesson.

Im Internet boxes, with provocative questions and photos, feature additional cultural explorations online.

Supersite

- **Kultur** reading
- **Im Internet** research activity expands on the chapter theme
- Textbook activities
- Chat activities for conversational skill-building and oral practice

Grammar
as a tool not a topic

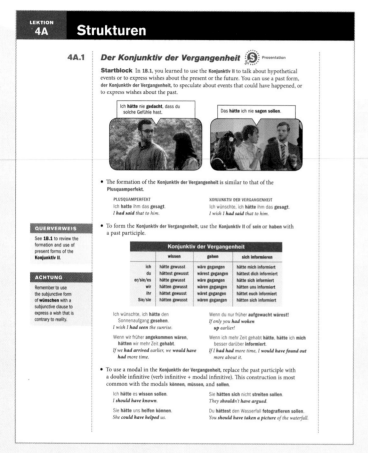

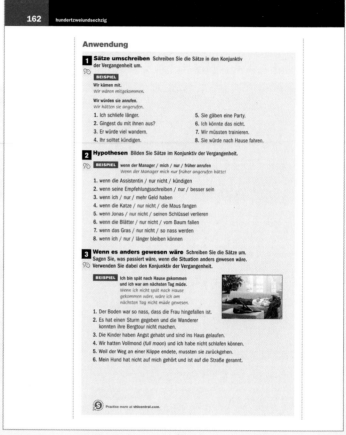

Startblock eases into each grammar explanation, with definitions of grammatical terms and reminders about grammar concepts which are already familiar.

Querverweis boxes call out information covered in earlier lessons or provide cross-references to related topics that will be covered in future lessons.

Achtung boxes clarify potential sources of confusion and provide supplementary information.

Jetzt sind Sie dran! is the first opportunity to practice the new grammar point.

Anwendung offers a wide range of guided activities that combine lesson vocabulary and previously learned material with the new grammar point.

Kommunikation activities provide opportunities for self-expression using the lesson grammar and vocabulary. These activities feature interaction with a partner, in small groups, or with the whole class.

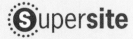upersite

- Grammar presentations
- Textbook activities

- Additional online-only practice activities
- Chat activities for conversational skill-building and oral practice

Carefully scaffolded
lesson review

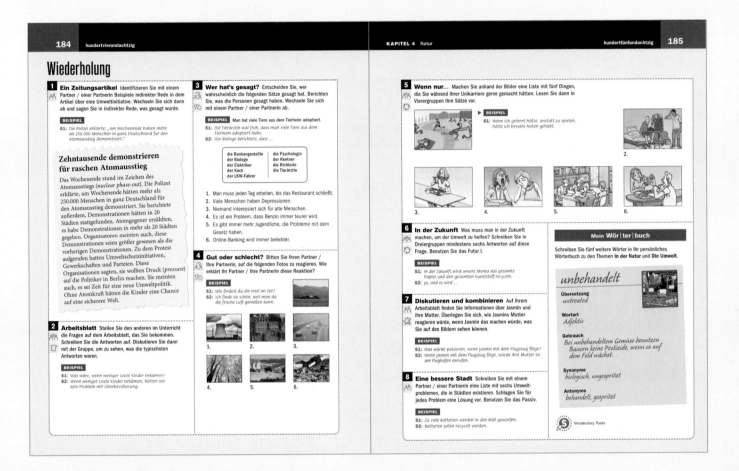

Wiederholung activities integrate the lesson's grammar points and vocabulary with previously learned vocabulary and structures, providing consistent, built-in review.

Pair and group icons indicate communicative activities—such as role play, games, personal questions, interviews, and surveys for interpersonal and presentational practice.

Information gap activities, identified by interlocking puzzle pieces, engage partners in problem-solving situations.

Recycling icons call out activities that practice the lesson's grammar and vocabulary along with previously learned material.

Mein Wörterbuch in the B lesson of each chapter offers the opportunity to increase vocabulary comprehension and the contextualization of new words.

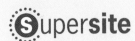upersite

- Chat activities for conversational skill-building and oral practice

Authentic cultural media
for interpretive communication

Zapping in Chapter 1 presents a TV commercial from the German-speaking world. Post-viewing activities check comprehension.

Kurzfilm in Chapters 2, 3, and 4 features short films from contemporary German-speaking filmmakers.

Summary provides context for each film.

Vorbereitung pre-viewing activities set the stage for the short films and provide key information to facilitate comprehension.

Analyse post-viewing activities encourage exploration of the broader themes presented in each film.

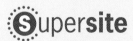upersite

- Streaming video of the TV clip or short film with teacher-controlled subtitle options
- Textbook activities

Perspective
through geography

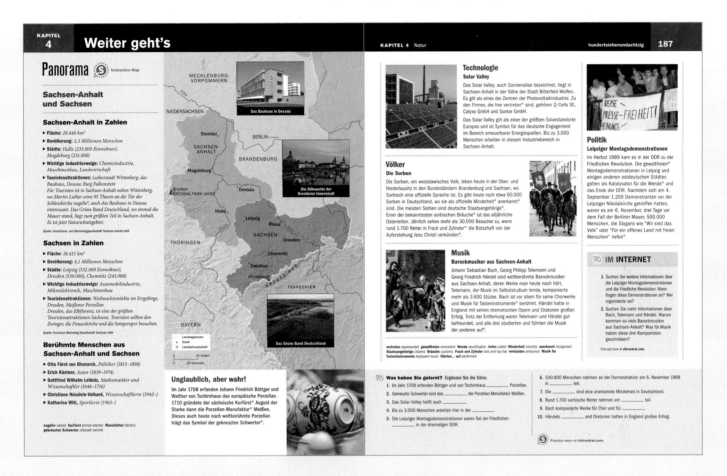

Panorama offers interesting facts about the featured city, region, or country.

Maps point out major geographical features and situate the featured region in the context of its immediate surroundings.

Readings explore different aspects of the featured region's culture, such as history, landmarks, fine art, literature, and insight into everyday life.

Unglaublich, aber wahr! highlights an intriguing fact about the featured region.

Comprehension questions check understanding of key ideas.

Supersite

- Map with statistics and cultural notes
- **Im Internet** research activity
- Textbook activities

Reading skills
developed in context

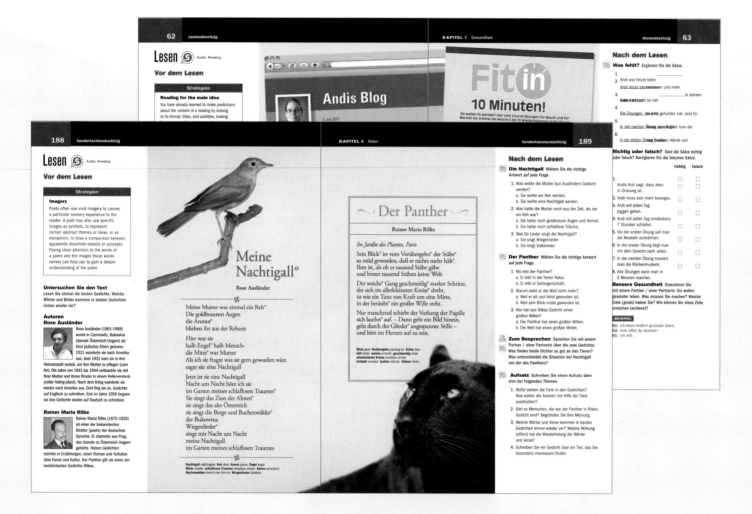

Vor dem Lesen presents useful strategies and activities that help develop stronger reading abilities.

Readings are tied to the lesson theme and recycle vocabulary and grammar previously learned. The selection in Chapter 1 features a cultural reading, while those in Chapters 2, 3, and 4 are authentic literary texts.

Nach dem Lesen consists of post-reading activities that check comprehension.

Supersite

- Audio-sync reading that highlights text as it is being read
- Textbook activities

- Chat activities for conversational skill-building and oral practice

Listening and writing skills
developed in context

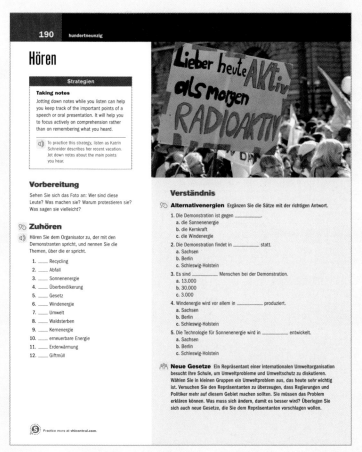

Hören

Strategien

Taking notes

Jotting down notes while you listen can help you keep track of the important points of a speech or oral presentation. It will help you to focus actively on comprehension rather than on remembering what you heard.

To practice this strategy, listen as Katrin Schneider describes her recent vacation. Jot down notes about the main points you hear.

Vorbereitung

Sehen Sie sich das Foto an: Wer sind diese Leute? Was machen sie? Warum protestieren sie? Was sagen sie vielleicht?

Zuhören

Hören Sie dem Organisator zu, der mit den Demonstranten spricht, und nennen Sie die Themen, über die er spricht.

1. _____ Recycling
2. _____ Abfall
3. _____ Sonnenenergie
4. _____ Überbevölkerung
5. _____ Gesetz
6. _____ Windenergie
7. _____ Umwelt
8. _____ Waldsterben
9. _____ Kernenergie
10. _____ erneuerbare Energie
11. _____ Erderwärmung
12. _____ Giftmüll

Practice more at vhlcentral.com.

Verständnis

Alternativenergien Ergänzen Sie die Sätze mit der richtigen Antwort.

1. Die Demonstration ist gegen _____.
   a. die Sonnenenergie
   b. die Kernkraft
   c. die Windenergie

2. Die Demonstration findet in _____ statt.
   a. Sachsen
   b. Berlin
   c. Schleswig-Holstein

3. Es sind _____ Menschen bei der Demonstration.
   a. 13.000
   b. 30.000
   c. 3.000

4. Windenergie wird vor allem in _____ produziert.
   a. Sachsen
   b. Berlin
   c. Schleswig-Holstein

5. Die Technologie für Sonnenenergie wird in _____ entwickelt.
   a. Sachsen
   b. Berlin
   c. Schleswig-Holstein

Neue Gesetze Ein Repräsentant einer internationalen Umweltorganisation besucht Ihre Schule, um Umweltprobleme und Umweltschutz zu diskutieren. Wählen Sie in kleinen Gruppen ein Umweltproblem aus, das heute sehr wichtig ist. Versuchen Sie den Repräsentanten zu überzeugen, dass Regierungen und Politiker mehr auf diesem Gebiet machen sollten. Sie müssen das Problem erklären können. Was muss sich ändern, damit es besser wird? Überlegen Sie sich auch neue Gesetze, die Sie dem Repräsentanten vorschlagen wollen.

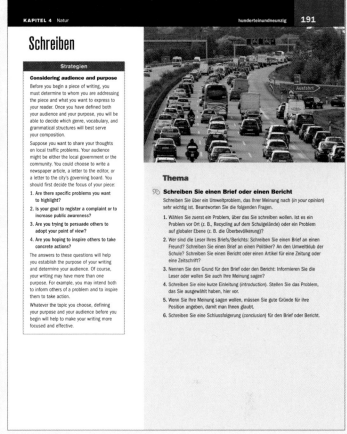

Schreiben

Strategien

Considering audience and purpose

Before you begin a piece of writing, you must determine to whom you are addressing the piece and what you want to express to your reader. Once you have defined both your audience and your purpose, you will be able to decide which genre, vocabulary, and grammatical structures will best serve your composition.

Suppose you want to share your thoughts on local traffic problems. Your audience might be either the local government or the community. You could choose to write a newspaper article, a letter to the editor, or a letter to the city's governing board. You should first decide the focus of your piece:

1. Are there specific problems you want to highlight?

2. Is your goal to register a complaint or to increase public awareness?

3. Are you trying to persuade others to adopt your point of view?

4. Are you hoping to inspire others to take concrete actions?

The answers to these questions will help you establish the purpose of your writing and determine your audience. Of course, your writing may have more than one purpose. For example, you may intend both to inform others of a problem and to inspire them to take action.

Whatever the topic you choose, defining your purpose and your audience before you begin will help to make your writing more focused and effective.

Thema

Schreiben Sie einen Brief oder einen Bericht

Schreiben Sie über ein Umweltproblem, das Ihrer Meinung nach (*in your opinion*) sehr wichtig ist. Beantworten Sie die folgenden Fragen.

1. Wählen Sie zuerst ein Problem, über das Sie schreiben wollen. Ist es ein Problem vor Ort (z. B., Recycling auf dem Schulgelände) oder ein Problem auf globaler Ebene (z. B. die Überbevölkerung)?

2. Wer sind die Leser Ihres Briefs/Berichts: Schreiben Sie einen Brief an einen Freund? Schreiben Sie einen Brief an einen Politiker? An den Umweltklub der Schule? Schreiben Sie einen Bericht oder einen Artikel für eine Zeitung oder eine Zeitschrift?

3. Nennen Sie den Grund für den Brief oder den Bericht: Informieren Sie die Leser oder wollen Sie auch Ihre Meinung sagen?

4. Schreiben Sie eine kurze Einleitung (*introduction*). Stellen Sie das Problem, das Sie ausgewählt haben, hier vor.

5. Wenn Sie Ihre Meinung sagen wollen, müssen Sie gute Gründe für Ihre Position angeben, damit man Ihnen glaubt.

6. Schreiben Sie eine Schlussfolgerung (*conclusion*) für den Brief oder den Bericht.

Hören uses a recorded conversation or narration to develop listening skills in German, while **Strategien** and **Vorbereitung** are preparation for an audio listening activity.

Zuhören serves as a guide to the recorded segment, and **Verständnis** checks comprehension.

In the **Schreiben** section, **Strategien** provides useful preparation for the writing task presented in **Thema.**

Thema presents a writing topic and includes suggestions for approaching it. It also provides words and phrases that may be useful in writing about the topic.

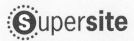upersite

- Audio for **Hören** activities
- Textbook activities
- Additional online-only practice activity
- Composition writing activity for **Schreiben**
- Chat activities for conversational skill-building and oral practice

Vocabulary

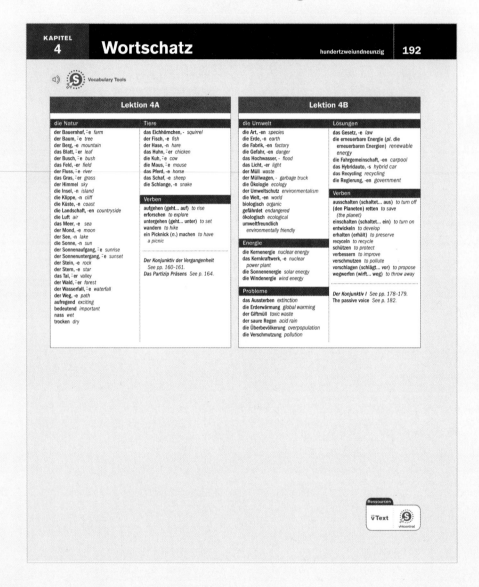

KAPITEL 4 | **Wortschatz** | hundertzweiundneunzig | **192**

🔊 ⑤ Vocabulary Tools

Lektion 4A

die Natur
der Bauernhof, ⁻e *farm*
der Baum, ⁻e *tree*
der Berg, -e *mountain*
das Blatt, ⁻er *leaf*
der Busch, ⁻e *bush*
das Feld, -er *field*
der Fluss, ⁻e *river*
das Gras, ⁻er *grass*
der Himmel *sky*
die Insel, -n *island*
die Klippe, -n *cliff*
die Küste, -n *coast*
die Landschaft, -en *countryside*
die Luft *air*
das Meer, -e *sea*
der Mond, -e *moon*
der See, -n *lake*
die Sonne, -n *sun*
der Sonnenaufgang, ⁻e *sunrise*
der Sonnenuntergang, ⁻e *sunset*
der Stein, -e *rock*
der Stern, -e *star*
das Tal, ⁻er *valley*
der Wald, ⁻er *forest*
der Wasserfall, ⁻e *waterfall*
der Weg, -e *path*
aufregend *exciting*
bedeutend *important*
nass *wet*
trocken *dry*

Tiere
das Eichhörnchen, - *squirrel*
der Fisch, -e *fish*
der Hase, -n *hare*
das Huhn, ⁻er *chicken*
die Kuh, ⁻e *cow*
die Maus, ⁻e *mouse*
das Pferd, -e *horse*
das Schaf, -e *sheep*
die Schlange, -n *snake*

Verben
aufgehen (geht... auf) *to rise*
erforschen *to explore*
untergehen (geht... unter) *to set*
wandern *to hike*
ein Picknick (n.) machen *to have a picnic*

Der Konjunktiv der Vergangenheit
See pp. 160–161.
Das Partizip Präsens See p. 164.

Lektion 4B

die Umwelt
die Art, -en *species*
die Erde, -n *earth*
die Fabrik, -en *factory*
die Gefahr, -en *danger*
das Hochwasser, - *flood*
das Licht, -er *light*
der Müll *waste*
der Müllwagen, - *garbage truck*
die Ökologie *ecology*
der Umweltschutz *environmentalism*
die Welt, -en *world*
biologisch *organic*
gefährdet *endangered*
ökologisch *ecological*
umweltfreundlich
  environmentally friendly

Energie
die Kernenergie *nuclear energy*
das Kernkraftwerk, -e *nuclear power plant*
die Sonnenenergie *solar energy*
die Windenergie *wind energy*

Probleme
das Aussterben *extinction*
die Erderwärmung *global warming*
der Giftmüll *toxic waste*
der saure Regen *acid rain*
die Überbevölkerung *overpopulation*
die Verschmutzung *pollution*

Lösungen
das Gesetz, -e *law*
die erneuerbare Energie (*pl. die erneuerbaren Energien*) *renewable energy*
die Fahrgemeinschaft, -en *carpool*
das Hybridauto, -s *hybrid car*
das Recycling *recycling*
die Regierung, -en *government*

Verben
ausschalten (schaltet... aus) *to turn off*
(den Planeten) retten *to save (the planet)*
einschalten (schaltet... ein) *to turn on*
entwickeln *to develop*
erhalten (erhält) *to preserve*
recyceln *to recycle*
schützen *to protect*
verbessern *to improve*
verschmutzen *to pollute*
vorschlagen (schlägt... vor) *to propose*
wegwerfen (wirft... weg) *to throw away*

Der Konjunktiv I See pp. 178–179.
The passive voice See p. 182.

Ressourcen
v̄Text ⑤
vhlcentral

Wortschatz presents the chapter's active vocabulary in logical groupings, including notation of plural forms. Words are separated by corresponding A and B lessons.

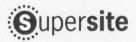

- Audio recordings of all vocabulary items
- My Vocabulary

World-Readiness Standards
for Learning Languages

Mosaik blends the underlying principles of ACTFL's World-Readiness Standards with features and strategies tailored specifically to build students' language and cultural competencies.

THE FIVE C'S OF FOREIGN LANGUAGE LEARNING	
Communication	**Students:** 1. Interact and negotiate meaning in spoken, signed, or written conversations to share information, reactions, feelings, and opinions. (Interpersonal mode) 2. Understand, interpret, and analyze what is heard, read, or viewed on a variety of topics. (Interpretive mode) 3. Present information, concepts, and ideas to inform, explain, persuade, and narrate on a variety of topics using appropriate media and adapting to various audiences of listeners, readers, or viewers. (Presentational mode)
Cultures	**Students use German to investigate, explain, and reflect on:** 1. The relationship of the practices and perspectives of the culture studied. 2. The relationship of the products and perspectives of the culture studied.
Connections	**Students:** 1. Build, reinforce, and expand their knowledge of other disciplines while using German to develop critical thinking and to solve problems creatively. 2. Access and evaluate information and diverse perspectives that are available through German and its cultures.
Comparisons	**Students use German to investigate, explain, and reflect on:** 1. The nature of language through comparisons of the German language and their own. 2. The concept of culture through comparisons of the cultures studied and their own.
Communities	**Students:** 1. Use German both within and beyond the school to interact and collaborate in their community and the globalized world. 2. Set goals and reflect on their progress in using languages for enjoyment, enrichment, and advancement.

Adapted from ACTFL's *Standards for Foreign Language Learning in the 21st Century*

Six-step instructional design

Take advantage of the unique, powerful six-step instructional design in **Mosaik**. With a focus on personalization, authenticity, cultural immersion, and the seamless integration of text and technology, language learning comes to life in ways that are meaningful to each and every student.

 STEP 1 →

Context

Begin each lesson by asking students to provide from their own experience words, concepts, categories, and opinions related to the theme. Spend quality time evoking words, images, ideas, phrases, and sentences; group and classify concepts. You are giving students the "hook" for their learning, focusing them on their most interesting topic—themselves—and encouraging them to invest personally in their learning.

 STEP 2 →

Vocabulary

Now turn to the vocabulary section, inviting students to experience it as a new linguistic code to express what they already know and experience in the context of the lesson theme. Vocabulary concepts are presented in context, carefully organized, and frequently reviewed to reinforce student understanding. Involve students in brainstorming, classifying and grouping words and thoughts, and personalizing phrases and sentences. In this way, you will help students see German as a new tool for self-expression.

 STEP 3 →

Media

Once students see that German is a tool for expressing their own ideas, bridge their experiences to those of German speakers through the **Fotoroman** section. The **Fotoroman** storyline video presents and reviews vocabulary and structure in accurate cultural contexts for effective training in both comprehension and personal communication.

STEP 4

Culture

Now bring students into the experience of culture as seen from the perspective of those living in it. Here we share German-speaking cultures' unique geography, history, products, perspectives, and practices. Through **Zapping** and **Kurzfilm** (authentic video) students experience and reflect on cultural experiences beyond their own.

STEP 5

Structure

Through context, media and culture, students have incorporated both previously learned and new grammatical structures into their personalized communication. Now a formal presentation of relevant grammar demonstrates that grammar is a tool for clearer and more effective communication. Clear presentations and invitations to compare German to English build confidence, fluency, and accuracy.

STEP 6

Skill synthesis

Pulling all their learning together, students now integrate context, personal experience, communication tools, and cultural products, perspectives, and practices. Through extended reading, writing, listening, speaking, and cultural exploration in scaffolded progression, students apply all their skills for a rich, personalized experience of German.

Learning to Use Your **Teacher's Edition**

Mosaik offers you a comprehensive, thoroughly developed Teacher's Edition (TE). It features student text pages overprinted with answers to all activities with discrete responses. Each page also contains annotations for a few selected activities that were written to complement and support varied teaching styles, to extend the already rich contents of the student textbook, and to save you time in class preparation and course management.

Because the **Mosaik** TE is different from teacher's editions available with other German programs, this section is designed as a quick orientation to the principal types of teacher annotations it contains. As you familiarize yourself with them, it is important to know that the annotations are suggestions only. Any German question, sentence, model, or simulated teacher-student exchange is not meant to be prescriptive or limiting. You are encouraged to view these suggested "scripts" as flexible points of departure that will help you achieve your instructional goals.

For the Chapter Opening Page

- **Suggestion** A discussion topic idea, based on the Chapter Opener photo

For the Lessons

- **Suggestion** Teaching suggestions for working with on-page materials, carrying out specific activities, and presenting new vocabulary or grammar

- **Expansion** Expansions and variations on activities

- **Vorbereitung** Suggestions for talking about the **Fotoroman** pages before students have watched the video or studied the pages

- **Nützliche Ausdrücke** A list of expressions taken from the **Fotoroman** that students may need to study before watching the episode

- **Partner and Virtual Chats** Assignments that develop students' communication skills with the convenience of the Supersite

- **Communication Icons** are tagged to activities that engage students in one of the three different modes of communication:

  Interpretive communication Exercises that target students' reading or listening skills and assess their comprehension

  Presentational communication Ideas and contexts that require students to produce a written or verbal presentation in the target language

  Interpersonal communication Activities that provide students with opportunities to carry out language functions in simulated real-life contexts or engage in personalized communication with others

 Please check the **Mosaik** Supersite at **vhlcentral.com** for additional teaching support.

Differentiation

Knowing how to appeal to learners of different abilities and learning styles will allow you to foster a positive teaching environment and motivate all your students. Here are some strategies for creating inclusive learning environments. Extension and expansion activities are also suggested.

Learners with Special Needs

Learners with special needs include students with attention priority disorders or learning disabilities, slower-paced learners, at-risk learners, and English language learners. Some inclusion strategies that work well with such students are:

Clear Structure By teaching concepts in a predictable order, you can help students organize their learning. Encourage students to keep outlines of materials they read, classify words into categories such as colors, or follow prewriting steps.

Frequent Review and Repetition Preview material to be taught and review material covered at the end of each lesson. Pair proficient learners with less proficient ones to practice and reinforce concepts. Help students retain concepts through continuous practice and review.

Multi-sensory Input and Output Use visual, auditory, and kinesthetic tasks to add interest and motivation, and to achieve long-term retention. For example, vary input with the use of audio recordings, video, guided visualization, rhymes, and mnemonics.

Additional Time Consider how physical limitations may affect participation in special projects or daily routines. Provide additional time and recommended accommodations.

Different Learning Styles

Visual Learners learn best by seeing, so engage them in activities and projects that are visually creative. Encourage them to write down information and to think in pictures as a long-term retention strategy. Reinforce their learning through visual displays such as diagrams, videos, and handouts.

Auditory Learners best retain information by listening. Engage them in discussions, debates, and role-playing. Reinforce their learning by playing audio versions of texts or reading aloud passages and stories. Encourage them to pay attention to voice, tone, and pitch to infer meaning.

Kinesthetic Learners learn best through moving, touching, and doing hands-on activities. Involve such students in skits and dramatizations; to infer or convey meaning, have them observe or model gestures such as those used for greeting someone or getting someone's attention.

Advanced Learners

Advanced Learners have the potential to learn language concepts and complete assignments at an accelerated pace. They may benefit from assignments that are more challenging than the ones given to their peers. The key to differentiating for advanced learners is adding a degree of rigor to a given task. Examples include sharing perspectives on texts they have read with the class, retelling detailed stories, preparing analyses of texts, or adding to discussions. Here are some other strategies for engaging advanced learners:

Timed Answers Have students answer questions within a specified time limit.

Persuading Adapt activities so students have to write or present their points of view in order to persuade an audience. Pair or group advanced learners to form debating teams.

Best Practices

The creators of **Mosaik** understand that there are many different approaches to successful language teaching and that no one method works perfectly for all teachers or all learners. These strategies and tips may be applied to any language-teaching method.

Maintain the Target Language

As much as possible, create an immersion environment by using German to *teach* German. Encourage the exclusive use of the target language in your classroom, employing visual aids, mnemonics, circumlocution, or gestures to complement what you say. Encourage students to perceive meaning directly through careful listening and observation, and by using cognates and familiar structures and patterns to deduce meaning.

Cultivate Critical Thinking

Prompt students to reflect, observe, reason, and form judgments in German. Engaging students in activities that require them to compare, contrast, predict, criticize, and estimate will help them to internalize the language structures they have learned.

Encourage Use of Circumlocution

Prompt students to discover various ways of expressing ideas and of overcoming potential blocks to communication through the use of circumlocution and paraphrasing.

Assessment

As you use the **Mosaik** program, you can employ a variety of assessments to evaluate progress. The program provides comprehensive, discrete answer assessments as well as more communicative assessments that elicit open-ended, personalized responses.

Diagnostic Testing

The **Wiederholung** section in each lesson provides you with an informal opportunity to assess students' readiness for the listening, reading, and writing activities in the **Weiter geht's** section. If some students need additional practice or instruction in a particular area, you can identify this before students move on.

Writing Assessment

At the end of each chapter, the **Weiter geht's** section includes a **Schreiben** page that introduces a writing strategy, which students apply as they complete the writing activity. These activities include suggestions that will focus students' attention on what is important for attaining clarity in written communication.

Testing Program

The **Mosaik** Testing Program offers two quizzes for each **Lektion**, one test per chapter, one cumulative exam per level, IPAs with rubrics for every chapter, oral testing suggestions with grading rubrics, audioscripts for listening comprehension activities, and all answer keys. The quizzes, tests, and exams may administered online, and may be customized by adding, eliminating, or moving items according to your classroom and student needs. Editable RTFs are also available in the Resources area of the Supersite and on the Teacher Resources DVD.

Portfolio Assessment

Portfolios can provide further valuable evidence of your students' learning. They are useful tools for evaluating students' progress in German and also suggest to students how they are likely to be assessed in the real world. Since portfolio activities often comprise classroom tasks that you would assign as part of a lesson or as homework, you should think of the planning, selecting, recording, and interpreting of information about individual performance as a way of blending assessment with instruction.

You may find it helpful to refer to portfolio contents, such as drafts, essays, and samples of presentations when writing student reports and conveying the status of a student's progress to his or her parents.

Ask students regularly to consider which pieces of their own work they would like to share with family and friends, and help them develop criteria for selecting representative samples of essays, stories, poems, recordings of plays or interviews, mock documentaries, and so on. Prompt students to choose a variety of media in their activities wherever possible to demonstrate development in all four language skills. Encourage them to seek peer and parental input as they generate and refine criteria to help them organize and reflect on their own work.

Strategies for Differentiating Assessment

Here are some strategies for modifying tests and other forms of assessment according to your students' needs and your own purposes for administering the assessment.

Adjust Questions Direct complex or higher-level questions to students who are equipped to answer them adequately and modify questions for students with greater needs. Always ask questions that elicit thinking, but keep in mind the students' abilities.

Provide Tiered Assignments Assign tasks of varying complexity depending on individual student needs.

Promote Flexible Grouping Encourage movement among groups of students so that all learners are appropriately challenged. Group students according to interest, oral proficiency levels, or learning styles.

Adjust Pacing Pace the sequence and speed of assessments to suit your students' learning needs. Time advanced learners to challenge them and allow slower-paced learners more time to complete tasks or answer questions.

Integrated
Performance Assessment

Integrated Performance Assessments (IPA) begin with a real-life task that engages students' interest. To complete the task, students progress through the three modes of communication: they read, view, and listen for information (interpretive mode); they talk and write with classmates about what they have experienced (interpersonal mode); and they share formally what they have learned (presentational mode).

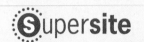 **Supersite** | Editable worksheets in the **Content > Resources** area of the Supersite

Integrated Performance Activity **Kapitel 4**

Context

You and your classmates would like to take an ecotourism trip and are investigating different destinations. You are going to compare three different locations and then choose the destination you like the best.

Interpretive Task

First, read the Kultur article in Lesson 4A, pages 156–157. As you read, make a list of reasons why you would like to visit these German national parks. Use facts mentioned in the article, as well as your own opinion.

Interpersonal Task

Compare your list with a partner's. Take turns talking about different reasons to choose one of the destinations for your trip. Then, each of you should describe one of the other destinations included in the article and why it would be a good place for your class trip. You will discuss all three destinations. Between the two of you, decide which destination is the best for your trip.

Presentational Task

Prepare a brief oral presentation in which you describe the destination you recommend for the class trip. Give at least three facts about it, and two reasons why you think it's the best choice among the three destinations that you considered. Be sure to include the criteria you used to make your decision.

	5 points	3 points	1 point
Interpretive	The student can easily identify interesting facts or reasons to visit their chosen destination.	The student can identify interesting facts or reasons to visit their chosen destination.	The student has difficulty identifying interesting facts or reasons to visit their chosen destination.
Interpersonal	The student can complete a basic conversation demonstrating mutual understanding. The result of the conversation is a clear list of reasons to visit the destination of the student's choice.	The student can complete a basic conversation with only some difficulty in mutual understanding. The result of the conversation is a list of reasons to visit the destination of the student's choice.	The student can complete a basic conversation but does not reach mutual understanding. The student is not able to prepare a list of reasons to visit a certain destination.
Presentational	The student can provide clear, relevant information about 3 positive features of the destination of his or her choice and 2 reasons why he or she chose it.	The student can provide some information about the positive features of his or her choice and why he or she chose it.	The presentation lacks detail, and the information about the destination and reason for picking it is unclear.

"I Can" Statements

Students can assess their own progress by using "I Can" (or "Can-Do") Statements. Use customizable "I Can" Worksheets provided for each chapter of **Mosaik** to guide student learning, and to train students to assess their progress.

Editable worksheets in the **Content > Resources** area of the Supersite

---

"I Can" Statements

STUDENT OBJECTIVES
Lektion 4A Mosaik 3

Name _____   Datum _____

Ziele: Kontext	Datum	Was kann ich schon?
1. I can recognize expressions related to nature.		
2. I name a variety of animals.		

Was kann ich schon?

4 *Ausgezeichnet!* I know this well enough to teach it to someone.

3 *Sehr gut!* I can do this with almost no mistakes.

2 *Mehr oder weniger!* I can do much of this but I have questions.

1 *Nicht so gut:* I can do this only with help.

0 *Hilfe!* I do not understand this, even with help.

Notizen: _____
_____
_____
_____
_____

Engage all students

Learning German isn't all about grammar and memorization. **Mosaik** provides multiple ways to get students excited about the language and culture of German-speaking people.

Make It Personal

- Find out why students decided to learn German. Is it to speak to relatives? To interact with German-speaking friends on social media? To learn more about a particular element of German culture, film, or literature? Keep students motivated by helping them see how individual tasks lead to the larger goal of communicating with German-speaking people. Take the time to explore (and expand on) the **Kultur** and **Panorama** sections to engage students with daily life and geography, as well as fine and performing arts.

- Have students talk about themselves! The Teacher's Edition interpersonal communication annotations point out activities where students ask each other questions about their own lives. Personalizing the discussion helps keep students engaged with the material they are practicing in German.

Get Students Talking

Look for icons calling out pair and group work. Some great speaking activities include:

Supersite Virtual and Partner Chat activities:

- Offer opportunities for spoken production beyond the face-to-face classroom

- Help reduce students' affective filter and build confidence

- Provide a recorded portfolio of students' spoken work that can be easily graded

Info Gap activities: Give students these worksheets either electronically or in print, and have them work to get information from a partner.

Textbook Activity Worksheets: Get the whole class on their feet to participate in activities, such as surveys, using the language they have just been learning.

Take Advantage of Multimedia

For students:

- Are your students on YouTube every minute of their free time? Engage them with the TV advertisements in **Zapping**.

- Do your students want to study abroad in a German-speaking area of Europe? Get them engaged with the **Fotoroman** series featuring George, an American studying abroad in Berlin. Younger students are fascinated by what older students are doing, so the situations with university students should hold their interest.

- Make learning vocabulary engaging and effective for students with the My Vocabulary on the Supersite. They can focus on the vocabulary for each lesson or customize flashcard banks to study only those words they need to learn for an upcoming quiz. The flashcard tool is ideal for student self-study of vocabulary.

For teachers:

- Assign or use the audio-enabled Vocabulary Presentations on the Supersite to give students an interactive experience while they hear the new terms spoken by a native speaker of German.

- Use the Digital Image Bank to enliven your own digital or print activities.

- Have students follow along in their text as the selections in **Lesen** are read aloud by a native German speaker.

- Keep grammar instruction focused by using the Grammar Slides. Breaking up the instructional points into slides helps make the lesson more digestible.

- Don't forget to use the summaries of the **Fotoroman** to reinforce grammar instruction.

Addressing the Modes of Communication

Interpretive Skills

One of **Mosaik**'s greatest strengths is in fostering students' interpretive communication skills. The **Lesen** sections provide various types of authentic written texts and the **Zapping** and **Kurzfilm** videos feature German spoken at a natural pace. Encourage students to interact with as much authentic language as possible, as this will lead to long-term success.

- Audio activities
- **Fotoroman**
- **Kultur**
- **Zapping** and **Kurzfilm**
- **Panorama**
- **Lesen**
- **Hören**

Presentational Skills

Scaffolded writing tasks help students build solid writing skills in German. Many activities can be turned into either spoken or written presentations to create additional opportunities for students to practice in this mode.

- **Schreiben**
- **Wiederholung**

Interpersonal Skills

With the inclusion of abundant activities for classroom interaction as well as Partner and Virtual Chats online, students can practice their speaking skills by sharing personal information throughout each lesson.

- Pair and group activities
- Partner and Virtual Chats

General Suggestions for Using the *Fotoroman* Video Episodes

The **Fotoroman** section in each lesson and the **Fotoroman** video were created as interlocking pieces. All photos in **Fotoroman** are actual video stills from the corresponding video episode, while the printed conversations are abbreviated versions of the dramatic segment. Both the **Fotoroman** conversations and their expanded video versions represent comprehensible input at the discourse level; they were purposely written to use language from the corresponding lesson's **Kontext** and **Strukturen** sections. Thus, they recycle known language, preview grammar points students will study later in the lesson, and, in keeping with Krashen's concept of "i + 1," contain some amount of unknown language.

Because the **Fotoroman** textbook sections and the dramatic episodes of the **Fotoroman** video are so closely connected, you may use them in many different ways. For instance, you can use **Fotoroman** as a preview, presenting it before showing the video episode. You can also show the video episode first and follow up with **Fotoroman**. You can even use **Fotoroman** as a stand-alone, video-independent section.

Depending on your teaching preferences and school facilities, you might decide to show all video episodes in class or to assign them solely for viewing outside the classroom. You could begin by showing the first one or two episodes in class to familiarize yourself and students with the characters, storyline, style, and **Summary** sections. After that, you could work in class only with **Fotoroman** and have students view the remaining video episodes outside of class. No matter which approach you choose, students have ample materials to support viewing the video independently and processing it in a meaningful way. For each video episode, there are activities in the **Fotoroman** section of the corresponding textbook lesson, as well as additional activities in the **Mosaik** Video Manual section of the Student Activities Manual.

You might also want to use the **Fotoroman** video in class when working with the **Strukturen** sections. You could play the parts of the dramatic episode that correspond to the video stills in the grammar explanations or show selected scenes and ask students to identify certain grammar points.

You could also focus on the **Zusammenfassung** sections that appear at the end of each episode to summarize the key language functions and grammar points used. In class, you could play the parts of the **Zusammenfassung** section that exemplify individual grammar points as you progress through each **Strukturen** section. You could also wait until you complete a **Strukturen** section and review it and the lesson's **Kontext** section by showing the corresponding **Summary** section in its entirety.

On the **Mosaik** Supersite, teachers can control what, if any, subtitles students can see. They are available in German or in English, and in transcript format.

About **Zapping TV Clips** and Short Films

A TV clip or a short film from the German-speaking world appears in the first **Lektion** of each **Kapitel**. The purpose of this feature is to expose students to the language and culture contained in authentic media pieces. The following list of the television commercials and short films is organized by **Kapitel**.

MOSAIK 1

Kapitel 1
Deutsche Bahn
(29 seconds)

Kapitel 2
TU Berlin
(1 minute, 15 seconds)

Kapitel 3
Bauer Joghurt
(33 seconds)

Kapitel 4
Yello Strom
(39 seconds)

MOSAIK 2

Kapitel 1
Penny
(35 seconds)

Kapitel 2
Hausarbeit
(1 minute, 13 seconds)

Kapitel 3
Urlaub im grünen Binnenland
(3 minutes, 41 seconds)

Kapitel 4
Mercedes Benz
(35 seconds)

MOSAIK 3

Kapitel 1
Central Krankenversicherung
(23 seconds)

Kurzfilm

Kapitel 2
Fanny
(13 minutes, 45 seconds)

Kapitel 3
Die Berliner Mauer
(15 minutes)

Kapitel 4
Bienenstich ist aus
(15 minutes)

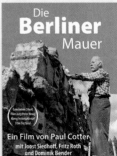

DAY	WARM-UP / ACTIVATE	PRESENT / PRACTICE / COMMUNICATE	REFLECT / CONCLUDE / CONNECT
1 Context for Communication	• Evoke student experiences and vocabulary for context; orient to **Kontext** 5 minutes	• Present vocabulary through illustrations, Digital Image Bank (**Supersite**), phrases, categories, association [15] • Student pairs begin **Anwendung** [15] 30 minutes	• Students restate context for vocabulary [5] • Introduce homework: select **Anwendung** (text/**Supersite**) [5] 10 minutes
2 Vocabulary as a Tool	• Student groups review **Anwendung** from previous day and homework 5 minutes	• Students complete **Anwendung** [15] • Students begin **Kommunikation** [15] 30 minutes	• Introduce homework: **Supersite** flashcards, context illustrations and audio; end-of-chapter list with audio; remaining **Supersite** activities (as applicable) [5] • Students do select **Kommunikation** activities [5] 10 minutes
3 Vocabulary as a Tool	• Student groups review **Anwendung** and **Kommunikation** activities 5 minutes	• Students complete **Kommunikation** activities and/or do select **Info Gap** activities (**Supersite: Resources**) [15] • Present **Aussprache und Rechtschreibung** (**Supersite**) [15] 30 minutes	• Students review vocabulary for assessment preparation [5] • Introduce homework: select **Aussprache und Rechtschreibung** (**Supersite**) activities [5] 10 minutes
4 Media as a Bridge	• Reflection and preparation: **Kontext** assessment 5 minutes	• Assessment: **Kontext** [20] • Clarity check on **Aussprache und Rechtschreibung** [5] • Orient students to **Fotoroman** through video stills [10] 35 minutes	• Introduce homework: review stills for **Fotoroman** (text/**Supersite**) 5 minutes
5 Media as a Bridge	• Review results of Assessment: **Kontext** 10 minutes	• Orient students to **Nützliche Ausdrücke** [10] • View and discuss **Fotoroman** [20] 30 minutes	• Introduce homework: select **Fotoroman** (text/**Supersite**) **Übungen** 5 minutes
6 Media as a Bridge	• Review **Fotoroman Übungen**, as applicable 10 minutes	• Use **Fotoroman** and **Nützliche Ausdrücke** for communication practice [20] • Pair/group work with **Fotoroman Übungen** [10] 30 minutes	• Introduce homework: complete **Fotoroman** (text/**Supersite**) **Übungen** 5 minutes
7 Culture for Communication	• Review **Fotoroman Übungen**, as applicable 5 minutes	• Present select **Kultur** features in whole class or small groups, jigsaw, numbered heads together, etc. 35 minutes	• Introduce homework: select **Kultur** (text/**Supersite**) **Übungen** 5 minutes
8 Culture for Communication	• Student pairs/groups review **Kultur Übungen** 5 minutes	• Focus on select **Kultur** items to confirm understanding [10] • Class, group, pair or individual research using **Im Internet** (**Supersite**) [25] 35 minutes	• Introduce homework: complete **Im Internet** (**Supersite**) 5 minutes
9 Structure as a Tool	• Whole class review of **Im Internet** research 10 minutes	• Present grammar point A.1 using text, **Supersite** (presentations, grammar slides in **Resources**), and corresponding **Fotoroman** segments [15] • Student pairs/groups do A.1 **Jetzt sind Sie dran**, begin **Anwendung** [15] 30 minutes	• Introduce homework: select **Anwendung** (text/**Supersite**) 5 minutes
10 Structure as a Tool	• Student pairs share results of completed items in **Anwendung** 5 minutes	• Students complete and/or review **Anwendung** [15] • Students begin A.1 **Kommunikation** [20] 35 minutes	• Introduce homework: complete and/or review **Kommunikation** (text/**Supersite**) 5 minutes

DAY	WARM-UP / ACTIVATE	PRESENT / PRACTICE / COMMUNICATE	REFLECT / CONCLUDE / CONNECT
11 Structure as a Tool	• Student pairs/groups review and/or present select **Kommunikation** **10 minutes**	• Lead discussion, review, or practice of grammar point A.1 [5] • Present grammar point A.2 using text, **Supersite** (presentations, grammar slides in **Resources**), and corresponding **Fotoroman** segments [15] • Student pairs/groups do A.2 **Jetzt sind Sie dran**, begin **Anwendung** [10] **30 minutes**	• Introduce homework: select **Anwendung** (text/**Supersite**) **5 minutes**
12 Structure as a Tool	• Student pairs share results of completed items in **Anwendung** **5 minutes**	• Students complete and/or review **Anwendung** [15] • Students begin A.2 **Kommunikation** [20] **35 minutes**	• Introduce homework: complete and/or review **Kommunikation** (text/**Supersite**) **5 minutes**
13 Structure as a Tool	• Student pairs/groups review and/or present select **Kommunikation** **10 minutes**	• Lead discussion, review, or practice of grammar point A.2 [5] • Present grammar point A.3 using text, **Supersite** (presentations, grammar slides in **Resources**), and corresponding **Fotoroman** segments [15] • Student pairs/groups do A.3 **Jetzt sind Sie dran**, begin **Anwendung** [10] **30 minutes**	• Introduce homework: select **Anwendung** (text/**Supersite**) **5 minutes**
14 Structure as a Tool	• Student pairs share results of completed items in **Anwendung** **5 minutes**	• Students complete and/or review **Anwendung** [15] • Students begin A.3 **Kommunikation** [20] **35 minutes**	• Introduce homework: complete and/or review **Kommunikation** (text/**Supersite**) **5 minutes**
15 Structure as a Tool	• Student pairs/groups review and/or present select **Kommunikation** **10 minutes**	• Student pairs/groups do **Wiederholung** **30 minutes**	• Introduce homework: prepare for assessment on **Strukturen** **5 minutes**
16 Authentic Media	• Students reflect in preparation for assessment on **Strukturen** **5 minutes**	• Assessment on grammar points [20] • Introduce and guide discussion of **Zapping** or **Kurzfilm**; show clip via **Supersite**; do **Verständnis** as a class [15] **35 minutes**	• Introduce homework: prepare for **Diskussion** from **Zapping** or **Kurzfilm** **5 minutes**
17 Context for Communication	• Class/groups/pairs engage in **Diskussion** from **Zapping** or **Kurzfilm** **5 minutes**	• Present vocabulary through illustrations, Digital Image Bank (**Supersite**), phrases, categories, association [15] • Student pairs begin **Anwendung** [15] **30 minutes**	• Students restate context of vocabulary [5] • Introduce homework: select **Anwendung** (text/**Supersite**) [5] **10 minutes**
18 Vocabulary as a Tool	• Student groups review **Anwendung** from previous day and homework **5 minutes**	• Students complete **Anwendung** **30 minutes**	• Students review and personalize key vocabulary in context [5] • Introduce homework: **Supersite** flashcards, context illustrations and audio; end-of-chapter list with audio; remaining **Supersite** activities (as applicable) [5] **10 minutes**
19 Vocabulary as a Tool	• Student groups review **Anwendung** from previous day and homework **5 minutes**	• Students do select **Kommunikation** activities [20] • Students do select **Info Gap** activities (**Supersite: Resources**) [10] **30 minutes**	• Students review and personalize key vocabulary in context [5] • Introduce homework: **Supersite** flashcards, context illustrations and audio; end-of-chapter list with audio; select **Kommunikation** activities (as applicable) [5] **10 minutes**

DAY		WARM-UP / ACTIVATE	PRESENT / PRACTICE / COMMUNICATE	REFLECT / CONCLUDE / CONNECT
20	Vocabulary as a Tool	• Student groups review **Kommunikation** from previous day and homework **5 minutes**	• Present **Aussprache und Rechtschreibung** (**Supersite**) [10] • Invite students to reflect on their pronunciation accuracy in preceding activities [15] **25 minutes**	• Students review vocabulary for assessment preparation [10] • Introduce homework: select **Aussprache und Rechtschreibung** (**Supersite**) activities [5] **15 minutes**
21	Media as a Bridge	• Reflection and preparation: **Kontext** assessment **5 minutes**	• Assessment: **Kontext** [20] • Clarity check on **Aussprache und Rechtschreibung** [5] • Orient students to **Fotoroman** through video stills [10] **35 minutes**	• Introduce homework: review stills for **Fotoroman** (text/**Supersite**) **5 minutes**
22	Media as a Bridge	• Review results of Assessment: **Kontext** **10 minutes**	• Orient students to **Nützliche Ausdrücke** [10] • View and discuss **Fotoroman** [20] **30 minutes**	• Introduce homework: select **Fotoroman** (text/**Supersite**) **Übungen** **5 minutes**
23	Media as a Bridge	• Review **Fotoroman Übungen**, as applicable **10 minutes**	• Use **Fotoroman** and **Nützliche Ausdrücke** for communication practice [20] • Pair/group work with **Fotoroman Übungen** [10] **30 minutes**	• Introduce homework: complete **Fotoroman** (text/**Supersite**) **Übungen** **5 minutes**
24	Culture for Communication	• Review **Fotoroman Übungen**, as applicable **5 minutes**	• Present select **Kultur** features in whole class or small groups, jigsaw, numbered heads together, etc. **35 minutes**	• Introduce homework: select **Kultur** (text/**Supersite**) **Übungen** **5 minutes**
25	Culture for Communication	• Student pairs/groups review **Kultur Übungen** **5 minutes**	• Focus on select **Kultur** items to confirm understanding [10] • Class, group, pair or individual research using **Im Internet** (**Supersite**) [25] **35 minutes**	• Introduce homework: complete **Im Internet** (**Supersite**) **5 minutes**
26	Structure as a Tool	• Whole class review of **Im Internet** research **10 minutes**	• Present grammar point B.1 using text, **Supersite** (presentations, grammar slides in **Resources**), and corresponding **Fotoroman** segments [15] • Student pairs/groups do B.1 **Jetzt sind Sie dran**, begin **Anwendung** [15] **30 minutes**	• Introduce homework: select **Anwendung** (text/**Supersite**) **5 minutes**
27	Structure as a Tool	• Student pairs share results of completed items in **Anwendung** **5 minutes**	• Students complete and/or review **Anwendung** [15] • Students begin B.1 **Kommunikation** [20] **35 minutes**	• Introduce homework: complete and/or review **Kommunikation** (text/**Supersite**) **5 minutes**
28	Structure as a Tool	• Student pairs/groups review and/or present select **Kommunikation** **10 minutes**	• Lead discussion, review, or practice of grammar point B.1 [5] • Present grammar point B.2 using text, **Supersite** (presentations, grammar slides in **Resources**), and corresponding **Fotoroman** segments [15] • Student pairs/groups do B.2 **Jetzt sind Sie dran**, begin **Anwendung** [10] **30 minutes**	• Introduce homework: select **Anwendung** (text/**Supersite**) **5 minutes**
29	Structure as a Tool	• Student pairs share results of completed items in **Anwendung** **5 minutes**	• Students complete and/or review **Anwendung** [15] • Students begin B.2 **Kommunikation** [20] **35 minutes**	• Introduce homework: complete and/or review **Kommunikation** (text/**Supersite**) **5 minutes**

DAY	WARM-UP / ACTIVATE	PRESENT / PRACTICE / COMMUNICATE	REFLECT / CONCLUDE / CONNECT
30 Structure as a Tool	• Student pairs/groups review and/or present select **Kommunikation** **10 minutes**	• Lead discussion, review, or practice of grammar point B.2 [5] • Present grammar point B.3 using text, **Supersite** (presentations, grammar slides in **Resources**), and corresponding **Fotoroman** segments [15] • Student pairs/groups do B.3 **Jetzt sind Sie dran**, begin **Anwendung** [10] **30 minutes**	• Introduce homework: select **Anwendung** (text/**Supersite**) **5 minutes**
31 Structure as a Tool	• Student pairs share results of completed items in **Anwendung** **5 minutes**	• Students complete and/or review **Anwendung** [15] • Students begin B.3 **Kommunikation** [20] **35 minutes**	• Introduce homework: complete and/or review **Kommunikation** (text/**Supersite**) **5 minutes**
32 Structure as a Tool	• Student pairs/groups review and/or present select **Kommunikation** **10 minutes**	• Student pairs/groups do **Wiederholung** **30 minutes**	• Introduce homework: prepare for assessment on **Strukturen** **5 minutes**
33 Skill Synthesis: Culture and Geography	• Students reflect in preparation for assessment on **Strukturen** **5 minutes**	• Assessment on **Strukturen** [20] • Present select **Weiter geht's - Panorama** features in whole class or small groups, jigsaw, numbered heads together, etc. [15] **35 minutes**	• Introduce homework: **Panorama - Was haben Sie gelernt?** activity/activities and/or initial research using **Im Internet** **5 minutes**
34 Skill Synthesis: Interpretive (Reading)	• Student pairs review homework from **Panorama** **10 minutes**	• Class review and discussion from **Panorama** [15] • Guide students through **Vor dem Lesen**, including **Strategien** [15] **30 minutes**	• Introduce homework: select **Vor dem Lesen** activities (text/**Supersite**) **5 minutes**
35 Skill Synthesis: Interpretive (Reading)	• Student pairs review homework from **Vor dem Lesen** **5 minutes**	• Students read **Lesen** (whole class or small groups) [25] • Students begin **Nach dem Lesen** [10] **35 minutes**	• Introduce homework: complete **Nach dem Lesen** activities (text/**Supersite**) **5 minutes**
36 Skill Synthesis: Interpretive (Listening)	• Share and discuss results from **Nach dem Lesen** **10 minutes**	• Guide students through **Strategien** and **Vorbereitung** in **Hören**; present selection [20] • Students (individuals, pairs, or small groups) do select **Verständnis** activities [10] **30 minutes**	• Introduce homework: complete **Verständnis** from **Hören** (text or **Supersite**) **5 minutes**
37 Skill Synthesis: Presentational (Writing)	• Student pairs check results from **Verständnis** **10 minutes**	• Guide students through **Schreiben**, including **Strategien** and **Thema** [15] • Review and preparation through use of communication activities, additional Partner Chat or Virtual Chat activities (**Supersite**) and **Wortschatz** (text/**Supersite**) [10] **25 minutes**	• Introduce homework: first draft of **Schreiben - Thema** • Review content and concepts for chapter assessment **10 minutes**
38 Skill Synthesis and Review	• Student pairs/groups do initial peer review of drafts of **Schreiben - Thema** **15 minutes**	• Review and preparation through use of communication activities, additional Partner Chat or Virtual Chat activities (**Supersite**) and **Wortschatz** (text/**Supersite**) and/or begin IPA (**Supersite: Resources**) **25 minutes**	• Confirm understanding of assessment content (and/or grading rubric if using IPA) • **Schreiben - Thema** due **5 minutes**
39 Assessment	• Confirm all students submitted **Schreiben - Thema** (text/**Supersite**) **5 minutes**	• Written or digital chapter assessment (from **Resources** section or **Assessment** section of **Supersite**, respectively) and/or complete IPA **40 minutes**	

DAY	WARM-UP / ACTIVATE	PRESENT / PRACTICE / COMMUNICATE
1 Context for Communication	• Present and practice first half of review section 1 (of 4) 25 minutes	• Evoke student experiences and vocabulary for context; orient to **Kontext** [10] • Present vocabulary through illustrations, Digital Image Bank (**Supersite**), phrases, categories, association [15] 25 minutes
2 Vocabulary as a Tool	• Present and practice second half of review section 1 (of 4) 15 minutes	• Student pairs/groups review **Anwendung** from previous day and homework [10] • Students do **Kommunikation** activities [10] 20 minutes
3 Media as a Bridge	• Present and practice first half of review section 2 (of 4) 20 minutes	• Reflection and preparation: **Kontext** assessment [5] • Assessment: **Kontext** [20] 25 minutes
4 Media as a Bridge	• Present and practice second half of review section 2 (of 4) 15 minutes	• Review **Fotoroman** [5] • Second viewing and discussion/communication using **Fotoroman** [10] • Student pairs/groups complete **Fotoroman Übungen** [10] 25 minutes
5 Culture for Communication	• Present and practice first half of review section 3 (of 4) 20 minutes	• Student pairs/groups review **Kultur Übungen** [5] • Class, group, pair or individual research using **Im Internet** (**Supersite**) [20] 25 minutes
6 Structure as a Tool	• Present and practice second half of review section 3 (of 4) 15 minutes	• Student pairs share results of completed items in A.1 **Anwendung** [5] • Students complete A.1 **Anwendung** and **Kommunikation** [20] 25 minutes
7 Structure as a Tool	• Present and practice first half of review section 4 (of 4) 20 minutes	• Student pairs share results of completed items in A.2 **Anwendung** [5] • Students complete A.2 **Anwendung** and **Kommunikation** [15] 20 minutes
8 Structure as a Tool	• Present and practice second half of review section 4 (of 4) 15 minutes	• Student pairs share results of completed items in A.3 **Anwendung** [5] • Students complete A.3 **Anwendung** and **Kommunikation** [20] 25 minutes
9 Authentic Media	• Students reflect in preparation for assessment on **Strukturen** 10 minutes	• Assessment on **Strukturen** 35 minutes
10 Context for Communication	• Evoke student experiences and vocabulary for context 5 minutes	• Present vocabulary through illustrations, Digital Image Bank (**Supersite**), phrases, categories, association 35 minutes

REFLECT	PRESENT / PRACTICE / COMMUNICATE	REFLECT / CONCLUDE / CONNECT
• Student pairs restate context of vocabulary **5 minutes**	• Students do **Anwendung** (individual, pairs, small groups) **25 minutes**	• Introduce homework: **Supersite** flashcards, context illustrations and audio; end-of-chapter list with audio; remaining **Supersite** activities (as applicable) **5 minutes**
• Students reflect on and take note of personal areas of strength and challenge **5 minutes**	• Students do select **Info Gap** activities (**Supersite**: **Resources**) [25] • Present **Aussprache und Rechtschreibung** (**Supersite**) [15] **40 minutes**	• Students review vocabulary for assessment preparation • Introduce homework: select **Aussprache und Rechtschreibung** (**Supersite**) activities **5 minutes**
• Students individually review points in **Aussprache und Rechtschreibung** **5 minutes**	• Orient students to **Fotoroman** through video stills [5] • Orient students to **Nützliche Ausdrücke** [15] • First viewing of **Fotoroman** [10] **30 minutes**	• Introduce homework: select **Fotoroman** (text/**Supersite**) **Übungen** **5 minutes**
• Students individually review and consolidate **Nützliche Ausdrücke** **5 minutes**	• Present select **Kultur** features in whole class or small groups, jigsaw, numbered heads together, etc. **35 minutes**	• Introduce homework: select **Kultur** (text/**Supersite**) **Übungen** **5 minutes**
• Students individually review and consolidate understanding of cultural information **5 minutes**	• Present grammar point A.1 using text, **Supersite** (presentations, grammar slides in **Resources**), and corresponding **Fotoroman** segments [15] • Student pairs/groups do A.1 **Jetzt sind Sie dran**, begin **Anwendung** [15] **30 minutes**	• Introduce homework: select A.1 **Anwendung** (text/**Supersite**) **5 minutes**
• Students individually reflect on and take note of personal areas of strength and challenge with regard to the grammar point and its use **5 minutes**	• Present grammar point A.2 using text, **Supersite** (presentations, grammar slides in **Resources**), and corresponding **Fotoroman** segments [25] • Student pairs/groups do A.2 **Jetzt sind Sie dran**, begin **Anwendung** [10] **35 minutes**	• Introduce homework: select A.2 **Anwendung** (text/**Supersite**) **5 minutes**
• Students individually reflect on and take note of personal areas of strength and challenge with regard to the grammar point and its use **5 minutes**	• Present grammar point A.3 using text, **Supersite** (presentations, grammar slides in **Resources**), and corresponding **Fotoroman** segments [25] • Student pairs/groups do A.3 **Jetzt sind Sie dran**, begin **Anwendung** [10] **35 minutes**	• Introduce homework: select A.3 **Anwendung** (text/**Supersite**) **5 minutes**
• Students individually reflect on and take note of personal areas of strength and challenge with regard to the grammar point and its use **5 minutes**	• Student pairs/groups do **Wiederholung** **35 minutes**	• Introduce homework: prepare for assessment on **Strukturen** **5 minutes**
	• Introduce and guide discussion of **Zapping** or **Kurzfilm**; show clip via **Supersite**; do **Verständnis** and **Diskussion** as a class **35 minutes**	• Introduce homework: preview **Kontext B** through pictures and word lists (text/**Supersite**) **5 minutes**
• Student pairs restate context of vocabulary **5 minutes**	• Students do **Anwendung** (individual, pairs, small groups) **35 minutes**	• Introduce homework: **Supersite** flashcards, context illustrations and audio; end-of-chapter list with audio; remaining **Supersite** activities (as applicable) **5 minutes**

DAY	WARM-UP / ACTIVATE	PRESENT / PRACTICE / COMMUNICATE
11 Vocabulary as a Tool	• Student pairs/groups review **Anwendung** from previous day and homework 5 minutes	• Students do **Kommunikation** activities 30 minutes
12 Media as a Bridge	• Reflection and preparation: **Kontext** assessment 5 minutes	• Assessment: **Kontext** 35 minutes
13 Media as a Bridge	• Review **Fotoroman Übungen** 10 minutes	• Second viewing and discussion/communication using **Fotoroman** [15] • Student pairs/groups complete **Fotoroman Übungen** [15] 30 minutes
14 Culture for Communication	• Student pairs/groups review **Kultur Übungen** 10 minutes	• Focus on select **Kultur** items to confirm understanding [10] • Class, group, pair or individual research using **Im Internet** (**Supersite**) [25] 35 minutes
15 Structure as a Tool	• Student pairs share results of completed items in B.1 **Anwendung** 5 minutes	• Students complete B.1 **Anwendung** and **Kommunikation** 35 minutes
16 Structure as a Tool	• Student pairs share results of completed items in B.2 **Anwendung** 5 minutes	• Students complete B.2 **Anwendung** and **Kommunikation** 35 minutes
17 Structure as a Tool	• Student pairs share results of completed items in B.3 **Anwendung** 5 minutes	• Students complete B.3 **Anwendung** and **Kommunikation** 35 minutes
18 Skill Synthesis: Culture and Geography	• Assessment on **Strukturen** 25 minutes	• Present select **Weiter geht's - Panorama** features in whole class or small groups, jigsaw, numbered heads together, etc. [25] • Class review and discussion from **Panorama** [10] 35 minutes
19 Skill Synthesis: Interpretive (Reading and Listening)	• Student pairs review homework from **Vor dem Lesen** 5 minutes	• Students read **Lesen** (whole class or small groups) [25] • Students do **Nach dem Lese**n [15] 40 minutes
20 Skill Synthesis: Presentational (Writing)	• Student pairs check results from **Verständnis** 10 minutes	• Guide students through **Schreiben**, including **Strategien** and **Thema**, and connect to chapter context [10] • Students prepare writing plan in discussion with partner [15] 25 minutes
21 Assessment	• Peer review of **Schreiben - Thema** 5 minutes	

REFLECT	PRESENT / PRACTICE / COMMUNICATE	REFLECT / CONCLUDE / CONNECT
• Students reflect on and take note of personal areas of strength and challenge	• Students do select **Info Gap** activities (**Supersite: Resources**) [25] • Present **Aussprache und Rechtschreibung** (**Supersite**) [15]	• Students review vocabulary for assessment preparation • Introduce homework: select **Aussprache und Rechtschreibung** (**Supersite**) activities
5 minutes	**40 minutes**	**5 minutes**
• Students individually review points in **Aussprache und Rechtschreibung**	• Orient students to **Fotoroman** through video stills [10] • Orient students to **Nützliche Ausdrücke** [15] • First viewing of **Fotoroman** [10]	• Introduce homework: select **Fotoroman** (text/**Supersite**) **Übungen**
5 minutes	**35 minutes**	**5 minutes**
• Students individually review and consolidate **Nützliche Ausdrücke**	• Present select **Kultur** features in whole class or small groups, jigsaw, numbered heads together, etc.	• Introduce homework: select **Kultur** (text/**Supersite**) **Übungen**
5 minutes	**35 minutes**	**5 minutes**
• Students individually review and consolidate understanding of cultural information	• Present grammar point B.1 using text, **Supersite** (presentations, grammar slides in **Resources**), and corresponding **Fotoroman** segments [15] • Student pairs/groups do B.1 **Jetzt sind Sie dran**, begin **Anwendung** [15]	• Introduce homework: select **Anwendung** (text/**Supersite**)
5 minutes	**30 minutes**	**5 minutes**
• Students individually reflect on and take note of personal areas of strength and challenge with regard to the grammar point and its use	• Present grammar point B.2 using text, **Supersite** (presentations, grammar slides in **Resources**), and corresponding **Fotoroman** segments [25] • Student pairs/groups do B.2 **Jetzt sind Sie dran**, begin **Anwendung** [10]	• Introduce homework: select **Anwendung** activities
5 minutes	**35 minutes**	**5 minutes**
• Students individually reflect on and take note of personal areas of strength and challenge with regard to the grammar point and its use	• Present grammar point B.3 using text, **Supersite** (presentations, grammar slides in **Resources**), and corresponding **Fotoroman** segments [25] • Student pairs/groups do B.3 **Jetzt sind Sie dran**, begin **Anwendung** [10]	• Introduce homework: select **Anwendung** (text/**Supersite**)
5 minutes	**35 minutes**	**5 minutes**
• Students individually reflect on and take note of personal areas of strength and challenge with regard to the grammar point and its use	• Student pairs/groups do **Wiederholung**	• Introduce homework: prepare for assessment on **Strukturen**
5 minutes	**35 minutes**	**5 minutes**
• Each student reviews what has just been presented from **Panorama**	• Guide students through **Vor dem Lesen**, including **Strategien**	• Introduce homework: **Panorama - Was haben Sie gelernt** activity/activities and/or initial research using **Im Internet**; and/or **Vor dem Lesen** activities (text/**Supersite**)
5 minutes	**15 minutes**	**5 minutes**
• Students individually reflect on understanding of **Lesen**	• Guide students through **Strategien** and **Vorbereitung** in **Hören**; present selection [20] • Students (individuals, pairs, or small groups) do **Verständnis** activities [10]	• Introduce homework: complete **Verständnis** from **Hören** (text/**Supersite**)
5 minutes	**30 minutes**	**5 minutes**
• Confirm understanding of assessment content and/or grading rubric if using IPA (**Supersite: Resources**) [5]	• Students work on **Schreiben - Thema** and/or review chapter content	• Introduce homework: prepare for chapter assessment and/or complete **Thema** (text/**Supersite**)
10 minutes	**35 minutes**	**5 minutes**

• Written or digital chapter assessment (from **Resources** section or **Assessment** section of **Supersite**, respectively) and/or complete **IPA**

40 minutes

AP® German Themes & Contexts

Long-term success in language learning starts in the first year of instruction. **Mosaik** incorporates AP® themes and contexts into all **Kultur**, **Zapping**, **Kurzfilm**, and **Weiter geht's** sections. **Mosaik** exposes students to the themes early in their language learning career. This will allow them to build the broad background they need to succeed on the AP® German Language and Culture Exam.

The numbers following each entry can be understood as follows:

(2)115 = **(Volume)** page
As shown, the entry above would be found in Volume 2, page 115.

MOSAIK 3

German Language and Culture

VISTA®
HIGHER LEARNING

Boston, Massachusetts

On the cover: Oval offices, Cologne, Germany

Publisher: José A. Blanco

Professional Development Director: Norah Lulich Jones

Editorial Development: Brian Contreras, Sharla Zwirek

Project Management: Sally Giangrande

Rights Management: Ashley Dos Santos, Annie Pickert Fuller

Technology Production: Fabián Montoya, Paola Ríos Schaaf, Erica Solari

Design: Radoslav Mateev, Gabriel Noreña, Andrés Vanegas

Production: Manuela Arango, Oscar Díez, Adriana Jaramillo Ch.

Student Text ISBN: 978-1-68005-135-3
Library of Congress Control Number: 2016947899

1 2 3 4 5 6 7 8 9   WC   21 20 19 18 17 16

MOSAIK 3

German Language and Culture

Überblick

KONTEXT

FOTOROMAN

KAPITEL 1

Gesundheit

KAPITEL 2

Stadtleben

KULTUR

STRUKTUREN

WEITER GEHT'S

KONTEXT

FOTOROMAN

KULTUR

STRUKTUREN

WEITER GEHT'S

The *Fotoroman* Episodes

Fully integrated with your textbook, the **Mosaik Fotoroman** contains 8 dramatic episodes—one for each lesson of the text. The episodes relate the adventures of four students who are studying in Berlin.

The **Fotoroman** dialogues in the printed textbook lesson are an abbreviated version of the dramatic episode featured in the video. Therefore, each **Fotoroman** section can be used as preparation before you view the corresponding video episode, as post-viewing reinforcement, or as a stand-alone section.

As you watch the video, you will see the characters interact using the vocabulary and grammar you are studying. Their conversations incorporate new vocabulary and grammar with previously taught language. At the conclusion of each episode, the **Zusammenfassung** segment summarizes the key language functions and grammar points used in the episode.

The Cast

Learn more about each of the characters you'll meet in **Mosaik Fotoroman**:

George
is from Milwaukee, Wisconsin.
He is studying Architecture.

Meline
is from Vienna.
She is studying Business.

Hans
is from Straubing, in Bavaria.
He studies Political Science and History.

Sabite
is from Berlin.
She studies Art.

About **Zapping TV Clips** and **Kurzfilm Short Films**

A TV clip or a short film from the German-speaking world appears in the first **Lektion** of each **Kapitel**. The purpose of this feature is to expose students to the language and culture contained in authentic media pieces. The following list of the television commercials and short films is organized by **Kapitel**.

Zapping

Kapitel 1

Central Krankenversicherung

(25 seconds)

Kurzfilm

Kapitel 2	**Kapitel 3**	**Kapitel 4**
Fanny	*Die Berliner Mauer*	*Bienenstich ist aus*
(13 minutes, 45 seconds)	(15 minutes)	(15 minutes)

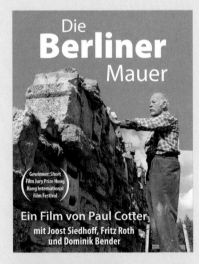

Ancillaries

- **Student Activities Manual (SAM)**

  The Student Activities Manual consists of three sections: the Workbook, the Video Manual, and the Lab Manual. The Workbook activities provide additional practice of the vocabulary and grammar for each textbook lesson. The Video Manual section includes activities for the **Mosaik Fotoroman**, and the Lab Manual activities focus on building your listening comprehension, speaking, and pronunciation skills in German.

- **Lab Audio MP3s**

  The Lab Audio MP3 files on the Supersite contain the recordings needed to complete the Lab Manual activities in the Student Activities Manual.

- **Textbook Audio MP3s**

  The Textbook Audio MP3 files contain the recordings needed to complete the listening activities in **Kontext**, **Aussprache und Rechtschreibung**, **Hören**, and **Wortschatz** sections. The files are available on the **Mosaik** Supersite.

- **Fotoroman Video**

  All episodes of the **Fotoroman** are available for streaming on the **Mosaik** Supersite.

- **Online Student Activities Manual (WebSAM)**

  Completely integrated with the **Mosaik** Supersite, the WebSAM provides online access to the SAM activities with instant feedback and grading. The complete audio program is online and features record-submit functionality for select activities.

- **Mosaik Supersite**

  The Supersite (**vhlcentral.com**) gives you access to a wide variety of interactive activities for each section of every lesson of the student text, including: auto-graded activities for extra practice with vocabulary, grammar, video, and cultural content; teacher-graded Partner Chat, Virtual Chat, and composition activities; reference tools; the **Zapping** TV commercials and **Kurzfilm** short films; the **Fotoroman** episodic videos; the Textbook Audio MP3 files, the Lab Program MP3 files, and more.

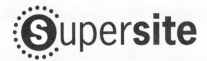

Each section of your textbook comes with activities on the **Mosaik** Supersite, many of which are auto-graded with immediate feedback. Plus, the Supersite is iPad®-friendly*, so it can be accessed on the go! Visit **vhlcentral.com** to explore the wealth of exciting resources.

KONTEXT	• Image-based vocabulary activities with audio • Additional activities for extra practice • **Aussprache und Rechtschreibung** presentation followed by record-compare activities	• Textbook activities • Chat activities for conversational skill-building and oral practice
FOTOROMAN	• Streaming video for all episodes of the **Fotoroman** with teacher-controlled options for subtitles • Textbook activities	• **Zusammenfassung** section with key vocabulary and grammar from the episode • Additional activities for extra practice
KULTUR	• Culture reading • Internet search activity	• Textbook activities • Additional activities for extra practice
STRUKTUREN	• Grammar presentations • Chat activities for conversational skill-building and oral practice • Streaming video of **Zapping** TV clip or short film **Kurzfilm**	• Textbook activities • Additional activities for extra practice
WEITER GEHT'S	**Panorama** • Interactive map with statistics and cultural notes • Additional activity for extra practice **Im Internet** • Internet search activity • Textbook activity with auto-grading **Lesen** • Audio-sync reading • Additional activities for extra practice • Textbook activities	**Hören** • Textbook activities • Additional activities for extra practice **Schreiben** • Submit your writing assignment online
WORTSCHATZ	• Audio recordings of all vocabulary items	• My Vocabulary to create lists and flashcards

Plus! Also found on the Supersite:

- All textbook and lab audio MP3 files
- Communication center for teacher notifications and feedback
- A single gradebook for all Supersite activities

- WebSAM online Workbook/Video Manual and Lab Manual
- vText online, interactive student edition with access to Supersite activities, audio, and video

*Students must use a computer for audio-recording.

Icons

Familiarize yourself with these icons that appear throughout **Mosaik**.

Online Activities

The mouse icon indicates when an activity is also available on the Supersite.

Pair Activities

Two heads indicate a pair activity.

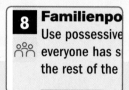

Group Activities

Three heads indicate a group activity.

Recycle

The recycling icon indicates that you will need to use vocabulary and grammar learned in previous lessons.

Partner and Virtual Chat Activities

Two heads with a speech bubble indicate that the activity may be assigned as a Partner Chat or a Virtual Chat activity on the Supersite.

Listening

The listening icon indicates that audio is available on the Supersite.

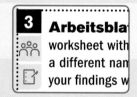

Worksheets

The activities marked with these icons require worksheets that your teacher will provide for you to complete the activity in a group.

Info Gap Activities

Two heads with a puzzle piece indicate an activity which will be done with a partner using a handout your teacher will provide.

Ressourcen

Ressourcen boxes tell you exactly what print and digital resources you can use to reinforce and expand on every section of the textbook lesson with page numbers where applicable.

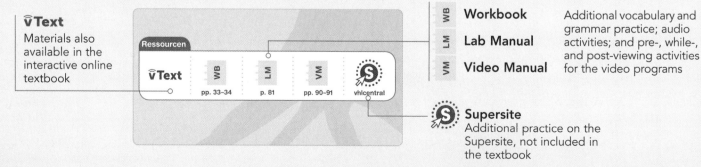

v̂Text
Materials also available in the interactive online textbook

WB Workbook
LM Lab Manual
VM Video Manual

Additional vocabulary and grammar practice; audio activities; and pre-, while-, and post-viewing activities for the video programs

Supersite
Additional practice on the Supersite, not included in the textbook

Why Learn German?

Explore Your Future

Are you already planning your future career? Employers in today's global economy look for workers who know different languages and understand other cultures. Your knowledge of German will make you a valuable job candidate, especially if you want to work abroad in the European Union.

In addition, studying a foreign language can improve your ability to analyze and interpret information and help you succeed in many other subject areas. When you first begin learning German, your studies will focus mainly on reading, writing, grammar, listening, and speaking skills. Many people who study a foreign language claim that they gained a better understanding of English. German can even help you understand the origins of many English words and expand your own vocabulary in English. Then, when you travel to a German-speaking country, you'll be able to converse freely with the people you meet. You'll find that speaking to people in their native language is the best way to bridge any culture gap.

The German-Speaking World

The German language is spoken primarily in Germany, Austria, and Switzerland and holds official status in Belgium, Liechtenstein, Luxembourg, and the European Union. The United States has the largest German-speaking population outside of Europe. After English and Spanish, German is the third most commonly spoken language in over a dozen states in the nation. After Hispanics, German descendants are the largest ethnic group in the U.S., making up about one third of the German diaspora worldwide.

German culture has a broad historical past dating back more than two thousand years. From Goethe to Mozart and from Gutenberg to Einstein, German language and culture has influenced the spheres of arts and sciences. Today, the German-speaking population has major economic and political importance in the European Union and beyond.

How to Learn German

Start with the Basics

As with anything you want to learn, start with the basics and remember that learning takes time! The basics are vocabulary, grammar, and culture.

Vocabulary | Every new word you learn in German will expand your vocabulary and ability to communicate. The more words you know, the better you can express yourself. Focus on sounds and think about ways to remember words. Use your knowledge of English and other languages to figure out the meaning of and memorize words like **Wasser, Apfel, Buch, Karte,** and **Fisch.**

Grammar | Grammar helps you put your new vocabulary together. By learning the rules of grammar, you can use new words correctly and speak in complete sentences. As you learn verbs and tenses, you will be able to speak about the past, present, or future, express yourself with clarity, and be able to persuade others with your opinions. Pay attention to structures and use your knowledge of English grammar to make connections with German grammar.

Culture | Culture provides you with a framework for what you may say or do. As you learn about the culture of German-speaking communities, you'll improve your knowledge of German. Think about a word like **Kindergarten**, and how it relates to the level of education and who attends it. Think about and explore customs like **die Sternsinger** ("Star Singers" who dress up in costume on Epiphany) and how they are similar to celebrations with which you're familiar. Observe customs—watch people greet each other or say good-bye. Listen for idioms and sayings that capture the spirit of what you want to communicate.

Die Sternsinger in traditional costumes.

Listen, Speak, Read, and Write

Listening | Listen for sounds and for words you can recognize. Listen for inflections and watch for key words that signal a question such as **wie** (*how*), **wo** (*where*), or **was** (*what*). Get used to the sound of German. Play German pop songs or watch German movies. Borrow audiobooks from your local library. Don't worry if you don't understand every single word. If you focus on key words and phrases, you'll get the main idea. The more you listen, the more you'll understand!

Speaking | Practice speaking German as often as you can. As you talk, work on your pronunciation, and read aloud texts so that words and sentences flow more easily. Don't worry if you don't sound like a native speaker, or if you make some mistakes. Time and practice will help you get there. Participate actively in German class. Try to speak German with classmates, especially native speakers (if you know any), as often as you can.

Reading | Read the lyrics of a song as you listen to it, or read books you've already read in English translated into German. Use reading strategies that you know to understand the meaning of a text that looks unfamiliar. Look for cognates, or words that are related in English and German, to guess the meaning of some words. Read as often as you can, and remember to read for fun.

Writing | German has standardized and largely phonetic rules for spelling. You'll need to learn how to interpret the sounds of the German language, but once you do, you can become a proficient speller. Write for fun—make up poems or songs, write e-mails or instant messages to friends, or start a journal or blog in German.

Tips for Learning German

- Listen to German radio shows. Write down words that you can't recognize or don't know and look up the meaning.

- Watch German TV shows or movies. Read subtitles to help you grasp the content.

- Read German-language newspapers, magazines, or blogs.

- Listen to German songs that you like —anything from contemporary pop music to traditional **Volksmusik**. Sing along and concentrate on your pronunciation.

Beatrice Egli, Swiss pop singer

- Seek out German speakers. Look for cultural centers where German might be spoken in your community. Order from a menu at a Viennese restaurant in German.

- Pursue language exchange opportunities (**Schüleraustausch**) in your school or community. Join language clubs or cultural societies, and explore opportunities for studying abroad or hosting a student from a German-speaking country in your home or school.

- Connect your learning to everyday experiences. Research naming the ingredients of your favorite dish in German. Research the origins of German place names in the U.S., like Anaheim, California and Bismarck, North Dakota, or of common English words like *pretzel, hamster, pumpernickel, rucksack, waltz, dachshund, glitz,* and *strudel.*

- Use mnemonics, or a memorizing device, to help you remember words. Make up a saying in English to remember the order of the days of the week in German by using their abbreviations (Mo, Di, Mi, Do, Fr, Sa, So).

- Visualize words. Try to associate words with images to help you remember meanings. For example, think of different sorts of **Wurst** as you learn the names of different types of meat. Visualize a national park and create mental pictures of the landscape as you learn names of animals, plants, and habitats.

- Enjoy yourself! Try to have as much fun as you can learning German. Take your knowledge beyond the classroom and find ways to make the learning experience your own.

KOMMUNIKATIONSZIELE

I will be able to:

- Talk about celebrations
- Describe my home and living arrangements
- Talk about vacations and travel
- Discuss transportation and technology

1A.1   The *Perfekt* (Part 1)

- To form the Perfekt, use a present tense form of **haben** or **sein** with the *past participle* of the verb that expresses the action.

- Form the past participle of a *weak* verb by adding **ge-** before the verb stem and **-t** or **-et** after the stem.

Hast Du einen neuen Rucksack **gekauft?**   Er **hat** am Montag **gearbeitet?**

common strong verbs			
infinitive	past participle	infinitive	past participle
essen	ge**g**essen	schlafen	geschlafen
finden	gef**u**nden	schreiben	geschr**ie**ben
geben	ge**g**eben	sprechen	gesprochen
heißen	ge**h**eißen	tragen	getragen
helfen	ge**h**olfen	treffen	getroffen
lesen	ge**l**esen	trinken	getrunken
nehmen	ge**n**ommen	waschen	gewaschen

1A.2   Accusative pronouns

- An accusative pronoun replaces a noun that functions as a direct object.

Er ruft **seinen Freund** an. ⟶ Er ruft **ihn** an.

personal pronouns			
	nominative	accusative	dative
singular	ich du Sie er/sie/es	mich dich Sie ihn/sie/es	mir dir Ihnen ihm/ihr/ihm
plural	wir ihr Sie sie	uns euch Sie sie	uns euch Ihnen ihnen

1A.3   Dative pronouns

- Use dative pronouns in place of dative nouns to indicate to *whom* or *for whom* an action is done.

Das gefällt **mir** sehr gut.   Wir wollen **euch** die Stadt zeigen.

- In German, some verbs always take an object in the dative case.

danken folgen	gefallen (gefällt) gehören	glauben gratulieren	helfen passen

1 Die letzte Party
Ergänzen Sie die Sätze mit den richtigen Formen der Hilfsverben und der Partizipien.

1. Er ___hat___ Kekse ___gebacken___. (backen)
2. Ihr ___habt___ viel Cola ___getrunken___. (trinken)
3. Sie ___haben___ laute Musik ___gemacht___. (machen)
4. ___Hat___ er sie ___geküsst___? (küssen)
5. Du ___hast___ den Termin nicht ___gewusst___. (wissen)
6. Sicher ___habt___ ihr viel ___gelacht___. (lachen)

2 Feiertage
Was haben Sie an den letzten Feiertagen unternommen? Benutzen Sie das jeweils entsprechende Hilfsverb sowie die angegebenen Verben im Partizip um Ihre Erlebnisse wiederzugeben.

1. Wir ___haben___ (sein / haben) gemeinsam Eis ___gegessen___. (essen)
2. Ich ___habe___ (sein / haben) mit den Nachbarn ___gesprochen___. (sprechen)
3. Auf dem Geburtstag ___seid___ (sein / haben) ihr durch das ganze Zimmer ___gesprungen___? (springen)
4. Er ___hat___ (sein / haben) wieder nicht an den Jahrestag ___gedacht___. (denken)
5. Am Weihnachtsabend ___ist___ (sein / haben) sie auf dem Weg ___gestürzt___. (stürzen)
6. Du ___hast___ (sein / haben) die Tageszeitung ausführlich ___gelesen___. (lesen)

3 Eine super Silvesterparty
Sie haben Ihren Eltern von der Silvesterfeier in einem Restaurant erzählt. Beantworten Sie ihre Fragen unter Anwendung von Akkusativpronomen.

1. —Habt Ihr das Restaurant vorher besichtigt?
   —Ja, wir haben ___es___ (es) vorher besichtigt.
2. —Hat Heike das Essen geschmeckt?
   —Das müsst ihr ___sie___ (sie) selbst fragen.
3. —Haben sich alle verkleidet?
   —Ja, wir haben ___uns___ (wir) nur bunte Kleidung angezogen.
4. —Hast du deinen Bruder eingeladen?
   —Ich habe ___ihn___ (er) angerufen, aber er war nicht erreichbar.
5. —Wo wollt Ihr im nächsten Jahr feiern?
   —Wir möchten bei ___euch___ (ihr) feiern.
6. —Habt ihr die beliebte Eiscreme zum Nachtisch gegessen?
   —Nein, wir haben ___sie___ (sie) nicht gekostet, dafür aber die heiße Schokolade.
7. —Es sollen auch einige Life-Musiker aufgetreten sein. Stimmt das?
   —Na klar. Was wäre eine Party ohne ___sie___ (sie)?
8. —Wie hat dir die Feier insgesamt gefallen?
   —Super. Ich habe ___mich___ (ich) köstlich amüsiert.

4 Danke schön
Wählen Sie den richtigen Fall für die unterstrichenen Wörter: Nominativ (N), Akkusativ (A), oder Dativ (D).

1. ___D___ Ich danke euch für die Fotos von der Hochzeit.
2. ___A___ Tomke besucht dich am Wochenende, nicht wahr?
3. ___N___ Wir bringen Käse zur Party mit.
4. ___A___ Hast du sie zu Weihnachten besucht?
5. ___D___ Er hat ihr eine Blume gegeben.
6. ___D___ Das Geschenk ist von ihr.

5 Besuch steht an
Bald bekommen Sie Besuch von Freunden. Besprechen Sie Ihre Pläne hierfür unter Anwendung von Dativpronomen.

1. Wir wollen ___euch___ (ihr) das Viertel zeigen.
2. Ihr könntet mit ___uns___ (wir) ins Theater gehen.
3. Euer Besuch wird ___ihr___ (sie) sehr gefallen.
4. Wollt ihr mit ___uns___ (wir) Eis essen gehen?
5. Wenn die Sonne scheint, würde ich mit ___euch___ (ihr) baden gehen.
6. ___Mir___ (ich) ist es recht, dass ihr euren Nachbarn mitbringt.
7. Wir können ___ihm___ (er) das Sofa zum Schlafen anbieten.
8. Das passt ___euch___ (ihr) sicherlich gut in eure Pläne.

6 Dialog
Führen Sie ein Gespräch mit einem Freund über das letzte gefeierte Fest. Answers will vary.

BEISPIEL

S1: Hast du deinen Geburtstag mit der Familie gefeiert?
S2: Nein, ich habe ihn mit meiner Freundin verbracht. Sie hat mich überrascht.

7 Schreiben
Erzählen Sie von der letzten Party, auf der Sie gewesen sind, und schreiben Sie einen kleinen Bericht darüber. Was haben Sie gemacht? Mit wem haben Sie gesprochen? Was hatten Sie und Ihre Freunde an? Was gab es zu essen und zu trinken? Answers will vary.

1B.1   The *Perfekt* (Part 2)

- Certain types of verbs form the **Perfekt** with **sein**. They are all verbs that indicate a change of condition or location.

Seid ihr im Sommer viel **gereist**?   Vor zwei Jahren **ist** er in Frankfurt **gewesen**.

verbs that form the *Perfekt* with *sein*			
infinitive	past participle	infinitive	past participle
bleiben	geblieben	reisen	gereist
fahren	gefahren	sein	gewesen
fallen	gefallen	steigen (*to climb*)	gestiegen
gehen	gegangen	sterben (*to die*)	gestorben
kommen	gekommen	wachsen (*to grow*)	gewachsen
laufen	gelaufen	wandern	gewandert
passieren (*to happen*)	passiert	werden	geworden

1B.2   *Wissen* and *kennen*

wissen *and* kennen			
kenne	*I know*	kennen	*we know*
kennst	*you know*	kennt	*you know*
kennt	*he/she/it knows*	kennen	*you/they know*

- Use **wissen** to express the idea of *knowing a fact* or piece of information.

Michael **weiß** die Antwort nicht.   **Weißt** du, wo mein Badeanzug ist?

- In the **Perfekt**, both **kennen** and **wissen** are mixed verbs; their past participles end in **-t**, but their stems are irregular.

Ich **habe** ihn nicht gut **gekannt**.   Mein Opa **hat** viel über Kunst **gewusst**.

1B.3   Two-way prepositions

two-way prepositions					
an	*at, on*	in	*in, into*	unter	*under*
auf	*on, on top of*	neben	*next to*	vor	*in front of*
hinter	*behind*	über	*above, over*	zwischen	*between*

- If the verb indicates *movement toward* a destination, use an object in the accusative to follow a two-way preposition. If the verb does *not* indicate movement toward a destination, use an object in the dative case.

Ich **fahre** das Auto **in die** Garage.   Das Auto **ist in der** Garage.

- Here are some common contractions of two-way prepositions and definite articles.

ans   aufs   ins   am   im

1 Das Leben ist Veränderung
Beschreiben Sie verschiedene Veränderungen in Ihrem Leben unter Zuhilfenahme des Perfekts mit „sein" sowie der angegebenen Verben.

1. Ich __bin__ in Berlin zur Schule __gegangen__. (gehen)
2. Danach __sind__ mein Bruder und ich nach Wien __gezogen__. (ziehen)
3. Unsere Eltern __sind__ im Norden __geblieben__. (bleiben)
4. Ihr __seid__ zu Besuch __gewesen__. (sein)
5. Du __bist__ niemals nach New York __geflogen__ (fliegen)?
6. Sie __ist__ wieder zurück __gekommen__. (kommen)
7. __Ist__ der Kuchen schon __gegessen__? (essen)
8. Ihr __seid__ nicht viel __gelaufen__. (laufen)

2 Wissen ist Macht
George und Meline diskutieren über dies und das. Ergänzen Sie die folgenden Sätze mit dem Verb *wissen* in der korrekten Form.

Du **weißt** viel über Architektur.

1. Was __weißt__ du schon über Kunst?
2. Über deutsche Geschichte __weiß__ er viel von seinen Großeltern.
3. Man __weiß__ es nie genau.
4. Sie __wissen__ alles über die Gesetze des Landes.
5. __Wisst__ ihr, wie spät es ist?
6. Wir __wissen__ gar nichts über ihren Freund.
7. Ich __weiß__, ich kann das.
8. Wo die Toilette ist, __wissen__ sie nicht.

3 Bekanntschaften
Erzählen Sie von den Menschen in ihrer Umgebung. Benutzen Sie dazu die jeweils entsprechende Form des Verbes „kennen".

1. Meine Nachbarn __kenne__ ich gut.
2. __Kennt__ ihr den neuen Lehrer?
3. So __kennen__ wir ihn noch überhaupt nicht.
4. Michael __kennt__ Heike schon seit vielen Jahren.
5. Du __kennst__ den letzten Freund deiner Schwester nur wenig.
6. __Kennt__ er sie aus der Universität?
7. Es ist gut, wenn ich deine Freunde gut __kenne__.

4 Beim Einkaufen
Sie haben mit Freunden ein Einkaufszentrum besucht. Fügen Sie in die folgenden Sätze des Berichts jeweils *„wissen"* oder *„kennen"* im Perfekt ein.

1. Wir haben die Neuigkeiten __gekannt__.
2. Michaela hat ihre Kleidergröße nicht __gewusst__.
3. Es gab Stiefel im Angebot. Habt ihr das __gewusst__?
4. Gestreifte Handschuhe habe ich nie __gekannt__.
5. __Gewusst__ haben sie von der Sonnenbrille erst später.
6. Habt ihr von der Verkäuferin __gewusst__ oder sie __gekannt__?

5 Anziehen bitte!
Ergänzen Sie die Sätze mit den entsprechenden Wechselpräpositionen (*two-way prepositions*).

1. Der Hut kommt __auf__ den Kopf.
2. __Über__ den Pullover zieht Henri eine Jacke.
3. Nicole legt einen Handschuh __neben__ den anderen.
4. Die Schuhe stehen __vor__ der Wohnungstür.
5. __Zwischen__ den Kindern gibt es Streit um einen Turnschuh.
6. Julia versteckt sich __hinter__ dem aufgehängten Mantel.

6 Wo und wohin
Beantworten Sie die folgenden Fragen unter Einsatz der Verbindungen von Wechselpräpositionen und dem entsprechenden Objekt im Dativ oder Akkusativ.

1. Wo hängt mein Anzug? Er hängt __im / in dem__ Kleiderschrank.
2. Wohin hast du den Anzug gehängt? Ich habe ihn __ins / in das__ Zimmer gehängt.
3. Wohin habe ich nur meine Schuhe gestellt? Du hast sie __aufs / auf das__ Fensterbrett gestellt.
4. Wo steht mein zweiter Turnschuh? Er steht __am / an dem__ anderen Fenster.
5. Wo liegt meine Hose? Sie liegt __an / auf dem / am__ Boden.
6. Wo steht mein Koffer? Er steht __an / hinter / neben / vor der__ Tür.
7. Wo sind meine neuen Socken? Sie sind __hinterm / hinter dem__ Schrank.
8. Wohin hat sie meine Unterwäsche gelegt? Die Unterwäsche hat sie __ins / in das__ Regal gelegt.

7 Schreiben
Verfassen Sie einen Bericht im Perfekt über ein Ereignis, das eine bedeutende Veränderung in Ihrem Leben bewirkt hat. Was haben Sie vorher gewusst? Was wissen Sie danach besser? Wen kennen Sie seitdem? Wo befanden Sie sich zum Zeitpunkt des Geschehens? Wohin sind Sie danach gegangen? Answers will vary.

2A.1 The *Präteritum*

Präteritum of weak verbs			
	sagen	**wohnen**	**arbeiten**
ich	sag**te**	wohn**te**	arbeite**te**
du	sag**test**	wohn**test**	arbeite**test**
er/sie/es	sag**te**	wohn**te**	arbeite**te**
wir	sag**ten**	wohn**ten**	arbeite**ten**
ihr	sag**tet**	wohn**tet**	arbeite**tet**
Sie/sie	sag**ten**	wohn**ten**	arbeite**ten**

Die Kinder **spielten** in ihren Zimmern.   Ich **mietete** eine kleine Wohnung.

irregular verb stems in the *Präteritum*					
bleiben	blieb	helfen	half	sehen	sah
essen	aß	kommen	kam	sprechen	sprach
fahren	fuhr	lesen	las	sterben	starb
finden	fand	nehmen	nahm	tragen	trug
geben	gab	schlafen	schlief	trinken	trank
gehen	ging	schreiben	schrieb	verstehen	verstand

Wir **blieben** gestern zu Hause.   Sie **fuhren** nach Berlin.

- The verbs **sein**, **haben**, and **werden** do not follow the pattern of the other irregular verbs.

sein	**haben**	**werden**
ich war	ich hatte	ich wurde
du warst	du hattest	du wurdest
er/sie/es war	er/sie/es hatte	er/sie/es wurde
wir waren	wir hatten	wir wurden
ihr wart	ihr hattet	ihr wurdet
Sie/sie waren	Sie/sie hatten	Sie/sie wurden

Es **wurde** schnell dunkel.   Als Kinder **hatten** wir viele Haustiere.

2A.2 *Da-, wo-, hin-,* and *her-* compounds

- You learned to use personal pronouns to refer to the object of a preposition. When the object is a thing or an idea, use a **da-** compound instead.

Wo ist der Teddybär? Das Baby will **damit** spielen.

- Use **wen** or **wem** to ask about the object of a preposition when it refers to a person. When you ask about a thing or idea, use a **wo**-compound.

Womit spielen die Kinder?   **Woran** denkst du jetzt?

2A.3 Coordinating conjunctions

- The most common coordinating conjunctions are **aber**, **denn**, **oder**, **sondern**, and **und**.

Lola braucht einen Schrank **oder** eine Kommode für ihre Kleider.

1 Die alte Wohnung
Nach dem Umzug in das neue Haus erzählen Sie von Ihrer alten Wohnung im Erdgeschoss. Ergänzen Sie die folgenden Sätze unter Verwendung schwacher Verben im Präteritum.

1. Wir __wohnten__ (wohnen) dort über sechs Jahre.
2. Ich __arbeitete__ (arbeiten) von zu Hause aus.
3. Wer __sagte__ (sagen) den Besuch ab?
4. Sie __besuchten__ (besuchen) uns sehr oft.
5. Ihr __blicktet__ (blicken) durch das Fenster auf den Hof.
6. Sie __putzte__ (putzen) nur das Wohnzimmer.
7. Aber wer __wischte__ (wischen) Bad und Küche?
8. Jeden Tag __fegtest__ (fegen) du den Flur.

2 Einen Haushalt führen
Beschreiben Sie Ihren Kindern, wie früher der Haushalt geführt wurde. Benutzen Sie die angegebenen Verben in der korrekten Form des Präteritums.

1. Wir __sollten__ (sollen) immer beim Hausputz mithelfen.
2. Regelmäßig __wusch__ (waschen) ich meine eigenen Socken.
3. Den Müll __brachte__ (bringen) normalerweise meine Schwester nach draußen.
4. Unser Vater __half__ (helfen) nie beim Tischdecken.
5. Und wer __durfte__ (dürfen) sich um die Wäsche kümmern?
6. Da __kamt__ (kommen) ihr aber nur selten zum Spielen, oder?
7. Sie __wussten__ (wissen), wie man bügelt.
8. Das __gefiel__ (gefallen) uns Kindern nicht sehr gut.

3 Sein, werden und haben
Beschreiben Sie, was sie auf den Fotos sehen, und benutzen Sie dazu das Präteritum eines der drei Verben.

1. Die Blätter __hatten__ die gelbe Farbe angenommen.
2. Der Kellner kam. Das __wurde__ aber auch Zeit.

3. Auf dem Baum __war__ der Junge vor dem Hund sicher.
4. Herr Meier __hatte__ in der Metzgerei großen Hunger.

4 Unterhaltung
Ergänzen Sie die Sätze. Verwenden Sie in Ihren Antworten für das jeweilige Objekt der Präposition eines der Komposita da- oder wo-.

1. —Wo ist deine Wohnung?
   —Sie ist in Berlin, mitten __darin / drin__ (in).
2. —Gibt es neben deiner Wohnung eine Garage?
   —Nein, sie ist __darunter / drunter__ (unter).
3. —__Womit__ (mit) beschäftigst du dich den ganzen Tag?
   —Ich wasche Wäsche.
4. —Gab es in deiner alten Küche eine Mikrowelle?
   —__Daran__ (an) kann ich mich nicht erinnern.
5. —__Wofür__ (für) hast du einen Besen im Badezimmer?
   —__Damit__ (mit) ich fegen kann.
6. —__Wozu__ (zu) dient der Raum in der zweiten Etage?
   —Er ist da, um Gäste __darin / drin__ (in) unterzubringen.

5 Konjunktionen.
Verbinden Sie die angegebenen Teilsätze zu einem vollständigen Satz. Benutzen Sie dazu die korrekten Konjunktionen. Schreiben Sie ein Komma vor der Konjunktion wenn notwendig.

1. Klaus sucht ein Haus __und__ (und / oder) eine Garage in Hamburg.
2. Wir kochen sehr gern __, aber__ (aber / oder) wir waschen ungern das Geschirr.
3. Ich schlafe nie im Wohnzimmer __, sondern__ (denn / sondern) immer im Schlafzimmer.
4. Ihr streicht die Küche __, denn__ (und / denn) die Wände sind sehr schmutzig.
5. Seine Schwester hat einen braunen Sessel __und__ (denn / und) ein blaues Sofa im Wohnzimmer.
6. Ich liebe Schokolade __, aber__ (aber / denn) ich bin leider auf Diät.

6 Dialog
Führen Sie mit einem Freund ein Gespräch über die Wohnung Ihrer Träume. Verwenden Sie Konjunktionen, um Ihre Wünsche zu begründen. Answers will vary.

BEISPIEL

S1: *Was muss die Wohnung deiner Träume unbedingt haben?*
S2: *Ich brauche ein sehr großes Wohnzimmer, denn ich habe viele Möbel. Und du?*
S1: *Das Wichtigste ist nicht das Wohnzimmer, sondern ein Keller, damit ich mein Fahrrad abstellen kann.*

1. Was ist das Wichtigste für Sie?
2. Warum ist es wichtig?
3. Worauf könntest du gern verzichten?
4. Wie müsste das Badezimmer deiner Träume aussehen?
5. Wen würdest du in diese Wohnung einladen?
6. Mit wem würdest du in dieser Wohnung leben wollen?

2B.1 · *Perfekt versus Präteritum*

Most Germans use the **Präteritum** of **sein, haben**, and modal verbs rather than the **Perfekt**.

Meine alte Wohnung **war** ein Saustall.

Hattet ihr am Mittwoch keine Hausaufgaben?

- The **Perfekt** tense is most often used in conversation and in informal writing, such as e-mails, blog entries, personal letters, or diaries.

Habt ihr den Tisch **gedeckt**?
Nein, aber wir **haben** den Boden **gewischt**.

- The **Präteritum** is generally used in formal or literary writing, such as novels or newspaper articles, or in other formal contexts, such as news reports or speeches.

Es **war** einmal eine junge Frau mit dem Namen Aschenputtel.

- Here are the principal parts of some of the verbs you have learned.

infinitive	*Präteritum*	past participle
bringen	brachte	gebracht
denken	dachte	gedacht
essen (isst)	aß	gegessen
helfen (hilft)	half	geholfen
laufen (läuft)	lief	ist gelaufen
nehmen (nimmt)	nahm	genommen
schlafen (schläft)	schlief	geschlafen
sehen (sieht)	sah	gesehen
sitzen	saß	gesessen
verstehen	verstand	verstanden
waschen (wäscht)	wusch	gewaschen
wissen (weiß)	wusste	gewusst

2B.2 · Separable and inseparable prefix verbs in the Perfekt

Remind students that the Präteritum is also preferred by most speakers after the subordinating conjuction **als**.

Als wir Kinder **waren**, haben wir viel Hausarbeit gemacht.

Als ich die Garage **aufräumte**, habe ich viele alte Bücher gefunden.

- To form the past participle of a separable prefix verb, add the separable prefix to the past participle of the root verb, before the -**ge**- prefix.

infinitive	participle	infinitive	participle
anrufen	an**ge**rufen	rausbringen	raus**ge**bracht
aufräumen	auf**ge**räumt	umtauschen	um**ge**tauscht
ausgehen	(ist) aus**ge**gangen	umziehen	(ist) um**ge**zogen
einkaufen	ein**ge**kauft	vorstellen	vor**ge**stellt
mitbringen	mit**ge**bracht	wegräumen	weg**ge**räumt

Prefixed verbs that indicate a change in condition or location and do not take a direct object are conjugated with **sein**.

Wir **sind** mit unseren Großeltern in die Schweiz **mitgefahren**.

Wolfgang **ist** gestern Abend **ausgegangen**.

- The past participle of inseparable prefix verbs are formed like those of separable prefix verbs, but without the -**ge**- prefix.

infinitive	participle	infinitive	participle
bedeuten	**be**deutet	erklären	**er**klärt
beginnen	**be**gonnen	gehören	**ge**hört
besuchen	**be**sucht	verkaufen	**ver**kauft
bezahlen	**be**zahlt	verschmutzen	**ver**schmutzt
entdecken	**ent**deckt	verstehen	**ver**standen

1 Bilder beschreiben
Erzählen Sie einem Freund, welche Ereignisse die Bilder jeweils wiedergeben. Benutzen Sie das Perfekt als Ausdruck einer informellen Unterhaltung.

1. Hilde __hat__ mit Anna __telefoniert__.
2. Mein Fahrrad __hat__ im Flur __gestanden__.
3. Die Schuhe __haben__ ihm nicht __gepasst__.
4. Ich __habe__ mein Zimmer __gereinigt__.
5. Meine Schwester und ihre Freundin __haben__ an der Bar __gesessen__.
6. Ich glaube, sie __hat__ von mir __geträumt__.

2 Vergangenheit
Setzen Sie in den folgenden Sätzen das angegebene Verb konjugiert in die Lücke.

1. Wir __brachten__ (bringen) Claudia nach Hause, denn es war schon spät.
2. Was __schenkten__ (schenken) sie ihren Kindern im letzten Jahr zu Weihnachten?
3. Monika __wusch__ (waschen) ihrem Sohn die Füße.
4. Während du __schliefst__ (schlafen), regnete es heftig.
5. Sie __saß__ (sitzen) allein in der Küche.
6. Wie __hieß__ (heißen) der Held der Geschichte?
7. Ihr __fuhrt__ (fahren) in den Sonnenuntergang hinein.
8. Sie __deckten__ (decken) sämtliche Karten auf.

3 Wie war das noch?
Verwenden Sie Hilfs- oder Modalverben im Präteritum, um die Sätze zu vervollständigen.

1. Das __konnten__ (können) nur Freunde sein.
2. Nein, dazu __hatte__ (haben) ich noch keine Zeit.
3. Ihr __durftet__ (dürfen) nicht im Hof spielen.
4. Er __sollte__ (sollen) das vergessen.
5. Weiße Schokolade __mochte__ (möchten) er überhaupt nicht.
6. __Warst__ (sein) du schon mal in unserer neuen Wohnung?
7. Das Zimmer __musste__ (müssen) immer ordentlich sein.
8. Die Eltern __wollten__ (wollen) immer nur das Beste für ihren Sohn.

4 Was haben Sie gestern gemacht?
Vervollständigen Sie die Sätze mit dem Partizip der trennbaren Verben.

1. Ich habe das Geschirr __abgewaschen__. (abwaschen)
2. Sie haben die leeren Flaschen gemeinsam __heruntergebracht__. (herunterbringen)
3. Hast du das Geburtstagslied __mitgesungen__? (mitsingen)
4. Die Uhren haben wir heute früh alle __umgestellt__. (umstellen)
5. __Staub gesaugt / Gestaubsaugt__ (staubsaugen) hat sie nach der Feier erst heute Vormittag.
6. Seine Mutter hat ihn abends noch __zugedeckt__. (zudecken)
7. Seid ihr nicht gestern __umgezogen__? (umziehen)
8. Sie hatte es sich ganz anders __vorgestellt__. (vorstellen)

5 Dialog
Sprechen Sie mit einem anderen Studenten über die täglich notwendige Hausarbeit. Answers will vary.

BEISPIEL

S1: *Wie sieht es bei dir mit der Hausarbeit aus? Hast du viel zu tun?*
S2: *Bei uns in der Wohngemeinschaft sind sämtliche Arbeiten aufgeteilt. Ich wasche dreimal in der Woche das Geschirr ab. Und du?*
S1: *Ich wohne noch bei meinen Eltern. Geschirr spülen muss ich nicht, sondern nur mein Zimmer aufräumen.*
S2: *Schön für dich.*

6 Veränderungen mit *sein*
Formen Sie aus den gegebenen Wörtern Aussagen zu vollzogenen Änderungen.

1. ich / umziehen / nach München
   Ich bin nach München umgezogen.
2. aufstehen / 10 Uhr / gestern / ihr
   Ihr seid gestern um 10 Uhr aufgestanden.
3. uns / das Geld / ausgehen
   Uns ist das Geld ausgegangen.
4. losgehen / unsere Party / spät abends
   Spät abends ist unsere Party losgegangen.
5. krank werden / letzter Monat / Eva
   Eva ist letzten Monat krank geworden.
6. meine Eltern / vorgestern / wegfahren / für eine Woche
   Meine Eltern sind vorgestern für eine Woche weggefahren.
7. einschlafen / das Kind / gegen 19 Uhr
   Das Kind ist gegen 19 Uhr eingeschlafen.
8. das Flugzeug / vor kurzem / abfliegen
   Das Flugzeug ist vor kurzem abgeflogen.
9. mitfahren / wir / mit unseren Großeltern
   Wir sind mit unseren Großeltern mitgefahren.
10. Herbert und Bärbel / vor einem Jahr / umziehen
    Herbert und Bärbel sind vor einem Jahr umgezogen.

3A.1

Separable and inseparable prefix verbs (*Präteritum*)

- In the **Präteritum**, just like the **Präsens**, some prefixes are always attached to the verb, and others can be separated from it. When using a separable prefix verb in the **Präteritum**, move the prefix to the end of the sentence or clause.

> Jan **verbrachte** den Sommer in der Schweiz.
> Einmal **brachten** wir unseren Hund zur Schule **mit**.

- In a negative sentence, put **nicht** before the separable prefix.

> Ute **rief** mich gestern **nicht an**.
> Die Kinder **räumten** ihre Sachen **nicht auf**.

- The **Präteritum** of a verb with a prefix is the same as the **Präteritum** of its base verb.

- When you talk about past events using a modal and a verb with a prefix, put the modal verb in the **Präteritum**. The prefixed verb goes at the end of the sentence in the infinitive form.

> Frau Müller **musste** den kaputten Regenschirm **umtauschen**.
> Frank **wollte** sein altes Fahrrad **verkaufen**.

3A.2

Prepositions of location
Prepositions in set phrases

- Use two-way prepositions with the dative to indicate location and with the accusative to show movement toward a destination.

Verb phrases with the dative	Verb phrases with the accusative
Angst haben vor	antworten auf
arbeiten an	denken an
erzählen von	schreiben an
fragen nach	sprechen/reden über
handeln von	warten auf
helfen bei	

> Meine Nichte **hat Angst vor** Hunden.
> Wir haben lange **auf den Bus gewartet**.

> Der Autor Weiss **arbeitet an** einem neuen Buch.
> **Antworte** bitte **auf** die Frage.

- Use **auf** with the dative to indicate that something is located on a horizontal surface or to describe a location in a public building or open space.

> Deine Bücher liegen **auf dem Tisch**.

> Ich **war** gestern **auf der Bank**.

- Use **an** with the dative to indicate a location on or at a border, wall, or body of water.

> **An der Wand** hängt ein schöner Kalender.

- Use **in** with the dative to indicate a location on or in an enclosed space.

> Die Sonnenbrille ist **in meiner Handtasche**.

1 In den Süden

Erzählen Sie von Ihrem letzten Flug in den Urlaub. Füllen Sie die Lücken mit den entsprechenden trennbaren (*with a prefix*) Verben und achten Sie dabei auf eine mögliche Trennung von Verb und Präfix im Präteritum.

1. Unseren letzten Urlaub _verbrachten_ wir in Spanien. (verbringen)
2. Am Anfang _hob_ das Flugzeug fast ohne uns _ab_. (abheben)
3. Bevor wir an Bord gingen, _packte_ Heike noch ihren gesamten Rucksack _aus_ (auspacken).
4. Sie _erklärte_, dass sie den Pass nicht finden könne. (erklären)
5. Alle Leute _schauten_ sie fragend _an_. (anschauen)
6. Am Ende _fand_ sie jedoch _heraus_, wo er war. (herausfinden)
7. Sie _bedachte_ nicht, dass man sie nach dem Dokument fragen würde. (bedenken)
8. Am Ende _flogen_ wir wegen ihr verspätet _ab_, (abfliegen)

2 Schlechte Erlebnisse

Zählen Sie die Kontrapunkte Ihres letzten Sommerurlaubs auf. Verneinen Sie die angegebenen präfigierten Verben.

1. Das Wetter _spielte nicht mit_. (mitspielen)
2. Das Geschäft _tauschte_ den kaputten Badeanzug _nicht um_. (umtauschen)
3. Unser Flugzeug _flog nicht_ rechtzeitig _ab_. (abfliegen)
4. _Kauften_ Sie dem Händler seine Souvenirs _nicht ab_? (abkaufen)
5. Unsere Eltern _buchten_ das Hotel _nicht um_. (umbuchen)
6. Unser Gepäck _kam nicht_ mit uns zusammen _an_. (ankommen)
7. Die Sommerkleidung _hielt_ dem kalten und regnerischen Wetter _nicht stand_. (standhalten)
8. Wegen des Lärms auf der Straße _schlief_ ich abends _nicht ein_. (einschlafen)

3 Dialog

Sie sprechen mit einem Freund über das Wetter der letzten Tage. Setzen Sie Modalverben in Verbindung mit präfigierten Verben ein, um Ihren Standpunkt zu erläutern. Answers will vary.

BEISPIEL

S1: *Wir wollten übrigens neulich an den Strand fahren, aber es war zu kalt dafür.*
S2: *Stimmt. Man musste sich richtig warm anziehen.*
S1: *Vergangene Nacht konnte ich aber das Fenster offen lassen.*
S2: *Und ich musste die Heizung abschalten.*

4 Orte

Verwenden Sie den Dativ zur Angabe von festen Orten. Ergänzen Sie die folgenden Sätze mit den entsprechenden Präpositionen.

1. Die Ferien verbrachten wir _am_ Strand.
2. Der Badeanzug befindet sich _im_ Koffer.
3. Lagst du _in der_ Sonne?
4. Gleich _neben dem_ Hotel ist der Pool.
5. _Auf der_ anderen Straßenseite befindet sich eine Jugendherberge.
6. Ihre Pässe sind noch _auf dem_ Tisch im Zimmer.

5 Feste Formulierungen I

Bilden Sie Fragen mit den angegebenen Wörtern.

1. welcher / Fluss / liegen an / die Stadt
   An welchem Fluss liegt die Stadt?
2. wer / verbringen mit / ihr Ferien
   Mit wem verbringt ihr die Ferien?
3. suchen nach / du / dein Zimmer
   Wonach suchst du in deinem Zimmer?
4. erzählen von / seine Oma / viel / ihre Kindheit
   Erzählt seine Oma viel von ihrer Kindheit?

6 Feste Formulierungen II

Benutzen Sie die angegebenen Wörter und formen Sie Sätze.

1. mein Vater / schreiben an / Beschwerde / das Amt
   Mein Vater schreibt eine Beschwerde an das Amt.
2. unsere Freunde / warten auf / nicht lange / U-Bahn
   Unsere Freunde warten nicht lange auf die U-Bahn.
3. der Professor / sprechen über / mit uns / Klausur
   Der Professor sprach mit uns über die Klausur.
4. die Eltern / fahren in / im Urlaub / ein anderes Land
   Die Eltern fahren im Urlaub in ein anderes Land.

7 Schreiben.

Verfassen Sie einen Text über Ihren letzten Urlaub in einer großen Stadt. Erzählen Sie von den Sehenswürdigkeiten, die Sie besucht haben. Beschreiben Sie auch, wie Sie an diese Orte gekommen sind und was genau Sie dort gemacht haben. Answers will vary.

3B.1   Infinitive expressions and clauses

- When you use a non-modal verb with an infinitive clause, add the preposition **zu** before the infinitive.

> Ich hatte keine Zeit, Postkarten **zu schreiben**.
> Es macht viel Spaß **zu reisen!**

- When using a double verb expression like **spazieren gehen**, put the preposition **zu** between the two verbs.

> Die Kinder haben Angst, **schwimmen zu gehen**.
> Es ist uns zu teuer, jeden Abend **essen zu gehen**.

- Infinitive constructions with **zu** often occur after the verbs **anfangen, beginnen, vergessen, helfen,** and **finden**; the expressions **Lust haben, Angst haben,** and **Spaß machen**; and adjectives like **einfach, wichtig,** and **schön**.

- The expressions **um... zu, ohne... zu,** and **anstatt... zu** are frequently used in infinitive clauses.

3B.2   Time expressions

- German has two main concepts related to expressions of time. **Zeit** describes a span of time, while **Mal** refers to specific occurrences and repetitions.

> Ich habe noch **50 Minuten Zeit** vor meinem Flug.
> Ich war nur **einmal** in Hamburg.

diesmal	*this time*	manchmal	*sometimes*
das erste Mal	*the first time*	niemals	*never*
einmal	*once*	zum ersten/letzten Mal	*for the first/last time*

- Use the accusative case to talk about a particular span of time or point in time.

> Die Kreuzfahrt dauerte **einen Monat**.
> **Nächsten Sommer** fahren wir an den Strand.

- Use the present tense with **seit** plus a dative time expression or **schon** plus an accusative time expression to indicate how long something has been going on.

> **Seit einem Monat** wohnt Patrick in Frankfurt.
> Er studiert **schon zwei Jahre** in Deutschland.

- Use the dative case with the time expressions **am, in,** and **vor**.

> **Vor einem Jahr** studierte ich im Ausland.
> Mein Geburtstag ist **am 18. Februar**.

3B.3   Indefinite pronouns

- Two indefinite pronouns that refer to people are **jemand** and **niemand**. Use the ending **-en** for the accusative case and **-em** for the dative.

- To talk about indefinite things, use **alles, etwas,** or **nichts**.

- Use the pronoun **man** to talk about people in general.

1 Mit und ohne *zu*

Bilden Sie mit den angegebenen Wörtern und mithilfe von Modal- und anderen Verben Infinitiv-Sätze. Benutzen Sie die Präposition **zu** dort, wo es angebracht ist, und achten Sie auf mögliche Kommas.

1. dürfen / wir / langsam / laufen / nur
   Wir dürfen nur langsam laufen.

2. Spaß machen / es / liegen / am Strand
   Es macht Spaß, am Strand zu liegen.

3. er / sollen / besuchen / seine Oma
   Er soll seine Oma besuchen.

4. Geld haben / kein / schlecht sein / es
   Es ist schlecht, kein Geld zu haben.

5. Hausaufgaben / machen/ müssen / ihr
   Ihr müsst Hausaufgaben machen.

6. Sie / erreichen / das gesetzte Ziel / können
   Sie können das gesetzte Ziel erreichen.

2 Infinitive mit *zu*

Verbinden Sie die unterstrichenen Verben und Verbkombinationen mit den restlichen Wörtern zu Fragen.

1. Spazieren gehen / Schön sein / finden / du
   Findest du es schön, spazieren zu gehen?

2. Spaß haben / Kinderzimmer / aufräumen / er
   Hatte er Spaß, sein Kinderzimmer aufzuräumen?

3. Lust haben / essen gehen / Ihr / heute Abend
   Habt ihr Lust, heute Abend essen zu gehen?

4. Hinbringen / wichtig sein / sie/ Kindergarten
   Ist es wichtig, sie zum Kindergarten hinzubringen?

5. Oma / anrufen / vergessen/ dürfen / nie / er
   Darf er niemals vergessen, seine Oma anzurufen?

6. Ball spielen / Eva / Müll / rausbringen / anstatt
   Spielt Eva Ball, anstatt den Müll rauszubringen?

3 Wann war das noch genau?

Genaue Zeitangaben verlangen besondere Zeitausdrücke. Vervollständigen Sie diese kurze Erzählung entsprechend.

____Vor____ einem halben Jahr im Winterurlaub hatte ich ein besonderes Erlebnis. Es war ___am___ 14. Februar, als wir den Valentinstag feierten. ___Zuerst___ luden wir unsere neuen Freunde ein, die wir ___während___ des Skifahrens kennen gelernt hatten. Es kamen immer mehr Leute, aber ___zuletzt___ auch ein nettes Mädchen. Wir nahmen uns eine Cola, setzten uns auf die Terrasse und ___manchmal___ unterhielten wir uns. Leider war der Urlaub rasch vorüber, und wir verloren uns ___danach___ aus den Augen. Nächste Woche treffe ich sie aber nun ___endlich___ wieder.

4 Wohnen in Deutschland.

Bilden Sie Sätze mit den folgenden Wörtern. Setzen Sie „seit" oder „schon" ein, so dass ein Zeitaussage im jeweils angegebenen Fall entsteht.

1. wir / ein halbes Jahr / wohnen / Frankfurt (Dativ)
   Seit einem halben Jahr wohnen wir in Frankfurt.

2. vor zwei Wochen / kommen / nach Bayern (Akkusativ)
   Schon vor zwei Wochen kam er nach Bayern.

3. in Berlin / leben / ich / sein / 5 Jahre alt (Dativ)
   In Berlin lebe ich, seit ich 5 Jahre alt war.

4. umziehen / fünfmal / sein / Susi / in Deutschland (Akkusativ)
   In Deutschland ist Susi schon fünfmal umgezogen.

5 Was ist passiert?

Antworten Sie auf die Fragen unter Zuhilfenahme eines der unbestimmten Pronomen „jemand", „niemand", „alles", „etwas" oder „nichts".

1. Was ist denn im Hotel passiert, Harald? Ich glaube, ___etwas___ sehr Schlimmes.
2. Waren noch Menschen am Strand? Da es spät und kalt war, ___niemand___ mehr.
3. Wem gehört dieser Liegestuhl? Er gehört ___jemand___ anderem.
4. Wie war denn eure Sommerparty gestern Abend? Ach, es war ___nichts___ Besonderes.
5. Hattet ihr im Urlaub jeden Tag gutes Wetter? Man kann nicht ___alles___ haben.
6. Ihr habt also wirklich im Sommer an eurem Haus gebaut? Irgend ___etwas___ mussten wir ja machen.

6 Dialog.

Im Urlaub unterhalten Sie sich mit einem Freund über einen Vorfall im Hotel. Versuchen Sie, Einzelheiten von ihm zu erfahren. Setzen Sie unbestimmte Pronomen ein. Answers will vary.

BEISPIEL

S1: *Gestern ist dem Gast aus Zimmer Nr. 143 alles gestohlen worden. Weißt du das schon?*

S2: *Ja, ich habe etwas gehört.*

S1: *Ich hätte nicht gedacht, dass jemand so etwas tun würde, und du?*

7 Text.

Schreiben Sie eine kurze allgemeine Empfehlung für einen Sommerurlaub. Benutzen Sie das unbestimmte Pronomen „man" um zu erklären, wohin die Leser Ihres Schreibens verreisen sollten, was sie sich ansehen können und was Sie Besonderes beachten müssen. Strukturieren Sie Ihren Text auch mit den in dieser Lektion gelernten Zeitangaben. Answers will vary.

4A.1 | ## *Das Plusquamperfekt*

- To form the **Plusquamperfekt**, use the **Präteritum** form of **haben** or **sein** with the past participle of the verb that expresses the action.

  Ich **hatte vergessen**, die Tür zu schließen.
  Jasmin **war** noch nicht nach Zürich **gefahren**.

- Use the subordinating conjunctions **als**, **bevor**, and **nachdem** to indicate the sequence in which two past events occurred.

  Als Jan ins Restaurant **kam**, **hatte** seine Freundin schon **bestellt**.
  Unsere Eltern kamen spät nach Hause, **nachdem** wir schon ins Bett **gegangen waren**.

- Since the **Plusquamperfekt** refers to a past event that was completed prior to another past event, both events are often described in the same sentence.

  Bevor Stefan in die Stadt **zog**, **hatte** er nie öffentliche Verkehrsmittel **benutzt**.

  Wir **hatten** über Kunst **geredet** und danach **verstand** ich die Gemälde besser.

- If the clause with **bevor**, **nachdem**, or **als** is first in the sentence, the main clause after the comma begins with the verb. If that verb is in the **Plusquamperfekt** or **Perfekt**, the helping verb is first and the past participle at the end.

  Als wir am Flughafen **ankamen**, **war das Flugzeug** schon **abgeflogen**.

  Das Flugzeug **war** schon **abgeflogen**, als wir am Flughafen **ankamen**.

4A.2 | ## Comparatives and superlatives

- When describing similarities between two people or things, use the expression **so... wie** or **genauso... wie** with the Grundform of an adjective or adverb.

  Dieser LKW ist **so groß wie** ein Bus.
  Der Zug fährt **genauso schnell wie** ein Auto.

- To describe differences between two people or things, you can use the expression **nicht so ... wie**, or you can use the **Komparativ**. Form the **Komparativ** by adding the ending **-er** to the Grundform of an adjective or adverb, followed by the word **als**.

  Inga fährt **nicht so langsam wie** Sara.
  Sara fährt **langsamer als** Inga.

GRUNDFORM	KOMPARATIV	SUPERLATIV
gern	lieber	liebst-
groß	größer	größt-
gut	besser	best-
hoch	höher	höchst-
viel	mehr	meist-

- A small number of adjectives and adverbs have irregular comparative forms. When a comparative adjective precedes a noun, the appropriate case ending after the **-er** ending should be used.

  Ich fahre **lieber** mit der U-Bahn als mit dem Bus.

  Benzin kostet in Deutschland **mehr** als in den USA.

1 Mit öffentlichen Verkehrsmitteln Bilden Sie mit den gegebenen Wörtern Sätze im Plusquamperfekt. Verwenden Sie die Hilfsverben „haben" oder „sein".

1. ich / benutzen / die U-Bahn / Berlin / immer
   Ich hatte in Berlin immer die U-Bahn benutzt.

2. Harald / sagen / damals / das Auto / bevorzugen
   Harald sagte, er hatte damals das Auto bevorzugt.

3. ihr / fahren / Bus / ohne Fahrschein
   Ihr wart ohne Fahrschein Bus gefahren.

4. vor 20 Jahren / öffentliche Nahverkehr (*local traffic*) / Deutschland / billig sein
   Vor 20 Jahren war der öffentliche Nahverkehr in Deutschland billig gewesen.

5. der Zug / warten / sie / zu spät kommen
   Der Zug, auf den sie warteten, war zu spät gekommen.

2 Viel Verkehr Verbinden Sie zwei vergangene Ereignisse mithilfe einer der Konjunktionen „als", „bevor", „da", „obwohl" oder „nachdem" zu einem Satz.

1. Gerhard zog auf das Land. / Er benutzte immer Bus und Bahn.
   Bevor Gerhard auf das Land zog, hatte er immer Bus und Bahn benutzt.

2. Wir standen an der Haltestelle. / Der Bus kam.
   Wir hatten an der Haltestelle gestanden, als der Bus kam.

3. Ihr kamt am Bahnhof an. / Die S-Bahn fuhr schon ab.
   Als ihr am Bahnhof ankamt, war die S-Bahn schon abgefahren.

4. Er begann zu studieren. / Niemals mehr fuhr er Auto.
   Nachdem er begonnen hatte zu studieren, fuhr er niemals mehr Auto.

5. Wir kauften eine Fahrkarte. / Wir durften mit dem Zug fahren.
   Da wir eine Fahrkarte gekauft hatten, durften wir mit dem Zug fahren.

3 Lückentext Ergänzen Sie den folgenden Text mit Verben im Plusquamperfekt.

(1.) Vor drei Jahren __bin__ ich nach Hamburg __umgezogen__ (umziehen). (2.) Seitdem ich hier wohnte, __hatte__ ich stets die öffentlichen Verkehrsmittel __benutzt__ (benutzen). (3.) Da jedoch mein neues Büro außerhalb der Stadt lag, __war__ ich __gezwungen__ (zwingen), mir etwas Neues einfallen zu lassen. (4.) Ein Auto war für mich nicht erschwinglich, da ich bisher noch nicht ausreichend __gespart__ __hatte__ (sparen). (5.) Obwohl mir ein gutes Angebot vorlag, __hatte__ ich mich dagegen __entschieden__ (entscheiden). (6.) Als ich noch an der Universität studierte, __war__ ich Mitglied bei den Grünen __geworden__ (werden). (7.) Jetzt war es an mir zu beweisen, dass mich die damalige Entscheidung __geprägt__ __hatte__ (prägen). (8.) Obwohl der Weg zu meinem neuen Job weit war, __hatte__ ich mir eine Monatskarte für den öffentlichen Nahverkehr __gekauft__ (kaufen). Man musste doch etwas für die Umwelt tun.

4 Fotos Bilden Sie zu jedem Bild einen entsprechenden Satz im Plusquamperfekt.

1. Obwohl sich das Pärchen __gestritten hatte__ (sich streiten), liebte es sich noch immer.
2. Da sie lange __gefeiert hatte__ (feiern), tat der jungen Frau nun der Kopf weh.
3. Da er über einen spitzen Stein __gefahren war__ (fahren), hatte er nun einen platten Reifen.
4. Nachdem sie den ganzen Tag über __gewandert waren__ (wandern), verbrachten sie den Abend am Lagerfeuer.
5. Seitdem man bei ihrem Hund Flöhe __festgestellt hatte__ (feststellen), wuschen sie ihn täglich.
6. Obwohl der Herr laut __gesungen hatte__ (singen), bekam er keinen Applaus.

5 Das Beste Komplettieren Sie die Sätze mit den korrekten Formen der angegeben Adjektive. Geben Sie jeweils an, ob es sich um einen Komparativ oder um einen Superlativ handelt.

1. Dieser Weg ist der __kürzeste__ (kurz) den ich kenne.
   Superlativ
2. __Einfacher__ (einfach) als mit der U-Bahn wirst du nicht hinkommen. *Komparativ*
3. Mein eigenes Auto ist mir das __liebste__ (lieb).
   Superlativ
4. Der __angenehmste__ (angenehm) Platz im Zug ist am Fenster.
   Superlativ
5. Das dichte Netz von Bussen und Bahnen ist das __beste__ (gut) an der Stadt. *Superlativ*.

6 Dialog Unterhalten Sie sich mit einem anderen Studenten über die Vor- und Nachteile des Autos gegenüber den öffentlichen Verkehrsmitteln. Benutzen Sie Komparativ und Superlativ.. Answers will vary.

BEISPIEL

S1: *Ich finde den öffentlichen Nahverkehr besser als das Auto. Was meinst du dazu?*
S2: *Naja, das Auto ist am angenehmsten.*

4B.1 The genitive case

articles	masculine	feminine	neuter	plural
dative	dem Drucker einem Drucker	der Festplatte einer Festplatte	dem Handy einem Handy	den E-Mails keinen E-Mails
genitive	des Druckers eines Druckers	der Festplatte einer Festplatte	des Handys eines Handys	der E-Mails keiner E-Mails

Was ist der Preis **der Spielkonsole**?
Ich kann die Telefonnummer **meiner Schwester** nicht finden.

- In the genitive case, an adjective *preceded by* an **ein**-word or a **der**-word always ends in **-en**. *Unpreceded* adjectives in the genitive case have the endings: **-en**, **-er**, **-en**, and **-er**.

  Ich mag das Aroma **schwarzen Kaffees**.   Mögen Sie den Geschmack **grüner Paprikas**?

- Use the genitive question word **wessen** to ask *whose*?

  Wessen Telefon klingelt?   Ich glaube, es ist **Josefs** Handy.

prepositions with the genitive			
(an)statt	*instead of*	trotz	*despite, in spite of*
außerhalb	*outside of*	während	*during*
innerhalb	*inside of, within*	wegen	*because of*

4B.2 Demonstratives

demonstrative pronouns	masculine	feminine	neuter	plural
nominative	der	die	das	die
accusative	den	die	das	die
dative	dem	der	dem	denen
genitive	dessen	deren	dessen	deren

- **Der**-words include the demonstrative adjectives **dieser**, **jeder**, **mancher**, and **solcher**, as well as the question word **welcher**.

- The chart below shows only **dieser**, but all the other **der**-words have the same endings.

der-words	masculine	feminine	neuter	plural
nominative	dieser Mann	diese Frau	dieses Kind	diese Kinder
accusative	diesen Mann	diese Frau	dieses Kind	diese Kinder
dative	diesem Mann	dieser Frau	diesem Kind	diesen Kindern
genitive	dieses Mannes	dieser Frau	dieses Kindes	dieser Kinder

1 Unsere technischen Geräte

Vervollständigen Sie die Sätze, indem Sie die angegebenen Substantive im Genitiv einfügen.

1. Wie hoch ist der Stromverbrauch _der Waschmaschine_ (die Waschmaschine)?
2. Ich kann die Fernbedienung _des Fernsehers_ (der Fernseher) nicht finden.
3. Leider ist mir die Nummer _des Faxgerätes_ (das Faxgerät) nicht bekannt.
4. Die maximale Lautstärke _der Stereoanlage_ (die Stereoanlage) ist immens.
5. Das Handy befindet sich im Kofferraum _des Autos_ (das Auto).
6. Beim Umzug ging die Tastatur _des Computers_ (der Computer) verloren.

2 Wessen Gerät ist das?

Sehen Sie sich die Bilder an und antworten Sie auf die Fragen.

1. Wessen neues Handy ist das? (Harald)
   Das ist Haralds neues Handy.
2. Wessen Kopfhörer hängen am Haken? (Heike)
   Heikes Kopfhörer hängen am Haken.
3. Wessen Camcorder ist zu verkaufen? (meine Schwester)
   Der Camcorder meiner Schwester ist zu verkaufen.
4. Wessen Computers Tastatur ist kaputt? (Karla)
   Die Tastatur von Karlas Computer ist kaputt.
5. Wessen Notebook ist geöffnet? (James)
   James' Notebook ist geöffnet.
6. Wessen Fernseher ist den ganzen Tag eingeschaltet? (Mutter)
   Mutters Fernseher ist den ganzen Tag eingeschaltet.

3 Schreiben

Verfassen Sie einen Text über die technischen Geräte, die sich in Ihrer Wohnung befinden. Erklären Sie, was die einzelnen Apparate machen, ob sie funktionieren oder irgendwelche Besonderheiten haben. Stellen Sie verschiedene Geräte einander gegenüber und vergleichen Sie die Häufigkeit deren Nutzung, ihr Funktionieren sowie das Design.

4 Genüsse

Bilden Sie Sätze, indem Sie das angegebene Adjektiv und sein Bezugssubstantiv im Genitiv einsetzen. Geben Sie jeweils die Möglichkeit mit und ohne Einsatz eines **ein**-Wortes oder **der**-Wortes an.

1. ich / mögen / Geschmack / grüner Tee.
   Ich mag den Geschmack eines / des grünen Tees.
   Ich mag den Geschmack grünen Tees.
2. wir / lieben / der Duft (*smell*) / frisch Gras
   Wir lieben den Duft eines / des frischen Grases.
   Wir lieben den Duft frischen Grases.
3. du / fürchten / die Kraft / starke Winde
   Du fürchtest die Kraft der starken Winde.
   Du fürchtest die Kraft starker Winde.
4. ihr / erwarten / die Wirkung / sanfte Massage / auf dem Rücken
   Ihr erwartet die Wirkung einer / der sanften Massage auf dem Rücken.
   Ihr erwartet die Wirkung sanfter Massage auf dem Rücken.
5. ich / brauchen / Harmonie / die absolute Ruhe (*calm*)
   Ich brauche die Harmonie einer / der absoluten Ruhe.
   Ich brauche die Harmonie absoluter Ruhe.

5 Genitiv-Präpositionen

Wählen Sie die passenden Präpositionen.

1. Wir stehen (außerhalb / trotz) der Gruppe.
2. Deutschland befindet sich (während / innerhalb) Europas.
3. (Trotz / Innerhalb) des guten Wetters blieb sie zu Hause.
4. (Wegen / Innerhalb) der guten Noten bekommst du ein Lob.
5. (Trotz / Innerhalb) des Ladens ist das Essen verboten.

6 Dialog I

Führen Sie ein Gespräch mit einem anderen Schüler. Benutzen Sie die Demonstrativ-Pronomen „dieser", „jeder", mancher", „solcher" oder „welcher", um auf die Besonderheiten der Autos dritter Personen einzugehen. Answers will vary.

BEISPIEL

S1: Es gibt jene, die ihr Auto pflegen, und es gibt solche, denen deren gutes Aussehen nichts bedeutet.
S2: Diese Windschutzscheibe hier ist zum Beispiel voller Schmutz. Das muss jeder säubern.
S1: Das hängt aber vom Wetter ab. Welches Auto wird denn bei Regen nicht nass?
S2: Dann soll eben jeder sein Auto behandeln, wie er will.

1. Wem gehört das alte Auto dort?
2. Welches Auto ist denn eigentlich [Heikos]?
3. Wer braucht täglich ein Auto?
4. Wen nahm [Christina] im Auto mit?

7 Freizeit Wählen Sie das korrekte Demonstrativ-Pronomen, um den Antworten auf die Fragen Sinn zu geben.

1. Kennen Sie schon das neueste Betriebssystem? Ja, ___das___ kenne ich schon seit letzter Woche.
2. Werden gebrauchte Handys zurückgenommen? Nein, denn ___deren___ Batterie ist nicht mehr leistungsfähig.
3. Welcher ist der richtige Knopf zum Anschalten des Fernsehers? ___Jener___ da.
4. Was machen die Kinder in ihrer Freizeit? So ___mancher___ Junge spielt nur mit der Konsole.
5. Was für eine Digitalkamera willst du dir denn kaufen? Ich denke, ___diese___ hier.
6. Wissen Sie, wer der beste Mechaniker in dieser Werkstatt ist? Ja, es ist ___der___, der am Fenster steht.
7. Nimmst du deinen Laptop mit auf die Reise? Natürlich, ___den___ brauche ich ja dringend zum Arbeiten.
8. Haben Sie die Kamera auf dem Markt gekauft? Niemals, ___solchen___ Leuten kann man nicht vertrauen.

8 Dialog II Führen Sie ein Gespräch mit einem Freund. Bilden Sie Antworten mithilfe von Demonstrativ-Pronomen. Verwenden Sie in Ihren Antworten die Adjektive aus der Liste. Bei Fragen und Antworten sollten Sie sich abwechseln.

BEISPIEL

S1: *Was denkst du über die E-Mail vom Chef?*
S2: *Die finde ich schrecklich.*

Wählen Sie aus den folgenden Adjektiven Ihre jeweiligen Antworten.

schrecklich	lächerlich
beunruhigend	immens
super	unüberschaubar
sehr interessant	einzigartig

Was denkst du über: Answers will vary.

1. ...das letzte Programm im Fernsehen?
2. ...das kostenlose Herunterladen von Filmen oder Musik?
3. ...den Preis der neuen Konsole?
4. ...die Bedienungsanleitung des Fernsehers?
5. ...das stundenlange Surfen im Internet?
6. ...die vielen notwendigen Passwörter?
7. ...den Spruch auf dem Anrufbeantworter?
8. ...die erhaltene Nachricht?

9 Besuchsvorbereitung Vor dem Besuch der Freunde müssen noch ein paar Einzelheiten geklärt werden. Tun Sie dies mithilfe der korrekten Pronomen und geben Sie an, ob diese dem Dativ oder dem Akkusativ entsprechen.

1. Der Hund— (Dativ) / Akkusativ
   Müsst ihr ___ihm___ (er) unbedingt diese Reise antun?
2. Die Geburtstagsparty— (Dativ) / Akkusativ
   Ihr könnt ___mir___ (ich) bei ihrer Vorbereitung helfen.
3. Essen und Trinken—Dativ / (Akkusativ)
   Sollen wir zum Abendessen etwas Besonderes für ___ihn___ (er) vorbereiten?
4. Geschenke—Dativ / (Akkusativ)
   ___Mich___ (ich) dürft ihr gern überraschen.
5. Die Ankunftszeit— (Dativ) / Akkusativ
   Bitte schreibt ___ihr___ (sie) eine E-Mail dazu.
6. Ein paar freie Tage— (Dativ) / Akkusativ
   Ich werde sie ___mir___ (ich) nehmen.
7. Gegenbesuch—Dativ / (Akkusativ)
   Mit Vergnügen besuchen wir ___euch___ (ihr) demnächst auch.
8. Tagesplan— (Dativ) / Akkusativ
   Wir haben Euer Wochenende mit ___uns___ (wir) komplett verplant.

10 Noch mehr Fragen Die folgenden Aussagen korrespondieren mit den entsprechenden Bildern. Formen Sie dazugehörige Fragen unter Anwendung des Kompositums mit wo-, jedoch getrennt von „hin" oder „her".

1. Das Paar kommt aus dem Theater. ___Wo___ kommt das Paar ___her___?

2. Maria und ihr Freund waren im Restaurant essen. ___Wo___ fuhren sie ___hin___?

3. Peter kommt gerade nach Hause. ___Wo___ kommt Peter so spät noch ___her___?

4. Die Frau im schwarzen Kleid rutschte aus. ___Wo___ führte die Eisglätte ___hin___?

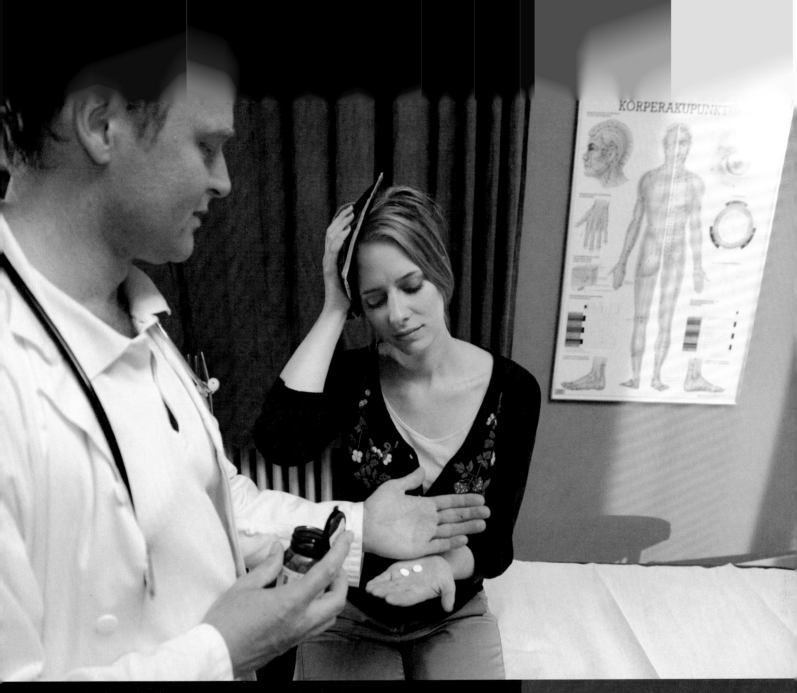

KÖRPERAKUPUNKTUR

Suggestion Ask students: **Wo ist Meline? Warum ist sie da? Wer ist der Mann neben ihr? Was macht er?**

Teaching Tip Look for icons indicating activities that address the modes of communication. Follow this key:

→⌂←	Interpretive communication
←⌂→	Presentational communication
⌂↔⌂	Interpersonal communication

Communicative Goals

You will learn how to:

- talk about morning routines
- discuss personal hygiene

Die Alltagsroutine

Vocabulary Tools

AP* Theme: Contemporary Life
Context: Health & Well-Being

Wortschatz

im Badezimmer	*in the bathroom*
der Haartrockner, -	*hair dryer*
das Shampoo, -s	*shampoo*
der Körper, -	***body***
die Augenbraue, -n	*eyebrow*
der Bart, ⁻e	*beard*
das Gesicht, -er	*face*
das Haar, -e	*hair*
die Hand, ⁻e	*hand*
die Lippe, -n	*lip*
der Rücken, -	*back*
die Schulter, -n	*shoulder*
Verben	***verbs***
aufwachen (wacht...auf)	*to wake up*
(sich) duschen	*to take a shower*
ins Bett gehen	*to go to bed*
sich anziehen (zieht sich...an)	*to get dressed*
sich die Haare bürsten	*to brush one's hair*
sich die Zähne putzen	*to brush one's teeth*

ACHTUNG

The pronoun **sich** is used with reflexive verbs. You will learn more about reflexive verbs in the **Strukturen** for this lesson.

Suggestion Remind students that they learned to use the verb **anziehen** without a reflexive pronoun in 5B. Ex.: **Ich ziehe das Hemd an. Er zieht die Jacke an.**

Er rasiert sich.
(sich rasieren)

Sie schminkt sich.
(sich schminken)

das Handtuch, ⁻er

der Lippenstift, -e

die Bürste, -n

der Rasierer, -

der Kamm, ⁻e

die Seife, -n

die Zahnbürste, -n

die Zahnpasta

der Rasierschaum, ⁻e

der Hausschuh, -e

der Bademantel, ⁻

Anwendung

1 Was passt nicht? Welches Wort passt nicht zu den anderen?

BEISPIEL Bart, Mund, Lippe, (Rücken)

1 Expansion Ask students to explain why each word doesn't belong.

1. Ohr, (Bauch), Auge, Nase
2. Zahnbürste, Mundwasser, (Mineralwasser), Zahnpasta
3. (Handtuch), Schlafanzug, Nachthemd, Bademantel
4. duschen, schminken, rasieren, (anziehen)
5. Shampoo, Seife, (Haar), Duschgel
6. (Gesicht), Lippenstift, Mascara, Make-up
7. Haartrockner, (Rasierer), Bürste, Kamm
8. Bein, Fuß, Zeh, (Schulter)

2 Bild beschriften Wie heißen die verschiedenen Körperteile (*parts of the body*)?

Suggestion Tell students that the variants **Ellbogen** and **Ellenbogen** are used interchangeably to refer to the elbow.

1. ___der Kopf___   5. ___der Rücken___
2. ___der Mund___   6. ___das Bein___
3. ___die Schulter___ 7. ___das Knie___
4. ___die Hand___   8. ___der Fuß___

3 Paulas Morgenroutine Hören Sie sich an, was Paula über ihre Morgenroutine erzählt. Bringen Sie danach ihre morgendlichen Aktivitäten in die richtige Reihenfolge.

1. __2__ Ich dusche mich.
2. __5__ Ich ziehe mich an.
3. __4__ Ich schminke mich.
4. __1__ Ich frühstücke.
5. __3__ Ich putze mir die Zähne.

3 Expansion Have students put the items in order according to their own morning routines.

Suggestion Call out the names of various body parts and have students point to each body part. Then move to "active recall" by pointing to a body part and asking: **Was ist das?**

der Kopf, ¨e
die Nase, -n
das Auge, -n
der Mund, ¨er
das Ohr, -en
der Hals, ¨e
der Arm, -e
der Finger, -
der Ell(en)bogen, -
der Bauch, ¨e
der Schlafanzug, ¨e
das Bein, -e
das Knie, -
der Fuß, ¨e
der Zeh, -en

4 Was haben wir? Fragen Sie Ihren Partner / Ihre Partnerin, welche Badezimmer- und Kosmetikartikel er/sie besitzt und wie viele davon er/sie hat. Answers will vary.

▶ **BEISPIEL**
S1: Hast du einen Spiegel?
S2: Ja, ich habe einen. Wie viele Spiegel hast du?

4 Suggestion Quickly review the plural form of each noun by asking: **Was ist das? Und wenn ich zwei davon habe, wie heißt das denn?**

4 Partner Chat You can also assign activity 4 on the Supersite. Students work in pairs to record the activity online. The pair's recorded conversation will appear in your gradebook.

1.

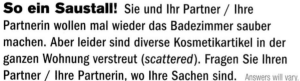

2.

3.

4.

5.

6.

7.

8.

5 Diskutieren und kombinieren Sie und Ihr Partner / Ihre Partnerin bekommen zwei verschiedene Bilder Außerirdischer (extraterrestrials) von Ihrem Lehrer / Ihrer Lehrerin. Finden Sie die sieben Unterschiede auf den Bildern.

BEISPIEL
S1: Wie viele Augen hat dein Außerirdischer?
S2: Mein Außerirdischer hat drei Augen.
S1: Aha! Mein Außerirdischer hat nur ein Auge.

6 So ein Saustall! Sie und Ihr Partner / Ihre Partnerin wollen mal wieder das Badezimmer sauber machen. Aber leider sind diverse Kosmetikartikel in der ganzen Wohnung verstreut (scattered). Fragen Sie Ihren Partner / Ihre Partnerin, wo Ihre Sachen sind. Answers will vary.

6 Suggestion Remind students to use the dative with two-way prepositions when describing location.

BEISPIEL
S1: Wo ist mein Rasierer?
S2: Den habe ich in der Küche neben der Spüle gesehen. Aber wo ist mein...

5 Expansion Model the pronunciation of **Außerirdischer**. Have students come up with a fictional profile for their aliens. Have them ask one another: **Wie heißt dein Außerirdischer? Woher kommt er? Was sind seine Hobbys?** etc.

7 Berühmte Leute Wählen Sie eine berühmte Person und schreiben Sie sechs Dinge über das Aussehen dieser Person. Lesen Sie Ihre Aussagen zwei Mitschülern vor, die erraten müssen, von welcher Person Sie sprechen. Answers will vary.

BEISPIEL
S1: Er ist Spanier, 1,85 Meter groß, hat dunkle Augen und dunkelbraune Haare. Er ist Linkshänder und hat die schnellsten Beine auf dem Tennisplatz.
S2: Ist es Rafael Nadal?
S1: Ja, genau!

7 Suggestion Circulate around the class to make sure students stay on task and to offer vocabulary support.

Aussprache und Rechtschreibung

Vocalic *r*

After a vowel, the German **r** often sounds more like a vowel than a consonant. When the syllable **er** occurs at the end of a word, it is pronounced with the *vocalic* **r** sound, similar to the letter *a* in the English word *sofa*.

Schulter	Pfleger	Schwester	guter	Badezimmer

The vocalic **r** also appears in unstressed prefixes, such as **er-**, **ver-** or **zer-**. In these prefixes, the sound of the **e** and the vocalic **r** are pronounced as separate sounds, blended together in a single syllable.

Verletzung	Erkältung	zerbrechen	verstauchen	erklären

The vocalic **r** also appears at the end of words after a long vowel sound. After a long **a** sound, the vowel and the vocalic **r** blend together. Otherwise, the long vowel and the vocalic **r** are pronounced as two separate sounds in a single syllable.

Ohr	vier	sehr	Haar	Bart

1 **Aussprechen** Wiederholen Sie die Wörter, die Sie hören.

1. Mutter	4. schwanger	7. zerstechen	10. schwer
2. Vater	5. verstopft	8. verstehen	11. hier
3. Rasierer	6. erkälten	9. Paar	12. Fahrt

2 **Nachsprechen** Wiederholen Sie die Sätze, die Sie hören.

1. Mir tut das rechte Ohr weh.
2. Die Krankenschwester und der Krankenpfleger suchen den Rasierer.
3. Mein kleiner Bruder hatte eine verstopfte Nase und Fieber.
4. Ohne Haar und ohne Bart friert man im Winter sehr.
5. Wie konnte Oliver mit dem verstauchten Fuß den 400-Meter-Lauf gewinnen?
6. Der erkältete Busfahrer hat eine lange Fahrt vor sich.

3 **Sprichwörter** Wiederholen Sie die Sprichwörter, die Sie hören.

Verbotene Früchte schmecken am besten.[2]

Es ist alles in Butter.[1]

[1] Everything is just great. (lit. *Everything is in butter.*)

[2] Forbidden fruit tastes the sweetest.

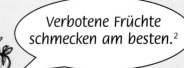

Guten Morgen, Herr Professor! Video

Meline schläft beim Lernen ein und hat einen interessanten Traum.
Er spielt in der Zukunft und wir begegnen einem guten Bekannten.

Vorbereitung Before showing students this episode, draw their attention to the reflexive verbs and other expressions used to talk about daily routines. Explain that reflexive pronouns always correspond to their subject pronouns. Ex.: **ich - mich/mir, du - dich/dir**, etc.

MELINE Schatz... es ist Zeit, dass du aufwachst und dich anziehst. Hase, ich habe um halb zehn eine Besprechung. Du musst dich für deinen ersten Unterrichtstag noch duschen und rasieren. Du darfst nicht zu spät kommen.

MELINE Da ist ja mein schöner Ehemann. Guten Morgen, Herr Professor.
HANS Wie haben wir uns nur so ineinander verliebt?
MELINE Tja, wahrscheinlich einfach Glück gehabt.

SABITE Meline? Meline, ist alles in Ordnung?
MELINE Hans?
SABITE Meline? Meline, beweg dich nicht. George? George!

MELINE Ich erinnere mich, du warst noch ein Junge. Dein Vater und ich – ist er schon aufgewacht? – dein Vater und ich haben uns diesen Tag immer vorgestellt. Wir haben nur nicht gedacht, dass er so schnell kommt. Heute machst du deinen Universitätsabschluss.

HANS Guten Morgen, mein Sohn.
WOLFGANG Paps.
HANS Mein Liebling.
WOLFGANG Mama, Paps, mir dreht sich der Magen um. Hört bitte auf, euch zu küssen.

MELINE Eines Tages, Wolfgang, wirst du erstaunt sein, wie es sich anfühlt, sich in jemanden zu verlieben. Ach Hans, putz dir die Zähne!
HANS Für dich tu ich doch alles, mein Liebling. Dann dusche ich mich, rasiere mich und wasche mir die Haare.

ÜBUNGEN

1

Was fehlt? Ergänzen Sie die Sätze mit den richtigen Informationen.

1. (Meline / Hans) hat um halb zehn eine Besprechung.
2. Hans muss sich noch duschen und (schminken / rasieren).
3. Er darf nicht zu (früh / spät) kommen.
4. Meline begrüßt ihren schönen (Schwiegervater / Ehemann).
5. In Melines Traum ist Hans (Professor / Ingenieur).
6. Wolfgang macht heute seinen (Universitätsabschluss / Urlaub).

7. Nach dem Frühstück geht Hans sich duschen, rasieren und die (Haare / Füße) waschen.
8. Als Meline aufwacht, liegt sie auf dem (Sofa / Boden).
9. Im Traum hat Meline gesagt, dass sie Hans (liebt / heiratet).
10. Sabite und George wollen Meline zum (Friseur / Arzt) bringen.

7

> **HANS** Heute ist ein besonderer Tag. Genießen wir ihn.

8

> **MELINE** Besonderer Tag. Hans, ich liebe dich. Hans?
> **GEORGE** Meline! Wach auf, Meline.
> **MELINE** Hans?
> **GEORGE** Ich bin's, George.

9

> **MELINE** Oh, mein Kopf. Was ist passiert? Warum bin ich am Boden?
> **GEORGE** Okay, Meline. Jetzt ganz langsam. Versuche, aufzustehen.

10

> **SABITE** Sollen wir Hans holen?
> **MELINE** Was? Nein. Warum wollt ihr ihn holen?
> **GEORGE** Ähm, du hast gesagt, du liebst ihn.
> **MELINE** Das ist nicht lustig. Jetzt wird mir erst recht schlecht.
> **SABITE** Komm, wir bringen dich zum Arzt.

Nützliche Ausdrücke

- **Besprechung**
  meeting
- **Du darfst nicht zu spät kommen.**
  You don't want to be late.
- **Meline, beweg dich nicht.**
  Meline, don't move.
- **sich erinnern**
  to remember
- **sich vorstellen**
  to imagine
- **Mama, Paps, mir dreht sich der Magen um.**
  Mom, Dad, my stomach is churning.
- **Hört bitte auf, euch zu küssen.**
  Please stop kissing each other.
- **Eines Tages, Wolfgang, wirst du erstaunt sein, wie es sich anfühlt, sich in jemanden zu verlieben.**
  One day, Wolfgang, you will be amazed at what it feels like to fall in love with someone.
- **Heute ist ein besonderer Tag.**
  Today is a special day.
- **der Arzt**
  doctor

1A.1
- **Du musst dich für deinen ersten Unterrichtstag noch duschen und rasieren.**
  You need to shower and shave for your first day of classes.

1A.2
- **Ach Hans, putz dir die Zähne!**
  Oh, Hans, brush your teeth!

1A.3
- **Wie haben wir uns nur so ineinander verliebt?**
  How did we get to be so in love with each other?

---

2 **Zum Besprechen** Wählen Sie zu zweit eine Person aus dem Fotoroman und beschreiben Sie seinen/ihren Morgen im Badezimmer. Benutzen Sie Informationen dieser Episode und Ihre Fantasie. Answers will vary.

2 Suggestion Before students begin this activity, ask them to brainstorm words and expressions used to talk about daily routines. Write these suggestions on the board for reference.

3 **Vertiefung** Im Deutschen gibt es viele Sprichwörter, die sich auf den Körper beziehen (*refer to*), zum Beispiel „Das geht mir nicht aus dem Kopf" (*It's always on my mind*). Finden Sie drei Sprichwörter mit Wörtern aus dieser Lektion. Answers will vary.

3 Suggestion Encourage students to share their selected proverbs. As a class, discuss the meaning of each proverb.

Die Kur°

AP* Theme: Contemporary Life
Context: Health & Well-Being

 Reading

IN DEUTSCHLAND GIBT ES UNGEFÄHR 300 Kurorte. An diesen Orten können Patienten sich erholen°. Nach einem schweren Unfall, bei psychischer Erschöpfung° oder wegen schwerer gesundheitlicher Probleme brauchen Patienten oft längere Pflege°: Kuraufenthalte° dauern normalerweise zwischen drei und sechs Wochen. Deutsche Krankenkassen° bezahlen einen großen Teil dieser Kurbesuche.

Kurorte in Deutschland bieten saubere Luft° und viel Ruhe°, damit Patienten sich auf ihre Gesundheit konzentrieren können. Patienten sollen in einer Kur physisch fit werden, indem sie wandern, schwimmen oder Rad fahren. Patienten sollen auch lernen, ihr Leben gesünder zu gestalten: Was kann man anders machen, damit man nicht wieder krank wird?

Einige der berühmtesten Kurorte in Deutschland sind Oberstdorf (Bayern), Bad Wörishofen (Bayern), Baden-Baden (Baden-Württemberg) und Westerland (Schleswig-Holstein). Oberstdorf liegt im Allgäu und ist die südlichste Gemeinde Deutschlands. Die Luft ist so klar, dass Patienten mit Allergien hier wenige Probleme haben. Hier hat man auch fantastische Wintersportmöglichkeiten. Das bayerische Bad Wörishofen im Allgäu ist berühmt wegen Sebastian Kneipp (1821–1897), einem katholischen Priester, der hier die Kneipp-Kur erfand. Teil der Kur ist Wassertreten° in einem kalten Wasserbad.

Baden-Baden liegt im Schwarzwald in der Nähe von Karlsruhe. Es ist bekannt für seine Thermalquellen°. Die Römer° haben die Stadt bereits im Jahr 80 nach Christus gegründet. Westerland liegt auf der Insel Sylt. Es ist ein sehr bekanntes Seeheilbad. Für Patienten ist die Nähe zur Nordsee und die Faszination des Wattenmeers interessant.

Anzahl an Kurorten pro Bundesland	
Baden-Württemberg – 56	Nordrhein-Westfalen – 34
Bayern – 53	Rheinland-Pfalz – 21
Brandenburg – 8	Saarland – 4
Hessen – 31	Sachsen – 11
Mecklenburg-Vorpommern – 30	Sachsen-Anhalt – 5
	Schleswig-Holstein – 45
Niedersachsen – 46	Thüringen – 16

QUELLE: Portal Bäderland Deutschland

Kur *health spa treatment* **sich erholen** *recover* **Erschöpfung** *exhaustion* **Pflege** *care* **Kuraufenthalte** *spa visits* **Krankenkassen** *health insurance* **Luft** *air* **Ruhe** *quiet* **Wassertreten** *treading water* **Thermalquellen** *hot springs* **Römer** *Romans*

ÜBUNGEN

1 **Richtig oder falsch?** Sagen Sie, ob die Sätze richtig oder falsch sind. Korrigieren Sie die falschen Sätze.

1. An etwa 300 Orten kann man in Deutschland eine Kur machen. Richtig.
2. Eine Kur dauert zwischen drei und sechs Wochen. Richtig.
3. Patienten müssen selber für eine Kur bezahlen. Falsch. Deutsche Krankenkassen bezahlen einen Teil einer Kur.
4. Kurorte bieten Patienten Ruhe und saubere Luft. Richtig.
5. In Bad Wörishofen wurde die Kneipp-Kur erfunden. Richtig.
6. In Oberstdorf ist das Klima so gut, dass Patienten wenige Probleme mit Allergien haben. Richtig.
7. Baden-Baden liegt in Baden-Württemberg. Richtig.
8. Westerland ist ein Seeheilbad in der Ostsee. Falsch. Westerland liegt auf Sylt in der Nordsee.
9. Die meisten Kurorte gibt es in Bayern. Falsch. Die meisten Kurorte gibt es in Baden-Württemberg.
10. Viele Kurorte gibt es im Saarland. Falsch. Die wenigsten Kurorte gibt es im Saarland.

 Practice more at vhlcentral.com.

Ausdrücke mit Körperteilen

Hand und Fuß haben	*to make sense*
jemandem ins Auge springen	*to catch somebody's eye*
sich die Augen aus dem Kopf weinen	*to cry one's eyes out*
Hals- und Beinbruch!	*Break a leg!*
Hand aufs Herz!	*Cross my heart!*

Öffentliche Schwimmbäder

Das erste öffentliche Schwimmbad° in Deutschland wurde 1860 in Marburg eröffnet. Heute gibt es viele verschiedene Arten von Schwimmbädern. Fast jede deutsche Stadt besitzt ein Freibad, das an warmen Sommertagen normalerweise voll ist. Dann gibt es auch noch Hallenbäder°, wo man das ganze Jahr über baden kann. Schwimmbäder mit moderneren Anlagen° wie Wellenbad°, Rutschen° und Saunen heißen entweder Spaßbad oder Erlebnisbad. Entlang der Meeresküsten gibt es Strandbäder, wo man in Meerwasser schwimmt, aber auch Flüsse und Seen, besonders Baggerseen°, sind sehr beliebt.

AP* Theme: Families & Communities
Context: Urban, Suburban, & Rural Life

Schwimmbad *swimming pool* **Hallenbäder** *indoor swimming pools* **Anlagen** *facilities* **Wellenbad** *wave pool* **Rutschen** *slides* **Baggerseen** *quarry ponds*

Nivea

Suggestion Ask students if they use any Nivea products. Tell them that Germany's cosmetics industry is the third largest in the world, after the U.S. and Japan.

Die Marke Nivea gibt es schon seit 1911. Sie ist Teil der deutschen Firma Beiersdorf. Ihr bekanntestes Produkt ist die Nivea-Hautcreme°. Seit 1925 verkauft Nivea diese Hautcreme in der bekannten, blauen Dose°. Neben der traditionellen weißen Hautcreme gibt es heute auch viele andere Produkte, zum Beispiel Cremes für Babys, Rasiercremes, Aftershaves und verschiedene Sonnenschutzmittel°. Wichtig ist auch, dass bei der Entwicklung und Produktion von Nivea-Produkten keine Tierversuche° gemacht werden. Heute kann man Nivea auf allen Kontinenten und in fast allen Ländern kaufen. **AP* Theme:** Science & Technology
Context: Ethical Considerations

Hautcreme *skin cream* **Dose** *jar* **Sonnenschutzmittel** *sunscreen* **Tierversuche** *animal testing*

🔗 IM INTERNET

Suchen Sie im Internet den Katalog eines öffentlichen Schwimmbads. Was kann man hier alles machen? Wie viel kostet der Eintritt?

Find out more at **vhlcentral.com**.

---

2 **Was fehlt?** Ergänzen Sie die Sätze.

1. In Magdeburg wurde das erste deutsche Schwimmbad ____1860____ eröffnet.
2. Ein ___Freibad/Schwimmbad___ hat fast jede deutsche Stadt.
3. ___Strandbäder___ gibt es entlang der Meeresküsten.
4. Die Marke Nivea gibt es seit ____1911____.
5. Die Nivea-Hautcreme kommt in einer blauen ____Dose____.
6. Für Nivea-Produkte finden keine ____Tierversuche____ statt.

3 **Ein Kurbesuch** Planen Sie mit einem Partner / einer Partnerin einen Besuch bei einer Kur. Was machen Sie jeden Tag? Was essen und trinken Sie? Was machen Sie in Ihrer Freizeit?

Ressourcen

v̂Text   vhlcentral

Reflexive verbs with accusative reflexive pronouns

 Presentation

Startblock A reflexive verb indicates an action you do to yourself or for yourself. The subject of a reflexive verb is also its object.

Du musst **dich** zum ersten Unterrichtstag **duschen** und **rasieren**.

Ich **erinnere mich**, du warst noch ein Junge.

ACHTUNG

The accusative reflexive pronouns are the same as the accusative personal pronouns, except that all of the third person pronouns and **Sie** are replaced by **sich**. Note that **sich** is never capitalized, even when it refers to **Sie**.

Suggestion Ask students: "If my subject is **ich**, what reflexive pronoun will I use?" etc.

- Reflexive verbs always use reflexive pronouns. When the subject of a reflexive verb is also its direct object, it takes an accusative reflexive pronoun.

personal pronouns						
nominative	ich	du	er/sie/es	wir	ihr	Sie/sie
accusative reflexive	mich	dich	sich	uns	euch	sich

- When a reflexive verb is conjugated, the verb and the reflexive pronoun must both agree with the subject. In the infinitive, reflexive verbs are always listed with the third person reflexive pronoun.

sich rasieren	
ich rasiere mich	wir rasieren uns
du rasierst dich	ihr rasiert euch
er/sie/es rasiert sich	Sie/sie rasieren sich

ACHTUNG

Verbs that are reflexive in German do not always have reflexive equivalents in English: **Ich frage mich, wo meine Schlüssel sind.** *I wonder where my keys are.*

Suggestion Note that students will learn to use **sich (etwas) vorstellen** to mean *to imagine (something)* in **1A.2**.

- Some verbs can be used both non-reflexively and reflexively. Note that certain verbs have a change in meaning when they are used reflexively.

non-reflexive verbs		reflexive verbs	
anziehen	*to put on*	sich anziehen	*to get dressed*
legen	*to put; to lay*	sich (hin)legen	*to lie down*
setzen	*to put; to set*	sich (hin)setzen	*to sit down*
fragen	*to ask*	sich fragen	*to wonder, ask oneself*
vorstellen	*to introduce*	sich vorstellen	*to introduce oneself*
umziehen	*to move*	sich umziehen	*to change clothes*
waschen	*to wash (something)*	sich waschen	*to wash (oneself)*

Ich **ziehe** den Mantel **an**.
I'm putting on my coat.

Ich **ziehe mich an**.
I'm getting dressed.

- A number of verbs related to daily routines, personal hygiene, and health take an accusative reflexive pronoun.

common reflexive verbs			
sich abtrocknen	*to dry oneself off*	sich entspannen	*to relax*
sich ausruhen	*to rest*	sich erkälten	*to catch a cold*
sich ausziehen	*to get undressed*	sich (wohl) fühlen	*to feel (well)*
(sich) baden	*to bathe, take a bath*	sich rasieren	*to shave*
sich beeilen	*to hurry*	sich schminken	*to put on makeup*
(sich) duschen	*to take a shower*	sich verspäten	*to be late*

Ich **fühle mich** nicht **wohl**.
I don't feel well.

Wir **haben uns** am Wochenende **entspannt**.
We relaxed this weekend.

- When the subject is the first word in a sentence, put the reflexive pronoun after the conjugated verb. When the verb and subject are inverted, put the reflexive pronoun after the subject.

Klara schminkt **sich** jeden Morgen.
Klara puts on makeup every morning.

Heute Morgen schminkt sie **sich** nicht.
She's not putting on makeup this morning.

Ziehst du **dich** an?
Are you getting dressed?

Setzen Sie **sich**, bitte!
Please be seated.

- In informal imperatives, since the pronoun **du** or **ihr** is dropped, the reflexive pronoun comes immediately after the verb.

Zieh **dich** bitte an!
Get dressed, please.

Setzt **euch**, bitte!
Please sit down.

- When the conjugated verb is a modal, the reflexive pronoun comes immediately after the modal, or immediately after the subject, if the word order is inverted.

Wir müssen **uns** beeilen.
We need to hurry up.

Möchtet ihr **euch** hier setzen?
Would you like to sit here?

- Use the auxiliary verb **haben** with reflexive verbs in the **Perfekt** and **Plusquamperfekt**.

Ich **habe mich** heute Morgen **rasiert**.
I shaved this morning.

Wir **hatten uns** schon **geduscht**.
We had already showered.

Suggestion Emphasize the point that *any* verb used reflexively takes **haben** in the perfect and the past perfect.

ACHTUNG

The verbs **baden** and **duschen** can also be used non-reflexively, with no difference in meaning: **Ich dusche jeden Morgen**.

Expansion Have students work in pairs to write a short text about getting ready for an evening out, using common reflexive verbs.

Suggestion You might want to refer students to **Vol. 1, 3B.3** to review the formation of imperatives.
Also, **Vol. 1, 3B.1** to review the use of modals.
Also, **Vol. 2, 1A.1** to review the **Perfekt** with **haben**.
Also, **Vol. 2, 4A.1** to review the **Plusquamperfekt**.

Ressourcen

v̂Text

WB
pp. 3–4

LM
p. 55

vhlcentral

Jetzt sind Sie dran!   Ergänzen Sie die Tabelle mit den fehlenden Formen.

		sich fragen	sich beeilen	sich ausziehen
1.	ich	ich frage mich	ich beeile mich	ich ziehe mich aus
2.	du	du fragst dich	du beeilst dich	du ziehst dich aus
3.	er/sie/es	er/sie/es fragt sich	er/sie/es beeilt sich	er/sie/es zieht sich aus
4.	wir	wir fragen uns	wir beeilen uns	wir ziehen uns aus
5.	ihr	ihr fragt euch	ihr beeilt euch	ihr zieht euch aus
6.	sie	sie fragen sich	sie beeilen sich	sie ziehen sich aus
7.	Sie	Sie fragen sich	Sie beeilen sich	Sie ziehen sich aus

Anwendung

1 Suggestion You may wish to provide a context for this activity. Ex.: **Es ist Montag um 6 Uhr 30, und die Familie Bauer ist gerade aufgestanden. Wie bereiten sich alle auf den Tag vor?**

1 **Reflexive Verben** Ergänzen Sie die Sätze mit den richtigen Reflexivformen der Verben in Klammern.

1. Birgit ist müde und __legt sich__ (sich legen) aufs Sofa.
2. Wie __fühlen__ Sie __sich__ (sich fühlen) heute, Frau Neumann?
3. Bei dem schlechten Wetter __erkälten sich__ (sich erkälten) manche Leute.
4. __Beeil dich__ (sich beeilen)! Du musst vor 17 Uhr noch einkaufen.
5. Torsten __duscht sich__ (sich duschen) schnell.
6. Ich __schminke mich__ (sich schminken) nur, wenn ich ausgehe.
7. Jana! Erik! __Setzt euch__ (sich setzen) hier zu uns an den Tisch!
8. Wir __fragen uns__ (sich fragen), wie das passieren konnte.

2 **Sätze bilden** Bilden Sie Sätze und achten Sie dabei auf die Wortstellung. Answers may vary. Sample answers provided.

> **BEISPIEL** Zuerst / Herr Bauer / sich duschen
> *Zuerst duscht sich Herr Bauer.*

1. Danach / er / sich rasieren / langsam
   Danach rasiert er sich langsam.
2. Seine Frau / sich schminken / vor dem Spiegel
   Seine Frau schminkt sich vor dem Spiegel.
3. Dann / sie / sich umziehen / schnell
   Dann zieht sie sich schnell um.
4. Die Kinder / sich anziehen / für die Schule
   Die Kinder ziehen sich für die Schule an.
5. Heute / alle in der Familie / sich verspäten
   Heute verspäten sich alle in der Familie.
6. Später / der Hund / sich legen / auf das Bett
   Später legt sich der Hund auf das Bett.

3 Suggestion To verify comprehension, ask students: **Hat Claudia den Job bekommen? Warum nicht?**

3 **Ein schlechter Tag** Gestern hat Claudia einen sehr schlechten Tag gehabt. Schreiben Sie ihre Geschichte ins Perfekt um.

> **BEISPIEL** Claudia steht erst um halb zehn auf.
> Sie fühlt sich nicht wohl.
> *Claudia ist erst um halb zehn aufgestanden.*
> *Sie hat sich nicht wohl gefühlt.*

1. Sie duscht sich, und dann schminkt sie sich. Sie hat sich geduscht, und dann hat sie sich geschminkt.
2. Sie zieht sich schön an. Sie hat sich schön angezogen.
3. Sie beeilt sich, zur U-Bahn zu kommen. Sie hat sich beeilt, zur U-Bahn zu kommen.
4. Um 10.15 Uhr stellt sie sich bei der Firma *Werner Elektronik* vor.
   Um 10.15 Uhr hat sie sich bei der Firma *Werner Elektronik* vorgestellt.
5. Sie verspätet sich, und deshalb (*for that reason*) bekommt sie den Job nicht.
   Sie hat/hatte sich verspätet, und deshalb hat sie den Job nicht bekommen.
6. Sie geht traurig nach Hause, und dann legt sie sich aufs Sofa.
   Sie ist traurig nach Hause gegangen, und dann hat sie sich aufs Sofa gelegt.

 Practice more at **vhlcentral.com.**

Kommunikation

4 **Bilder beschreiben** Beschreiben Sie mit einem Partner / einer Partnerin, was die Personen auf den Bildern gerade machen. Benutzen Sie reflexive Verben. Sample answers are provided.

▶ **BEISPIEL**

Er zieht sich an.

1.
Er duscht sich.

2.
Das Kind wäscht sich.

3.
Sie schminkt sich.

4.
Er rasiert sich.

5.
Sie legt sich hin.

6.
Er beeilt sich.

5 **Pantomimen** Sie spielen eine Tätigkeit (*activity*) aus der Liste vor und Ihre zwei Mitschüler erraten, was Sie vorgespielt haben (*mimed*). Wechseln Sie sich ab. Answers will vary.

BEISPIEL

S1: (spielt „sich rasieren" vor)
S2: Du hast dich rasiert!

sich abtrocknen	sich umziehen
sich erkälten	sich vorstellen
sich hinsetzen	sich (nicht) wohl fühlen
sich rasieren	

6 **Machst du das?** Fragen Sie Ihre Mitschüler, ob (*whether*) sie diese Sachen machen. Finden Sie für jede Frage eine Person, die das macht. Answers will vary.

BEISPIEL

S1: Verspätest du dich oft?
S2: Nein, ich verspäte mich nie!
S3: Ja, ich verspäte mich immer am Montagmorgen.

Tätigkeiten	Name
sich oft verspäten	
sich vor einer Prüfung entspannen	
sich zweimal am Tag duschen	
sich nachmittags hinlegen	
sich am Abend duschen	
sich im Winter immer erkälten	

7 **Was soll ich machen?** Geben Sie Ihrem Partner / Ihrer Partnerin Ratschläge (*advice*) für seine/ihre Probleme. Wechseln Sie sich ab. Answers will vary.

BEISPIEL

S1: Ich fühle mich so schmutzig!
S2: Du musst dich duschen.

Die Probleme:

1. Ich bin sehr müde.

2. Ich kenne meinen Klassenkameraden nicht und möchte mit ihm sprechen.

3. Ich habe in fünf Minuten Schule und muss mich noch anziehen.

4. Ich habe beim Essen mein neues T-Shirt verschmutzt.

4 **Suggestion** You may want to do this activity as a class. Ask: **Was macht der Mann? Was macht das Kind?** etc.

4 **Virtual Chat** You can also assign activity 4 on the Supersite. Students record individual responses that appear in your gradebook.

5 **Suggestion** Act out a few reflexive verbs yourself, such as **sich kämmen** or **sich anziehen**. Ask: **Was habe ich gerade gemacht?**

6 **Suggestion** Formulate the questions together before students begin circulating.

7 **Virtual Chat** You can also assign activity 7 on the Supersite. Students record individual responses that appear in your gradebook.

Reflexive verbs with dative reflexive pronouns

 Presentation

Startblock In **1A.1**, you learned that when the subject of a reflexive verb is also its direct object, it takes an accusative reflexive pronoun. When the subject of a reflexive verb is not its direct object, it takes a dative reflexive pronoun.

Dann dusche ich mich, rasiere ich mich und **wasche mir** die Haare.

Ach Hans, **putz dir** die Zähne!

- The dative reflexive pronouns are the same as the dative personal pronouns, except that all of the third person pronouns and the formal **Sie** are replaced by **sich**. Remember that the pronoun **sich** is never capitalized, even when it refers to the formal **Sie**.

personal pronouns						
nominative	ich	du	er/sie/es	wir	ihr	Sie/sie
accusative reflexive	mich	dich	sich	uns	euch	sich
dative reflexive	mir	dir	sich	uns	euch	sich

- Many verbs take an accusative reflexive pronoun when used on their own but a dative reflexive pronoun when used with a different direct object.

reflexive verbs used with direct objects	
sich (die Hände) abtrocknen	*to dry (one's hands)*
sich (eine Jacke) anziehen	*to put on (a jacket)*
sich (einen Mantel) ausziehen	*to take off (a coat)*
sich die Haare bürsten	*to brush one's hair*
sich die Haare färben	*to dye one's hair*
sich die Haare kämmen	*to comb one's hair*
sich die Zähne putzen	*to brush one's teeth*
sich (die Beine) rasieren	*to shave (one's legs)*
sich (die Augen) schminken	*to put on (eye) makeup*
sich (das Gesicht) waschen	*to wash (one's face)*
sich etwas vorstellen	*to imagine something (for oneself)*
sich etwas wünschen	*to wish for something (for oneself)*

Ich wasche **mich**.
I'm washing (myself).

Ich wasche **mir** das Gesicht.
I'm washing my face.

- Note that the meaning of the verb **sich vorstellen** changes when it is used with a direct object and a dative reflexive pronoun.

Hast du **dich** vorgestellt?	Kannst du **dir** das vorstellen?
Did you introduce yourself?	*Can you imagine that?*

- To refer to a part of the body or a particular piece of clothing after a reflexive verb in German, use a definite article where you would use a possessive adjective in English.

Ela putzt sich **die** Zähne.	Habt ihr euch **die** Haare gebürstet?
*Ela is brushing **her** teeth.*	*Did you brush **your** hair?*
Ich ziehe mir **den** Mantel aus.	Zieh dir **die** Schuhe schnell an!
*I'm taking off **my** coat.*	*Put **your** shoes on quickly!*

Suggestion You may want to translate these phrases literally into English, to humorously emphasize the pattern. Ex: *She brushes herself the teeth. Did you brush yourself the hair?*

- Some verbs can be used reflexively to emphasize that the subject of the verb is also its indirect object.

Ich **bestelle (mir)** einen Kaffee.	**Hast** du **(dir)** eine Jacke **gekauft**?
*I'm ordering **(myself)** a coffee.*	*Did you buy **(yourself)** a jacket?*

ACHTUNG

When the verbs **anziehen** and **ausziehen** are used with a direct object, the reflexive pronoun is optional: **Zieh (dir) die Schuhe aus!**

- If the direct object is a *noun*, put the dative reflexive pronoun before it. If the direct object is a *pronoun*, put the dative reflexive pronoun after it.

Machst du **dir** eine Tasse Tee?	Ja, ich habe sie **mir** schon gemacht.
*Are you making **(yourself)** a cup of tea?*	*Yes, I've already made it **(for myself)**.*

Suggestion You might want to refer students to **Vol. 1, 4B.1** for a note on word order with dative and accusative objects.

Suggestion You may want to translate these phrases literally into English, to humorously emphasize the pattern. Ex: *She brushes herself the teeth. Did you brush yourself the hair?*

- In a sentence with more than one object, the dative object comes before the accusative object. However, when one object is a pronoun, the pronoun comes first. If there are two pronouns, the accusative pronoun comes before the dative.

Ich kaufe **meiner Schwester einen Hund**.	Ich kaufe **ihn meiner Schwester**.
*I'm buying **my sister a dog**.*	*I'm buying **it** for my sister.*
Ich kaufe **ihr** einen Hund.	Ich kaufe **ihn ihr**.
*I'm buying **her** a dog.*	*I'm buying **it** for her.*

Ressourcen

v̂Text

WB
pp. 5–6

LM
p. 56

Ⓢ
vhlcentral

 **Jetzt sind Sie dran!** **Ergänzen Sie die Sätze mit den richtigen Reflexivpronomen.**

1. Niklas kauft (sich / ihm) ein Sandwich.
2. Hast du (dich / dir) einen Salat gemacht?
3. Wir haben (euch / uns) ein kleines Auto gemietet.
4. Max und Lara haben (sich / ihnen) eine Pizza bestellt.
5. Nina wünscht (sich / ihm) eine Spielkonsole zum Geburtstag.
6. Ich backe (mich / mir) einen Schokoladenkuchen.

Anwendung

1 Suggestion Do the first few items as a class to verify that students understand the pattern.

1 **Körperteile und Kleidung** Bilden Sie Sätze mit den reflexiven Verben in Klammern. Achten Sie (*Pay attention*) auf die Artikel!

> **BEISPIEL** ihre Beine (sich rasieren)
> Jasmin _rasiert sich die Beine_.

1. meine Nase (sich putzen)
   Ich _putze mir die Nase_.

2. deine Hände (sich abtrocknen)
   Du _trocknest dir die Hände ab_.

3. seine Uniform (sich anziehen)
   Julius _zieht sich die Uniform an_.

4. eure Füße (sich waschen)
   Ihr _wascht euch die Füße_.

5. deine Jacke (sich ausziehen)
   Du _ziehst dir die Jacke aus_.

6. meine Handschuhe (sich anziehen)
   Ich _ziehe mir die Handschuhe an_.

2 **Was machen sie?** Schreiben Sie die Sätze um.

> **BEISPIEL** Putzt du dir die Zähne? (ihr)
> _Putzt ihr euch die Zähne?_

1. Kauft David sich neue Hausschuhe? (du)
   Kaufst du dir neue Hausschuhe?

2. Sie machen sich eine Tasse Tee. (ich)
   Ich mache mir eine Tasse Tee.

3. Hat Anna sich die Haare gefärbt? (du)
   Hast du dir die Haare gefärbt?

4. Ich bestelle mir etwas zu trinken. (Ben und Lisa)
   Ben und Lisa bestellen sich etwas zu trinken.

5. Stell dir das vor! (Sie)
   Stellen Sie sich das vor!

3 **Sätze mit Dativ** Schreiben Sie zu jedem Bild einen Satz. Benutzen sie ein reflexives Verb mit einem Reflexivpronomen im Dativ. Sample answers are provided.

 ▶ **BEISPIEL**
Lina
Lina schminkt sich den Mund.

1. Fabian
Fabian rasiert sich das Gesicht.

2. du
Du wäschst dir die Haare.

3. wir
Wir waschen uns das Gesicht.

4. Nils
Nils bürstet sich die Haare.

5. ich
Ich putze mir die Zähne.

Practice more at **vhlcentral.com**.

Kommunikation

4 **Was macht man damit?** Ihr kleiner Bruder möchte wissen, was man mit den Sachen unten macht. Schreiben Sie gemeinsam einen Dialog. Answers will vary.

BEISPIEL Haartrockner
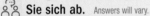
S1: Was ist das?
S2: Das ist ein Haartrockner.
S1: Und was machst du damit?
S2: Damit trocke ich mir die Haare.

1. ein Lippenstift
2. ein Rasierer
3. ein Kamm
4. eine Zahnbürste
5. Shampoo
6. eine Kaffeemaschine

5 **Und nun?** Ihr Partner / Ihre Partnerin hat Probleme. Helfen Sie ihm/ihr mit guten Ratschlägen (*advice*). Benutzen Sie den Imperativ und wechseln Sie sich ab. Answers will vary.

BEISPIEL

S1: Ich habe kalte Hände.
S2: Zieh dir doch Handschuhe an!

> sich die Füße waschen
> sich die Haare kämmen
> sich einen Pullover anziehen
> sich etwas zu essen machen

1. Meine Füße sind sehr schmutzig.
2. Meine Haare hängen mir ins Gesicht.
3. Ich habe so einen Hunger!
4. Mir ist kalt.

6 **Wann machst du das?** Fragen Sie Ihren Partner / Ihre Partnerin, wann oder wie oft er/sie diese Dinge macht. Answers will vary.

BEISPIEL

S1: Wann wäschst du dir die Haare?
S2: Ich wasche mir jeden zweiten Tag die Haare.

> jeden Tag/Morgen/Abend | wenn ich Lust habe
> ein/zwei Mal am Tag | jeden zweiten Tag
> vor/nach dem Essen | wenn ich kalte Füße habe
> nie | bevor ich ins Bett gehe

1. sich die Haare waschen
2. sich die Zähne putzen
3. sich etwas zu essen machen
4. sich die Hände waschen
5. sich die Haare föhnen
6. sich Hausschuhe anziehen

7 **Gewonnen** Sie haben 500.000 Dollar gewonnen! Sagen Sie, was Sie sich zuerst kaufen, und dann fragen Sie Ihre Mitschüler, was sie sich kaufen wollen. Answers will vary.

BEISPIEL

S1: Ich kaufe mir ein großes Boot. Und was kaufst du dir, Tim?
S2: Ich kaufe mir ein Flugticket nach Sydney. Was kaufst du dir, Sophie?
S3: Ich gehe ins Restaurant und bestelle mir...

---

4 **Suggestion** Have students act out their dialogues for the class.

4 **Virtual Chat** You can also assign activity 4 on the Supersite. Students record individual responses that appear in your gradebook.

5 **Virtual Chat** You can also assign activity 5 on the Supersite. Students record individual responses that appear in your gradebook.

6 **Partner Chat** You can also assign activity 6 on the Supersite. Students work in pairs to record the activity online. The pair's recorded conversation will appear in your gradebook.

7 **Suggestion** Circulate and provide vocabulary help, if needed. Set a time limit for this activity. As a follow-up, have students share answers, using the 3rd person. Ex.: **Sophie kauft sich einen Roboter.**

1A.3 | **Reciprocal verbs and reflexives used with prepositions**  Presentation

Startblock Reciprocal verbs express an action done by two or more people or things to or for one another.

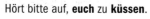

> Hört bitte auf, **euch** zu **küssen**.

> Torsten und ich **haben uns gestritten**.

Reciprocal verbs

- Because reciprocal verbs refer to more than one person, they are only used with the plural reflexive pronouns **uns**, **euch**, and **sich**.

Wir rufen **uns** jeden Tag an.
*We call **each other** every day.*

Meine Großeltern lieben **sich** sehr.
*My grandparents love **each other** very much.*

Woher kennt **ihr euch**?
*How do **you** know **each other**?*

Sie schrieben **sich** zweimal im Monat.
*They wrote to **one another** twice a month.*

- Here are some common verbs with reciprocal meanings.

common reciprocal verbs	
sich anrufen	*to call each other*
sich kennen	*to know each other*
sich kennen lernen	*to meet (each other) for the first time*
sich küssen	*to kiss (each other)*
sich lieben	*to love each other*
sich schreiben	*to write to one another*
sich streiten	*to argue (with one another)*
sich trennen	*to separate, split up*
sich treffen	*to meet up*
sich unterhalten	*to chat, have a conversation*
sich verlieben	*to fall in love (with one another)*

Wir **kennen uns** schon seit Jahren.
*We've **known each other** for years.*

Habt ihr **euch** gestern **gestritten**?
*Did you **argue (with each other)** yesterday?*

Unsere Eltern **haben sich** vor fünfundzwanzig Jahren **verliebt**.
*Our parents **fell in love** twenty-five years ago.*

Die Schüler **treffen sich** gern im Restaurant, um **sich zu unterhalten**.
*Students like to **meet (each other)** at the restaurant **to talk (with one another)**.*

- In some cases, it may be unclear whether a verb is being used reflexively or reciprocally. To clarify or emphasize a verb's reciprocal meaning, use the expression **einander** (*each other, one another*) instead of, or in addition to, a reflexive pronoun.

Sie haben **sich** vorgestellt.
They introduced themselves (to one another, or to someone else).

Sie haben sich **einander** vorgestellt.
They introduced themselves to one another.

Reflexive verbs with prepositions

- Some reflexive verbs are typically used in set phrases with a preposition. Use accusative reflexive pronouns with these verbs. The prepositions in the following fixed expressions also take the accusative case.

common reflexive verbs with prepositions	
sich ärgern über	*to get angry about*
sich erinnern an	*to remember*
sich freuen auf	*to look forward to*
sich freuen über	*to be happy about*
sich gewöhnen an	*to get used to*
sich informieren über	*to find out about*
sich interessieren für	*to be interested in*
sich verlieben in	*to fall in love with*
sich vorbereiten auf	*to prepare oneself for*

Mama **hat sich über** mein unordentliches Zimmer **geärgert**.
*Mom **got mad about** my messy room.*

Nach der Reise **freuten** wir **uns auf** ein warmes Bad.
*After our trip, we **were looking forward to** a warm bath.*

Meine kleine Schwester **interessiert sich für** Computer.
*My little sister **is interested in** computers.*

Ich **habe mich an** das kalte Wetter **gewöhnt**.
*I've **gotten used to** the cold weather.*

ACHTUNG

When using **einander** with a preposition, attach it to the end of the preposition to form a single word: **Die Kinder spielen immer so schön <u>miteinander</u>.**

Klara und Paul haben sich <u>ineinander</u> verliebt.

QUERVERWEIS

Note that **erinnern**, **gewöhnen**, and **verlieben** all have inseparable prefixes. The verb **vorbereiten** has a separable prefix, but because its root verb, **bereiten**, has an inseparable prefix, there is no **-ge-** added to its past participle: **Ich bereite mich auf einen Marathon vor. Wie hast du dich auf die Prüfung vorbereitet?**

Suggestion You might want to refer students to **Vol. 2, 2B.2** to review how to form the past participles of verbs with separable and inseparable prefixes. Also, **Vol. 2, 3A.2** to review other verbs that are used in set phrases with prepositions.

Suggestion Tell students that in some cases, reflexive pronouns can be used after prepositions to mean myself, herself, etc. Ex.: **Mein Freund denkt nur an *sich*.**

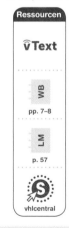

Ressourcen

v̂Text

WB
pp. 7–8

LM
p. 57

vhlcentral

Jetzt sind Sie dran! Geben Sie an, ob die Verben in den Sätzen eine reflexive oder reziproke Bedeutung (*meaning*) haben.

	reflexiv	reziprok		reflexiv	reziprok
1. Wir treffen uns um 16 Uhr im Café.	☐	☑	5. Seht ihr euch heute Abend?	☐	☑
2. Max und ich kennen uns seit drei Jahren.	☐	☑	6. Tom verliebte sich in Lena.	☑	☐
3. Die Schüler freuten sich auf die Ferien.	☑	☐	7. Lena freute sich sehr darüber.	☑	☐
4. Sara und Felix schreiben einander über 100 SMS am Tag.	☐	☑	8. Dana und ihr Freund streiten sich nur selten.	☐	☑

Anwendung

1 **Was fehlt?** Ergänzen Sie die Sätze mit den passenden Reflexivpronomen.

> **BEISPIEL** Mira und Hasan rufen ___sich___ dreimal pro Tag an.

1. Heute küssten sie ___sich___ zum ersten Mal.
2. Unsere Großeltern kennen ___sich___ seit 60 Jahren.
3. Es ist klar, dass ihr ___euch___ liebt.
4. Philip und Daniel unterhalten ___sich___ gern.
5. Wo sollen wir ___uns___ treffen?
6. Ich kann ___mich___ nicht an seinen Namen erinnern.
7. Hast du ___dich___ über den neuen Film informiert?
8. Ihr sollt ___euch___ vorstellen.

2 **Bilder beschreiben** Beschreiben Sie die Bilder mit reziproken reflexiven Verben. Benutzen Sie das Perfekt.

> **BEISPIEL** die Geschäftsleute
> *Die Geschäftsleute haben sich getroffen.*

sich jeden Tag anrufen	sich streiten
sich küssen	sich treffen
sich oft schreiben	sich unterhalten

Tobias und ich
1. haben uns geküsst.

Klara und Mia
2. haben sich jeden Tag angerufen.

Ihr
3. habt euch gestritten.

Wir
4. haben uns oft geschrieben.

Sie
5. haben sich unterhalten.

3 **Sätze schreiben** Schreiben Sie mindestens (*at least*) sechs logische Sätze mit Wörtern aus jeder Spalte.

> **BEISPIEL** *Die Studenten bereiten sich auf das Abschlussexamen vor.*

Julia	sich ärgern über	das Abschlussexamen
der Hotelgast	sich aufregen über	sein ehemaliger (*former*) Lehrer
die Enkelkinder	sich erinnern an	die Geburt ihres Enkelkindes
Simon	sich freuen auf	die Laptopangebote im Internet
Oma und Opa	sich freuen über	der schlechte Zimmerservice
die Passagierin	sich informieren über	ihr verlorenes (*lost*) Handgepäck
die Studenten	sich vorbereiten auf	die vielen Geschenke

3 **Suggestion** Remind students that the objects of these prepositions should be in the accusative case.

3 **Expansion** Have students write sentences about *themselves* using the verbs provided.

3 **Suggested answers:**
Julia informiert sich über die Laptopangebote im Internet.

Der Hotelgast ärgert sich über den schlechten Zimmerservice.

Die Enkelkinder freuen sich über die vielen Geschenke.

Simon erinnert sich an seinen ehemaligen Lehrer.

Oma und Opa freuen sich auf die Geburt ihres Enkelkindes.

Die Passagierin regt sich über ihr verlorenes Handgepäck auf.

 Practice more at **vhlcentral.com**.

Kommunikation

4 **Beste Freunde** Stellen Sie Ihrem Partner / Ihrer Partnerin Fragen über seinen besten Freund / ihre beste Freundin. Antworten Sie in ganzen Sätzen und wechseln Sie sich ab. Answers will vary.

BEISPIEL

S1: Seit wann kennt ihr euch schon?
S2: Wir kennen uns schon seit 10 Jahren.

1. Seit wann kennt ihr euch schon?
2. Wo und wie habt ihr euch kennen gelernt?
3. Wie oft seht ihr euch?
4. Wo trefft ihr euch meistens?

5. Schreibt ihr euch viele SMS?
6. Ruft ihr euch an? Wie oft?
7. Worüber unterhaltet ihr euch?
8. Streitet ihr euch manchmal? Worüber?

5 **Eine Liebesgeschichte** Schreiben Sie mit Ihrem Partner / Ihrer Partnerin eine Liebesgeschichte über Lisa und David. Verwenden Sie die reflexiven Verben aus der Liste und benutzen Sie das Perfekt. Answers will vary.

▶ **BEISPIEL** Lisa und David haben sich auf einer Party kennen gelernt.

sich anrufen	sich treffen
sich kennen lernen	sich trennen
sich küssen	sich unterhalten
sich schreiben	sich verlieben
sich streiten	sich vorstellen

6 **Interessen** Wofür interessieren sich Ihre Klassenkameraden? Machen Sie eine kurze Umfrage in Ihrer Klasse. Answers will vary.

BEISPIEL

S1: Ich interessiere mich für Technologie. Und du, Max, wofür interessierst du dich?
S2: Ich interessiere mich für Musik. Und du, Hanna, wofür interessierst du dich?
S3: Ich interessiere mich für...

7 **Fragen über Fragen** Stellen Sie Fragen an Ihre Klassenkameraden. Finden Sie für jede Frage mindestens eine Person, die sie mit ja beantwortet. Answers will vary.

BEISPIEL

S1: Freust du dich auf das Schuljahrsende?
S2: Ja, ich freue mich total auf das Schuljahrsende. Und du, freust du dich auf das Schuljahrsende?
S1: Nein, gar nicht! Ich muss in den Ferien arbeiten.

	Name
sich auf das Schuljahrsende freuen	
sich gern an den letzten Sommer erinnern	
sich für Politik interessieren	
sich über das Essen in der Cafeteria aufregen	
sich über schlechte Noten ärgern	

4 **Suggestion** As a class project, compile the stories into a "class book" of **Liebesgeschichten**.

4 **Virtual Chat** You can also assign activity 4 on the Supersite. Students record individual responses that appear in your gradebook.

7 **Suggestion** Formulate the questions as a class before students begin the group activity.

Wiederholung

1 Welches Bild?

Beschreiben Sie sich gegenseitig die Bilder und erraten Sie, welches Bild Ihr Partner / Ihre Partnerin beschreibt. Answers will vary.

BEISPIEL

S1: Es ist im Badezimmer...
S2: Auf Bild eins?
S1: Nein, es ist im Badezimmer vor dem Spiegel ...

1 **Partner Chat** You can also assign activity 1 on the Supersite. Students work in pairs to record the activity online. The pair's recorded conversation will appear in your gradebook.

1.

2.

3.

4.

5.

6.

2 Lebensregeln

Schreiben Sie eine Regelliste (*list of rules*) für Ihre Familie. Benutzen Sie reflexive Verben und Reflexivpronomen. Answers will vary.

2 **Expansion** Have the groups compare their lists and decide which rules are most important.

BEISPIEL

Alle in der Familie müssen einander jeden Tag helfen...

3 Arbeitsblatt

Schreiben Sie drei Aktivitäten auf, die Sie diese Woche gemacht haben. Dann fragen Sie vier Personen im Unterricht, was sie gemacht haben. Answers will vary.

BEISPIEL

S1: Hast du dich diese Woche über etwas geärgert?
S2: Ja.
S1: Worüber hast du dich geärgert?
S2: Über das schlechte Essen in der Cafeteria.

4 Körperteile

Arbeiten Sie mit einem Partner / einer Partnerin und beschreiben Sie Tätigkeiten, die mit den verschiedenen Körperteilen zu tun haben. Benutzen Sie die reflexiven und reziproken Verben aus der Liste. Answers will vary.

4 **Expansion** Have students come up with additional statements involving parts of the body and reflexive verbs.

BEISPIEL

S1: Wir schreiben einander mit den Händen.
S2: Wir kämmen uns die Haare.

A	B
Gesicht	sich anrufen
Haare	sich kämmen
Hände	sich küssen
Lippen	sich rasieren
Mund	sich schminken
Ohren	sich schreiben
	sich sprechen

5 Diskutieren und kombinieren

Sie und Ihr Partner / Ihre Partnerin bekommen zwei verschiedene Blätter mit Jasmins Alltagsroutine. Wechseln Sie sich ab und fragen Sie, was Jasmin jeden Abend und jeden Morgen macht. Answers will vary.

BEISPIEL

S1: Um 23 Uhr zieht sich Jasmin aus und zieht ihren Schlafanzug an. Was macht sie danach?
S2: Danach...

6 In der Stadt

Schreiben Sie mit einem Partner / einer Partnerin einen kurzen Text über eine Shoppingtour, die Sie zusammen am Wochenende machen wollen. Beantworten Sie die Fragen. Answers will vary.

6 **Virtual Chat** You can also assign activity 6 on the Supersite.

BEISPIEL

S1: Wir treffen uns am Samstagmorgen um 9 Uhr auf dem Markt vor der Bank.
S2: Wir haben uns einen Monat lang nicht gesehen. Wir freuen uns auf den Tag zusammen.

- Wo und wann treffen Sie sich?
- Worauf freuen Sie sich?
- Was kaufen Sie sich?
- Worüber ärgern Sie sich?
- Gehen Sie in ein Restaurant oder in ein Café?
- Was bestellen Sie sich?
- Worüber unterhalten Sie sich?
- Was machen Sie noch?

Zapping Video

AP* Theme: Science & Technology
Context: Healthcare & Medicine

Gesundheit bewegt uns

Deutschland hat ein duales Krankenversicherungssystem°. Zum einen gibt es die gesetzliche° Krankenversicherung. Sie ist eine verpflichtende° Versicherung für alle Personen in Deutschland. Zum anderen gibt es private Unternehmen, die Krankenversicherungen anbieten.

Die Central Krankenversicherung ist so eine private Krankenversicherung. Sie wurde 1913 als Aktiengesellschaft° in Köln gegründet und ist die älteste private Krankenversicherung Deutschlands. Die Central hat mehr als 1,75 Millionen Versicherte und bietet, neben der vollen Krankenversicherung, auch verschiedene Zusatzmodelle° an. Sie zählt mit mehr als 1.000 Mitarbeitern zu den führenden° privaten Krankenversicherungen in Deutschland.

Es gibt Spezialisten für die Gesundheit Ihrer Knochen°, ...

Ihres Herz-Kreislaufsystems°...

und Ihren Spezialisten für die private Krankenversicherung.

Krankenversicherungssystem *health insurance system* **gesetzliche** *compulsory* **verpflichtende** *obligatory* **Aktiengesellschaft** *corporation* **Zusatzmodelle** *additional plans* **führenden** *leading* **Knochen** *bones* **Herz-Kreislaufsystem** *cardiovascular system*

 Verständnis Beantworten Sie die Fragen mit den Informationen aus dem Video.

1. Wofür wirbt (*advertises*) der Mann?
   a. eine Arztpraxis   b. ein Krankenhaus
   c. eine Krankenversicherung

2. Wofür ist Central Spezialist?
   a. für Knochen   b. für die private Krankenversicherung
   c. für das Herz-Kreislaufsystem

 Diskussion Diskutieren Sie die folgenden Fragen mit einem Partner / einer Partnerin. Answers will vary.

1. Welche Unterschiede gibt es zwischen den Krankenversicherungen in Deutschland und denen in Ihrem Land?

2. Was macht Ihrer Meinung nach eine gute Krankenversicherung aus? Erarbeiten Sie ein Modell.

Communicative Goals

You will learn how to:

- talk about health
- talk about remedies and well-being

Beim Arzt  Vocabulary Tools

AP* Theme: Contemporary Life
Context: Health & Well-Being

Suggestion Point out that when reporting symptoms, it's common to say: **Ich *habe* Husten und Schnupfen**, rather than using the conjugated verbs.

Suggestion Model pronunciation of **Patient** and **Patientin**.

Wortschatz

die Gesundheit	*health*
die Allergie, -n	*allergy*
die Apotheke, -n	*pharmacy*
allergisch sein (gegen)	*to be allergic (to)*
krank/gesund werden	*to get sick/better*
in guter/schlechter Form sein	*to be in/out of shape*
sich verletzen	*to hurt oneself*
zum Arzt gehen	*to go to the doctor*
Symptome	*symptoms*
der Schmerz, -en	*pain*
die verstopfte Nase	*stuffy nose*
Zahnschmerzen (*pl.*)	*toothache*
leicht	*mild*
schwer	*serious*
schwindlig	*dizzy*
übel	*nauseous*
im Krankenhaus	*at the hospital*
der Arzt, ⸚e / die Ärztin, -nen	*doctor*
das Medikament, -e	*medicine*
die Grippe, -n	*flu*
der Krankenwagen, -	*ambulance*
die Notaufnahme, -n	*emergency room*
das Pflaster, -e	*adhesive bandage*
das Rezept, -e	*prescription*
das Thermometer, -	*thermometer*
der Zahnarzt, ⸚e / die Zahnärztin, -nen	*dentist*
sich (das Handgelenk / den Fuß) verstauchen	*to sprain (one's wrist/ankle)*
sich (den Arm / das Bein) brechen	*to break (an arm / a leg)*
weh tun (tut...weh)	*to hurt*
weinen	*to cry*
krank	*sick*

Expansion Ask students: **Wer hier studiert Medizin? Möchte jemand Arzt oder Krankenpfleger werden? Hat jemand hier sich schon mal was gebrochen, einen Arm oder ein Bein?** etc.

Ressourcen

vText | WB pp. 9–10 | LM p. 58 | vhlcentral

Er hat Fieber.

Sie hustet. (husten)

Sie gibt ihm eine Spritze.

Sie hat Rückenschmerzen.

der Patient, -en (die Patientin, -nen *f.*)

Sie ist schwanger.

die Tablette, -n

das Taschentuch, ⸚er

Er hat eine Erkältung.

Sie ist gesund.

HATSCHI!

Er niest. (niesen)

die Verletzung, -en

der Krankenpfleger, -

Sie treibt Sport.
(Sport treiben)

die Krankenschwester, -n

Sie hat Kopfschmerzen.

Er hat Bauchschmerzen.

RAUCHEN VERBOTEN

Anwendung

1 Assoziationen Wählen Sie ein Wort aus der Liste, das Sie mit einem der Ausdrücke assoziieren.

die Allergie	die Notaufnahme
die Apotheke	das Thermometer
das Ibuprofen	die Zahnschmerzen

1. sich den Arm brechen ___die Notaufnahme___
2. eine verstopfte Nase haben ___die Allergie___
3. zum Zahnarzt gehen ___die Zahnschmerzen___
4. 39 Grad Celsius Fieber haben ___das Thermometer___
5. Kopfschmerzen haben ___das Ibuprofen___
6. Medikamente kaufen ___die Apotheke___

1 Expansion Have students create four additional associations for a partner to complete.

2 Bilder beschriften Finden Sie ein passendes Wort oder einen passenden Ausdruck für jedes Bild. Sample answers are provided.

1. weinen

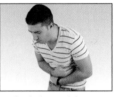

2. Bauchschmerzen haben

3. Fieber haben

4. die Ärztin

5. schwanger sein

6. in schlechter Form sein

3 Beim Arzt Hören Sie sich das Gespräch zwischen Elias und seinem Arzt an und markieren Sie dabei die Ausdrücke, die Sie hören.

1. Ich habe Halsschmerzen. ☑
2. Mir ist übel. ☐
3. Ich habe Fieber. ☑
4. Mein Bauch tut weh. ☐
5. Ich schlafe schlecht. ☑
6. Mir tut alles weh. ☑
7. Ich habe eine Erkältung. ☐
8. Meine Nase ist verstopft. ☑
9. Ich treibe Sport. ☐
10. Ich huste. ☑

3 Suggestion To prepare for the listening activity, ask students to be your "doctor." Provide a list of symptoms and have them diagnose the problem.

Kommunikation

4 Ratschläge geben

Sehen Sie sich mit einem Partner / einer Partnerin die Bilder an. Was ist passiert und welche Ratschläge (*advice*) geben Sie den Personen auf den Bildern, so dass es ihnen dann besser geht? Answers will vary.

▶ **BEISPIEL** Hanna
S1: *Hanna hat Zahnschmerzen*
S2: *Sie soll den Zahnarzt anrufen.*

4 Partner Chat You can also assign activity 4 on the Supersite. Students work in pairs to record the activity online. The pair's recorded conversation will appear in your gradebook.

1. Emma

2. Frau Schmidt

3. Jasmin

4. Moritz

5. Herr Meyer

6. Michaela

7. Klara

8. Jonas

5 Fragen und Antworten

Beantworten Sie mit einem Partner / einer Partnerin die Fragen. Answers will vary.

BEISPIEL

5 Virutal Chat You can also assign activity 5 on the Supersite.

S1: *Was machst du bei Kopfschmerzen?*
S2: *Ich lege mich ins Bett.*

1. Bist du gegen etwas allergisch?
2. Bekommst du jedes Jahr eine Spritze gegen die Grippe?
3. Hast du dir schon mal etwas gebrochen?
4. Wie oft gehst du zum Arzt?
5. Was machst du, um fit zu bleiben?

6 Diskutieren und kombinieren

Sie und Ihr Partner / Ihre Partnerin bekommen zwei verschiedene Blätter von Ihrem Lehrer / Ihrer Lehrerin. Fragen Sie Ihren Partner / Ihre Partnerin nach den Patienten, die in der Notaufnahme sind. Answers will vary.

BEISPIEL

S1: *Wer hat sich den Arm gebrochen?*
S2: *Frau Zimmermann hat sich den Arm gebrochen. Welches Problem hat Herr Arslan?*
S1: *Er hat...*

7 Wörter erraten

Erraten Sie mit zwei Mitschülern zusammen Wörter aus Ihrer neuen Vokabelliste. Eine Person beschreibt ein Wort und die anderen zwei müssen es erraten. Wechseln Sie sich ab. Answers will vary.

BEISPIEL

S1: *Man putzt sie sich, wenn sie verstopft ist.*
S2: *Die Nase!*

7 Suggestion Give students a few minutes beforehand to prepare their definitions.

Aussprache und Rechtschreibung

 Audio

Syllabic Stress

When a syllable in a word is stressed, it is pronounced with more emphasis than the other syllables. In German, the main stress is usually on the first syllable of a word.

Seife	**Na**se	**Au**ge	**Tech**niker	**fern**sehen

You have already learned that separable prefixes are always stressed, while inseparable prefixes are never stressed.

aufwachen	**an**kommen	be**spre**chen	Ver**kehr**	**wie**dersehen

In compound words, the first part of the compound is usually stressed.

Schlafanzug	**Spei**sekarte	**Bade**mantel	**Zahn**pasta	**Haus**schuh

In words borrowed from other languages, the placement of stress varies. In nouns ending with **–ei** or **-ie**, the final syllable is stressed. In verbs ending in **–ieren**, the stress is on the **ie** sound.

Com**pu**ter	Stu**dent**	Bäcke**rei**	Aller**gie**	ra**sie**ren

Expansion Give students examples of words that change meaning if stress is placed on the prefix: wieder**holen** *to repeat*, **wieder**holen *to fetch*; über**fahren** *to run over*, **über**fahren *to ferry*; durch**schlagen** *to smash*; **durch**schlagen *to split in two*.

1 **Aussprechen** Wiederholen Sie die Wörter, die Sie hören.

1. Rücken
2. duschen
3. anziehen
4. Einkauf
5. Gesicht
6. verlieren
7. überraschen
8. Handtuch
9. Bauchschmerzen
10. Hotel
11. Metzgerei
12. Psychologie

2 **Nachsprechen** Wiederholen Sie die Sätze, die Sie hören.

1. Ich nehme immer eine Zahnbürste, Zahnpasta und saubere Unterwäsche mit.
2. Mein Arzt verschreibt mir solche Medikamente nicht.
3. Robert rasiert sich nur mit Rasierschaum.
4. Die Studenten lernen am liebsten in der Bäckerei.
5. In den Ländern war die Demokratie nicht nur Theorie.
6. Wenn ich zu früh aufstehe, bekomme ich Kopfschmerzen.

3 **Sprichwörter** Wiederholen Sie die Sprichwörter, die Sie hören.

Was du heute kannst besorgen, das verschiebe nicht auf morgen.[1]

Aller Anfang ist schwer.[2]

[1] Never put off till tomorrow what you can do today.

[2] The first step is always the hardest. (lit. *Every beginning is hard.*)

Ressourcen

vText | LM p. 59 | vhlcentral

Im Krankenhaus Video

George und Sabite haben Meline ins Krankenhaus gebracht. Der Arzt möchte sie eine Nacht dabehalten und Meline beginnt wieder, von Hans zu träumen. Oder ist es gar kein Traum?

NATIONAL communication cultures STANDARDS

Vorbereitung Have students look at the video stills and guess what the episode will be about.

1

GEORGE Sie wird wieder gesund, Sabite. Sie ist auf den Kopf gefallen. Der Arzt untersucht sie gleich und dann gehen wir wieder nach Hause. Mein Bruder ist einmal aus einem Baum gefallen, ohne schwere Verletzungen zu haben.

5

ARZT Haben Sie ein Schwindelgefühl?
MELINE Ein bisschen.
ARZT Übelkeit?
MELINE Ahhh. Ja.
ARZT Ohrgeräusche?
MELINE Haben vor einer Stunde aufgehört.
ARZT Gut. Haben wir noch andere Symptome?
MELINE Außer Kopfschmerzen? Nein.

2

SABITE Was ist passiert?
GEORGE Er hat sich den Knöchel verstaucht. Und den Arm gebrochen. Und ihm war mehrere Stunden lang schlecht und schwindlig. Tage. Aber jetzt ist er gesund, in toller Form und schmerzfrei. Aber er meidet Bäume.

ARZT Okay. Hier ist ein Schmerzmittel. Lassen Sie mich die Schwester holen, damit wir eine Computertomographie machen können. Sie bleiben heute Nacht bei uns.
MELINE Och, Herr Doktor. Ich...
ARZT Frau... Meline. Es sieht so aus, als hätten Sie eine leichte Gehirnerschütterung.

3

ARZT Das ist eine schöne Beule auf Ihrem Kopf. Erinnern Sie sich, was passiert ist?
MELINE Ich habe gelernt und bin eingeschlafen. Und dann bin ich aufgewacht und vom Stuhl gefallen.
ARZT Und nachdem Sie das Bewusstsein wiedererlangt hatten?
MELINE Ich bin am Boden gelegen und meine Freunde haben mich gefunden.

4

MELINE Es geht mir gut, Dr. Klompenhouwer. Ist das holländisch?

---

1 **Richtig oder falsch?** Entscheiden Sie, ob die folgenden Sätze richtig oder falsch sind.

1. Meline ist auf ihren Arm gefallen. Falsch.

2. Georges Bruder ist einmal von der Garage gefallen. Falsch.

3. Georges Bruder hat sich einmal den Arm gebrochen. Richtig.

4. Meline hat eine Beule am Kopf. Richtig.

5. Sie ist aufgewacht und aus dem Bett gefallen. Falsch.

6. Jetzt hat sie ein Schwindelgefühl, Ohrgeräusche und Fieber. Falsch.

7. Dr. Klompenhouwer gibt Meline eine Spritze. Falsch.

8. Er will die Krankenschwester rufen, um eine CT zu machen. Richtig.

9. Meline hat wahrscheinlich eine leichte Gehirnerschütterung. Richtig.

10. Hans trägt einen Mundschutz (face mask), weil er Schnupfen und Husten hat. Richtig.

Expansion Point out that Meline says **bin am Boden gelegen** instead of **habe am Boden gelegen**. Explain that in Southern Germany and Austria, **sein** is used with **liegen** instead of **haben**. Explain also that the use of **am Boden** implies that she fell to the floor, whereas **auf dem Boden** would imply that she lay down intentionally.

7

ARZT George Bachman, Sabite Yilmaz?
ARZT Wir würden Meline heute Nacht gern im Krankenhaus behalten. Es geht ihr gut. Wir möchten auf Nummer sicher gehen.
SABITE Können wir sie sehen?
ARZT Sie würde heute lieber keine Besucher mehr haben.

8

MELINE Dr. Klompenhouwer? Sind Sie Chirurg? Ich verstehe das nicht.
HANS Ich musste mit meinen eigenen Augen sehen, dass es dir gut geht.
MELINE Hans, ich liebe dich!

9

ARZT Ihre Freunde sind hier, um Sie abzuholen.
MELINE Oh, Dr. Klompenhouwer, ganz herzlichen Dank. Sie haben mein Leben gerettet. Sie sind ein ausgezeichneter Arzt.
ARZT Danke, Meline. Wenn Sie Symptome haben, dann rufen Sie uns bitte auf jeden Fall an.

10

MELINE Wo ist George?
SABITE Er wäre hier, wenn er keine Uni hätte. Hans ist mit mir gekommen.
HANS Na, wie geht es unserer Patientin heute morgen? Das hier hat mir die Schwester gegeben, weil ich Schnupfen und Husten habe. Ich soll ja niemanden anstecken.

Nützliche Ausdrücke

- **untersuchen**
  to examine
- **der Baum**
  tree
- **der Knöchel**
  ankle
- **meiden**
  to avoid
- **die Beule**
  bump
- **Und nachdem Sie das Bewusstsein wiedererlangt hatten?**
  And after you regained consciousness?
- **das Schmerzmittel**
  painkiller
- **die Gehirnerschütterung**
  concussion
- **der Chirurg**
  surgeon
- **abholen**
  to pick (someone) up
- **ausgezeichnet**
  excellent

1B.1
- **Er wäre hier, wenn er keine Uni hätte.**
  He would have come if he weren't in class.

1B.2
- **Wir würden Meline heute Nacht gern im Krankenhaus behalten.**
  We would like to keep Meline in the hospital tonight.

2 **Zum Besprechen** Stellen Sie sich vor, Meline hat andere Symptome, als sie ins Krankenhaus kommt. Spielen Sie einen Dialog zwischen Meline und Dr. Klompenhouwer. Answers will vary.

2 **Expansion** Have students act out their dialogues for the class.

2 **Partner Chat** You can also assign activity 2 on the Supersite.

3 **Vertiefung** Wilhelm Conrad Röntgen hat etwas erfunden, das heute in jedem Krankenhaus täglich benutzt wird. Finden Sie heraus, was es ist und wie er es erfunden hat. Answers may include X-rays or electromagnetic radiation.

Apotheken Reading

AP* Theme: Contemporary Life
Context: Health & Well-Being

Suggestion Tell students that in Germany, supermarkets are not allowed to sell over-the-counter drugs. Before they read the article, have students skim for familiar words and cognates.

TIPP

Die Medizin refers to the practice of medicine, while **das Medikament** refers to medication.

In jeder Stadt ist immer mindestens eine Apotheke geöffnet. Das bedeutet, dass die Menschen 24 Stunden am Tag wichtige Medikamente bekommen können.

Apotheken sind Geschäfte, in denen man nicht nur Medikamente, sondern auch andere gesundheitsfördernde° Produkte kaufen kann. Neben Medikamenten findet man normalerweise auch Nahrungsergänzungsmittel° wie zum Beispiel Vitamine, Kosmetikprodukte, sowie Produkte für Diäten, Haut- und Fußpflege° und für die Kontaktlinsenpflege.

In Deutschland gibt es neben der traditionellen Medizin auch viele Menschen, die homöopathische Mittel° benutzen. Beide Medikamentensorten kann man in Apotheken kaufen, aber manche Ärzte und Apotheken spezialisieren sich auf die traditionelle Medizin oder auf die homöopathische Medizin.

DEUTSCHLAND IST DER GRÖSSTE Apothekenmarkt in Europa. Hier gibt es etwa 21.500 Apotheken. Jede Apotheke muss von einem staatlich geprüften° Apotheker geleitet werden°. Apotheken sind keine Ketten°, daher darf ein Apotheker höchstens vier davon besitzen. Die Medikamentenpreise werden von der Regierung° reglementiert. Relativ neu sind Versandapotheken°, bei denen man im Internet Medikamente bestellen kann.

Typische homöopathische Mittel	
Belladonna	Fieber und Kopfschmerzen
Kamille	Ohren- und Zahnschmerzen
Echinacea	Erkältung und Fieber
Hopfen	Schlafstörung°

staatlich geprüften state certified **geleitet werden** headed **Ketten** chains **Regierung** government **Versandapotheken** mail-order pharmacies **gesundheitsfördernde** health promoting **Nahrungsergänzungsmittel** dietary supplements **Fußpflege** foot care **Mittel** remedy **Schlafstörung** insomnia

Expansion Have students compare and contrast German pharmacies with their local drugstores.

---

1 **Richtig oder falsch?** Sagen Sie, ob die Sätze richtig oder falsch sind. Korrigieren Sie die falschen Sätze.

1. Die Schweiz ist der größte Apothekenmarkt in Europa.
   Falsch. Deutschland ist der größte Apothekenmarkt in Europa.
2. In Deutschland gibt es etwa 23.400 Apotheken.
   Falsch. In Deutschland gibt es etwa 21.500 Apotheken.
3. Es dürfen nicht mehr als vier Apotheken zusammengehören. Richtig.
4. Die deutsche Regierung reglementiert den Apothekerberuf. Richtig.
5. Bei Versandapotheken kann man online Medikamente bestellen. Richtig.

6. In deutschen Städten ist immer mindestens eine Apotheke geöffnet. Richtig.
7. In Apotheken kann man keine Vitamine kaufen.
   Falsch. In Apotheken kann man Vitamine kaufen.
8. Deutsche Apotheken verkaufen traditionelle und homöopathische Medikamente. Richtig.
9. Echinacea ist ein homöopatisches Mittel gegen Erkältung und Fieber. Richtig.
10. Ein homöopatisches Mittel gegen Schlafstörung ist Kamille.
    Falsch. Ein homöopatisches Mittel gegen Schlafstörung ist Hopfen.

Practice more at **vhlcentral.com**.

DEUTSCH IM ALLTAG

Ausdrücke zur Gesundheit

der Blutdruck	*blood pressure*
der blaue Fleck	*bruise*
der Hitzschlag	*heat stroke*
der Muskelkater	*sore muscles*
der Sonnenbrand	*sunburn*
der steife Hals	*stiff neck*

DIE DEUTSCHSPRACHIGE WELT

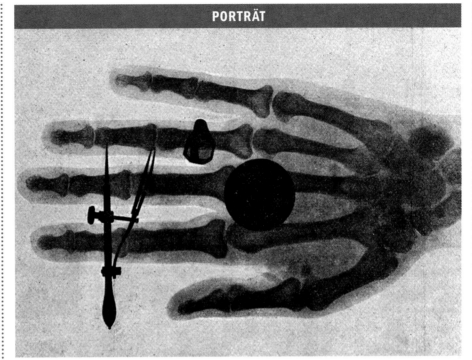

10°C   20°C

AP* Theme: Global Challenges
Föhn **Context:** Geography

Föhn heißt ein Windsystem in den Alpen.
Dieser Wind, auch Fallwind genannt, ist sehr
trocken°, weil er beim Aufsteigen° auf der
Südseite der Alpen Wasser in der Form von
Regen verliert. Wenn er von den Gipfeln°
der Alpen nach Norden ins Voralpengebiet°
weht°, ist die Luftmasse° trocken und warm.
Das Wetter in Bayern ist bei Föhn sonnig und
trocken. Aber viele Menschen haben bei
Föhn Kopfschmerzen.

trocken *dry* **Aufsteigen** *rising* **Gipfeln** *peaks* **Voralpengebiet**
foothills of the Alps **weht** *blows* **Luftmasse** *air mass*

PORTRÄT

Suggestion Tell students that **der Föhn, -e** is   **AP* Theme:** Science & Technology
Röntgen also used as a synonym for **Haartrockner**.   **Context:** Inventions as Catalysts of Change

Wilhelm Conrad Röntgen (1845–1923) war ein deutscher Physiker. Er arbeitete als
Professor an der Universität Würzburg, als er 1895 zufällig° eine besondere Art von
Strahlen° entdeckte: die X-Strahlen. Mit diesen Strahlen konnte man durch viele Materialien
hindurchsehen. Für diese Entdeckung° bekam Röntgen 1901 als erster Wissenschaftler
den Nobelpreis für Physik. Vor allem für die Medizin war diese Entdeckung sehr wichtig:
Ärzte konnten mit den X-Strahlen zum Beispiel Knochenbrüche° diagnostizieren. In seinem
Testament° schrieb Röntgen, dass die Strahlen nicht seinen Namen tragen dürfen.
Trotzdem nennt man die X-Strahlen heute in Deutschland und in Polen Röntgenstrahlen.

zufällig *accidentally* **Strahlen** *rays* **Entdeckung** *discovery* **Knochenbrüche** *bone fractures* **Testament** *will*

IM INTERNET

Suchen Sie im Internet eine deutsche Versandapotheke. Was kann man bei der Versandapotheke
bestellen? Kann man hier homöopathische
Mittel kaufen?

Find out more at **vhlcentral.com**.

---

2 **Was fehlt?** Ergänzen Sie die Sätze.

1. Föhn ist ein Windsystem in den ___Alpen___.
2. Bei Föhn ist das Wetter sonnig, warm und ___trocken___.
3. Viele Menschen haben bei Föhn ___Kopfschmerzen___.
4. Wilhelm Conrad Röntgen war ein deutscher ___Physiker___.
5. Er entdeckte die ___X-Strahlen___.
6. In Deutschland und Polen heißen die X-Strahlen ___Röntgenstrahlen___.

3 **Leben Sie gesund?** Diskutieren Sie mit einem Partner / einer
Partnerin: Was machen Sie, damit Sie gesund bleiben? Sollten Sie
mehr machen?

3 Suggestion Have students prepare a list of
their healthy and unhealthy habits before they
speak with their partners.

3 Partner Chat You can also assign activity 3
on the Supersite. Students work in pairs to record
the activity online. The pair's recorded
conversation will appear in your gradebook.

Ressourcen

v̂ Text   vhlcentral

Der Konjunktiv II S Presentation

Startblock Use the subjunctive, also called the **Konjunktiv II**, to talk about hypothetical or unreal conditions, to express wishes, and to make polite requests.

Könnte es auch schlimmer sein?

Er **wäre** hier, wenn er keinen Unterricht **hätte**.

Suggestion Run through the formation of the subjunctive with **sollen**, **wollen** and a few weak verbs, such as **machen**. Point out that **würden** + infinitive is often used in place of the subjunctive of weak verbs, to avoid confusion with the **Präteritum**. Students will learn about **würden** + infinitive in **1B.2**.

Suggestion You might want to remind students that they learned the subjunctive form of **mögen** and its uses in **Vol. 1, 4A.1**.

QUERVERWEIS

See **Appendix A** for a complete list of strong verbs and their **Präteritum** forms.

Suggestion Have students review the **Präteritum** of weak verbs, modals, mixed verbs, and strong verbs, taught in **Vol. 2, 2A.1**.

ACHTUNG

In conversation, German speakers often shorten the **du** and **ihr** subjunctive endings to **-st** and **-t**: **du gingst, ihr gingt; du wärst, ihr wärt.**

- To form the subjunctive of weak verbs and the modal verbs **sollen** and **wollen**, add the subjunctive endings **-e, -est, -e; -en, -et, -en** to the **Präteritum** stem. The subjunctive forms of these verbs are identical to their **Präteritum** forms.

wünschen (*to wish*)	
Präteritum	**Konjunktiv II**
ich wünschte	ich wünschte
du wünschtest	du wünschtest
er/sie/es wünschte	er/sie/es wünschte
wir wünschten	wir wünschten
ihr wünschtet	ihr wünschtet
Sie/sie wünschten	Sie/sie wünschten

Wir **sollten** vier Mal pro Woche Sport treiben.
*We **should** exercise four times a week.*

Ich **wünschte**, ich **spielte** besser Fußball.
*I **wish** I **played** soccer better.*

- To form the subjunctive of strong verbs, add the subjunctive endings to the **Präteritum** stem. If the stem vowel is **a**, **o**, or **u**, add an **Umlaut**. The verbs **sein** and **haben** and the modals **dürfen**, **können**, **mögen**, and **müssen** also follow this pattern.

Infinitiv	Präteritum	Konjunktiv II
bleiben	ich blieb	ich bliebe
geben	du gabst	du gäbest
gehen	er/sie/es ging	er/sie/es ginge
kommen	wir kamen	wir kämen
lassen	ihr ließt	ihr ließet
tun	Sie/sie taten	Sie/sie täten

Infinitiv	Präteritum	Konjunktiv II
dürfen	ich durfte	ich dürfte
können	du konntest	du könntest
mögen	er/sie/es mochte	er/sie/es möchte
müssen	wir mussten	wir müssten
haben	ihr hattet	ihr hättet
sein	Sie/sie waren	Sie/sie wären

- The only mixed verb commonly used in the subjunctive is **wissen**. Its subjunctive forms are the same as its **Präteritum** forms, but with an added **Umlaut** on the stem vowel.

Wüssten Sie, wo die Apotheke ist?
***Would** you **happen to know** where the pharmacy is?*

Wenn ich das nur **wüsste**!
*If only I **knew** that!*

Suggestion Point out that the red endings in the **Konjunktiv II** chart for **wünschen** are the same endings used with strong verbs. Have students practice deriving the full subjunctive conjugations of a few strong verbs, as well as **dürfen**, **können**, and **müssen**.

- Modals and the verbs **haben** and **sein** are often used in the subjunctive to make polite requests or ask questions.

  Hätten Sie Lust, diesen Film mit mir zu sehen?
  Do you feel like seeing this movie with me?

  Könntest du mir bitte ein Taschentuch reichen?
  Could you hand me a tissue, please?

- To express a wish that is contrary to reality, use the subjunctive form of **wünschen** with another clause in the subjunctive.

  Ich wünschte, wir hätten mehr Zeit!
  I wish we had more time!

  Ich wünschte, ich könnte heute schwimmen gehen.
  I wish I could go swimming today!

- The conjunction **wenn** (*if*) is often used with **nur** to mean *if only*. Move the conjugated verb to the end of a clause beginning with **wenn**.

  Wenn wir **nur** mehr Zeit **hätten**!
  If only we had more time!

  Wenn ich heute **nur** schwimmen gehen **könnte**!
  If only I could go swimming today!

- To express a condition that is hypothetical or contrary to fact, use a **wenn**-clause with a second clause that indicates what would happen if the **wenn**-clause were true.

  Wenn du Zeit **hättest, könnten** wir heute Abend ins Konzert gehen.
  *If you **had** time, we **could** go to a concert this evening.*

  Wenn mir die Füße nicht so **weh täten, käme** ich **gern** mit euch wandern.
  *If my feet didn't **hurt** so much, I'd **be happy to come** hiking with you.*

- You can use the conjunction **dann** to introduce the second clause in a hypothetical statement.

  Wenn du nicht so spät ins Bett **gingest**...
  *If you **didn't go** to bed so late,...*

  dann wärest du nicht so müde.
  *then you **wouldn't be** so tired.*

- Use **als ob** with the subjunctive, instead of **wenn**, to mean *as if*.

  Er tut, **als ob** er krank **wäre**.
  *He's acting **as if** he **were** sick.*

  Du siehst aus, **als ob** du eine Grippe **hättest**.
  *You look **as if** you **had** the flu.*

  Es hört sich an, **als ob** Paul Husten und Schnupfen **hätte**.
  *It sounds **like** Paul **has** a cough and the sniffles.*

  Sara tut so, **als ob** sie am besten Tennis **spielte**.
  *Sara's acting **like** she's the best tennis player.*

Suggestion Have students review the use of the subjunctive forms of **mögen**, taught in **Vol. 1, 4A.1**.

QUERVERWEIS

Wenn and **als ob** are subordinating conjunctions.

You will learn more about subordinating conjunctions in **2A.3**.

Suggestion Have students review the subordinating conjunctions **bevor**, **nachdem**, and **als**, taught in **Vol. 2, 4A.1**.

ACHTUNG

Ich möchte is typically used instead of **ich wollte** as the polite equivalent of **ich will**. **Ich hätte gern** is also frequently used for ordering in a restaurant.

Ressourcen

v̂ Text

WB
pp. 11–12

LM
p. 60

S
vhlcentral

Jetzt sind Sie dran! Wählen Sie die passenden Verbformen.

1. Ich (habe / hätte) gern einen Kaffee, bitte.
2. (Soll / Sollte) man immer wegen Rückenschmerzen zum Arzt gehen?
3. Ihr tut immer, als ob ihr keine Zeit zum Rad fahren (hättet / habt).
4. Wenn ich dagegen nicht allergisch (bin / wäre), (könnte / kann) ich Erdbeeren essen.
5. Ich (will / wollte), mein Computer (funktionierte / funktioniert) besser!
6. Wenn ich nur (wüsste / weiß), wo das Rezept für die Tabletten ist!
7. Die Zahnärztin (wünscht / wünschte), dass nicht so viele Patienten vor ihr Angst (haben / hätten).
8. Wenn Sie mehr Sport (treiben / trieben), dann (sind / wären) Sie in besserer Form.
9. (Könnten / Können) Sie die Krankenschwester rufen, bitte?
10. Wenn Roland kein Fieber (hätte / hat), (kommen / käme) er mit uns ins Restaurant.
11. (Dürfte / Darf) ich bitte die Tabletten und ein Glas Wasser haben?
12. Wenn es Lina nur nicht so schlecht (geht / ginge)!

Anwendung

1 **Expansion** Have students work in pairs to write about a hypothetical situation using the verbs from this activity.

1 **Konjunktivformen** Ergänzen Sie die Tabelle mit den fehlenden Verbformen im Präteritum und im Konjunktiv II.

Präsens	Präteritum	Konjunktiv II
wir kommen	wir kamen	wir kämen
ich gebe	ich gab	ich gäbe
sie will	sie wollte	sie wollte
ihr arbeitet	ihr arbeitetet	ihr arbeitetet
du hast	du hattest	du hättest
er geht	er ging	er ginge

2 **Hypothesen** Ergänzen Sie die Sätze mit den richtigen Konjunktivformen der Verben in Klammern.

BEISPIEL Wenn ich das _____wüsste_____ (wissen), könnte ich dir helfen.

1. Wenn Jan nicht krank wäre, _____könnte_____ (können) er ins Konzert gehen.
2. Wenn das Baby nicht so laut _____weinte_____ (weinen), könnte die Ärztin ihm eine Spritze geben.
3. Wenn Julian Zeit hätte, _____ginge_____ (gehen) er mit uns zum Fußballspiel.
4. Es sieht aus, als ob Sophia sehr unglücklich _____wäre_____ (sein).
5. Ali sieht aus, als ob er Fieber _____hätte_____ (haben).

3 **Suggestion** Remind students of how the conjunction **wenn** impacts word order. Do the first few sentences together as a class.

3 **Wünsche** Was würden (*would*) die Personen sagen? Schreiben Sie zu jedem Bild einen Satz im Konjunktiv II und benutzen Sie die angegebenen Verben.

▶ **BEISPIEL**

Kopfschmerztabletten haben
Wenn ich nur Kopfschmerztabletten hätte!

1. nicht so früh aufwachen
   müssen Wenn ich nur nicht so früh aufwachen müsste!

2. ihre Handynummer
   wissen Wenn ich nur ihre Handynummer wüsste!

3. Tennis spielen können
   Wenn ich nur Tennis spielen könnte!

4. nicht so viele Patienten
   haben Wenn ich nur nicht so viele Patienten hätte!

 Practice more at **vhlcentral.com**.

Kommunikation

4 Drei Wünsche Fragen Sie einander, was Sie sich wünschen. Benutzen Sie dabei den Konjunktiv II. Answers will vary.

BEISPIEL

S1: *Was hättest du am liebsten?*
S2: *Ich hätte am liebsten ein Motorrad.*

1. Was hättest du am liebsten?
2. Wo wärest du am liebsten?
3. Was wüsstest du am liebsten?
4. Was möchtest du am liebsten?

4 Virtual Chat You can also assign activity 4 on the Supersite. Students record individual responses that appear in your gradebook.

5 Stell dir mal vor... Fragen Sie Ihren Partner / Ihre Partnerin, was er/sie wäre, wenn er/sie eine andere Person, ein Tier oder ein Ding sein könnte. Answers will vary.

BEISPIEL

S1: *Wenn du ein Tier wärest, welches Tier wärest du und warum?*
S2: *Ich wäre ein Vogel, denn dann könnte ich fliegen. Und welches Tier wärest du?*

1. ein Tier
2. eine berühmte Person
3. ein Möbelstück
4. eine Person aus einem Film/Buch

5 Expansion Have students report what they learned about their partners to the class.

5 Virtual Chat You can also assign activity 5 on the Supersite. Students record individual responses that appear in your gradebook.

6 Wenn es nur anders wäre! Erzählen Sie einander, was Sie stört (*bothers*) und was Sie sich wünschen. Benutzen Sie den Konjunktiv II. Answers will vary.

BEISPIEL

S1: *Ich habe nicht viel Zeit für meine Hobbys. Ich wünschte, ich hätte mehr Zeit!*
S2: *Mein Computer ist so langsam. Ich wünschte, mein Computer wäre schneller!*

6 Partner Chat You can also assign activity 6 on the Supersite. Students work in pairs to record the activity online. The pair's recorded conversation will appear in your gradebook.

7 Rollenspiel: Im Restaurant Sie sind im Restaurant. Fragen Sie den Kellner / die Kellnerin, was er/sie Ihnen empfehlen kann. Answers will vary.

BEISPIEL

S1: *Guten Tag, was möchten Sie trinken?*
S2: *Ich hätte gern ein Mineralwasser.*
S3: *Und könnte ich bitte Apfelsaft bekommen?*

Kellner(in)	Gäste
Möchten Sie etwas trinken/essen?	Dürfte/Könnte ich bitte...
Was hätten Sie gern?	Hätten Sie vielleicht...?
	Ich hätte gern...
	Könnten Sie etwas empfehlen?
	Könnten Sie mir/uns bitte sagen...?
	Wir möchten bitte...
	Was / Wie viel macht das?

7 Suggestion Have students repeat the items in the word bank after you to practice pronunciation. Remind them to use the accusative with **Ich hätte gern...** and **Ich möchte...**

Speisekarte

Vorspeisen

Tomatensuppe	€4,80
Großer Salatteller	€9,50
Kleiner Salatteller	€3,60
Brotteller (Wurst oder Käse)	€6,80

Nachspeisen

Schokoladentorte	€6,45
Apfelkuchen	€5,80
Gemischtes Eis	€5,30
Obstsalat mit Pfirsich, Melone, Erdbeeren und Birne	€4,10

Hauptspeisen

Currywurst mit Pommes frites	€8,20
Hähnchen mit Reis, Pilzen und Gemüse	€18,80
Wiener Schnitzel mit Kartoffeln und kleinem Salat	€15,60
Thunfisch mit Bratkartoffeln und grünen Bohnen	€21,30
Scampi: Garnelen mit Reis und Knoblauch	€20,50

Getränke

Mineralwasser 0,2 l	€1,50
Limonade (Cola, Orange, Zitrone) 0,2 l	€1,80
Saft (Apfel, Ananas, Orange) 0,2 l	€2,20
Tasse Kaffee, Tee	€1,50

Würden with the infinitive  Presentation

Startblock The subjunctive of **werden** is **würden**. It is the subjunctive form used most commonly in conversation.

> Wir **würden** Meline heute Nacht gern im Krankenhaus behalten.

> Sie **würde** heute lieber keine Besucher mehr haben.

- The subjunctive forms of **werden** are the same as its **Präteritum** forms, but with an added **Umlaut** on the stem vowel.

QUERVERWEIS

You will learn about other uses of **werden** in **4B.2**.

werden		
Indikativ	**Präteritum**	**Konjunktiv II**
ich werde	ich wurde	ich würde
du wirst	du wurdest	du würdest
er/sie/es wird	er/sie/es wurde	er/sie/es würde
wir werden	wir wurden	wir würden
ihr werdet	ihr wurdet	ihr würdet
Sie/sie werden	Sie/sie wurden	Sie/sie würden

- **Würden** functions like a modal verb. When you use it with an infinitive, place **würden** in the position of the conjugated verb and place the infinitive at the end of the clause.

Würden Sie mir bitte **helfen?**
Would you help me, please?

An deiner Stelle **würde** ich zum Arzt **gehen**.
If I were you, I would go to the doctor.

Ich glaube, ich **würde** mit ihr **gehen**.
I think I would go with her.

Wenn er nur **mitkommen würde**!
If only he would come with us!

- Since all weak verbs, and some strong and mixed verbs, have identical subjunctive and **Präteritum** forms, German speakers typically use **würden** with the infinitive to express a subjunctive meaning for those verbs.

Sie **rannte** nach Hause.
She ran home. / She would run home.

Sie **würde** nach Hause rennen.
She would run home.

Ich **fragte** die Krankenschwester nach einem Pflaster.
I asked the nurse for a bandage. / I would ask the nurse for a bandage.

Ich **würde** die Krankenschwester nach einem Pflaster **fragen**.
I would ask the nurse for a bandage.

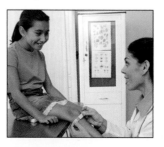

- Use **würden** + *infinitive* with a **wenn**-clause in the subjunctive to describe a hypothetical situation.

Wenn du vorsichtiger **wärest**, **würdest** du dich nicht so oft **verletzen**.
*If you **were** more careful, you **wouldn't hurt** yourself so much.*

Wenn ich Zahnschmerzen **hätte**, **würde** ich zum Zahnarzt **gehen**.
*If I **had** a toothache, I **would go** to the dentist.*

Wenn du mehr **Sport treiben würdest**, **wärst** du in besserer Form.
*If you **exercised more**, you'd **be** in better shape.*

Wenn Jan und Susanna **sich** nicht so oft **streiten würden**, **dann würden** sie sich **nicht trennen**.
*If Jan and Susanna **didn't fight** with each other so much, they **wouldn't be splitting up**.*

ACHTUNG

The subjunctive forms of **haben**, **sein**, **wissen**, and the modal verbs are commonly used in conversation. These verbs are rarely used as infinitives with **würden**.

- Use **würden** + *infinitive* to express wishes, give advice, make polite requests, or ask questions.

ACHTUNG

To give advice, use the expression **An deiner/Ihrer Stelle**, meaning *In your place...* or *If I were you...*

Ich **würde** gern in die Türkei **reisen**.

An Ihrer Stelle **würde** ich die Wahrheit **sagen**.

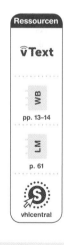

Ressourcen

v̂ Text

WB
pp. 13–14

LM
p. 61

vhlcentral

Sie **würden gern** nach Bern **fahren**.
*They'd **love** to go to Bern.*

An deiner Stelle **würde** ich das nicht **tun**.
*I **wouldn't do** that if I were you.*

Würdest du bitte das Fenster **schließen?**
*Would you **close** the window, please?*

Wir **würden** das nie **tun**.
*We **would** never **do** that.*

Expansion Have students pick a famous person and give them a few words of advice: **An Ihrer Stelle würde ich...**

Jetzt sind Sie dran! Geben Sie an, wie der Konjunktiv mit **würden** in jedem Satz verwendet wird (*is used*):
a. Frage b. Wunsch c. Ratschlag (*advice*) d. hypothetische Situation

1. _a_ Würden Sie die Tür bitte schließen?
2. _a_ Würdest du dich auf einen Besuch freuen?
3. _c_ An Ihrer Stelle würde ich mehr Gemüse essen.
4. _b_ Sie würden gern Musik hören.
5. _a_ Würden Sie bitte den Arzt rufen?
6. _c_ An seiner Stelle würde ich keinen Kaffee trinken.
7. _d_ Er würde sich nicht verletzen.
8. _d_ Wenn ich Rückenschmerzen hätte, würde ich mich hinlegen.
9. _b_ Ich würde gern nach Hause gehen.
10. _c_ An deiner Stelle würde ich zum Zahnarzt gehen.
11. _a_ Würdest du mir bitte das Thermometer geben?
12. _a_ Würden Sie lieber mit der Ärztin oder dem Arzt sprechen?

Anwendung

1 **Konjunktivformen** Schreiben Sie die Verben in die Konjunktivform mit **würden** + *Infinitiv* um.

> **BEISPIEL** ich käme _ich würde kommen_

1. sie sagte _sie würde sagen_
2. du nähmest _du würdest nehmen_
3. ich gäbe _ich würde geben_
4. wir zögen um _wir würden umziehen_
5. er lernte _er würde lernen_
6. ihr schriebet _ihr würdet schreiben_
7. sie arbeitete _sie würde arbeiten_
8. sie informierten sich _sie würden sich informieren_

2 **Was tun?** Was würden Sie an Stelle dieser Personen machen? Schreiben Sie zu jedem Bild einen Satz mit **würden** + *Infinitiv*. Benutzen Sie die Wörter im Wortschatz.

> den Automechaniker anrufen | an Land schwimmen
> Brille tragen | sehr still bleiben
> ein Boot bauen

▶ **BEISPIEL**
An seiner Stelle
würde ich ein Boot bauen.

1. **An seiner Stelle**
   würde ich eine Brille tragen.

2. **An ihrer Stelle**
   würde ich sehr still bleiben.

3. **An seiner Stelle**
   würde ich den Automechaniker anrufen.

4. **An ihrer Stelle**
   würde ich an Land schwimmen.

3 **Sätze umschreiben** Schreiben Sie die Sätze mit **würden** + *Infinitiv* um. Sample answers are provided.

> **BEISPIEL** Öffnen Sie bitte die Tür!
> *Würden Sie bitte die Tür öffnen?*

1. Räumt bitte eure Zimmer auf! Würdet ihr bitte eure Zimmer aufräumen?
2. Mach bitte den Fernseher aus! Würdest du bitte den Fernseher ausmachen?
3. Fahr bitte langsamer! Würdest du bitte langsamer fahren?
4. Zeigen Sie mir Ihre Bordkarte, bitte! Würden Sie mir Ihre Bordkarte zeigen, bitte?
5. Ladet dieses Dokument für mich herunter! Würdet ihr dieses Dokument für mich herunterladen?

Kommunikation

4 An deiner Stelle würde ich... Erzählen Sie Ihrem Partner / Ihrer Partnerin von Ihren Gesundheitsproblemen. Er/Sie sagt dann, was er/sie an Ihrer Stelle machen würde. Answers will vary.

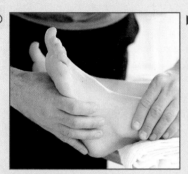

▶ **BEISPIEL**

S1: Mir tun die Füße weh.
S2: An deiner Stelle würde ich mich öfter hinsetzen.

Probleme	Ratschläge (Advice)
Ich bin immer müde.	früher ins Bett gehen
Ich habe Rückenschmerzen.	mehr Sport treiben
Ich bin in schlechter Form.	sich öfter hinsetzen
Mir ist schwindlig.	sich hinlegen
Mir tun die Füße weh.	Tabletten nehmen
Ich bin allergisch gegen...	zum Arzt gehen

5 Wenn es so wäre, ... Erzählen Sie einander, was Sie machen würden, wenn diese Situationen echt wären. Answers will vary.

BEISPIEL

S1: Wenn ich mehr Zeit hätte, würde ich öfter ausgehen. Und du?
S2: Ich würde mehr Sport treiben.

1. Wenn es jetzt Sommer wäre, ...
2. Wenn ich wieder ein Kind wäre, ...
3. Wenn ich den ganzen Tag frei hätte, ...
4. Wenn ich eine Zeitmaschine hätte, ...
5. Wenn ich fliegen könnte, ...
6. Wenn ich viel Geld hätte, ...

6 Austauschschüler Zwei Austauschschüler (exchange students) aus Deutschland sind für ein paar Tage bei Ihnen. Diskutieren Sie, was Sie in der Zeit alles zusammen machen könnten. Benutzen Sie den Konjunktiv II. Answers will vary.

BEISPIEL

S1: Sollten wir vielleicht ins Kino gehen?
S2: Das wäre okay, aber ich würde lieber ein Museum besuchen.
S3: Wir könnten auch...

Wir könnten vielleicht...	Das wäre toll/langweilig/schön/okay...
Möchtet ihr...	Ich hätte nicht so viel Lust auf...
Sollten wir vielleicht...	Es würde bestimmt viel/keinen Spaß machen, zu...
Ich würde gern / lieber / am liebsten...	

7 Ein neues Konzept Was würden Sie an Ihrer Schule anders machen? Machen Sie einen Plan und überzeugen (convince) Sie dann Ihre Mitschülern von den Vorteilen (advantages) Ihres Konzepts. Answers will vary.

BEISPIEL

S1: Wir würden zuerst allen Schülern einen Tag frei geben.
S2: Und Klassen würden niemals vor 10 Uhr beginnen.

4 Suggestion Tell students they don't have to stick to the **Ratschläge** in the word bank, as long as they use the **würde** + infinitive construction.

4 Expansion Have students repeat the activity, this time coming up with **schlechte Ratschläge**.

4 Virtual Chat You can also assign activity 4 on the Supersite. Students record individual responses that appear in your gradebook.

5 Virtual Chat You can also assign activity 5 on the Supersite. Students record individual responses that appear in your gradebook.

6 Suggestion Give students a few minutes to brainstorm ideas before they begin working in groups.

7 Expansion Have pairs share some of their suggestions with the class, and have students vote on whether or not the suggestions should be implemented.

Wiederholung

1 **Suggestion** Point out that although some speakers still treat **backen** (item 2) as a strong verb, it is more frequently conjugated as a weak verb in current usage.

1 Als ob!
Diese Leute tun, als ob sie alles machen könnten. Beschreiben Sie mit einem Partner / einer Partnerin, was sie machen und wie sie sich benehmen (*act*). Sample answers are provided.

BEISPIEL Florian / vom Tennisspielen sprechen

S1: Florian spricht immer vom Tennisspielen.
S2: Als ob er am besten spielte!

1 **Virtual Chat** You can also assign activity 1 on the Supersite.

1. Tim / vom Singen sprechen
   Als ob er am besten sänge!
2. Antonia und Jan / vom Backen sprechen
   Als ob sie am besten backten!
3. Simon / von seinen Reisen sprechen
   Als ob er am meisten reiste!
4. Mia / vom Laufen sprechen
   Als ob sie am schnellsten liefe!
5. Herr und Frau Schulz / vom Tanzen sprechen
   Als ob sie am schönsten tanzten!
6. Sara / vom Schreiben sprechen
   Als ob sie am schönsten schriebe!

2 Diskutieren und kombinieren
Sie und Ihr Partner / Ihre Partnerin bekommen zwei Blätter mit verschiedenen Informationen über Familie Weber. Was hat jedes Familienmitglied gemacht und was ist danach passiert? Finden Sie für jede Wirkung (*effect*) eine Ursache (*cause*). Answers will vary.

BEISPIEL

S1: Wie hat David sich den Arm gebrochen?
S2: Er ist beim Baseballspiel gefallen.

3 Wenn nur...
Schauen Sie sich mit einem Partner / einer Partnerin die Bilder an. Sagen Sie, was die Personen alles machen würden, wenn sie gesund wären. Answers will vary.

BEISPIEL

3 **Partner Chat** You can also assign activity 3 on the Supersite.

S1: Wenn Emma kein gebrochenes Bein hätte, könnte sie Fußball spielen.
S2: Auch könnte sie...

1. Emma

2. Herr Yildirim

3. Frau Krüger

4. Michael

4 Sätze bilden
Bilden Sie mit einem Partner / einer Partnerin logische Sätze. Verwenden Sie den Konjunktiv II für den Satzanfang und **würden** + *Infinitiv* für das Satzende. Sample answers are provided.

BEISPIEL ich / Zahnschmerzen haben / den Zahnarzt anrufen

Wenn ich Zahnschmerzen hätte, würde ich den Zahnarzt anrufen.

1. ich / mehr Geld haben / dir ein Geschenk mitbringen
   Wenn ich mehr Geld hätte, würde ich dir ein Geschenk mitbringen.

2. ihr / nicht so erkältet sein / campen gehen
   Wenn ihr nicht so erkältet wärt, würdet ihr campen gehen.

3. er / nicht arbeiten müssen / Zeit mit seiner Familie verbringen
   Wenn er nicht arbeiten müsste, würde er Zeit mit seiner Familie verbringen.

4. wir / spät ausgehen / morgen lange schlafen
   Wenn wir spät ausgingen, würden wir morgen lange schlafen.

5. du / nicht so viele Hausaufgaben haben / mehr Sport treiben
   Wenn du nicht so viele Hausaufgaben hättest, würdest du mehr Sport treiben.

5 Kritische Meinungen
Schauen Sie sich mit einem Partner / einer Partnerin die Bilder an. Fragen Sie ihn/sie, wie er/sie die Geräte findet. Answers will vary.

BEISPIEL

5 **Virtual Chat** You can also assign activity 5 on the Supersite. Students record individual responses that appear in your gradebook.

S1: Wie findest du das Handy?
S2: Ich fände es besser, wenn es nicht so alt wäre. Wie findest du es?

6 Arbeitsblatt
Wählen Sie eine schwierige Situation aus der Liste. Fragen Sie vier Personen, was sie in der Situation machen würden. Answers will vary.

BEISPIEL

S1: Was würdest du machen, wenn du einen Unfall sähest?
S2: Wenn ich einen Unfall sähe, würde ich den Krankenwagen rufen.

Im Kleidergeschäft Sie sind Verkäufer/Verkäuferin in einem Kleidergeschäft und versuchen Ihrem Partner / Ihrer Partnerin etwas zu verkaufen, aber ihm/ihr gefällt das Kleidungsstück nicht. Answers will vary.

BEISPIEL

S1: Hätten Sie gern das rote Kleid?
S2: Vielleicht... wenn es nur nicht so rot wäre.

7 Suggestion Bring in photos from fashion magazines and have students use them for this activity.

7 Partner Chat You can also assign activity 7 on the Supersite. Students work in pairs to record the activity online. The pair's recorded conversation will appear in your gradebook.

---

8 Ich wünschte, ... Sprechen Sie in der Klasse über Ihre Wünsche. Verwenden Sie den Konjunktiv II mit **sein**, **haben**, **können**, **müssen** oder **dürfen**. Answers will vary.

BEISPIEL

S1: Ich wünschte, ich müsste nicht so früh aufwachen. Was wünschst du dir?
S2: Ich wünschte, ich wäre in wirklich guter Form.

9 Mir geht's nicht gut Sagen Sie Ihrem Partner / Ihrer Partnerin, warum Sie sich nicht wohl fühlen. Beschreiben Sie alle Symptome. Der Partner / Die Partnerin sagt Ihnen, was Sie machen sollen, um sich besser zu fühlen. Answers will vary.

BEISPIEL

S1: Ich fühle mich nicht gut. Ich habe eine verstopfte Nase, und ich huste. Ich glaube, ich habe auch Fieber.
S2: Es hört sich an, als ob du eine schwere Erkältung hättest. Du solltest...

9 Partner Chat You can also assign activity 9 on the Supersite.

8 Expansion As a final project on the subjunctive, have students work in groups to prepare a poster with 10 statements about a hypothetical topic of their choice, such as their ideal world, what it would be like to be a cat, etc. Encourage them to use **würde** + infinitive constructions, except with the modals and **haben**, **sein**, **wissen**, **wünschen**.

Mein Wör|ter|buch

Schreiben Sie noch fünf weitere Wörter in Ihr persönliches Wörterbuch zu den Themen **Tagesroutine** und **Gesundheit**.

sich ankleiden

Übersetzung
to get dressed

Wortart
Verb

Gebrauch
Ich kleide mich nach der Dusche an.
Im Winter sollen die Kinder sich warm ankleiden.

Synonyme
sich anziehen, sich Kleidung anlegen

Antonyme
sich ausziehen, sich auskleiden

 Vocabulary Tools

Panorama

Mecklenburg-Vorpommern und Brandenburg

Mecklenburg-Vorpommern in Zahlen

NATIONAL connections cultures STANDARDS

- ▶ **Fläche:** *23.193 km²*
- ▶ **Bevölkerung:** *1,6 Millionen Menschen*
- ▶ **Städte:** *Rostock (204.000 Einwohner), Schwerin (96.000), Neubrandenburg (63.000)*
- ▶ **Wichtige Industriezweige:** *Schiffbau°, Reedereien°, Energiesektor, Tourismus*
- ▶ **Touristenattraktionen:** *Usedom, Rügen, Hiddensee, Greifswald, Stralsund*

Mecklenburg-Vorpommern zieht jedes Jahr viele Touristen an, die die Ostseeinseln° Usedom, Rügen und Hiddensee oder die historischen Hafenstädte° Rostock und Schwerin besuchen wollen.

QUELLE: Landesportal Mecklenburg-Vorpommern

Suggestion Tell students that **Buchenwald** was a concentration camp during the Nazi regime.

Brandenburg in Zahlen

- ▶ **Fläche:** *29.654 km²*
- ▶ **Bevölkerung:** *2,5 Millionen Menschen*
- ▶ **Städte:** *Potsdam (163.000 Einwohner), Cottbus (99.000), Brandenburg (71.000)*
- ▶ **Wichtige Industriezweige:** *Holzgewerbe°, Ernährungsindustrie°, Landwirtschaft°, Tourismus*
- ▶ **Touristenattraktionen:** *Potsdam, Schloss Sanssouci, Buchenwald im Grumsiner Forst*

Viele Touristen besuchen Potsdam mit seinen kaiserlichen Schlössern und Parkanlagen°.

QUELLE: Landesportal Brandenburg

Berühmte Menschen aus Mecklenburg-Vorpommern und Brandenburg

- ▶ **Heinrich von Kleist,** *Autor (1777–1811)*
- ▶ **Marie Christine Eleonora Prochaska,** *Soldatin (1785–1813)*
- ▶ **Heinrich Schliemann,** *Archäologe und Entdecker der Ruinen von Troja (1822–1890)*
- ▶ **Otto Lilienthal,** *Flugpionier (1848–1898)*
- ▶ **Gerhart Hauptmann,** *Autor und Literaturnobelpreisträger (1862–1946)*

Schiffbau shipbuilding **Reedereien** shipping companies **Ostseeinseln** Baltic Sea islands **Hafenstädte** port cities **Holzgewerbe** wood industry **Ernährungsindustrie** food industry **Landwirtschaft** agriculture **Parkanlagen** parks **Innere** inside

DÄNEMARK

OSTSEE

NATIONALPARK VORPOMMERSCHE BODDENLANDSCHAFT

RÜGEN

Stralsund

Schloss Güstrow

MECKLENBURGER BUCHT

SCHLESWIG-HOLSTEIN

Greifswald

POMMERSCHE BUCHT

Rostock

USEDOM

Wismar

MECKLENBURG-VORPOMMERN

Neubrandenburg

Schwerin

NATIONALPARK MÜRITZ

Müritz

Elbe

Oder

Havel

BRANDENBURG

POLEN

NIEDERSACHSEN

Oranienburg

BERLIN

Berlin

Frankfurt an der Oder

Havel

Brandenburg

Potsdam

Oder

Hafen von Rostock

Spree

Neiße

SACHSEN-ANHALT

Cottbus

SACHSEN

Segeln in Brandenburg

—— Landesgrenzen
• Stadt
⊙ Landeshauptstadt
✪ Hauptstadt

0 ——— 25 Meilen
0 ——— 25 Kilometer

Suggestion You may want to mention the comedian Loriot as another example of a **berühmte Brandenburger**. Many of his classic sketches, such as **Die Nudel** or **Die Jodelschule**, can be found online.

TSCHECHIEN

Unglaublich, aber wahr!

Auf Rügen gibt es seit 2010 eine neue Touristenattraktion: Das „Haus-Kopf-über". Hier kann man ein Haus besuchen, das auf dem Dach steht. Besucher stehen auf der Unterseite des Hauses und können sich das Innere° des Hauses ansehen. **AP* Theme:** Beauty & Aesthetics
Context: Architecture

AP* Theme: Beauty & Aesthetics
Context: Architecture

Architektur

Schloss Sanssouci

Suggestion Before they read about the Potsdam Conference, have students briefly share what they know about the situation in Germany in 1945.

Schloss Sanssouci war der Lieblingsort von Friedrich dem Großen, König von Preußen. Das Schloss war seine Sommerresidenz, in der er sein Privatleben genießen wollte. Der Name Sanssouci bedeutet „ohne Sorge°". Es wurde von 1745 bis 1747 von Georg Wenzeslaus von Knobelsdorff nach den Ideen des Königs auf einem terrassierten Weinberg° gebaut°. Es gilt als Hauptwerk deutscher Rokokoarchitektur. Die prächtigen° und eleganten Räume sind noch original ausgestattet°. Das Schloss und die Parks sind eine der größten Touristenattraktionen Brandenburgs.

Geographie
AP* Theme: Global Challenges
Context: Geography

Rügen

Die Ostseeinsel Rügen ist mit 926 km² die größte deutsche Insel und gehört zum Bundesland Mecklenburg-Vorpommern. 70.000 Menschen leben hier ständig. Dazu kommen rund 800.000 Urlauber, die die Insel jedes Jahr besuchen.

Zu den meistbesuchten Touristenattraktionen zählen die Kreidefelsen° im Nationalpark Jasmund und die rund 80 km langen Sand- und Naturstrände.

Archäologie
AP* Theme: Families & Communities
Context: Family Structure

Megalithgräber°

In Mecklenburg-Vorpommern bauten Menschen während der Jungsteinzeit° fast 5.000 große Grabmonumente. Diese Gräber heißen auch Megalithgräber. Die ersten Gräber stammen aus der Zeit um 3.500 vor Christus. Anfangs waren diese Gräber nur für Familienoberhäupter°, später wurden sie immer größer, und ganze Familien wurden in den Gräbern beerdigt°. Etwa 1.000 dieser Grabanlagen° gibt es noch, und wenn man durch die flache Landschaft Mecklenburg-Vorpommerns fährt, kann man sie heute noch gut erkennen.

AP* Theme: Global Challenges
Context: Political Issues

Geschichte

Die Potsdamer Konferenz

Zwischen dem 17. Juli und dem 2. August 1945 trafen sich in Potsdam die Alliierten Großbritannien, USA und UdSSR. Sie berieten°, was mit dem ehemaligen Kriegsgegner° Deutschland passieren sollte. An der Konferenz nahmen der sowjetische Diktator Josef Stalin, der US-Präsident Harry S. Truman und die britischen Premierminister Winston Churchill und Clement Attlee teil. Sie entschieden°, dass Deutschland eine Demokratie werden sollte, alle Naziparteien verboten werden und Deutschland eine wirtschaftliche Einheit° werden sollte. Konflikte zwischen Stalin und den anderen Alliierten führten aber später zur Teilung° Deutschlands.

 IM INTERNET

1. Suchen Sie Informationen über die Potsdamer Konferenz: Warum traf man sich in Potsdam? Was wollten die Alliierten mit Deutschland machen?

2. Suchen Sie Informationen über Schloss Sanssouci: Welche Gärten sind Teil der Parkanlage?

Find out more at **vhlcentral.com**.

Sorge *worry* **Weinberg** *vineyard* **wurde... gebaut** *was built* **prächtigen** *grand* **ausgestattet** *furnished*
berieten *deliberated* **Kriegsgegner** *wartime enemy* **entschieden** *decided* **Einheit** *unity* **Teilung** *division*
Kreidefelsen *chalk rocks* **Megalithgräber** *megalith graves* **Jungsteinzeit** *New Stone Age*
Familienoberhäupter *patriarchs* **wurden... beerdigt** *were buried* **Grabanlagen** *burial sites*

Was haben Sie gelernt? Ergänzen Sie die Sätze.

1. Auf Rügen gibt es ein Haus, das auf dem ___Kopf___ steht.

2. Wenn man das ___Innere___ des Hauses sehen will, muss man auf der Unterseite des Hauses stehen.

3. Schloss Sanssouci war das Schloss von ___Friedrich dem Großen___.

4. Die Architektur von Sanssouci ist ein Beispiel der ___Rokokoarchitektur___.

5. Die Potsdamer Konferenz fand im Jahre ___1945___ statt.

6. An der Konferenz nahmen Churchill, Truman und ___(Josef) Stalin___ teil.

7. Rügen ist die ___größte___ deutsche Insel.

8. Sie liegt an der ___Ostsee___.

9. Die großen Grabmonumente in Mecklenburg-Vorpommern heißen auch ___Megalithgräber___.

10. Die größeren Gräber sind nicht nur für ___Familienoberhäupter___, sondern auch für die ganze Familie.

 Practice more at **vhlcentral.com**.

Lesen Audio: Reading

Vor dem Lesen

AP* Theme: Contemporary Life
Context: Health & Well-Being

Strategien

Reading for the main idea

You have already learned to make predictions about the content of a reading by looking at its format, titles, and subtitles, looking for cognates, skimming to get the gist, and scanning for specific information. Reading for the main idea involves locating the topic sentences of each paragraph to determine the author's purpose. Topic sentences can provide clues about the content of each paragraph, as well as the general organization of the reading. Your choice of which reading strategies to use will depend on the style and format of the reading selections you encounter.

 Untersuchen Sie den Text

Sehen Sie sich beide Texte kurz an. Welche Ähnlichkeiten (*similarities*) und Unterschiede (*differences*) können Sie erkennen? Welche Strategien können Sie benutzen, um die Art (*type*) der Texte zu identifizieren? Vergleichen Sie Ihre Ideen mit denen eines Partners / einer Partnerin.

Vergleichen Sie die Texte

- Analysieren Sie das Format des ersten Texts. Gibt es eine Überschrift (*heading*)? Gibt es viele Abschnitte (*sections*)? Wie ist der Text gegliedert (*structured*)? Sehen Sie sich jetzt den Inhalt an. Was für Vokabeln benutzt man? Was ist die Hauptidee von jedem Abschnitt?

- Ist der zweite Text genauso gegliedert wie der erste? Gibt es Überschriften und verschiedene Abschnitte? Ist die Information ähnlich der im ersten Text? Welche Vokabeln werden benutzt? Was für eine Art Text ist es? Was ist die Hauptidee von jedem Abschnitt? Haben beide Texte das gleiche Thema?

Andis Blog

Kommentare

Vorheriger Eintrag

Nächster Eintrag

Archiv

3. Juni 2012

Meine Gesundheitspläne

Heute war ich beim Arzt für eine allgemeine Untersuchung°. Er hat mir gesagt, dass ich in keiner guten Form bin! Meine Blutdruckwerte sind zu hoch. Ich muss gesünder leben! Besser essen und mehr Sport treiben. Das soll ich machen:

Als Erstes muss ich mehr schlafen. Jeden Tag mindestens sieben Stunden. Vielleicht kann ich ja weniger Videospiele spielen!

Vor allem muss ich mich mehr bewegen°. Auf der Arbeit werde ich jeden Tag zum Büro Treppen steigen und nicht mit dem Aufzug° fahren! Ich bin früher immer gerne gelaufen. Also werde ich wieder anfangen zu joggen. Drei Mal die Woche möchte ich eine halbe Stunde joggen. Das wäre super! Ich habe einen tollen Artikel gefunden, der zeigt, wie man drei kurze Übungen machen kann, um fit zu werden. Ich möchte diese Übungen auch drei Mal die Woche machen.

Im Allgemeinen darf ich nicht so viel Stress in meinem Leben haben. Schlafen, Bewegung und besser essen sind ein guter Start. So hoffe ich, bald wieder gesünder zu sein.

Andi

Untersuchung *check-up* **mich... bewegen** *move around* **Aufzug** *elevator*

Fit in 10 Minuten!

Sie wollen fit werden? Hier sind 3 kurze Übungen für Bauch und Po°.
Machen Sie dreimal die Woche 5 bis 10 Wiederholungen jeder Übung.

Aufwärmen

Stehen sie aufrecht°, die Füße hüftweit° auseinander.
Gehen Sie 2 Minuten lang auf der Stelle. Die Arme schwingen mit.

Obere Bauchmuskeln

Übung 1

Legen Sie sich mit dem Rücken auf ein Handtuch. Ziehen Sie jetzt die Knie an. Fassen Sie das Handtuch mit den Händen an den Enden hinter dem Kopf. Rollen Sie nun den Oberkörper° langsam auf. Halten Sie kurz die Position und rollen Sie langsam wieder in die erste Position.

Schräge° Bauchmuskeln

Legen Sie sich auf den Rücken und ziehen Sie die Knie an. Heben Sie die Unterschenkel°, bis diese parallel zum Boden sind. Verschränken° Sie nun die Hände hinter dem Kopf. Jetzt heben Sie den linken Ellenbogen zum rechten Knie und zurück, ohne dass die rechte Schulter den Boden berührt°. Der Rücken bleibt auf dem Boden. Wiederholen Sie die Übung mit der anderen Seite.

Übung 2

Po

Übung 3

Hände und Knie berühren den Boden. Heben Sie nun das linke Knie, bis Oberschenkel und Boden etwa parallel sind. Halten Sie kurz diese Position und senken Sie das Knie langsam wieder zum Boden. Wiederholen Sie die Übung auch mit der anderen Seite.

Suggestion If you have a lively class and a suitable space, have students try out the exercises described.

Po glutes **aufrecht** upright **hüftweit** hip-wide **Oberkörper** upper body **Schräge** Oblique
Unterschenkel lower leg **Verschränken** Cross **berührt** touches

---

Nach dem Lesen

Was fehlt? Ergänzen Sie die Sätze.

1. Andi war heute beim _____Arzt_____.
2. Andi muss besser essen und mehr _____Sport_____ treiben.
3. Andi darf nicht so viel _____Stress_____ in seinem Leben haben.
4. Die Übungen, die Andi gefunden hat, sind für _____Bauch_____ und Po.
5. In der zweiten Übung verschränkt man die _____Hände_____ hinter dem Kopf.
6. In der dritten Übung berühren Hände und _____Knie_____ den Boden.

Richtig oder falsch? Sind die Sätze richtig oder falsch? Korrigieren Sie die falschen Sätze.

Sample answers are provided.

	richtig	falsch
1. Andis Arzt sagt, dass alles in Ordnung ist. Der Arzt sagt, dass Andi gesünder leben muss.	☐	☑
2. Andi muss sich mehr bewegen.	☑	☐
3. Andi will jeden Tag joggen gehen. Andi will 3 Mal die Woche joggen gehen.	☐	☑
4. Andi will jeden Tag mindestens 7 Stunden schlafen.	☑	☐
5. Vor der ersten Übung soll man die Muskeln aufwärmen.	☑	☐
6. In der ersten Übung liegt man mit dem Gesicht nach unten. In der ersten Übung liegt man auf dem Rücken.	☐	☑
7. In der zweiten Übung trainiert man die Rückenmuskeln. In der zweiten Übung trainiert man die Bauchmuskeln.	☐	☑
8. Alle Übungen kann man in 5 Minuten machen. Alle Übungen kann man in 10 Minuten machen.	☐	☑

Bessere Gesundheit Diskutieren Sie mit einem Partner / einer Partnerin: Sie wollen gesünder leben. Was müssen Sie machen? Welche Ziele (*goals*) haben Sie? Wie können Sie diese Ziele erreichen (*achieve*)?

BEISPIEL

S1: *Ich muss endlich gesünder leben.*
S2: *Was willst du machen?*
S1: *Ich will...*

Partner Chat You can also assign this activity on the Supersite. Students work in pairs to record the activity online. The pair's recorded conversation will appear in your gradebook.

Hören

Vorbereitung

Wie ist es, mit anderen Menschen zusammenzuwohnen? Schreiben Sie vier Dinge auf, die man mit Mitbewohnern planen oder diskutieren muss, damit das Zusammenwohnen ohne Probleme funktioniert. Answers will vary.

 ## Zuhören

Hören Sie sich den Dialog zwischen Marco, Annette und Simone an. Worüber diskutieren sie? Schreiben Sie mindestens sechs Sachen auf. Sample answers are provided.

| Frühstück machen |
| Küche sauber machen |
| Badezimmer benutzen |
| Abfall raustragen |
| Zeitung lesen |
| Geschirr spülen |

Verständnis

 Richtig oder falsch Sind die Sätze richtig oder falsch? Korrigieren Sie die falschen Sätze. Sample answers are provided.

1. Marco, Simone und Annette wohnen in einer Wohnung zusammen.
   Richtig.

2. Marco möchte um 7 Uhr ins Badezimmer.
   Falsch. Simone möchte um 7 Uhr ins Badezimmer.

3. Alle Personen bleiben 20 Minuten im Badezimmer.
   Falsch. Marco bleibt nur 15 Minuten im Badezimmer.

4. Simone wird sich nicht im Badezimmer schminken.
   Richtig.

5. Annette muss das Frühstück um 7 Uhr machen.
   Falsch. Annette muss das Frühstück vor 7 Uhr machen.

6. Um 7.20 Uhr darf Annette ins Badezimmer.
   Richtig.

7. Simone muss den Abfall runterbringen.
   Falsch. Annette muss den Abfall runterbringen.

8. Marco liest jeden Morgen Zeitung.
   Richtig.

 Morgenroutine Sie und Ihre Partner / Partnerinnen wohnen in einer Wohngemeinschaft (WG) zusammen. Wie funktioniert das Zusammenleben? Wer benutzt wann das Bad? Wie lange? Wie organisieren Sie das Frühstück? Wer räumt auf? Planen Sie die WG-Regeln.

BEISPIEL

S1: *Zuerst müssen wir über das Badezimmer sprechen.*
S2: *Ich möchte als Erster ins Badezimmer.*
S3: *Und wann?*
S1: *Kann ich es um 7 Uhr benutzen?*

Schreiben

Strategien

Using linking words

You can make your writing more sophisticated by using linking words (**Verbindungswörter**) to connect simple sentences or clauses, creating more complex sentences.

Consider these two passages.

> Heute Morgen war ich beim Arzt. Ich hatte starke Kopfschmerzen. Ich hatte einen schlimmen Schnupfen. Es waren viele Leute im Wartezimmer. Ich musste über eine Stunde warten. Der Arzt hat mich behandelt. Er hat gesagt, dass ich eine Grippe habe.

> Heute Morgen war ich beim Arzt, **denn** ich hatte starke Kopfschmerzen und einen schlimmen Schnupfen. Es waren viele Leute im Wartezimmer. **Deshalb** musste ich über eine Stunde warten. **Endlich** hat der Arzt mich behandelt. Er hat gesagt, dass ich eine Grippe habe.

Expansion Have students work in groups to create a plan and then pitch it to the rest of the class in a Q & A session.

Bio-Produkte haben's drauf.

Thema

 Unsere neue Firma

Sie wollen eine Firma im Bereich Gesundheit gründen und brauchen einen Businessplan. Die neue Firma kann ein Fitness-Center, ein Wellness-Center, ein Bioladen (*health-food store*) oder etwas Ähnliches sein.

Schreiben Sie einen Businessplan für potentielle Investoren. Bevor Sie anfangen, überlegen Sie sich Antworten auf die folgenden Fragen:

- Warum gibt es Ihre Firma?
- Welche Art von Service oder welche Produkte bieten Sie an (*offer*)?
- Warum braucht man diesen Service oder diese Produkte?
- Wer sind die Kunden Ihrer Firma?
- Wie erfüllt Ihre Firma die Bedürfnisse (*needs*) Ihrer Kunden?
- Wie ist Ihre Firma anders als ähnliche Firmen?
- Wie heißt Ihre Firma?

Benutzen Sie Verbindungswörter, damit die Präsentation Ihrer Geschäftsidee überzeugend (*persuasive*) wird.

Verbindungswörter			
aber	*but*	**deswegen**	*that's why*
als erstes	*first*	**endlich**	*finally*
also	*so*	**manchmal**	*sometimes*
außerdem	*moreover*	**normalerweise**	*usually*
danach	*then, after that*	**oder**	*or*
dann	*then*	**oft**	*often*
denn	*because*	**sondern**	*however*
deshalb	*so*	**sowie**	*as well as*

Lektion 1A

der Körper

der Arm, -e *arm*
das Auge, -n *eye*
die Augenbraue, -n *eyebrow*
der Bart, ⁼e *beard*
der Bauch, ⁼e *belly*
das Bein, -e *leg*
der Ell(en)bogen, - *elbow*
der Finger, - *finger*
der Fuß, ⁼e *foot*
das Gesicht, -er *face*
das Haar, -e *hair*
der Hals, ⁼e *neck*
die Hand, ⁼e *hand*
das Knie, - *knee*
der Kopf, ⁼e *head*
die Lippe, -n *lip*
der Mund, ⁼er *mouth*
die Nase, -n *nose*
das Ohr, -en *ear*
der Rücken, - *back*
die Schulter, -n *shoulder*
der Zeh, -en *toe*

Verben

aufwachen (wacht...auf) *to wake up*
(sich) duschen *to take a shower*
ins Bett gehen *to go to bed*
sich anziehen (zieht sich...an)
   to get dressed
sich die Haare bürsten *to brush
   one's hair*
sich die Zähne putzen *to brush
   one's teeth*
sich rasieren *to shave*
sich schminken *to put on makeup*

im Badezimmer

der Bademantel, ⁼ *bathrobe*
die Bürste, -n *brush*
der Haartrockner, - *hair dryer*
das Handtuch, ⁼er *towel*
der Hausschuh, -e *slipper*
der Kamm, ⁼e *comb*
der Lippenstift, -e *lipstick*
der Rasierer, - *razor*
der Rasierschaum *shaving cream*
der Schlafanzug, ⁼e *pajamas*
die Seife, -n *soap*
das Shampoo, -s *shampoo*
die Zahnbürste, -n *toothbrush*
die Zahnpasta
   (*pl.* Zahnpasten) *toothpaste*

Accusative reflexive pronouns
   See pp. 28–29.
Dative reflexive pronouns
   See pp. 32–33.
Reflexives used with prepositions
   See pp. 36–37.

Lektion 1B

im Krankenhaus

der Arzt, ⁼e / die Ärztin, -nen *doctor*
die Grippe, -n *flu*
der Krankenpfleger, - *nurse (m.)*
die Krankenschwester, -n *nurse (f.)*
der Krankenwagen, - *ambulance*
das Medikament, -e *medicine*
die Notaufnahme, -n *emergency room*
der Patient, -en / die Patientin, -nen
   patient
das Pflaster, -e *adhesive bandage*
das Rezept, -e *prescription*
die Tablette, -n *pill*
das Taschentuch, ⁼er *tissue*
das Thermometer, - *thermometer*
die Verletzung, -en *injury*
der Zahnarzt, ⁼e / die Zahnärztin, -nen
   dentist
sich (das Handgelenk / den Fuß)
   verstauchen *to sprain (one's
   wrist/ankle)*
sich (den Arm / das Bein) brechen *to
   break (an arm / a leg)*
eine Spritze geben *to give a shot*
weh tun (tut...weh) *to hurt*
weinen *to cry*
gesund *healthy*
krank *sick*
schwanger *pregnant*

Der Konjunktiv II

wünschen *to wish*

die Gesundheit

die Allergie, -n *allergy*
die Apotheke, -n *pharmacy*
die Erkältung, -en *cold*
allergisch sein (gegen) *to be
   allergic (to)*
krank/gesund werden *to get sick/better*
in guter/schlechter Form sein *to be in/
   out of shape*
sich verletzen *to hurt oneself*
Sport treiben *to exercise*
zum Arzt gehen *to go to the doctor*

Symptome

die Bauchschmerzen (*pl.*) *stomachache*
die Kopfschmerzen (*pl.*) *headache*
die Rückenschmerzen (*pl.*) *backache*
der Schmerz, -en *pain*
die verstopfte Nase *stuffy nose*
die Zahnschmerzen (*pl.*) *toothache*
Fieber haben *to have a fever*
husten *to cough*
niesen *to sneeze*
leicht *mild*
schwer *serious*
schwindlig *dizzy*
übel *nauseous*

Der Konjunktiv II See pp. 50–51.
würden See pp. 54–55.

Suggestion Have students brainstorm a list of things they associate with city life. Ask them which of those things they can identify in the picture.

Teaching Tip Look for icons indicating activities that address the modes of communication. Follow this key:

→ⵡ←	Interpretive communication
←ⵡ→	Presentational communication
ⵡ↔ⵡ	Interpersonal communication

Communicative Goals

You will learn how to:

- talk about errands and banking
- talk about places and businesses in town

Wortschatz

Orte	places
das Blumengeschäft, -e	flower shop
die Drogerie, -n	drugstore
das Kino, -s	movie theater
die Polizeiwache, -n	police station
das Rathaus, ̈er	town hall
der Waschsalon, -s	laundromat

Suggestion Model the pronunciation of **Waschsalon**.

geöffnet	open
geschlossen	closed
die Post	**mail**
die Adresse, -n	address
die Briefmarke, -n	stamp
der Briefumschlag, ̈e	envelope
die Postkarte, -n	postcard
auf der Bank	**at the bank**
das Geld	money
das Kleingeld	change
das Konto (pl. die Konten)	bank account
die Münze, -n	coin
Geld abheben	to withdraw money
Geld einzahlen	to deposit money
Ausdrücke	**expressions**
das Bargeld	cash
bar bezahlen	to pay in cash
Besorgungen machen	to run errands
ein Formular ausfüllen	to fill out a form
mit der Karte bezahlen	to pay by (credit) card
unterschreiben	to sign

ACHTUNG

Post is short for **das Postamt, ̈er** or **die Postfiliale, -n**. It is also used to refer to the mail in general: **Wann kommt die Post?** *When does the mail arrive?*

Suggestion Ask students if they ever send or receive letters. Tell them that a pen pal is a **Brieffreund** or **Brieffreundin**.

Ressourcen

vText · WB pp. 15–16 · LM p. 62 · vhlcentral

Besorgungen   Vocabulary Tools

Suggestion Point out the separable-prefix verbs on this page: **abschicken, abheben, einzahlen, ausfüllen.** Remind students that these are listed in the end-of-unit **Wortschatz** with their 3rd-person forms in parentheses. Tell students that **unterschreiben** is an inseparable-prefix verb, and ask them to guess its past-tense forms.

AP* Theme: Families & Communities
Context: Urban, Suburban, & Rural Life

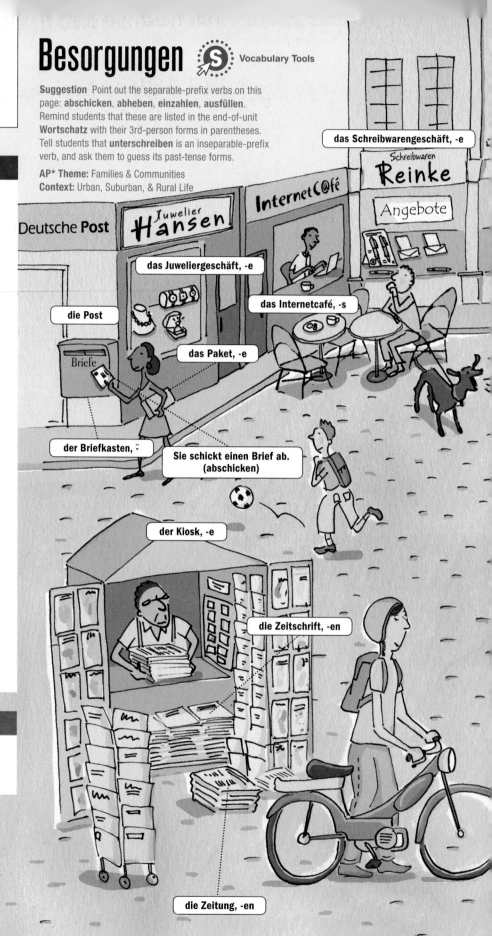

das Schreibwarengeschäft, -e

das Juweliergeschäft, -e

das Internetcafé, -s

die Post

das Paket, -e

der Briefkasten, ̈

Sie schickt einen Brief ab. (abschicken)

der Kiosk, -e

die Zeitschrift, -en

die Zeitung, -en

der Kosmetiksalon, -s

der Briefträger, -
(die Briefträgerin, -nen *f.*)

der Brief, -e

die Bank, -en

der Geldschein, -e

der Geldautomat, -en

Suggestion Tell students that **Euro** bills come in different sizes so that they can be easily identified by the visually impaired.

Anwendung

1 Was passt nicht? Welches Wort passt nicht zu den anderen?

BEISPIEL Briefumschlag, (Kleingeld,) Briefmarke, Paket

1. Geldschein, Münze, Bank, (Briefkasten)
2. Zeitschrift, (Rathaus,) Kiosk, Zeitung
3. einzahlen, bezahlen, (abschicken), abheben
4. Heft, (Konto,) Bleistift, Schreibwaren
5. Blumen, Pflanzen, Blumengeschäft, (Polizeiwache)

1 **Expansion** Have students explain *why* each word doesn't belong.

2 Assoziationen Wohin geht man, um diese Dinge zu bekommen?

1. auf die ___Bank___
2. ins ___Blumengeschäft___
3. ins ___Schreibwarengeschäft___

4. ins ___Juweliergeschäft___
5. an den ___Kiosk___
6. auf die ___Post___

3 Kombinieren Finden Sie zu jeder Aussage eine passende Erwiderung (*response*).

3 **Expansion** Have students add one line to each exchange and read the resulting dialogues out loud.

__b__ 1. Ich habe nicht genug Geld bei mir.

__c__ 2. Ich möchte meiner Oma alles Gute zum Geburtstag wünschen.

__e__ 3. Wo finde ich wohl eine italienische Zeitung?

__a__ 4. Ich muss meinen Pass (*passport*) erneuern.

__d__ 5. Ich habe Lust, einen Film zu sehen.

a. Da musst du zum Rathaus gehen.

b. Dort an der Ecke ist ein Geldautomat.

c. Im Schreibwarengeschäft haben sie nette Geburtstagskarten.

d. Also gehen wir heute Abend ins Kino!

e. Am Kiosk am Bahnhof.

4 Richtig oder falsch? Hören Sie sich die acht Aussagen an und entscheiden Sie, ob sie richtig oder falsch sind.

4 **Expansion** Have students correct the false statements.

	richtig	falsch		richtig	falsch
1.	✓		5.		✓
2.		✓	6.	✓	
3.		✓	7.		✓
4.	✓		8.	✓	

Kommunikation

4 Expansion Have two volunteers act out the dialogue.

5 Besorgungen
Bringen Sie mit Ihrem Partner / Ihrer Partnerin die folgenden Sätze in eine logische Reihenfolge.

___7___ **MICHAELA** Ja, ich muss dir nämlich unbedingt erzählen, wen ich im Juweliergeschäft gesehen habe.

___3___ **MICHAELA** Weißt du was? Ich gehe mit dir auf die Post. Ich brauche sowieso Briefmarken. Und danach gehe ich dann auf die Bank, Geld abheben.

___6___ **JULIA** Klar, für einen Kaffee immer. Dann können wir uns dabei auch noch ein bisschen unterhalten.

___2___ **JULIA** Ich muss ein paar Besorgungen machen. Ich muss auf die Post, ein Paket an meine Freundin abschicken, und dann wollte ich noch nach einem Geburtstagsgeschenk für meinen Bruder suchen.

___1___ **MICHAELA** Hallo Julia! Was machst du heute Schönes in der Stadt?

___4___ **JULIA** Du, dort auf der anderen Straßenseite ist ein Geldautomat. Ich will auch noch Bargeld holen.

___8___ **JULIA** Ach ja?! Da bin ich jetzt aber neugierig. Also komm!

___5___ **MICHAELA** Okay, dann lass uns das schnell machen und dann können wir ja noch im Wiener Café einen Kaffee trinken. Hast du Zeit und Lust?

6 Definitionen
Schreiben Sie zuerst zu jedem Begriff eine Definition und lesen Sie sie Ihrem Partner / Ihrer Partnerin vor. Er/sie muss dann den passenden Begriff aus der unten stehenden Liste identifizieren.
Suggested answers provided.

BEISPIEL

5 Partner Chat You can also assign activity 5 on the Supersite.

S1: Es ist ein Automat, wo man Geld abheben kann.
S2: Ein Geldautomat!

1. **Internetcafé** Es ist kein Café, wo man nur Kaffee trinkt, sondern wo man im Internet surft.
2. **Briefmarken** Man macht sie auf einen Umschlag, um einen Brief abzuschicken.
3. **Kiosk** Hier kauft man Zeitungen und Magazine.
4. **Kreditkarte** Mit ihr kann man ohne Bargeld bezahlen.
5. **Briefträger** Diese Person bringt die Post ans Haus.
6. **Waschsalon** Hier stehen viele Waschmaschinen und Wäschetrockner.

7 Diskutieren und kombinieren
Sie und Ihr Partner / Ihre Partnerin bekommen zwei verschiedene Blätter von Ihrem Lehrer / Ihrer Lehrerin. Erzählen Sie abwechselnd, wohin Anna geht und was sie macht.
Suggested answers provided.

BEISPIEL

S1: Um zehn Uhr geht Anna auf die Post, um Briefmarken zu kaufen.
S2: Danach…

6 Expansion Ask students to compare their day with Anna's. Ex.: **Haben Sie etwas gemacht, was Anna gemacht hat? Sind Sie auf die Post gegangen?**

8 Die perfekte Stadt
Wählen Sie mit zwei Mitschülern mindestens (*at least*) sechs Orte und Geschäfte, die Ihrer Meinung nach zu einer perfekten Stadt gehören. Answers will vary.

BEISPIEL

S1: Für mich muss es in einer perfekten Stadt ein Internetcafé geben.
S2: Gute Idee. Ich hätte auch gern eine leckere Konditorei.
S3: Ach, das ist doch nicht so wichtig! Was ich brauche, ist …

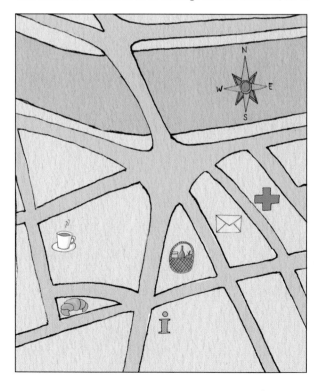

Aussprache und Rechtschreibung

  Audio

The Glottal Stop

The glottal stop is the sound you hear in the middle of the English phrase *uh oh*. In German, there is a glottal stop before all words that begin with a vowel.

obwohl   **A**mpel   **I**nnenstadt   **a**bbiegen   **e**inkaufen

Glottal stops occur within words, when one syllable ends with a vowel and the next syllable begins with a vowel. They also occur in compound words, when the second part of the compound begins with a vowel.

gerade**a**us   bee**i**len   Geld**a**utomat   Zahn**a**rzt   Wochen**e**nde

A glottal stop also occurs when one syllable of a word ends with a consonant and the next syllable begins with a vowel.

nach**a**hmen   über**a**ll   neben**a**n   über**a**us   berg**a**b

Suggestion Point out that the glottal stop is also used in English before words beginning with vowel sounds. Write the sentence *I eat an egg at eight*. Have students try saying it without using glottal stops between the words.

1 **Aussprechen** Wiederholen Sie die Wörter, die Sie hören.

1. abheben
2. Orte
3. einzahlen
4. Ecke
5. bearbeiten
6. Schlafanzug
7. Hausaufgaben
8. Freizeitaktivität
9. Mittagessen
10. hinab
11. fortan
12. bergauf

2 **Nachsprechen** Wiederholen Sie die Sätze, die Sie hören.

1. Auch am Abend kann man Geld vom Geldautomaten abheben.
2. Am Wochenende arbeitet Amanda in der Apotheke.
3. Im Internetcafé essen acht Engländer Erdbeereis.
4. Auf dem Briefumschlag steht die Adresse allerdings nicht.
5. Fortan bearbeitet ihr alles vor Ort.
6. Das Nadelöhr am Autobahndreieck wird ab morgen ausgebaut.

3 **Sprichwörter** Wiederholen Sie die Sprichwörter, die Sie hören.

Erst die Arbeit, dann das Vergnügen.[1]

Unkraut vergeht nicht.[2]

[1] Business before pleasure.
[2] Bad weeds grow tall. (*lit.,* Weeds don't die.)

Ressourcen

vText   LM   
p. 63   vhlcentral

Gute Neuigkeiten

 Video

Sabite bekommt einen Anruf vom Manager der Galerie. Die Freunde wollen die guten Neuigkeiten feiern. Dann erzählt George von seinem Kuss mit Sabite...

communication cultures
NATIONAL STANDARDS

Vorbereitung Have students read the title of the episode and discuss in pairs what they think will happen in the episode.

HANS Sind wir an einer Bank vorbeigekommen? Ich muss Geld vom Bankautomaten abheben.

GEORGE Ich zahle nie bar. Ich zahle mit meiner Bankkarte.

HANS Immer wenn ich eine Zeitung oder einen Kaffee kaufe, zahle ich bar. Ich vergesse immer, die kleinen Artikel aufzuschreiben, und dann geht mir das Geld auf dem Bankkonto aus. Ich gebe jede Woche gleich viel aus.

GEORGE Ich habe auf der anderen Straßenseite eine Bank gesehen, dort.

HANS Was musst du heute Nachmittag sonst noch erledigen?

GEORGE Ich muss zur Post gehen und diese Karten abschicken. Als ich die USA verlassen habe, habe ich meiner kleinen Schwester Olivia versprochen, ihr Postkarten zu schicken. Ich habe sie schon geschrieben, habe sie aber noch nicht in den Briefkasten geworfen.

HANS Das müssen um die 20 Karten sein. ... Potsdamer Platz, Alexanderplatz, Brandenburger Tor, Jüdisches Museum, Checkpoint Charlie...

GEORGE Ich werde sie in ein Päckchen legen mit etwas Schokolade und diesem hier.

SABITE Es geht ihr jetzt wieder gut. Ja, was komisch ist, ist, dass sie nach Hans gefragt hat, als sie aufgewacht ist. Ich weiß. Ich weiß. Oh, Mama, ich muss auflegen. Ich habe auf diesen Anruf gewartet. Ok, ich gebe dir Bescheid. Tschüss. Hallo, hier ist Sabite. Guten Tag, Herr Kleinedler, wie geht es Ihnen?

MELINE Hallo? Oh, hallo Sabite. Was gibt's Neues? Gutes oder Schlechtes? Okay, okay. Ich komme gerade aus dem Salon und treffe dich in einer Stunde im Biergarten. Bis dann. „Ich sage es dir, wenn ich dich sehe." Künstler sind so dramatisch.

GEORGE Hallo Sabite. Hat er angerufen? Okay... okay. Wir sehen uns dann im Biergarten. Das brauchst du nicht, er steht direkt hier. Alles klar. Tschüss. Sabite hat Neuigkeiten von der Galerie in der Torstraße bekommen. Sie wollte sie nicht am Telefon sagen. Wir werden beim Blumengeschäft Halt machen müssen.

---

1 Wer ist das? Welche Person(en) beschreiben die folgenden Sätze: George, Hans, Meline oder Sabite?

1. __Hans__ muss Geld vom Bankautomaten abheben.
2. __George__ zahlt nie bar, sondern immer mit der Karte.
3. __Hans__ gibt jede Woche gleich viel Geld aus.
4. __George__ muss zur Post gehen und Karten abschicken.
5. __George__ will ein Päckchen mit Schokolade abschicken.

6. __Sabite__ bekommt einen Anruf von Herrn Kleinedler.
7. __Meline__ kommt gerade aus dem Salon.
8. __George__ möchte beim Blumengeschäft Halt machen.
9. __George__ erzählt Hans von dem Kuss.
10. __Sabite__ hat gute Neuigkeiten von der Galerie.

George
 Hans
 Meline
 Sabite

7

HANS Immer wenn etwas passiert, ruft sie dich an.
GEORGE Wir sind Freunde.
HANS Mehr nicht?
GEORGE Nein. Als wir uns geküsst haben, da wussten wir beide...
HANS Als ihr was?

8

GEORGE Wenn ich richtig rate, hast du gute Neuigkeiten. Komisch, ich habe es in deiner Stimme gehört, als du angerufen hast.
MELINE Herzlichen Glückwunsch, Sabite!

9

SABITE Danke. Wow. Wo ist Hans?
GEORGE Er, ähm...
MELINE Er hat ein Problem mit der Beziehung zwischen... dir und George.
SABITE Welche Beziehung? Wir sind Freunde.
GEORGE Ich habe ihm aus Versehen von unserem Kuss erzählt.

10

MELINE Von was?
SABITE Oh, George, wie konntest du nur?
GEORGE Frauen bringen mich ganz durcheinander.
MELINE So soll es ja auch sein. Hast du Hunger? Lass uns bestellen.

Nützliche Ausdrücke

- **vorbeikommen**
  to pass
- **aufschreiben**
  to write down
- **erledigen**
  to run an errand
- **verlassen**
  to leave
- **versprechen**
  to promise
- **einen Brief einwerfen**
  to mail a letter
- **das Päckchen**
  little package
- **auflegen**
  to hang up
- **Halt machen**
  to stop by
- **raten**
  to guess
- **die Beziehung**
  relationship
- **aus Versehen**
  by mistake
- **durcheinanderbringen**
  to confuse

2A.1
- **Ich werde sie in ein Päckchen legen mit etwas Schokolade und diesem hier.**
  I'm going to put them all in a little package with some chocolate and this.

2A.2
- **Was gibt's Neues? Gutes oder Schlechtes?**
  What's the news? Is it good or bad?

2A.3
- **Wenn ich richtig rate, hast du gute Neuigkeiten.**
  If I'm right, you have good news.

---

 2 **Zum Besprechen** Machen Sie zu zweit Pläne für einen Tag in der Stadt. Entscheiden Sie, wohin Sie gehen und was Sie machen wollen. Erklären Sie Ihre Entscheidungen. Answers will vary.

2 Expansion Have students act out their dialogue in front of the class.

3 **Vertiefung** In den deutschsprachigen Ländern wird der Begriff ‚Kreditkarte' anders verwendet als in den USA. Benutzen Sie das Internet, um herauszufinden, wo genau die Unterschiede (*differences*) liegen.
Suggested answer: In German-speaking countries, the term refers to real credit cards as well as debit, prepaid, or charge cards.

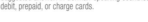

Ressourcen

 vText | VM p. 89 | vhlcentral

Fußgängerzonen°

S Reading

Suggestion Have students describe the photo before they read the article. Ask them if anything in the image strikes them as surprising or unusual.

IN VIELEN EUROPÄISCHEN STÄDTEN findet man im Stadtzentrum oder in der historischen Altstadt eine Fußgängerzone, in der man nur zu Fuß gehen darf. Radfahrer müssen langsam fahren oder das Fahrrad schieben°, und Autos dürfen hier nur fahren, wenn sie Geschäfte in der Fußgängerzone beliefern° oder zur Polizei, Feuerwehr oder anderen Notdiensten° gehören. Aber auch sie müssen hier Schritttempo° fahren und sehr vorsichtig sein.

Viele Leute kommen in die Fußgängerzone, weil man in den vielen Geschäften gut einkaufen und in schönen Cafés oder Restaurants im Freien sitzen kann.

Die erste Fußgängerzone Europas gibt es seit 1953 in der Lijnbaan im holländischen Rotterdam. Im selben Jahr eröffnete man in der Kasseler Treppenstraße, die erste Fußgängerzone Deutschlands. Nachdem große Teile Kassels während des Zweiten Weltkriegs zerstört wurden°, gab es einen Wiederaufbauwettbewerb°, um die Innenstadt Kassels neu zu gestalten°. 1961 folgte in Klagenfurt die erste Fußgängerzone in Österreich: die Kramergasse.

Historische Innenstädte° in Deutschland	
Dresden	Im 2. Weltkrieg wurde Dresden fast komplett zerstört. Heute kann man in der Altstadt wieder die Semperoper, den Zwinger und die Frauenkirche besuchen.
Heidelberg	Heidelberg, die Stadt mit der ältesten Universität im heutigen Deutschland, hat die längste Fußgängerzone Deutschlands.
Köln	Die Schildergasse in Köln ist die meistbesuchte Einkaufsmeile Europas.
Regensburg	Die Regensburger Altstadt geht auf die Römer° zurück. Das Schloss der Familie von Thurn und Taxis, die die erste Post in Deutschland gründete, ist Teil dieser Altstadt.

AP* Theme: Families & Communities
Context: Urban, Suburban, & Rural Life

Fußgängerzonen *traffic-free zones* **schieben** *push* **beliefern** *supply* **Notdiensten** *emergency services* **Schritttempo** *walking pace* **zerstört wurden** *were destroyed* **Wiederaufbauwettbewerb** *reconstruction competition* **gestalten** *design* **Innenstädte** *city centers* **Römer** *Romans*

1 Richtig oder falsch? Sagen Sie, ob die Sätze richtig oder falsch sind. Korrigieren Sie die falschen Sätze.

1. Fußgängerzonen findet man meistens in der Innenstadt. Richtig.

2. Viele Menschen besuchen die Fußgängerzonen einer Stadt. Richtig.

3. In Fußgängerzonen gibt es nur Straßen mit vielen Geschäften.
Falsch. In Fußgängerzonen gibt es auch viele Cafés, Restaurants, Bänke, Brunnen und Bäume.

4. In einer Fußgängerzone dürfen keine Autos fahren.
Falsch. Nur wenige Autos dürfen in einer Fußgängerzone fahren.

5. In Cafés und Restaurants kann man draußen sitzen. Richtig.

6. In Kassel baute man eine Fußgängerzone nach dem Zweiten Weltkrieg, weil große Teile der Innenstadt zerstört waren. Richtig.

7. Die Fußgängerzone in Kassel heißt Kramergasse.
Falsch. Die Fußgängerzone in Kassel heißt Treppenstraße.

8. Die erste Fußgängerzone in Europa gab es in Klagenfurt.
Falsch. Die erste Fußgängerzone in Europa gab es in Rotterdam.

9. Die längste Fußgängerzone in Deutschland ist in Dresden.
Falsch. Die längste Fußgängerzone in Deutschland ist in Heidelberg.

10. Die meistbesuchte Fußgängerzone ist in Köln. Richtig.

 Practice more at **vhlcentral.com**.

Geschäfte

der Antiquitätenladen	antiques shop
der Buchladen	bookshop
der Makler	real estate agent
der Schneider	tailor
der Schuster	shoemaker
das Spielwarengeschäft	toy store

Heimat
AP* Theme: Personal & Public Identities
Context: National Identity

Für Deutsche, Österreicher und Schweizer ist Heimat ein sehr wichtiger Begriff°. Es ist der Ort, wo man geboren und aufgewachsen ist. Oft haben an diesem Ort schon mehrere Generationen einer Familie gelebt. Heimat bedeutet aber auch die Sprache, die man spricht, und zwar nicht nur Deutsch, sondern auch den Dialekt der Region. Heimat sind auch die Traditionen der Region. Im Allgemeinen ist Heimat ein sehr emotionales Konzept. Man kann dieses Wort nicht direkt ins Englische übersetzen. Oft sagt man *home* oder *homeland*.

Suggestion Ask students what
Begriff *term*   place they consider home and why.

Die Deutsche Post
AP* Theme: Families & Communities
Context: Urban, Suburban, & Rural Life

Die Post hat in Deutschland eine lange Tradition. Seit 1615 organisierte die Familie Thurn und Taxis in Deutschland den Postverkehr. Aus dieser Zeit stammt° auch das Symbol der Post: das Posthorn. Reiter benutzten es, wenn sie in Städte oder über Grenzen ritten. Ab 1660 führte die Familie Thurn und Taxis eine Fahrpost ein°, mit der sie Briefe und Personen beförderte°. Die erste Strecke führte von Halle über Magdeburg nach Hamburg. Ab 1710 gab es die ersten Briefträger in Deutschland und ab 1874 gab es dann in ganz Deutschland auch Briefkästen an Häusern. Heute ist die Deutsche Post kein staatliches Unternehmen° mehr, sondern eine private Aktiengesellschaft°.

Suggestion Point out that the **Deutsche Post** has become one of the world's largest courier companies.
stammt *stems* **führte ... ein** *instituted* **beförderten** *transported* **Unternehmen** *organization*
Aktiengesellschaft *corporation*

🔗 IM INTERNET

Suchen Sie im Internet Informationen über eine bekannte Innenstadt in Deutschland. Was können Touristen und Besucher hier alles machen? Welche Geschäfte gibt es? Welche anderen Attraktionen?

Find out more at **vhlcentral.com**.

---

2 **Was fehlt?** Ergänzen Sie die Sätze.

1. Den Begriff Heimat gibt es vor allem in <u>deutschsprachigen</u> Ländern.
2. Heimat ist der Ort, wo man <u>geboren</u> und aufgewachsen ist.
3. Für viele Menschen ist Heimat ein sehr <u>emotionales</u> Konzept.
4. Die Familie <u>Thurn und Taxis</u> hat in Deutschland die erste Post organisiert.
5. Briefträger gibt es in Deutschland seit <u>1710</u>.
6. Die erste Poststrecke war von Halle über Magdeburg nach <u>Hamburg</u>.

3 **Traumstadt** Diskutieren Sie mit einem Partner / einer Partnerin: Wo möchten Sie gerne leben? In einer großen Stadt? In einer kleinen Stadt? Was muss eine Stadt für Sie bieten (*offer*)?

3 **Expansion** Ask students whether they would prefer to live in a big city or a small town.

3 **Partner Chat** You can also assign activity 3 on the Supersite. Students work in pairs to record the activity online. The pair's recorded conversation will appear in your gradebook.

Ressourcen

v̂ Text
vhlcentral

Subordinating conjunctions  Presentation

Startblock Coordinating conjunctions combine two independent clauses in a single sentence. Use subordinating conjunctions to combine a subordinate clause with a main clause.

„Ich sage es dir, **wenn** ich dich sehe."

Wenn ich richtig rate, hast du gute Neuigkeiten.

- A subordinate clause explains, how, when, why, or under what circumstances the action in the main clause occurs. Subordinate clauses always begin with a subordinating conjunction and normally end with the conjugated verb. Always use a comma to separate the subordinate clause from the main clause.

MAIN CLAUSE	SUBORDINATE CLAUSE
Ich lese die Zeitung,	**wenn** ich Zeit **habe**.
I read the newspaper	*when I **have** the time.*

- Here is a list of commonly used subordinating conjunctions:

subordinating conjunctions			
als	*as, when*	ob	*whether, if*
bevor	*before*	obwohl	*although*
bis	*until*	seit	*since*
damit	*so that*	während	*while; whereas*
dass	*that*	weil	*because*
nachdem	*after*	wenn	*when; whenever; if*

Vergiss nicht, **dass** wir nächste Woche ins Konzert **gehen**.
*Don't forget **that** we're going to a concert next week.*

Ich bezahle immer bar, **weil** ich keine Kreditkarte **habe**.
*I always pay cash, **because** I don't **have** a credit card.*

- When you begin a sentence with a subordinate clause, the entire clause is treated as the first element of the sentence. The verb in the main clause moves to second position, after the comma, and is followed by its subject.

SUBORDINATE CLAUSE	MAIN CLAUSE
Wenn ich nach Deutschland fahre,	**spreche** ich immer Deutsch.
Weil meine Familie deutsch ist,	**habe** ich als Kind Deutsch gelernt.
Obwohl ich Deutsch spreche,	**möchte** ich lieber in Italien wohnen.

- When using a separable prefix verb in a subordinate clause, attach the prefix to the beginning of the conjugated verb.

Ich **rufe dich** heute Abend **an**.
*I'll **call** you tonight.*

Ich warte, **bis** du mich **anrufst**.
*I'll wait **until** you **call** me.*

- When using a modal verb in a subordinate clause, put the conjugated form of the modal at the end of the clause, after the infinitive of the verb it modifies.

Wir **müssen** heute Nachmittag
Briefmarken **kaufen**.
*We **need to buy** stamps
this afternoon.*

Wir gehen zur Post, **weil** wir Briefmarken
kaufen müssen.
*We're going to the post office **because** we
need to buy stamps.*

- For a subordinate clause in the **Perfekt** or **Plusquamperfekt**, move the conjugated form of **sein** or **haben** to the end of the clause, after the past participle.

Ich **bin** heute früher nach
Hause **gegangen**.
*I **went** home early today.*

Ich habe Besorgungen gemacht, **bevor** ich
nach Hause **gegangen bin**.
*I ran some errands **before** I **went** home.*

- Use **als** to refer to a one-time event or continuing situation in the past. Use **wenn** to refer to a one-time event in the present or future. Use **(immer) wenn** to refer to a recurring event in the past, present, or future.

Als wir Kinder waren, gab uns Papa
Münzen aus anderen Ländern.
***When** we were kids, Dad used to give
us coins from other countries.*

Wenn du nächsten Sommer nach Hannover fährst,
musst du mir eine Postkarte schicken.
***When** you go to Hannover next summer, you'll
have to send me a postcard.*

Indirect questions

- Indirect questions are a type of subordinate clause. They are introduced by a main clause beginning with a phrase such as **Weißt du**, **Ich möchte wissen**, **Kannst du mir sagen**, **Ich weiß nicht**, or **Ich frage mich**.

Ich möchte wissen, **ob** ich ein
Formular ausfüllen muss.
*I'd like to know **whether** I need
to fill out a form.*

Ich frage mich, **warum** es so viele
Internetcafés in Berlin gibt.
*I wonder **why** there are so many Internet
cafés in Berlin.*

Erzähl uns bitte, **was** passiert ist.
*Please tell us **what** happened.*

Sag mir, **wie viele** Briefmarken du brauchst.
*Tell me **how many** stamps you need.*

- Use the subordinating conjunction **ob** to ask indirect yes-or-no questions.

Wissen Sie, **ob** man hier mit der
Karte bezahlen kann?
*Do you know **if** I can pay by card here?*

Weißt du, **ob** die Post schon
da ist?
*Do you know **if** the mail has come yet?*

- For all other indirect questions, use the question words as subordinating conjunctions.

Sie wissen, **wohin** man gehen soll.
*They know **where** to go.*

Ich weiß, **wie** du dich fühlst.
*I know **how** you feel.*

Suggestion You might refer your students to **Vol. 1, 1B.2** to review basic word order. Also, **Vol. 1, 2A.2** to review question words. Also, **Vol. 2, 1B.2** to review the conjugations of the verb **wissen**.

ACHTUNG

Both **ob** and **wenn** are sometimes translated as *if*, but only **ob** is used in indirect yes-or-no questions. Use **wann**, rather than **als** or **wenn**, to mean *when* in an indirect question.

Expansion Write on the board: **ob** = *whether*. Then, have students complete the sentence, **Ich möchte wissen, ob…** and share their sentences.

Expansion Write two simple sentences, putting each word on a separate card. In class, distribute the cards and have students stand in the correct order to form the sentences. Then, add a card with a subordinating conjunction. Have students place the card between the sentences and rearrange themselves accordingly.

Ressourcen

v̂Text

WB
pp. 17–18

LM
p. 64

S
vhlcentral

Jetzt sind Sie dran!
Wählen Sie die richtigen Konjunktionen.

1. Lara geht zur Post, (**weil**/ ob) sie Briefmarken braucht.
2. Der Kunde erklärte der Verkäuferin, (**dass**/ ob) er kein Kleingeld hat.
3. Ich habe ein Paket bekommen, (**obwohl**/ ob) ich nichts bestellt habe.
4. (Damit /**Nachdem**) die Touristen im Internetcafé ihre E-Mails gelesen hatten, sind sie zum Hotel gegangen.
5. (Als /**Bevor**) man einen Brief abschickt, muss man die Adresse auf den Briefumschlag schreiben.
6. Weißt du, (**ob**/ damit) es beim Kiosk noch Zeitungen gibt?

Anwendung

1 Ausflug nach München Ergänzen Sie die Sätze mit **als** oder **wenn**.

BEISPIEL _Wenn_ wir nach München fahren, besuchen wir die Frauenkirche.

1. _Wenn_ es 12 Uhr mittags ist, sollte man am Münchner Rathaus das Glockenspiel anschauen.

2. _Als_ wir das letzte Mal in München waren, hat es nur geregnet.

3. _Wenn_ wir Ende September hier wären, könnten wir auch aufs Oktoberfest gehen.

4. Das erste Oktoberfest hat man 1810 gefeiert, _als_ Kronprinz Ludwig Prinzessin Therese heiratete.

5. Vielleicht fahren wir morgen zum Schloss Neuschwanstein, _wenn_ wir Zeit haben.

6. Ludwig II baute Schloss Neuschwanstein, _als_ er 1864 König (king) von Bayern wurde.

2 Suggestion Tell students that **Klatsch** means gossip.

2 Klatsch Schreiben Sie, was Petra sagt, und verbinden Sie die Sätze mit der Konjunktion **dass**.

BEISPIEL Mein kleiner Bruder will immer etwas kaputt machen.
Anna sagt, _dass ihr kleiner Bruder immer etwas kaputt machen will._

1. Max hat noch nie Sushi gegessen.
Anna sagt, _dass Max noch nie Sushi gegessen hat._

2. Simon und Greta freuen sich nicht auf ihre Reise.
Anna sagt, _dass Simon und Greta sich nicht auf ihre Reise freuen._

3. Die Katze hat eine Ratte im Garten gefangen.
Anna sagt, _dass die Katze eine Ratte im Garten gefangen hat._

4. Die Eltern von Antonia haben sich getrennt.
Anna sagt, _dass die Eltern von Antonia sich getrennt haben._

5. Mia kommt wegen Nina nicht auf die Feier mit.
Anna sagt, _dass Mia wegen Nina nicht auf die Feier mitkommt._

3 Ein kurzes Interview Ändern Sie die direkten Fragen in indirekte Fragen um und verwenden Sie dabei die Ausdrücke aus der Liste. Sample answers provided.

BEISPIEL Warum lernst du Deutsch und nicht Spanisch?
Darf ich dich fragen, warum du Deutsch und nicht Spanisch lernst?

Darf ich dich fragen	Ich weiß nicht
Erzähl mir bitte	Kannst du mir sagen
Ich frage mich	Sag mir
Ich möchte gern wissen	Weißt du

1. Kommen deine Großeltern aus Deutschland?
Weißt du, ob deine Großeltern aus Deutschland kommen?

2. Hast du Geschwister?
Ich frage mich, ob du Geschwister hast.

3. Wie oft bist du schon nach Europa geflogen?
Sag mir, wie oft du schon nach Europa geflogen bist.

4. Welches Land möchtest du gern mal besuchen?
Erzähl mir bitte, welches Land du gern mal besuchen möchtest.

 Practice more at **vhlcentral.com**.

Kommunikation

4 **Besorgungen** Fragen Sie Ihren Partner / Ihre Partnerin, wohin er/sie geht, um die folgenden Besorgungen zu machen. Answers will vary.

einen schönen
Ring kaufen

> **BEISPIEL**
> **S1:** Wohin gehst du, wenn du einen schönen Ring kaufen willst?
> **S2:** Ich gehe zum Juweliergeschäft.

1. Geld abheben

2. schöne Rosen kaufen

3. ein Paket abschicken

4. eine Zeitung kaufen

5. schmutzige Wäsche waschen

5 **Was und wenn** Fragen Sie Ihren Partner / Ihre Partnerin, was er/sie normalerweise in den folgenden Situationen macht. Achten Sie auf die Wortstellung. Answers will vary.

BEISPIEL

S1: Was machst du normalerweise, wenn du richtig Hunger hast?
S2: Wenn ich richtig Hunger habe, esse ich einen Hamburger.

1. Hunger haben
2. sich schlecht fühlen
3. müde sein

4. sich verspäten
5. ein Paket abschicken wollen
6. traurig sein

6 **Was weißt du?**
A. Schreiben Sie vier Dinge auf, die Sie schon über die deutschsprachigen Länder gelernt haben. Beginnen Sie jede Aussage mit „**Ich weiß, dass...**". Answers will vary.

BEISPIEL

Ich weiß, dass Berlin die Hauptstadt Deutschlands ist.

B. Machen Sie jetzt ein kleines Quiz, um herauszufinden, ob Ihr Partner / Ihre Partnerin dasselbe Wissen hat. Beginnen Sie jede Frage mit **Weißt du, ...** und einem passenden Fragewort – **wer, was, wann, wo, wie**. Answers will vary.

BEISPIEL

S1: Weißt du, was die Hauptstadt Deutschlands ist?
S2: Natürlich! Berlin ist die Hauptstadt Deutschlands!

4 **Partner Chat** You can also assign activity 4 on the Supersite. Students work in pairs to record the activity online. The pair's recorded conversation will appear in your gradebook.

5 **Suggestion** Tell students that they can be creative with their answers.

5 **Virtual Chat** You can also assign activity 5 on the Supersite. Students record individual responses that appear in your gradebook.

6 **Expansion** After students complete part B, have everyone switch partners and repeat the quiz.

Adjectives used as nouns  Presentation

Startblock Many adjectives in German can also be used as nouns.

Herr Miller ist ein sehr **alter** Mann.
*Mr. Miller is a very **old** man.*

Was sollen wir machen, um **den Alten** zu helfen?
*What should we do to help **the elderly**?*

- The endings for adjectival nouns change depending on the gender, number, or case of the noun, and whether it is preceded by a **der**-word or an **ein**-word. When you use an adjective as a noun, add the same ending that you would add to the adjective form.

adjective	noun after a *der*-word	noun after an *ein*-word
arbeitslos *unemployed*	**der/die Arbeitslose** *unemployed person*	**ein Arbeitsloser / eine Arbeitslose**
bekannt *(well-)known*	**der/die Bekannte** *acquaintance*	**ein Bekannter / eine Bekannte**
erwachsen *grown(-up)*	**der/die Erwachsene** *adult*	**ein Erwachsener / eine Erwachsene**
jugendlich *young, youthful*	**der/die Jugendliche** *young person*	**ein Jugendlicher / eine Jugendliche**
verlobt *engaged*	**der/die Verlobte** *fiancé(e)*	**ein Verlobter / eine Verlobte**
verwandt *related*	**der/die Verwandte** *relative*	**ein Verwandter / eine Verwandte**

- When adjectival nouns refer to people, the gender of the noun matches the gender of the person. When they refer to previously mentioned objects, the gender of the noun matches the gender of the object.

Marias **Verlobter** ist sehr nett.
*Maria's **fiancé** is very nice.*

Seine **Verwandten** habe ich nicht so gern.
*I'm not so crazy about his **relatives**.*

Welche **Krawatte** hast du gekauft?
*Which **tie** did you buy?*

Ich habe die **Blaue** gekauft.
*I bought the **blue one**.*

- Adjectival nouns that refer to concepts are always neuter and are only used in the singular. They often follow indefinite words such as **alles**, **etwas** and **nichts**, or the quantity words **viel** and **wenig** (*little, not much*). For adjectival nouns after **etwas**, **nichts**, **viel**, or **wenig**, use the endings for unpreceded neuter adjectives. After **alles**, use the endings you would use after a **der**-word. **Suggestion** Have students memorize the phrase **Alles Gute!** as a reminder that adjectival nouns after **alles** take the -e ending.

Wir wünschen dir **alles Gute**!
*We wish you **all the best**!*

Möchtest du **etwas Kaltes** trinken?
*Do you want **something cold** to drink?*

Jetzt sind Sie dran! Wählen Sie das Wort, das in jedem Satz am besten passt.

1. Meine __c__ sind alle sportlich, vor allem mein Onkel.
2. Ich will dir etwas __a__ erzählen.
3. Du __e__! Hast du dich schwer verletzt?
4. Dein __b__ hat dir einen wunderschönen Ring geschenkt.
5. Amila bestellt alles __d__, das sie auf der Speisekarte sieht.

a. Lustiges
b. Verlobter
c. Verwandten
d. Leckere
e. Arme

Anwendung und Kommunikation

1 **Was fehlt?** Ergänzen Sie die Sätze mit den richtigen Endungen der substantivierten Adjektive.

1. Wer ist die hübsche Rothaarig_e___ dort drüben?

2. Ich finde, dass Tom nichts Interessant_es___ zu sagen hat.

3. Er ist ein Bekannt_er___, aber kein Freund.

4. In dem Gestreift_en___ siehst du wirklich gut aus.

5. Macht ihr heute noch etwas Besonder_es___?

2 **Interview** Stellen Sie Fragen mit einem passenden Paar aus der Liste. Answers will vary.

BEISPIEL

S1: *Was isst du lieber, etwas Süßes oder etwas Scharfes?*
S2: *Ich esse lieber etwas Scharfes.*

einfach / kompliziert	kalt / warm
fantastisch / realistisch	lecker / gesund
hell / dunkel	modern / klassisch
italienisch / mexikanisch	süß / scharf

1. Was isst du lieber, ... ?

2. Was trinkst du am häufigsten, ... ?

3. Was schaust du dir im Fernsehen lieber an, ... ?

4. Welche Musik hörst du dir meistens an, ... ?

5. Welche Kleidung steht dir besser, ... ?

3 **Bilder beschreiben** Beschreiben Sie mit einem Partner / einer Partnerin die Bilder und verwenden Sie dabei substantivierte Adjektive aus der Liste. Answers will vary.

dick	klein	verlobt
jugendlich	krank	verwandt

▶ **BEISPIEL**

Die Kleine hat einen Brief an den Weihnachtsmann geschrieben.

1.

2.   3.   4.

1 **Suggestion** Do the first few items as a class. After students have completed the activity, have them explain how they chose the correct endings.

2 **Partner Chat** You can also assign activity 2 on the Supersite. Students work in pairs to record the activity online. The pair's recorded conversation will appear in your gradebook.

3 **Suggestion** Have students work through this activity twice: first orally, with an emphasis on communication and content; then in writing, with an emphasis on accuracy.

Das Futur I  Presentation

Startblock You have already learned to make statements about the future using the present tense with future meaning. You can also use the future tense (**das Futur I**) to talk about the future, especially when the future meaning might not otherwise be clear from context.

QUERVERWEIS

See **1B.2** to review the present tense forms of **werden**.

In **3B.1**, you will learn about the future perfect tense, **das Futur II**.

Suggestion You might want students to review the use of present tense with future meaning, taught in **Vol. 1, 2B.2**.

ACHTUNG

Do not confuse the modal **wollen** with the future auxiliary **werden**: **Ich will gehen**. *I want to go.* BUT: **Ich werde gehen**. *I will go. / I'm going to go.*

In a subordinate clause, the infinitive of the modal comes at the end of the clause, preceded by the infinitive of the verb it modifies. The conjugated form of **werden** comes *before* both infinitives.: **Er weiß nicht, wie lange er wird arbeiten müssen**.

Suggestion Since this is a common mistake among students, you may want to have your class highlight the first note in the **Achtung** box. Write on board: **Ich will** is NOT *I will!*

Er **wird** bald hier **sein**.

Wir **werden** beim Blumengeschäft Halt machen **müssen**.

- To form the **Futur I**, use a present tense form of the verb **werden** with the infinitive of the verb that expresses the action.

Wir **werden** uns in einer Woche wieder **treffen**.
We'll meet again in one week.

Werdet ihr am Wochenende Zeit **haben?**
Will you have time on the weekend?

- In subordinate clauses, move the conjugated form of **werden** to the end of the clause, unless the clause contains a modal verb. When using a modal verb in the **Futur**, place the infinitive of the modal verb at the end of the clause, *after* the infinitive of the verb it modifies.

  Suggestion Tell students that a trick for remembering verb order with modals in future subordinate clauses is the acronym **AIM**: Auxiliary Infinitive Modal.

Wir **werden** unsere Hausaufgaben **machen**, nachdem wir etwas essen.
We'll do our homework after we eat something.

Ich verspreche dir, dass ich dich immer **lieben werde**.
I promise you that I will always love you.

Bald **wird** man überall mit der Karte **bezahlen können**.
Soon, you'll be able to pay by credit card everywhere.

Sie **werden** ein Formular bei der Post **ausfüllen müssen**.
You will have to fill out a form at the post office.

- The **Futur I** is commonly used to talk about assumptions or expectations concerning the present *or* future. Such sentences often include the words **wohl**, **wahrscheinlich**, **sicher**, or **schon**, all of which mean *probably* when used with the **Futur**.

Daniel **wird wohl** noch bei der Ärztin **sein**.
Daniel is probably still at the doctor's office.

In 100 Jahren **wird** die Welt **sicher** sehr anders **aussehen**.
In 100 years, the world will probably look very different.

Ressourcen

v̂Text

WB
pp. 21–22

LM
p. 66

S
vhlcentral

Jetzt sind Sie dran! Bilden Sie Sätze im Futur.

1. ich / bar bezahlen *Ich werde bar bezahlen.*
2. wir / machen keine Besorgungen
   Wir werden keine Besorgungen machen.
3. du / jetzt ins Bett gehen / ?
   Wirst du jetzt ins Bett gehen?
4. ihr / wahrscheinlich Hunger haben
   Ihr werdet wahrscheinlich Hunger haben.
5. ich / müssen / sich schnell anziehen
   Ich werde mich schnell anziehen müssen.

6. Nina / wohl / auf der Post / sein
   Nina wird wohl auf der Post sein.
7. das Kind / schon / schlafen
   Das Kind wird schon schlafen.
8. es / heute noch / regnen
   Es wird heute noch regnen.
9. wir / müssen / früh aufstehen
   Wir werden früh aufstehen müssen.
10. Onkel Gerhard / Diät machen
    Onkel Gerhard wird Diät machen.

Anwendung und Kommunikation

1 **Sätze schreiben** Schreiben Sie die Sätze um. Benutzen Sie das Futur.

> **BEISPIEL** Wir kommen um 10 Uhr an.
> *Wir werden um 10 Uhr ankommen.*

1. Ich koche morgen Abend. Ich werde morgen Abend kochen.
2. Müsst ihr am Abend noch lernen? Werdet ihr am Abend noch lernen müssen?
3. Andreas ärgert sich wohl darüber. Andreas wird sich wohl darüber ärgern.
4. Das Wetter wird bald besser. Das Wetter wird bald besser werden.
5. Das Flugzeug hat vier Stunden Verspätung. Das Flugzeug wird vier Stunden Verspätung haben.
6. Bist du nächstes Jahr schon 21? Wirst du nächstes Jahr schon 21 sein?
7. Will Michaela ein Zimmer buchen? Wird Michaela ein Zimmer buchen wollen?
8. Sie ziehen im Herbst in eine größere Wohnung um. Sie werden im Herbst in eine größere Wohnung umziehen.

2 **Meine Zukunftspläne** Fragen Sie einander nach Ihren Zukunftsplänen (*plans for the future*). Benutzen Sie die Futurformen. Answers will vary.

> **BEISPIEL**
> **S1:** *Was wirst du heute Abend machen?*
> **S2:** *Heute Abend werde ich Deutsch lernen.*

1. heute Abend
2. am Wochenende
3. im Sommer
4. im Winter
5. nach dem Studium

3 **Und dann** Schauen Sie sich mit Ihrem Partner / Ihrer Partnerin zusammen die Fotos an und entscheiden Sie, was wohl in den nächsten Minuten passieren wird. Benutzen Sie das Futur. Answers will vary.

> ▶ **BEISPIEL**
> **S1:** *Ich glaube, der Mann wird einen Käsekuchen kaufen.*
> **S2:** *Ich glaube, er wird Brötchen fürs Frühstück kaufen.*

1.

2.

3.

4.

2 Expansion Ask pairs to prepare a list of predictions about what they and their classmates will be doing in 10 years.

2 Virtual Chat You can also assign activity 2 on the Supersite. Students record individual responses that appear in your gradebook.

3 Partner Chat You can also assign activity 3 on the Supersite. Students work in pairs to record the activity online. The pair's recorded conversation will appear in your gradebook.

 Practice more at **vhlcentral.com.**

Wiederholung

 2 Suggestion Verify that students recall the names and genders of all items pictured on their activity sheets. Write model adjective endings on the board for reference during the activity, ex.: **einen roten Rock, eine rote Ratte, ein rotes Rad, rote Rosen.**

1 Wer ist's?

Wählen Sie drei Adjektive aus der Liste und beschreiben Sie Ihrem Partner / Ihrer Partnerin zu jedem Adjektiv eine Person. Ihr Partner / Ihre Partnerin sagt, was für eine Person Sie beschreiben. *Answers will vary.*

BEISPIEL

S1: Dieser Mann hat seine Katze verloren. Er weint den ganzen Tag.
S2: Ist das der Traurige?
S1: Ja.

1 Expansion Have students act out the characteristics described by the adjectival nouns.

dreckig	langweilig
intelligent	lustig
sportlich	nervös

1 Partner Chat You can also assign activity 1 on the Supersite.

2 Diskutieren und kombinieren

Sie und Ihr Partner / Ihre Partnerin bekommen verschiedene Arbeitsblätter. Fragen Sie Ihren Partner / Ihre Partnerin, welche Gegenstände die einzelnen Personen in dem Kaufhaus möchten.

BEISPIEL

S1: Was für einen Pulli möchte Paul?
S2: Er möchte einen Roten.

3 Unglaublich!

Wechseln Sie sich mit einem Partner / einer Partnerin ab: Was ist den Personen in den Bildern passiert? Beginnen Sie jede Beschreibung mit „Hast du gehört, dass ..." oder „Weißt du, dass ...". Ihr Partner / Ihre Partnerin wird auf die Neuigkeiten (*news*) reagieren. *Answers will vary.*

3 Expansion Bring in additional pictures for students to work with.

BEISPIEL

S1: Hast du gehört, dass Maria einen Autounfall hatte?
S2: Nein! Unglaublich! Sie fährt aber doch immer so langsam.

1. Maria

2. Anna und Jonas

3. Emma und Felix

4. Max

5. Jan

6. Lisa und Erik

3 Partner Chat You can also assign activity 3 on the Supersite.

4 Versprechungen

Wählen Sie eine Person aus der linken Spalte und einen Zeitraum aus der rechten. Erzählen Sie Ihrem Partner / Ihrer Partnerin, was Sie jeder Person für diese Zeiträume versprochen haben. *Answers will vary.*

BEISPIEL

4 Suggestion Remind students that **versprechen** takes a dative object.

S1: Ich habe meinen Eltern versprochen, dass ich nach dem Abschluss einen Job finden werde.
S2: Gute Idee. Meinen Eltern habe ich versprochen, dass ...

die Eltern	in drei Wochen
der Freund	im Sommer
der Professor	nach dem Studium
du	in fünf Jahren
die Schwester	vor dem 65. Lebensjahr
die Freundin	in 15 Jahren

4 Partner Chat You can also assign activity 4 on the Supersite.

5 Arbeitsblatt

Formulieren Sie in Dreiergruppen drei Fragen für eine Umfrage (*poll*): Wohin gehen andere Personen im Unterricht, wenn sie in die Stadt gehen? Was machen sie dort? Seien Sie höflich (*polite*), wenn Sie fragen! *Answers will vary.*

5 Suggestion Remind students to use the subjunctive for polite requests.

BEISPIEL

S1: Entschuldigung, ich möchte gern wissen, wie oft du im Monat auf die Bank gehst.
S2: Vielleicht ein- oder zweimal im Monat.
S1: Aha, und könntest du mir sagen, ob ...

6 Die Zukunft

Diskutieren Sie mit einem Partner / einer Partnerin, wie die Stadt der Zukunft aussehen wird. *Answers will vary.*

S1: In der Zukunft wird wohl kein Mensch mehr Auto fahren.
S2: Das stimmt. Wahrscheinlich werden Computer bald Auto fahren können.

6 Partner Chat You can also assign activity 6 on the Supersite.

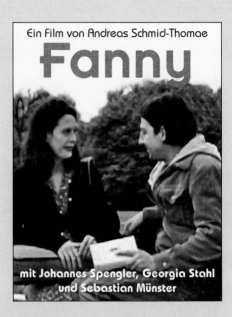

Ein Film von Andreas Schmid-Thomae

Fanny

mit Johannes Spengler, Georgia Stahl und Sebastian Münster

Nützliche Ausdrücke

- **leben**
  to live
- **die Probe**
  rehearsal
- **sich (etwas) merken**
  to remember (something)
- **Halt die Klappe!**
  Shut your mouth!
- **fassen**
  to understand
- **Das soll nicht dein Ernst sein!**
  You can't be serious!
- **Rate mal!**
  Guess!
- **verrückt**
  crazy
- **eigentlich**
  actually

Über den Film sprechen

- **der Regenschauer**
  rain shower
- **malen**
  to paint
- **sich trennen (von)**
  to break up (with)
- **sich verabreden (mit)**
  to make a date (with)

Kurzfilm

Video: Short Film

AP* Theme: Families & Communities
Context: Relationships

Fanny

Fanny erkennt Al im Park wieder und sie verabreden sich. Aber Al verliert ihre Telefonnummer. Fannys Mitbewohnerin Nora und Als Freund Max lernen einander kennen, als sie Fanny und Al helfen, zueinander zu finden.

Vorbereitung

1 **Fragen und Antworten** Verbinden Sie jede Frage mit der logischsten Antwort.

_c_ 1. Hast du dich mit Sophie zum Abendessen verabredet?

_e_ 2. Soll man jeden Tag leben, als ob es der letzte wäre?

_d_ 3. Rate mal, wen ich heute im Supermarkt getroffen habe!

_a_ 4. Könnt ihr uns helfen, die Wohnung anzumalen?

_b_ 5. Soll ich dir meine Telefonnummer aufschreiben?

a. Heute können wir leider nicht, weil wir Probe haben.

b. Nein, danke! Ich kann sie mir merken.

c. Nein. Eigentlich habe ich mich gestern von ihr getrennt.

d. Das weiß ich nicht. Du musst es mir sagen.

e. Das ist verrückt! Wenn man so lebte, könnte man niemals seine Zukunft planen.

2 **Besprechen Sie** Diskutieren Sie die folgenden Sprichwörter mit einem Partner / einer Partnerin. Glauben Sie an diese Sprichwörter? Warum oder warum nicht?

Liebe macht blind.

Die Zeit vergeht - die Liebe bleibt.

2 **Partner Chat** You can also assign activity 2 on the Supersite. Students work in pairs to record the activity online. The pair's recorded conversation will appear in your gradebook.

Szenen: Fanny

FANNY: Al!
AL: Fanny! Hallo!
FANNY: Hallo.
AL: Was machst du hier?
FANNY: Ich lebe hier.
AL: Das kann nicht sein.

MAX: Und? Was wirst du jetzt tun?
AL: Hier hab' ich sie wiedergetroffen.
MAX: Ja, und?
AL: Hier werd' ich auf sie warten.

AL: Sie ist nicht allein!
MAX: Ja und?
AL: Und sie hat dieses lebende° Paket geküsst.
MAX: Ja, aber das heißt doch gar nichts°.

NORA: Ich wohn' mit ihr zusammen.
MAX: Mit Fanny?
NORA: Ja.
MAX: Zeig mir, wo ihr wohnt!

AL: Hab' ich für dich gepflückt°.

FANNY: Jean... Ich liebe dich nicht mehr.
JEAN: Ich hab' wohl einige Dinge° falsch gemacht. Gelächelt hast du aber. Dann werde ich wohl den Rest meiner Tage im Kloster° verbringen.

einige Dinge *some things* **Kloster** *monastery* **lebende** *living* **gar nichts** *nothing* **gepflückt** *picked*

Analyse

3 Wer ist das? Welche Personen beschreiben die folgenden Sätze?

a. Al

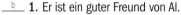

b. Max

c. Fanny

d. Nora

e. Jean

f. der Hausmeister

_b_ 1. Er ist ein guter Freund von Al.

_e_ 2. Er hat sich als lebendes Paket verkleidet.

_d_ 3. Max hat sie im Park erkannt.

_c_ 4. Sie ist Noras Mitbewohnerin.

_a_ 5. Er hat für Fanny Blumen angemalt.

_f_ 6. Er will nicht, dass Jean bei ihm klingelt.

4 Und wie geht's weiter? Entscheiden Sie mit einem Partner / einer Partnerin, was die Personen aus diesem Film in Zukunft machen werden. Werden sowohl Fanny und Al als auch Nora und Max für immer zusammen bleiben? Wird Jean endlich seine große Liebe finden? Schreiben Sie zusammen mindestens fünf Sätze darüber.

5 Beziehungsgespräch In diesem Film erfährt (learns) man, dass Fanny und Jean sich vor einem Jahr getrennt haben. Erfinden Sie ein Gespräch zwischen Fanny und Jean, das vor der Trennung stattfindet.

6 Diskutieren Sie Wenn Sie verliebt wären, hätten Sie auch wie Al im Film gehandelt? Wenn Sie Max oder Nora wären, hätten Sie auch Fanny und Nora geholfen? Besprechen Sie diese Fragen mit Ihren Partnern.

Communicative Goals

You will learn how to:

- ask for and give directions
- talk about parts of a city

In der Stadt 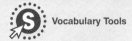 Vocabulary Tools

AP* Theme: Families & Communities
Context: Urban, Suburban, & Rural Life

Wortschatz

die Innenstadt	*downtown*
das Einkaufszentrum, (pl. Einkaufszentren)	*mall; shopping center*
das Gebäude, -	*building*
das Kaufhaus, ¨er	*department store*
die Kirche, -n	*church*
die Stadt, ¨e	*town*
das Viertel, -	*neighborhood*
Verkehr	*traffic*
die Allee, -n	*avenue; boulevard*
der Bürgersteig, -e	*sidewalk*
die Ecke, -n	*corner*
die Hauptstraße, -n	*main road*
der Zebrastreifen, -	*crosswalk*
Menschen	*people*
der Bürgermeister, - / die Bürgermeisterin, -nen	*mayor*
der Fußgänger, - / die Fußgängerin, -nen	*pedestrian*
Wo ist ...?	*Where is ...?*
abbiegen (biegt... ab)	*to turn*
folgen	*to follow*
bis zu	*until; up to*
gegenüber von	*across from*
geradeaus	*straight*
in der Nähe von	*close to*
in Richtung	*toward*
nah(e)	*near; nearby*
weit von	*far from*
Ausdrücke	*expressions*
(jemanden) mitnehmen	*to give (someone) a ride*
(die Straße) überqueren	*to cross (the street)*

Suggestion
Remind students that they encountered the numerical meaning of **Viertel** when they learned to tell time in **2A.3**. Ex: **Es ist Viertel nach vier**. Point out that the English word quarter can also refer to a neighborhood or section of a city, as in the French Quarter of New Orleans.

die Brücke, -n

Sie geht die Treppe hoch.
(hochgehen)

die Statue, -n

Er geht die Treppe herunter.
(heruntergehen)

der Brunnen, -

Osten

Süden

Norden

Westen

Er hat sich verlaufen.
(sich verlaufen)

Sie findet sich zurecht.
(sich zurechtfinden)

ACHTUNG

Folgen is used with an object in the dative case: **Folge mir! Folgen Sie dem Bus!** To tell someone to follow a road, use **entlanggehen** if the person is on foot or **entlangfahren** for someone in a vehicle: **Gehen Sie die Hauptstraße entlang, bis Sie zur ersten Kreuzung kommen.**

Ressourcen

 v̂Text   **WB** pp. 23–24   **LM** p. 67 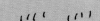 vhlcentral

Anwendung

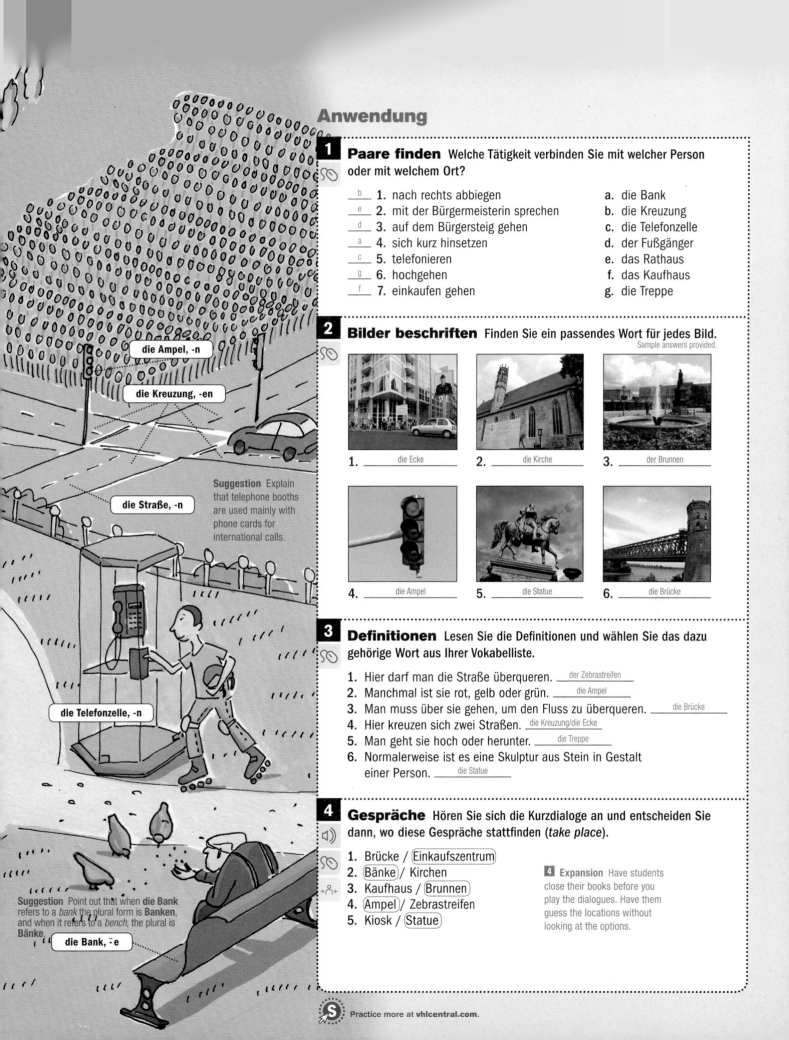

die Ampel, -n

die Kreuzung, -en

die Straße, -n

Suggestion Explain that telephone booths are used mainly with phone cards for international calls.

die Telefonzelle, -n

Suggestion Point out that when **die Bank** refers to a *bank* the plural form is **Banken**, and when it refers to a *bench*, the plural is **Bänke**.

die Bank, ¨e

1 **Paare finden** Welche Tätigkeit verbinden Sie mit welcher Person oder mit welchem Ort?

- b 1. nach rechts abbiegen
- e 2. mit der Bürgermeisterin sprechen
- d 3. auf dem Bürgersteig gehen
- a 4. sich kurz hinsetzen
- c 5. telefonieren
- g 6. hochgehen
- f 7. einkaufen gehen

a. die Bank
b. die Kreuzung
c. die Telefonzelle
d. der Fußgänger
e. das Rathaus
f. das Kaufhaus
g. die Treppe

2 **Bilder beschriften** Finden Sie ein passendes Wort für jedes Bild.

Sample answers provided.

1. _die Ecke_   2. _die Kirche_   3. _der Brunnen_

4. _die Ampel_   5. _die Statue_   6. _die Brücke_

3 **Definitionen** Lesen Sie die Definitionen und wählen Sie das dazu gehörige Wort aus Ihrer Vokabelliste.

1. Hier darf man die Straße überqueren. _der Zebrastreifen_
2. Manchmal ist sie rot, gelb oder grün. _die Ampel_
3. Man muss über sie gehen, um den Fluss zu überqueren. _die Brücke_
4. Hier kreuzen sich zwei Straßen. _die Kreuzung/die Ecke_
5. Man geht sie hoch oder herunter. _die Treppe_
6. Normalerweise ist es eine Skulptur aus Stein in Gestalt einer Person. _die Statue_

4 **Gespräche** Hören Sie sich die Kurzdialoge an und entscheiden Sie dann, wo diese Gespräche stattfinden (*take place*).

1. Brücke / (Einkaufszentrum)
2. (Bänke) / Kirchen
3. Kaufhaus / (Brunnen)
4. (Ampel) / Zebrastreifen
5. Kiosk / (Statue)

4 **Expansion** Have students close their books before you play the dialogues. Have them guess the locations without looking at the options.

5 Wegbeschreibungen
Sehen Sie sich den Stadtplan an und fragen Sie Ihren Partner / Ihre Partnerin, wie Sie zu den angegebenen Orten kommen. Ihre Ausgangsposition (*starting point*) ist mit einem "X" gekennzeichnet. Wechseln Sie sich ab. Answers will vary.

BEISPIEL

S1: *Entschuldigen Sie bitte, können Sie mir sagen, wie man zur Peterskirche kommt?*

S2: *Gehen Sie auf der Karolinenstraße geradeaus bis zum Bismarckplatz! Dann…*

1. die Peterskirche
2. der Tiergarten
3. die Universitätsbibliothek
4. der Herkulesbrunnen
5. das Einkaufszentrum "Königsarkaden"
6. die Post

Suggestion Review the phrases listed on p. 434 under the headings **Wo ist…?** and **Ausdrücke**. To help students use these phrases correctly, begin with a listening task: Have students start at the "X" and move along the map as you give directions to different locations. Repeat a few times before having them work in pairs.

5 Virtual Chat You can also assign activity 5 on the Supersite. Students record individual responses that appear in your gradebook.

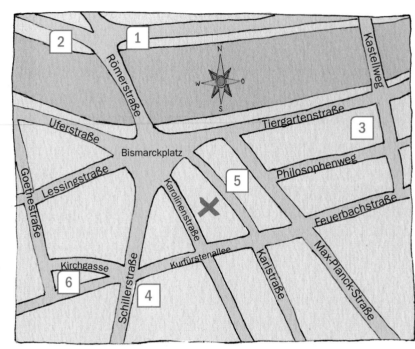

6 Nach der Ankunft
Schreiben Sie zusammen mit Ihrem Partner / Ihrer Partnerin eine E-Mail an Toni, eine Freundin aus Österreich, die Sie nächste Woche besuchen kommt. Erklären Sie ihr, wie man am besten zu Ihnen nach Hause findet. Answers will vary.

Von:	Vogel.Scheuche@online.de
An:	toni.meltzer@epost.au
Betreff:	Dein Besuch

Hallo Toni!

Wir freuen uns schon sehr auf deinen Besuch. Wenn du am Flughafen ankommst, solltest du erst mit dem Bus 51 in die Stadtmitte fahren. Dann…

7 Diskutieren und kombinieren
Sie und Ihr Partner / Ihre Partnerin bekommen zwei verschiedene Versionen des- selben Kreuzworträtsels (*crossword puzzle*). Geben Sie einander die Definitionen der fehlenden Wörter, um die beiden Versionen des Kreuzworträtsels auszufüllen.

BEISPIEL

S1: *Eins waagerecht: Hier treffen sich vier Straßen.*

S2: *Das ist eine Kreuzung.*

8 Mein Viertel
Zeichnen Sie zuerst eine Karte Ihres Viertels und beschreiben Sie es danach Ihrem Partner / Ihrer Partnerin. Er/Sie versucht eine eigene Karte zu zeichnen. Answers will vary.

BEISPIEL

S1: *Ich wohne um die Ecke, zwischen der Hauptstraße und dem Park. Wenn du bei mir aus der Haustür rausgehst und dann gleich nach rechts, dann…*

Aussprache und Rechtschreibung

 Audio

Loan Words (Part 1)

Some German words borrowed from other languages retain elements of their original pronunciation. For example, the German consonant **v** is normally pronounced like the *f* in the English word *fan*. But in certain loan words, the **v** is pronounced like the *v* in *van*.

Investor	**Universität**	**Ventilator**	**Advokat**	**Vegetarier**

The **ch** letter combination has a variety of pronunciations in loan words. Depending on the word, it may be pronounced like the *k* in *kitten*, like the *sh* in *shop*, or with a sound similar to the *j* in *jungle*. In some loan words, it is pronounced like the **ch** in the word **ich**.

Charakter	**Ch**ef	che**ck**en	**Ch**emie	**Ch**ina

The **sk** in the German word **Ski** and related compound words is pronounced like the *sh* in *shirt*.

Skilift	**Sk**ier	**Sk**iläufer	**Sk**ipiste	**Sk**iurlaub

Suggestion Point out to students that many borrowed words are pronounced with standard German pronunciation, ex.: **informativ**, **aktiv**.

Suggestion Tell students about regional variations in pronunciation of **ch** at the beginning of loanwords. For example, an Austrian would typically pronounce **China**, "keen ah," while someone from Wuppertal might say "sheen ah."

1 Aussprechen Wiederholen Sie die Wörter, die Sie hören.

1. Interview
2. Vase
3. Video
4. investieren
5. Chaos
6. Champignon
7. Charter
8. Chance
9. chinesisch
10. Skifahrer
11. Skihütte
12. Skispringen

Suggestion Have students refer to the **Aussprache** and **Rechtschreibung** sections of **5B** and **6A** to review the pronunciation of **ch** in German words.

2 Nachsprechen Wiederholen Sie die Sätze, die Sie hören.

1. Der kreative und aktive Vegetarier war in Wirklichkeit ein Vampir.
2. Mit den chaotischen Zuständen in China kommt der Chef nicht zurecht.
3. Die Skiläufer fahren mit dem Skilift zu den Skipisten.
4. Das Interview mit dem Investor von der Bank war sehr informativ.
5. Auch im Winter essen wir oft Vanilleeis in unserer Villa in Venedig.
6. Der charmante Chemiker war ein Mann von Charakter.

3 Sprichwörter Wiederholen Sie die Sprichwörter, die Sie hören.

Auf dem Vulkan tanzen.[1]

„Wer nichts als Chemie versteht, versteht auch die nicht recht."[2]
—Georg Christoph Lichtenberg

[1] To laugh in the face of danger. (*lit.*, To dance on the volcano.)
[2] Whoever understands nothing other than chemistry, does not truly understand even that.

Ressourcen

v̂ Text | **LM** p. 68 | vhlcentral

Sabites Nacht  Video

Die Freunde wollen ausgehen, um Sabites Erfolg zu feiern. Leider ist Berlin ziemlich groß. Wo war nochmal dieses spanische Restaurant?

NATIONAL communication cultures STANDARDS

Vorbereitung Have students look at scenes 5 and 6 and try to predict what the characters are reacting to. After they have watched the video, have them review their predictions.

1

GEORGE Hans? Hans! Du verlierst noch das Gehör, wenn du diese Dinger die ganze Zeit auf den Ohren trägst. Es sind jetzt schon drei Tage, Hans. Könntest du bitte mit mir darüber reden?
HANS Ich kann dich nicht hören.
GEORGE Geh heute Abend mit uns aus. Idiot.

2

GEORGE Sabite, ich bin's, George!
SABITE Ich komme! Kein Hans?
MELINE Hallo! Lass mal sehen. Sehr europäisch. Spricht Hans immer noch nicht mit dir? Idiot. Gib mir deine Schlüssel.

3

MELINE Hans, ich sage es nur einmal – hör also gut zu. Die Galerie in der Torstraße stellt Sabites Kunst in ein paar Wochen aus. Heute Abend feiern wir diese Neuigkeiten. Wir laufen nach Charlottenburg, um in einem spanischen Restaurant zu Abend zu essen. Und danach gehen wir in einen Club tanzen. George und Sabite sind nur Freunde. Das musst du einfach kapieren.

4

GEORGE Kommst du mit?
HANS Ich muss mich noch umziehen. Wir sehen uns dann in Kreuzberg.
SABITE Ich habe Melines Handtasche. Beeil dich. Wir treffen dich dann dort.

5

MELINE Du bist Berlinerin, Sabite! Wie kann man sich denn hier verlaufen?
SABITE Ich bin noch nie in diesem Stadtteil gewesen.
GEORGE Ich habe zwei Häuserblocks weiter unten an der Kreuzung mit der Straßenampel ein koreanisches Restaurant gesehen. Wir sollten umkehren.
SABITE Ich will kein koreanisches Essen essen, ich wollte doch spanisches Essen. Es ist mein Abend.

6

MELINE Mir ist es egal, wo wir essen gehen.
SABITE Hallo Hans. Wo bist du? Beweg dich nicht. Wir treffen dich dort in ein paar Minuten.

---

1 **Was fehlt?** Ergänzen Sie die Sätze mit den richtigen Informationen.

1. (George / Hans) spricht seit drei Tagen mit niemandem.
2. Die Galerie in der Torstraße will Sabites Kunst (kaufen / ausstellen).
3. Alle möchten diese Neuigkeiten in Charlottenburg (erzählen / feiern).
4. Sie wollen in einem (italienischen / spanischen) Restaurant essen gehen.
5. Anschließend wollen sie in einem Club (tanzen / singen).
6. George hat an der (Kreuzung / Brücke) ein koreanisches Restaurant gesehen.

7. Sabite möchte kein (koreanisches / spanisches) Essen.
8. Hans hat eine (Notiz / Karte) ausgedruckt, bevor er die Wohnung verlassen hat.
9. Sie müssen an der Kreuzung abbiegen und Richtung (Brücke / Tankstelle) gehen.
10. Das Restaurant ist gegenüber von einer (Telefonzelle / Statue).

7

SABITE Er ist an der U-Bahn-Station Görlitzer Bahnhof. Wir sind nicht weit weg davon. Ich kann mich erinnern, sie gesehen zu haben. Sie ist einen Häuserblock von der Falckensteinstraße entfernt. Wir sollten über diese Straße gehen und dann in diese Richtung weitergehen.

8

HANS Ich hatte es online nachgesehen, bevor ich die Wohnung verlassen habe. Ich habe uns eine Karte ausgedruckt. So, wir sind nicht weit vom Restaurant entfernt. Wir gehen einen Häuserblock weiter, biegen an der Kreuzung ab und gehen in Richtung Brücke. Es ist gegenüber von einer Statue.

9

GEORGE Es tut mir leid, Sabite.
SABITE Mir auch.
HANS Ich... Ich muss gehen.

10

SABITE Hans, warte! Hans! Geh ihm hinterher!
MELINE Ich laufe Jungen nicht hinterher, Sabite, Jungen laufen mir hinterher. Lass nicht zu, dass er uns den Spaß verdirbt. Essen und Tanzen warten auf dich. Es ist Sabites Nacht!

Nützliche Ausdrücke

- **das Gehör verlieren**
  to lose one's hearing
- **kapieren**
  to understand
- **umkehren**
  to turn around
- **sich bewegen**
  to move
- **Ich laufe Jungen nicht hinterher, Sabite, Jungen laufen mir hinterher.**
  I don't chase boys, Sabite; they chase me.
- **Lass nicht zu, dass er uns den Spaß verdirbt.**
  Don't let him ruin our fun.

2B.1
- **Wir sollten über diese Straße gehen und dann in diese Richtung weitergehen.**
  We should cross this street, and continue in this direction.

2B.2
- **Ich will kein koreanisches Essen essen, ich wollte doch spanisches Essen.**
  I don't want Korean food, I wanted Spanish food.

---

2 **Zum Besprechen** Stellen Sie sich vor, Hans kommt als Tourist in Ihre Stadt. Spielen Sie einen Dialog, in dem Sie ihm drei Orte empfehlen, die er sehen sollte. Erklären Sie ihm den Weg von Ihrer Schule oder Uni aus. Answers will vary.

2 **Expansion** Ask each pair of students what their three favorite places in town are and have them describe how you can get there.

3 **Vertiefung** Hans, George, Meline und Sabite wollen im Berliner Stadtteil (*district*) Charlottenburg spanisch essen gehen. Finden Sie weitere Stadtteile von Berlin.

Possible answers: Mitte, Tiergarten, Wedding, Prenzlauer Berg, Friedrichshain, Wilmersdorf, Kreuzberg, Spandau, Zehlendorf, Schöneberg, Steglitz, Tempelhof, Neukölln, Treptow, Köpenick, Lichtenberg, Weißensee, Pankow, Reinickendorf.

3 **Expansion** Have students identify which districts were formerly part of East Berlin.

AP* Theme: Beauty & Aesthetics
Context: Performing Arts

Kabarett  Reading

Suggestion As a pre-reading activity, have students ask each other about their favorite comedians, late-night TV shows, and theater acts. Do any of these engage in social criticism or political satire?

KABARETT IST EINE FORM DES THEATERS. Es wird auch Kleinkunst genannt. Beim Kabarett kombinieren und verbinden° Künstler Monologe, Dialoge, Pantomime und schauspielerische Szenen. Auch Aspekte der Lyrik (Gedichte° und Balladen) und Musik sind Teil° des Kabaretts. Im Kabarett kritisieren Künstler oft Aspekte der Gesellschaft°, indem sie Satire, Parodie, Sarkasmus und Ironie für diese Kritik benutzen. Dabei wollen sie auch das Publikum unterhalten° und zum Lachen bringen. Man kann Kabarett vor allem auf kleinen Bühnen° sehen. Die deutsche Kultshow „Mitternachtsspitzen", moderiert vom Kabarettisten Jürgen Becker, ist ein Beispiel dafür, dass es Kabarett auch im Fernsehen gibt.

Kabarett begann ursprünglich in Frankreich. 1901, etwa 20 Jahre später, gründete° Ernst von Wolzogen in Berlin das Kabarett „Überbrettl". Während des Kaiserreichs am Anfang des 20. Jahrhunderts und während des Dritten Reichs hatten Kabarettisten große politische Probleme. Erst nach dem 2. Weltkrieg durften Künstler im Kabarett wieder sagen, was sie wollten, und freie Kritik an Politik und Gesellschaft üben. In Mainz kann man heute das Deutsche Kabarettarchiv finden, wo es für die herausragenden° deutschen Kaberettisten ähnlich dem° *Hollywood Walk of Fame* einen Weg „Sterne der Satire" gibt.

Expansion One of the more accessible **Kabarett** artists for first-year students is the American Gayle Tufts, who performs in a language of her own invention: "Denglisch."

verbinden *combine* Gedichte *poems* Teil *part* Gesellschaft *society* unterhalten *entertain* Bühnen *stages* gründete *founded* herausragenden *outstanding* ähnlich dem *similar to the* Mitbegründer *co-founder*

Berühmte Kabarettisten	
Dieter Hallervorden (1935–)	Gründete 1960 das Kabarett *Die Wühlmäuse* und ist berühmt für die Figur *Didi*. In dem Film „Didi und die Rache der Enterbten" spielt Hallervorden sieben Rollen!
Dieter Hildebrandt (1927–2013)	Einer der wichtigsten Kaberettisten Deutschlands und Mitbegründer° der Münchner Lach- und Schießgesellschaft.
Urban Priol (1961–)	Berühmt für seine Arbeit im Kabarett und im Fernsehen. 2015 wurde ein Asteroid nach ihm benannt: (233880) Urbanpriol.

QUELLE: Das deutsche Kaberett Portal

ÜBUNGEN

1 **Richtig oder falsch?** Sind die Aussagen richtig oder falsch? Korrigieren Sie die falschen Aussagen mit einem Partner / einer Partnerin.

1. Ein anderer Name für Kabarett ist Kleinkunst. Richtig.

2. Kabarett ist eine Kombination von vielen Kunstformen. Richtig.

3. Kabarett kann man nur im Fernsehen sehen. Falsch. Kabarett kann man vor allem auf kleinen Bühnen sehen.

4. Das erste Kabarett in Deutschland hieß Überbrettl. Richtig.

5. Eine berühmte Kabarettshow im deutschen Radio heißt „Mitternachtsspitzen". Falsch. Die Show spielt im deutschen Fernsehen.

6. Das Deutsche Kabarettarchiv ist in Mainz. Richtig.

7. In Berlin gibt es einen Weg „Sterne der Satire". Falsch. Er ist in Mainz.

8. Urban Priol spielt auf der Bühne und im Fernsehen. Richtig.

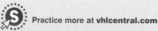

Orte der Kunst

die Freilichtbühne, -n	open air theater
die Galerie, -n	gallery
das Kabarett, -s	cabaret
das Museum, Museen	museum
die Oper, -n	opera
das Theater, -	theater

Religion

Die beiden größten Religionsgruppen in Deutschland sind der Katholizismus (die Römisch-Katholische Kirche) und der Protestantismus (Evangelische Landeskirchen). Etwa 30% der Deutschen sind römisch-katholisch und 35% evangelisch. Im Süden und Westen sind mehr Menschen katholisch. Im Norden sind mehr Menschen evangelisch. Diese Aufteilung° geht auf den Dreißigjährigen Krieg° zurück, als Länder im Norden die protestantische Seite unterstützten° und Länder im Süden die römisch-katholische Kirche. Neben den beiden Hauptreligionen ist der Islam mit 3% die drittgrößte Religionsgruppe, aber etwa ein Drittel der Bevölkerung (29%), vor allem in Ostdeutschland, ist konfessionslos.

Aufteilung *division* Krieg *war* unterstützten *supported*
AP* Theme: Global Challenges
Context: Philosophical Thought & Religion

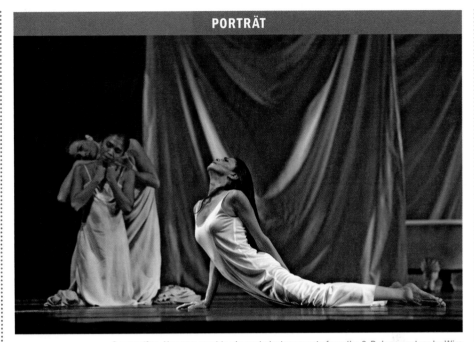

Pina Bausch

Suggestion You may want to show students excerpts from the 3-D documentary by Wim Wenders, *Pina*, 2012. Other clips that showcase Bausch's choreography are available online.

Pina Bausch (1940–2009) war neben Mary Wigman die bedeutendste° deutsche Choreographin der Gegenwart°. Sie begann ihre Ausbildung° als Tänzerin an der Folkwangschule in Essen. Sie studierte auch an der Juilliard School in New York. 1973 wurde sie choreographische Leiterin° bei den Wuppertaler Bühnen und das Tanzensemble wird schon bald in Tanztheater Wuppertal umbenannt.

AP* Theme: Beauty & Aesthetics
Context: Performing Arts

Bausch entwickelte° eine neue Tanzform, das Tanztheater, eine Kombination von Tanz, Gesang, Pantomime und Akrobatik. Es war sehr radikal und die Aufführungen° waren am Anfang oft kontrovers. Bausch war international anerkannt° und sie bekam Preise in Deutschland, England, Frankreich, Italien, Japan, Russland, der Türkei und den USA.

bedeutendste *most significant* Gegenwart *present times* Ausbildung *training* Leiterin *director* entwickelte *developed* Aufführungen *performances* anerkannt *recognized*

∞ IM INTERNET

Suchen Sie mehr Informationen zum Thema Religion in Deutschland: Welche Religionen gibt es in Deutschland? Welche religiösen Feste feiern die Deutschen? Welche offiziellen Feiertage gibt es?

Find out more at **vhlcentral.com**.

Suggestion Point out that the religious landscape of Germany is changing rapidly as immigrants bring their own beliefs with them.

---

2 **Was fehlt?** Ergänzen Sie die Sätze.

1. Etwa 35% der Deutschen sind _____evangelisch_____.
2. Mehr katholische Deutsche wohnen im _____Süden_____ und Westen.
3. Das Tanztheater Pina Bausch ist in _____Wuppertal_____.
4. Tanztheater ist eine neue _____Tanzform_____.
5. Pina Bauschs Tanztheater ist eine Kombination von Tanz, Gesang, Pantomime und _____Akrobatik_____.

3 **Kabarett!** Schreiben Sie mit einem Partner / einer Partnerin ein kurzes Kabarettstück, um es vor der Klasse zu spielen. Wählen Sie zuerst ein Thema. Überlegen Sie sich dann, was Sie darüber sagen oder zeigen wollen. Wollen Sie soziale oder politische Kommentare in Ihr Stück integrieren? Wollen Sie Satire oder Sarkasmus integrieren? Wie können Sie Ihre Ideen am besten zeigen: durch ein Gedicht (*poem*), mit Pantomime oder in der Form von Musik?

3 Suggestion Help students with planning a few days before the actual performance, and encourage them to rehearse. Clarify your expectations in terms of length of performance, props, etc. Ideally, students should memorize their lines instead of reading them.

Ressourcen

v̄Text
vhlcentral

Prepositions of direction  Presentation

QUERVERWEIS

You will learn more about country names in **2B.2**.

Suggestion You might want to direct students to **Vol. 1, 3B.3, 4B.2,** and **Vol. 2, 1B.3,** to review the use of prepositions with the accusative and dative cases.
Also, **Vol. 2, 3A.2,** to review the use of prepositions to indicate location.

ACHTUNG

Remember that **nach Hause** means *(to) home,* while **zu Hause** means *(at) home.* Note that you cannot use **zu Hause** to express going to someone else's home.

Remember that certain prepositions are typically combined with the definite article to form a contraction. You have already learned the accusative contractions **ans, aufs, durchs, fürs, ins, ums** and the dative contractions **am, beim, im, vom, zum, zur.**

Suggestion Tell students that the patterns described here are helpful as guidelines, but that the use of prepositions is not always clear cut. Point out, for example, that the phrases **zum Kunstmuseum** and **ins Kunstmuseum** are both acceptable, but that **ins** emphasizes going *inside* to look at exhibits. Point out that **in, auf,** and **an** are also sometimes used interchangeably.

Startblock Use prepositions to talk about where things are located. You can also use prepositions to talk about movement toward or away from a location.

Wir müssen **nach** Kreuzberg zurück.

Wir sollten **über** die Straße gehen und dann **in** diese Richtung weitergehen.

- Use **nach** with geographical place names to talk about traveling to a destination. Use **in** with the accusative if a place name includes a definite article.

Fliegt ihr morgen **nach** Istanbul?
*Are you flying **to** Istanbul tomorrow?*

Wir wollten schon immer **in** die Türkei fahren.
*We've always wanted to go **to** Turkey.*

- Use **zu** with the dative to talk about going to a destination within a town or city, such as a store or building. You can also use **zu** with a dative personal pronoun or a person's name or title to say that you are going to their home or business.

Dieser Bus fährt **zum** Einkaufszentrum.
*This bus goes **to** the shopping center.*

Die Fahrt **zu** meinen Großeltern dauert zwei Stunden.
*The drive **to** my grandparents' house takes two hours.*

Ich muss noch schnell **zu** Aldi, um Milch zu kaufen.
*I still have to go **to** Aldi to buy milk.*

Vergiss nicht, dass du morgen **zur** Zahnärztin gehen musst!
*Don't forget that you have to go **to** the dentist tomorrow!*

- Use **in** with the accusative to talk about going to a location inside a building, into a geographical area, or to a certain street.

Heute Abend gehe ich **in** die Bibliothek.
*I'm going **to** the library tonight.*

Am Wochenende fahren wir gern **in** die Berge.
*On weekends, we like to drive up **into** the mountains.*

Mia geht **in** den Waschsalon.
*Mia's going **into** the laundromat.*

Biegen Sie links ab **in** die Waldstraße!
*Take a left **onto** Wald Street!*

- Use **auf** with the accusative to talk about movement toward a horizontal surface, an open space, or a public building, and also in idiomatic expressions such as **auf eine Party gehen**.

Legen Sie die Papiere bitte **auf** meinen Schreibtisch.
*Please put the papers **on** my desk.*

Könntest du bitte **auf** die Post gehen und Briefmarken kaufen?
*Could you please go **to** the post office and buy some stamps?*

Am Sonntag gehen wir **auf** den Markt.
*On Sunday, we're going **to** the market.*

Morgen fahren Herr und Frau Maier **aufs** Land.
*Tomorrow, Mr. and Mrs. Maier are driving **out to** the country.*

- Use **an** with the accusative to talk about movement toward a vertical surface or a body of water.

Emma hängt ihre Poster **an** die Wand.
*Emma is putting her posters up **on** the wall.*

Fahren wir zusammen **ans** Meer!
*Let's go **to** the seaside together!*

Im Sommer gehen wir immer **an** den Strand.
*We always go **to** the beach in the summer.*

Sie fahren im Urlaub **an** die Nordsee.
*They're going **to** the North Sea on vacation.*

- Use **über** with the accusative to talk about movement over, across, or by way of something, such as a street, a bridge, or a mountain.

Radfahrer sollen ihre Fahrräder **über** die Straße schieben.
*Bicyclists are supposed to push their bikes **across** the street.*

Sie fahren **über** München nach Salzburg.
*They're driving to Salzburg **by way of** Munich.*

Nur bei Grün darf man **über** die Kreuzung fahren.
*You can only drive **through** the intersection when the light is green.*

Wir sind **über** die Berge nach Österreich gereist.
*We traveled **over** the mountains to Austria.*

- Use **aus** with place names to express where someone is from. If the place name includes a definite article, use the dative case.

Unsere Eltern kommen **aus** Österreich.
*Our parents are **from** Austria.*

Die beste Schokolade kommt **aus** der Schweiz.
*The best chocolate comes **from** Switzerland.*

- When using modals with prepositions of location, German speakers often omit the infinitive after the modal.

Wir müssen **nach Hause**.
*We have to **go home**.*

Ich will **ins Bett**.
*I want to **go to bed**.*

Suggestion Encourage students to create flash-cards to help them memorize some of the more common directional expressions as "sound bites." Ex.: **ins Kino, ins Restaurant, ins Café, in die Stadt, in den Park, auf die Bank, auf die Post, auf eine Party, auf den Markt, aufs Land, zur Schule, zur Uni, zur Arbeit, an den Strand, ans Meer.**

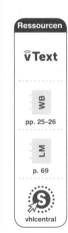

Ressourcen

v̂Text

WB
pp. 25–26

LM
p. 69

vhlcentral

🎧 **Jetzt sind Sie dran!** **Wählen Sie die passenden Präpositionen.**

1. Ich fliege morgen früh (nach / in / auf) Spanien.
2. Tim und Greta fahren (in / auf / an) den Strand.
3. In zwei Wochen fliegen wir alle (über / nach / zu) Hause.
4. Wie kommt man am schnellsten (an den / zum / in den) Deutschen Museum?
5. Ich fahre gern (in / über / auf) die Schweiz.
6. Geht ihr am Wochenende (an / nach / auf) Annikas Party?
7. Schaut in beide Richtungen, bevor ihr (nach / über / in) den Zebrastreifen lauft.
8. Der Lehrer hat seinen Namen (an / in / nach) die Tafel geschrieben.
9. Warst du schon (in / zu / auf) der Post?
10. Fahren Sie (an / in / auf) die Albstraße hinein und suchen Sie dort einen Parkplatz.
11. Mama, ich gehe (nach / über / zu) einer Freundin.
12. Der Mann ist bei Rot (zu / über / aus) die Kreuzung gefahren.
13. Ich fliege morgen (zu / nach / auf) München.
14. Wir gehen (zu / auf / an) den Markt.

Anwendung

1 **Was fehlt?** Ergänzen Sie die Sätze mit **nach** oder **in**.

 ▶ **BEISPIEL** Italien
Nächsten Freitag fahre ich
nach Italien.

die Fußgängerzone
1. Zum Einkaufen
geht man
in die Fußgängerzone.

Paris
2. Macht ihr
eine Reise
nach Paris?

die Schweiz
3. Jan und
Maria fahren
in die Schweiz.

Mexiko
4. Kiara würde gern
nach Mexiko
fliegen.

die Staatsbibliothek
5. Am Freitag
gehen wir
in die Staatsbibliothek.

2 **Kombinieren Sie** Ergänzen Sie die Sätze mit den passenden Präpositionen: **an, auf, in, über, zu.**

BEISPIEL Kommst du nach dem Konzert noch mit uns _zu_ Paul?

1. Mein Opa legt sich nach dem Mittagessen immer _auf_ das Sofa.
2. Um zu Sarah zu kommen, musst du _über_ die Brücke fahren und dann links abbiegen.
3. Wisst ihr, ob Annika und Lena _in_ die Bibliothek gegangen sind?
4. Ich muss noch schnell _auf_ die Bank gehen und Geld abheben.
5. Warum fährst du im Winter nie in die Berge, sondern immer nur _an_ den Strand?

3 **Persönliche Fragen** Beantworten Sie die Fragen in ganzen Sätzen. Achten Sie darauf, dass Sie die passenden Präpositionen bei Ihren Antworten benutzen. Sample answers provided.

BEISPIEL Wohin werden Sie am Ende des Semesters fahren?
Ich werde zu meinen Eltern fahren.

1. Wohin gehen Sie, wenn Sie richtig Spaß haben wollen? Ich gehe zu meinem besten Freund.
2. Wohin gehen Sie, wenn Sie mal ganz allein sein wollen? Ich gehe in den Wald.
3. Wohin gehen Sie, wenn Sie ein schönes Geschenk für Ihre Mutter suchen?
Ich gehe in ein Juweliergeschäft.
4. Wohin gehen Sie, wenn Sie Briefmarken brauchen? Ich gehe auf die Post.
5. Wohin fahren Sie lieber: in die Berge oder an den Strand? Ich fahre lieber an den Strand.
6. Wohin möchten Sie in Urlaub fahren? Ich möchte gern in die Schweiz in Urlaub fahren.

Kommunikation

4 **Wohin?** Wohin sind die Leute in den Bildern gegangen, gefahren oder geflogen? Schreiben Sie Sätze mit einem Partner / einer Partnerin und benutzen Sie dabei das Perfekt und die passenden Präpositionen. Answers will vary.

> | Italien | der See | der Supermarkt |
> | das Konzert | der Strand | |

▶ **BEISPIEL** Simone und Emil

Simone und Emil sind an den See gefahren.

1. Herr und Frau Kaymaz

2. Julian

3. Mira

4. Familie Lehmann

5 **Wie oft...?** Fragen Sie Ihren Partner / Ihre Partnerin, wie oft er/sie zu den angegebenen Orten geht. Answers will vary.

BEISPIEL

S1: Wie oft gehst du ins Theater?
S2: Vielleicht einmal im Jahr. Und wie oft gehst du auf eine Party?
S1: Jedes Wochenende.

1. das Kino
2. das Einkaufszentrum
3. der Arzt
4. die Großeltern
5. die Bank

6 **Spielen im Unterricht** Zwei Schüler verlassen (*leave*) das Klassenzimmer. Der Rest der Klasse ändert die Position von ein paar Sachen im Klassenzimmer. Die zwei Schüler kommen wieder herein und müssen herausfinden, was die anderen Schüler gemacht haben. Answers will vary.

BEISPIEL

S1: Ihr habt Bücher unter den Tisch gelegt.
S2: Und ihr habt einen Rucksack an die Wand gehängt.

5 Suggestion Write the questions as a class, to verify that students are forming the prepositional phrases correctly.

5 Partner Chat You can also assign activity 5 on the Supersite. Students work in pairs to record the activity online. The pair's recorded conversation will appear in your gradebook.

Talking about nationality  Presentation

Startblock In German, both nouns and adjectives are used to talk about nationality.

- Unlike in English, German adjectives of nationality are never capitalized and are rarely used to refer to people. To describe a person's nationality, use **sein** with a noun of nationality, dropping the article before the noun.

Suggestion Point out that one can also form nouns and adjectives from city names. Ex: **Er ist Münchner. Ich esse gern Wiener Würstchen.**

Magst du **deutsches** Essen?
*Do you like **German** food?*

Sarah ist **Deutsche**.
*Sarah is **German**.*

countries and nationalities		
Amerika	der Amerikaner,- / die Amerikanerin,-nen	amerikanisch
China	der Chinese,-n / die Chinesin,-nen	chinesisch
Deutschland	der Deutsche,-n / die Deutsche,-n	deutsch
England	der Engländer,- / die Engländerin,-nen	englisch
Frankreich	der Franzose,-n / die Französin,-nen	französisch
Indien	der Inder,- / die Inderin,-nen	indisch
Italien	der Italiener,- / die Italienerin,-nen	italienisch
Japan	der Japaner, - / die Japanerin, -nen	japanisch
Kanada	der Kanadier,- / die Kanadierin,-nen	kanadisch
Korea	der Koreaner,- / die Koreanerin,-nen	koreanisch
Mexiko	der Mexikaner,- / die Mexikanerin,-nen	mexikanisch
Österreich	der Österreicher,- / die Österreicherin,-nen	österreichisch
Russland	der Russe,-n / die Russin,-nen	russisch
die Schweiz	der Schweizer,- / die Schweizerin,-nen	schweizerisch, Schweizer
Spanien	der Spanier,- / die Spanierin,-nen	spanisch
die Türkei	der Türke,-n / die Türkin,-nen	türkisch

- You can use either **nicht** or **kein** before a noun of nationality.

Marie **ist Französin**.
*Marie **is French**.*

Yasmin **ist keine Türkin**.
*Yasmin **isn't Turkish**.*

Max **ist nicht Kanadier**.
*Max **isn't Canadian**.*

- Most nouns referring to languages are identical to the corresponding adjective of nationality, but are capitalized and have no added endings. Nouns referring to a language are always neuter. They do not take definite articles.

Ben spricht fließend **Deutsch**.
*Ben speaks **German** fluently.*

Wir sprechen **kein Italienisch**.
*We don't speak **Italian**.*

Ihr **Französisch** ist sehr gut.
*Your **French** is very good.*

Ich spreche nicht so gut **Russisch**.
*I don't speak **Russian** very well.*

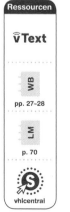
Jetzt sind Sie dran! Wählen Sie das passende Wort.

1. Niklas spricht (deutsch / (Deutsch)).
2. Ich finde (Chinesisches / (chinesisches)) Essen sehr lecker.
3. Arnold Schwarzenegger ist (Österreich / (Österreicher)).
4. Karl studiert seit zwei Jahren in Rom und spricht fließend ((Italienisch)/ italienisch).

5. Die (Deutsche / (deutsche)) Flagge ist schwarz, rot und gold.
6. Lara kommt aus der Türkei und ist (eine Türkin / (Türkin)).
7. Daniela wohnt in Madrid und ist (spanisch / (Spanierin)).
8. In Kanada spricht man (englisch / (Englisch)) und Französisch.

1 **Nationalitäten** Geben Sie die Nationalitäten und die Muttersprachen dieser Personen an.

> **BEISPIEL** Marie / Frankreich
> *Marie ist Französin. Sie spricht wohl Französisch.*

1. Manfred / Deutschland   Manfred ist Deutscher. Er spricht (wohl) Deutsch.
2. Francesca / Italien   Francesca ist Italienerin. Sie spricht (wohl) Italienisch.
3. Jasmin / Türkei   Jasmin ist Türkin. Sie spricht (wohl) Türkisch.
4. Sergio / Spanien   Sergio ist Spanier. Er spricht (wohl) Spanisch.
5. Emily / die USA   Emily ist Amerikanerin. Sie spricht (wohl) Englisch.

2 **Was fehlt?** Ergänzen Sie die Sätze mit den Adjektiven, die zu den Orten in Klammern gehören. Benutzen Sie die richtigen Adjektivendungen.

> **BEISPIEL** (Türkei) Im Pergamonmuseum kann man etwas über die ___türkische___ Geschichte lernen.

1. (Österreich) Das Wiener Schnitzel ist eine ___österreichische___ Spezialität.
2. (Spanien) Das Guggenheim-Museum in der ___spanischen___ Stadt Bilbao ist sehr modern.
3. (die Schweiz) Emmentaler und Münster sind ___Schweizer___ Käse.
4. (Korea) Ich esse sehr gern ___koreanisches___ Essen.
5. (Deutschland) Der ___deutsche___ Journalist ist sehr neugierig.

3 **Aus aller Welt** Fragen Sie Ihren Partner / Ihre Partnerin, welche Sachen aus verschiedenen Ländern er/sie (nicht) gern mag. Benutzen Sie die Wörter aus der Liste oder Ihre eigenen. Answers will vary.

> **BEISPIEL**
> **S1:** *Isst du gern Käse aus Holland?*
> **S2:** *Ja, ich esse gern holländischen Käse.*
> *Am liebsten esse ich aber französischen Käse.*

Architektur (*f.*)	Musik (*f.*)
Essen (*n.*)	Olivenöl (*n.*)
Filme (*pl.*)	Schokolade (*f.*)
Käse (*m.*)	Tee (*m.*)
Kaffee (*m.*)	Würstchen (*n.*)
Literatur (*f.*)	Zeitungen (*pl.*)

3 Partner Chat You can also assign activity 3 on the Supersite. Students work in pairs to record the activity online. The pair's recorded conversation will appear in your gradebook.

Wiederholung

1

Diskutieren und kombinieren Sie und Ihr Partner / Ihre Partnerin bekommen Blätter mit ähnlichen Bildern einer Straße. Suchen Sie die Unterschiede und notieren Sie sie. Answers will vary.

BEISPIEL

S1: *Auf meinem Bild gibt es zwei Zeitungskioske. Wie viele hast du?*
S2: *Ich habe nur einen.*

2

Geografie Fragen Sie Ihren Partner / Ihre Partnerin, in welches Land man fahren muss, um die abgebildeten Sehenswürdigkeiten zu besichtigen. Sample answers are provided.

BEISPIEL

S1: *Wohin reist man, wenn man den Eiffelturm sehen will?*
S2: *Wenn man den Eiffelturm sehen will, muss man nach Frankreich reisen.*

der Eiffelturm in Paris
Nach Frankreich.

die Brooklyn-Brücke
in New York   In die USA.

der Westminster-Palast
in London   Nach England.

die Sultan-Ahmed-Moschee
in Istanbul   In die Türkei.

das Matterhorn in
den Alpen   In die Schweiz.

das Brandenburger Tor
in Berlin   Nach Deutschland.

2 Expansion Have students name additional landmarks from other countries for their partners to guess.

2 Virtual Chat You can also assign activity 2 on the Supersite. Students record individual responses that appear in your gradebook.

3

In der Stadt Wählen Sie eine Aktivität aus der Liste. Sagen Sie Ihrem Partner / Ihrer Partnerin, was Sie in der Stadt machen wollen. Er/Sie sagt Ihnen, wohin Sie gehen müssen, um das zu machen. Answers will vary.

BEISPIEL   **3** Virtual Chat You can also assign activity 3 on the Supersite.

S1: *Ich möchte mit dem Bürgermeister sprechen.*
S2: *Hmmm, da musst du ins Rathaus.*

> mit dem Bürgermeister sprechen
> schwimmen gehen
> eine Sportzeitschrift kaufen
> frisches Obst und Gemüse kaufen
> Blumen kaufen
> Wäsche waschen
> im Grünen spazieren gehen
> im Internet surfen

4

Wer isst das? Erzählen Sie Ihrem Partner / Ihrer Partnerin, was Sie gerne essen würden. Ihr Partner / Ihre Partnerin sagt, in welches Restaurant Sie gehen sollen. Answers will vary.

BEISPIEL   **4** Partner Chat You can also assign activity 4 on the Supersite.

S1: *Ich würde gern Pasta oder Pizza essen.*
S2: *Gehen wir doch in ein italienisches Restaurant!*

5

Arbeitsblatt Wählen Sie drei Orte in Ihrer Stadt aus. Fragen Sie zwei Personen, wie man von der Bibliothek zu jedem Ort kommt. Schreiben Sie die Antwort auf, und entscheiden Sie, welche Antwort besser ist. Answers will vary.

BEISPIEL

S1: *Wie kommt man am besten von der Bibliothek zu Martins Waschsalon?*
S2: *Wenn du vor der Bibliothek stehst, geh erst nach links und dann geradeaus bis zum Broadway, dann...*

6 **Ein Festessen** Sie und Ihr Partner / Ihre Partnerin haben Ihre Eltern zu einem schönen Abendessen eingeladen. Planen Sie erst das Menü und was Sie alles dazu brauchen. Dann schauen Sie auf das Bild und sagen Sie, was Sie in jedem Geschäft kaufen. Answers will vary.

> **BEISPIEL**
>
> **S1:** *Mein Vater will immer Brot zum Abendessen. Ich kaufe es in der Bäckerei.*
> **S2:** *Und wie wär's mit Garnelen? Ich kann dafür ins Fischgeschäft gehen.*

6 Suggestion Verify that students remember the genders of the shops shown in the drawing.

6 Partner Chat You can also assign activity 6 on the Supersite. Students work in pairs to record the activity online. The pair's recorded conversation will appear in your gradebook.

METZGEREI   BÄCKEREI   FEINKOST   FISCHGESCHÄFT   KONDITOREI

---

7 **Stadtführer** Wählen Sie mit einem Partner / einer Partnerin fünf Orte in Ihrer Stadt, die Besucher unbedingt sehen sollen. Beschreiben Sie jeden Ort. Besprechen Sie dann, wie man von einem Ort zum nächsten kommt.
Answers will vary.

> **BEISPIEL**
> **7 Partner Chat** You can also assign activity 7 on the Supersite.
> **S1:** *Ich finde, Besucher sollten das Kunstmuseum sehen.*
> **S2:** *Du hast recht! Da kann man...*

8 **Wer und woher?** Beschreiben Sie Ihrem Partner / Ihrer Partnerin eine berühmte Person. Er/Sie rät, wer das ist, und sagt, woher er/sie kommt. Answers will vary.

> **BEISPIEL**
> **8 Partner Chat** You can also assign activity 8 on the Supersite.
> **S1:** *Man kennt diesen Mann durch seine Opern und Symphonien. Er war Österreicher und lebte im 18. Jahrhundert und ist jung gestorben.*
> **S2:** *Das ist Mozart, der österreichische Musiker.*

Mein Wör | ter | buch

Schreiben Sie fünf weitere Wörter in Ihr persönliches Wörterbuch zu den Themen **Besorgungen** und **In der Stadt**.

Schmuckgeschäft

Übersetzung
jewelry store

Wortart
Substantiv

Gebrauch
Im Schmuckgeschäft will ich mir eine neue Halskette aussuchen.

Synonyme
Juweliergeschäft, Juwelier

Antonyme

 Vocabulary Tools

Panorama

Niedersachsen und Nordrhein-Westfalen

Niedersachsen in Zahlen

Suggestion Tell students that the people of Hannover are thought to speak the "purest" form of **Hochdeutsch.**

▶ **Fläche:** *47,634 km²*

▶ **Bevölkerung:** *7,9 Millionen Menschen*

▶ **Städte:** *Hannover (514.000 Einwohner), Braunschweig (249.000), Osnabrück (160.000)*

▶ **Wichtige Industriezweige:** *Automobil, Stahl°, Windenergie, Messen°*

▶ **Touristenattraktionen:** *Cuxhaven, Ostfriesische Inseln, Hannover, Otterndorf, Lüneburger Heide*

Touristen können in Niedersachsen Urlaub an der Nordseeküste machen oder die Natur in der Lüneburger Heide oder im Harz genießen. Die Industrie wird vor allem durch den Autohersteller VW mit seinem Sitz in Wolfsburg dominiert.

QUELLE: Landesportal Niedersachsen

Suggestion Have students find some of the places mentioned on the map.

Nordrhein-Westfalen in Zahlen

▶ **Fläche:** *34,088 km²*

▶ **Bevölkerung:** *17,6 Millionen Menschen*

▶ **Städte:** *Köln (1.039.500 Einwohner), Düsseldorf (601.000), Dortmund (578.000)*

▶ **Wichtige Industriezweige:** *Maschinenbau, Elektroindustrie, Banken, Tourismus*

▶ **Touristenattraktionen:** *Teutoburger Wald, Siegerland, Wittgensteiner Land*

Viele Touristen besuchen Nordrhein-Westfalen wegen der schönen Natur und der vielen Bäder im Teutoburger Wald. Nordrhein-Westfalen ist nicht nur das Bundesland mit der größten Bevölkerung, sondern auch mit der stärksten Wirtschaft°.

Suggestion Tell students that the Teutoburger Wald was the site of a famous
QUELLE: Landesportal Nordrhein-Westfalen battle in 9 A.D., in which the Germanic tribes ambushed the Roman army.

Berühmte Menschen aus Niedersachsen und Nordrhein-Westfalen

▶ **Wilhelm Busch,** *Autor (1832–1908)*

▶ **Lena Meyer-Landrut,** *Sängerin (1991–)*

▶ **Baron Münchhausen,** *Aristokrat (1720–1797)*

▶ **Michael Schumacher,** *Formel-1-Rennfahrer (1969–)*

▶ **Werner von Siemens,** *Erfinder° (1816–1892)*

Stahl *steel* **Messen** *trade shows* **Wirtschaft** *economy* **Erfinder** *inventor* **Würfen** *throws* **eine bestimmte Strecke schaffen** *complete a predetermined route* **freien Feldern** *open fields*

Karnevalskostüm in Köln

VW-Werk in Wolfsburg

HAMBURG

NATIONALPARK NIEDERSÄCHSISCHES WATTENMEER

Bremerhaven

Lüneburg

BREMEN

Elbe

LÜNEBURGER HEIDE

Oldenburg

NIEDERSACHSEN

Weser

Ems

Wolfsburg

NIEDERLANDE

Osnabrück

Hannover

WESERBERGLAND

Braunschweig

Münster

Bielefeld

NATIONALPARK HARZ

SACHSEN-ANHALT

Paderborn

Wurmberg

HARZ

Lippe

Göttingen

NORDRHEIN-WESTFALEN

Ruhr

Langenberg

SAUERLAND

ROTHAARGEBIRGE

HESSEN

Rhein

Düsseldorf

Köln

BERGISCHES LAND

Aachen

Bonn

BELGIEN

EIFEL

RHEINLAND-PFALZ

Der Harz liegt in Niedersachsen, Sachsen-Anhalt und Thüringen

RUHRGEBIET

Gelsenkirchen

Dortmund

Essen

Bochum

Duisburg

Ruhr

Rhein

— Landesgrenzen
● Stadt
◎ Landeshauptstadt

0   50 Meilen
0   50 Kilometer

0   25 Meilen
0   25 Kilometer

Unglaublich, aber wahr!

Boßeln ist ein Ballsport in Norddeutschland. Ein Spieler muss mit einem Ball in so wenig Würfen° wie möglich eine bestimmte Strecke schaffen°. Man kann auf freien Feldern° oder auf Straßen spielen. Normalerweise ist Boßeln ein Mannschaftssport.

Suggestion Tell students that Lena Meyer-Landrut is famous for winning the 2010 Eurovision Song Contest for her song *"Satellite."*

AP* **Theme:** Contemporary Life
Context: Health & Well-Being

AP* Theme: Beauty & Aesthetics
Context: Architecture

Landschaftsarchitektur

Landschaftspark Duisburg-Nord

Als die Stahlproduktion unrentabel° wurde, veränderte sich die gesamte Region. Aus dem Stahlwerk° in Duisburg-Meiderich ist so der Landschaftspark Duisburg-Nord geworden. Viele Industrieelemente sind im Park noch erhalten, aber sie wurden mit Bäumen, Blumen und Freizeitgeländen° kombiniert. Das Resultat ist eine bemerkenswerte Integration von Industriestrukturen und Landschaft. Der Landschaftspark gilt als eins der wichtigsten Projekte der Landschaftsarchitektur der Jahrtausendwende°.

Natur

Lüneburger Heide

Die Lüneburger Heide° ist eine Naturlandschaft in Niedersachsen. Sie liegt zwischen Hamburg, Bremen und Hannover. Die Heide ist eine der wichtigsten Touristenattraktion in Niedersachsen: mehr als vier Millionen Touristen besuchen die Heide jedes Jahr. In dieser flachen Region kann man Wald- und Heidelandschaften finden. Im Naturschutzgebiet° darf man nicht mit dem Auto fahren. Selbst die Polizisten reiten auf Pferden°. Besonders interessant für Touristen sind die vielen Heidschnuckenherden°, die es auf der Heide gibt.

AP* Theme: Contemporary Life
Context: Entertainment, Travel, & Leisure

Berühmte Personen

Karl der Große°

Karl der Große (circa 747–814) gilt als einer der bedeutendsten Herrscher° Europas. Er war ab dem Jahr 768 König des fränkischen Reiches° und ab dem Jahr 800 Römischer Kaiser. Er regierte das heutige Deutschland, Frankreich, die Niederlande, Belgien, Italien und Polen. Er gilt als der erste Europäer, weil er in dieser Region eine Art europäische Kultur geprägt° hat. Zum Beispiel war Latein die wichtigste Sprache in dem gesamten Reich. Nach seinem Tod wurde er in der Pfalzkapelle in seiner Residenzstadt Aachen, die heute in Nordrhein-Westfalen liegt, begraben°.

AP* Theme: Personal & Public Identities
Context: National Identity

Öffentlicher Verkehr

Schwebebahn° Wuppertal

In Wuppertal gibt es nicht nur Busse für den öffentlichen Verkehr, sondern auch eine Schwebebahn, die seit 1901 Menschen zwischen Vohwinkel und Oberbarmen transportiert. Sie ist das Wahrzeichen° der Stadt Wuppertal und steht seit 1997 unter Denkmalschutz. Im Jahr 1950 sollte der Elefant Tuffi zwischen zwei Stationen mit der Schwebebahn fahren. Als der Elefant erschrak°, sprang er aus der Schwebebahn und landete in der Wupper. Dem Tier passierte dabei nichts, aber die Stadt ist seither dafür berühmt.

AP* Theme: Science & Technology
Context: Transportation

🔗 IM INTERNET

1. Suchen Sie Touristeninformationen über die Lüneburger Heide: Was kann man hier machen? Wo kann man wohnen?

2. Suchen Sie mehr Informationen zu Karl dem Großen: Was weiß man über seine Familie? Warum war sein Reich so wichtig für Europa?

Find out more at **vhlcentral.com**.

---

unrentabel *unprofitable* **Stahlwerk** *steel mill* **Freizeitgeländen** *recreational facilities* **Jahrtausendwende** *turn of the millennium*
Heide *heath* **Naturschutzgebiet** *protected landscape* **Pferden** *horses* **Heidschnuckenherden** *flocks of moorland sheep*
Schwebebahn *suspended monorail* **Wahrzeichen** *landmark* **erschrak** *became scared* **Karl der Große** *Charlemagne*
Herrscher *rulers* **des fränkischen Reiches** *of the Frankish Empire* **geprägt** *shaped* **begraben** *buried*

🔗 **Was haben Sie gelernt?** Ergänzen Sie die Sätze.

1. Boßeln ist ein ___Ballsport___ in Norddeutschland.

2. Normalerweise spielt man Boßeln als ___Mannschaft___.

3. Aus einem Stahlwerk hat man im Ruhrgebiet einen ___Park___ gemacht.

4. Der Landespark Duisburg-Nord ist eine Kombination aus ___Industrieelementen___ und Landschaft.

5. Die Lüneburger Heide liegt zwischen ___Hamburg___, Bremen und Hannover.

6. Mehr als ___vier Millionen___ Touristen besuchen die Heide jedes Jahr.

7. Die Wuppertaler Schwebebahn gibt es seit ___1901___.

8. 1950 sprang ein ___Elefant___ aus der Schwebebahn.

9. Karl der Große hat in seinem Reich eine europäische ___Kultur___ geprägt.

10. Karl der Große ist in ___Aachen___ begraben.

 Practice more at **vhlcentral.com**.

Lesen Audio: Reading

Vor dem Lesen
AP* Theme: Beauty & Aesthetics
Context: Language & Literature

Strategien

Repetition

Poets often use repetition of sounds, syllables, words, rhymes, or rhythms to emphasize certain images or themes, to establish a particular mood or tone, or to create a musical effect. A poet may also repeat a particular verse or phrase with slight variations, using these subtle differences to create a shift in tone or change of focus. Paying attention to the effects of recurring words, phrases, and sounds will help you gain insight into the meaning of a poem.

Suggestion Explain to students that a fugue refers to a musical piece built around a repeating theme.

Untersuchen Sie den Text

Sehen Sie sich diese beiden Gedichte (*poems*) an. Beachten Sie die Wiederholung von Wörtern und Zeilen. Gibt es auch Wiederholungen mit kleinen Unterschieden (*differences*)?

Suggestion Ask students if they are familiar with any of Hesse's work, such as the novels *Steppenwolf* and *Demian*.

Autoren
Hermann Hesse

Der deutsche Schriftsteller (*writer*) Hermann Hesse (1877–1962) war weit gereist. In einigen Werken (z.B. seinem Roman *Siddhartha*) merkt man den Einfluss der indischen Kultur. Während beider Weltkriege wohnte Hesse in der Schweiz, wo er viel über Pazifismus schrieb.

Paul Celan

Paul Celan (1920–1970) wurde in Rumänien geboren. Seine Familie waren deutschsprachige Juden (*Jews*). 1941 deportierten die Nazis Celans Familie in ein Konzentrationslager. Beide Eltern sind dort gestorben. Celan überstand (*survived*) das Konzentrationslager. Nach dem Krieg ging er nach Paris, wo er sich niederließ (*settled*). In vielen Gedichten schrieb er über die Vernichtung der Juden im Zweiten Weltkrieg.

Suggestion Let students know that in Switzerland, only **ss** is used and not **ß**.

Allein

Hermann Hesse

Es führen° über die Erde°
Strassen und Wege° viel,
Aber alle haben
Dasselbe Ziel°

Du kannst reiten und fahren
Zu zwein und zu drein°,
Den letzten Schritt°
Mußt du gehen allein.
Drum° ist kein Wissen
Noch Können so gut,
Als daß man alles Schwere
Alleine tut.

führen *lead* Erde *earth* Wege *paths*
Ziel *goal* Zu zwein...zu drein *in twos and threes*
Schritt *step* Drum *Because of that* Todesfuge *death fugue*
schaufeln *shovel* Grab *grave* Lüften *air* Schlangen *snakes*
tritt *steps* blitzen *flash* Sterne *stars* pfeift *whistles*
Rüden *hounds* Erde *earth* befiehlt *commands*
aschenes *ash-colored* stecht *stab* tiefer *deeper*
Eisen *iron* Gurt *belt* Spaten *shovels* Meister *master*
streicht *play* Geigen *violins* Rauch *smoke* Wolken *clouds*
bleierner Kugel *lead bullet* genau *exactly* hetzt...auf *stirs up*

Todesfuge

Paul Celan

Schwarze Milch der Frühe wir trinken sie abends
wir trinken sie mittags und morgens wir trinken sie nachts
wir trinken und trinken
wir schaufeln° ein Grab° in den Lüften° da liegt man nicht eng
Ein Mann wohnt im Haus der spielt mit den Schlangen° der schreibt
der schreibt wenn es dunkelt nach Deutschland dein goldenes Haar Margarete
er schreibt es und tritt° vor das Haus und es blitzen° die Sterne° er pfeift°
    seine Rüden° herbei
er pfeift seine Juden hervor läßt schaufeln ein Grab in der Erde°
er befiehlt° uns spielt auf nun zum Tanz

Schwarze Milch der Frühe wir trinken dich nachts
wir trinken dich morgens und mittags wir trinken dich abends
wir trinken und trinken
Ein Mann wohnt im Haus der spielt mit den Schlangen der schreibt
der schreibt wenn es dunkelt nach Deutschland dein goldenes Haar Margarete
Dein aschenes° Haar Sulamith wir schaufeln ein Grab in den Lüften da liegt
    man nicht eng

Er ruft stecht° tiefer° ins Erdreich ihr einen ihr andern singet und spielt
er greift nach dem Eisen° im Gurt° er schwingts seine Augen sind blau
stecht tiefer die Spaten° ihr einen ihr andern spielt weiter zum Tanz auf

Schwarze Milch der Frühe wir trinken dich nachts
wir trinken dich mittags und morgens wir trinken dich abends
wir trinken und trinken
ein Mann wohnt im Haus dein goldenes Haar Margarete
dein aschenes Haar Sulamith er spielt mit den Schlangen

Er ruft spielt süßer den Tod der Tod ist ein Meister° aus Deutschland
er ruft streicht° dunkler die Geigen° dann steigt ihr als Rauch° in die Luft
dann habt ihr ein Grab in den Wolken° da liegt man nicht eng

Schwarze Milch der Frühe wir trinken dich nachts
wir trinken dich mittags der Tod ist ein Meister aus Deutschland
wir trinken dich abends und morgens wir trinken und trinken
der Tod ist ein Meister aus Deutschland sein Auge ist blau
er trifft dich mit bleierner Kugel° er trifft dich genau°
ein Mann wohnt im Haus dein goldenes Haar Margarete
er hetzt seine Rüden auf° uns er schenkt uns ein Grab in der Luft
er spielt mit den Schlangen und träumet der Tod ist ein Meister aus Deutschland

dein goldenes Haar Margarete
dein aschenes Haar Sulamith

Nach dem Lesen

Verständnis Antworten Sie auf die folgenden Fragen. Sample answers are provided.

1. Worüber führen laut Hesse die Straßen und die Wege? Sie führen über die Erde.

2. Wie geht man den letzen Schritt?
Den letzten Schritt geht man allein.

3. Was machen die Juden in dem Gedicht von Celan?
Sie schaufeln ein Grab (in den Lüften/in der Erde).

4. Welche Farbe haben die Augen des Mannes?
Seine Augen sind blau.

5. Womit spielt der Mann? Er spielt mit Schlangen.

6. Wann schreibt der Mann nach Deutschland?
Er schreibt nach Deutschland, wenn es dunkelt.

Diskutieren Sie Suchen Sie mit einem Partner/einer Partnerin alle Wörter in dem Gedicht „Allein", die ähnliche Geräusche (*similar sounds*) oder Bedeutungen haben. Suchen Sie auch alle Zeilen (*lines*) in „Todesfuge", die sich wiederholen. Wie benutzt jeder Dichter (*poet*) diese Wiederholungen (*repetitions*)?

Fragen Sie einander Was sind laut Hermann Hesse sowohl dasselbe Ziel als auch der letzte Schritt? Hat Hesse Recht? Ist man immer allein, wenn man stirbt? Sind die Juden in Celans Gedicht allein vor ihrem Tod, wie Hesse glaubt? Warum oder warum nicht?

Partner Chat You can also assign this activity on the Supersite.

Schreiben Sie Sie haben hier zwei Arten von Gedichten: Ein Gedicht hat Verse und Strophen (*stanzas*) und hält sich an die Regeln (*rules*) der Interpunktion (*punctuation*) und der Rechtschreibung. Das zweite Gedicht hat zwar Verse und Strophen, hält sich aber nicht an die Regeln. Welche Wirkung (*effect*) haben diese verschiedenen Stile? Welches Gedicht gefällt Ihnen besser? Warum?

Expansion Hand out photocopies of **Todesfuge** and have students fill in punctuation, adding quotation marks, periods, and capitalization at the beginning of sentences. Ask them how the addition of punctuation changes the effect of the poem.

Suggestion Explain to students that **Margarete** is a common German women's name, while **Sulamith** (or **Shulamite**) is a Jewish woman's name meaning "peace." In the biblical Song of Solomon, it is the name of Solomon's beloved.

Hören

Strategien

Guessing the meaning of words from context

When you hear an unfamiliar word, you can often guess its meaning based on the context in which it is used...

🔊 To practice this strategy, you will listen to a tour guide talking about Bonn. Jot down some of the familiar words or place names that you hear. Then, listen again and try to guess the meaning of two unfamiliar words based on context. Suggested answers.

Hilfreiche Wörter	Unbekannte Wörter
Haupstadt, Berlin	Regierungssitz
Politiker, gearbeitet	Abgeordnetenhaus

Vorbereitung

Sehen Sie sich das Bild an. Was meinen Sie; welchen Beruf hat die Frau in der weißen Bluse?

🔊 ## Zuhören

Hören Sie sich den Dialog an. Benutzen Sie den Kontext, um die Wörter in Spalte A zu verstehen. Welche Wörter in Spalte B passen zu den Wörtern in Spalte A?

Spalte A	Spalte B
1. __c__ Büro	a. Viertel
2. __d__ Umbau	b. Geschäfte
3. __b__ Läden	c. Arbeitszimmer für Geschäftsleute
4. __a__ Nachbarschaft	d. Renovierung eines Hauses
5. __e__ Tiefgarage	e. Parkplätze unter einem Haus

Suggestion Have students match the concepts in columns A and B *before* listening to the audio. Play the dialogue 2-3 times, and have students complete the true/false questions in **Verständnis**. Then, have them reevaluate their answers in **Zuhören**.

Verständnis

Richtig oder falsch Sind die Sätze richtig oder falsch? Korrigieren Sie die falschen Sätze. Sample answers are provided.

1. Das renovierte Gebäude soll nur für Büros sein.
   Falsch. Das Gebäude soll für Läden, Büros und Wohnungen sein.

2. Das Gebäude soll 100 Büros haben.
   Falsch. Das Gebäude soll 200 Büros haben.

3. Der Umbau soll ein Jahr dauern.
   Richtig.

4. Es wird definitiv einen Supermarkt und ein Fitnessstudio in dem Gebäude geben.
   Falsch. Es könnten ein Supermarkt und ein Fitnessstudio in dem Gebäude sein.

5. Es wird Drei- und Vier-Zimmer-Wohnungen geben.
   Falsch. Es wird Zwei-, Drei- und Vier-Zimmer-Wohnungen geben.

6. Die Architektur ist eine Kombination aus alt und neu.
   Richtig.

7. Es werden neue Parkplätze neben dem Gebäude gebaut.
   Falsch. Man baut eine Tiefgarage.

8. Die Renovierung soll den Charakter der Nachbarschaft nicht verändern.
   Richtig.

Neue Architektur Identifizieren Sie in einer Gruppe ein Gebäude in Ihrer Stadt, das man renovieren oder neu bauen sollte. Was sind die Vor- und Nachteile (*advantages and disadvantages*) einer Renovierung oder eines Neubaus? Was ist für die Bewohner und Nutzer des Gebäudes besser? Was ist effizienter? Was ist für die Nachbarschaft am besten?

Suggestion Play the **Strategien** recording once and ask comprehension questions: **Wie lange war Bonn die Hauptstadt Westdeutschlands? Wer hat früher in dem Alten Abgeordnetenhaus gearbeitet?** Then, play it again, and have students compile their word lists.

Schreiben

Strategien

Using note cards

When you write, note cards can help you organize and sequence the information you wish to present.

For example, if you were going to write an article about a new apartment complex being built in your town, you would jot down notes about each feature of the development on a different note card. Then you could easily organize the cards once you decide how you want to present the information. For example, you could include the best and worst features of the apartment complex, the different uses incorporated into the design, the size of the various facilities, etc.

Here are some helpful techniques:

- Label the top of each card with a general subject, such as **Geschäfte** or **Wohnungen**.

- Use only the front side of each note card so that you can easily flip through them to find information.

- On each card, jot down only those specifics that correspond to the topic of the card.

- As a last step, number the cards in each subject category in the upper right corner to help you organize them.

Wohnungskriterien　　　6

- *2–3 Schlafzimmer*
- *2 Badezimmer*
- *Einbauküche*
- *große Fenster*
- *Fitnesscenter im Haus*
- *Einkaufsmöglichkeiten im Haus*

Thema

 ### Eine virtuelle Stadttour

 Wählen Sie eine Stadt, die Sie kennen und mögen. Schreiben Sie einen Text für eine virtuelle Stadttour für deutschsprechende Besucher. Schreiben Sie für jede Besonderheit (*feature*) der Stadt eine Notizkarte mit einigen Details, die Sie beschreiben wollen.

- Jede Notizkarte soll ein allgemeines Thema und eine spezifische Sehenswürdigkeit (*point of interest*) haben. Ein allgemeines (*general*) Thema kann auf verschiedene Karten verteilt sein, jede mit einer anderen Sehenswürdigkeit. Wenn die Stadt zum Beispiel mehrere Viertel hätte, wäre „Viertel" das allgemeine Thema und jedes Viertel hätte seine eigene Karte mit einer Beschreibung.

- Benutzen Sie die Notizkarten, um die Tour zu organisieren. Sie können sie nach Nähe (*proximity*), Zweck (Wohnen, Geschäfte, Industrie, Unterhaltung), historischer Entwicklung (ältester Teil bis neuester Teil), saisonalen Interessen oder Art der Bewohner (Studenten, Geschäftsleute, Künstler (*artists*), Rentner (*retirees*)) organisieren.

- Wenn Sie die Tour beginnen, heißen Sie die Besucher willkommen und geben Sie eine allgemeine Übersicht (*orientation*) über die Stadt. Wenn Sie die Tour beenden, sagen Sie den Besuchern, dass Sie hoffen, dass ihnen die Tour gefallen hat und dass sie bald wiederkommen.

Lektion 2A

Orte

das Blumengeschäft, -e *flower shop*
die Drogerie, -n *drugstore*
das Internetcafé, -s *internet café*
das Juweliergeschäft, -e *jewelry store*
das Kino, -s *movie theater*
der Kiosk, -e *newspaper kiosk*
der Kosmetiksalon, -s *beauty salon*
die Polizeiwache, -n *police station*
das Rathaus, ⁻er *town hall*
das Schreibwarengeschäft, -e
  paper-goods store
der Waschsalon, -s *laundromat*
geöffnet *open*
geschlossen *closed*

die Post

die Adresse, -n *address*
der Brief, -e *letter*
der Briefkasten, ⁻ *mailbox*
die Briefmarke, -n *stamp*
der Briefträger, - / die Briefträgerin,
  -nen *mail carrier*
der Briefumschlag, ⁻e *envelope*
das Paket, -e *package*
die Post *post office*
die Postkarte, -n *postcard*
abschicken (schickt... ab) *to mail*

in der Bank

die Bank, -en *bank*
das Geld *money*
der Geldautomat, -en *ATM*
der Geldschein, -e *bill*
das Kleingeld *change*
das Konto (*pl.* die Konten) *bank account*
die Münze, -n *coin*
abheben (hebt... ab) *to withdraw*
einzahlen (zahlt... ein) *to deposit*

Ausdrücke

das Bargeld *cash*
das Formular, -e *form*
die Zeitschrift, -en *magazine*
die Zeitung, -en *newspaper*
bar bezahlen *to pay in cash*
Besorgungen machen *to run errands*
ausfüllen (füllt... aus) *to fill out*
mit der Karte bezahlen *to pay by
  (credit) card*
unterschreiben *to sign*

....

Subordinating conjunctions *See p. 76.*
Adjectives as nouns *See p. 80.*
Das Futur I See p. 82.

Lektion 2B

die Innenstadt

das Einkaufszentrum,
  (*pl.* Einkaufszentren) *mall;
  shopping center*
das Gebäude, - *building*
das Kaufhaus, ⁻er *department store*
die Kirche, -n *church*
die Stadt, ⁻e *town*
die Telefonzelle, -n *phone booth*
das Viertel, - *neighborhood*

Verkehr

die Allee, -n *avenue; boulevard*
die Ampel, -n *traffic light*
die Bank, ⁻e *bench*
die Brücke, -n *bridge*
der Brunnen, - *fountain*
der Bürgersteig, -e *sidewalk*
die Ecke, -n *corner*
die Hauptstraße, -n *main road*
die Kreuzung, -en *intersection*
die Statue, -n *statue*
die Straße, -n *street*
die Treppe, -n *stairs*
der Zebrastreifen, - *crosswalk*

Menschen

der Bürgermeister, - / die
  Bürgermeisterin, -nen *mayor*
der Fußgänger, - / die Fußgängerin,
  -nen *pedestrian*

Wo ist...?

abbiegen (biegt... ab) *to turn*
folgen *to follow*
bis zu *until; up to*
gegenüber von *across from*
geradeaus *straight*
in der Nähe von *close to*
in Richtung *toward*
nah(e) *near; nearby*
weit von *far from*

Ausdrücke

mitnehmen (nimmt... mit) *to give a ride*
überqueren *to cross*
hochgehen (geht... hoch) *to go up/climb*
heruntergehen (geht... herunter) *to
  go down*
sich verlaufen *to be/get lost*
sich zurechtfinden (findet sich...
  zurecht) *to find one's way*

....

Prepositions of direction
  See pp. 96–97.
Talking about nationality *See p. 100.*

Suggestion Have students look at the photo. Ask: **Wo ist Meline? Was macht sie?**

Teaching Tip Look for icons indicating activities that address the modes of communication. Follow this key:

→◌←	Interpretive communication
←◌→	Presentational communication
◌↔◌	Interpersonal communication

Communicative Goals

You will learn how to:
- talk about jobs and qualifications
- talk about job applications and interviews

Im Büro

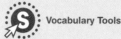 Vocabulary Tools

Wortschatz

eine Stelle suchen	*looking for a job*
die Ausbildung, -en	*education*
der Beruf, -e	*profession*
die Berufsausbildung, -en	*professional training*
die Besprechung, -en	*meeting*
der Bewerber, - / die Bewerberin, -nen	*applicant*
das Empfehlungsschreiben, -	*letter of recommendation*
die Erfahrung, -en	*experience*
das (hohe/niedrige) Gehalt (*pl.* die (hohen/niedrigen) Gehälter)	*(high/low) salary*
das Geschäft, -e	*business*
das Praktikum (*pl.* die Praktika)	*internship*
die Referenz, -en	*reference*
die Stelle, -n	*position; job*
der Termin, -e	*appointment*
der Vertrag, -e	*contract*
Arbeit finden	*to find a job*
einen Termin vereinbaren	*to make an appointment*
sich bewerben um (bewirbt sich)	*to apply for*
Büromaterial	*office supplies*
die Büroklammer, -n	*paperclip*
das Büromaterial, -ien	*office supplies*
die Pinnwand, ¨e	*bulletin board*
der Hefter, -	*stapler*
am Telefon	*on the phone*
Wer spricht?	*Who's calling?*
Bleiben Sie bitte am Apparat.	*Please hold.*
eine Nachricht hinterlassen	*to leave a message*

Suggestion Tell students that **sich bewerben** is typically used with the preposition **um** (+ *acc.*). Ex.: **Julius bewirbt sich um eine Stelle bei einer Bank in Frankfurt**. However, some speakers also use it with **auf** or **für**. You may want to provide past tense forms: **bewarb sich, hat sich beworben**. Also remind students that complete conjugations for all verb types are listed in **Appendix A.**

Ressourcen

vText | WB pp. 29–30 | LM p. 71 | vhlcentral

Sie legt auf. (auflegen)

die Telefonnummer, -n

Ja, (022)) 1 23 45 67

Hallo

Sie nimmt einen Anruf entgegen. (entgegennehmen)

Er ist in der Warteschleife.

der Geschäftsführer, - (die Geschäftsführerin, -nen f.)

die Angestellte, -n (der Angestellte, -n m.)

ACHTUNG

In the singular, **Stellenangebot** typically refers to a specific job offer: **Die Firma macht dem Bewerber ein Stellenangebot.** In the plural, it usually refers to job listings: **Der Arbeitslose liest jeden Tag die Stellenangebote in der Zeitung.**

die Personalchefin, -nen
(der Personalchef, -s *m.*)

der Lebenslauf, -̈e

Personalbüro

das Vorstellungsgespräch, -e

die Assistentin, -nen
(der Assistent, -en *m.*)

der Hörer, -

das Stellenangebot, -e

Lotmeyer GmbH

die Firma (*pl.* die Firmen)

Suggestion Explain that **GmbH** stands for **Gesellschaft mit beschränkter Haftung**, a type of limited partnership, similar to "*Ltd.*" in English.

Anwendung

1 Bilder beschriften Wählen Sie das richtige Wort für jedes Foto.

1. (die Büroklammer) / die Stellen

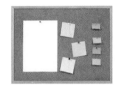

2. der Bewerber / (die Pinnwand)

3. (die Besprechung) / der Vertrag

4. die Referenz / (der Hefter)

5. das Praktikum / (der Hörer)

6. (der Lebenslauf) / das Gehalt

2 Definitionen Finden Sie die passende Definition.

1. __c__ die Personalchefin
2. __e__ der Beruf
3. __b__ das Praktikum
4. __f__ die Warteschleife
5. __a__ die Stellenangebote
6. __d__ das Empfehlungsschreiben

2 Expansion Have students write additional definitions and have classmates guess the words they refer to. Ex.: **In diesem Dokument steht meine Berufserfahrung. Was ist das? (der Lebenslauf)**

a. Die liest man, wenn man eine neue Stelle sucht.
b. Studenten oder Schüler machen das, um praktische Erfahrungen in einem Beruf zu bekommen.
c. Mit dieser Person führt man ein Vorstellungsgespräch.
d. Das schickt man zusammen mit einer Bewerbung ab.
e. Das ist die Arbeit, die man jeden Tag macht.
f. Hier bleibt man oft lange, wenn zu viele Telefonanrufe zur selben Zeit ankommen.

3 Das Vorstellungsgespräch Hören Sie sich den Dialog an und zeigen Sie die Worte an, die die Bewerberin spricht.

1. Empfehlungsschreiben ☐
2. Gehaltshöhe ☑
3. Praktikum ☑
4. Chefassistentin ☐
5. Bewerbung ☐
6. Ausbildung ☑
7. Berufserfahrungen ☐
8. Vorstellungsgespräch ☑

3 Expansion After they complete the listening activity, ask students if they think Frau Mellert will get the job and why. Have them come up with additional interview questions to ask her.

Kommunikation

4 **Virtual Chat** You can also assign activity 4 on the Supersite. Students record individual responses that appear in your gradebook.

4 Bewerber

Bewerber Verwenden Sie die angegebenen Vorschläge (*suggestions*) und berichten Sie in ganzen Sätzen, welche Qualifikationen die Bewerber für die aufgelisteten Stellen brauchen. Sample answers are provided.

BEISPIEL

Für die Stelle als Fußballtrainer braucht der Bewerber mindestens fünf Jahre Erfahrung als Fußballspieler in der Bundesliga.

1. _f_ Fußballtrainer
2. _b_ Journalistin
3. _a_ Koch
4. _e_ Kosmetikerin
5. _d_ Mechaniker
6. _c_ Polizistin

a. fünf Jahre Berufserfahrung in einem Restaurant
b. ein abgeschlossenes (*completed*) Studium und ein Praktikum bei einer Zeitung, einer Zeitschrift oder einem Fernsehsender
c. eine zweijährige juristische (*legal*) Ausbildung in Praxis und Theorie
d. eine abgeschlossene technische Lehre (*apprenticeship*)
e. mindestens eine dreijährige Ausbildung in einer Drogerie oder einem Kosmetiksalon
f. mindestens fünf Jahre Erfahrung als Fußballspieler in der Bundesliga

5 Diskutieren und kombinieren

Diskutieren und kombinieren Sie und Ihr Partner / Ihre Partnerin bekommen zwei verschiedene Blätter. Jedes Blatt hat fünf Schritte, die für jede Bewerbung notwendig sind. Bringen Sie alle zehn Schritte in die richtige Reihenfolge. Answers will vary.

5 **Suggestion** Make sure students understand all vocabulary before beginning the activity.

BEISPIEL

S1: *Als Erstes würde ich eine Liste mit Namen und Adressen einiger Firmen aufstellen. Was meinst du?*

S2: *Ich würde mich zuerst mal über mögliche Stellenangebote informieren, bevor ich eine Liste der Firmen aufstelle.*

5 **Expansion** Ask students questions about their personal experience with job searches. Ex.: Haben *Sie* jemals eine Stelle gesucht? Haben Sie die Stelle bekommen? Was für eine Stelle war sie?

6 Stellenangebote

Stellenangebote Wählen Sie in Dreiergruppen zwei der abgebildeten Fotos aus und schreiben Sie zu jedem Foto ein Stellenangebot. Es sollte Informationen über gewünschte Qualifikationen enthalten (*contain*), sowie über das Gehalt und die Anzahl der bezahlten Urlaubstage. Machen Sie Ihr Stellenangebot so attraktiv wie möglich. Answers will vary.

BEISPIEL

S1: *Wir suchen einen Piloten/eine Pilotin.*
S2: *Der/die ideale Bewerber (-in) sollte...*
S3: *Unsere Firma ist...*

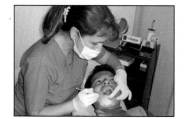

Aussprache und Rechtschreibung  Audio

Loan words (Part 2)

You have already learned that the main stress in German words usually falls on the first syllable. However, in words borrowed from other languages, the first syllable may not be stressed.

Kandidat   **Immo**bi**lien**   **Karri**e**re**   **Poli**ti**ker**   **Fa**b**rik**

....

Some loan words in German are pronounced similarly to their English equivalents.

Computer   **Sek**tor   **Kom**ma   **Seme**s**ter**

....

In other loan words, the stress falls on a different syllable in German than it does in English.

Referenz   **Assis**tent   **Psycho**lo**ge**   **Mate**rial

....

The stress in a loan word may shift to a different syllable in the plural form of a word, or in the feminine form of a noun.

Doktor   **Dok**to**rin**   **Dok**to**ren**   **Sek**tor   **Sek**to**ren**

---

1 Aussprechen Wiederholen Sie die Wörter, die Sie hören.

1. Jurist
2. Kosmetik
3. Identität
4. Hotel
5. Laptop
6. Thermometer
7. Sekretär
8. Temperatur
9. Akrobat
10. Student
11. Faktor
12. Faktoren

2 Nachsprechen Wiederholen Sie die Sätze, die Sie hören.

1. Am Computer sitzt der Student im ersten Semester.
2. Die Kandidaten werden vor der Wahl sehr nervös.
3. Der Atlas, den du suchst, liegt unter den anderen Atlanten.
4. In dem Sektor findet man weniger Arbeitslosigkeit als in den anderen Sektoren.
5. Die Assistentin kocht sich oft eine Tomatensuppe im Labor.
6. Aus diesem Katalog kann man sehr günstig Büromaterial bestellen.

3 Sprichwörter Wiederholen Sie die Sprichwörter, die Sie hören.

Je ärgrer Student, je frömmerer Pastor.[1]

Schlaf ist die beste Medizin.[2]

Sag niemals nie Video

Hans hat Meline seit Tagen nicht mehr gesehen. Er besucht sie, um sich für den Kuss zu entschuldigen. Aber dann kommt alles ganz anders.

NATIONAL communication cultures STANDARDS

Vorbereitung Have students preview the images and write down 3 questions they want to have answered in the video.

SABITE Ich habe euch nicht mehr gesehen seit... Was macht ihr hier?
HANS Der Reichstag verkörpert deutsche Geschichte.

HANS Der Reichstag war bis 1918 Sitz des Parlamentes im Deutschen Kaiserreich. Hier verabschiedeten die Abgeordneten Gesetze, erließen Beschlüsse und wählten ihren Präsidenten. Nach dem Ersten Weltkrieg rief Philipp Scheidemann hier die Weimarer Republik aus. Ich habe vor, mich für ein Praktikum zu bewerben. Was genau machst du denn hier?

SABITE Der Reichstag bietet eine große Sammlung zeitgenössischer deutscher Kunst, die ich mir gern anschaue. Als ich ein Kind war, hat der Künstler Christo das gesamte Gebäude in Stoff verpackt. Ich schreibe darüber eine Hausarbeit.

HANS Hast du Meline gesehen?
SABITE Ich weiß, dass sie viel zu tun hat und in Wien nach Arbeit sucht und Lebensläufe und Bewerbungsschreiben abgeschickt hat. Ich glaube, sie hat nächste Woche ein Vorstellungsgespräch. Ich habe sie nicht mehr gesehen seit...

GEORGE Hans, mein Freund, vergiss es. Sie flirtet mit Männern, bekommt ihre Nummern und schmeißt sie danach in den Abfall.
SABITE Oh, George, du hast doch keine Ahnung von der Liebe. Hans, wenn Meline mit dir nicht geredet hat, ist es deshalb, weil sie Angst hat, dass ihr Herz gebrochen wird.

MELINE Hallo?
HANS Hallo, Meline. Ich bin's, Hans. Leg bitte nicht auf. Ich bin draußen. Ich wollte mit dir reden über...

ÜBUNGEN

1 **Richtig oder falsch?** Entscheiden Sie, ob die folgenden Sätze **richtig** oder **falsch** sind.

1. Der Reichstag war bis 1918 Sitz des Parlamentes im Deutschen Kaiserreich. Richtig.

2. Philipp Scheidemann rief im Reichstag die Weimarer Republik aus. Richtig.

3. Hans möchte sich als Geschäftsführer bewerben. Falsch.

4. Als Sabite ein Kind war, hat der Künstler Christo das Reichstagsgebäude in Stoff verpackt. Richtig.

5. Sie schreibt darüber ihr Examen. Falsch.

6. Meline sucht in Berlin nach Arbeit. Falsch.

7. Sie flirtet mit Männern, bekommt ihre Nummern und ruft sie an. Falsch.

8. Hans schreibt Meline eine SMS. Falsch.

9. Hans möchte sich für sein Verhalten entschuldigen. Richtig.

10. George glaubt, dass Meline und Hans zu unterschiedlich sind. Richtig.

PERSONEN

 George   Hans   Meline   Sabite

7

HANS Also, ich bin hierhergekommen, um dir zu sagen, dass das, was neulich Abend passiert ist, nie wieder passieren wird. Ich möchte mich für mein Verhalten entschuldigen.

MELINE Ich bin froh, dass du das so siehst. Wir hätten das nicht tun sollen.

8

HANS Dann haben wir also eine Abmachung?

MELINE Ja.

HANS Du siehst hübsch aus, wenn du nicht total... fabelhaft aussiehst.

MELINE Danke, Hans. Das ist sehr nett von dir.

9

GEORGE Du liegst falsch, Sabite. Es würde zwischen den beiden niemals klappen. Sie sind zu unterschiedlich.

SABITE Glaubst du nicht, dass sich Gegensätze anziehen?

GEORGE Ich glaube nicht, dass Hans und Meline... Was ich gemeint habe, ist...

10

MELINE Genug. Alle raus. Ich muss arbeiten. Ja. Du auch, Sabite.

Nützliche Ausdrücke

- **verkörpern**
  to embody
- **ein Gesetz verabschieden**
  to pass a law
- **einen Beschluss erlassen**
  to adopt a resolution
- **ausrufen**
  to proclaim
- **das Gebäude**
  building
- **schmeißen**
  to throw
- **Oh, George, du hast doch keine Ahnung von der Liebe.**
  Oh, George, you don't know anything about love.
- **jemandem das Herz brechen**
  to break someone's heart
- **eine Abmachung haben**
  to have a deal
- **fabelhaft**
  fabulous
- **der Gegensatz**
  opposite

3A.1
- **Der Reichstag bietet eine große Sammlung zeitgenössischer deutscher Kunst, die ich mir gern anschaue.**
  The Reichstag holds a large collection of contemporary German art, which I like looking at.

3A.2
- **Der Reichstag war bis 1918 Sitz des Parlamentes im Deutschen Kaiserreich.**
  Until 1918, the Reichstag housed the parliament of the German Reich.

---

2 **Zum Besprechen** Was passiert zwischen Hans und Meline? Schreiben Sie in kleinen Gruppen einen kurzen Absatz darüber, wie es mit den beiden weitergehen wird. Bereiten Sie sich darauf vor, Ihre Prognose der Klasse zu präsentieren. Answers will vary.

2 Suggestion Have all the groups read their predictions to the class. Ask them to keep their paragraphs until they watch the last episode, so that they can find out which predictions were correct.

3 **Vertiefung** Hans sagt, dass der Reichstag deutsche Geschichte verkörpert. Finden Sie mehr über das Reichstagsgebäude heraus. Wann wurde es gebaut? Welche historischen Ereignisse fanden hier statt? Possible answers: The Reichstag was built between 1884 and 1894. Philipp Scheidemann proclaimed the Weimarer Republik from the balcony in 1918. In 1990, the official German reunification ceremony took place in the Reichstag.

3 Suggestion Have students present their findings to the class.

Ressourcen

 v̂Text   VM p. 91   vhlcentral

Suggestion As a pre-reading activity, have pairs of students find the long compound words in the article and break them down into their component parts.

AP* **Theme:** Global Challenges
Context: Economic Issues

Familienunternehmen Reading

LAUT EINER STUDIE DES INSTITUTS für Mittelstandsforschung sind etwa 3 Millionen deutsche Firmen in Familienbesitz. Diese Familienunternehmen sind ungefähr 95% aller Firmen und Betriebe. Über 41% des Umsatzes° aller Firmen wird von Familienunternehmen erwirtschaftet°. Bei diesen Zahlen ist es kein Wunder, dass Experten Familienunternehmen den wichtigsten Aspekt der deutschen Wirtschaft nennen.

Die Liste bekannter deutscher Familienunternehmen ist lang. Die Familie Quandt besitzt zum Beispiel fast 50% des Automobilbauers BMW. Auch die Familie Bertelsmann ist mit dem größten deutschen Medienkonzern sehr erfolgreich. Die Familie Heraeus besitzt Heraeus Holding GmbH, die im Bereich Edelmetall° jährlich über 22 Milliarden Euro erwirtschaftet. Andere berühmte Familienunternehmen sind Henkel (Reinigungsmittel), Marquard und Bahls (Mineralöl) und Fresenius (Arzneimittel).

Neben diesen großen Unternehmen findet sich in ganz Deutschland eine große Anzahl kleinerer Familieunternehmen, die oft auf eine lange Tradition zurückschauen° können. Das Familienunternehmen Hipp produziert Babynahrung. Die Gebrüder Mehler produzieren Stoffe° im Bayerischen Wald. Und das Familieunternehmen Rombach & Haas stellt in vierter Generation im Schwarzwald Kuckucksuhren° her.

Bekannte deutsche Familienunternehmen	
Meggle	(Butter) Gründer°: Josef Anton Meggle (1877)
Oetker	(Pudding) Gründer: August Oetker (1891)
Porsche	(Autos) Gründer: Ferdinand Porsche (1931)
Ritter Sport	(Schokolade) Gründer: Clara und Alfred E. Ritter (1912)
Steiff	(Plüschtiere°) Gründerin: Margarete Steiff (1880)

Umsatzes *sales* **erwirtschaftet** *generated*
Edelmetall *precious metal* **zurückschauen** *look back*
Stoffe *fabrics* **Kuckucksuhren** *cuckoo clocks*
Gründer *founder* **Plüschtiere** *stuffed animals*

Expansion Have students "go shopping" online, searching for products mentioned in the text.

ÜBUNGEN

1 Richtig oder falsch Sagen Sie, ob die Sätze richtig oder falsch sind. Korrigieren Sie die falschen Sätze.

1. Etwa 5 Millionen deutsche Firmen sind in Familienbesitz.
   Falsch. Etwa 3 Millionen Firmen sind in Familienbesitz.
2. Familienunternehmen sind etwa 95% aller deutschen Firmen. Richtig.
3. Mehr als 50% des Umsatzes aller Firmen wird von Familienunternehmen erwirtschaftet.
   Falsch. Etwa 41% des Umsatzes aller Firmen wird von Familienunternehmen erwirtschaftet.
4. Familienunternehmen sind der wichtigste Teil der deutschen Wirtschaft. Richtig.
5. Die Firma BMW ist zu über 50% im Besitz der Familie Quandt. Richtig.

6. Die Familie Heraeus verdient viel Geld durch den Handel mit Edelmetallen. Richtig.
7. In allen Teilen Deutschlands gibt es Familienunternehmen mit einer langen Tradition. Richtig.
8. Eine bekannte Firma für Babynahrung ist Hipp. Richtig.
9. Die Firma Rombach & Haas produziert Kuckucksuhren. Richtig.
10. Die Firma Mehler produziert Stoffe Im Schwarzwald.
    Falsch. Die Firma Mehler ist im Bayerischen Wald.

 Practice more at **vhlcentral.com**.

DEUTSCH IM ALLTAG

Im Büro

der Arbeitgeber	employer
der Arbeitnehmer	employee
die Abteilung	department
das Bewerbungsschreiben	cover letter
die Stellenanzeige	job advertisement
die Visitenkarte	business card

DIE DEUTSCHSPRACHIGE WELT

Kuckucksuhren

Kuckucksuhren haben in Deutschland und vor allem im Schwarzwald große Tradition. Die meisten Kuckucksuhren sind Wanduhren aus Holz. Jede volle Stunde° kommt ein Kuckuck mechanisch aus der Uhr und man kann einen Kuckucksruf° hören. Traditionelle Kuckucksuhren müssen alle 24 Stunden bis 8 Tage aufgezogen° werden, damit sie funktionieren. Im Schwarzwald werden heute noch viele dieser Uhren von Hand gemacht. Die ältesten Kuckucksuhren stammen aus dem 18. Jahrhundert.

volle Stunde top of the hour Kuckucksruf call of a cuckoo aufgezogen wound up
AP* Theme: Beauty & Aesthetics
Context: Cultural Perspectives

PORTRÄT

Robert Bosch

AP* Theme: Science & Technology
Context: Inventions as Catalysts of Change

Robert Bosch, 1861 in Albeck geboren und 1942 in Stuttgart gestorben, war ein deutscher Erfinder°, Unternehmer°, Sozialreformer und Philanthrop. Seine bedeutendste Erfindung war die Zündkerze°, mit der man Autos leichter starten konnte. Diese Zündkerzen und andere Erfindungen machten sein Unternehmen bald zu einem multinationalen Unternehmen. Bosch war aber auch ein deutscher Philanthrop und Sozialreformer. In seinen Firmen mussten Arbeiter zum Beispiel nur acht Stunden am Tag arbeiten. Außerdem war ihm wichtig, dass es viel Licht und frische Luft in den Fabriken° gab. Bosch war auch ein spendabler Stifter°. Im Jahr 1910 schenkte er der Technischen Hochschule Stuttgart 1.000.000 Mark, um die Forschung zu unterstützen°. Suggestion Ask students whether they think Robert Bosch was a good boss, and why.

Erfinder inventor Unternehmer entrepreneur Zündkerze spark-plug Fabriken factories spendabler Stifter generous donor Forschung zu unterstützen to support research

∞ IM INTERNET

Suchen Sie im Internet mehr Informationen über ein deutsches Familienunternehmen: Welche Informationen können Sie über die Familie finden?

Find out more at vhlcentral.com.

---

2 **Was fehlt?** Ergänzen Sie die Sätze.

1. Kuckucksuhren haben vor allem im __Schwarzwald__ große Tradition.

2. Die meisten Kuckucksuhren sind aus __Holz__.

3. Die ältesten Kuckucksuhren stammen aus dem __18. Jahrhundert__.

4. Die bedeutendste Erfindung von Robert Bosch war die __Zündkerze__.

5. Eine soziale Reform für Arbeiter von Robert Bosch war, dass sie nur acht __Stunden__ am Tag arbeiten mussten.

3 Partner Chat You can also assign activity 3 on the Supersite.

3 **Vorbereitung auf ein Vorstellungsgespräch** Diskutieren Sie mit einem Partner / einer Partnerin, wie man sich am besten auf ein Vorstellungsgespräch vorbereitet. Was muss man vor dem Gespräch alles wissen? Welche Fragen sind typisch für ein Bewerbungsgespräch?

BEISPIEL

3 Expansion Have pairs compile a list of tips for a successful interview and share them with the class.

S1: Wenn ich mich auf ein Vorstellungsgespräch vorbereite, will ich alles Mögliche über die Firma wissen.
S2: Wo findest du die Informationen?

Ressourcen

3A.1

QUERVERWEIS

See **2A.1** to review subordinate clauses.

ACHTUNG

Relative pronouns are not optional in German, even though they are sometimes omitted in English.

Suggestion Point out that the relative pronouns are identical to the definite articles except in the dative plural (**denen**) and the genitive forms (**dessen** and **deren**).

Relative pronouns  Presentation

Startblock Demonstrative pronouns refer to someone or something mentioned in a previous sentence. Demonstratives can also be used as relative pronouns, to introduce a subordinate clause that refers to someone or something mentioned in the main clause.

Er ist der Künstler, **der** im Central Park in New York das Kunstwerk „The Gates" errichtet hat.

Sie ist eine Frau, **die** mit Typen flirtet, ihre Telefonnummern bekommt und sie dann in den Abfall wirft.

- Use relative pronouns to combine two statements about the same subject into a single sentence. German relative pronouns correspond to the English relative pronouns *who, whom, whose, that,* and *which*.

relative pronouns				
	masculine	**feminine**	**neuter**	**plural**
nominative	der	die	das	die
accusative	den	die	das	die
dative	dem	der	dem	denen
genitive	dessen	deren	dessen	deren

Ich arbeite bei **einer** kleinen **Firma**.
*I work for **a** small **company**.*

Die Firma verkauft Möbel.
***The company** sells furniture.*

Ich arbeite bei einer kleinen Firma, **die** Möbel verkauft.
*I work for a small company **that** sells furniture.*

- Separate a relative clause from the main clause with a comma, and put the conjugated verb at the end. As in English, a relative clause may come in the middle of a main clause. In this case, put commas both before and after the relative clause.

Wer hat den Hefter genommen, **der** auf meinem Schreibtisch stand?
*Who took the stapler **that** was on my desk?*

Die Personalchefin, **die** meinen Anruf entgegengenommen hat, war sehr nett.
*The HR manager **who** took my call was very nice.*

- The gender and number of a relative pronoun matches the gender and number of the noun it refers to. The case depends on whether the relative pronoun is functioning as a subject, direct object, indirect object, or possessive in the relative clause.

Ich habe eine gute Freundin, **die** eine Stelle sucht.
*I have a good friend **who** is looking for a job.*

Der Lebenslauf, **den** wir gestern bekommen haben, hatte viele Schreibfehler.
*The résumé **(that)** we received yesterday had a lot of spelling mistakes.*

Die Bewerberin, **der** wir die Stelle anbieten, hat sehr gute Referenzen.
*The applicant **to whom** we're offering the job has very good references.*

Das ist der Geschäftsführer, **dessen** Tochter ein Praktikum bei unserer Firma macht.
*That's the manager **whose** daughter is doing an internship at our company.*

- Use **was** as the relative pronoun if the noun in the main clause is an indefinite pronoun such as **alles, etwas, nichts, viel,** or **wenig**.

Ist das alles, **was** du mir sagen wolltest?
*Is that all **(that)** you wanted to say to me?*

Das ist etwas, **was** nur die Geschäftsführerin entscheiden darf.
*That's something **(that)** only the manager can decide.*

- If a relative pronoun is the object of a preposition, put the preposition at the beginning of the clause, *before* the relative pronoun. Remember to use a relative pronoun in the appropriate case for the preposition that precedes it.

Der Kalender, **auf den** ich meine Termine schreibe, ist hinter den Schreibtisch gefallen.
*The calendar **on which** I write my appointments fell behind the desk.*

Wie heißt die Firma, **für die** Sie gerne arbeiten würden?
*What's the name of the company **(that)** you'd like to work **for**?*

- You may also use **wo** instead of a prepositional phrase to indicate location in a relative clause.

In dem Gebäude, **wo** ich arbeite, gibt es ein gutes Restaurant.
*There's a good restaurant in the building **where** I work.*

Ich kenne ein Geschäft, **wo** man Schweizer Schokolade kaufen kann.
*I know a shop **where** you can buy Swiss chocolate.*

Ressourcen

v̂ Text

WB
pp. 31–32

LM
p. 73

vhlcentral

1. Hast du das Paket bekommen, (das/ dem) ich dir letzte Woche geschickt habe?

2. Die Telefonnummer, (der/ die) er mir gegeben hat, funktioniert nicht.

3. Die Firma, bei (die/ der) Franz sich beworben hat, hat viele Angestellte.

4. Ich kenne den Geschäftsführer, mit (dem/ der) du sprichst, schon seit Jahren.

5. Ich muss den Lebenslauf, an (dem/ das) ich jetzt arbeite, bis morgen abschicken.

6. Ist das die Assistentin, (der/ die) dir bei der Arbeit hilft?

7. Kennen Sie die Angestellten, (der/ die) ihre Ausbildung in Wien gemacht haben?

8. Herr Vögele, (dessen/ der) Frau Geschäftsführerin ist, arbeitet als Personalchef.

9. Wie heißt die Bewerberin, mit (die/ der) Sie gesprochen haben?

10. Das ist die nette Frau, (der/ die) im Schreibwarengeschäft arbeitet.

11. Das Paket, auf (das/ dem) ich seit Wochen warte, ist heute angekommen.

12. Die Assistenten, (den/ denen) der Personalchef gute Referenzen gegeben hat, freuten sich sehr.

Anwendung

1 Suggestion Have students write their answers on the board. Correct any mistakes and explain the correct answers.

1 Falschbestellungen
Sie haben einige neue Artikel im Internet bestellt, aber bei der Bestellung gab es ein Durcheinander (*mix-up*). Sagen Sie, dass Sie diese Artikel nicht bestellt haben.

▶ **BEISPIEL** Computer

Das ist nicht der Computer, den ich bestellt habe.

Stuhl

1. Das ist nicht der Stuhl, den ich bestellt habe.

Uhr

2. Das ist nicht die Uhr, die ich bestellt habe.

Fahrrad

3. Das ist nicht das Fahrrad, das ich bestellt habe.

Schuhe

4. Das sind nicht die Schuhe, die ich bestellt habe.

Haartrockner

5. Das ist nicht der Haartrockner, den ich bestellt habe.

2 Suggestion Remind students that **was** is used as the relative pronoun when the antecedent is **alles**, **etwas**, **nichts**, **viel**, or **wenig**.

2 Relativpronomen
Ergänzen Sie die Sätze mit den Relativpronomen aus der Liste.

das	den	dessen	was
dem	der	die	wo

BEISPIEL Dort ist der Student, *dessen* Eltern Immobilienmakler sind.

1. Meine Schwester hat einen neuen Freund, __den__ ich nicht mag.
2. Das Geschichteprojekt, an __dem__ die Studenten arbeiten, ist sehr interessant.
3. Die alte Frau, __der__ Martin immer beim Einkaufen hilft, ist heute krank.
4. An der Ecke ist eine Eisdiele, __wo__ es leckeres italienisches Eis gibt.
5. Die Brücke, über __die__ man gehen muss, um in die Altstadt zu kommen, ist für den Fahrverkehr geschlossen.
6. Es gibt nicht viel, __was__ mein Mann nicht isst.
7. Das ist das neue Handy, __dessen__ Display die Größe von einem Tablet-Computer hat.
8. Wo ist das Silberbesteck, __das__ wir zur Hochzeit bekommen haben?

3 Die Tierarztpraxis
Ergänzen Sie den Dialog mit der richtigen Form der passenden Relativpronomen.

BEISPIEL JASMIN: Hanna, kennst du den Tierarzt, bei __dem__ Nina ihr Praktikum macht?

HANNA: Ja, ist das nicht der, (1) __dessen__ Büro gegenüber vom Juweliergeschäft Wagner ist?

JASMIN: Meinst du das Geschäft, (2) __wo / in dem__ es die tollen Halsketten gibt?

HANNA: Ja, genau. Und was sagt Nina so über die Arbeit, (3) __die__ sie da machen muss?

JASMIN: Sie sagt, sie lernt viele Dinge, von (4) __denen__ sie vorher nichts wusste.

Kommunikation

4 **Was passt zusammen?** Finden Sie mit einer Partnerin / einem Partner die richtige Definition für jeden Begriff und ergänzen Sie dann das passende Relativpronomen.

> **BEISPIEL**
>
> *Ein Geschäftsführer ist eine Person,*
> *die die Angestellten leitet.*

1. Ein Geschäftsführer ist eine Person, _f_.
2. Ein Praktikum ist eine Arbeit, _c_.
3. Ein Gehalt ist Geld, _e_.
4. Ein Personalchef ist ein Mann, _b_.
5. Ein Bewerber ist eine Person, _a_.
6. Ein Lebenslauf ist ein Dokument, _d_.

a. _die_ sich um eine Stelle bewirbt.
b. _der_ Vorstellungsgespräche vereinbart.
c. _die_ oft unbezahlt ist.
d. _das_ zu einer Bewerbung gehört.
e. _das_ man für seine Arbeit bekommt.
f. _die_ die Angestellten leitet.

5 **Definitionen** Erfinden Sie mit einem Partner / einer Partnerin Ihre eigenen Definitionen und benutzen Sie Relativpronomen. Sample answers provided.

> **BEISPIEL** Büromaterialien sind Sachen, *die man bei der Arbeit benutzt*.

1. Ein Terminkalender ist ein Kalender, in den man wichtige Termine und Besprechungen schreibt.
2. Ein Vorstellungsgespräch ist ein Interview, das ein Bewerber mit einem Personalchef oder einem Geschäftsführer hat.
3. Arzt ist ein Beruf, für den man lange studieren muss.
4. Ein Kosmetiksalon ist ein Geschäft, in dem / wo man einen neuen Haarschnitt bekommen kann.
5. Ein Briefträger ist ein Mann, der die Post bringt.

6 **Stadt, Land, Fluss** Denken Sie sich mit Ihrem Partner / Ihrer Partnerin fünf Fragen zu den Themen Geografie, Sprachen, bekannte Leute und Architektur aus. Machen Sie dann ein Quiz mit zwei Mitschülern. Benutzen Sie Relativsätze. Answers will vary.

> **BEISPIEL**
>
> **S1:** *Wie heißt der Fluss, der in Deutschland beginnt*
> *und ins Schwarze Meer fließt?*
> **S2:** *Das ist die Donau. Wie heißt der berühmteste*
> *Tennisspieler, der aus der Schweiz kommt?*
> **S3:** *Das ist Roger Federer.*

7 **Im Konferenzzimmer** Beschreiben Sie mit einem Partner / einer Partnerin, was in dieser Szene passiert. Verwenden Sie auch Ihre Fantasie dabei. Benutzen Sie Relativsätze. Answers will vary.

> **BEISPIEL**
>
> *Die Angestellten sind in einer Besprechung,*
> *in der sie über die Bewerberin für die Stelle*
> *als Chefsektretärin reden. Frau Weber, die*
> *eine der Bewerbungen liest, arbeitet schon*
> *lange in der Firma und hat ein Gehalt, das...*

7 **Partner Chat** You can also assign activity 7 on the Supersite. Students work in pairs to record the activity online. The pair's recorded conversation will appear in your gradebook.

3A.2

The past tenses (review) Presentation

Startblock You have learned to use weak, strong, and mixed verbs, including verbs with separable and inseparable prefixes, in both the **Perfekt** and the **Präteritum**.

- The **Perfekt** tense is used in conversation and informal writing to talk about the past. It is formed with a conjugated form of **haben** or **sein** and a past participle. **Suggestion** Make sure students remember the meanings of the verbs reviewed in this section.

Hat Herr Schwartz eine Nachricht **hinterlassen**?
*Did Mr. Schwartz **leave** a message?*

Wir **sind** gestern erst sehr spät **angekommen**.
*We **got here** very late yesterday.*

- To form the **Perfekt** of a reflexive verb, place the reflexive pronoun between the conjugated form of **haben** or **sein** and the past participle.

Ich **habe mich** um fünfzehn Stellen **beworben**.
*I **applied** for fifteen jobs.*

Hast du **dir** die Zähne **geputzt**?
*Did you **brush** your teeth?*

- The **Präteritum** is used to talk about the past in writing or in formal spoken contexts. **Präteritum** forms of **sein**, **haben**, **werden**, and the modal verbs are used more commonly than **Perfekt** forms, even in informal speech.

Sie **suchten** Arbeit.
*They **were looking for** work.*

Lena **blieb** am Apparat.
*Lena **stayed** on the line.*

- The **Plusquamperfekt** is used to talk about an action that happened before another event in the past. It is formed with the **Präteritum** of **haben** or **sein** and a past participle.

Jasmin **hatte vergessen**, das Telefon aufzulegen.
*Jasmin **had forgotten** to hang up the phone.*

Sie **war** eine halbe Stunde in der Warteschleife **gewesen**.
*She **had been** on hold for half an hour.*

verb type	*Infinitiv*	*Präteritum*	*Perfekt*	*Plusquamperfekt*
weak	suchen besuchen	suchte besuchte	hat gesucht hat besucht	hatte gesucht hatte besucht
modal	dürfen wollen	durfte wollte	hat gedurft hat gewollt	hatte gedurft hatte gewollt
mixed	bringen mitbringen	brachte brachte mit	hat gebracht hat mitgebracht	hatte gebracht hatte mitgebracht
strong	kommen ankommen	kam kam an	ist gekommen ist angekommen	war gekommen war angekommen

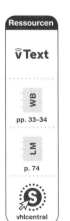
Jetzt sind Sie dran!   Ergänzen Sie die Tabelle mit den fehlenden Verbformen.

	Präteritum (er/sie/es)	Perfekt (er/sie/es)	Plusquamperfekt (er/sie/es)
abheben	*hob ab*	*hat abgehoben*	*hatte abgehoben*
sich anziehen	zog sich an	hat sich angezogen	hatte sich angezogen
haben	hatte	hat gehabt	hatte gehabt
nehmen	nahm	hat genommen	hatte genommen
sein	war	ist gewesen	war gewesen
mitbringen	brachte mit	hat mitgebracht	hatte mitgebracht
gehen	ging	ist gegangen	war gegangen

Anwendung und Kommunikation

1 Was fehlt? Ergänzen Sie die Sätze mit den Verben in Klammern. Benutzen Sie die richtigen Präteritumsformen.

1. Ben __bewarb sich__ (sich bewerben) um eine Stelle bei einer Bank.

2. Er __stand auf__ (aufstehen) und zog seinen besten Anzug an.

3. Nach dem Frühstück __wurde__ (werden) es Zeit, dass er sich auf den Weg machte.

4. Er __hatte__ (haben) nur noch fünfzehn Minuten, um zu seinem Termin zu kommen.

5. Er __wollte__ (wollen) einen guten Eindruck (*impression*) machen.

6. Aber als er die Kreuzung __überquerte__ (überqueren), hatte er einen Unfall!

7. Als er Stunden später bei seinem Vorstellungsgespräch __ankam__ (ankommen), sagte man ihm, dass er wieder gehen konnte.

8. Er __war__ (sein) sehr traurig.

2 Sätze umschreiben Schreiben Sie die Sätze um. Benutzen Sie das Perfekt anstelle des Präsens und das Plusquamperfekt anstelle des Perfekt.

1. Ich habe vier Karten für ein Konzert bekommen, also lade ich drei Freunde dazu ein.
   Ich hatte vier Karten für ein Konzert bekommen, also habe ich drei Freunde dazu eingeladen.
2. Nachdem wir im Restaurant gegessen haben, fahren wir zusammen zum Konzert.
   Nachdem wir im Restaurant gegessen hatten, sind wir zusammen zum Konzert gefahren.
3. Obwohl Jan die Wegbeschreibung (*directions*) im Internet heruntergeladen hat, biegen wir zweimal falsch ab.
   Obwohl Jan die Wegbeschreibung im Internet heruntergeladen hatte, sind wir zweimal falsch abgebogen.
4. Als wir endlich in der Konzerthalle ankommen, hat das Konzert schon begonnen.
   Als wir endlich in der Konzerthalle angekommen sind, hatte das Konzert schon begonnen.

3 Im Märchenland Wählen Sie mit Ihrem Partner / Ihrer Partnerin eine Märchenfigur (*fairy-tale character*). Auf was für eine Stelle würde diese Figur sich bewerben und wie würde ihr Lebenslauf aussehen? Schreiben Sie aus der Ich-Perspektive und benutzen Sie das Präteritum. *Answers will vary.*

3 Expansion Have students role-play a job interview with their fairy-tale character.

> **BEISPIEL**
>
> **Aschenputtels Lebenslauf:**
>
> Meine Mutter starb, als ich sehr jung war. Ich musste also viele Jahre lang die ganze Hausarbeit für meine Stiefmutter und zwei Stiefschwestern machen. Ich putzte täglich das ganze Haus, kochte das Essen und hatte nie einen freien Tag …

4 Wer hat das gemacht? Benutzen Sie die Verben aus der Liste und erfinden Sie mit einem Partner / einer Partnerin sechs Quizfragen zu dem Thema, was berühmte Leute gemacht haben. Stellen Sie Ihre Fragen dann zwei anderen Mitschülern. Verwenden Sie das Perfekt und das Plusquamperfekt. Wechseln Sie sich ab. *Answers will vary.*

4 Partner Chat You can also assign activity 4 on the Supersite. Students work in pairs to record the activity online. The pair's recorded conversation will appear in your gradebook.

> **BEISPIEL**
>
> **S1:** Wer hat *Der Steppenwolf* geschrieben?
> **S2:** Hermann Hesse.

bauen	gewinnen	singen
bekommen	heiraten	(mit)spielen
entdecken	landen	sterben
erfinden	schreiben	verlieren

Wiederholung

1 Die Familie

Wählen Sie eine Person von der Liste aus. Beschreiben Sie die Person mit einem Relativsatz. Ihr Partner / Ihre Partnerin muss die Person erraten, die Sie beschreiben. Answers will vary.

1 Partner Chat You can also assign activity 1 on the Supersite.

BEISPIEL

S1: Das ist der junge Mann, dessen Vater mein Onkel ist.
S2: Ist es dein Cousin?

die Mutter	die Schwester
der Onkel	die Cousine
die Schwiegertochter	die Nichte
der Urgroßvater	die Tante

2 Diskutieren und kombinieren

Sie und Ihr Partner / Ihre Partnerin bekommen unterschiedliche Blätter. Fragen Sie Ihren Partner / Ihre Partnerin, was jede Person gemacht hat. Answers will vary.

BEISPIEL

S1: Was wollte die Geschäftsführerin?
S2: Sie wollte, dass die Assistentin Anrufe entgegennimmt.

3 Was trägst du?

Beschreiben Sie abwechselnd die Kleidung der Personen in Ihrer Gruppe. Die anderen erraten, wen Sie beschreiben. Verwenden Sie möglichst viele Relativsätze. Answers will vary.

BEISPIEL

S1: Ich denke an eine Frau, die eine schwarze Hose und eine weiße Bluse trägt.
S2: Denkst du an Sarah?

3 Expansion Have students describe the attributes of a famous person and have group members guess who is being described.

4 Arbeitsblatt

Fragen Sie drei Personen in der Gruppe, über welches Thema sie viel, alles, ein bisschen oder nichts wissen. Schreiben Sie die Antworten auf. Answers will vary.

BEISPIEL

S1: Worüber weißt du viel?
S2: Ich weiß viel über alles, was mit Mathematik zu tun hat.

5 Arbeitsuchender

Felix sucht eine neue Stelle. Sehen Sie mit einem Partner / einer Partnerin seinen Terminkalender an und besprechen Sie, was er gestern morgen gemacht hat, um eine Stelle zu finden. Benutzen Sie das Präteritum und das Plusquamperfekt. Answers will vary.

BEISPIEL

Felix hatte die Stellenangebote schon gelesen, bevor er gefrühstückt hat...

8.00	Stellenangebote lesen
9.00	Frühstück
10.00	dem Personalchef der Computerfirma meinen Lebenslauf schicken
11.00	mich aufs Vorstellungsgespräch vorbereiten
12.00	Vorstellungsgespräch bei „Maxifirma"
13.00	Mittagessen

6 Generationen

Diskutieren Sie mit einem Partner / einer Partnerin, wie das Leben der älteren Generationen war. Answers will vary.

BEISPIEL

S1: Meine Eltern sind beide 1978 geboren. Als sie Kinder waren, gab es kein Internet. Sie haben meistens Musik im Radio gehört.
S2: Das war bei meinen Eltern genauso. Aber meine Großeltern...

Arbeit	Kochen
Familie	Schule
Freizeit	Technologie
Gesundheit	Urlaub
Hausarbeit	

6 Suggestion Have students prepare notes individually, before they begin working with a partner.

6 Partner Chat You can also assign activity 6 on the Supersite. Students work in pairs to record the activity online. The pair's recorded conversation will appear in your gradebook.

Die **Berliner** Mauer

Gewinner: Short Film Jury Prize Hong Kong International Film Festival

Ein Film von Paul Cotter
mit Joost Siedhoff, Fritz Roth
und Dominik Bender

Nützliche Ausdrücke

- **anscheinend**
  apparently
- **der Ärger, -**
  trouble
- **Das reicht!**
  That's enough!
- **erlaubt**
  allowed
- **eingreifen**
  to intervene
- **ermutigen**
  to encourage
- **das Grundstück, -e**
  piece of land
- **der Grund, ⸚e**
  reason
- **die Steuer, -n**
  tax
- **zustimmen**
  to approve; to agree

Über den Film sprechen

- **der Ausländer, - / Ausländerin, -nen**
  foreigner
- **die Diskriminierung, -en**
  discrimination
- **einsam**
  lonely
- **feindlich (zu)**
  hostile (to)
- **der Nachbar, -n / Nachbarin, -nen**
  neighbor
- **hassen**
  to hate

Suggestion Point out that
Nachbar is an **n**-noun.

Kurzfilm

Video: Short Film

AP* Theme: Personal & Public Identities
Context: Alienation & Integration

Die Berliner Mauer

Nach dem Tod seiner Ehefrau baut ein alter Mann eine Mauer (*wall*), wo die Berliner Mauer früher in seinem Dorf stand. Niemand weiß warum. Die Kinder in der Nachbarschaft (*neighborhood*) helfen ihm, während die Erwachsenen über die Bedeutung der neuen Mauer für Westdeutsche, Ostdeutsche und Ausländer diskutieren.

Vorbereitung

1 **Was fehlt?** Schreiben Sie die Wörter aus den zwei Listen, die die Sätze unten ergänzen.

1. Die Witwe war sehr ____einsam____ nach dem Tod ihres Ehemannes.
2. Wir wollen keinen ____Ärger____ mit der Polizei.
3. Viele Menschen glauben, dass sie zu hohe ____Steuern____ zahlen.
4. Sich nicht sicher zu sein ist kein ____Grund____, etwas nicht zu tun.
5. Ich weiß nicht, ob sie freundlich oder ____feindlich____ sind.
6. In diesem Land gibt es manchmal ____Diskriminierung____ von Ausländern.
7. Ist das Rauchen (*smoking*) ____erlaubt____ in diesem Gebäude?
8. Sie waren ____anscheinend____ glücklich, obwohl sie viele Probleme gehabt hatten.

2 **Diskutieren** Sprechen Sie über die folgenden Themen.

1. Was wissen Sie schon über die Berliner Mauer und die Wiedervereinigung (*reunification*) Deutschlands? Welche Probleme kann es geben, wenn Menschen, die sehr unterschiedliche Lebenserfahrungen gehabt haben, zusammenleben müssen?

2. Erzählen Sie einander über etwas, was Ihnen nicht erlaubt war, das Sie aber trotzdem getan haben. Glauben Sie, dass Sie das Richtige getan haben, obwohl es verboten war?

Szenen: Die Berliner Mauer

MANN: Sie wird in Frieden ruhen°.

Suggestion You may want to explain some of the slang used in the film. For example, tell students that **Ossi** is a negative slang term used to refer to East Germans.

KATJA: Was macht er da?
KATJAS MANN: Ich hab' keine Ahnung°. Da macht er schon seit über einer Stunde 'rum.
KATJAS MANN: Werden wir auch so, wenn wir alt sind? Drehst du auch durch°, wenn ich sterbe?
KATJA: Der arme alte Mann. Sieht aus, als hätte er nicht mehr alle Tassen im Schrank.

HELMUT: Herr Schlömerkemper, was machen Sie denn da? Sie können doch hier nicht einfach die Mauer wieder aufbauen. Die ist ja aus gutem Grund abgerissen worden°, nicht wahr? Sicher, es gibt schon Momente... da hätte ich sie auch schon gerne wieder, schon allein wegen des Gesindels° da, nicht wahr? Aber... Herr Schlömerkemper, das kann man nicht machen... Das ist nicht erlaubt!

POLIZIST: Okay! Stoppt, stoppt! Das reicht! Genug° jetzt! Die Mauer wird abgerissen! Räumen sie alle Ihre Gerätschaften° hier weg! Sie auch! Das muss hier alles weg!

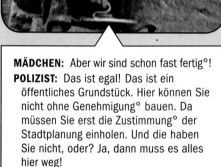

MÄDCHEN: Aber wir sind schon fast fertig°!
POLIZIST: Das ist egal! Das ist ein öffentliches Grundstück. Hier können Sie nicht ohne Genehmigung° bauen. Da müssen Sie erst die Zustimmung° der Stadtplanung einholen. Und die haben Sie nicht, oder? Ja, dann muss es alles hier weg!

HELMUT: Tut mir leid, Werner. Wir haben es versucht°.

in Frieden ruhen *rest in peace* keine Ahnung *no idea* Drehst du...durch *Will you go crazy*
ist... abgerissen worden *was torn down* Gesindels *scum* Genug *Enough* Gerätschaften *equipment*
fertig *finished* Genehmigung *permit* Zustimmung *approval* haben...versucht *tried*

Analyse

3 **Verständnis** Lesen Sie die folgenden Sätze aus dem Film und bringen Sie sie in die richtige Reihenfolge (1-8).

___3___ „Werden wir auch so, wenn wir alt sind?"

___6___ „Aber wir sind fast fertig!"

___2___ „Ihr sollt nicht mal mit diesen Kindern spielen!"

___4___ „Herr Schlömerkemper, das kann man nicht machen."

___5___ „Die Mauer wird abgerissen!"

___8___ „Tut mir leid, Werner."

___7___ „Können wir das kleine Stückchen Mauer nicht einfach stehen lassen?"

___1___ „Sie wird in Frieden ruhen."

4 **Dialoge** Erfinden Sie mit einem Partner / einer Partnerin einen Dialog zu einer der folgenden Situationen.

- Stellen Sie sich vor, dass Sie Katja und ihr Ehemann sind. Was besprechen Sie zusammen, nachdem die Polizei die Mauer zerstört (*destroyed*) hat? Wollen Sie Herrn Schlömerkemper und die anderen Nachbarn besser kennen lernen?

- Spielen Sie die Szene von dem Tag im Jahre 1962, als Werner Schlömerkemper und Theresa ihre Namen in den Stein eingeritzt (*carved*) haben. Welche Gedanken über die Zukunft hatten Sie? Was waren Ihre Träume für Ihr Leben zusammmen?

5 **Zum Besprechen** Diskutieren Sie die folgenden Sprichwörter. Glauben Sie an diese Sprichwörter? Welche Verbindung haben sie zu dem Film?

Stille Wasser sind tief.

Liebe deinen Nachbarn, reiß aber den Zaun (*fence*) nicht ein (*tear down*).

Suggestion Ask students if they can think of contemporary examples where the building of a wall or fence has been a source of controversy.

Berufe

Communicative Goals

You will learn how to:

- talk about professions
- talk about work

Suggestion To help students personalize the new vocabulary, have them think of people they know who work in each of the professions listed.

Suggestion Tell students that **scheitern** takes **sein** as its auxiliary in the **Perfekt**. Point out that **entlassen** is a strong verb, and provide its past tense forms. You may want to note that **feuern** is often used in place of **entlassen** in informal speech.

Wortschatz

auf der Arbeit	*at work*
die Beförderung, -en	*promotion*
das Büro, -s	*office*
der Chef, -s / die Chefin, -nen	*boss*
der Erfolg, -e	*success*
die Gehaltserhöhung, -en	*raise*
die Gewerkschaft, -en	*labor union*
die Karriere, -n	*career*
anspruchsvoll	*demanding*
fertig	*ready; finished*
ganztags	*full-time*
halbtags	*part-time*
zuverlässig	*reliable*
Berufe	*occupations*
der Fabrikarbeiter, - / die Fabrikarbeiterin, -nen	*factory worker*
der Gärtner, - / die Gärtnerin, -nen	*gardener*
der Hausmann, ¨er / die Hausfrau, -en	*homemaker*
der Hausmeister, - / die Hausmeisterin, -nen	*caretaker; custodian*
der Klempner, - / die Klempnerin, -nen	*plumber*
der Politiker, - / die Politikerin, -nen	*politician*
der Rentner, - / die Rentnerin, -nen	*retiree*
der Richter, - / die Richterin, -nen	*judge*
Ausdrücke	*expressions*
arbeitslos sein	*to be unemployed*
entlassen	*to fire; to lay off*
kündigen	*to resign*
leiten	*to manage*
scheitern	*to fail*
Urlaub nehmen	*to take time off*
verdienen	*to earn*

Suggestion Have students guess the meaning of the suffix **-los**.

Ressourcen

vText | WB pp. 35–36 | LM p. 75 | vhlcentral

**die Wissenschaftlerin, -nen
(der Wissenschaftler, - *m.*)**

$H_2O + C_2...$

**die Tierärztin, -nen
(der Tierarzt, ¨e *m.*)**

**die LKW-Fahrerin, -nen
(der LKW-Fahrer, - *m.*)**

**die Buchhalterin, -nen
(der Buchhalter, - *m.*)**

**der Feuerwehrmann; *pl.*
die Feuerwehrleute
(die Feuerwehrfrau, -en *f.*)**

**der Taxifahrer, -
(die Taxifahrerin, -nen *f.*)**

**der Koch, ¨e
(die Köchin, -nen *f.*)**

Suggestion Remind students not to confuse the meaning of the words **Chef** and **Koch**. Point out that the compound **Chefkoch** means *head chef*.

der Bankangestellte, -n
(die Bankangestellte, -n _f._)

die Immobilienmaklerin, -nen
(der Immobilienmakler, - _m._)

der Bauer, -n
(die Bäuerin, -nen _f._)

die Elektrikerin, -nen
(der Elektriker, - _m._)

der Psychologe, -n
(die Psychologin, -nen _f._)

Suggestion Explain that **Bankangestellte(r)** is a compound adjectival noun, derived from the adjective **angestellt** (_employed_). Remind students that the ending of an adjectival noun changes depending on the article that precedes it.

Anwendung

1 **Assoziationen** Wählen Sie die Berufsbezeichnung, die Sie mit jedem Foto assoziieren.

_c_ 1. Feuerwehrmann	_e_ 3. LKW-Fahrer	_d_ 5. Bankangestellter
_f_ 2. Richterin	_a_ 4. Gärtnerin	_b_ 6. Tierärztin

a.

b.

c.

d.

e.

f.

2 **Vergleiche** Ergänzen Sie die Vergleiche mit einem passenden Wort.

Suggested answers provided.

1. Garten : Gärtner :: Fabrik : _____Fabrikarbeiter_____
2. Küche : Koch :: Labor (_lab_) : _____Wissenschaftler_____
3. LKW : LKW-Fahrer :: Taxi : _____Taxifahrer_____
4. Auto : Mechaniker :: Toilette : _____Klempner_____
5. Musik : Musiker :: Politik : _____Politiker_____
6. Friseurin : Friseur :: Hausfrau : _____Hausmann_____

2 **Expansion** Have students explain which of these jobs they would or would not like to have, and why.

3 **Die Beförderung** Hören Sie sich das Gespräch zwischen Lukas und seinem Chef an, und entscheiden Sie dann, ob die folgenden Aussagen richtig oder falsch sind.

	richtig	falsch
1. Der Chef hatte eine Besprechung mit dem Geschäftsführer.	☑	☐
2. Er bietet Lukas eine Halbtagsstelle an.	☐	☑
3. Lukas hat ein abgeschlossenes Studium.	☑	☐
4. Lukas nimmt das Angebot nicht an.	☐	☑
5. Der Buchhalter schickt Lukas einen neuen Vertrag.	☐	☑
6. Lukas bekommt eine Stelle als Assistent.	☑	☐
7. Die neue Stelle ist nicht sehr anspruchsvoll.	☐	☑
8. Der Chef denkt, dass Lukas eine große Karriere machen wird.	☑	☐

3 **Expansion** Have groups of students write a conversation between a manager and an employee and then act it out.

Kommunikation

 Definitionen Schreiben Sie mit einem Partner / einer Partnerin zu jedem Begriff eine Definition. Sample answers are provided.

1. die Gehaltserhöhung — Man bekommt ein höheres Gehalt.
2. halbtags arbeiten — Man arbeitet nur zwanzig Stunden die Woche.
3. arbeitslos sein — Man hat keine Arbeitsstelle und muss eine suchen.
4. die Gewerkschaft — Das ist eine Organisation, die sich für die Interessen der Arbeiter oder Angestellten stark macht.
5. Urlaub nehmen — Man nimmt sich ein paar Tage frei.
6. die Beförderung — Man bekommt eine bessere Stelle.

4 Expansion Have partners play a guessing game. One student says the definition, and the other guesses the correct word.

---

5 **Berufe raten** Wählen Sie aus der Vokabelliste einen Beruf und beschreiben Sie, was man in diesem Beruf macht. Ihr Partner / Ihre Partnerin muss erraten, um welchen Beruf es geht. Answers will vary.

BEISPIEL

S1: Diese Frau arbeitet an biologischen, chemischen oder physikalischen Experimenten.
S2: Ist sie Wissenschaftlerin?

5 Partner Chat You can also assign activity 5 on the Supersite. Students work in pairs to record the activity online. The pair's recorded conversation will appear in your gradebook.

---

6 **Diskutieren und kombinieren** Sie und Ihr Partner / Ihre Partnerin bekommen zwei unterschiedliche Bilder. Finden Sie die sieben Unterschiede auf den Bildern. Wechseln Sie sich bei Ihren Fragen und Antworten ab.

BEISPIEL

S1: Sind auf deinem Bild Taxifahrer zu sehen?
S2: Ja, drei. Und auf deinem?
S1: Auf meinem sind zwei.

---

7 **Heute im Büro** Wählen Sie zwei der Zeichnungen und erfinden Sie eine Geschichte, in der Sie erzählen, was diesen Personen heute alles passiert ist. Sie können über die zwei Zeichnungen getrennt erzählen oder sie zu einer Geschichte verbinden. Answers will vary.

BEISPIEL

S1: Heute Morgen hat Lisa zu lange geschlafen.
S2: Sie kam eine halbe Stunde zu spät zur Arbeit.
S3: Im Büro hat sie dann …

Aussprache und Rechtschreibung

 Audio

Recognizing near-cognates

Because English and German belong to the same language family, the two languages share some related sounds. Knowing these relationships makes it easier to recognize English and German cognates. For example, for many English words that contain a *d* sound, the German equivalent has a **t** in the same position.

Tag	**un**t**er**	**Bro**t	**ro**t	**Tür**

For many English words that contain a *p* sound, the German equivalent has an **f** or **pf** in the same position, while a *t* sound in an English word may correspond to a German **z** or **s** sound.

Pfanne	**Schiff**	**zwei**	**aus**	**essen**

In some German words, the **ch** corresponds to an English *k* or *gh*.

mach**en**	**Bu**ch	**la**ch**en**	**Na**ch**t**	**ho**ch

In many German words, the **d** corresponds to the English *th* sound, and in a few words, the **g** corresponds to an English *y*.

Brud**er**	**Don**ner	**Le**d**er**	**g**estern	**g**elb

---

1 **Aussprechen** Wiederholen Sie die Wörter, die Sie hören.

1. trinken
2. Wort
3. sitzen
4. zu
5. Pfeffer
6. Apfel
7. helfen
8. brechen
9. denken
10. Bad
11. recht
12. Garn

2 **Nachsprechen** Wiederholen Sie die Sätze, die Sie hören.

1. Der alte Koch arbeitet nur noch halbtags.
2. Die Gärtnerin findest du unter einem großen Baum im Hinterhof.
3. Ich suche gerade seine Telefonnummer in meinem Adressbuch.
4. Wir wollen nicht den ganzen Tag vor einem Computer sitzen.
5. Es ist besser länger zu schlafen, als soviel Kaffee zu trinken.
6. Seit einer Woche leitet sie das Büro.

3 **Sprichwörter** Wiederholen Sie die Sprichwörter, die Sie hören.

Wo sich Fuchs und Hase gute Nacht sagen.[1]

Die Nacht zum Tage machen.[2]

[1] In the middle of nowhere. (lit. Where the fox and hare say "good night" to each other.)
[2] To party all night. (lit. To turn the night into day.)

Schlechte Nachrichten Video

Sabite bekommt schlechte Nachrichten aus der Galerie. Zum Glück ist Hans gut in Wirtschaft und kann Sabite trösten.

Vorbereitung Have students look at scene 1, and discuss with a partner why they think Sabite is sad. After they have watched the episode, have students get together with their partners again and check their predictions.

1

HERR KLEINEDLER Danke, dass Sie zu dieser Besprechung in die Galerie gekommen sind, Sabite. Ich hoffe, Sie mussten dafür nicht Ihre Uni ausfallen lassen.
SABITE Ich hatte heute nur einen Kurs. Dies ist die erste Ausstellung meiner Karriere, drum möchte ich... Herr Kleinedler, es gibt doch noch eine Ausstellung, oder?

2

HERR KLEINEDLER Sabite, sie sind eine junge und talentierte Künstlerin, aber es gibt noch so viele ausgezeichnete Künstler mit vielen neuen aufregenden Werken. Wir werden den Schwerpunkt unserer Ausstellung ändern auf Berlins Nachwuchskünstler. Wir werden nur zwei Ihrer Werke anstatt zehn brauchen.

3

SABITE Aber nur zwei Werke? Das ist nicht fair.
HERR KLEINEDLER Diese beiden Werke werden fünf Wochen in der Ausstellung sein, zusammen mit den Werken aller anderen Künstler. Dadurch werden viel mehr Leute Ihre Kunst sehen. Es ist die bessere Lösung.

4

MELINE Also, Hans, jetzt wohne ich schon seit fast einem Jahr neben dir, und ich weiß immer noch nicht einmal, was du studierst.
HANS Geschichte und Politik.
MELINE Willst du Politiker werden?
HANS Ich glaube nicht, dass ich ein guter Politiker wäre.

5

HANS Mein Vater ist Forscher und Wissenschaftler. Meine Mutter arbeitet in einer Versicherungsagentur. Sie ist Buchhalterin. Und Max plant eine Karriere als Psychologe.

MELINE Ich möchte, dass bereits etwas organisiert ist, wenn ich nach Wien komme.
HANS Ich war noch nie in Wien.
MELINE Wien ist eine wunderschöne Kulturstadt. Du solltest Wien besuchen kommen...

6

1 **Wer ist das?** Welche Person(en) beschreiben die folgenden Sätze: George, Hans, Meline, Sabite oder Herr Kleinedler?

1. Er/Sie hat die erste Ausstellung seiner/ihrer Karriere. Sabite

2. Er/Sie muss den Schwerpunkt der Ausstellung ändern. Herr Kleinedler

3. Er/Sie wird nur zwei seiner/ihrer Werke ausstellen können. Sabite

4. Er/Sie weiß nicht, was Hans studiert. Meline

5. Er/Sie glaubt nicht, dass er/sie ein guter Politiker/eine gute Politikerin wäre. Hans

6. Seine/Ihre Mutter arbeitet in einer Versicherungsagentur als Buchhalterin. Hans

7. Sein/Ihr Bruder möchte Psychologe werden. Hans

8. Er/Sie möchte eine Stelle in Wien finden. Meline

9. Er/Sie hatte in den letzten Monaten sehr viele Notfälle. Sabite

10. Es tut ihm/ihr leid, dass er/sie so anstrengend ist. Sabite

PERSONEN

Herr Kleinedler

Hans

Meline

Sabite

George

7

MELINE Hallo Sabite. Gut. Wir treffen dich dann in einer halben Stunde da. Mann. Sabite hatte in den letzten drei Monaten mehr Notfälle als ich in meinem ganzen Leben.

8

SABITE Und das alles, nachdem ich allen, die ich kenne, davon erzählt habe. Könnt ihr das glauben?

HANS Sabite, wir sind deine Freunde, die dich immer unterstützen. Aber Kleinedlers Idee ist wirklich nicht schlecht. Die Nachfrage nach deiner Kunst wird sich erhöhen, wenn weniger Werke über einen längeren Zeitraum ausgestellt werden.

9

MELINE VWL, Einführungskurs. Hans hat recht.

HANS Es werden auch Leute wegen der anderen Künstler kommen. Und die werden dann wieder deine Kunst gesehen haben, wenn sie wieder gehen.

10

SABITE Danke, Hans. Du überraschst mich immer wieder aufs Neue. Es tut mir leid, dass ich so anstrengend bin.

HANS Ist schon okay, Sabite.

MELINE Wenn ich es mir so recht überlege, Hans, könntest du doch auch ein guter Politiker sein.

Nützliche Ausdrücke

- **die Ausstellung**
  exhibition
- **der Künstler / die Künstlerin**
  artist
- **der Schwerpunkt**
  focus
- **der Nachwuchskünstler**
  emerging artist
- **die Lösung**
  solution
- **die Versicherungsagentur**
  insurance agency
- **Wien ist eine wunderschöne Kulturstadt.**
  Vienna is a beautiful cultural city.
- **der Notfall**
  emergency
- **die Nachfrage**
  demand
- **unterstützen**
  support
- **der Zeitraum**
  period of time
- **VWL, Einführungskurs.**
  Economics 101.

3B.1
- **Und die werden dann wieder deine Kunst gesehen haben, wenn sie wieder gehen.**
  Plus, they will have seen your art, too, by the time they leave.

3B.2
- **Sabite, sie sind eine junge und talentierte Künstlerin, aber es gibt noch so viele ausgezeichnete Künstler mit vielen neuen aufregenden Werken.**
  Sabite, you are a talented young artist, but there are so many new exciting works by other fine artists as well.

---

2 **Zum Besprechen** Zuerst ist Sabite sehr enttäuscht (*disappointed*), dass Herr Kleinedler nur zwei ihrer Werke ausstellen kann. Schreiben Sie zu zweit einen Absatz, in dem Sie Sabite erklären, dass es besser ist, weniger Werke länger auszustellen. Answers will vary.

2 **Suggestion** Students can also write a conversation between Sabite and her friends.

3 **Vertiefung** Meline sagt, dass Wien eine wunderschöne Kulturstadt ist. Finden Sie heraus, warum. Was gibt es in Wien zu sehen? Für welche Art von Kultur ist Wien besonders berühmt? Answers will vary.

3 **Suggestion** On the board, make a list of the cultural highlights that students identified.

IM FOKUS

AP* Theme: Families & Communities
Context: Citizenship

Sozialversicherungen  Reading

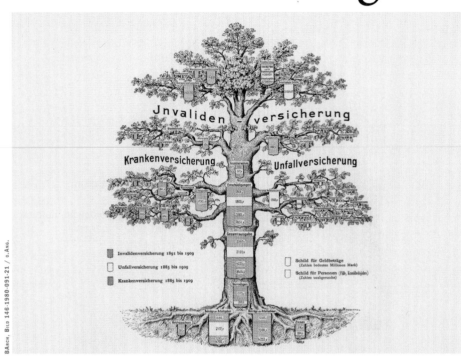

BArch, Bild 146-1980-091-21 / o.Ang.

GESETZLICHE SOZIALVERSICHERUNGEN° gibt es in Deutschland schon seit Ende des 19. Jahrhunderts. Im Jahr 1883 führte° der deutsche Reichskanzler Otto von Bismarck die gesetzliche Krankenversicherung ein. Er wollte soziale Unruhen verhindern° und den Sozialismus bekämpfen°. Später kamen die Rentenversicherung und die Arbeitslosenversicherung. Diese drei Versicherungen bilden heute die gesetzliche Sozialversicherung. Dieses System wird nicht durch Steuern°, sondern durch geteilte Beiträge° von Arbeitgebern und Arbeitnehmern° finanziert.

In Österreich und in der Schweiz ist dieses System sehr ähnlich. In Österreich sind Unfall- Kranken-, Pensions- und Arbeitslosenversicherung Teil der gesetzlichen Sozialversicherungen. In der Schweiz gibt es eine Kranken- und eine Arbeitslosenversicherung so wie auch die Altersversicherung und die Invalidenversicherung. Anders als in Österreich und in Deutschland gibt es eine separate Versicherung für Erwerbsersatz° für den Fall, dass man Militär- oder Zivildienst leisten muss oder Erziehungsurlaub° machen muss.

Neben diesen Sozialversicherungen gibt es noch andere Ähnlichkeiten: festgelegte Wochenarbeitsstunden, ein gesetzliches Rentenalter° eine bestimmte Anzahl an Urlaubstagen und Feiertage, an denen nicht gearbeitet wird.

Zusatzleistungen° in deutschsprachigen Ländern			
	Deutschland	**Österreich**	**Schweiz**
Wochenarbeitszeit (Stunden pro Woche)	35–42	40	42
gesetzliches Rentenalter	Männer: 67 Frauen: 67	Männer: 65 Frauen: 60	Männer: 65 Frauen: 64
Urlaubstage pro Jahr	30	28	20
gesetzliche Feiertage	9–13	17–18	8–14

Sozialversicherungen *social security* **führte... ein** *established* **soziale Unruhen verhindern** *avoid social unrest* **bekämpfen** *combat* **Steuern** *taxes* **geteilte Beiträge** *shared contributions* **Arbeitgebern und Arbeitnehmern** *employers and employees* **Erwerbsersatz** *compensation for loss of income* **Erziehungsurlaub** *maternity leave* **gesetzliches Rentenalter** *legal retirement age* **Zusatzleistungen** *job benefits*

Expansion Have students compare these statistics to the corresponding data for their home country.

ÜBUNGEN

1 **Richtig oder falsch?** Sagen Sie, ob die Sätze richtig oder falsch sind. Korrigieren Sie die falschen Sätze.

1. Die gesetzliche Sozialversicherung hat in Deutschland keine lange Tradition. Falsch. Sie hat eine lange Tradition.

2. Otto von Bismarck führte die gesetzliche Krankenversicherung in Deutschland ein. Richtig.

3. Das Sozialversicherungssystem wird durch Steuern finanziert. Falsch. Es wird durch Beiträge finanziert.

4. Österreicher haben auch die Unfallversicherung. Richtig.

5. In der Schweiz gibt es eine Erwerbsersatzversicherung, wenn man Militärdienst leisten muss. Richtig.

6. Das Sozialversicherungssystem in Deutschland, Österreich und der Schweiz ist sehr ähnlich. Richtig.

7. In Deutschland können Männer vor Frauen in Rente gehen. Falsch. In Deutschland können beide mit 67 Jahren in Rente gehen.

8. In der Schweiz gibt es die meisten gesetzlichen Feiertage. Falsch. In Österreich gibt es die meisten gesetzlichen Feiertage.

 Practice more at **vhlcentral.com.**

Berufe

der Fotograf, -en / die Fotografin, -nen	photographer
der Künstler, - / die Künstlerin, -nen	artist
der Optiker, - / die Optikerin, -nen	optician
der Schauspieler, - / die Schauspielerin, -nen	actor
der Schreiner, - / die Schreinerin, -nen	carpenter

Angestellte, Arbeiter, Beamte

Angestellte, Arbeiter und Beamte: Diese drei Wörter bezeichnen° Personen, die arbeiten. Was sind aber die Unterschiede zwischen diesen Bezeichnungen? Angestellte sind Personen, die vor allem in Büros arbeiten. In Firmen haben sie oft auch eine leitende° Funktion. Sie bekommen ein festes monatliches Gehalt. Arbeiter sind Personen, die Lohn° bekommen. Es kann zum Beispiel ein Stück- oder Stundenlohn sein. Arbeiter verrichten typischerweise manuelle Tätigkeiten°. Beamte sind Personen, die für die Regierung arbeiten, wie zum Beispiel Polizisten und Lehrer.

AP* Theme: Contemporary Life
Context: Education & Career

bezeichnen designate **leitende** managerial
Lohn wage **Tätigkeiten** tasks

Der Marshallplan

Suggestion Tell students that in today's dollars, the Marshall Plan would cost around $137.5 billion.

Nach dem Zweiten Weltkrieg war Europa zu großen Teilen zerstört°. Am 3. April 1948 verabschiedete° der amerikanische Kongress einen Plan, den Marshallplan oder auch *European Recovery Program*, um Westeuropa wieder aufzubauen°. Teil des Plans war es, Kredite, Rohstoffe°, Lebensmittel und Waren nach Westeuropa zu schicken. Die drei Gründe für den Marshallplan waren Hilfe für Westeuropa, Eindämmung° der Sowjetunion und des Kommunismus, und Erschaffung° eines Marktes für amerikanische Waren. Das Volumen des Plans betrug 1948 13,1 Milliarden Dollar. Der Plan war nach dem US-Außenminister George C. Marshall benannt, der 1953 den Friedensnobelpreis bekam. **AP* Theme:** Global Challenges
Context: Political Issues

zerstört destroyed **verabschiedete** passed **aufzubauen** rebuild **Rohstoffe** raw materials
Eindämmung containment **Erschaffung** creation

🔗 IM INTERNET

Suchen Sie im Internet weitere Informationen zum Marshallplan. Wie war die wirtschaftliche Situation 1948 in Deutschland? Was war die Reaktion auf den Marshallplan in Europa?

Find out more at **vhlcentral.com**.

Suggestion Point out that the differences between **Angestellte, Arbeiter,** and **Beamter** are similar to the distinction in English between "blue-collar" and "white-collar" workers.

---

2 Was fehlt? Ergänzen Sie die Sätze.

1. Angestellte kann man vor allem in ____Büros____ finden.
2. Für den Staat arbeiten ____Beamte____.
3. Beispiele von Beamten sind ____Polizisten____ und Lehrer.
4. Der amerikanische Kongress verabschiedete 1948 den ____Marshallplan____.
5. Europa war nach dem Zweiten ____Weltkrieg____ zu großen Teilen zerstört.
6. 1953 bekam George C. Marshall den ____Friedensnobelpreis____.

3 Arbeitsbedingungen Diskutieren Sie mit einem Partner / einer Partnerin: Was wäre Ihnen am Arbeitsplatz wichtig? Wo möchten Sie arbeiten? Mit wie vielen Mitarbeitern möchten Sie arbeiten? Wie sollte die Hierarchie an Ihrem Arbeitsplatz sein? Welche Sozialleistungen (*benefits*) wären Ihnen wichtig?

3 Expansion Have students describe their dream boss. Ask them what a good boss does or doesn't do.

3 Virtual Chat You can also assign activity 3 on the Supersite.

Ressourcen

v̂Text · S vhlcentral

Das Futur II  Presentation

Startblock In **2A.3** you learned about the future tense (**das Futur I**). Although it is rarely used, German also has a future perfect tense (**das Futur II**).

> Bis zum Ende des Tages **werde** ich mit vier weiteren Künstlern **gesprochen haben**.

> Die **werden** dann auch deine Kunst **gesehen haben**, wenn sie wieder gehen.

- Use the **Futur II** to indicate that an event is expected to have happened by or before a particular point in the future.

  Ich arbeite an einem Brief, den meine Chefin heute Nachmittag abschicken will.
  I'm working on a letter that my boss wants to send this afternoon.

  Bis heute Nachmittag **werde** ich den Brief **geschrieben haben**.
  *By this afternoon, I **will have written** the letter.*

- To form the **Futur II**, use the present tense of **werden** with the past participle of the verb that expresses the action plus the infinitive of **haben** or **sein**.

  Wir **werden** Urlaub **genommen haben**.
  *We **will have taken** time off.*

  Nils **wird** im Büro **geblieben sein**.
  *Nils **will have stayed** at the office.*

- Standard word order rules apply in the **Futur II**. Use **bis** to indicate the time by which a future action will have happened.

  Herr Mauer **wird bis** morgen die Arbeit **beendet haben**.
  *Herr Mauer **will have completed** the work **by** tomorrow.*

  Ich denke, dass er die ganze Nacht **gearbeitet haben wird**.
  *I think that he **will have worked** the whole night.*

- Use the **Futur II** with **wohl**, **wahrscheinlich**, **schon**, or **sicher**, to express the likelihood that something has happened or will have happened by or before a particular time.

  Peter wird **wahrscheinlich** heute gekündigt haben.
  *Peter **probably** (will have) quit today.*

  Bis nächste Woche wird er **wohl** eine neue Stelle gefunden haben.
  *By next week he will **likely** have found a new job.*

Jetzt sind Sie dran! Formulieren Sie die folgenden Sätze ins Futur II um.

1. Wir werden früh ins Bett gehen.
   Wir werden früh ins Bett gegangen sein.
2. Ich werde Arbeit finden.
   Ich werde Arbeit gefunden haben.
3. Die Assistentin wird kündigen.
   Die Assistentin wird gekündigt haben.
4. Ihr werdet einen wichtigen Termin haben.
   Ihr werdet einen wichtigen Termin gehabt haben.
5. Wie viele Fabrikarbeiter werden sie wohl entlassen?
   Wie viele Fabrikarbeiter werden sie wohl entlassen haben?
6. Dieses Projekt wird wohl scheitern.
   Dieses Projekt wird wohl gescheitert sein.

Anwendung und Kommunikation

1 **Was fehlt?** Ergänzen Sie die Sätze mit den Verben in Klammern. Benutzen Sie das **Futur II**.

> **BEISPIEL** Bis morgen Abend ___werden___ wir den Film schon ___gesehen haben___. (sehen)

1. Bis heute Nachmittag ___werdet___ ihr schon die Besprechung mit eurem Chef ___gehabt haben___. (haben).

2. Bevor ich eine gute Stelle finde, ___werde___ ich schon bei vielen Vorstellungsgesprächen ___gewesen sein___. (sein)

3. Vor Ende der Woche ___wirst___ du bestimmt schon vom Personalchef ___gehört haben___. (hören)

4. Bis nächstes Frühjahr ___wird___ die Zahl (*number*) der Stellenangebote schon ___gestiegen sein___. (steigen)

5. Bis zum Ende des Jahres ___werden___ wohl viele Angestellte schon ___gekündigt haben___. (kündigen)

6. Vor Anfang September ___werden___ viele Geschäfte schon alle Sommerkleidung ___verkauft haben___. (verkaufen)

7. In zehn Jahren ___wird___ mein Vater schon in Rente ___gegangen sein___. (gehen)

8. Bis Dienstagnachmittag ___werden___ wir schon in unseren Urlaubsort ___abgeflogen sein___. (abfliegen)

2 **Bis zum 30. Geburtstag** Fragen Sie Ihren Partner / Ihre Partnerin, was er/sie wohl bis zum 30. Geburtstag alles gemacht haben wird. Benutzen Sie das **Futur II**. Answers will vary.

> **BEISPIEL**
>
> **S1:** *Wirst du bis zu deinem 30. Geburtstag geheiratet haben?*
> **S2:** *Nein, ich werde nicht bis zu meinem 30. Geburtstag geheiratet haben. Und du, wirst du geheiratet haben?*

> den Uni-Abschluss machen
> heiraten
> Kinder bekommen
> in ein anderes Land umziehen
> deinen Traumberuf (*dream job*) finden
> viel Geld verdienen
> nach Europa reisen

3 **Vor nächster Woche** Sagen Sie Ihrem Partner / Ihrer Partnerin vier Sachen, die Sie diese Woche machen müssen oder wollen. Benutzen Sie dabei das **Futur I**. Danach sagen Sie dem Rest der Klasse, was Sie voneinander gelernt haben. Benutzen Sie dabei das **Futur II**. Answers will vary.

> **BEISPIEL**
>
> **S1:** *Ich werde diese Woche zwei Referate schreiben. Ich werde auch ein neues Handy kaufen.*
> **S2:** *Paul wird bis nächste Woche zwei Referate geschrieben haben. Er wird auch ein neues Handy gekauft haben...*

 Practice more at **vhlcentral.com**.

2 **Suggestion** Before students begin the activity, ask them which verbs in the word bank take **sein**, and verify that they know all of the past participles.

2 **Partner Chat** You can also assign activity 2 on the Supersite. Students work in pairs to record the activity online. The pair's recorded conversation will appear in your gradebook.

3 **Expansion** Ask students to make realistic predictions about what you will have done by the end of the week. Tell them whether or not their predictions are correct.

3B.2

Adjective endings (review)  Presentation

Startblock Adjectives that precede a noun take different endings depending on the case, gender, and number of the noun and whether they are preceded by a **der**-word, an **ein**-word, or neither.

- Adjectives that are preceded by **der**-words have the following endings.

<table>
<tr><th colspan="5">adjective endings after der-words</th></tr>
<tr><th></th><th>masculine</th><th>feminine</th><th>neuter</th><th>plural</th></tr>
<tr><td>nom.</td><td>der gute Chef</td><td>die gute Chefin</td><td>das gute Geschäft</td><td>die guten Stellen</td></tr>
<tr><td>acc.</td><td>den guten Chef</td><td>die gute Chefin</td><td>das gute Geschäft</td><td>die guten Stellen</td></tr>
<tr><td>dat.</td><td>dem guten Chef</td><td>der guten Chefin</td><td>dem guten Geschäft</td><td>den guten Stellen</td></tr>
<tr><td>gen.</td><td>des guten Chefs</td><td>der guten Chefin</td><td>des guten Geschäfts</td><td>der guten Stellen</td></tr>
</table>

- Adjectives that are preceded by **ein**-words have the following endings.

<table>
<tr><th colspan="5">adjective endings after ein-words</th></tr>
<tr><th></th><th>masculine</th><th>feminine</th><th>neuter</th><th>plural</th></tr>
<tr><td>nom.</td><td>ein guter Chef</td><td>eine gute Chefin</td><td>ein gutes Geschäft</td><td>keine guten Stellen</td></tr>
<tr><td>acc.</td><td>einen guten Chef</td><td>eine gute Chefin</td><td>ein gutes Geschäft</td><td>keine guten Stellen</td></tr>
<tr><td>dat.</td><td>einem guten Chef</td><td>einer guten Chefin</td><td>einem guten Geschäft</td><td>keinen guten Stellen</td></tr>
<tr><td>gen.</td><td>eines guten Chefs</td><td>einer guten Chefin</td><td>eines guten Geschäfts</td><td>keiner guten Stellen</td></tr>
</table>

Thomas hat eine sehr **gute** Stelle gefunden.
*Thomas found a really **good** job.*

Hast du mein **kleines** Adressbuch gesehen?
*Have you seen my **little** address book?*

- Unpreceded adjectives have the following endings.

<table>
<tr><th colspan="5">unpreceded adjective endings</th></tr>
<tr><th></th><th>masculine</th><th>feminine</th><th>neuter</th><th>plural</th></tr>
<tr><td>nom.</td><td>warmer Regen</td><td>helle Sonne</td><td>schönes Wetter</td><td>farbige Blumen</td></tr>
<tr><td>acc.</td><td>warmen Regen</td><td>helle Sonne</td><td>schönes Wetter</td><td>farbige Blumen</td></tr>
<tr><td>dat.</td><td>warmem Regen</td><td>heller Sonne</td><td>schönem Wetter</td><td>farbigen Blumen</td></tr>
<tr><td>gen.</td><td>warmen Regens</td><td>heller Sonne</td><td>schönen Wetters</td><td>farbiger Blumen</td></tr>
</table>

Suggestion Have students review the use of **der**-words, taught in **Vol. 2, 4B.2**, and **ein**-words, taught in **Vol. 1, 2B.3**.

Suggestion Point out that since **der**-words already carry information about case and gender, the adjective ending doesn't have to.

ACHTUNG

Remember that these endings are used with comparatives and superlatives, as well as with adjectival nouns.

———

Remember that adjectives that come directly after **sein**, **bleiben**, or **werden** do not have added endings.

———

Remember that adjectives ending in **-el** and **-er** drop the **-e-** when they take a case ending:
teuer → teure, teuren, teurer, teures

Suggestion Remind students that unpreceded adjectives and those after **ein**-words have "strong" endings because they must carry the case information that is not shown by the article.

Jetzt sind Sie dran! **Wählen Sie die passenden Adjektivformen.** Suggestion Before students select the adjective endings, have them determine whether the article is a **der**-word or an **ein**-word, or if there is no article.

1. Ein Gärtner muss auch bei (schlechtes / schlechte / schlechtem) Wetter oft draußen arbeiten.

2. Wissenschaftler machen (wichtig / wichtige / wichtigen) Entdeckungen.

3. Ein (kaputter / kaputten / kaputte) Wäschetrockner ist für einen Elektriker kein Problem.

4. Die Immobilienmaklerin hat das Haus trotz des (hohes / hoch / hohen) Preises verkaufen können.

5. Unser Hausmeister geht nicht gern in den (dunkle / dunklen / dunkler) Keller.

6. Ingrid arbeitet seit (kurze / kurzen / kurzer) Zeit als Buchhalterin.

Anwendung und Kommunikation

1 Beim Vorstellungsgespräch Ergänzen Sie die Sätze mit den richtigen Formen der Adjektive in Klammern.

1. Wer träumt nicht von einer __erfolgreichen__ Karriere? (erfolgreich)
2. Auf ein __persönliches__ Vorstellungsgespräch sollte man sich gut vorbereiten. (persönlich).
3. Suchen Sie sich __nützliche__ Informationen über die Firma aus dem Internet. (nützlich)
4. Machen Sie dem Personalchef klar, dass Sie ein __zuverlässiger__ Mitarbeiter sind. (zuverlässig)
5. Sagen Sie, dass Sie an einer __längeren__ Zusammenarbeit interessiert sind. (länger)
6. Bleiben Sie immer freundlich und locker trotz __stressiger__ Fragen. (stressig)
7. Ziehen Sie sich lieber konservativ an und kommen Sie in __sauberer__ Kleidung zu Ihrem Termin. (sauber)
8. Zeigen Sie sich von Ihrer __besten__ Seite. (best-)

1 Expansion For more practice, bring in assorted postcards and have students work in pairs to describe what they see on each card, using complete sentences and as many adjectives as possible. Collect the descriptions and correct any mistakes in adjective endings.

2 Lebensläufe Beschreiben Sie mit einem Partner / einer Partnerin die drei Personen auf dem Bild und erfinden Sie zu jeder Person einen kurzen Lebenslauf: Wer sind sie, woher kommen sie, was haben sie gemacht und so weiter. Verwenden Sie attributive Adjektive. Answers will vary.

BEISPIEL

S1: Die Frau in dem roten Kleid ist eine berühmte Musikerin.
S2: Sie kommt aus einer kleinen Stadt in der Schweiz...

2 Partner Chat You can also assign activity 2 on the Supersite. Students work in pairs to record the activity online. The pair's recorded conversation will appear in your gradebook.

3 Mein Traumjob Fragen Sie einander, was Sie sich von Ihrem Traumberuf (nicht) erhoffen. Answers will vary.

BEISPIEL

S1: Was für eine Stelle möchtest du?
S2: Ich möchte eine interessante, anspruchsvolle Stelle.

anspruchsvoll	großzügig	modern
dynamisch	intelligent	ordentlich
ernst	interessant	schön
freundlich	kreativ	zuverlässig

1. Was für eine Arbeitsstelle möchtest du (nicht)?
2. Was für ein Gehalt möchtest du (nicht)?
3. Was für einen Chef oder eine Chefin möchtest du (nicht)?
4. In was für einem Büro möchtest du (nicht) arbeiten?
5. Mit was für Mitarbeitern möchtest du (nicht) arbeiten?

3 Expansion Allow students to focus on communication and content during the activity, but follow up by having them write down a few of their answers with a focus on accuracy. Have them trade with a partner and check each other's adjective endings.

3 Virtual Chat You can also assign activity 3 on the Supersite. Students record individual responses that appear in your gradebook.

 Practice more at **vhlcentral.com**.

Wiederholung

1 Diskutieren und kombinieren
Sie und Ihr Partner / Ihre Partnerin haben einige Personen, die Arbeit suchen, und einige Stellenangebote. Sprechen Sie über die Arbeitssuchenden und die Stellenangebote und entscheiden Sie, wer zu welcher Stelle passt. *Answers will vary.*

BEISPIEL

S1: *Martin Richter hat sieben Jahre lang als Feuerwehrmann in Hamburg gearbeitet.*

S2: *Ich habe die perfekte Stelle für ihn. In Dresden gibt es einige Stellen für Feuerwehrleute.*

1 Expansion Have students write a "want ad" together using the texts as models.

2 Schuljahrsende
Was werden Sie vor Ende des Jahres gemacht haben? Vergleichen Sie Ihre Antworten mit denen Ihres Partners / Ihrer Partnerin. *Answers will vary.*

2 Partner Chat You can also assign activity 2 on the Supersite.

BEISPIEL

S1: *Bis Ende des Jahres werde ich noch zwei Stücke auf dem Saxophon gelernt haben. Und du?*

S2: *Ich werde …* **2 Suggestion** Remind students to use the **Futur II**.

> Projekte fertig machen
> für die Prüfungen lernen
> ein Referat halten
> einen Ferienjob finden
> Aufsätze schreiben
> eine Sportveranstaltung besuchen
> Prüfungen schreiben
> mein Zimmer aufräumen

3 Weltpolitik
Sagen Sie, was mit jedem der Länder auf der Liste in der Zukunft passieren wird. Sagen Sie auch, wann das passieren wird. Vergleichen Sie Ihre Antworten mit denen Ihres Partners / Ihrer Partnerin. *Answers will vary.*

BEISPIEL

S1: *Bis 2035 wird China sicher eine Demokratie geworden sein.*

S2: *Ich glaube, dass es wohl ein kommunistisches Land geblieben sein wird.*

> | Kanada | Russland |
> |--------|----------|
> | Österreich | Deutschland |
> | die USA | die Schweiz |

3 Partner Chat You can also assign activity 3 on the Supersite. Students work in pairs to record the activity online. The pair's recorded conversation will appear in your gradebook.

4 Der schönste Geburtstag
Beschreiben Sie Ihrem Partner / Ihrer Partnerin den schönsten Geburtstag Ihres Lebens. Benutzen Sie Adjektive, um den Tag zu beschreiben. *Answers will vary.*

4 Partner Chat You can also assign activity 4 on the Supersite.

BEISPIEL

Als ich neun wurde, habe ich den schönsten Geburtstag meines Lebens gehabt. Der Tag begann mit einem leckeren Frühstück. Wir aßen…

5 Kleine Geschichte
Schreiben Sie mit Ihrem Partner / Ihrer Partnerin die Geschichte von Frank, der in seinem Beruf nicht immer erfolgreich war. Gebrauchen Sie die angegebenen Worte. Beachten Sie den Gebrauch des Präteritums. *Answers will vary.*

> eine Gehaltserhöhung bekommen
> eine große Überraschung sein
> die Firma verlassen
> ins Büro kommen
> eine Beförderung anbieten
> entlassen
> an der Qualität der Arbeit scheitern
> sich um eine neue Stelle bewerben

6 Arbeitsblatt
Fragen Sie drei Mitschüler nach ihrer Lieblingsfarbe. Bitten Sie sie, zwei Dinge, die sie in dieser Farbe besitzen, detailliert zu beschreiben. *Answers will vary.*

BEISPIEL

S1: *Was ist deine Lieblingsfarbe?*

S2: *Meine Lieblingsfarbe ist Grün.*

S1: *Was hast du alles in Grün?*

S2: *Ich habe eine warme, grüne Bettdecke, die mir meine Großmutter geschenkt hat…*

6 Expansion Conduct a poll to find out students' favorite colors and the most common items they have in those colors.

7 Berufsberatung

Arbeiten Sie mit einem Partner / einer Partnerin. Beschreiben Sie was für eine Person Sie sind, Ihre Erfahrungen und die Art Arbeit, die Sie gerne machen wollen. Ihr Partner / Ihre Partnerin wird die Rolle des Berufsberaters / der Berufsberaterin (*career counselor*) spielen, Ihnen Fragen stellen und Sie beraten, welche Berufe für Sie in Frage kommen. Wechseln Sie dann die Rollen. Answers will vary.

BEISPIEL

S1: *Ich bin ein kreativer Mensch und ich bin auch sehr logisch.*
S2: *Arbeiten Sie lieber allein oder mit anderen?*
S1: *Lieber allein, aber nicht immer...*

7 Suggestion Before they begin the role-play, give students time to jot down relevant information and potential questions.

7 Partner Chat You can also assign activity 7 on the Supersite. Students work in pairs to record the activity online. The pair's recorded conversation will appear in your gradebook.

8 Beim Immobilienmakler

Beschreiben Sie Ihrem Partner / Ihrer Partnerin das Haus, das Sie suchen. Er/Sie wird die Rolle des Immobilienmaklers / der Immobilienmaklerin spielen und Ihnen einige Häuser anbieten. Entscheiden Sie, welches Haus für Sie am besten ist. Beachten Sie die folgenden Fragen. Answers will vary.

BEISPIEL

S1: *Ich suche ein kleines Haus auf dem Land nicht weit vom Meer. Ich brauche ein ziemlich großes Grundstück für meine drei Hunde.*
S2: *Hmmm... Ich habe hier drei Häuser, die Ihnen gefallen könnten.*

- Wo möchten Sie gerne wohnen?
- Wie groß soll das Haus sein?
- Was für einen Stil soll das Haus haben?
- Wer wird in dem Haus wohnen?
- Wie viele Zimmer brauchen Sie?
- Brauchen Sie besondere Zimmer oder Einrichtungen (*features*)?
- Wie muss das Haus ausgestattet (*equipped*) sein?
- Würden Sie sich für ein Haus interessieren, das renoviert werden muss?
- Wie viel wollen Sie maximal bezahlen?

8 Virtual Chat You can also assign activity 8 on the Supersite.

Mein Wör|ter|buch

Schreiben Sie noch fünf weitere Wörter in Ihr persönliches Wörterbuch zu den Themen **Im Büro** und **Berufe**.

der Ferienjob

Übersetzung
vacation job

Wortart
Substantiv

Gebrauch
Fast alle Studenten suchen für den Sommer einen Ferienjob, damit sie etwas Geld verdienen können.

Synonyme
die Ferienarbeit

Antonyme
fester Arbeitsplatz

 Vocabulary Tools

Baden-Württemberg, das Saarland und Rheinland-Pfalz

Baden-Württemberg in Zahlen

▶ **Fläche:** *35.751 km²*

▶ **Bevölkerung:** *10,7 Millionen Menschen*

▶ **Städte:** *Stuttgart (603.000 Einwohner), Mannheim (314.000), Karlsruhe (300.000)*

▶ **Wichtige Industriezweige:** *Maschinenbau, Automobilindustrie, Metallerzeugnisse°*

▶ **Touristenattraktionen:** *Schwarzwald, Bodensee, Baden-Baden*

QUELLE: Tourismusportal Baden-Württemberg

Das Saarland in Zahlen

▶ **Fläche:** *2.569 km²*

▶ **Bevölkerung:** *1 Million Menschen*

▶ **Städte:** *Saarbrücken (177.000 Einwohner), Neunkirchen (46.000)*

▶ **Wichtige Industriezweige:** *Automobilbau, Keramikindustrie, Informatik*

▶ **Touristenattraktionen:** *Ludwigskirche in Saarbrücken, Völklinger Hütte, römische Villa in Borg*

QUELLE: Tourismus Zentrale Saarland GmbH

Rheinland-Pfalz in Zahlen

▶ **Fläche:** *19.853 km²*

▶ **Bevölkerung:** *4 Millionen Menschen*

▶ **Städte:** *Mainz (203.000 Einwohner), Ludwigshafen (167.000), Koblenz (110.000)*

▶ **Wichtige Industriezweige:** *Weinanbau°, chemische Industrie, pharmazeutische Industrie, Tourismus*

▶ **Touristenattraktionen:** *Speyerer Dom, Kulturlandschaft Oberes Mittelrheintal, Limes*

QUELLE: Rheinland-Pfalz Tourismus GmbH

Expansion Divide the class into small groups and assign each student one of these famous people to research and present to their group. You may want to provide additional names, ex.: **Hildegard von Bingen, Gottlieb Daimler, Oskar Lafontaine**.

Suggestion Tell students that the Limes was a protective wall built by the ancient Romans to secure their territory and hold back Germanic invaders.

Berühmte Baden-Württemberger, Saarländer und Rheinland-Pfälzer

▶ **Friedrich Schiller,** *Dichter° (1759–1805)*

▶ **Nicole (Seibert),** *Sängerin (1964–)*

▶ **Helmut Kohl,** *Politiker (1930–)*

Metallerzeugnisse *metal products* Weinanbau *vineyards* Dichter *poet* Dom *cathedral* Kelten *Celts* Grab *grave* Fürstin *princess* starb *died* ausweichen *yield*

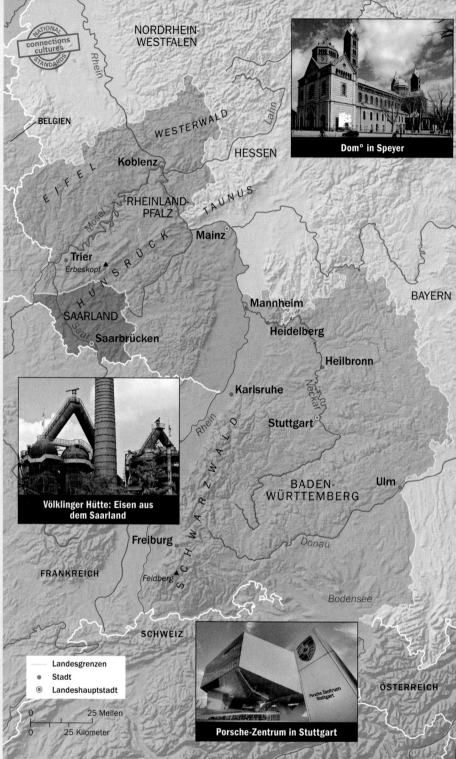

Dom° in Speyer

Völklinger Hütte: Eisen aus dem Saarland

Landesgrenzen
● Stadt
◉ Landeshauptstadt

0 ————— 25 Meilen
0 ————— 25 Kilometer

Porsche-Zentrum in Stuttgart

Unglaublich aber wahr!

Die Kelten° lebten früher in der Nähe der Donau im heutigen Baden-Württemberg, dem östlichen Frankreich und der Schweiz. Das älteste Grab° einer keltischen Fürstin° fand man 2010 in Ludwigsburg. Die Fürstin starb° etwa im Jahr 600 vor Christus. Erst später mussten die Kelten ins westliche Europa der britischen Inseln ausweichen°. **AP* Theme:** Personal & Public Identities
Context: National Identity

AP* Theme: Global Challenges
Context: Geography

Geographie

Rhein

Expansion Tell students that the castles built along the river served a defensive purpose, but also functioned as a means of extracting tolls from passing ships.

Der Rhein ist der längste Fluss Deutschlands. Er ist 1.233 Kilometer lang, 865 Kilometer davon fließen° durch Deutschland zwischen dem Bodensee im Süden und Holland im Norden. Er ist eine der verkehrsreichsten Wasserstraßen der Welt. Er ist auch eine wichtige Grenze° zwischen Deutschland und Frankreich. Die vielen Schlösser°, die man bei einer Bootsfahrt durch das Obere Mittelrheintal zwischen Bingen und Koblenz sehen kann, sind historische Beispiele der Grenzfunktion des Flusses.

AP* Theme: Personal & Public Identities
Context: National Identity

Sport

Das Saarland bei Olympischen Spielen

An der Grenze zwischen Deutschland, Luxemburg und Frankreich liegt das Saarland, wegen seiner Bodenschätze ein oft umstrittenes° Land. 1952 war das Saarland politisch unabhängig°, gehörte wirtschaftlich aber zu Frankreich. Bei den ersten Olympischen Sommerspielen nach dem Zweiten Weltkrieg im finnischen Helsinki trat zum einzigen Mal eine saarländische Mannschaft bei der Olympiade an°. Sechsunddreißig saarländische Sportler fuhren nach Finnland, gewannen dort aber keine Medaille. Ab 1956 waren die Saarländer dann Teil der deutschen Mannschaft.

Kultur

Trier

Suggestion Tell students that the name of the Igeler Säule (which is topped with an eagle) comes from the Latin word for eagle: aquila.

Trier ist eine Stadt in Rheinland-Pfalz. Sie gilt als älteste Stadt Deutschlands. Vor mehr als 2000 Jahren gründeten die Römer die Stadt unter dem Namen Augusta Treverorum. Aus der Zeit der Römer kann man noch das Amphitheater, die Thermen°, die Konstantinbasilika und die Igeler Säule° besuchen. Die Römerbrücke ist die älteste Brücke Deutschlands. Das bekannteste Bauwerk° ist aber die Porta Nigra, ein römisches Stadttor° und Wahrzeichen° der Stadt. Alle diese Bauwerke sind Teil des UNESCO-Weltkulturerbes.

AP* Theme: Beauty & Aesthetics
Context: Architecture

fließen flow **Grenze** border **Schlösser** castles **umstrittenes** disputed **unabhängig** independent **trat...an** took part **beweglichen Metalllettern** movable metal type **mitteilen** communicate **Thermen** thermal baths **Säule** column **Bauwerk** building **Stadttor** city gate **Wahrzeichen** landmark

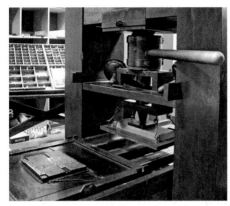

AP* Theme: Science & Technology
Context: Inventions as Catalysts of Change

Technologie

Gutenberg

Johannes Gutenberg (1400–1468) gilt als Erfinder des Buchdrucks mit beweglichen Metalllettern° in Europa. Diese Erfindung startete eine Medienrevolution. Bücher und andere Publikationen wie zum Beispiel Pamphlete konnten mit der neuen Erfindung wesentlich schneller und billiger produziert werden. Mit Hilfe von Pamphleten konnte Martin Luther (1483–1546), der 1517 mit seinen 95 Thesen in direkte Konfrontation zur römisch-katholischen Kirche getreten war, seine neuen Ideen schnell und billig den Menschen mitteilen°. Ohne diese technische Neuerung wäre er isoliert und ohne Publikum gewesen.

🔗 IM INTERNET

1. Suchen Sie weitere Informationen über die Kelten in Deutschland: Wo genau haben sie gelebt? Was weiß man über sie?

2. Suchen Sie mehr Informationen über Johannes Gutenberg: Wer war er? Was hat er noch gemacht?

Find out more at **vhlcentral.com**.

🔗 **Was haben Sie gelernt?** Ergänzen Sie die Sätze.

1. Das älteste Grab einer keltischen Fürstin fand man in ___Ludwigsburg___.

2. Die Kelten lebten in Baden-Württemberg und Teilen Frankreichs, bevor sie auf die britischen Inseln ausweichen mussten.

3. Im Süden Deutschlands beginnt der Rhein am ___Bodensee___.

4. Der Rhein war schon immer eine ___Grenze___ zwischen Deutschland und Frankreich.

5. Die saarländische Mannschaft gewann keine ___Medaille___.

6. Nach 1952 waren die Saarländer Teil der ___deutschen___ Mannschaft.

7. Johannes Gutenberg erfand den ___Buchdruck___ mit beweglichen Metalllettern.

8. Luthers ___Pamphlete___ konnte man schneller und billiger produzieren.

9. Trier hieß früher ___Augusta Treverorum___.

10. Das bekannteste Bauwerk Triers ist die ___Porta Nigra___.

Vor dem Lesen
AP* **Theme:** Beauty & Aesthetics
Context: Language & Literature

Strategien

Perspective

Identifying the narrator's perspective can help you make sense of a story. The perspective of the narrator may be limited to that of a single character, or the narrator may be omniscient, describing the thoughts and actions of all the characters in a story. By employing an omniscient narrator, the author can create distance between the reader and the characters, revealing aspects of a situation that the characters themselves cannot see. The author may use this distance to create a humorous contrast between the perspective of the characters and the perspective provided by the narrator.

Untersuchen Sie den Text

Sehen Sie den Titel und die Bilder an. Was wissen Sie sofort über diese Geschichte? Lesen Sie die ersten Sätze der Geschichte. Glauben Sie, dass der Erzähler dieser Geschichte allwissend (*omniscient*) ist?

Autor

Peter Bichsel

Peter Bichsel ist Schweizer. Er wurde 1935 in Luzern geboren. Er hat als Lehrer in einer Grundschule, als freier Journalist, und als Berater in der Politik gearbeitet. Jetzt ist er freier Schriftsteller. Er schreibt Kurzgeschichten und Essays. Oft schreibt er humorvolle Erzählungen aus der Perspektive junger Kinder. Bichsel hat einige Literaturpreise gewonnen. Er hat viele Einladungen an amerikanische Universitäten bekommen, wo er weitere Texte verfasst und seine Werke vorgelesen hat. Peter Bichsel wohnt heute im schweizerischen Solothurn.

Suggestion Point out to students that Bichsel uses pre-reform spelling on some words, ex.: **Mikrophon**, instead of **Mikrofon**.

Der Erfinder
(Ausschnitt°)

Erfinder ist ein Beruf, den man nicht lernen kann; deshalb ist er selten; heute gibt es ihn überhaupt nicht mehr.

Früher aber gab es noch Erfinder. Einer von ihnen hieß Edison. Er erfand das Mikrophon und baute einen Apparat, mit dem man die Filme abspielen konnte.

1931 starb er.

1890 wurde zwar noch einer geboren, und der lebt noch. Niemand kennt ihn, weil er jetzt in einer Zeit lebt, in der es keine Erfinder mehr gibt. Seit dem Jahre 1931 ist er allein. Das weiß er nicht, weil er schon damals nicht mehr hier in der Stadt wohnte und nie unter die Leute ging; denn Erfinder brauchen Ruhe°.

Er berechnete° und zeichnete° den ganzen Tag. Er saß stundenlang da, legte seine Stirn° in Falten°, fuhr sich mit der Hand immer wieder übers Gesicht und dachte nach.

Dann nahm er seine Berechnungen, zerriss° sie und warf sie weg und begann wieder von neuem, und abends war er mürrisch° und schlecht gelaunt°, weil die Sache wieder nicht gelang.

Er ging früh zu Bett, stand früh auf und arbeitete den ganzen Tag. Er bekam keine Post, las keine Zeitungen und wusste nichts davon, dass es Radios gibt.

Und nach all den Jahren kam der Abend, an dem er nicht schlecht gelaunt war, denn er hatte seine Erfindung erfunden, und er legte sich jetzt überhaupt nicht mehr schlafen. Tag und Nacht saß er über seinen Plänen und prüfte sie nach, und sie stimmten°.

Dann rollte er sie zusammen und ging nach Jahren zum ersten Mal in die Stadt. Sie hatte sich völlig verändert°. Wo es früher Pferde gab, da gab es jetzt Automobile, und im Warenhaus° gab es eine Rolltreppe°, und die Eisenbahnen° fuhren nicht mehr mit Dampf°. Der Erfinder staunte°. Aber weil er ein Erfinder war, begriff er alles sehr schnell. Er sah einen Kühlschrank und sagte: „Aha." Er sah ein Telefon und sagte: „Aha." Und als er rote und grüne Lichter sah, begriff er, dass man bei Rot warten muss und bei Grün gehen darf.

Ausschnitt *excerpt* **Ruhe** *quiet* **berechnete** *calculated* **zeichnete** *sketched* **Stirn** *forehead* **Falten** *wrinkles* **zerriss** *tore* **mürrisch** *grumpy* **schlecht gelaunt** *in a bad mood* **stimmten** *were correct*

Und er begriff alles, aber er staunte, und fast hätte er dabei seine eigene Erfindung vergessen.

Als sie ihm wieder einfiel, ging er auf einen Mann zu, der eben bei Rot wartete und sagte: „Entschuldigen Sie, mein Herr, ich habe eine Erfindung gemacht." Und der Herr war freundlich und sagte: „Und jetzt, was wollen Sie?" Und der Erfinder wusste es nicht. „Es ist nämlich eine wichtige Erfindung", sagte der Erfinder, aber da schaltete die Ampel auf Grün, und sie mussten gehen.

Was hätten die Leute sagen sollen, zu denen der Erfinder sagte: „Ich habe eine Erfindung gemacht."

Er sprang auf in der Straßenbahn, breitete seine Pläne zwischen den Beinen der Leute auf den Boden aus und rief: „Hier schaut mal, ich habe einen Apparat erfunden, in dem man sehen kann, was weit weg geschieht°." „Der hat das Fernsehen erfunden", rief jemand, und alle lachten. „Warum lachen Sie?" fragte der Mann, aber niemand antwortete, und er stieg aus, ging durch die Straßen, blieb bei Rot stehen und ging bei Grün weiter, setzte sich in ein Restaurant und bestellte einen Kaffee, und als sein Nachbar° zu ihm sagte: „Schönes Wetter heute", da sagte der Erfinder: „Helfen Sie mir doch, ich habe das Fernsehen erfunden, und niemand will es glauben – alle lachen mich aus." „Sie lachen", sagte der Mann, „weil es das Fernsehen schon lange gibt und weil man das nicht mehr erfinden muss", und er zeigte in die Ecke des Restaurants, wo ein Fernsehapparat stand, und fragte: „Soll ich ihn einstellen°?"

Aber der Erfinder sagte: „Nein, ich möchte das nicht sehen." Er stand auf und ging.

Er ging durch die Stadt, achtete nicht mehr auf Grün und Rot, und die Autofahrer schimpften° und tippten mit dem Finger an die Stirn.

Seither kam der Erfinder nie mehr in die Stadt.

Er ging nach Hause und erfand jetzt nur noch für sich selbst.

Er nahm einen Bogen Papier, schrieb darauf „Das Automobil", rechnete und zeichnete wochenlang und monatelang und erfand das Auto noch einmal, dann erfand er die Rolltreppe, er erfand das Telefon, und er erfand den Kühlschrank. Alles, was er in der Stadt gesehen hatte, erfand er noch einmal. Und jedes Mal, wenn er eine Erfindung gemacht hatte, zerriss er die Zeichnungen, warf sie weg und sagte: „Das gibt es schon."

Doch er blieb sein Leben lang ein richtiger Erfinder, denn auch Sachen, die es gibt, zu erfinden, ist schwer und nur Erfinder können es.

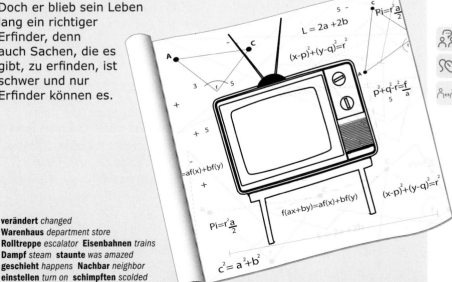

verändert *changed*
Warenhaus *department store*
Rolltreppe *escalator* **Eisenbahnen** *trains*
Dampf *steam* **staunte** *was amazed*
geschieht *happens* **Nachbar** *neighbor*
einstellen *turn on* **schimpften** *scolded*

Nach dem Lesen

Richtig oder falsch? Laut dieser Geschichte sind die Sätze richtig oder falsch?

	Richtig	Falsch
1. Man kann den Beruf Erfinder lernen.	☐	☑
2. Thomas Edison erfand das Mikrofon.	☑	☐
3. Der Erfinder wurde 1931 geboren.	☐	☑
4. Der Erfinder war selten gut gelaunt.	☑	☐
5. Eisenbahnen in der Stadt fuhren noch mit Dampf.	☐	☑
6. Der Erfinder wollte, dass der Nachbar im Restaurant den Fernsehapparat einstellt.	☐	☑
7. Der Erfinder wartete immer bei Rot und ging immer bei Grün.	☐	☑
8. Der Erfinder zeichnete ein Automobil auf das Papier.	☑	☐

Fragen Antworten Sie auf die folgenden Fragen.
Sample answers provided.
1. Was erfand Edison? Er erfand das Mikrophon und einen Apparat, mit dem man die Filme abspielen konnte.
2. Was erfand der Erfinder? Er erfand das Fernsehen.
3. Was gibt es nicht mehr in der Stadt? Pferde gibt es nicht mehr in der Stadt.
4. Was sind die neuen Erfindungen in der Stadt? Automobile, Rolltreppe und Eisenbahnen sind die neuen Erfindungen in der Stadt.
5. Was will der Erfinder den Leuten in der Straßenbahn zeigen? Er will den Leuten seine Pläne zeigen.

Schreiben Wie finden Sie diese Geschichte? Beschreiben Sie, was Sie davon denken. Ist die Geschichte traurig oder lustig? Warum?

Zum Besprechen Sprechen Sie mit einem Partner / einer Partnerin über vier Erfindungen, die Sie für wichtig halten (*consider important*). Wozu benutzen Sie diese vier Geräte? Warum sind diese Dinge wichtig in Ihrem Leben?

Hören

Strategien

Listening for linguistic clues

You can enhance your listening comprehension by listening for specific cues. For example, if you listen for the endings of conjugated verbs or for familiar constructions, such as the **Perfekt**, **Futur**, or **Konjunktiv**, you can find out whether a person did something in the past, is going to do something in the future, or would do something under certain conditions.

 To practice this strategy, you will listen to questions and statements from an interview. As you listen, note whether each question or statement refers to a past, present, or future action.

Vorbereitung

Sehen Sie sich das Bild an. Welche Art von Arbeit sucht wohl der Bewerber? Läuft das Bewerbungsgespräch gut oder schlecht? Glauben Sie, dass der Mann die Stelle bekommen wird?

Zuhören

Hören Sie sich das Gespräch zweimal an. Machen Sie sich Notizen über den Bewerber, nachdem Sie das Gespräch ein zweites Mal gehört haben.

Name des Bewerbers: _Herr Huber_

Stelle: _Programmierer_

Studienabschluss: _Informatik_

Arbeitserfahrung: _keine_

Praktika: _zwei: Softwarefirmen in Karlsruhe und Mannheim_

Forschung (*research*): _Computerspiele_

Teilzeitarbeit: _Studentenjobs_

Suggestion Have students listen to the conversation again, before they complete the **richtig oder falsch** activity.

Verständnis

Richtig oder falsch Sind die Sätze richtig oder falsch?

1. Herr Huber ist gerade erst mit dem Studium fertig geworden.
   Richtig.

2. Herr Huber hat sein Studium mit der Note 1,5 beendet.
   Richtig.

3. Das erste Praktikum von Herrn Huber dauerte zwei Monate.
   Falsch.

4. Das erste Praktikum war bei einer Firma in Stuttgart.
   Falsch.

5. Das zweite Praktikum hat Herr Huber bei einer Softwarefirma gemacht.
   Richtig.

6. Das zweite Praktikum dauerte drei Monate lang.
   Richtig.

7. In seiner Forschung konzentrierte sich Herr Huber auf Softwareprogramme für die Buchhaltung.
   Falsch.

8. Herr Huber wird erst in zwei Wochen wieder von der Firma hören.
   Falsch.

Brief an den Interviewer Stellen Sie sich vor, dass Sie sich für ein Praktikum bei einer deutschen Firma beworben haben. Es war ein gutes Bewerbungsgespräch und Sie wollen sich bei der Firma bedanken. Schreiben Sie mit einem Partner / einer Partnerin einen Brief an den Interviewer: Bedanken Sie sich für das Interview und das Interesse der Firma. Wiederholen Sie nochmal Ihre Qualifikationen für die Stelle. Verwenden Sie die Sie-Form.

Suggestion Teach students formal letter openers and closers such as **Sehr geehrte Frau/geehrter Herr...** and **Mit freundlichen Grüßen**.

Schreiben

Writing strong introductions and conclusions

Introductions and conclusions serve a similar purpose: both are intended to focus the reader's attention on the topic being discussed. The introduction presents a brief preview of the topic and informs the reader of the important points that will be covered in the body of the text. The conclusion reaffirms those points and concisely sums up the information that has been provided.

If you were writing a cover letter for a job application, you might start by identifying the job posting to which you are responding. The rest of your introductory paragraph could outline the areas you will cover in the body of your letter, such as your work experience and your reasons for wanting the job. In your conclusion, you might sum up the most important and convincing points of your letter and tie them together in a way that would leave your reader impressed and curious to learn more. You could, for example, use your conclusion to state why your qualifications make you the ideal candidate for the job and convince your reader of your enthusiasm for the position.

Suggestion You may want to share a few sample **Bewerbungsschreiben** with the class. Examples can be found online by searching with the keywords **Beispiele Bewerbungsschreiben** or **Muster Bewerbungsschreiben**.

Thema

Bewerbungsschreiben

 Schreiben Sie eine Bewerbung, um sich auf Ihren Traumjob zu bewerben. Der Brief sollte drei Teile haben: Einleitung (*introduction*), Hauptteil (*body*) und Schluss (*conclusion*). Nennen Sie in der Einleitung kurz den Grund (*reason*) für den Brief. Beschreiben Sie dann im Detail Ihre Qualifikationen und Interessen. Fassen Sie am Ende die diversen Aspekte zusammen und erklären Sie, warum Sie ein guter Bewerber / eine gute Bewerberin für die Stelle sind.

Einleitung

- Nennen Sie den Titel der Stelle, auf die Sie sich bewerben.
- Erklären Sie, warum Sie sich auf die Stelle bewerben.

Hauptteil

- Fassen Sie Ihre (Schul-)Ausbildung und Erfahrungen zusammen.
- Beschreiben Sie, was Sie dadurch gelernt haben.
- Erklären Sie, warum Sie wegen dieser Erfahrungen für die Stelle qualifiziert sind.
- Beschreiben Sie, welche von Ihren Eigenschaften (*characteristics*) für die Firma wichtig sein könnten.

Schluss

- Bestätigen Sie (*Confirm*) Ihren Enthusiasmus für diese Stelle und Ihr Interesse daran.
- Erklären Sie, warum diese Stelle Ihrer Karriere helfen kann und auch, wie Sie dem Arbeitgeber nützen (*be of use*) können.

 **Vocabulary Tools**

Lektion 3A

eine Stelle suchen

der/die Angestellte, -n *employee*
der Assistent, -en / die Assistentin,
  -nen *assistant*
die Ausbildung, -en *education*
der Beruf, -e *profession*
die Berufsausbildung, -en *professional
  training*
die Besprechung, -en *meeting*
der Bewerber, - / die Bewerberin,
  -nen *applicant*
das Empfehlungsschreiben, -
  letter of recommendation
die Erfahrung, -en *experience*
die Firma (*pl.* die Firmen) *firm;
  company*
das Geschäft, -e *business*
der Geschäftsführer, - / die
  Geschäftsführerin, -nen *manager*
das (hohe/niedrige) Gehalt (*pl.* die
  (hohen/niedrigen) Gehälter (*high/
  low*) *salary*
der Lebenslauf, -̈e *résumé; CV*
der Personalchef, -s / die
  Personalchefin, -nen *human
  resources manager*
das Praktikum (*pl.* die
  Praktika) *internship*
die Referenz, -en *reference*
die Stelle, -n *position; job*
das Stellenangebot, -e *job opening*
der Termin, -e *appointment*
der Vertrag, -̈e *contract*
das Vorstellungsgespräch, -e *job
  interview*
Arbeit finden *to find a job*
einen Termin vereinbaren *to make
  an appointment*
sich bewerben um (bewirbt sich) *to
  apply for*

Büromaterial

die Büroklammer, -n *paperclip*
das Büromaterial, -ien *office supplies*
die Pinnwand, -̈e *bulletin board*
der Hefter, - *stapler*

am Telefon

der Hörer, - *receiver*
die Telefonnummer, -n *telephone
  number*
Wer spricht? *Who's calling?*
Bleiben Sie bitte am Apparat. *Please
  hold.*
auflegen *to hang up*
einen Anruf entgegennehmen *to
  answer the phone*
eine Nachricht hinterlassen *to leave
  a message*
in der Warteschleife sein *to be on hold*

Relative pronouns *See pp. 120–121.*
Perfekt versus *Präteritum* (review)
  See p. 124.

Lektion 3B

Berufe

der/die Bankangestellte, -n *bank
  employee*
der Bauer, -n / die Bäuerin,
  -nen *farmer*
der Buchhalter, - / die Buchhalterin,
  -nen *accountant*
der Elektriker, - / die Elektrikerin,
  -nen *electrician*
der Fabrikarbeiter, - / die
  Fabrikarbeiterin, -nen *factory worker*
der Feuerwehrmann (*pl.* die
  Feuerwehrleute) / die Feuerwehrfrau,
  -en *firefighter*
der Gärtner, - / die Gärtnerin,
  -nen *gardener*
der Hausmann, -̈er / die Hausfrau,
  -en *homemaker*
der Hausmeister, - / die Hausmeisterin,
  -nen *caretaker; custodian*
der Immobilienmakler, - / die
  Immobilienmaklerin, -nen *real
  estate agent*
der Klempner, - / die Klempnerin,
  -nen *plumber*
der Koch, -̈e / die Köchin, -nen
  cook, chef
der LKW-Fahrer, - / die LKW-Fahrerin,
  -nen *truck driver*
der Politiker, - / die Politikerin,
  -nen *politician*
der Psychologe, -n / die Psychologin,
  -nen *psychologist*
der Rentner, - / die Rentnerin,
  -nen *retiree*
der Richter, - / die Richterin,
  -nen *judge*
der Taxifahrer, - / die Taxifahrerin,
  -nen *taxi driver*
der Tierarzt, -̈e / die Tierärztin,
  -nen *veterinarian*
der Wissenschaftler, - / die
  Wissenschaftlerin, -nen *scientist*

auf der Arbeit

die Beförderung, -en *promotion*
das Büro, -s *office*
der Chef, -s / die Chefin, -nen *boss*
der Erfolg, -e *success*
die Gehaltserhöhung, -en *raise*
die Gewerkschaft, -en *labor union*
die Karriere, -n *career*
anspruchsvoll *demanding*
fertig *ready; finished*
ganztags *full-time*
halbtags *part-time*
zuverlässig *reliable*

Ausdrücke

arbeitslos sein *to be unemployed*
entlassen *to fire; to lay off*
kündigen *to resign*
leiten *to manage*
scheitern *to fail*
Urlaub nehmen *to take time off*
verdienen *to earn*

Das Futur II *See p. 138.*
Adjective endings (review) *See p. 140.*

Suggestion Ask students: Who are the people in the photo and what are they doing?

Teaching Tip Look for icons indicating activities that address the modes of communication. Follow this key:

→🛉←	Interpretive communication
←🛉→	Presentational communication
🛉↔🛉	Interpersonal communication

In der Natur  Vocabulary Tools

Suggestion Have students brainstorm nature-related vocabulary they have already learned: **Blume, Pflanze, Park, Vogel, klettern, spazieren**, etc.

AP* Theme: Global Challenges
Context: Environmental Issues

Wortschatz

die Natur	*nature*
der Bauernhof, ⸚e	*farm*
der Berg -e	*mountain*
das Blatt, ⸚er	*leaf*
das Feld, -er	*field*
der Fluss, ⸚e	*river*
die Küste, -n	*coast*
die Landschaft, -en	*countryside*
die Luft	*air*
das Meer, -e	*sea*
die Sonne, -n	*sun*
der Sonnenaufgang, ⸚e	*sunrise*
der Sonnenuntergang, ⸚e	*sunset*
der Wasserfall, ⸚e	*waterfall*
der Weg, -e	*path*
nass	*wet*
trocken	*dry*
Tiere	***animals***
der Fisch, -e	*fish*
das Huhn, ⸚er	*chicken*
die Maus, ⸚e	*mouse*
das Pferd, -e	*horse*
das Schaf, -e	*sheep*
Verben	***verbs***
aufgehen (geht...auf)	*to rise (sun)*
erforschen	*to explore*
untergehen (geht...unter)	*to set (sun)*
wandern	*to hike*

Suggestion Provide students with the past tense forms of the new verbs.

ACHTUNG

Kaninchen (*rabbits*) in the German-speaking world are almost exclusively domesticated. Their cousins **Hasen** (*hares*) are found in the wild.

Suggestion Point out that **aufgehen** and **untergehen** are used with other celestial bodies besides the sun.

der Himmel

der Baum, ⸚e

der Busch, ⸚e

das Tal, ⸚er

der Wald, ⸚er

Sie machen ein Picknick (*n.*).

das Eichhörnchen, -

die Kuh, ⸚e

das Gras

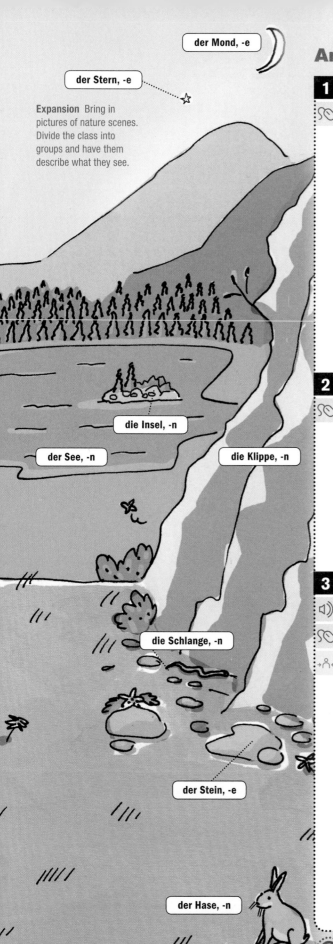

der Mond, -e

der Stern, -e

Expansion Bring in pictures of nature scenes. Divide the class into groups and have them describe what they see.

die Insel, -n

der See, -n

die Klippe, -n

die Schlange, -n

der Stein, -e

der Hase, -n

Anwendung

1 Was passt zusammen? Wählen Sie das richtige Wort zu jedem Foto.

1. __b__ der Baum

2. __f__ der Wasserfall

3. __e__ das Feld

4. __a__ der Sonnenaufgang

5. __d__ die Klippe

6. __c__ der Berg

a.    b.

c.    d.

e.    f.

2 Kategorien Geben Sie zu jeder Kategorie drei passende Begriffe an.

Sample answers are provided.

BEISPIEL Waldtiere *der Hase, die Maus, das Eichhörnchen*

2 Expansion Have students come up with additional words for each category.

1. Pflanzen der Baum, das Gras, der Busch

2. Landschaftliche Formationen die Klippen, die Insel, das Tal

3. Lebensräume (*habitats*) von wilden Tieren der Wald, der Fluss, das Feld

4. Gewässer (*bodies of water*) das Meer, der See, der Wasserfall

5. Tiere auf dem Bauernhof die Kuh, das Schaf, das Pferd

6. Himmelskörper (*celestial bodies*) der Mond, die Sterne, die Sonne

3 Momentaufnahmen Hören Sie sich die Dialoge an und entscheiden Sie, welches Bild am besten zu jeder Situation passt. Schreiben Sie außerdem zu allen Bildern einen kurzen Satz darüber, was jedes Paar in diesem Moment gerade macht oder gemacht hat.

Sample answers are provided.

BEISPIEL Sie hören:

— Wie rosa der Himmel ist!
— Ja, da hinten am Horizont geht die Sonne unter.

Gespräch __1__
Sie schauen sich einen Sonnenuntergang an.

1. Gespräch __4__

Sie machen ein Picknick.

2. Gespräch __3__

Sie schwimmen im See.

3. Gespräch __2__
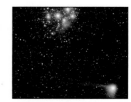
Sie sehen sich die Sterne an.

Suggestion Point out to students that **Hase** is an **n**-noun.

S Practice more at **vhlcentral.com.**

Kommunikation

4 Ein schöner Urlaub
Bringen Sie zusammen mit Ihrem Partner / Ihrer Partnerin die Sätze in eine logische Reihenfolge.

___5___ **FABIAN** Ja, nur gut, dass wir den Stall gefunden haben, wo wir uns unterstellen konnten. Wir wären sonst bis auf die Knochen *(to the bone)* nass geworden.

___1___ **FABIAN** Ich habe gerade nochmal die Fotos von unserem letzten Urlaub angeschaut. Ich glaube, das war der schönste Urlaub, den wir bis jetzt gemacht haben.

___4___ **LINA** Nicht nur an den. Auch an den Bergsee. Das Blau des Wassers—einfach unbeschreiblich! Und die vielen Tiere: die Kühe, die Schafe, die Hasen und die süßen Eichhörnchen! Leider zog dann am Nachmittag plötzlich ein Gewitter auf.

___3___ **FABIAN** Was waren wir kaputt am nächsten Tag! Denk mal an die vielen Kilometer, die wir gelaufen sind! Durch die Täler, über die Felder und dann auf den Berg hoch. Erinnerst du dich noch an den Wasserfall, der da senkrecht nach unten ging?

___2___ **LINA** Ich erinnere mich auch gern daran. Wir hatten so viel Spaß und haben so viel unternommen und gesehen. Die Wanderung, die wir gleich am zweiten Tag gemacht haben, war beeindruckend.

5 Richtig oder falsch?
Entscheiden Sie mit einem Partner / einer Partnerin, ob die folgenden Aussagen richtig oder falsch sind. Korrigieren Sie die falschen Aussagen. Answers to false items may vary.

	richtig	falsch
1. Der Mond ist ein braves Haustier.	☐	☑
2. Die Sonne geht im Osten unter.	☐	☑
3. Aus Schafsmilch macht man Käse.	☑	☐
4. Der Rhein ist ein europäischer Fluss.	☑	☐
5. Hasen sind Pflanzenfresser.	☑	☐
6. Schafe sind kleiner als Mäuse.	☐	☑
7. Eichhörnchen wohnen auf Bäumen.	☑	☐
8. Steine verlieren im Herbst ihre Blätter.	☐	☑

5 Expansion Have pairs of students write four more true-false statements to exchange with another pair.

6 Diskutieren und kombinieren
Sie und Ihr Partner / Ihre Partnerin bekommen zwei verschiedene Bilder. Finden Sie die sieben Unterschiede auf den Bildern. Wechseln Sie sich bei Ihren Fragen und Antworten ab. Sample answers are provided.

BEISPIEL

S1: *Wie viele Flüsse sind auf deinem Bild zu sehen?*
S2: *Ein Fluss. Und auf deinem?*
S1: *Auf meinem Bild ist auch nur ein Fluss.*

7 Der perfekte Tag
Beschreiben Sie mit einem Partner / einer Partnerin, wie ein perfekter Tag in der freien Natur aussehen würde. Wie ist die Landschaft? Was würden Sie um sich herum sehen? Mit wem würden Sie den Tag verbringen? Was würden Sie machen? Und warum mögen Sie gerade diese Landschaft? Answers may vary.

BEISPIEL

S1: *Mein perfekter Tag beginnt in den Bergen. Ich würde bei Sonnenaufgang aufstehen und ein großes Bauernfrühstück mit meiner Familie essen.*
S2: *Und was macht ihr nach dem Frühstück?*
S1: *Danach…*

7 Expansion Have students take notes and describe their partner's perfect day to the class. Have the class identify similarities and differences.

7 Virtual Chat You can also assign activity 7 on the Supersite. Students record individual responses that appear in your gradebook.

Aussprache und Rechtschreibung

Intonation

Intonation refers to the rise and fall of the voice in speaking. In German, different intonation is used for different types of questions and statements.

Es regnet.   **Es regnet?**   **Wenn es regnet…**

In general, statements and commands end with a drop in pitch. A speaker may use rising intonation at the end of a command or statement to communicate a friendly or encouraging tone.

Werfen Sie das nicht weg!   **Bring doch deine Schwester mit.**

Yes-or-no questions typically end with a rising intonation. Questions that begin with a question word end with falling intonation. In questions where multiple options are presented, the pitch rises before each pause and falls at the end of the last option.

Schwimmst du gern?   **Wo liegt diese Insel?**   **Ist das gut oder schlecht?**

The pitch neither rises nor falls at the end of incomplete sentences. It remains flat or neutral. This is also the case before a comma in a complex sentence. The final clause in a complex sentence usually ends with a drop in pitch.

Und wenn die Blätter bunt werden…   **Wenn die Sonne scheint, fahren wir.**

Suggestion Write an English sentence on the board to demonstrate how pitch functions in English. Have students say the sentence with different stress patterns to express questioning intonation, insistence, hesitation, friendliness, etc.

---

1 **Aussprechen** Wiederholen Sie die Sätze die Sie hören.

1. Der Müllwagen kommt zweimal in der Woche.
2. Wie retten wir uns vor der Erderwärmung?
3. Schlagen Sie eine bessere Lösung vor!
4. Warst du schon mal auf einem Bauernhof?
5. Willst du die Schafe, Kühe oder die Pferde sehen?
6. Wenn du nicht gleich ins Bett gehst, geht bald die Sonne auf.

2 **Nachsprechen** Wiederholen Sie die Sätze, die Sie hören.

1. Machen wir heute ein Picknick im Wald?
2. Ich weiß nicht, ob ich kommen kann.
3. Bleib stehen! Siehst du die Schlange nicht?
4. Wohnst du lieber in den Bergen oder an der Küste?

3 **Sprichwörter** Wiederholen Sie die Sprichwörter, die Sie hören.

Wo ein Wille ist, ist auch ein Weg.[1]

Es ist noch kein Meister vom Himmel gefallen.[2]

Ressourcen

vText   LM   vhlcentral
        p. 80

In der Kunstgalerie

 Video

Endlich ist der Tag für Sabites Ausstellung gekommen. Sabite und Karl, ein anderer Künstler, kommen sich näher, aber Meline und Hans haben Probleme.

Vorbereitung Have students scan the script to find words and expressions related to nature.

1

KARL Ich finde deine Werke toll.

SABITE Danke, aber deine Kunst ist auch nicht schlecht. Und Herr Kleinedler hat mir gesagt, dass du noch nicht einmal eine formelle Ausbildung hast.

2

KARL Danke. Du bist sehr liebenswürdig. Erschaffen ist das, worin ich am besten bin. Durch die Arbeit mit meinen Händen erforsche ich meine Gefühle. Sag mir, liebst du die Natur? Ich gehe oft bei Sonnenaufgang in den Tiergarten, um unter den Eichen zu spazieren. Möchtest du mich morgen begleiten?

3

HANS Ciao, meine Damen! Na, wie geht's uns heute Abend?

SABITE Hans? Was trägst du da? Und deine Haare... sind sie... kürzer?

HANS Ich probiere einen eleganteren Look aus. Also, was meint ihr?

SABITE Ich glaube, du solltest du selbst sein. Wer immer das auch sein mag.

4

GEORGE Meline, was meinst du?

MELINE Fast so schön wie Lederhosen.

HANS Was ist an Lederhosen auszusetzen? Das Tragen von Lederhosen ist eine stolze urbayrische Tradition. Die Österreicher... ja, dein Großvater trug sicher auch Lederhosen! Diese Intoleranz macht mich rasend.

5

MELINE Hans, du verstehst nicht, worum es geht. Schon wieder nicht. Du bist manchmal so schwierig.

HANS Ich? Du bist die schwierigste Person, die ich jemals kennen gelernt habe!

MELINE Das stimmt nicht!

HANS Du hast recht. Es gibt schon etwas, das dir gefällt: du selbst!

MELINE Entschuldigt mich bitte.

6

---

1 **Was fehlt?** Ergänzen Sie die Sätze mit den richtigen Informationen.

1. Karl hat keine (Erfahrung / Ausbildung) als Künstler.

2. Durch die Arbeit mit seinen Händen erforscht er seine (Probleme / Gefühle).

3. Er geht oft in den Tiergarten, um unter den (Sternen zu schlafen / Eichen zu spazieren).

4. Hans probiert einen neuen (eleganteren / sportlicheren) Look aus.

5. Das Tragen von Lederhosen ist eine (bayrische / norddeutsche) Tradition.

6. Für Hans ist Meline die (schwierigste / schönste) Person, die er jemals kennen gelernt hat.

7. George findet, dass Hans sich (rasieren / entschuldigen) sollte.

8. Er denkt, Hans sollte Meline Zeit geben, sich zu (schminken / beruhigen).

9. Meline möchte nicht über (Hans / Kunst) reden.

10. Karl hat früher die Wälder erkundet und ist im (See / Fluss) geschwommen.

George

Hans

Meline

Sabite

Faik

Karl

Herr Kleinedler

Nützliche Ausdrücke

- **liebenswürdig**
  amiable
- **erschaffen**
  to create
- **erforschen**
  to explore
- **die Eiche**
  oak tree
- **begleiten**
  to accompany
- **Wer immer das auch sein mag.**
  Whoever that may be.
- **Was ist an Lederhosen auszusetzen?**
  What's wrong with lederhosen?
- **rasend**
  furious
- **sich beruhigen**
  to calm down

4A.1
- **Ich hätte das nicht sagen sollen?**
  I shouldn't have said that?

4A.2
- **Es war eine herrliche Landschaft mit singenden Vögeln und blühenden Blumen.**
  It was a beautiful countryside with singing birds and blooming flowers.

7

HANS Ich hätte das nicht sagen sollen? Ich muss mich entschuldigen?
SABITE Noch nicht. Du würdest es nur schlimmer machen.
GEORGE Lass sie sich erst einmal beruhigen!
HANS Ich gehe nach Hause.

8

GEORGE Wer war das?
MELINE Mikhail Zagoruychenko.
GEORGE Russe?
MELINE Ja.
GEORGE Langweilig? Und Hans?
MELINE Ich möchte nicht darüber reden.

9

SABITE Hallo.
KARL Hallo. Schön, dass wir uns treffen.
SABITE Ich liebe diesen Ort.

10

SABITE Woher kommst du?
KARL Wir kommen aus einem Tal in der Nähe von Zürich. Wir haben die Wälder erkundet und sind im See geschwommen. Es war eine herrliche Landschaft mit singenden Vögeln und blühenden Blumen.

---

2 **Zum Besprechen** Organisieren Sie ein Picknick für das nächste Wochenende. Wohin soll es gehen? Wann geht es los? Wie kommen Sie dorthin? Was gibt es zu essen? Wen laden Sie ein? Besprechen Sie die Pläne Ihrer Gruppe mit dem Rest der Klasse. Answers will vary.

2 **Expansion** Ask students which group's picnic they would most like to attend and why.

3 **Vertiefung** Karl kommt aus einem Tal in der Nähe von Zürich. Finden Sie heraus, welche Freizeitaktivitäten unter freiem Himmel (*outdoors*) dieser Teil der Schweiz bietet. Was würden Sie dort am liebsten tun?
Answers will vary.

Ressourcen

v̂Text

VM
p. 93

vhlcentral

Landschaften Deutschlands Reading

AP* Theme: Global Challenges
Context: Environmental Issues

connections
cultures

VOM WATTENMEER° IM HOHEN Norden bis zu den bayerischen Alpen: Deutschland ist ein Land mit vielen verschiedenen Landschaften und einer Vielzahl an heimischen Tieren. Besonders in den Nationalparks findet man seltene Tiere, Vögel und Pflanzen.

Nationalpark Bayerischer Wald

Der Nationalpark Bayerischer Wald ist der älteste Nationalpark Deutschlands. Nirgendwo zwischen Atlantik und Ural gibt es einen so großen Wald, der sich ganz natürlich entwickeln° darf. Es ist ein wilder Wald, in dem es 17 Fledermausarten° gibt. Außerdem kann man Luchse° in freier Natur sehen und acht verschiedene Spechtarten° entdecken.

Biosphärenreservat Spreewald

Dieses Reservat in Brandenburg ist mit 500 Quadratkilometern eine der größten Fluss- und Auenlandschaften° Mitteleuropas. Die Flüsse und Kanäle sind hier etwa 1.500 Kilometer lang: ein Traum für Kanu- und Kajakfreunde. Wer Tiere mag, kann hier Otter, Biber°, Eisvogel° und Prachtlibelle° bewundern. Auch zu sehen sind etwa 1.600 Pflanzenarten wie zum Beispiel diverse Orchideen, Schwertlilien° und die Kuckuckslichtnelke°.

Nationalpark Sächsische Schweiz

Der Nationalpark Sächsische Schweiz, der in Sachsen liegt und an die Tschechische Republik angrenzt°, ist erst 20 Jahre alt. Er ist ein Paradies für Kletterfans und Wanderer. Seltene Pflanzen gibt es hier; das Gelbe Veilchen° ist noch ein Relikt aus der Eiszeit°. Vogelfans können hier Schwarzstörche, Uhus° und Wanderfalken° sehen. Außerdem gibt es Feuersalamander und Fischotter.

Gefährdete° Arten Deutschlands			
Säugetiere°:	6	Fische:	21
Vögel:	6	Weichtiere°:	9
Reptilien:	0	Pflanzen:	12

QUELLE: Rote Liste gefährdeter Arten (2009)

Suggestion Remind students that they read about another bio-diverse landscape, **National Park Niedersächsisches Wattenmeer**, in **Vol. 2, Kapitel 3.**

Wattenmeer *intertidal zone* **entwickeln** *develop* **Fledermausarten** *bat species* **Luchse** *lynxes* **Spechtarten** *woodpecker species* **Auenlandschaften** *meadow landscapes* **Biber** *beaver* **Eisvogel** *kingfisher* **Prachtlibelle** *banded damselfly* **Schwertlilien** *irises* **Kuckuckslichtnelke** *ragged robin* **angrenzt** *borders* **Gelbe Veilchen** *twoflower violet* **Eiszeit** *Ice Age* **Uhus** *eagle owls* **Wanderfalken** *peregrine falcons* **Gefährdete** *Endangered* **Säugetiere** *mammals* **Weichtiere** *molluscs*

Expansion Ask students: **Welche Nationalparks haben Sie besucht? Was hat Ihnen da gefallen? Was haben Sie alles gesehen? Gibt es da irgendwelche besonderen Tiere, Pflanzen usw?**

ÜBUNGEN

1 **Richtig oder falsch?** Sagen Sie, ob die Sätze richtig oder falsch sind. Korrigieren Sie die falschen Sätze.

1. Der älteste deutsche Nationalpark ist der Nationalpark Bayerischer Wald.
   Richtig.
2. Der Nationalpark Bayerischer Wald ist der größte wilde Wald in Europa.
   Richtig.
3. Das Biosphärenreservat Spreewald liegt in Sachsen.
   Falsch. Es liegt in Brandenburg.
4. Kanu- und Kajakfreunde finden Flüsse und Kanäle im Bayerischen Wald.
   Falsch. Man findet sie im Biosphärenreservat Spreewald.
5. Schwertlilien findet man in der Sächsischen Schweiz.
   Falsch. Man findet sie im Biosphärenreservat Spreewald.

6. Der Nationalpark Sächsische Schweiz liegt in der Nähe der Tschechischen Republik. Richtig.

7. Der Nationalpark Sächsische Schweiz ist noch sehr jung. Richtig.

8. Eine der ältesten Blumenarten im Nationalpark Sächsische Schweiz ist das Gelbe Veilchen. Richtig.

9. Es gibt in Deutschland keine gefährdeten Fischarten.
   Falsch. Es gibt in Deutschland 21 gefährdete Fischarten.
10. Es gibt in Deutschland sechs gefährdete Vogelarten. Richtig.

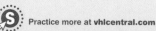

Naturkatastrophen

das Erdbeben, -	*earthquake*
die Lawine, -en	*avalanche*
der Tornado, -s	*tornado*
der Treibsand	*quicksand*
der Vulkan, -e	*volcano*

Der Weißstorch

Der Weißstorch ist ein mitteleuropäischer Vogel, den man vor allem in Deutschland, Österreich, Polen und der Schweiz finden kann. Er ist weiß mit schwarzen Flügeln°. Beine und Schnabel° sind rot. Er überwintert in Afrika. Der Storch kehrt jedes Jahr zum gleichen Nest zurück, und so kann es nach vielen Jahren über eine Tonne wiegen. In Deutschland gelten Störche als Glücksbringer°. Der Sage° nach bringen sie auch die neugeborenen Kinder.

Flügeln *wings* **Schnabel** *beak* **Glücksbringer** *good luck charms* **Sage** *legend*
AP* Theme: Beauty & Aesthetics
Context: Cultural Perspectives

Alexander von Humboldt

Suggestion You may want to read students an excerpt from Daniel Kehlmann's popular book *Die Vermessung der Welt*, which offers a fictionalized account of Humboldt's travels through South America.

Friedrich Wilhelm Heinrich Alexander von Humboldt wurde am 14. September 1769 in Berlin geboren und starb dort am 6. Mai 1859. Er war Naturforscher und Begründer° der heutigen Geographie. Vor allem durch seine Reise nach Amerika, auf der er zwischen 1799 und 1804 das heutige Venezuela, Peru, Mexiko und die USA besuchte, wurde er weltweit berühmt. Seine Entdeckungen in den Bereichen der Botanik, Zoologie, Klimatologie und Ozeanographie dokumentierte er in seinem Werk *Kosmos*. Wegen seines großen Einflusses auf Botanik und Zoologie tragen heute eine Orchideen-, eine Lilien-, eine Kaktus°-, eine Pinguin-, eine Fledermaus- und mehrere Affenarten° seinen Namen. Allein in den USA heißen acht Städte Humboldt und der wichtige Humboldtstrom fließt entlang der Küste Südamerikas.

Begründer *founder* **Kakteen** *cactus* **Affenarten** *monkey species*

AP* Theme: Science & Technology
Context: Social Impacts

🔊 IM INTERNET

Suchen Sie im Internet eine europäische Pflanze oder ein europäisches Tier, über das Sie gerne mehr wissen möchten: Wie sieht es aus? Wo kann man es finden? Was frisst es?

Find out more at **vhlcentral.com**.

---

2 **Was fehlt?** Ergänzen Sie die Sätze.

1. Der Weißstorch hat schwarze ___Flügel___.
2. Der Weißstorch fliegt im Winter nach ___Afrika___.
3. Weißstörche benutzen jedes ___Jahr___ dasselbe Nest.
4. Alexander von Humboldt hat die heutige ___Geographie___ begründet.
5. Die Erlebnisse seiner Reise dokumentierte er in seinem Werk ___Kosmos___.
6. Viele Pflanzen und Tiere tragen seinen ___Namen___.

3 **Die Natur** Diskutieren Sie mit einem Partner / einer Partnerin Ihre Einstellung (*attitude*) zur Natur. Sind Sie gerne in der Natur oder nicht? Warum? Was sind einige positive und negative Aspekte der Natur?

3 **Partner Chat** You can also assign activity 3 on the Supersite. Students work in pairs to record the activity online. The pair's recorded conversation will appear in your gradebook.

Ressourcen

v̂Text · vhlcentral

Der Konjunktiv der Vergangenheit  Presentation

Startblock In **1B.1**, you learned to use the **Konjunktiv II** to talk about hypothetical events or to express wishes about the present or the future. You can use a past form, **der Konjunktiv der Vergangenheit**, to speculate about events that could have happened, or to express wishes about the past.

Ich **hätte** nie **gedacht**, dass du solche Gefühle hast.

Das **hätte** ich nie **sagen sollen**.

- The formation of the **Konjunktiv der Vergangenheit** is similar to that of the **Plusquamperfekt**.

PLUSQUAMPERFEKT	KONJUNKTIV DER VERGANGENHEIT
Ich **hatte** ihm das **gesagt**.	Ich wünschte, ich **hätte** ihm das **gesagt**.
*I **had said** that to him.*	*I wish I **had said** that to him.*

- To form the **Konjunktiv der Vergangenheit**, use the **Konjunktiv II** of **sein** or **haben** with a past participle.

Konjunktiv der Vergangenheit			
	wissen	**gehen**	**sich informieren**
ich	hätte gewusst	wäre gegangen	hätte mich informiert
du	hättest gewusst	wärest gegangen	hättest dich informiert
er/sie/es	hätte gewusst	wäre gegangen	hätte sich informiert
wir	hätten gewusst	wären gegangen	hätten uns informiert
ihr	hättet gewusst	wäret gegangen	hättet euch informiert
Sie/sie	hätten gewusst	wären gegangen	hätten sich informiert

Ich wünschte, ich **hätte** den Sonnenaufgang **gesehen**.
*I wish I **had seen** the sunrise.*

Wenn wir früher **angekommen wären**, **hätten** wir mehr Zeit **gehabt**.
*If we **had arrived** earlier, we **would have had** more time.*

Wenn du nur früher **aufgewacht wärest**!
*If only you **had woken up** earlier!*

Wenn ich mehr Zeit gehabt **hätte**, **hätte** ich mich besser darüber **informiert**.
*If I **had had** more time, I **would have found out** more about it.*

- To use a modal in the **Konjunktiv der Vergangenheit**, replace the past participle with a double infinitive (verb infinitive + modal infinitive). This construction is most common with the modals **können**, **müssen**, and **sollen**.

Ich **hätte** es **wissen sollen**.
*I **should have known**.*

Sie **hätte** uns **helfen können**.
*She **could have helped** us.*

Sie **hätten sich** nicht **streiten sollen**.
*They **shouldn't have argued**.*

Du **hättest** den Wasserfall **fotografieren sollen**.
*You **should have taken a picture** of the waterfall.*

- In a subordinate clause with a modal, place the conjugated form of **haben** *before* the double infinitive at the end of the clause.

> Die Lehrerin hat Paul gesagt, dass er seine Hausaufgabe **hätte machen sollen**.
> *The teacher told Paul that he **should have done** his homework.*

> Wir wussten nicht, dass wir hier ein Picknick **hätten machen können**.
> *We didn't know that we **could have had** a picnic here.*

- When a modal is used without an accompanying infinitive, the **Konjunktiv der Vergangenheit** is formed as with other verbs.

> Er **hätte** das nicht **gekonnt**.
> *He **wouldn't have been able to do** that.*

> Wir **hätten** das nicht **gewollt**.
> *We **wouldn't have wanted** that.*

- Use the **Konjunktiv der Vergangenheit** to express wishes about events that are already past.

> Ich wünschte, ich **hätte** mehr Zeit **gehabt**, um den Wald zu erforschen.
> *I wish I **had had** more time to explore the forest.*

> Wenn wir nur länger auf der Insel **hätten bleiben können**!
> *If only we **could have stayed** on the island longer!*

- Use the **Konjunktiv der Vergangenheit** to make statements or ask questions about hypothetical situations in the past.

> Was **wäre passiert**, wenn ich dort nicht pünktlich **angekommen wäre**?
> *What **would have happened** if I **hadn't gotten** there in time?*

> Was **hättet** ihr an seiner Stelle **gemacht**?
> *What **would** you **have done** in his place?*

> Wenn das Wetter schön **gewesen wäre**, **hätten wir** ein Picknick **gemacht**.
> *If the weather **had been** nice, we **would have had** a picnic.*

> Wenn sie sehr krank **gewesen wäre**, **hätten** wir sie ins Krankenhaus **bringen müssen**.
> *If she **had been** really sick, we **would have had to take** her to the hospital.*

 Jetzt sind Sie dran!   Wählen Sie die passenden Wörter.

1. Wenn ich nur nichts gesagt (hätte / wäre)!

2. Wir wünschten, wir (wären / hätten) am Wochenende wandern gegangen.

3. Wenn er keinen Unfall (gehabt / haben) hätte, hätte er sein Fahrrad nicht reparieren müssen.

4. Wenn die Klippe nicht so hoch (gewesen / sein) wäre, wären wir hinaufgeklettert.

5. Ich wünschte, ich (haben / hätte) als Kind ein Kaninchen gehabt.

6. Er wusste nicht, dass er den Hausmeister hätte (anrufen sollen / sollen anrufen).

7. Wenn wir den Bauernhof (wären / hätten) finden können, hätten wir frische Milch gekauft.

8. Welchen Weg (hättest / wärest) du durch den Wald genommen?

9. Was für ein Wasserfall! Wenn ihr ihn nur hättet (sehen / gesehen) können!

10. Ich (wäre / hätte) gern mit euch aufs Land gefahren.

Anwendung

1 Sätze umschreiben
Schreiben Sie die Sätze in den Konjunktiv der Vergangenheit um.

BEISPIEL

Wir kämen mit.
Wir wären mitgekommen.

Wir würden sie anrufen.
Wir hätten sie angerufen.

1. Ich schliefe länger. Ich hätte länger geschlafen.
2. Gingest du mit ihnen aus? Wärest du mit ihnen ausgegangen?
3. Er würde viel wandern. Er wäre viel gewandert.
4. Ihr solltet kündigen. Ihr hättet kündigen sollen.
5. Sie gäben eine Party. Sie hätten eine Party gegeben.
6. Ich könnte das nicht. Ich hätte das nicht gekonnt.
7. Wir müssten trainieren. Wir hätten trainieren müssen.
8. Sie würde nach Hause fahren. Sie wäre nach Hause gefahren.

2 Hypothesen
Bilden Sie Sätze im Konjunktiv der Vergangenheit. Suggested answers provided.

BEISPIEL wenn der Manager / mich / nur / früher anrufen
Wenn der Manager mich nur früher angerufen hätte!

1. wenn die Assistentin / nur nicht / kündigen
Wenn die Assistentin nur nicht gekündigt hätte!
2. wenn seine Empfehlungsschreiben / nur / besser sein
Wenn seine Empfehlungsschreiben nur besser gewesen wären!
3. wenn ich / nur / mehr Geld haben Wenn ich nur mehr Geld gehabt hätte!
4. wenn die Katze / nur nicht / die Maus fangen Wenn die Katze nur nicht die Maus gefangen hätte!
5. wenn Jonas / nur nicht / seinen Schlüssel verlieren
Wenn Jonas nur nicht seinen Schlüssel verloren hätte!
6. wenn die Blätter / nur nicht / vom Baum fallen
Wenn die Blätter nur nicht vom Baum gefallen wären!
7. wenn das Gras / nur nicht / so nass werden Wenn das Gras nur nicht so nass geworden wäre!
8. wenn ich / nur / länger bleiben können Wenn ich nur länger hätte bleiben können!

3 Wenn es anders gewesen wäre
Schreiben Sie die Sätze um.
Sagen Sie, was passiert wäre, wenn die Situation anders gewesen wäre.
Verwenden Sie dabei den Konjunktiv der Vergangenheit. Suggested answers provided.

BEISPIEL Ich bin spät nach Hause gekommen und ich war am nächsten Tag müde.
Wenn ich nicht spät nach Hause gekommen wäre, wäre ich am nächsten Tag nicht müde gewesen.

1. Der Boden war so nass, dass die Frau hingefallen ist.
Wenn der Boden nicht so nass gewesen wäre, wäre die Frau nicht hingefallen.
2. Es hat einen Sturm gegeben und die Wanderer konnten ihre Bergtour nicht machen.
Wenn es keinen Sturm gegeben hätte, hätten die Wanderer ihre Bergtour machen können.
3. Die Kinder haben Angst gehabt und sind ins Haus gelaufen.
Wenn die Kinder keine Angst gehabt hätten, wären sie nicht ins Haus gelaufen.
4. Wir hatten Vollmond (*full moon*) und ich habe nicht schlafen können.
Wenn wir keinen Vollmond gehabt hätten, hätte ich schlafen können.
5. Weil der Weg an einer Klippe endete, mussten sie zurückgehen.
Wenn der Weg nicht an einer Klippe geendet hätte, hätten sie nicht zurückgehen müssen.
6. Mein Hund hat nicht auf mich gehört und ist auf die Straße gerannt.
Wenn mein Hund auf mich gehört hätte, wäre er nicht auf die Straße gerannt.

2 Suggestion Quickly review the **Partizipien** of the verbs provided and have students identify which verbs take **hätte** and which take **wäre**.

2 Expansion Have students choose one sentence, build a scenario around it, and turn it into a short dialogue to share with the class.

Kommunikation

4 **Ich nicht** Schauen Sie sich die Bilder an und erzählen Sie sich, was Sie anders gemacht hätten. Benutzen Sie den Konjunktiv der Vergangenheit. Answers will vary.

> **BEISPIEL**
>
> **S1:** Ich wäre nicht so schnell gefahren!
> **S2:** Ich hätte länger an der Kreuzung gewartet!

---

5 **Wenn nur!** Was wäre wenn? Arbeiten Sie mit einem Partner / einer Partnerin und diskutieren Sie, was im letzten Jahr passiert wäre, wäre die Situation anders gewesen. Verwenden Sie dazu den Konjunktiv der Vergangenheit. Answers will vary.

BEISPIEL

S1: Was wäre (passiert), wenn ich fleißiger gelernt hätte?
S2: Du hättest vielleicht eine bessere Note bekommen!
S1: Was wäre passiert, wenn der Winter nicht so kalt gewesen wäre?
S2: Dann hätte ich nicht so viel gefroren.

---

6 **Was hättest du lieber gemacht?** Berichten Sie Ihrem Partner / Ihrer Partnerin von zwei Aktivitäten, die Sie letztes Wochenende gemacht haben. Erzählen Sie sich, was Sie lieber gemacht hätten, und verwenden Sie dabei den Konjunktiv der Vergangenheit. Answers will vary.

BEISPIEL

S1: Was hast du am Wochenende gemacht?
S2: Am Samstag habe ich ein Referat für Geschichte geschrieben und am Sonntag bin ich zum Waschsalon gefahren.
S1: Und was hättest du lieber gemacht?
S2: Ich hätte lieber länger geschlafen. Ich wäre auch lieber ins Kino gegangen.

---

7 **Vor 100 Jahren** Was hätten Sie (nicht) machen können, müssen oder dürfen, wenn Sie vor hundert Jahren gelebt hätten? Answers will vary.

BEISPIEL

S1: Ich hätte nicht im Internet surfen können.
S2: Ich hätte keinen Minirock tragen dürfen.

4 Suggestion If students have difficulty spontaneously producing the past subjunctive in this activity, have them prepare their answers as written homework, and then share them with a partner during the next class.

4 Partner Chat You can also assign activity 4 on the Supersite. Students work in pairs to record the activity online. The pair's recorded conversation will appear in your gradebook.

5 Partner Chat You can also assign activity 5 on the Supersite. Students work in pairs to record the activity online. The pair's recorded conversation will appear in your gradebook.

6 Virtual Chat You can also assign activity 6 on the Supersite. Students record individual responses that appear in your gradebook.

7 Partner Chat You can also assign activity 7 on the Supersite. Students work in pairs to record the activity online. The pair's recorded conversation will appear in your gradebook.

4A.2   *Das Partizip Präsens*  Presentation

QUERVERWEIS

See **3B.2** to review adjective endings.

Suggestion Have students review the formation of comparatives and superlatives, taught in **Vol. 2, 4A.2.**

Suggestion Explain that while an English present participle may be used as a noun (*smoking is prohibited*), German present participles cannot.

Startblock The present participle (**das Partizip Präsens**) can be used as an adjective or an adverb. It is used more often in writing than in spoken German.

... es gibt auch von anderen ausgezeichneten Künstlern so viele neue **aufregende** Werke.

Es war eine herrliche Landschaft mit **singenden** Vögeln und **blühenden** Blumen.

- To form the present participle in German, add **-d** to the infinitive.

Suggestion Emphasize to students that *any* infinitive can be turned into an adjective or adverb by adding **-d**, followed by an adjective ending where necessary.

present participle	
klingelnd	*ringing*
lachend	*laughing*
wachsend	*growing*

Suggestion Point out that the second example sentence is a **Sprichwort**, similar to the English proverb, "Let sleeping dogs lie."

- When you use present participles as adjectives, follow the normal rules for adjective endings.

Der **aufgehende** Mond war sehr schön.
*The **rising** moon was beautiful.*

Schlafende Hunde soll man nicht wecken.
*You shouldn't wake a **sleeping** dog.*

Michael Hanekes Filme sind **bedeutend**.
*Michael Haneke's films are **important**.*

- Present participles can also be used as adverbs. When used as adverbs, they do not have added endings.

Nachdem der Junge vom Baum gefallen war, lief er **weinend** nach Hause.
*After the boy fell out of the tree, he ran home **crying**.*

Er sah ihr **suchend** in die Augen.
*He looked **searchingly** into her eyes.*

Suggestion Point out that a present participle and a past participle can be used together as attributive adjectives. Ex.: **die folgenden vergessenen historischen Orte.**

Jetzt sind Sie dran!   **Wählen Sie die passenden Wörter.**

1. Peter ist ein gut (aussehend / (aussehender) / aussehenden) Bauer.

2. Die (spielend / (spielenden) / spielende) Eichhörnchen sind niedlich (*cute*).

3. Wir fahren am (kommend / (kommenden) / kommendes) Wochenende an den See.

4. Hast du auch die (passend / passende / (passenden)) Schuhe zu diesem Kleid?

5. Das Mädchen lief ((singend) / singende / singender) durch den Wald.

6. Wo ist hier ein (funktionierend / (funktionierender) / funktionierenden) Drucker?

7. Die Kinder laufen ((lachend) / lachende / lachendes) durch das Feld.

8. Das war ein (überraschend / überraschenden / (überraschender)) Besuch!

9. ((Anschließend) / Anschließende / Anschließenden) gingen wir alle ins Kino.

10. Bitte beantworten Sie die (folgend / (folgenden) / folgende) Fragen.

Anwendung und Kommunikation

1 Partizipien
Ergänzen Sie die richtigen Partizipendungen. Wenn Sie keine Endung brauchen, machen Sie einen Strich (*slash*).

> **BEISPIEL** Der Zirkus hatte einen tanzend__en__ Bären (*bear*).
> Sein Tanzen war überraschend_____ gut.

1. Die laufend__en__ Kosten sind circa 120 Euro monatlich.
2. Sie hat das weinend__e__ Baby nicht beruhigen (*calm down*) können.
3. Wir fahren in der kommend__en__ Woche an den Strand.
4. Der Film war aufregend_____.
5. Wegen stark steigend__er__ Ölpreise wird alles teurer.
6. Ein schlafend__er__ Hund liegt vor der Tür.
7. Die Prüfung war überraschend_____ einfach.
8. Sein klingelnd__es__ Handy ist allen auf die Nerven gegangen.

2 Bilder beschreiben
Beschreiben Sie bei jedem Bild, was gerade passiert. Benutzen Sie dabei die Verben aus der Liste. Danach wiederholt Ihr Partner / Ihre Partnerin den Satz, aber er/sie muss das Verb in ein Partizip umändern (*change*). Answers will vary.

klingeln	spielen
scheinen	weinen
schlafen	

▶ **BEISPIEL**
S1: *Der Mond scheint hell diese Nacht.*
S2: *Ja, das ist ein hell scheinender Mond.*

Der Mond...

Die Katze...

Das Kind...

Der Wecker...

Die Mädchen...

3 Umweltprobleme
Schlagen Sie sich gegenseitig mögliche Lösungen (*solutions*) für die folgenden Probleme vor. Answers will vary.

S1: *Die Temperaturen steigen.*
S2: *Was können wir gegen die steigenden Temperaturen tun?*
S1: *Wir könnten weniger Auto fahren.*

1. Die Temperaturen steigen.
2. Der Müll stinkt.
3. Die Regenwälder (*rainforests*) sterben.
4. Die Wasserqualität sinkt.

 Practice more at **vhlcentral.com**.

1 Suggestion Make sure students understand that the participle ending **-d** has already been added, and they just need to decide what, if any, adjective ending is needed. Also, remind students that **wegen** (in item 5) is a genitive preposition. In item 7, point out that **überraschend** is being used as an adverb, not as an adjective.

2 Virtual Chat You can also assign activity 2 on the Supersite. Students record individual responses that appear in your gradebook.

3 Suggestion Remind students that since **gegen** is an accusative preposition, their participles will need accusative endings.

3 Partner Chat You can also assign activity 3 on the Supersite. Students work in pairs to record the activity online. The pair's recorded conversation will appear in your gradebook.

Wiederholung

1 Expansion Have students write down additional conditions. Collect them and have the class come up with logical conclusions.

1 Wie wäre es gewesen?
Wählen Sie eine Angabe (*condition*) aus der Liste und bilden Sie mit einem Partner / einer Partnerin eine logische Folgerung (*conclusion*) daraus. Benutzen Sie den Konjunktiv der Vergangenheit.

Answers will vary.

BEISPIEL

Wenn wir früh aufgestanden wären, hätten wir den Sonnenaufgang gesehen.

früh aufstehen	mehr regnen
das Feld nicht so klein sein	auf den Berg steigen
wandern gehen	ein Boot haben

2 Diskutieren und kombinieren
Auf Ihrem Blatt finden Sie Informationen über vier Personen und vier Urlaubsorte. Berichten Sie Ihrem Partner / Ihrer Partnerin, was Ihre Personen gerne im Urlaub machen.

Answers will vary.

2 Suggestion Give students time to read through each text and underline key words.

BEISPIEL

S1: *Julian Koch liebt das Leben in der Stadt. Aber er segelt auch gerne und geht gerne klettern.*
S2: *Er sollte Salzburg besuchen. Da gibt es viele Theater und Konzerte. Die Berge sind sehr nah und es gibt auch Seen in der Nähe.*

3 Was hätten Sie gemacht?
Sehen Sie sich mit einem Partner / einer Partnerin die Fotos an. Sagen Sie, was jede Person gemacht hat, und fragen Sie einander, was Sie in der gleichen Situation gemacht hätten. Benutzen Sie den Konjunktiv der Vergangenheit. Answers will vary.

3 Partner Chat You can also assign activity 3 on the Supersite.

BEISPIEL

S1: *Sarah ist auf diesem Weg gelaufen. Wärest du darauf gelaufen?*
S2: *Nein. Obwohl dieser Weg sehr schön aussieht, wäre ich dort nicht gelaufen, weil es zu viele Insekten im hohen Gras gibt.*

Sarah / laufen

David / spielen   Lara / schwimmen   Nina / nahekommen

Jonas / klettern gehen   Max / angeln gehen   Hanna / springen

4 Arbeitsblatt
Zeichnen Sie (*draw*) ein Bild mit Tieren, die etwas Unerwartetes (*unexpected*) machen. Bitten Sie drei Personen im Unterricht, das Bild mit Partizipien der Gegenwart zu beschreiben. Schreiben Sie die Antworten auf.

Answers will vary.

BEISPIEL

S1: *Was siehst du auf meinem Bild?*
S2: *Die sprechende Kuh fragt das stehende Pferd, was das singende Huhn sagt.*
S3: *Das singende Huhn erzählt dem denkenden Pferd ...*

5 Regeln
Schreiben Sie mit einem Partner / einer Partnerin Sicherheitsregeln für die folgenden Situationen.

Answers will vary.

5 Virtual Chat You can also assign activity 5 on the Supersite.

BEISPIEL in den Bergen wandern

S1: *Wenn man in den Bergen wandert, soll man auf das Wetter achten.*
S2: *Wenn man in den Bergen wandert, muss man Trinkwasser mitbringen.*

im Wald Fahrrad fahren	auf eine Klippe klettern
in einem See baden	unter einem Wasserfall baden
auf dem Meer segeln	ein Pferd reiten

6 Die Traumlandschaft
Beschreiben Sie einem Partner / einer Partnerin Ihre Traumlandschaft. Benutzen Sie so viele Details wie möglich für Ihre Beschreibung. Ihr Partner / Ihre Partnerin macht sich Notizen, um später allen diese Traumlandschaft beschreiben zu können.

Answers will vary.

BEISPIEL

Neulich habe ich einen komischen Traum gehabt. Ich wanderte in den Bergen und kam auf ein Feld. Beim aufgehenden Mond sah ich einen laufenden Hasen aus dem Wald kommen. Der Hase...

AP* Theme: Personal & Public Identities
Context: Alienation & Integration

Bienenstich
ist aus

Thilo Berndt, Renate Fuhrmann, Lotte Becker,
Eva Pliego und Lucius Woytt

Buch und Regie: Sarah Winkenstette

Eine Produktion der Kunsthochschule
für Medien Köln

© 2009 KHM/Winkenstette

Nützliche Ausdrücke

- **das Apfelmus, -e**
  apple sauce
- **erschrecken**
  to frighten
- **Ich muss dann mal los.**
  I have to go now.
- **der Kirschkuchen, -**
  cherry cake
- **das Lied, -er**
  song
- **das Mittagsschläfchen, -**
  mid-day nap
- **der Seemann, ¨er**
  sailor
- **verrückt**
  crazy
- **wasserscheu**
  afraid of water

Über den Film sprechen

- **der Schlaganfall**
  stroke
- **der Schrebergarten**
  community garden
- **stottern**
  to stutter
- **vermissen**
  to miss

Bienenstich ist aus

Paul stottert und weigert sich (*refuses*) zu sprechen. Seine Eltern reisen viel und Paul ist oft alleine. Er hat keine Freunde. Aber er hat seine Oma, die er sehr lieb hat. In ihrem Garten essen sie oft zusammen Kuchen, am liebsten Bienenstich (*cream-filled cake*). Dort lernt er auch Emma und ihren Hund Anton kennen, die seine Freunde werden.

Vorbereitung

Suggestion Tell students that **Bienenstich** (literally "bee sting" cake) is filled with vanilla cream and topped with caramelized almonds. You may want to bring in a recipe to share with the class.

1 **Was fehlt?** Ergänzen Sie die Sätze mit einem passenden Wort oder Ausdruck aus den Listen.

1. Der ____Kirschkuchen____ kommt frisch aus dem Ofen.
2. Lina geht nicht gern schwimmen, weil sie ____wasserscheu____ ist.
3. Frau Müller ist im Krankenhaus, weil sie letzte Woche einen ____Schlaganfall____ hatte.
4. Diese laute Musik macht mich ganz ____verrückt____.
5. Mit Äpfeln, die vom Baum gefallen sind, könnten wir ____Apfelmus____ machen.
6 Nach einem ____Mittagsschläfchen____ würdest du dich nicht so müde fühlen.
7. Wir haben heute einen Baum im ____Schrebergarten____ gepflanzt.
8. Paul spricht nicht gern, weil er ____stottert____.
9. Die Schlangen ____erschrecken____ mich sehr.
10. Ich habe gestern ein schönes ____Lied____ im Radio gehört.

2 **Partnerarbeit** Besprechen Sie mit einem Partner / einer Partnerin die folgenden Themen.

1. In vielen deutschen Städten gibt es Schrebergärten. Gibt es solche Gärten auch in ihrer Stadt? Wie unterscheiden sie sich von anderen Gärten?
2. In Deutschland kauft man Brot und Kuchen oft bei einem Bäcker und nicht im Supermarkt. Ist dies in ihrem Land auch so? Diskutieren Sie die Vor- und Nachteile der beiden Läden.

Szenen: Bienenstich ist aus

TIM: Ey... Hast du seit Neuestem auch was auf den Augen, oder was?
STEFAN: Lass ihn doch!
TIM: Was, lass ihn doch? Der hätte doch wohl mal eben den Ball aufheben können.
STEFAN: Du weißt doch, wie er ist ...

VERKÄUFERIN: Der Bienenstich ist leider schon aus, tut mir leid. Darf ich dir denn irgendwas anderes geben? Wie wär's denn mit Kirschkuchen? Der ist ganz frisch aus dem Ofen. Ja? Zwei Stück, wie immer?

NACHBARIN: Ach, vielleicht hat sie sich ja auch was gebrochen.
NACHBAR: Gebrochen?
NACHBARIN: Ich weiß nicht, was das ist...
HERR SCHULTE: Das muss ganz plötzlich°, offensichtlich°... Eben hat sie noch gestanden. Ich verstehe das nicht.

HERR SCHULTE: Jetzt reicht's!° Stellen Sie die Musik leiser, Frau Hoffmann!
OMA: (singend) ... deine Freunde sind die Sterne, über Rio und Shanghai, über Bali und Hawaii...
HERR SCHULTE: Ja, ein Seemann müsste man sein. Dann hätte man wenigstens seine Ruhe!

EMMA: Meinst du nicht, dass es deiner Oma stinklangweilig° ist, so alleine im Krankenhaus? Sie vermisst dich bestimmt.
PAUL: Kommst du mit?

OMA: Och, der sieht doch noch ganz gut aus.
PAUL: Bienenstich gab's nicht mehr.
OMA: Mmm, boah°, ist der lecker!

Jetzt reicht's! *That does it!* **boah** *wow* **plötzlich** *suddenly* **offensichtlich** *obviously* **stinklangweilig** *really boring*

Analyse

3 **Richtig oder falsch?** Entscheiden Sie, ob die folgenden Sätze richtig oder falsch sind.

	richtig	falsch
1. Paul hat etwas auf den Augen und sieht nicht gut.	☐	☑
2. Seine Eltern sind nicht oft zu Hause.	☑	☐
3. Pauls Oma singt nicht gern.	☐	☑
4. Paul kann nicht sprechen und auch nicht singen.	☐	☑
5. Emmas Hund heißt Anton.	☑	☐
6. Anton hat alle vier Würstchen aufgegessen.	☑	☐
7. Im Schrebergarten wird Pauls Oma von einer Biene (*bee*) gestochen.	☐	☑
8. Die Nachbarn haben den Krankenwagen gerufen.	☑	☐

4 **Fortsetzung** Überlegen Sie sich mit einem Partner / einer Partnerin, wie der Kurzfilm weitergehen könnte. Wird Pauls Oma wieder gesund? Wie können Paul und seine Eltern ihr dabei helfen? Wird Paul wieder sprechen und sein Stottern überwinden (*overcome*)? Schreiben Sie einen Dialog zwischen Paul und seinen Eltern sowie zwischen Paul und Emma.

5 **Diskutieren** Besprechen Sie die folgenden Themen im Kurs.

• Für Paul ist der Schrebergarten seiner Oma ein Ort, wo er sich gut und sicher fühlt. Haben Sie auch einen Ort, an dem Sie sich besonders gut fühlen? Ist es irgendwo in der freien Natur oder woanders?

• Großeltern spielen eine wichtige Rolle im Leben von vielen Kindern. Besprechen Sie, warum Pauls Oma so wichtig für ihn ist. Versteht er sich gut mit seinen Eltern?

• Werden Menschen diskriminiert, die stottern oder andere Sprachfehler haben? Was kann man tun, um einem Freund, der stottert, zu helfen?

6 **Nachgedacht** Lesen Sie die folgenden Zitate (*quotations*) des römischen Politikers Cicero und des schweizerischen Schriftstellers Curt Goetz. Welchen Bezug (*connection*) haben sie zum Film? Finden Sie, dass die beiden Zitate richtig sind? Begründen Sie Ihre Meinung. Besprechen Sie diese Fragen mit einem Partner / einer Partnerin.

„Reden lernt man nur durch Reden."
—Marcus Tullius Cicero

„Eine Gelegenheit (*opportunity*), den Mund zu halten, sollte man nie vorübergehen lassen."
— Curt Goetz

6 **Suggestion** Make sure students understand the meaning of the quotations before discussing them in pairs. Alternatively, you may wish to discuss them as a class.

 Practice more at **vhlcentral.com**.

Die Umwelt  Vocabulary Tools

AP* Theme: Global Challenges
Context: Environmental Issues

Suggestion Point out that environmental protection is an official national goal for Germany, and has been part of the German **Grundgesetz** since 1994. Ask students if they think environmental protection is a priority in their own country.

Suggestion Point out that Germany has announced plans to abandon nuclear energy by 2022, although some government officials have stated that this goal is unrealistic.

Wortschatz

die Umwelt	*environment*
die Art, -en	*species*
die Erde, -n	*earth*
die Gefahr, -en	*danger*
das Hochwasser, -	*flood*
das Licht, -er	*light*
die Ökologie	*ecology*
der Umweltschutz	*environmentalism*
die Welt, -en	*world*
biologisch	*organic*
gefährdet	*endangered*
ökologisch	*ecological*
umweltfreundlich	*environmentally friendly*
Energie	***energy***
die Windenergie	*wind energy*
Probleme	***problems***
das Aussterben	*extinction*
die Erderwärmung	*global warming*
der Giftmüll	*toxic waste*
die Überbevölkerung	*overpopulation*
Lösungen	***solutions***
das Gesetz, -e	*law*
die erneuerbare Energie (*pl.* die erneuerbaren Energien)	*renewable energy*
das Hybridauto, -s	*hybrid car*
die Regierung, -en	*government*
Verben	***verbs***
ausschalten (schaltet... aus)	*to turn off*
(den Planeten) retten	*to save (the planet)*
einschalten (schaltet... ein)	*to turn on*
entwickeln	*to develop*
erhalten	*to preserve*
schützen	*to protect*
verbessern	*to improve*
verschmutzen	*to pollute*
vorschlagen (schlägt... vor)	*to propose*
wegwerfen (wirft... weg)	*to throw away*

der saure Regen

die Kernenergie

die Sonnenenergie

das Kernkraftwerk, -e

Fabrik

die Fabrik, -en

die Verschmutzung

Sie bilden eine Fahrgemeinschaft.

der Müllwagen, -

Sie recycelt. (recyceln)

das Recycling

der Müll

Anwendung

1 Was passt nicht? Geben Sie an, welches Wort nicht zu den anderen passt.

1. Glas, Papier, (Gras), Plastik
2. erforschen, erfinden, entdecken, (einladen)
3. Smog, (Lösung), Wasserverschmutzung, Giftmüll
4. (Körperenergie), Windenergie, Sonnenenergie, Kernenergie
5. Regierung, Gesetz, Minister, (Gefahr)
6. biologisch, ökologisch, (gefährdet), umweltfreundlich

2 Bilder beschriften Beschriften Sie jedes Bild mit einem passenden Wort aus der Vokabelliste.

1. ___die Sonnenenergie___   2. ___der Müllwagen___   3. ___das Hochwasser___

4. ___das Kernkraftwerk___   5. ___der Müll___   6. ___die Windenergie___

3 Was ist richtig? Ergänzen Sie die Sätze mit einem passenden Ausdruck.

1. Um unsere Umwelt zu schützen, müssen wir alle mehr (recyceln) / wegwerfen).
2. Der saure Regen (verbessert / (verschmutzt)) die Wälder.
3. Viele Tierarten sind ((gefährdet) / erneuerbar).
4. Wenn es plötzlich zu viel regnet, haben die Flüsse (Giftmüll / (Hochwasser)).
5. Es ist wichtig, dass die Regierungen umweltfreundliche ((Gesetze) / Gefahren) vorschlägt.

4 Jeder muss seinen Teil tun Sie hören im Radio einen öffentlichen Aufruf (*public service announcement*) zum Thema Umweltschutz. Hören Sie zu und ergänzen Sie dann jeden Satz mit dem richtigen Wort.

1. Jeder muss seinen Teil (*part*) tun, um unsere ___Umwelt___ zu schützen.
2. Wir sollen Papier und ___Glas___ recyceln.
3. Wir können Strom (*electricity*) sparen, wenn wir nicht in allen Zimmern das ___Licht___ anlassen.
4. Man sollte weniger Produkte konsumieren, die ___Giftmüll___ produzieren.
5. Bio-Lebensmittel sind nicht nur gesünder, sondern auch ___umweltfreundlicher___.

Kommunikation

5 Ein Umweltproblem
Lesen Sie den folgenden Artikel und ergänzen Sie mit einem Partner / einer Partnerin die Sätze. Sample answers are provided.

1. Wir haben eine Krise, weil zu viel ___Energie___ verbraucht wird.
2. Alte Fabriken ___verschmutzen___ den Planeten.
3. Es gibt viele ___Lösungen___ für die Energiekrise.
4. Solar-, Wind- und Kernenergie sind ___erneuerbare___ Energiequellen.
5. Öffentliche Verkehrsmittel und ___Hybridautos___ verbrauchen weniger Energie pro Person.
6. Zusammen können wir den Planeten ___retten___.

5 Expansion Ask students: **Was kann man sonst noch machen um den Planeten zu retten?**

Fokus Umwelt

ENERGIEVERBRAUCH

Die Energiekrise wird zu einem immer ernsteren Problem, das wir so schnell wie möglich angehen (*address*) müssen. Unsere Fabriken sind alt, verbrauchen (*use*) zu viel Energie und tragen (*contribute*) zur Verschmutzung des Planeten bei. Unsere Autos verbrauchen zu viel Benzin und verursachen (*cause*) Smog. Man kann die Energiekrise auf verschiedene Art und Weise lösen (*solve*). Erstens müssen wir weitere erneuerbare Energiequellen wie Solar-, Wind- oder Kernenergie verwenden. In der Stadt könnten wir alle öffentliche Verkehrsmittel oder Hybridautos benutzen. In den Häusern sollten wir versuchen, weniger Energie zu verbrauchen und unseren Stromverbrauch zu kontrollieren. Wir müssen zusammenarbeiten, um den Planeten zu retten!

6 Diskutieren und kombinieren
Sie und Ihr Partner / Ihre Partnerin bekommen zwei verschiedene Arbeitsblätter. Jeder von Ihnen hat nur die Hälfte der Informationen über die verschiedenen Umweltprobleme auf der Welt. Finden Sie heraus, welche Information Ihnen fehlt. Sample answers are provided.

BEISPIEL

S1: *Welches Land auf deiner Karte hat Probleme mit Smog?*
S2: *Mexiko hat Probleme mit Smog. Und auf deiner Karte?*
S1: *Großbritannien hat auch Probleme damit.*

7 Sätze bilden
Bringen Sie die Sätze zu einem logischen Schluss. Vergleichen Sie danach Ihre Antworten mit denen Ihres Partners / Ihrer Partnerin. Answers will vary.

BEISPIEL Das Gute an Hybridautos ist,...

dass sie die Luftverschmutzung in den Städten reduzieren.

1. Die größten Umweltprobleme sind...
2. Die Überbevölkerung ist ein weltweites Problem,...
3. Viele Tierarten sind vom Aussterben bedroht,...
4. Recyceln ist wichtig,...
5. Erneuerbare Energien sind solche,...
6. Um unseren Planeten zu retten,...

8 Karrieren mit Zukunftschancen
Beschreiben Sie in Gruppen drei Berufe, die Ihrer Meinung nach große Zukunftschancen haben. Beschreiben Sie für jeden Beruf die Tätigkeit (*type of work*), den Nutzen in der heutigen Zeit, und warum Ihrer Meinung nach dieser Beruf in der Zukunft noch wichtiger sein wird. Answers will vary.

BEISPIEL

S1: *In der Zukunft wird die Erderwärmung weiter zunehmen.*
S2: *Ein nützlicher Beruf wäre deshalb einer, der...*

Aussprache und Rechtschreibung   Audio

Tongue Twisters

Zungenbrecher (*Tongue twisters*) are a part of German culture. Mastering a tongue twister means being able to say it quickly several times in a row. One popular type of tongue twister reverses sounds, syllables or words.

Rauchlachs mit Lauchreis.   **Allergischer Algerier, algerischer Allergiker.**

Other tongue twisters repeat syllables, words, or phrases that contain similar sounds.

In Ulm, um Ulm und um Ulm herum.   **Der dicke Dachdecker deckte das dicke Dach.**

German allows for the construction of very long compound words. Many such compounds appear in tongue twisters, sometimes as nonsense words.

Postkutschkasten   **Fichtendickicht**   **Kirschenmirschen**

---

1 **Aussprechen** Wiederholen Sie die Zungenbrecher, die Sie hören.

1. zwischen zwei Zwetschgenzweigen
2. ein krummer Krebs kroch
3. der Cottbuser Postkutscher
4. allergischer Algerier

Expansion Have students take turns trying to read these **Zungenbrecher** out loud. Have them search online for additional examples and variations.

2 **Nachsprechen** Wiederholen Sie die Sätze, die Sie hören.

1. Hinter Hermann Hansens Haus hängen hundert Hemden raus.
2. Esel essen Nesseln nicht, Nesseln essen Esel nicht.
3. Der Cottbuser Postkutscher putzt den Cottbuser Postkutschkasten blank.
4. Fischers Fritz fischt frische Fische, frische Fische fischt Fischers Fritz.
5. Zehn Ziegen zogen zehn Zentner Zucker zum Zoo.
6. Es klapperten die Klapperschlangen, bis ihre Klappern schlapper klangen.

3 **Sprichwörter** Wiederholen Sie die Sprichwörter, die Sie hören.

Blaukraut bleibt Blaukraut und Brautkleid bleibt Brautkleid.[1]

Zwischen zwei Zwetschgenzweigen zwitschern zwei Schwalben.[2]

[1] You can't make a silk purse out of a sow's ear. (lit. *Red cabbage remains red cabbage and a wedding dress remains a wedding dress.*)
[2] Between two plum branches twitter two swallows.

Ressourcen

vText   LM   p. 84   vhlcentral

Auf Wiedersehen, Berlin! Video

Zum letzten Mal treffen sich unsere Freunde im Biergarten, um den Abschied von George zu feiern.

Vorbereitung Have students read the title and discuss what they expect to happen in the episode.

NATIONAL communication cultures STANDARDS

HANS Hey, an was arbeitest du?

GEORGE Ich schreibe meine Hausarbeit über ökologische Architektur fertig. Damit der Planet gerettet werden kann, sollten erneuerbare Energien wie Solar- und Windenergie in neuen Gebäuden verwendet werden. Regierungen müssen Gesetze verabschieden, die die Umwelt erhalten. Die Bedrohung durch Abforstung und Verschmutzung darf nicht ignoriert werden. Außerdem...

HANS Ich habe meine Abschlussarbeit für das Semester gestern abgegeben.

GEORGE Ich schlage eine Lösung vor, die Fabriken helfen wird, weniger zu verschmutzen und mehr zu recyceln. Mein Professor sagt, es sei eine gute Sache.

HANS Meline, ich bin's. Bist du da? Es tut mir leid wegen neulich Abend in der Galerie. Können wir darüber reden? Meline?

SABITE Hans! Was machst du denn hier draußen? Oh, Mann.

HANS Meline?

SABITE Sie ist wohl nicht zu Hause.

HANS Sie ist mir immer noch böse, oder? Sie gibt mir gar keine Chance, mich zu entschuldigen. Manchmal verstehe ich sie überhaupt gar nicht. Ich glaube, George hatte recht, wir sind einfach zu unterschiedlich.

SABITE Vielleicht.

SABITE Bist du Hans immer noch böse? Es tut ihm wirklich leid.

MELINE Er hat sehr liebe Nachrichten hinterlassen. Ich bin ihm nicht böse. Ich glaube, dass er ein guter Mensch ist, aber ich... ja...

SABITE Du mochtest ihn mehr, als du ihn nicht mochtest.

MELINE Genau!

MELINE Hallo! George! Das ist für dich. Von uns.

HANS Öffne es, öffne es!

SABITE Vorsichtig!

GEORGE Das ist wunderbar. Habt vielen herzlichen Dank.

GEORGE Ich hätte keine besseren Freunde finden können. Wegen euch war das Jahr in Berlin so großartig.

ÜBUNGEN

1 **Richtig oder falsch?** Entscheiden Sie, ob die folgenden Sätze **richtig** oder **falsch** sind.

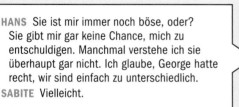

1. George schreibt eine Hausarbeit über Ökotourismus. Falsch.

2. Er schlägt vor, dass in neuen Gebäuden Solar- und Windenergie verwendet wird. Richtig.

3. Hans hat seine Abschlussarbeit für das Semester schon abgegeben. Richtig.

4. Georges Professor gefällt die Lösung nicht, die George vorschlägt. Falsch.

5. Meline versteckt sich in ihrem Zimmer, weil sie Hans nicht sehen möchte. Richtig.

6. Hans hat Meline einen Kuchen mitgebracht. Falsch.

7. Meline ist immer noch böse auf Hans. Falsch.

8. Seine Freunde schenken George einen Stadtplan von Milwaukee. Falsch.

9. Hans möchte mit George die nächsten paar Wochen verreisen. Falsch.

10. Meline und Hans möchten weiterhin Freunde sein. Richtig.

7

MELINE Ich hoffe, wir bleiben in Verbindung?
GEORGE Das werden wir. Ich möchte Wien besuchen.
HANS Ich habe gehört, es soll eine wunderschöne Kulturstadt sein.
SABITE Ähh, George, lass uns...
GEORGE Ja, definitiv.

Nützliche Ausdrücke

- **ein Gesetz verabschieden**
  to pass a law
- **neulich**
  the other day
- **unterschiedlich**
  different
- **eine Nachricht hinterlassen**
  to leave a message
- **in Verbindung bleiben**
  to stay in touch
- **falsch liegen**
  to be wrong

4B.1
- **Mein Professor sagt, es sei eine gute Sache.**
  My professor says it's a worthy cause.

4B.2
- **Die Bedrohung durch Abforstung und Verschmutzung darf nicht ignoriert werden.**
  The threat of deforestation and pollution shouldn't be ignored.

8

HANS Das war nicht nett von mir, tut mir leid. Und wegen neulich Abend, ich... ich war wütend und ich hätte diese Dinge nicht zu dir sagen sollen.
MELINE Es ist schon okay, Hans. Du hast vielleicht gar nicht so falsch gelegen. Es tut mir leid, dass ich dich nicht angerufen habe.

9

HANS Max und ich, wir werden die nächsten paar Wochen verreisen, bevor ich wieder nach Hause zurückkehre, und ich... ich möchte dir nicht weh tun, aber ich kann mich im Moment nicht binden. Ich hoffe, du hast Verständnis dafür.
MELINE Ja, das habe ich. Können wir weiterhin Freunde sein?

10

HANS Auf ein tolles Jahr in Berlin, und neue Freunde.
GEORGE Richtig! Bravo!

---

2 **Zum Besprechen** Am Ende dieser Episode trennen sich Hans und Meline. Denken Sie sich zu zweit ein alternatives Ende der Episode aus. Wie könnte es mit Hans und Meline weitergehen? Entwickeln Sie einen Dialog zwischen Hans und Meline und präsentieren Sie ihn Ihrer Klasse. Answers will vary.

2 **Expansion** Have students write a dialogue in which Hans and Meline meet again after Hans comes back from his vacation.

3 **Vertiefung** Suchen Sie im Internet nach dem „Grünen Punkt". Welches System steckt dahinter? Wann wurde es eingeführt (*introduced*)? In welchen Ländern gibt es den Grünen Punkt? Answers may include: recycling of packaging materials, Duales System Deutschland, introduced 1990 in Germany, most European countries participate.

Ressourcen

v̂ Text   VM   p. 94   vhlcentral

Grüne Berufe in Sachsen Reading

Bauernhöfe und landwirtschaftliche Betriebe haben heute viele verschiedene Funktionen. Sie produzieren nicht nur landwirtschaftliche Produkte wie Fleisch, Obst, Gemüse, Milch und Eier; sie sind auch für den Umweltschutz verantwortlich. Außerdem sind sie sowohl Kunden als auch Arbeitgeber im ländlichen Raum° und deshalb sehr wichtig für die wirtschaftliche Entwicklung einer Region.

Grüne Berufe geben jungen Menschen die Möglichkeit°, viele verschiedene berufliche Tätigkeiten zu lernen. Eine Ausbildung dauert normalerweise drei Jahre. In dieser Zeit sammeln Auszubildende° praktische Kenntnisse bei der Arbeit. Regelmäßig besuchen sie auch die Berufsschule, wo sie die theoretischen Aspekte ihres neuen Berufes lernen. Durch Fort- und Weiterbildungsmöglichkeiten° haben Berufstätige auch die Chance, später in ihrer Karriere eine bessere Perspektive als verantwortliche° Mitarbeiter oder selbstständige Unternehmer° zu bekommen.

GRÜNE BERUFE IN SACHSEN IST EINE Initiative der Regierung, um Jugendliche, die sich für Natur und Umwelt interessieren, in sogenannte „grüne Berufe" zu bringen. Warum sind grüne Berufe so wichtig? Moderne

AP* Theme: Contemporary Life
Context: Education & Career

ländlichen Raum *rural area* **Möglichkeit** *opportunity* **Auszubildende** *apprentices* **Fort- und Weiter bildungsmöglichkeiten** *continuing education* **verantwortliche** *responsible* **selbstständige Unternehmer** *independent entrepreneur* **ziehen... auf** *breed* **bedienen** *operate* **Abfüllanlagen** *bottling systems* **überwachen** *monitor* **hält** *keeps* **züchtet** *breeds*

Grüne Berufe	Stellenbeschreibungen
Fischwirt/ Fischwirtin	Fischwirte arbeiten an den vielen Seen und Flüssen in Deutschland: sie fangen Fische und ziehen sie in Seen auf°.
Milchtechnologe/ Milchtechnologin	Milchtechnologen bedienen° die modernen Produktions- und Abfüllanlagen° und überwachen° die Produktionsprozesse von Milch und Milchprodukten wie Käse oder Jogurt.
Pferdewirt/ Pferdewirtin	Pferdewirte lernen, wie man Pferde richtig hält°, wie man sie reitet und wie man sie züchtet°.

ÜBUNGEN

1 **Richtig oder falsch?** Sagen Sie, ob die Sätze richtig oder falsch sind. Korrigieren Sie die falschen Sätze.

1. In Sachsen gibt es viele grüne Berufe. Richtig.

2. Menschen in grünen Berufen tragen grüne Kleider.
Falsch. Sie arbeiten in Berufen, die mit Natur oder Umwelt zu tun haben.

3. Die Arbeit auf Bauernhöfen ist wichtig für den Umweltschutz. Richtig.

4. Auf Bauernhöfen werden Produkte wie Eier, Fleisch, Milch, Obst und Gemüse produziert. Richtig.

5. Eine Ausbildung dauert normalerweise zwei Jahre. Falsch. Sie dauert normalerweise drei Jahre.

6. Bauernhöfe sind nicht mehr so wichtig für die Wirtschaft im ländlichen Raum. Falsch. Sie sind sehr wichtig für die Wirtschaft im ländlichen Raum.

7. In der Ausbildung arbeitet man und geht in die Berufsschule. Richtig.

8. Ein Milchtechnologe holt die Milch von den Kühen.
Falsch. Ein Milchtechnologe produziert Milchprodukte.

9. Fischwirte fangen Fische und kochen sie.
Falsch. Sie fangen Fische und ziehen sie in Seen auf.

10. Pferdewirte lernen, wie man Pferde reitet. Richtig.

Suggestion Read the **Deutsch im Alltag** words together and ask students which of these things they recycle.

DEUTSCH IM ALLTAG

Abfall und Recycling

der Abfall, ⸚e	waste
die Altkleider	second-hand clothing
das Altpapier	used paper
der Gartenabfall, ⸚e	yard waste
der Schrott	scrap metal
der Verpackungsmüll	packaging waste

DIE DEUTSCHSPRACHIGE WELT

Umweltschutzorganisationen°

Deutschland AP* Theme: Families & Communities
Context: Community Service
Seit 1975 gibt es in Deutschland den Bund für
Umwelt und Naturschutz. Diese Organisation
engagiert° sich für ökologische Landwirtschaft,
gesunde Lebensmittel, den Klimaschutz und
den Ausbau° regenerativer Energien.

Österreich In Österreich gibt es seit 1913
den Naturschutzbund Österreich. Diese
Organisation war bei der Gründung° der
österreichischen Nationalparks sehr aktiv
und hilft auch bei der Erhaltung des Wiener
Waldes, der Krimmler Wasserfälle und der
Hainburger Au.

Die Schweiz In der Schweiz setzt sich die
Organisation Pro Natura seit 1909 für den
Naturschutz ein°. Zu den Erfolgen dieser
Organisation zählt ein Netz° von 600
Naturschutzgebieten°.

Umweltschutzorganisationen *ecology groups*
engagiert *gets involved in* **Ausbau** *development*
Gründung *founding* **setzt sich... ein** *advocates*
Netz *network* **Naturschutzgebieten** *nature reserves*

PORTRÄT

Michael Braungart

Suggestion Ask students: **Gibt es hier irgendwelche Organisationen, die sich für den Umweltschutz einsetzen? Wie heißen sie? Was tun sie alles?**

Michael Braungart, ein Chemiker aus Schwäbisch-Gmünd, arbeitet heute als Professor
an der Erasmus-Universität Rotterdam. In den 80er Jahren war er aktives Mitglied° von
Greenpeace Deutschland. Seither sucht er Antworten auf die folgenden Fragen: Wie
kann der Mensch sich in das Leben auf der Erde integrieren? Wie kann er nicht nur
wenig Schaden anrichten°, sondern wie kann er selbst einen Beitrag für die Umwelt
leisten? Braungart ist bekannt für die Entwicklung von Umweltschutz-Konzepten und
die Konzeption umweltverträglicher Produktionsverfahren°. AP* Theme: Science & Technology
Context: Ethical Considerations

Mitglied *member* **Schaden anrichten** *do damage* **umweltverträglicher Produktionsverfahren** *environmentally friendly production*

🔗 IM INTERNET

Wählen Sie einen Umweltaspekt aus, der Sie besonders interessiert. Suchen Sie Informationen darüber. Machen Sie eine Liste mit Initiativen, die es auf diesem Gebiet gibt.

Find out more at **vhlcentral.com**.

---

2 **Was fehlt?** Ergänzen Sie die Sätze.

1. Der Bund für Umwelt und Naturschutz engagiert sich für den Ausbau regenerativer ___Energien___.

2. Der Naturschutzbund Österreich war bei der Gründung der österreichischen ___Nationalparks___ aktiv.

3. Michael Braungart war in den 80er Jahren ein aktives ___Mitglied___ von Greenpeace Deutschland.

4. Braungart will vor allem Antworten auf zwei ___Fragen___ finden.

3 **Mein Umwelteinfluss** Diskutieren Sie mit einem Partner / einer Partnerin die folgenden Fragen: Was machen Sie, um der Umwelt zu helfen? In Ihrem Alltag? Bei besonderen Anlässen? Wie informieren Sie sich über Umweltprobleme?

3 **Virtual Chat** You can also assign activity 3 on the Supersite. Students record individual responses that appear in your gradebook.

Ressourcen

 vText

 vhlcentral

Der Konjunktiv I and indirect speech  Presentation

Startblock You learned in **1B.1** and **4A.1** about the **Konjunktiv II** and its present and past tense forms. There is another subjunctive, **der Konjunktiv I**, which is used to report what someone else has said.

Mein Professor sagt, es **sei** eine gute Sache.

Sie hat gesagt, sie **werde** sein Geschenk **mitnehmen**.

Der Konjunktiv I

- To form the present tense of the **Konjunktiv I**, add the endings **-e, -est, -e, -en, -et, -en** to the infinitive stem. Only the verb **sein** is irregular: its stem is **sei-** and the first and third person singular have no added endings.

Konjunktiv I Präsens				
	geben	**können**	**haben**	**sein**
ich	geb**e**	könn**e**	hab**e**	sei
du	geb**est**	könn**est**	hab**est**	sei(e)st
er/sie/es	geb**e**	könn**e**	hab**e**	sei
wir	geb**en**	könn**en**	hab**en**	sei**en**
ihr	geb**et**	könn**et**	hab**et**	sei**et**
Sie/sie	geb**en**	könn**en**	hab**en**	sei**en**

Herr Braun sagt, die Erde **sei** wegen Erderwärmung gefährdet.
*Herr Braun says the earth **is** in danger because of global warming.*

Er meint, dass er die Lösung dafür **habe**.
*He believes that he **has** the solution for it.*

- To form the past tense of the **Konjunktiv I**, use the **Konjunktiv I** of **haben** or **sein** with the past participle.

Der *Spiegel* berichtete, dass es gestern sauren Regen **gegeben habe**.
*Der Spiegel reported that acid rain **fell** yesterday.*

Papa sagte, das Paket **sei** heute Morgen **gekommen**.
*Dad said the package **came** this morning.*

- Use the **Konjunktiv I** of **werden** with an infinitive to report a statement someone else has made about the future.

Frau Müller sagte, sie **werde** ein Hybridauto **kaufen**.
*Ms. Müller said she **would buy** a hybrid car.*

Wissenschaftler sagen, sie **werden** eine Lösung für die Erderwärmung **finden**.
*Scientists say they **will find** a solution for global warming.*

Indirect Speech

Expansion Bring in German-language newspapers, or printouts from online newspapers, and have students find statements containing the **Konjunktiv I**.

- In conversation, you can report what someone else said using the **Indikativ**, especially when you want to show that you agree with what was said or that you believe it to be true. If you wish to express skepticism or doubt, however, use the **Konjunktiv I**.

Die Nachbarn sagten, sie **haben** eine Maus **gesehen**.
*The neighbors said they **saw** a mouse.*

Murat sagte, er **werde** später **wiederkommen**.
*Murat said he **would come back** later.*

- In more formal contexts, such as news reports, political speeches, and scientific writing, the **Konjunktiv I** is used to report what people have said without implying that the information is necessarily true or accurate. It is typically introduced with a verb that denotes speech or belief, such as **sagen, berichten** (*to report*), **behaupten** (*to claim*), **meinen** (*to mean, to opine*), or **glauben**.

Die *Zeit* berichtet, dass es einen Atomkraftwerkunfall **gegeben habe**.
*Die Zeit reports that there **was** a nuclear power plant accident.*

Wissenschaftler glauben, dass viele Menschen und Tiere in Gefahr **seien**.
*Scientists believe that many people and animals **are** in danger.*

- The **Konjunktiv I** is used mainly with modals, **wissen, sein**, and third-person singular verbs. In cases where the **Konjunktiv I** conjugation is identical to the present-tense indicative, it is more common to use the **Konjunktiv II** or **würden** + infinitive.

Thomas behaupte, er **habe** das nicht **gewusst**.
*Thomas claimed he **didn't know** that.*

Sarah sagte, dass sie uns vielleicht morgen **besuchen werde**.
*Sarah said that she **might visit** us tomorrow.*

Suggestion Show students an ambiguous sentence in which the indicative and **Konjunktiv II** forms are identical. Ex.: Natasha sagt, ich gebe Ihnen all mein Geld. Then, restate it using the **Konjunktiv II** to avoid the ambiguity: Natasha sagt, ich gäbe Ihnen all mein Geld.

- To express imperatives in indirect speech, use the **Konjunktiv I** or **II** of the modals **sollen** or **müssen**. **Suggestion** Mention that the modal mögen can be used in indirect speech describing polite requests. Ex.: Die Chefin sagte, der Bewerber möge jetzt eintreten.

Die Schüler meinen, die Schule **solle/sollte** nicht so viel Papier **verschwenden**.
*The students feel that the school **shouldn't waste** so much paper.*

Die Geschäftsführerin sagte, wir **müssten** mehr **recyceln**.
*Our manager said we **should recycle** more.*

- The tense of the verb in indirect speech is the same as the tense in the original direct speech.

Der Bundespräsident: „Unser Land **braucht** mehr Windenergie."
*The President: "Our country **needs** more wind energy."*

Der Bundespräsident meint, unser Land **brauche** mehr Windenergie.
*The President believes that our country **needs** more wind energy.*

QUERVERWEIS

See **2A.1** to review indirect questions.

ACHTUNG

When you are reporting what someone else said, personal pronouns, possessive adjectives, and adverbs of time and place may need to be changed accordingly:

Paul: „*Ich* freue *mich* auf *meinen* Urlaub."

Paul sagte, dass *er sich* auf *seinen* Urlaub freue.

QUERVERWEIS

See **1B.1** and **1B.2** to review **Konjunktiv II** and the **würden** + infinitive construction.

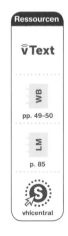

Ressourcen

v̂Text

WB
pp. 49–50

LM
p. 85

vhlcentral

Jetzt sind Sie dran! **Entscheiden Sie, ob die folgenden Sätze im Indikativ oder im Konjunktiv I stehen.**

Expansion Write two sentences on the board, one in the **Indikativ** and one in the **Konjunktiv I**. Ex.: **Er hat keine Schuhe. Er habe keine Schuhe**. Ask students to explain the difference in English.

	Indikativ	Konjunktiv I		Indikativ	Konjunktiv I
1. Maria sagte, sie sei krank.	☐	☑	7. Ihr sagt, ihr benutzt wenig Energie.	☑	☐
2. Du sagst, du fährst nur Hybridautos.	☑	☐	8. Er sagte, er werde Lösungen entwickeln.	☐	☑
3. Er meinte, die Umwelt bleibe in Gefahr.	☐	☑	9. Sie meinte, sie habe ihren Müll getrennt.	☐	☑
4. Sie sagte, sie habe eine Lösung vorgeschlagen.	☐	☑	10. Erika sagte, sie kaufe nur biologische Lebensmittel.	☐	☑
5. Max sagt, er wird Windenergie benutzen.	☑	☐	11. Alex sagt, er wird die Umwelt schützen.	☑	☐
6. Er glaubt, er werde den Planeten retten.	☐	☑	12. Ihr sagt, ihr habt keinen Giftmüll produziert.	☑	☐

Anwendung

1 **Was ist richtig?** Ihr Freund hat keine Lust mit Ihnen ins Konzert zu gehen. Berichten Sie Ihren anderen Freunden, was er gesagt hat. Wählen Sie die passenden Verbformen des Konjunktiv I.

BEISPIEL Er sagte, er (war /(sei)) zu müde, um ins Konzert zu gehen.

Er sagte, ...

1. er ((müsse)/ muss) noch für eine schwere Prüfung am nächsten Tag lernen.
2. er (hatte / (habe)) nicht genug Geld, eine Konzertkarte zu kaufen.
3. er (wollte / (wolle)) heute Abend früh ins Bett gehen.
4. das Konzert ((werde)/ wird) schon ausverkauft (*sold out*) sein.
5. ich ((solle)/ soll) jemand anders einladen.

2 **Welche Zeitform?** Markieren Sie die richtigen Zeitformen.

	Indikativ	Konjunktiv I Präsens	Konjunktiv I Vergangenheit	Konjunktiv I Zukunft
1. er habe nichts gemacht	☐	☐	☑	☐
2. sie werde ihn heiraten	☐	☐	☐	☑
3. ich dürfe das nicht	☐	☑	☐	☐
4. sie sind angekommen	☑	☐	☐	☐
5. du werdest kündigen	☐	☐	☐	☑
6. sie seien abgefahren	☐	☐	☑	☐
7. sie wollte umziehen	☑	☐	☐	☐
8. ihr habet eine Idee	☐	☑	☐	☐

3 **Suggestion** Do the first few items together as a class.

3 **Unsere Gegenwart** Formen Sie die Sätze in indirekte Rede um. Suggested answers provided.

BEISPIEL „Der Wasserspiegel (*water level*) der Weltmeere steigt."Der Wissenschaftler erklärte, dass *der Wasserspiegel der Weltmeere steige.*

1. „Die Regenwald (*rainforest*) muss gerettet werden."
   Die Wissenschaftlerin sagte, dass ____der Regenwald gerettet werden müsse____.
2. „Die Solarzellen werden Ihre Energiekosten reduzieren."
   Der Elektriker sagte dem Mann, dass ____die Solarzellen seine Energiekosten reduzieren würden____.
3. „Wollen Sie in dieser Firma ein Praktikum machen?"
   Der Personalchef fragte mich, ob ____ich in dieser Firma ein Praktikum machen wolle____.
4. „Warum recycelst du nicht deinen alten Computer?"
   Jan fragte seine Freundin, warum ____sie nicht ihren alten Computer recycle____.
5. „Die Papierfabrik hat seit Jahren die Luft verschmutzt."
   Der Bürgermeister klagte (*complained*), dass ____die Papierfabrik seit Jahren die Luft verschmutzt habe____.
6. „Ich weiß nicht, ob man diesen Nationalpark erhalten kann."
   Die Innenministerin sagte, ____sie wisse nicht, ob man diesen Nationalpark erhalten könne____.

S Practice more at **vhlcentral.com**.

Kommunikation

4 **Ein Streitgespräch** Schreiben Sie mit einem Partner / einer Partnerin einen kurzen Dialog zu dem Bild. Dann berichten Sie zwei anderen Studenten, was die Leute auf dem Bild gesagt haben. Verwenden Sie den Konjunktiv I. Answers will vary.

BEISPIEL

Dialog:
Mann: *Warum bist du so böse (angry) auf mich?*
Frau: *Weil du niemals bei der Hausarbeit hilfst.*
Mann: *Das ist nicht wahr! ...*

Bericht:
Der Mann hat die Frau gefragt, warum sie so böse auf ihn sei. Die Frau hat geantwortet, er helfe niemals bei der Hausarbeit. Der Mann hat dann gesagt, das sei nicht wahr. ...

5 **Glaubst du das?** Erzählen Sie zwei Partnern/Partnerinnen zwei Dinge über sich, die wahr oder eine Lüge (*lie*) sein könnten. Ein Partner / Eine Partnerin berichtet davon. Der andere Partner / Die andere Partnerin sagt, ob er/sie das glaubt oder nicht. Wechseln Sie sich ab. Answers will vary.

BEISPIEL

S1: *Ich bin 18 Jahre alt.*
S2: *Melanie hat gesagt, sie sei 18 Jahre alt. Glaubst du das?*
S3: *Nein, das glaube ich nicht. Ich glaube, sie ist 19.*

6 **Klatschkolumnen** Schreiben Sie mit Ihrem Partner / Ihrer Partnerin eine Klatschkolumne (*gossip column*) über einen Prominenten. Benutzen Sie Indikativformen. Tauschen Sie (*exchange*) Ihre Kolumne mit zwei Mitstudenten aus. Berichten Sie dem Rest der Klasse, was in der Kolumne Ihrer Mitstudenten steht. Verwenden Sie dabei den Konjunktiv I. Answers will vary.

BEISPIEL

S1/S2: *In der Klatschkolumne steht, dass die große Schauspielerin Tanja ihr ganzes Geld der Tierschutzorganisation „Ein Herz für Tiere" gegeben habe. Sie sei gestern in die Schweiz geflogen, habe das Geld abgehoben und dann ihre Konten gekündigt. Sie sei noch nie so glücklich gewesen, sagte Tanja.*

Die große Schauspielerin (*actress*) Tanja hat ihr ganzes Vermögen (*fortune*) der Tierschutzorganisation „Ein Herz für Tiere" gegeben. Sie ist gestern in die Schweiz geflogen, hat das Geld abgehoben und dann ihre Konten gekündigt. „Ich bin noch nie so glücklich gewesen", sagte Tanja.

4 **Virtual Chat** You can also assign activity 4 on the Supersite. Students record individual responses that appear in your gradebook.

5 **Suggestion** Tell students to use statements with **Ich bin...,** **Ich habe..., Ich will...,** or **Ich kann...** Provide model subjunctive forms on the board: **Sie sagt, sie sei... Er sagt, er habe... Sie sagt, sie wolle... Er sagt, er könne...** Circulate and provide help as needed.

6 **Suggestion** After they swap columns, give students time to convert the verbs into indirect speech. It may be helpful to have them underline all of the verbs first. Point out that since they'll be using the 3rd person throughout their reports, the pattern will be: *verb stem* + **-e**.

The passive voice  Presentation

Startblock Most sentences in German are in the *active* voice. Use the *passive* voice to put the focus on the action itself, or on the receiver of the action.

- To form a sentence using the passive voice, use a conjugated form of **werden** with the past participle of the verb that describes the action of the sentence. Sentences using the passive voice are usually in the present tense or the **Präteritum**.

  In diesem Land **wird** zu viel Müll **produziert**.
  *Too much trash **is being produced** in this country.*

  Im Jahr 2009 **wurden** 455 kg Müll pro Kopf **weggeworfen**.
  *In 2009, 455 kilos of trash per person **were thrown out**.*

- The subject of a passive sentence is the receiver of the action.

  Wir **schalten** immer die Lichter **aus**.
  *We always **turn out** the lights.*

  Die Lichter **werden ausgeschaltet**.
  *The lights **are being turned out**.*

- In a passive voice sentence, the doer of the action is often unidentified. To indicate who or what performed or is performing the action, use the preposition **von** after the conjugated form of **werden**, followed by a noun in the dative case.

  Neue Hybridautos werden (**von Wissenschaftlern**) entwickelt.
  *New hybrid cars are being developed **(by scientists)**.*

  Das Wasser wurde (**von der Fabrik**) verschmutzt.
  *The water was polluted **(by the factory)**.*

- In passive sentences with a modal verb, use the conjugated form of the modal and move the infinitive **werden** to the end of the sentence, after the past participle.

  Ein neues Gesetz **soll vorgeschlagen werden**.
  *A new law **needs to be proposed**.*

  Die Technologie **musste** erst **verbessert werden**.
  *The technology **had to be improved** first.*

- In an impersonal statement, where there is no specific subject, the sentence may begin with **es**, or with an adverb of time or place.

  Es wird hier nur Deutsch gesprochen.
  Only German is spoken here.

  Gestern wurde viel gearbeitet.
  *A lot of work was done **yesterday**.*

- You can often replace a statement in the passive voice with an active sentence using the indefinite pronoun **man** as the subject.

  In den USA **benutzt man** zu viel Benzin.
  ***People** in the U.S. **use** too much gasoline.*

  Man soll Energie sparen.
  ***We should save** energy.*

Jetzt sind Sie dran! Markieren Sie, ob die folgenden Sätze aktiv oder passiv sind.

	aktiv	passiv		aktiv	passiv
1. Es muss mehr getan werden.	☐	☑	4. Heute wird mehr wiederverwertet.	☐	☑
2. Viele Tierarten sind jetzt gefährdet.	☑	☐	5. Man muss mehr Wasser sparen.	☑	☐
3. Fahrgemeinschaften sollen oft benutzt werden.	☐	☑	6. Der Müll wurde von dem Müllfahrer abgeholt (*picked up*).	☐	☑

Anwendung und Kommunikation

1 **Was fehlt?** Ergänzen Sie die Sätze mit den Passivformen der Verben in Klammern.

> **BEISPIEL** In meiner Familie ___werden___ keine Batterien in den Müll _geworfen_. (werfen)

1. Innovative Ideen, unseren Planeten zu retten, ___werden___ dringend (*urgently*) ___gesucht___. (suchen)
2. Die Luft ___wird___ immer mehr ___verschmutzt___. (verschmutzen)
3. Stofftaschen (*Cloth bags*) statt Plastiktaschen sollen beim Einkaufen ___benutzt___ ___werden___. (benutzen)
4. Wasserreservoirs, um Trinkwasser zu speichern, müssen ___gebaut___ ___werden___. (bauen)
5. In welchem Land ___wird___ das meiste Altpapier ___recycelt___? (recyceln)
6. Die Tier- und Pflanzenwelt darf nicht ___vergessen___ ___werden___. (vergessen)

2 **Was wird hier gemacht?** Beschreiben Sie mit einem Partner / einer Partnerin, was auf den Bildern gerade passiert. Benutzen Sie die Präsensformen des Passivs. Answers will vary.

> **BEISPIEL**
>
> **S1:** *Hier wird Mathematik gelernt.*

1.

2.    3.    4.    5.

Bücher / verkaufen	Müll / recyceln
ein Hund / baden	Pizza / essen
Mathematik / lernen	die Umwelt / verschmutzen

3 **Lösungsvorschläge** Diskutieren Sie mit einem Partner / einer Partnerin, was (nicht) gemacht werden kann/muss/soll/darf, um unsere Umweltprobleme zu lösen. Gebrauchen Sie Modalverben im Passiv. Answers will vary.

> **BEISPIEL**
>
> **S1:** *Die Windenergie muss ausgebaut werden.*

ausbauen	das Kernkraftwerk / der Reaktor...
entwickeln	die Landschaft
erfinden	die Luft / das Wasser /...
finden	die Natur / die Flora / die Fauna...
recyceln	das Papier / das Glas / das Plastik / das Aluminium...
reduzieren	die Windenergie / die Solarenergie / die Kernenergie...
retten	die Wissenschaft
verbessern	

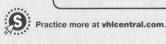

Practice more at **vhlcentral.com**.

2 **Virtual Chat** You can also assign activity 2 on the Supersite. Students record individual responses that appear in your gradebook.

3 **Expansion** Ask students if they think people will start living in a more environmentally aware manner in the near future. Are they optimistic or pessimistic about the environment?

3 **Partner Chat** You can also assign activity 3 on the Supersite. Students work in pairs to record the activity online. The pair's recorded conversation will appear in your gradebook.

Wiederholung

1 Ein Zeitungsartikel

1 Ein Zeitungsartikel Identifizieren Sie mit einem Partner / einer Partnerin Beispiele indirekter Rede in dem Artikel über eine Umweltinitiative. Wechseln Sie sich dann ab und sagen Sie in indirekter Rede, was gesagt wurde.

Answers will vary.

BEISPIEL

S1: Die Polizei erklärte: „Am Wochenende haben mehr als 250.000 Menschen in ganz Deutschland für den Atomausstieg demonstriert."

Zehntausende demonstrieren für raschen Atomausstieg

Das Wochenende stand im Zeichen des Atomausstiegs (*nuclear phase-out*). Die Polizei erklärte, am Wochenende hätten mehr als 250.000 Menschen in ganz Deutschland für den Atomausstieg demonstriert. Sie berichtete außerdem, Demonstrationen hätten in 20 Städten stattgefunden. Atomgegener erzählten, es habe Demonstrationen in mehr als 20 Städten gegeben. Organisatoren meinten auch, diese Demonstrationen seien größer gewesen als die vorherigen Demonstrationen. Zu dem Protest aufgerufen hatten Umweltschutzinitiativen, Gewerkschaften und Parteien. Diese Organisationen sagten, sie wollten Druck (*pressure*) auf die Politiker in Berlin machen. Sie meinten auch, es sei Zeit für eine neue Umweltpolitik. Ohne Atomkraft hätten die Kinder eine Chance auf eine sicherere Welt.

2 Arbeitsblatt

2 Arbeitsblatt Stellen Sie den anderen im Unterricht die Fragen auf dem Arbeitsblatt, das Sie bekommen. Schreiben Sie die Antworten auf. Diskutieren Sie dann mit der Gruppe, um zu sehen, was die typischsten Antworten waren. Answers will vary.

BEISPIEL

S1: Was wäre, wenn weniger Leute Kinder bekämen?
S2: Wenn weniger Leute Kinder bekämen, hätten wir kein Problem mit Überbevölkerung.

2 Suggestion Make sure that students understand they will be practicing **Konjunktiv II** in this activity, not **Konjunktiv I**.

3 Wer hat's gesagt?

3 Wer hat's gesagt? Entscheiden Sie, wer wahrscheinlich die folgenden Sätze gesagt hat. Berichten Sie, was die Personen gesagt haben. Wechseln Sie sich mit einem Partner / einer Partnerin ab. Sample answers are provided.

3 Virtual Chat You can also assign activity 3 on the Supersite.

BEISPIEL Man hat viele Tiere aus dem Tierheim adoptiert.

S1: Die Tierärztin war froh, dass man viele Tiere aus dem Tierheim adoptiert habe.
S2: Der Biologe berichtete, dass ...

die Bankangestellte	die Psychologin
der Biologe	der Rentner
der Elektriker	die Richterin
der Koch	die Tierärztin
der LKW-Fahrer	

1. Man muss jeden Tag arbeiten, bis das Restaurant schließt.
   Der Koch sagte, man müsse jeden Tag arbeiten, bis das Restaurant schließe.
2. Viele Menschen haben Depressionen.
   Die Psychologin berichtete, viele Menschen hätten Depressionen.
3. Niemand interessiert sich für alte Menschen.
   Der Rentner meinte, niemand interessiere sich für alte Menschen.
4. Es ist ein Problem, dass Benzin immer teurer wird.
   Der LKW-Fahrer sagte, es sei ein Problem, dass Benzin immer teurer werde.
5. Es gibt immer mehr Jugendliche, die Probleme mit dem Gesetz haben.
   Die Richterin sagte, es gebe immer mehr Jugendliche, die Probleme mit dem Gesetz hätten.
6. Online-Banking wird immer beliebter.
   Die Bankangestellte berichtete, Online-Banking werde immer beliebter.

4 Gut oder schlecht?

4 Gut oder schlecht? Bitten Sie Ihren Partner / Ihre Partnerin, auf die folgenden Fotos zu reagieren. Wie erklärt Ihr Partner / Ihre Partnerin diese Reaktion? Answers will vary.

BEISPIEL

S1: Wie findest du die Insel im See?
S2: Ich finde sie schön, weil man da die frische Luft genießen kann.

1.   2.   3.

4.   5.   6.

4 Expansion Have students describe each picture in detail before giving their reactions.

4 Partner Chat You can also assign activity 4 on the Supersite. Students work in pairs to record the activity online. The pair's recorded conversation will appear in your gradebook.

5 Wenn nur...
Machen Sie anhand der Bilder eine Liste mit fünf Dingen, die Sie während Ihrer Unikarriere gerne gemacht hätten. Lesen Sie dann in Vierergruppen Ihre Sätze vor. Answers will vary.

▶ **BEISPIEL**
S1: Wenn ich gelernt hätte, anstatt zu spielen, hätte ich bessere Noten gehabt.

2.

3.

4.

5.

6.

6 In der Zukunft
Was muss man in der Zukunft machen, um der Umwelt zu helfen? Schreiben Sie in Dreiergruppen mindestens sechs Antworten auf diese Frage. Benutzen Sie das Futur I. Answers will vary.

BEISPIEL

6 Suggestion Remind students to use **werden** with an infinitive to form the **Futur I**.

S1: In der Zukunft wird unsere Mensa das gesamte Papier und den gesamten Kunststoff recyceln.
S2: Ja, und es wird…

7 Diskutieren und kombinieren
Auf Ihrem Arbeitsblatt finden Sie Informationen über Jasmin und ihre Mutter. Überlegen Sie sich, wie Jasmins Mutter reagieren würde, wenn Jasmin das machen würde, was Sie auf den Bildern sehen können. Answers will vary.

BEISPIEL

7 Suggestion Remind students that **werden** can be used in its subjunctive form for hypotheses and contrary-to-fact situations.

S1: Was würde passieren, wenn Jasmin mit dem Flugzeug flöge?
S2: Wenn Jasmin mit dem Flugzeug flöge, würde ihre Mutter sie am Flughafen anrufen.

8 Eine bessere Stadt
Schreiben Sie mit einem Partner / einer Partnerin eine Liste mit sechs Umwelt-problemen, die in Städten existieren. Schlagen Sie für jedes Problem eine Lösung vor. Benutzen Sie das Passiv. Answers will vary.

BEISPIEL

S1: Zu viele Batterien werden in den Müll geworfen.
S2: Batterien sollen recycelt werden.

Mein Wör|ter|buch

Schreiben Sie fünf weitere Wörter in Ihr persönliches Wörterbuch zu den Themen **In der Natur** und **Die Umwelt**.

unbehandelt

Übersetzung
untreated

Wortart
Adjektiv

Gebrauch
Bei unbehandeltem Gemüse benutzen Bauern keine Pestizide, wenn es auf dem Feld wächst.

Synonyme
biologisch, ungespritzt

Antonyme
behandelt, gespritzt

S Vocabulary Tools

Panorama

Sachsen-Anhalt und Sachsen

NATIONAL STANDARDS — connections cultures

Sachsen-Anhalt in Zahlen

▶ **Fläche:** *20.446 km²*

▶ **Bevölkerung:** *2,3 Millionen Menschen*

▶ **Städte:** *Halle (233.000 Einwohner), Magdeburg (231.000)*

▶ **Wichtige Industriezweige:** *Chemieindustrie, Maschinenbau, Landwirtschaft*

▶ **Touristenattraktionen:** *Lutherstadt Wittenberg; das Bauhaus, Dessau; Burg Falkenstein*
Für Touristen ist in Sachsen-Anhalt neben Wittenberg, wo Martin Luther seine 95 Thesen an die Tür der Schlosskirche nagelte°, auch das Bauhaus in Dessau interessant. Das Grüne Band Deutschland, wo einmal die Mauer stand, liegt zum größten Teil in Sachsen-Anhalt. Es ist jetzt Naturschutzgebiet.

Quelle: Investitions- und Marketinggesellschaft Sachsen-Anhalt mbH

Sachsen in Zahlen

▶ **Fläche:** *18.415 km²*

▶ **Bevölkerung:** *4,1 Millionen Menschen*

▶ **Städte:** *Leipzig (532.000 Einwohner), Dresden (530.000), Chemnitz (243.000)*

▶ **Wichtige Industriezweige:** *Automobilindustrie, Mikroelektronik, Maschinenbau*

▶ **Touristenattraktionen:** *Weihnachtsmärkte im Erzgebirge, Dresden, Meißener Porzellan*
Dresden, das Elbflorenz, ist eine der größten Touristenattraktionen Sachsens. Touristen sollten den Zwinger, die Frauenkirche und die Semperoper besuchen.

Quelle: Tourismus Marketing Gesellschaft Sachsen mbH

Berühmte Menschen aus Sachsen-Anhalt und Sachsen

▶ **Otto Fürst von Bismarck,** *Politiker (1815–1898)*

▶ **Erich Kästner,** *Autor (1839–1974)*

▶ **Gottfried Wilhelm Leibniz,** *Mathematiker und Wissenschaftler (1646–1716)*

▶ **Christiane Nüsslein-Volhard,** *Wissenschaftlerin (1942–)*

▶ **Katharina Witt,** *Sportlerin (1965–)*

Expansion For homework, have students research one of these famous individuals and find one piece of information about them to share with the class.

nagelte *nailed* **Kurfürst** *prince-elector* **Manufaktur** *factory*
gekreuzten Schwerter *crossed swords*

Das Bauhaus in Dessau

Die Silhouette der Dresdener Innenstadt

MECKLENBURG-VORPOMMERN

NIEDERSACHSEN

Stendal

SACHSEN-ANHALT

BERLIN

BRANDENBURG

Magdeburg

Brocken
NATIONALPARK HARZ

Dessau

Halle

Saale

Leipzig

Riesa

SACHSEN

Elbe

Dresden

THÜRINGEN

Suggestion Tell students that the former no-man's land between East and West Germany remained relatively untouched for nearly 40 years and is now a protected area of rich biodiversity

Chemnitz

Zwickau

Fichtelberg

ERZGEBIRGE

TSCHECHIEN

BAYERN

Das Grüne Band Deutschland

— Landesgrenzen
• Stadt
◉ Landeshauptstadt

0   25 Meilen
0   25 Kilometer

Elbe

Unglaublich, aber wahr!

Im Jahr 1708 erfanden Johann Friedrich Böttger und Walther von Tschirnhaus das europäische Porzellan. 1710 gründete der sächsische Kurfürst° August der Starke dann die Porzellan-Manufaktur° Meißen. Dieses auch heute noch weltberühmte Porzellan trägt das Symbol der gekreuzten Schwerter°.

AP* Theme: Science & Technology
Context: Inventions as Catalysts of Change

Technologie

Solar Valley

Suggestion Tell students that, according to *National Geographic*, Germany is the world leader in solar power. On June 9, 2014, Germany became the first country to generate more than half of its electricity supply from solar energy.

Das Solar Valley, auch Sonnenallee bezeichnet, liegt in Sachsen-Anhalt in der Nähe der Stadt Bitterfeld-Wolfen. Es gilt als eines der Zentren der Photovoltaikindustrie. Zu den Firmen, die hier vertreten° sind, gehören Q-Cells SE, Calyxo GmbH und Sontor GmbH.

Das Solar Valley gilt als einer der größten Solarstandorte Europas und ist Symbol für das deutsche Engagement im Bereich erneuerbarer Energiequellen. Bis zu 3.000 Menschen arbeiten in diesem Industriebereich in Sachsen-Anhalt.

AP* Theme: Personal & Public Identities
Context: National Identity

Völker

Die Sorben

Die Sorben, ein westslawisches Volk, leben heute in der Ober- und Niederlausitz in den Bundesländern Brandenburg und Sachsen, wo Sorbisch eine offizielle Sprache ist. Es gibt heute noch etwa 60.000 Sorben in Deutschland, wo sie als offizielle Minderheit° anerkannt° sind. Die meisten Sorben sind deutsche Staatsangehörige°. Einer der bekanntesten sorbischen Bräuche° ist das alljährliche Osterreiten. Jährlich sehen mehr als 30.000 Besucher zu, wenn rund 1.700 Reiter in Frack und Zylinder° die Botschaft von der Auferstehung Jesu Christi verkünden°.

Musik

Suggestion Play students clips of music by Händel, Telemann, and Bach. Ask students whether they have heard these pieces before, and whether they can identify each piece's composer.

Barockmusiker aus Sachsen-Anhalt

Johann Sebastian Bach, Georg Philipp Telemann und Georg Friedrich Händel sind weltberühmte Barockmusiker aus Sachsen-Anhalt, deren Werke man heute noch hört. Telemann, der Musik im Selbststudium lernte, komponierte mehr als 3.600 Stücke. Bach ist vor allem für seine Chorwerke und Musik für Tasteninstrumente° berühmt. Händel hatte in England mit seinen dramatischen Opern und Oratorien großen Erfolg. Trotz der Entfernung waren Telemann und Händel gut befreundet, und alle drei studierten und führten die Musik der anderen auf°.

AP* Theme: Beauty & Aesthetics
Context: Performing Arts

AP* Theme: Global Challenges
Context: Political Issues

Politik

Leipziger Montagsdemonstrationen

Im Herbst 1989 kam es in der DDR zu der Friedlichen Revolution. Die gewaltfreien° Montagsdemonstrationen in Leipzig und einigen anderen ostdeutschen Städten galten als Katalysator für die Wende° und das Ende der DDR. Nachdem sich am 4. September 1.200 Demonstranten vor der Leipziger Nikolaikirche getroffen hatten, waren es am 6. November, drei Tage vor dem Fall der Berliner Mauer, 500.000 Menschen, die Slogans wie "Wir sind das Volk" oder "Für ein offenes Land mit freien Menschen" riefen°.

🖐 IM INTERNET

1. Suchen Sie weitere Informationen über die Leipziger Montagsdemonstrationen und die Friedliche Revolution: Wann fingen diese Demonstrationen an? Wer organisierte sie?

2. Suchen Sie mehr Informationen über Bach, Telemann und Händel. Warum kommen so viele Barockmusiker aus Sachsen-Anhalt? Was für Musik haben diese drei Komponisten geschrieben?

Find out more at **vhlcentral.com**.

---

vertreten *represented* **gewaltfreien** *nonviolent* **Wende** *reunification* **riefen** *called* **Minderheit** *minority* **anerkannt** *recognized* **Staatsangehörige** *citizens* **Bräuche** *customs* **Frack und Zylinder** *tails and top hat* **verkünden** *announce* **Musik für Tasteninstrumente** *keyboard music* **führten... auf** *performed*

 Was haben Sie gelernt? Ergänzen Sie die Sätze.

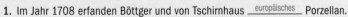

1. Im Jahr 1708 erfanden Böttger und von Tschirnhaus ___europäisches___ Porzellan.

2. Gekreuzte Schwerter sind das ___Symbol___ der Porzellan-Manufaktur Meißen.

3. Das Solar Valley heißt auch ___Sonnenallee___.

4. Bis zu 3.000 Menschen arbeiten hier in der ___Photovoltaikindustrie___.

5. Die Leipziger Montagsdemonstrationen waren Teil der Friedlichen ___Revolution___ in der ehemaligen DDR.

6. 500.000 Menschen nahmen an der Demonstration am 6. November 1989 in ___Leipzig___ teil.

7. Die ___Sorben___ sind eine anerkannte Minderheit in Deutschland.

8. Rund 1.700 sorbische Reiter nehmen am ___Osterreiten___ teil.

9. Bach komponierte Werke für Chor und für ___Tasteninstrumente___.

10. Händels ___Opern___ und Oratorien hatten in England großen Erfolg.

 Practice more at **vhlcentral.com**.

Lesen Audio: Reading

communication cultures NATIONAL STANDARDS

Vor dem Lesen
AP* Theme: Beauty & Aesthetics
Context: Language & Literature

Strategien

Imagery

Poets often use vivid imagery to convey a particular sensory experience to the reader. A poet may also use specific images as symbols, to represent certain abstract themes or ideas, or as metaphors, to draw a comparison between apparently dissimilar objects or concepts. Paying close attention to the words of a poem and the images those words convey can help you to gain a deeper understanding of the poem.

Untersuchen Sie den Text

Lesen Sie einmal die beiden Gedichte. Welche Wörter und Bilder kommen in beiden Gedichten immer wieder vor?

Autoren
Rose Ausländer

Rose Ausländer (1901–1988) wurde in Czernowitz, Bukowina (damals Österreich-Ungarn) als Kind jüdischer Eltern geboren. 1921 wanderte sie nach Amerika aus, aber 1931 kam sie in ihre Heimatstadt zurück, um ihre Mutter zu pflegen (*care for*). Die Jahre von 1941 bis 1944 verbrachte sie mit ihrer Mutter und ihrem Bruder in einem Kellerversteck (*cellar hiding-place*). Nach dem Krieg wanderte sie wieder nach Amerika aus. Dort fing sie an, Gedichte auf Englisch zu schreiben. Erst im Jahre 1956 begann sie ihre Gedichte wieder auf Deutsch zu schreiben.

Rainer Maria Rilke

Rainer Maria Rilke (1875–1926) ist einer der bekanntesten Dichter (*poets*) der deutschen Sprache. Er stammte aus Prag, das damals zu Österreich-Ungarn gehörte. Neben Gedichten schrieb er Erzählungen, einen Roman und Aufsätze über Kunst und Kultur. Der Panther gilt als eines der berühmtesten Gedichte Rilkes.

Meine Nachtigall°

Rose Ausländer

Meine Mutter war einmal ein Reh°
Die goldbraunen Augen
die Anmut°
blieben ihr aus der Rehzeit

Hier war sie
halb Engel° halb Mensch-
die Mitte° war Mutter
Als ich sie fragte was sie gern geworden wäre
sagte sie: eine Nachtigall

Jetzt ist sie eine Nachtigall
Nacht um Nacht höre ich sie
im Garten meines schlaflosen Traumes°
Sie singt das Zion der Ahnen°
sie singt das alte Österreich
sie singt die Berge und Buchenwälder°
der Bukowina
Wiegenlieder°
singt mir Nacht um Nacht
meine Nachtigall
im Garten meines schlaflosen Traumes

Nachtigall *nightingale* **Reh** *deer* **Anmut** *grace* **Engel** *angel*
Mitte *middle* **schlaflosen Traumes** *sleepless dream* **Ahnen** *ancestors*
Buchenwälder *beech tree forests* **Wiegenlieder** *lullabies*

～ Der Panther ～

Rainer Maria Rilke

Im Jardin des Plantes, Paris

Sein Blick° ist vom Vorübergehn° der Stäbe°
so müd geworden, daß er nichts mehr hält°.
Ihm ist, als ob es tausend Stäbe gäbe
und hinter tausend Stäben keine Welt.

Der weiche° Gang geschmeidig° starker Schritte,
der sich im allerkleinsten Kreise° dreht,
ist wie ein Tanz von Kraft um eine Mitte,
in der betäubt° ein großer Wille steht.

Nur manchmal schiebt der Vorhang der Pupille
sich lautlos° auf. – Dann geht ein Bild hinein,
geht durch der Glieder° angespannte Stille –
und hört im Herzen auf zu sein.

Blick *gaze* **Vorübergehn** *passing by* **Stäbe** *bars*
hält *holds* **weiche** *smooth* **geschmeidig** *sleek*
allerkleinsten Kreise *smallest circles*
betäubt *numbed* **lautlos** *silently* **Glieder** *limbs*

Nach dem Lesen

Die Nachtigall Wählen Sie die richtige Antwort auf jede Frage.

1. Was wollte die Mutter laut Ausländers Gedicht werden?
   a. Sie wollte ein Reh werden.
   b. Sie wollte eine Nachtigall werden.

2. Was hatte die Mutter noch aus der Zeit, als sie ein Reh war?
   a. Sie hatte noch goldbraune Augen und Anmut.
   b. Sie hatte noch schlaflose Träume.

3. Was für Lieder singt die Nachtigall?
   a. Sie singt Wiegenlieder.
   b. Sie singt Volkslieder.

Der Panther Wählen Sie die richtige Antwort auf jede Frage.

1. Wo lebt der Panther?
   a. Er lebt in der freien Natur.
   b. Er lebt in Gefangenschaft.

2. Warum sieht er die Welt nicht mehr?
   a. Weil er alt und blind geworden ist.
   b. Weil sein Blick müde geworden ist.

3. Wer hat laut Rilkes Gedicht einen großen Willen?
   a. Der Panther hat einen großen Willen.
   b. Die Welt hat einen großen Willen.

Zum Besprechen Sprechen Sie mit einem Partner / einer Partnerin über die zwei Gedichte. Was finden beide Dichter so gut an den Tieren? Was unterscheidet die Situation der Nachtigall von der des Panthers? Partner Chat You can also assign this activity on the Supersite.

Aufsatz Schreiben Sie einen Aufsatz über eins der folgenden Themen.

1. Wofür stehen die Tiere in den Gedichten? Was wollen die Autoren mit Hilfe der Tiere ausdrücken?

2. Gibt es Menschen, die wie der Panther in Rilkes Gedicht sind? Begründen Sie Ihre Meinung.

3. Welche Wörter und Verse kommen in beiden Gedichten immer wieder vor? Welche Wirkung (*effect*) hat die Wiederholung der Wörter und Verse?

4. Schreiben Sie ein Gedicht über ein Tier, das Sie besonders interessant finden.

Hören

Strategien

Taking notes

Jotting down notes while you listen can help you keep track of the important points of a speech or oral presentation. It will help you to focus actively on comprehension rather than on remembering what you heard.

 To practice this strategy, listen as Katrin Schneider describes her recent vacation. Jot down notes about the main points you hear. Suggested answers are provided.

Vorbereitung

Sehen Sie sich das Foto an: Wer sind diese Leute? Was machen sie? Warum protestieren sie? Was sagen sie vielleicht?

Zuhören

Hören Sie dem Organisator zu, der mit den Demonstranten spricht, und nennen Sie die Themen, über die er spricht.

1. ____ Recycling
2. __X__ Abfall
3. __X__ Sonnenenergie
4. ____ Überbevölkerung
5. ____ Gesetz
6. __X__ Windenergie
7. __X__ Umwelt
8. ____ Waldsterben
9. __X__ Kernenergie
10. __X__ erneuerbare Energie
11. ____ Erderwärmung
12. __X__ Giftmüll

Suggestion For the first round of listening, have students keep their books closed and jot down as many words as they can catch. Ask them to share their lists and make a projection about the purpose of the speech.

Verständnis

Alternativenergien Ergänzen Sie die Sätze mit der richtigen Antwort.

1. Die Demonstration ist gegen ___die Kernkraft___.
   a. die Sonnenenergie
   b. die Kernkraft
   c. die Windenergie

2. Die Demonstration findet in ___Berlin___ statt.
   a. Sachsen
   b. Berlin
   c. Schleswig-Holstein

3. Es sind ___30.000___ Menschen bei der Demonstration.
   a. 13.000
   b. 30.000
   c. 3.000

4. Windenergie wird vor allem in ___Schleswig-Holstein___ produziert.
   a. Sachsen
   b. Berlin
   c. Schleswig-Holstein

5. Die Technologie für Sonnenenergie wird in ___Sachsen___ entwickelt.
   a. Sachsen
   b. Berlin
   c. Schleswig-Holstein

Expansion Ask students to identify the rhetorical devices that they hear such as repetition of words, phrases, and structures, rhetorical questions, etc.

Suggestion Tell students that **Atomenergie** and **Solarenergie** are frequently used as synonyms for **Kernenergie** and **Sonnenenergie**, respectively.

Neue Gesetze Ein Repräsentant einer internationalen Umweltorganisation besucht Ihre Schule, um Umweltprobleme und Umweltschutz zu diskutieren. Wählen Sie in kleinen Gruppen ein Umweltproblem aus, das heute sehr wichtig ist. Versuchen Sie den Repräsentanten zu überzeugen, dass Regierungen und Politiker mehr auf diesem Gebiet machen sollten. Sie müssen das Problem erklären können. Was muss sich ändern, damit es besser wird? Überlegen Sie sich auch neue Gesetze, die Sie dem Repräsentanten vorschlagen wollen.

Schreiben

Strategien

Considering audience and purpose

Before you begin a piece of writing, you must determine to whom you are addressing the piece and what you want to express to your reader. Once you have defined both your audience and your purpose, you will be able to decide which genre, vocabulary, and grammatical structures will best serve your composition.

Suppose you want to share your thoughts on local traffic problems. Your audience might be either the local government or the community. You could choose to write a newspaper article, a letter to the editor, or a letter to the city's governing board. You should first decide the focus of your piece:

1. Are there specific problems you want to highlight?

2. Is your goal to register a complaint or to increase public awareness?

3. Are you trying to persuade others to adopt your point of view?

4. Are you hoping to inspire others to take concrete actions?

The answers to these questions will help you establish the purpose of your writing and determine your audience. Of course, your writing may have more than one purpose. For example, you may intend both to inform others of a problem and to inspire them to take action.

Whatever the topic you choose, defining your purpose and your audience before you begin will help to make your writing more focused and effective.

Suggestion Remind students of the techniques introduced in earlier chapters for organizing their ideas, such as idea-maps and note cards, as well as linking words such as adverbs and conjunctions for creating logical connections and emphasis.

Thema

 Schreiben Sie einen Brief oder einen Bericht

 Schreiben Sie über ein Umweltproblem, das Ihrer Meinung nach (*in your opinion*) sehr wichtig ist. Beantworten Sie die folgenden Fragen.

1. Wählen Sie zuerst ein Problem, über das Sie schreiben wollen. Ist es ein Problem vor Ort (z. B., Recycling auf dem Schulgelände) oder ein Problem auf globaler Ebene (z. B. die Überbevölkerung)?

2. Wer sind die Leser Ihres Briefs/Berichts: Schreiben Sie einen Brief an einen Freund? Schreiben Sie einen Brief an einen Politiker? An den Umweltklub der Schule? Schreiben Sie einen Bericht oder einen Artikel für eine Zeitung oder eine Zeitschrift?

3. Nennen Sie den Grund für den Brief oder den Bericht: Informieren Sie die Leser oder wollen Sie auch Ihre Meinung sagen?

4. Schreiben Sie eine kurze Einleitung (*introduction*). Stellen Sie das Problem, das Sie ausgewählt haben, hier vor.

5. Wenn Sie Ihre Meinung sagen wollen, müssen Sie gute Gründe für ihre Position angeben, damit man Ihnen glaubt.

6. Schreiben Sie eine Schlussfolgerung (*conclusion*) für den Brief oder Bericht.

Expansion Before leaving the topic of the environment, ask students for their closing thoughts: **Wie sieht die Zukunft unseres Planeten aus? Möchten Sie versuchen, umweltfreundlicher zu leben? Warum, warum nicht? Wie? Kann der Einzelne was bewirken?**

Lektion 4A

die Natur

der Bauernhof, -̈e *farm*
der Baum, -̈e *tree*
der Berg, -e *mountain*
das Blatt, -̈er *leaf*
der Busch, -̈e *bush*
das Feld, -er *field*
der Fluss, -̈e *river*
das Gras, -̈er *grass*
der Himmel *sky*
die Insel, -n *island*
die Klippe, -n *cliff*
die Küste, -n *coast*
die Landschaft, -en *countryside*
die Luft *air*
das Meer, -e *sea*
der Mond, -e *moon*
der See, -n *lake*
die Sonne, -n *sun*
der Sonnenaufgang, -̈e *sunrise*
der Sonnenuntergang, -̈e *sunset*
der Stein, -e *rock*
der Stern, -e *star*
das Tal, -̈er *valley*
der Wald, -̈er *forest*
der Wasserfall, -̈e *waterfall*
der Weg, -e *path*
aufregend *exciting*
bedeutend *important*
nass *wet*
trocken *dry*

Tiere

das Eichhörnchen, - *squirrel*
der Fisch, -e *fish*
der Hase, -n *hare*
das Huhn, -̈er *chicken*
die Kuh, -̈e *cow*
die Maus, -̈e *mouse*
das Pferd, -e *horse*
das Schaf, -e *sheep*
die Schlange, -n *snake*

Verben

aufgehen (geht... auf) *to rise*
erforschen *to explore*
untergehen (geht... unter) *to set*
wandern *to hike*
ein Picknick (*n.*) machen *to have a picnic*

Der Konjunktiv der Vergangenheit
See pp. 160–161.
Das Partizip Präsens See p. 164.

Lektion 4B

die Umwelt

die Art, -en *species*
die Erde, -n *earth*
die Fabrik, -en *factory*
die Gefahr, -en *danger*
das Hochwasser, - *flood*
das Licht, -er *light*
der Müll *waste*
der Müllwagen, - *garbage truck*
die Ökologie *ecology*
der Umweltschutz *environmentalism*
die Welt, -en *world*
biologisch *organic*
gefährdet *endangered*
ökologisch *ecological*
umweltfreundlich *environmentally friendly*

Energie

die Kernenergie *nuclear energy*
das Kernkraftwerk, -e *nuclear power plant*
die Sonnenenergie *solar energy*
die Windenergie *wind energy*

Probleme

das Aussterben *extinction*
die Erderwärmung *global warming*
der Giftmüll *toxic waste*
der saure Regen *acid rain*
die Überbevölkerung *overpopulation*
die Verschmutzung *pollution*

Lösungen

das Gesetz, -e *law*
die erneuerbare Energie (*pl.* die erneuerbaren Energien) *renewable energy*
die Fahrgemeinschaft, -en *carpool*
das Hybridauto, -s *hybrid car*
das Recycling *recycling*
die Regierung, -en *government*

Verben

ausschalten (schaltet... aus) *to turn off*
(den Planeten) retten *to save (the planet)*
einschalten (schaltet... ein) *to turn on*
entwickeln *to develop*
erhalten (erhält) *to preserve*
recyceln *to recycle*
schützen *to protect*
verbessern *to improve*
verschmutzen *to pollute*
vorschlagen (schlägt... vor) *to propose*
wegwerfen (wirft... weg) *to throw away*

Der Konjunktiv I See pp. 178–179.
The passive voice See p. 182.

Appendix A

Appendix B

Appendix C

die Welt

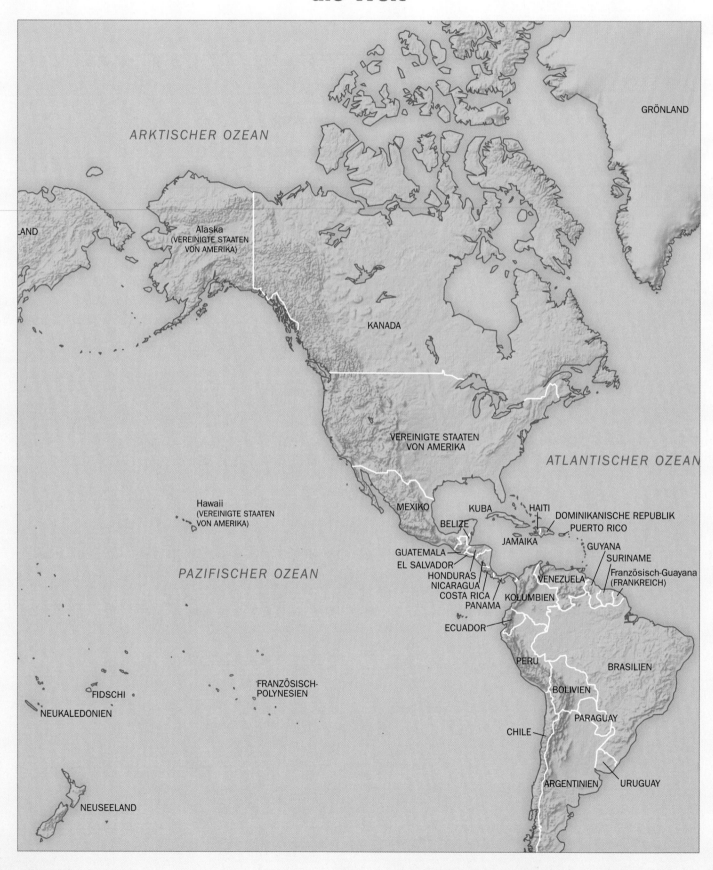

GRÖNLAND

ARKTISCHER OZEAN

LAND

Alaska
(VEREINIGTE STAATEN
VON AMERIKA)

KANADA

VEREINIGTE STAATEN
VON AMERIKA

ATLANTISCHER OZEAN

Hawaii
(VEREINIGTE STAATEN
VON AMERIKA)

MEXIKO

KUBA   HAITI

DOMINIKANISCHE REPUBLIK
PUERTO RICO

BELIZE

JAMAIKA

GUYANA
SURINAME
Französisch-Guayana
(FRANKREICH)

GUATEMALA
EL SALVADOR
HONDURAS
NICARAGUA
COSTA RICA
PANAMA

VENEZUELA

KOLUMBIEN

PAZIFISCHER OZEAN

ECUADOR

PERU

BRASILIEN

FIDSCHI

FRANZÖSISCH-
POLYNESIEN

BOLIVIEN

NEUKALEDONIEN

PARAGUAY

CHILE

ARGENTINIEN   URUGUAY

NEUSEELAND

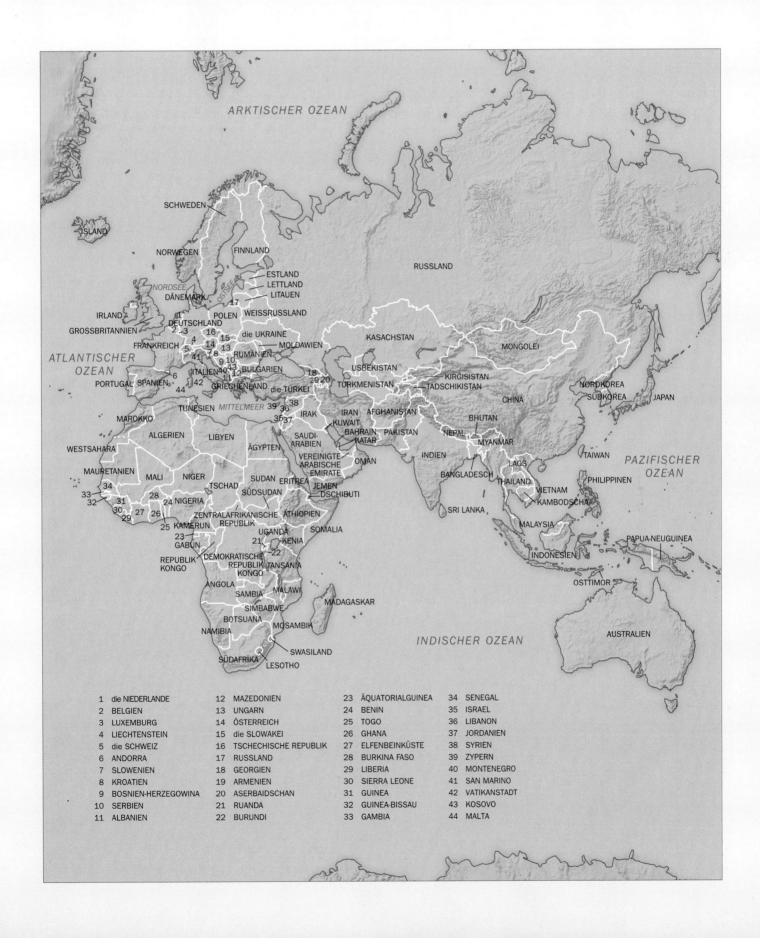

Europa

0 500 Meilen
0 500 Kilometer

Länder, in denen Deutsch eine Amtssprache ist

BARENTSSEE

ISLAND
Reykjavik

EUROPÄISCHES NORDMEER

SCHWEDEN
FINNLAND

NORWEGEN
Helsinki
RUSSLAND

Stockholm
Oslo

Tallinn
ESTLAND

OSTSEE

Riga
LETTLAND
Moskau

NORDSEE
DÄNEMARK

LITAUEN
Vilnius

ÖSTERREICH

LIECHTENSTEIN
Vaduz

Dublin
die NIEDERLANDE
Kopenhagen

RUSSLAND

Minsk
WEISSRUSSLAND

die SCHWEIZ

IRLAND
GROSS-BRITANNIEN

Amsterdam
Berlin
Warschau

London
POLEN
Kiew

Brüssel
LUXEMBURG
BELGIEN
DEUTSCHLAND

Prag
die SLOWAKEI

Luxemburg
TSCHECHISCHE REPUBLIK

die UKRAINE

Paris
Bratislava

MOLDAWIEN

LIECHTENSTEIN
Wien
Kischinau

FRANKREICH
Bern
Vaduz
ÖSTERREICH
Budapest

ATLANTISCHER OZEAN
die SCHWEIZ
SLOWENIEN
UNGARN

Ljubljana
Zagreb
RUMÄNIEN
SCHWARZES MEER

KROATIEN
Bukarest

ITALIEN
BOSNIEN
HERZEGOWINA
Belgrad

Monaco
SERBIEN
KOSOVO

SAN MARINO
Sarajevo
Pristina
BULGARIEN

Andorra la Vella
MONTENEGRO
Sofia

MONACO
Podgorica
Skopje
Ankara

PORTUGAL
ANDORRA
Rom
Tirana
MAZEDONIEN

Madrid
Korsika
VATIKANSTADT
ALBANIEN
die TÜRKEI

Lissabon
SPANIEN
GRIECHENLAND

Sardinien
Nicosia

Balearische Inseln
Sizilien
Athen
ZYPERN

Algier
Kreta

Tunis
Valletta
MALTA

Rabat
MITTELMEER

MAROKKO
TUNESIEN

ALGERIEN
Tripolis
Kairo

LIBYEN
ÄGYPTEN

Deutschland

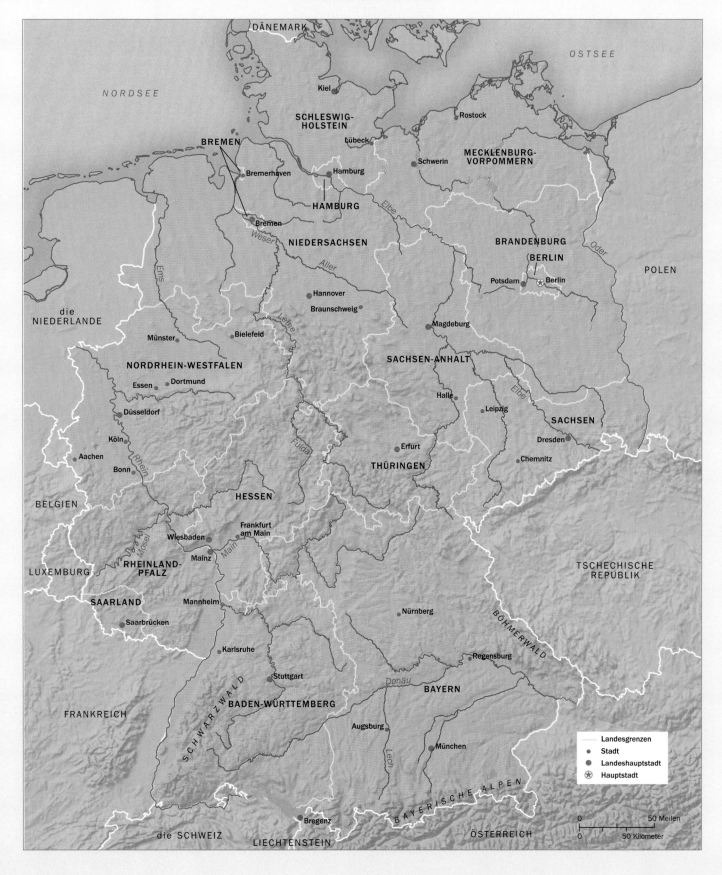

DÄNEMARK

OSTSEE

NORDSEE

Kiel

SCHLESWIG-
HOLSTEIN

Rostock

Lübeck

MECKLENBURG-
VORPOMMERN

BREMEN

Bremerhaven

Schwerin

Hamburg

Elbe

HAMBURG

Bremen

Weser

NIEDERSACHSEN

Aller

BRANDENBURG

BERLIN

Oder

Potsdam

Berlin

POLEN

Hannover

Braunschweig

Leine

Magdeburg

die
NIEDERLANDE

Münster

Bielefeld

Ems

SACHSEN-ANHALT

Elbe

NORDRHEIN-WESTFALEN

Essen

Dortmund

Halle

Leipzig

SACHSEN

Düsseldorf

Köln

Rhein

Fulda

Erfurt

Dresden

Chemnitz

Aachen

Bonn

THÜRINGEN

BELGIEN

HESSEN

Mosel

Wiesbaden

Frankfurt
am Main

Main

TSCHECHISCHE
REPUBLIK

LUXEMBURG

RHEINLAND-
PFALZ

Mainz

Saar

SAARLAND

Mannheim

Nürnberg

Saarbrücken

BÖHMERWALD

Karlsruhe

Regensburg

Stuttgart

Donau

BAYERN

SCHWARZWALD

BADEN-WÜRTTEMBERG

FRANKREICH

Augsburg

Lech

München

BAYERISCHE ALPEN

Bregenz

die SCHWEIZ

LIECHTENSTEIN

ÖSTERREICH

Landesgrenzen
Stadt
Landeshauptstadt
Hauptstadt

0   50 Meilen
0   50 Kilometer

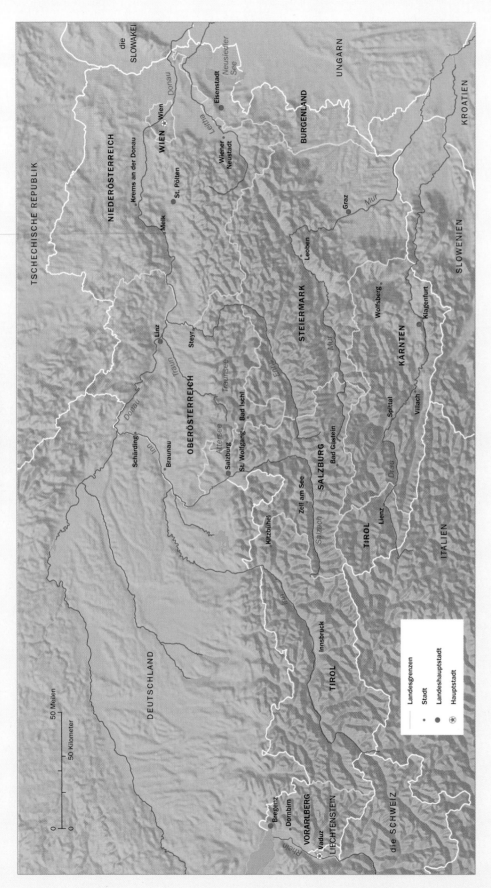

Österreich

Liechtenstein

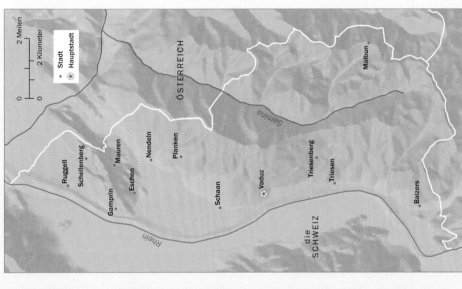

Stadt
Hauptstadt

2 Meilen
2 Kilometer
0
0

ÖSTERREICH

Samina

Malbun

Ruggell
Schellenberg
Mauren
Nendeln
Planken
Gamprin
Eschen
Triesenberg
Triesen
Schaan
Vaduz
Balzers

die
SCHWEIZ

Rhein

die Schweiz

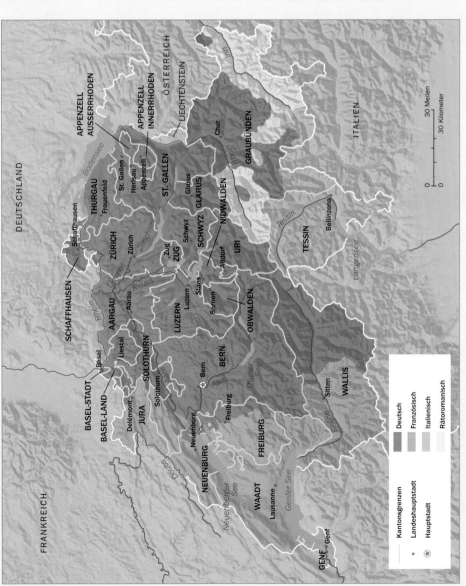

DEUTSCHLAND

FRANKREICH

ÖSTERREICH

ITALIEN

Inn

Bodensee

APPENZELL
AUSSERRHODEN

APPENZELL
INNERRHODEN

LIECHTENSTEIN

THURGAU
Frauenfeld

St. Gallen
Herisau
Appenzell

ST. GALLEN

Chur

GRAUBÜNDEN

Rhein

Schaffhausen

ZÜRICH
Zürich

GLARUS
Glarus

Schwyz

NIDWALDEN

SCHAFFHAUSEN

Limmat
Reuss
Zürichsee

Zug
ZUG

SCHWYZ

URI

TESSIN

Tessin

Bellinzona

AARGAU
Aarau

Luzern

Stans

Altdorf

Langensee

Basel

Liestal

SOLOTHURN

LUZERN

Sarnen

OBWALDEN

BASEL-STADT

BASEL-LAND

JURA
Delémont

Solothurn

BERN

Bern

Aare

Thuner
See

WALLIS
Sitten

Neuenburg

Freiburg

Rhone

NEUENBURG

FREIBURG

WAADT
Lausanne

Neuenberger
See

Genfer See

GENF
Genf

Doubs

Kantonsgrenzen
Landeshauptstadt
Hauptstadt

Deutsch
Französisch
Italienisch
Rätoromanisch

30 Meilen
30 Kilometer
0
0

Declension of articles

definite articles				
	masculine	**feminine**	**neuter**	**plural**
nominative	der	die	das	die
accusative	den	die	das	die
dative	dem	der	dem	den
genitive	des	der	des	der

der-words				
	masculine	**feminine**	**neuter**	**plural**
nominative	dieser	diese	dieses	diese
accusative	diesen	diese	dieses	diese
dative	diesem	dieser	diesem	diesen
genitive	dieses	dieser	dieses	dieser

indefinite articles				
	masculine	**feminine**	**neuter**	**plural**
nominative	ein	eine	ein	-
accusative	einen	eine	ein	-
dative	einem	einer	einem	-
genitive	eines	einer	eines	-

ein-words				
	masculine	**feminine**	**neuter**	**plural**
nominative	mein	meine	mein	meine
accusative	meinen	meine	mein	meine
dative	meinem	meiner	meinem	meinen
genitive	meines	meiner	meines	meiner

Declension of nouns and adjectives

nouns and adjectives with *der*-words				
	masculine	**feminine**	**neuter**	**plural**
nominative	der gute Rat	die gute Landschaft	das gute Brot	die guten Freunde
accusative	den guten Rat	die gute Landschaft	das gute Brot	die guten Freunde
dative	dem guten Rat	der guten Landschaft	dem guten Brot	den guten Freunden
genitive	des guten Rates	der guten Landschaft	des guten Brotes	der guten Freunde

nouns and adjectives with *ein*-words				
	masculine	**feminine**	**neuter**	**plural**
nominative	ein guter Rat	eine gute Landschaft	ein gutes Brot	meine guten Freunde
accusative	einen guten Rat	eine gute Landschaft	ein gutes Brot	meine guten Freunde
dative	einem guten Rat	einer guten Landschaft	einem guten Brot	meinen guten Freunden
genitive	eines guten Rates	einer guten Landschaft	eines guten Brotes	meiner guten Freunde

unpreceded adjectives				
	masculine	**feminine**	**neuter**	**plural**
nominative	guter Rat	gute Landschaft	gutes Brot	gute Freunde
accusative	guten Rat	gute Landschaft	gutes Brot	gute Freunde
dative	gutem Rat	guter Landschaft	gutem Brot	guten Freunden
genitive	guten Rates	guter Landschaft	guten Brotes	guter Freunde

Declension of pronouns

personal pronouns										
nominative	ich	du	Sie	er	sie	es	wir	ihr	Sie	sie
accusative	mich	dich	Sie	ihn	sie	es	uns	euch	Sie	sie
accusative reflexive	mich	dich	sich	sich	sich	sich	uns	euch	sich	sich
dative	mir	dir	Ihnen	ihm	ihr	ihm	uns	euch	Ihnen	ihnen
dative reflexive	mir	dir	sich	sich	sich	sich	uns	euch	sich	sich

Glossary of Grammatical Terms

ADJECTIVE Words that describe people, places, or things. An attributive adjective comes before the noun it modifies and takes an ending that matches the gender and case of the noun. A predicate adjective comes after the verb **sein**, **werden**, or **bleiben** and describes the noun that is the subject of the sentence. Predicate adjectives take no additional endings.

Thomas hat eine sehr **gute** Stelle gefunden.	Hast du mein **kleines** Adressbuch gesehen?
*Thomas found a really **good** job.*	*Have you seen my **little** address book?*
Mein Bruder ist **klein**.	Deine Schwester wird **groß**.
*My brother is **short**.*	*Your sister is getting **tall**.*

Possessive adjectives Words that are placed before a noun to indicate ownership or belonging. Each personal pronoun has a corresponding possessive adjective. Possessive adjectives take the same endings as the indefinite article **ein**.

Meine Schwester ist hier.	Wo ist **dein** Vater?
***My** sister is here.*	*Where is **your** father?*

ADVERB Words or phrases that modify a verb, an adjective, or another adverb. Adverbs and adverbial phrases describe *when*, *how*, or *where* an action takes place.

Der Kuchen ist **fast** fertig.	Du isst **viel zu** schnell.
*The cake is **almost** ready.*	*You eat **much too** quickly.*

ARTICLE A word that precedes a noun and indicates its gender, number, and case.

Definite article Equivalent to *the* in English. Its form indicates the gender and case of the noun, and whether it is singular or plural.

der Tisch (*m. s.*)	**die** Türen (*f. pl.*)
the table	*the doors*
die Tische (*m. pl.*)	**das** Fenster (*n. s.*)
the tables	*the window*
die Tür (*f. s.*)	**die** Fenster (*n. pl.*)
the door	*the windows*

Indefinite article Corresponds to *a* or *an* in English. It precedes the noun and matches its gender and case. There is no plural indefinite article in German.

ein Tisch (*m.*)	**ein** Fenster (*n.*)
a table	*a window*
eine Tür (*f.*)	
a door	

CASE There are four cases in German. The case indicates the function of each noun in a sentence. The case of a noun determines the form of the definite or indefinite article that precedes the noun, the form of any adjectives that modify the noun, and the form of the pronoun that can replace the noun.

Nominativ (*nominative*): **Der Professor** ist alt.
The professor is old.

Akkusativ (*accusative*): Ich verstehe **den Professor**.
I understand the professor.

Dativ (*dative*): Der Assistent zeigt **dem Professor** den neuen Computer.
The assistant is showing the professor the new computer.

Genitiv (*genitive*): Das ist der Assistent **des Professors**.
This is the professor's assistant.

The nominative case The grammatical subject of a sentence is always in the nominative case. The nominative case is also used for nouns that follow a form of **sein**, **werden**, or **bleiben**. In German dictionaries, nouns, pronouns, and numbers are always listed in their nominative form.

Das ist **eine gute Idee**.	**Die Kinder** schlafen.
*That's **a good idea**.*	***The kids** are sleeping.*

The accusative case A noun that functions as a direct object is in the accusative case.

Der Lehrer hat **den Stift**.	Ich kaufe **einen Tisch**.
*The teacher has **the pen**.*	*I'm going to buy **a table**.*
Sie öffnet **die Tür**.	Ich habe **ein Problem**.
*She's opening **the door**.*	*I have **a problem**.*

The dative case An object in the dative case indicates to whom or for whom an action is performed.

Ich bringe **dem Lehrer** einen Apfel.
*I'm bringing **the teacher** an apple.*

Zeig **der Professorin** deine Arbeit.
*Show your work **to the professor**.*

The genitive case A noun in the genitive case modifies another noun. The genitive case indicates ownership or a close relationship between the genitive noun and the noun it modifies, which may be a subject or an object.

Thorsten hat die Rede **des Bundespräsidenten** heruntergeladen.
*Thorsten downloaded **the president's** speech.*

Das Mikrofon **der Professorin** funktioniert nicht.
***The professor's** microphone doesn't work.*

CLAUSE A group of words that contains both a conjugated verb and a subject, either expressed or implied.

Main (or independent) clause A clause that can stand alone as a complete sentence.

Ich bezahle immer bar, weil ich keine Kreditkarte habe.
I always pay cash, because I don't have a credit card.

Subordinate clause A subordinate clause explains how, when, why, or under what circumstances the action in the main clause occurs. The conjugated verb of a subordinate clause is placed at the end of that clause.

Ich lese die Zeitung, **wenn** ich Zeit **habe**.
*I read the newspaper **when I have** the time.*

COMPARATIVE The form of an adjective or adverb that compares two or more people or things.

Meine Geschwister sind alle **älter** als ich.
*My siblings are all **older** than I am.*

Die Fahrt dauert mit dem Auto **länger** als mit dem Zug.
*The trip takes **longer** by car than by train.*

CONJUNCTION A word used to connect words, clauses, or phrases.

Coordinating conjunctions Words that combine two related sentences, words, or phrases into a single sentence. There are five coordinating conjunctions in German: **aber** (*but*), **denn** (*because; since*), **oder** (*or*), **sondern** (*but, rather*), **und** (*and*). All other conjunctions are subordinating.

Ich möchte eine große Küche, **denn** ich koche gern.
*I want a big kitchen, **because** I like to cook.*

Lola braucht einen Schrank **oder** eine Kommode.
*Lola needs a closet **or** a dresser.*

Subordinating conjunctions Words used to combine a subordinate clause with a main clause.

Ich lese die Zeitung, **wenn** ich Zeit **habe**.
*I read the newspaper **when I have** the time.*

DEMONSTRATIVE Pronouns or adjectives that refer to something or someone that has already been mentioned, or that point out a specific person or thing.

Ist Greta online? –Ja, **die** schreibt eine E-Mail.
*Is Greta online? –Yes, **she's** writing an e-mail.*

Gefällt dir dieser Sessel? –Ja, **der** ist sehr bequem!
*Do you like that chair? –Yes, **it's** very comfortable!*

DER-WORDS Words that take the same endings as the forms of the definite article **der**. These include the demonstrative pronouns **dieser** (*this; that*), **jeder** (*each, every*), **jener** (*that*), **mancher** (*some*), and **solcher** (*such*), and the question word **welcher** (*which*).

Welcher Laptop gefällt dir am besten?
***Which** laptop do you like best?*

Ich finde **diesen** Laptop am schönsten.
*I think **this** laptop is the nicest.*

DIRECT OBJECT A noun or pronoun that directly receives the action of the verb. Direct objects are in the accusative.

Kennst du **diesen Mann**?   Ich mache **eine Torte**.
*Do you know **that man**?*   *I'm making **a cake**.*

EIN-WORDS Words that take the same endings as the forms of the indefinite article **ein**. These include the negation **kein** and all of the possessive adjectives.

Hast du **einen** Hund?   Ich habe **keinen** Fußball.
*Do you have **a** dog?*   *I don't have **a** soccer ball.*

GENDER The grammatical categorization of nouns, pronouns, and adjectives as masculine, feminine, or neuter.

Masculine
articles: **der, ein**
pronouns: **er, der**
adjectives: **guter, schöner**

Feminine
articles: **die, eine**
pronouns: **sie, die**
adjectives: **gute, schöne**

Neuter
articles: **das, ein**
pronouns: **es, das**
adjectives: **gutes, schönes**

HELPING VERB *See* VERB, *Auxiliary verb*.

IMPERATIVE Imperatives are verb forms used to express commands, requests, suggestions, directions, or instructions.

Mach deine Hausaufgaben!   **Backen wir** einen Kuchen!
***Do** your homework!*   ***Let's bake** a cake!*

INDIRECT OBJECT A noun or pronoun that receives the action of the verb indirectly. The indirect object is often a person to whom or for whom the action of the sentence is performed. Indirect objects are in the dative case.

Manfred hat **seinem Bruder** ein Buch geschenkt.
*Manfred gave **his brother** a book.*

INFINITIVE The basic, unconjugated form of a verb. Most German infinitives end in **-en**. A few end in **-ern** or **-eln**.

sehen, essen, lesen, wandern, sammeln
to see, to eat, to read, to hike, to collect

NOUN A word that refers to one or more people, animals, places, things, or ideas. Nouns in German may be masculine, feminine, or neuter, and are either singular or plural.

der **Junge**, die **Katze**, das **Café**
the boy, the cat, the café

Compound noun Two or more simple nouns can be combined to form a compound noun. The gender of a compound noun matches the gender of the last noun in the compound.

die Nacht + das Hemd = **das Nachthemd**
night + shirt = nightshirt

NUMBER A grammatical term that refers to the quantity of a noun. Nouns in German are either singular or plural. The plural form of a noun may have an added umlaut and/or an added ending. Adjectives, articles, and verbs also have different endings, depending on whether they are singular or plural.

Singular:
der **Mann**, die **Frau**, das **Kind**
the man, the woman, the child

Plural:
die **Männer**, die **Frauen**, die **Kinder**
the men, the women, the children

NUMBERS Words that represent quantities.

Cardinal numbers Numbers that indicate specific quantities. Cardinal numbers typically modify nouns, but do not add gender or case endings.

zwei Männer, **fünfzehn** Frauen, **sechzig** Kinder
two men, fifteen women, sixty children

Ordinal numbers Words that indicate the order of a noun in a series. Ordinal numbers add the same gender and case endings as adjectives.

der **erste** Mann, die **zweite** Frau, das **dritte** Kind
the first man, the second woman, the third child

PARTICIPLE A participle is formed from a verb but may be used as an adjective or adverb. Present participles are used primarily in written German. Past participles are used in compound tenses, including the **Perfekt** and the **Plusquamperfekt**.

Der **aufgehende** Mond war sehr schön.
The rising moon was beautiful.

Habt ihr schon **gegessen**?
Have you already eaten?

PREPOSITION A preposition links a noun or pronoun to other words in a sentence. Combined with a noun or pronoun, it forms a prepositional phrase, which can be used like an adverb to answer the question *when, how,* or *where*. In German, certain prepositions are always followed by a noun in the accusative case, while others are always followed by a noun in the dative case. A small number of prepositions are used with the genitive case.

ohne das Buch   **mit** dem Auto
without the book   *by car*

trotz des Regens
in spite of the rain

Two-way prepositions can be followed by either the dative or the accusative, depending on the situation. They are followed by the accusative when used with a verb that indicates movement toward a destination. With all other verbs, they are followed by the dative.

Stell deine Schuhe nicht **auf den Tisch**!
Don't put your shoes on the table!

Dein Schal liegt **auf dem Tisch**.
Your scarf is lying on the table.

PRONOUN A word that takes the place of a noun.

Subject pronouns Words used to replace a noun in the nominative case.

Maria ist nett.   **Der Junge** ist groß.
Maria is nice.   *The boy is tall.*

Sie ist nett.   **Er** ist groß.
She is nice.   *He is tall.*

Accusative pronouns Words used to replace a noun that functions as the direct object.

Wer hat **die Torte** gebacken?   Ich habe **sie** gebacken.
Who baked the cake?   *I baked it.*

Dative pronouns Words used to replace a noun that functions as the indirect object.

Musst du **deiner Oma** eine E-Mail schicken?
Do you need to send an e-mail to your grandma?

Nein, ich habe **ihr** schon geschrieben.
No, I already wrote to her.

Indefinite pronouns Words that refer to an unknown or nonspecific person or thing.

Jemand hat seinen Personalausweis vergessen.
Someone forgot his I.D. card.

Herr Klein will mit **niemandem** sprechen.
Mr. Klein doesn't want to speak with anyone.

Reflexive pronouns The pronouns used with reflexive verbs. When the subject of a reflexive verb is also its direct object, it takes an accusative reflexive pronoun. When the subject of a reflexive verb is not its direct object, it takes a dative reflexive pronoun.

Ich wasche **mich**.	Ich wasche **mir** das Gesicht.
I'm washing (myself).	*I'm washing my face.*

SUBJUNCTIVE A verb form (**der Konjunktiv II**) used to talk about hypothetical, unlikely or impossible conditions, to express wishes, and to make polite requests. German also has an additional subjunctive tense, der **Konjunktiv I**, used to report what someone else has said without indicating whether the information is true or false.

Ich **hätte** gern viel Geld.
I'd like to have a lot of money.

Wenn er sportlicher **wäre**, **würde** er häufiger trainieren.
If he were more athletic, he would exercise more.

SUPERLATIVE The form of an adjective or adverb used to indicate that a person or thing has more of a particular quality than anyone or anything else.

Welches ist **das größte** Tier der Welt?
What's the biggest animal in the world?

Wie komme ich **am besten** zur Tankstelle?
What's the best way to get to the gas station?

TENSE A set of verb forms that indicates if an action or state occurs in the past, present, or future.

Compound tense A tense made up of an auxiliary verb and a participle or infinitive.

Wir **haben** ihren Geburtstag **gefeiert**.
We celebrated her birthday.

VERB A word that expresses actions or states of being. German verbs are classified as *weak*, *mixed*, or *strong*, based on the way their past participles are formed.

weak: Ich **habe** eine Torte **gemacht**.	strong: Wir **haben** Kekse **gegessen**.
I made a cake.	*We ate cookies.*

mixed: Er **hat** eine CD **gebrannt**.
He burned a CD.

Auxiliary verb A conjugated verb used with the participle or infinitive of another verb. The auxiliary verbs **haben** and **sein** are used with past participles to form compound tenses including the **Perfekt** and **Plusquamperfekt**. **Werden** is used with an infinitive to form the future tense, and with a past participle to form a passive construction. Modals are also frequently used as auxiliary verbs.

Habt ihr den Tisch **gedeckt**?
Did you set the table?

Jasmin **war** noch nie nach Zürich **gefahren**.
Jasmin had never been to Zurich.

Wir **werden** uns in einer Woche wieder **treffen**.
We'll meet again in one week.

Es **wird** hier nur Deutsch **gesprochen**.
Only German is spoken here.

Modal verbs Verbs that modify the meaning of another verb. Modals express an attitude toward an action, such as permission, obligation, ability, desire, or necessity.

Ich **muss** Französisch **lernen**.	Ich **will** Französisch **lernen**.
I have to study French.	*I want to learn French.*

Principal parts German verbs are usually listed in dictionaries by their *principal parts* (**Stammformen**): the infinitive, the third-person singular present tense form (if the verb is irregular in the present), the third-person singular **Präteritum** form, and the past participle. Knowing the principal parts of a verb allows you to produce all of its conjugations in any tense.

geben (gibt)	**gab**	**gegeben**
to give (gives)	*gave*	*given*

Reflexive verbs Verbs that indicate an action you do to yourself or for yourself. The subject of a reflexive verb is also its object.

Ich **fühle mich** nicht **wohl**.	Wir **haben uns entspannt**.
I don't feel well.	*We've been relaxing.*

Reciprocal reflexive verbs Verbs that express an action done by two or more people or things to or for one another.

Wir rufen **uns** jeden Tag an.	Meine Großeltern lieben **sich** sehr.
*We call **each other** every day.*	*My grandparents love **each other** very much.*

Verb conjugation tables

Here are the infinitives of all verbs introduced as active vocabulary in **Mosaik**. Each verb is followed by a model verb that follows the same conjugation pattern. The number in parentheses indicates where in the verb tables, pages **A16–A25**, you can find the conjugated forms of the model verb. The word (*sein*) after a verb means that it is conjugated with **sein** in the **Perfekt** and **Plusquamperfekt**. For irregular reflexive verbs, the list may point to a non-reflexive model verb. A full conjugation of the simple forms of a reflexive verb is presented in Verb table 6 on page **A17**. Verbs followed by an asterisk (*) have a separable prefix.

abbiegen* (*sein*) like schieben (42)
abbrechen* like sprechen (47)
abfahren* (*sein*) like tragen (51)
abfliegen* (*sein*) like schieben (42)
abheben* like heben (29)
abschicken* like machen (3)
abstauben* like machen (3)
(sich) abtrocknen* like arbeiten (1)
adoptieren like probieren (4)
anbieten* like schieben (42)
anfangen* like fangen (23)
angeln like sammeln (5)
ankommen* (*sein*) like kommen (32)
anmachen* like machen (3)
anrufen* like rufen (40)
anschauen* like machen (3)
anstoßen* like stoßen (50)
antworten like arbeiten (1)
(sich) anziehen* like schieben (42)
arbeiten (1)
(sich) ärgern like fordern (26)
aufgehen* (*sein*) like gehen (28)
auflegen* like machen (3)
aufmachen* like machen (3)
aufnehmen* like nehmen (38)
aufräumen* like machen (3)
aufstehen* (*sein*) like stehen (48)
aufwachen* (*sein*) like machen (3)
ausfüllen like machen (3)
ausgehen like gehen (28)
ausmachen like machen (3)
(sich) ausruhen like sich freuen (6)
ausschalten* like arbeiten (1)
(sich) ausziehen* like schieben (42)
backen like mahlen (37)
(sich) baden like arbeiten (1)
bauen like machen (3)
beantworten like arbeiten (1)
bedeuten like arbeiten (1)
bedienen like machen (3)
(sich) beeilen like sich freuen (6)
beginnen like schwimmen (44)
behaupten like arbeiten (1)
bekommen like kommen (32)
belegen like machen (3)
benutzen like machen (3)
berichten like arbeiten (1)

beschreiben like bleiben (20)
besprechen like sprechen (47)
bestehen like stehen (48)
bestellen like machen (3)
besuchen like machen (3)
(sich) bewegen like heben (29)
(sich) bewerben like helfen (31)
bezahlen like machen (3)
bieten like schieben (42)
bleiben (*sein*) (20)
braten like schlafen (43)
brauchen like machen (3)
brechen like sprechen (47)
brennen like rennen (17)
bringen like denken (16)
buchen like machen (3)
büffeln like sammeln (5)
bügeln like sammeln (5)
bürsten like arbeiten (1)
danken like machen (3)
decken like machen (3)
denken like denken (16)
drücken like machen (3)
drucken like machen (3)
durchfallen* (*sein*) like fallen (22)
durchmachen* like machen (3)
dürfen (10)
(sich) duschen like sich freuen (6)
einkaufen* like machen (3)
einladen* like tragen (51)
einschlafen* (*sein*) like schlafen (43)
einzahlen* like machen (3)
empfehlen like stehlen (49)
entdecken like machen (3)
entfernen like machen (3)
entgegennehmen* like nehmen (38)
entlassen like fallen (22)
(sich) entschließen like fließen (25)
(sich) entschuldigen like machen (3)
(sich) entspannen like sich freuen (6)
entwerten like arbeiten (1)
entwickeln like sammeln (5)
erfinden like trinken (52)
erforschen like machen (3)
ergänzen like machen (3)
erhalten like fallen (22)
(sich) erinnern like fordern (26)

(sich) erkälten like arbeiten (1)
erkennen like rennen (17)
erklären like machen (3)
erzählen like machen (3)
essen (21)
fahren (*sein*) like tragen (51)
fallen (*sein*) (22)
fangen (23)
(sich) färben like machen (3)
faulenzen like machen (3)
fegen like machen (3)
feiern (2)
fernsehen* like geben (27)
finden like trinken (52)
fliegen (*sein*) like schieben (42)
folgen (*sein*) like machen (3)
(sich) fragen like machen (3)
(sich) freuen (6)
(sich) fühlen like sich freuen (6)
füllen like machen (3)
funktionieren like probieren (4)
geben (27)
gefallen like fallen (22)
gehen (*sein*) (28)
gehören like machen (3)
genießen like fließen (25)
gewinnen like schwimmen (44)
(sich) gewöhnen like sich freuen (6)
glauben like machen (3)
gratulieren like probieren (4)
grüßen like machen (3)
haben like haben (7)
handeln like sammeln (5)
hängen like machen (3)
heiraten like arbeiten (1)
heißen (30)
helfen (31)
heruntergehen* (*sein*) like gehen (28)
herunterladen* like tragen (51)
(sich) hinlegen* like machen (3)
(sich) hinsetzen* like machen (3)
hinterlassen like fallen (22)
hochgehen* (*sein*) like gehen (28)
hören like machen (3)
husten like arbeiten (1)
(sich) informieren like probieren (4)
(sich) interessieren like probieren (4)

joggen (*sein*) like machen (3)
(sich) kämmen like machen (3)
kaufen like machen (3)
kennen like rennen (17)
klettern (*sein*) like fordern (26)
klingeln like sammeln (5)
kochen like machen (3)
kommen (*sein*) (32)
können (11)
korrigieren like probieren (4)
kosten like arbeiten (1)
küssen like machen (3)
lächeln like sammeln (5)
lachen like machen (3)
laden like tragen (51)
landen (*sein*) like arbeiten (1)
lassen like fallen (22)
laufen (*sein*) (33)
leben like machen (3)
legen like machen (3)
leiten like arbeiten (1)
lernen like machen (3)
lesen (34)
lieben like machen (3)
liegen (35)
löschen like tragen (51)
lügen (36)
machen (3)
meinen like machen (3)
mieten like arbeiten (1)
mitbringen* like denken (16)
mitkommen* (*sein*) like kommen (32)
mitmachen* like machen (3)
mitnehmen* like nehmen (38)
mögen (12)
müssen (13)
nachmachen* like machen (3)
nehmen (38)
(sich) nennen like rennen (17)
niesen like machen (3)
öffnen like arbeiten (1)
packen like machen (3)
parken like machen (3)
passen like machen (3)
passieren (*sein*) like probieren (4)
probieren (4)
putzen like machen (3)

(sich) rasieren like probieren (4)
rauchen like machen (3)
recyceln like sammeln (5)
reden like arbeiten (1)
regnen like arbeiten (1)
reisen (*sein*) like machen (3)
reiten (*sein*) like pfeifen (39)
rennen (*sein*) (17)
reparieren like probieren (4)
retten like arbeiten (1)
sagen like machen (3)
schauen like machen (3)
scheitern (*sein*) like fordern (26)
schenken like machen (3)
schicken like machen (3)
schlafen (43)
schmecken like machen (3)
(sich) schminken like machen (3)
schneien like machen (3)
schreiben like bleiben (20)
schützen like machen (3)
schwänzen like machen (3)
schwimmen (*sein*) (44)
sehen like lesen (34)
sein (*sein*) (8)
(sich) setzen like machen (3)
singen like trinken (52)
sitzen (46)

sollen (14)
sortieren like probieren (4)
spazieren (*sein*) like probieren (4)
speichern like fordern (26)
spielen like machen (3)
sprechen (47)
springen (*sein*) like trinken (52)
spülen like machen (3)
starten (*sein*) like arbeiten (1)
staubsaugen like saugen (41)
stehen (48)
stehlen (49)
steigen (*sein*) like bleiben (20)
stellen like machen (3)
sterben (*sein*) like helfen (31)
(sich) streiten like pfeifen (39)
studieren like probieren (4)
suchen like machen (3)
surfen (*sein*) like machen (3)
tanken like machen (3)
tanzen like machen (3)
tragen (51)
träumen like machen (3)
(sich) treffen (*sein*) like sprechen (47)
treiben (*sein*) like bleiben (20)
(sich) trennen like sich freuen (6)
trinken (52)
tun (53)

üben like machen (3)
(sich) überlegen like machen (3)
übernachten like arbeiten (1)
überqueren like machen (3)
überraschen like machen (3)
umtauschen* like machen (3)
(sich) umziehen* (*sein*) like schieben (42)
untergehen* (*sein*) like gehen (28)
(sich) unterhalten* like fallen (22)
unterschreiben like bleiben (20)
(sich) verbessern like fordern (26)
verbringen like denken (16)
verdienen like machen (3)
vereinbaren like machen (3)
vergessen like essen (21)
verkaufen like machen (3)
verkünden like arbeiten (1)
(sich) verlaufen like laufen (33)
(sich) verletzen like machen (3)
(sich) verlieben like machen (3)
verlieren like schieben (42)
verschmutzen (*sein*) like machen (3)
(sich) verspäten like sich freuen (6)
(sich) verstauchen like machen (3)
verstehen like stehen (48)
versuchen like machen (3)
(sich) vorbereiten* like arbeiten (1)

vormachen* like machen (3)
vorschlagen* like tragen (51)
(sich) vorstellen* like machen (3)
wachsen (*sein*) like waschen (54)
wandern (*sein*) like fordern (26)
warten like arbeiten (1)
(sich) waschen (54)
wegräumen* like machen (3)
wegwerfen* like helfen (31)
weinen like machen (3)
werden (*sein*) (9)
wettmachen* like machen (3)
wiederholen like machen (3)
wiegen like schieben (42)
wischen like machen (3)
wissen (55)
wohnen like machen (3)
wollen (15)
(sich) wünschen like machen (3)
zeigen like machen (3)
ziehen (*sein*) like schieben (42)
zubereiten* like arbeiten (1)
zumachen* like machen (3)
(sich) zurechtfinden* like trinken (52)
zurückkommen* (*sein*) like kommen (32)
zuschauen* like machen (3)

Regular verbs: simple tenses

Infinitiv Partizip I Partizip II Perfekt	INDIKATIV			KONJUNKTIV I	KONJUNKTIV II		IMPERATIV
	Präsens	Präteritum	Plusquamperfekt	Präsens	Präsens	Perfekt	
1 **arbeiten**	arbeite	arbeitete	hatte gearbeitet	arbeite	arbeitete	hätte gearbeitet	
(to work)	arbeitest	arbeitetest	hattest gearbeitet	arbeitest	arbeitetest	hättest gearbeitet	arbeite
	arbeitet	arbeitete	hatte gearbeitet	arbeite	arbeitete	hätte gearbeitet	
arbeitend	arbeiten	arbeiteten	hatten gearbeitet	arbeiten	arbeiteten	hätten gearbeitet	arbeiten wir
gearbeitet	arbeitet	arbeitetet	hattet gearbeitet	arbeitet	arbeitetet	hättet gearbeitet	arbeitet
gearbeitet haben	arbeiten	arbeiteten	hatten gearbeitet	arbeiten	arbeiteten	hätten gearbeitet	arbeiten Sie
2 **feiern**	feiere	feierte	hatte gefeiert	feiere	feierte	hätte gefeiert	
(to celebrate)	feierst	feiertest	hattest gefeiert	feierest	feiertest	hättest gefeiert	feiere
	feiert	feierte	hatte gefeiert	feiere	feierte	hätte gefeiert	
feiernd	feiern	feierten	hatten gefeiert	feiern	feierten	hätten gefeiert	feiern wir
gefeiert	feiert	feiertet	hattet gefeiert	feiert	feiertet	hättet gefeiert	feiert
gefeiert haben	feiern	feierten	hatten gefeiert	feiern	feierten	hätten gefeiert	feiern Sie
3 **machen**	mache	machte	hatte gemacht	mache	machte	hätte gemacht	
(to make; to do)	machst	machtest	hattest gemacht	machest	machtest	hättest gemacht	mache/mach
	macht	machte	hatte gemacht	mache	machte	hätte gemacht	
machend	machen	machten	hatten gemacht	machen	machten	hätten gemacht	machen wir
gemacht	macht	machtet	hattet gemacht	machet	machtet	hättet gemacht	macht
gemacht haben	machen	machten	hatten gemacht	machen	machten	hätten gemacht	machen Sie
4 **probieren**	probiere	probierte	hatte probiert	probiere	probierte	hätte probiert	
(to try)	probierst	probiertest	hattest probiert	probierest	probiertest	hättest probiert	probiere/probier
	probiert	probierte	hatte probiert	probiere	probierte	hätte probiert	
probierend	probieren	probierten	hatten probiert	probieren	probierten	hätten probiert	probieren wir
probiert	probiert	probiertet	hattet probiert	probieret	probiertet	hättet probiert	probiert
probiert haben	probieren	probierten	hatten probiert	probieren	probierten	hätten probiert	probieren Sie
5 **sammeln**	sammle	sammelte	hatte gesammelt	sammle	sammelte	hätte gesammelt	
(to collect)	sammelst	sammeltest	hattest gesammelt	sammlest	sammeltest	hättest gesammelt	sammle
	sammelt	sammelte	hatte gesammelt	sammle	sammelte	hätte gesammelt	
sammelnd	sammeln	sammelten	hatten gesammelt	sammlen	sammelten	hätten gesammelt	sammeln wir
gesammelt	sammelt	sammeltet	hattet gesammelt	sammlet	sammeltet	hättet gesammelt	sammelt
gesammelt haben	sammeln	sammelten	hatten gesammelt	sammlen	sammelten	hätten gesammelt	sammeln Sie

Reflexive verbs

Infinitiv	INDIKATIV			KONJUNKTIV I	KONJUNKTIV II		IMPERATIV
Partizip I Partizip II Perfekt	Präsens	Präteritum	Plusquamperfekt	Präsens	Präsens	Perfekt	
6 **sich freuen**	freue mich	freute mich	hatte mich gefreut	freue mich	freute mich	hätte mich gefreut	
(to be happy)	freust dich	freutest dich	hattest dich gefreut	freuest dich	freutest dich	hättest dich gefreut	freue/freu dich
	freut sich	freute sich	hatte sich gefreut	freue sich	freute sich	hätte sich gefreut	
sich freuend	freuen uns	freuten uns	hatten uns gefreut	freuen uns	freuten uns	hätten uns gefreut	freuen wir uns
sich gefreut	freut euch	freutet euch	hattet euch gefreut	freuet euch	freutet euch	hättet euch gefreut	freut euch
sich gefreut haben	freuen sich	freuten sich	hatten sich gefreut	freuen sich	freuten sich	hätten sich gefreut	freuen Sie sich

Auxiliary verbs

Infinitiv	INDIKATIV			KONJUNKTIV I	KONJUNKTIV II		IMPERATIV
Partizip I Partizip II Perfekt	Präsens	Präteritum	Plusquamperfekt	Präsens	Präsens	Perfekt	
7 **haben**	habe	hatte	hatte gehabt	habe	hätte	hätte gehabt	
(to have)	hast	hattest	hattest gehabt	habest	hättest	hättest gehabt	habe/hab
	hat	hatte	hatte gehabt	habe	hätte	hätte gehabt	
habend	haben	hatten	hatten gehabt	haben	hätten	hätten gehabt	haben wir
gehabt	habt	hattet	hattet gehabt	habet	hättet	hättet gehabt	habt
gehabt haben	haben	hatten	hatten gehabt	haben	hätten	hätten gehabt	haben Sie
8 **sein**	bin	war	war gewesen	sei	wäre	wäre gewesen	
(to be)	bist	warst	warst gewesen	seiest/seist	wärst/wärest	wärst/wärest gewesen	sei
	ist	war	war gewesen	sei	wäre	wäre gewesen	
seiend	sind	waren	waren gewesen	seien	wären	wären gewesen	seien wir
gewesen	seid	wart	wart gewesen	seiet	wärt/wäret	wärt/wäret gewesen	seid
gewesen sein	sind	waren	waren gewesen	seien	wären	wären gewesen	seien Sie
9 **werden**	werde	wurde	war geworden	werde	würde	wäre geworden	
(to become)	wirst	wurdest	warst geworden	werdest	würdest	wärst geworden	werde
	wird	wurde	war geworden	werde	würde	wäre geworden	
werdend	werden	wurden	waren geworden	werden	würden	wären geworden	werden wir
geworden	werdet	wurdet	wart geworden	werdet	würdet	wärt geworden	werdet
geworden sein	werden	wurden	waren geworden	werden	würden	wären geworden	werden Sie

Compound tenses

Hilfsverb	INDIKATIV				KONJUNKTIV I		KONJUNKTIV II	
	Perfekt		**Plusquamperfekt**		**Präsens**	**Perfekt**	**Präsens**	**Perfekt**
haben	habe		hatte		habe		hätte	
	hast	gemacht	hattest	gemacht	habest	gemach	hättest	gemach
	hat	gearbeitet	hatte	gearbeitet	habe	gearbeitet	hätte	gearbeitet
	haben	studiert	hatten	studiert	haben	studiert	hätten	studiert
	habt	gefeiert	hattet	gefeiert	habet	gefeiert	hättet	gefeiert
	haben	gesammelt	hatten	gesammelt	haben	gesammelt	hätten	gesammelt
sein	bin gegangen		war gegangen		sei gegangen		wäre gegangen	
	bist gegangen		warst gegangen		seiest/seist gegangen		wärst/wärest gegangen	
	ist gegangen		war gegangen		sei gegangen		wäre gegangen	
	sind gegangen		waren gegangen		seien gegangen		wären gegangen	
	seid gegangen		wart gegangen		seiet gegangen		wärt/wäret gegangen	
	sind gegangen		waren gegangen		seien gegangen		wären gegangen	

	Futur I/II	Futur I/II	Futur I/II
werden	werde machen / gemacht haben	werde machen / gemacht haben	würde machen / gemacht haben
	wirst machen / gemacht haben	werdest machen / gemacht haben	würdest machen / gemacht haben
	wird machen / gemacht haben	werde machen / gemacht haben	würde machen / gemacht haben
	werden machen / gemacht haben	werden machen / gemacht haben	würden machen / gemacht haben
	werdet machen / gemacht haben	werdet machen / gemacht haben	würdet machen / gemacht haben
	werden machen / gemacht haben	werden machen / gemacht haben	würden machen / gemacht haben

Modal verbs

Infinitiv	INDIKATIV			KONJUNKTIV I	KONJUNKTIV II		IMPERATIV
Partizip I Partizip II Perfekt	Präsens	Präteritum	Plusquamperfekt	Präsens	Präsens	Perfekt	
10 dürfen	darf	durfte	hatte gedurft	dürfe	dürfte	hätte gedurft	*Modal verbs are not used in the imperative.*
(to be permitted to)	darfst	durftest	hattest gedurft	dürfest	dürftest	hättest gedurft	
	darf	durfte	hatte gedurft	dürfe	dürfte	hätte gedurft	
dürfend	dürfen	durften	hatten gedurft	dürfen	dürften	hätten gedurft	
gedurft/dürfen	dürft	durftet	hattet gedurft	dürfet	dürftet	hättet gedurft	
gedurft haben	dürfen	durften	hatten gedurft	dürfen	dürften	hätten gedurft	
11 können	kann	konnte	hatte gekonnt	könne	könnte	hätte gekonnt	*Modal verbs are not used in the imperative.*
(to be able to)	kannst	konntest	hattest gekonnt	könnest	könntest	hättest gekonnt	
	kann	konnte	hatte gekonnt	könne	könnte	hätte gekonnt	
könnend	können	konnten	hatten gekonnt	können	könnten	hätten gekonnt	
gekonnt /können	könnt	konntet	hattet gekonnt	könnet	könntet	hättet gekonnt	
gekonnt haben	können	konnten	hatten gekonnt	können	könnten	hätten gekonnt	
12 mögen	mag	mochte	hatte gemocht	möge	möchte	hätte gemocht	*Modal verbs are not used in the imperative.*
(to like)	magst	mochtest	hattest gemocht	mögest	möchtest	hättest gemocht	
	mag	mochte	hatte gemocht	möge	möchte	hätte gemocht	
mögend	mögen	mochten	hatten gemocht	mögen	möchten	hätten gemocht	
gemocht /mögen	mögt	mochtet	hattet gemocht	möget	möchtet	hättet gemocht	
gemocht haben	mögen	mochten	hatten gemocht	mögen	möchten	hätten gemocht	
13 müssen	muss	musste	hatte gemusst	müsse	müsste	hätte gemusst	*Modal verbs are not used in the imperative.*
(to have to)	musst	musstest	hattest gemusst	müssest	müsstest	hättest gemusst	
	muss	musste	hatte gemusst	müsse	müsste	hätte gemusst	
müssend	müssen	mussten	hatten gemusst	müssen	müssten	hätten gemusst	
gemusst /müssen	müsst	musstet	hattet gemusst	müsset	müsstet	hättet gemusst	
gemusst haben	müssen	mussten	hatten gemusst	müssen	müssten	hätten gemusst	
14 sollen	soll	sollte	hatte gesollt	solle	sollte	hätte gesollt	*Modal verbs are not used in the imperative.*
(to be supposed to)	sollst	solltest	hattest gesollt	sollest	solltest	hättest gesollt	
	soll	sollte	hatte gesollt	solle	sollte	hätte gesollt	
sollend	sollen	sollten	hatten gesollt	sollen	sollten	hätten gesollt	
gesollt /sollen	sollt	solltet	hattet gesollt	sollet	solltet	hättet gesollt	
gesollt haben	sollen	sollten	hatten gesollt	sollen	sollten	hätten gesollt	
15 wollen	will	wollte	hatte gewollt	wolle	wollte	hätte gewollt	*Modal verbs are not used in the imperative.*
(to want to)	willst	wolltest	hattest gewollt	wollest	wolltest	hättest gewollt	
	will	wollte	hatte gewollt	wollev	wollte	hätte gewollt	
wollend	wollen	wollten	hatten gewollt	wollen	wollten	hätten gewollt	
gewollt/wollen	wollt	wolltet	hattet gewollt	wollet	wolltet	hättet gewollt	
gewollt haben	wollen	wollten	hatten gewollt	wollen	wollten	hätten gewollt	

Mixed verbs

Infinitiv Partizip I Partizip II Perfekt	INDIKATIV			KONJUNKTIV I	KONJUNKTIV II		IMPERATIV
	Präsens	Präteritum	Plusquamperfekt	Präsens	Präsens	Perfekt	
16 **denken**	denke	dachte	hatte gedacht	denke	dächte	hätte gedacht	
(to think)	denkst	dachtest	hattest gedacht	denkest	dächtest	hättest gedacht	denke/denk
	denkt	dachte	hatte gedacht	denke	dächte	hätte gedacht	
denkend	denken	dachten	hatten gedacht	denken	dächten	hätten gedacht	denken wir
gedacht	denkt	dachtet	hattet gedacht	denket	dächtet	hättet gedacht	denkt
gedacht haben	denken	dachten	hatten gedacht	denken	dächten	hätten gedacht	denken Sie
17 **rennen**	renne	rannte	war gerannt	renne	rennte	wäre gerannt	
(to run)	rennst	ranntest	warst gerannt	rennest	renntest	wärest gerannt	renne/renn
	rennt	rannte	war gerannt	renne	rennte	wäre gerannt	
denkend	rennen	rannten	waren gerannt	rennen	rennten	wären gerannt	rennen wir
gerannt	rennt	ranntet	wart gerannt	rennet	renntet	wärt gerannt	rennt
gerannt sein	rennen	rannten	waren gerannt	rennen	rennten	wären gerannt	rennen Sie
18 **senden**	sende	sandte	hatte gesandt	sende	sendete	hätte gesandt	
(to send)	sendest	sandtest	hattest gesandt	sendest	sendetest	hättest gesandt	sende
	sendet	sandte	hatte gesandt	sende	sendete	hätte gesandt	
sendend	senden	sandten	hatten gesandt	senden	sendeten	hätten gesandt	senden wir
gesendet	sendet	sandtet	hattet gesandt	sendet	sendetet	hättet gesandt	sendet
gesendet haben	senden	sandten		senden	sendeten	hätten gesandt	senden Sie

Irregular verbs

Infinitiv Partizip I Partizip II Perfekt	INDIKATIV			KONJUNKTIV I	KONJUNKTIV II		IMPERATIV
	Präsens	Präteritum	Plusquamperfekt	Präsens	Präsens	Perfekt	
19 **bitten**	bitte	bat	hatte gebeten	bitte	bäte	hätte gebeten	
(to ask)	bittest	batest	hattest gebeten	bittest	bätest	hättest gebeten	bitte
	bittet	bat	hatte gebeten	bitte	bäte	hätte gebeten	
bittend	bitten	baten	hatten gebeten	bitten	bäten	hätten gebeten	bitten wir
gebeten	bittet	batet	hattet gebeten	bittet	bätet	hättet gebeten	bittet
gebeten haben	bitten	baten	hatten gebeten	bitten	bäten	hätten gebeten	bitten Sie
20 **bleiben**	bleibe	bliebe	war geblieben	bleibe	bliebe	wäre geblieben	
(to stay)	bleibst	bliebst	warst geblieben	bleibest	bliebest	wärest geblieben	bleibe/bleib
	bleibt	blieb	war geblieben	bleibe	bliebe	wäre geblieben	
bleibend	bleiben	blieben	waren geblieben	bleiben	blieben	wären geblieben	bleiben wir
geblieben	bleibt	bliebt	wart geblieben	bleibet	bliebet	wärt geblieben	bleibt
geblieben sein	bleiben	blieben	waren geblieben	bleiben	blieben	wären geblieben	bleiben Sie

Infinitiv / Partizip I / Partizip II / Perfekt	INDIKATIV			KONJUNKTIV I	KONJUNKTIV II		IMPERATIV
	Präsens	Präteritum	Plusquamperfekt	Präsens	Präsens	Perfekt	
21 essen	esse	aß	hatte gegessen	esse	äße	hätte gegessen	
(to eat)	isst	aßest	hattest gegessen	essest	äßest	hättest gegessen	iss
	isst	aß	hatte gegessen	esse	äße	hätte gegessen	
essend	essen	aßen	hatten gegessen	essen	äßen	hätten gegessen	essen wir
gegessen	esst	aß	hattet gegessen	esset	äßet	hättet gegessen	esst
gegessen haben	essen	aßen	hatten gegessen	essen	äßen	hätten gegessen	essen Sie
22 fallen	falle	fiel	war gefallen	falle	fiele	wäre gefallen	
(to fall)	fällst	fielst	warst gefallen	fallest	fielest	wärest gefallen	falle/fall
	fällt	fiel	war gefallen	falle	fiele	wäre gefallen	
fallend	fallen	fielen	waren gefallen	fallen	fielen	wären gefallen	fallen wir
gefallen	fallt	fielt	wart gefallen	fallet	fielet	wäret gefallen	fallt
gefallen sein	fallen	fielen	waren gefallen	fallen	fielen	wären gefallen	fallen Sie
23 fangen	fange	fing	hatte gemacht	fange	finge	hätte gefangen	
(to catch)	fängst	fingst	hattest gemacht	fangest	fingest	hättest gefangen	fange/fang
	fängt	fing	hatte gemacht	fange	finge	hätte gefangen	
fangend	fangen	fingen	hatten gemacht	fangen	fingen	hätten gefangen	fangen wir
gefangen	fangt	fingt	hattet gemacht	fanget	finget	hättet gefangen	fangt
gefangen haben	fangen	fingen	hatten gemacht	fangen	fingen	hätten gefangen	fangen Sie
24 flechten	flechte	flocht	hatte geflochten	flechte	flöchte	hätte geflochten	
(to braid)	flichtst	flochtest	hattest geflochten	flechtest	flöchtest	hättest geflochten	flicht
	flicht	flocht	hatte geflochten	flechte	flöchte	hätte geflochten	
flechtend	flechten	flochten	hatten geflochten	flechten	flöchten	hätten geflochten	flechten wir
geflochten	flechtet	flochtet	hattet geflochten	flechtet	flöchtet	hättet geflochten	flechtet
geflochten haben	flechten	flochten	hatten geflochten	flechten	flöchten	hätten geflochten	flechten Sie
25 fließen	fließe	floss	war geflossen	fließe	flösse	wäre geflossen	
(to flow)	fließt	flossest/flosst	warst geflossen	fließest	flössest	wärest geflossen	fließe/fließ
	fließt	floss	war geflossen	fließe	flösse	wäre geflossen	
fließend	fließen	flossen	waren geflossen	fließen	flössen	wären geflossen	fließen wir
geflossen	fließt	flosst	wart geflossen	fließet	flösset	wärt geflossen	fließt
geflossen sein	fließen	flossen	waren geflossen	fließen	flössen	wären geflossen	fließen Sie
26 fordern	ford(e)re	forderte	hatte gefordert	fordere	forderte	hätte gefordert	
(to demand)	forderst	fordertest	hattest gefordert	forderest	fordertest	hättest gefordert	fordere/fordre
	fordert	forderte	hatte gefordert	fordere	forderte	hätte gefordert	
fordernd	fordern	forderten	hatten gefordert	forderen	forderten	hätten gefordert	fordern wir
gefordert	fordert	fordertet	hattet gefordert	forderet	fordertet	hättet gefordert	fordert
gefordert haben	fordern	forderten	hatten gefordert	forderen	forderten	hätten gefordert	fordern Sie
27 geben	gebe	gab	hatte gegeben	gebe	gäbe	hätte gegeben	
(to give)	gibst	gabst	hattest gegeben	gebest	gäbest	hättest gegeben	gib
	gibt	gab	hatte gegeben	gebe	gäbe	hätte gegeben	
gebend	geben	gaben	hatten gegeben	geben	gäben	hätten gegeben	geben wir
gegeben	gebt	gabt	hattet gegeben	gebet	gäbet	hättet gegeben	gebt
gegeben haben	geben	gaben	hatten gegeben	geben	gäben	hätten gegeben	geben Sie

Infinitiv Partizip I Partizip II Perfekt	INDIKATIV			KONJUNKTIV I	KONJUNKTIV II		IMPERATIV
	Präsens	Präteritum	Plusquamperfekt	Präsens	Präsens	Perfekt	
28 **gehen**	gehe	ging	war gegangen	gehe	ginge	wäre gegangen	
(to go)	gehst	gingst	warst gegangen	gehest	gingest	wärest gegangen	gehe/geh
	geht	ging	war gegangen	gehe	ginge	wäre gegangen	
gehend	gehen	gingen	waren gegangen	gehen	gingen	wären gegangen	gehen wir
gegangen	geht	gingt	wart gegangen	gehet	ginget	wäret gegangen	geht
gegangen sein	gehen	gingen	waren gegangen	gehen	gingen	wären gegangen	gehen Sie
29 **heben**	hebe	hob	hatte gehoben	hebe	höbe	hätte gehoben	
(to lift)	hebst	hobst	hattest gehoben	hebest	höbest/höbst	hättest gehoben	hebe/heb
	hebt	hob	hatte gehoben	hebe	höbe	hätte gehoben	
hebend	heben	hoben	hatten gehoben	heben	höben	hätten gehoben	heben wir
gehoben	hebt	hobt	hattet gehoben	hebet	höbet/höbt	hättet gehoben	hebt
gehoben haben	heben	hoben	hatten gehoben	heben	höben	hätten gehoben	heben Sie
30 **heißen**	heiße	hieß	hatte geheißen	heiße	hieße	hätte geheißen	
(to be called)	heißt	hießest	hattest geheißen	heißest	hießest	hättest geheißen	heiß/heiße
	heißt	hieß	hatte geheißen	heiße	hieße	hätte geheißen	
heißend	heißen	hießen	hatten geheißen	heißen	hießen	hätten geheißen	heißen wir
geheißen	heißt	hießt	hattet geheißen	heißet	hießet	hättet geheißen	heißt
geheißen haben	heißen	hießen	hatten geheißen	heißen	hießen	hätten geheißen	heißen Sie
31 **helfen**	helfe	half	hatte geholfen	helfe	hälfe	hätte geholfen	
(to help)	hilfst	halfst	hattest geholfen	helfest	hälfest/hälfst	hättest geholfen	hilf
	hilft	half	hatte geholfen	helfe	hälfe	hätte geholfen	
helfend	helfen	halfen	hatten geholfen	helfen	hälfen	hätten geholfen	helfen wir
geholfen	helft	halft	hattet geholfen	helfet	hälfet/hälft	hättet geholfen	helft
geholfen haben	helfen	halfen	hatten geholfen	helfen	hälfen	hätten geholfen	helfen Sie
32 **kommen**	komme	kam	war gekommen	komme	käme	wäre gekommen	
(to come)	kommst	kamst	warst gekommen	kommest	kämest	wärest gekommen	komme/komm
	kommt	kam	war gekommen	komme	käme	wäre gekommen	
kommend	kommen	kamen	waren gekommen	kommen	kämen	wären gekommen	kommen wir
gekommen	kommt	kamt	wart gekommen	kommet	kämet	wäret gekommen	kommt
gekommen sein	kommen	kamen	waren gekommen	kommen	kämen	wären gekommen	kommen Sie
33 **laufen**	laufe	lief	war gelaufen	laufe	liefe	wäre gelaufen	
(to run)	läufst	liefst	warst gelaufen	laufest	liefest	wärest gelaufen	laufe/lauf
	läuft	lief	war gelaufen	laufe	liefe	wäre gelaufen	
laufend	laufen	liefen	waren gelaufen	laufen	liefen	wären gelaufen	laufen wir
gelaufen	lauft	lieft	wart gelaufen	laufet	liefet	wäret gelaufen	lauft
gelaufen sein	laufen	liefen	waren gelaufen	laufen	liefen	wären gelaufen	laufen Sie
34 **lesen**	lese	las	hatte gelesen	lese	läse	hätte gelesen	
(to read)	liest	la(se)st	hattest gelesen	lesest	läsest	hättest gelesen	lies
	liest	las	hatte gelesen	lese	läse	hätte gelesen	
lesend	lesen	lasen	hatten gelesen	lesen	läsen	hätten gelesen	les en wir
gelesen	lest	last	hattet gelesen	leset	läset	hättet gelesen	lest
gelesen haben	lesen	lasen	hatten gelesen	lesen	läsen	hätten gelesen	lesen Sie

Infinitiv Partizip I Partizip II Perfekt	INDIKATIV			KONJUNKTIV I	KONJUNKTIV II		IMPERATIV
	Präsens	Präteritum	Plusquamperfekt	Präsens	Präsens	Perfekt	
35 liegen	liege	lag	hatte gelegen	liege	läge	hätte gelegen	
(to lie; to be lying)	liegst	lagst	hattest gelegen	liegest	lägest	hättest gelegen	liege/lieg
	liegt	lag	hatte gelegen	liege	läge	hätte gelegen	
liegend	liegen	lagen	hatten gelegen	liegen	lägen	hätten gelegen	liegen wir
gelegen	liegt	lagt	hattet gelegen	lieget	läget	hättet gelegen	liegt
gelegen haben	liegen	lagen	hatten gelegen	liegen	lägen	hätten gelegen	liegen Sie
36 lügen	lüge	log	hatte gelogen	lüge	löge	hätte gelogen	
(to lie)	lügst	logst	hattest gelogen	lügest	lögest	hättest gelogen	lüge/lüg
	lügt	log	hatte gelogen	lüge	löge	hätte gelogen	
lügend	lügen	logen	hatten gelogen	lügen	lögen	hätten gelogen	lügen wir
gelogen	lügt	logt	hattet gelogen	lüget	löget	hättet gelogen	lügt
gelogen haben	lügen	logen	hatten gelogen	lügen	lögen	hätten gelogen	lügen Sie
37 mahlen	mahle	mahlte	hatte gemahlt/gemahlen	mahle	mahlte	hätte gemahlt/gemahlen	
(to grind)	mahlst	mahltest	hattest gemahlt/gemahlen	mahlest	mahltest	hättest gemahlt/gemahlen	mahle/mahl
mahlend	mahlt	mahlte	hatte gemahlt/gemahlen	mahle	mahlte	hätte gemahlt/gemahlen	
gemahlt/gemahlen	mahlen	mahlten	hatten gemahlt/gemahlen	mahlen	mahlten	hätten gemahlt/gemahlen	mahlen wir
gemahlt/gemahlen	mahlt	mahltet	hattet gemahlt/gemahlen	mahlet	mahltet	hättet gemahlt/gemahlen	mahlt
haben	mahlen	mahlten	hatten gemahlt/gemahlen	mahlen	mahlten	hätten gemahlt/gemahlen	mahlen Sie
38 nehmen	nehme	nahm	hatte genommen	nehme	nähme	hätte genommen	
(to take)	nimmst	nahmst	hattest genommen	nehmest	nähmest	hättest genommen	nimm
	nimmt	nahm	hatte genommen	nehme	nähme	hätte genommen	
nehmend	nehmen	nahmen	hatten genommen	nehmen	nähmen	hätten genommen	nehmen wir
genommen	nehmt	nahmt	hattet genommen	nehmet	nähmet	hättet genommen	nehmt
genommen haben	nehmen	nahmen	hatten genommen	nehmen	nähmen	hätten genommen	nehmen Sie
39 pfeifen	pfeife	pfiff	hatte gepfiffen	pfeife	pfiffe	hätte gepfiffen	
(to whistle)	pfeifst	pfiffst	hattest gepfiffen	pfeifest	pfiffest	hättest gepfiffen	pfeife/pfeif
	pfeift	pfiff	hatte gepfiffen	pfeife	pfiffe	hätte gepfiffen	
pfeifend	pfeifen	pfiffen	hatten gepfiffen	pfeifen	pfiffen	hätten gepfiffen	pfeifen wir
gepfiffen	pfeift	pfifft	hattet gepfiffen	pfeifet	pfiffet	hättet gepfiffen	pfeift
gepfiffen haben	pfeifen	pfiffen	hatten gepfiffen	pfeifen	pfiffen	hätten gepfiffen	pfeifen Sie
40 rufen	rufe	rief	hatte gerufen	rufe	riefe	hätte gerufen	
(to call)	rufst	riefst	hattest gerufen	rufest	riefest	hättest gerufen	rufe/ruf
	ruft	rief	hatte gerufen	rufe	riefe	hätte gerufen	
rufend	rufen	riefen	hatten gerufen	rufen	riefen	hätten gerufen	rufen wir
gerufen	ruft	rieft	hattet gerufen	rufet	riefet	hättet gerufen	ruft
gerufen haben	rufen	riefen	hatten gerufen	rufen	riefen	hätten gerufen	rufen Sie
41 saugen	sauge	saugte/sog	hatte gesaugt/gesogen	sauge	saugte/söge	hätte gesaugt/gesogen	
(to suck)	saugst	saugtest/sogst	hattest gesaugt/gesogen	saugest	saugtest/sögest	hättest gesaugt/gesogen	sauge/saug
saugend	saugt	saugte/sog	hatte gesaugt/gesogen	sauge	saugte/söge	hätte gesaugt/gesogen	
gesaugt/gesogen	saugen	saugten/sogen	hatten gesaugt/gesogen	saugen	saugten/sögen	hätten gesaugt/gesogen	saugen wir
gesaugt/gesogen	saugt	saugtet/sogt	hattet gesaugt/gesogen	sauget	saugtet/söget	hättet gesaugt/gesogen	saugt
haben	saugen	saugten/sogen	hatten gesaugt/gesogen	saugen	saugten/sögen	hätten gesaugt/gesogen	saugen Sie

Infinitiv / Partizip I / Partizip II / Perfekt	INDIKATIV			KONJUNKTIV I	KONJUNKTIV II		IMPERATIV
	Präsens	Präteritum	Plusquamperfekt	Präsens	Präsens	Perfekt	
42 **schieben**	schiebe	schob	hatte geschoben	schiebe	schöbe	hätte geschoben	
(to push)	schiebst	schobst	hattest geschoben	schiebest	schöbest	hättest geschoben	schiebe/schieb
	schiebt	schob	hatte geschoben	schiebe	schöbe	hätte geschoben	
schiebend	schieben	schoben	hatten geschoben	schieben	schöben	hätten geschoben	schieben wir
geschoben	schiebt	schobt	hattet geschoben	schiebet	schöbet	hättet geschoben	schiebt
geschoben haben	schieben	schoben	hatten geschoben	schieben	schöben	hätten geschoben	schieben Sie
43 **schlafen**	schlafe	schlief	hatte geschlafen	schlafe	schliefe	hätte geschlafen	
(to sleep)	schläfst	schliefst	hattest geschlafen	schlafest	schliefest	hättest geschlafen	schlafe/schlaf
	schläft	schlief	hatte geschlafen	schlafe	schliefe	hätte geschlafen	
schlafend	schlafen	schliefen	hatten geschlafen	schlafen	schliefen	hätten geschlafen	schlafen wir
geschlafen	schlaft	schlieft	hattet geschlafen	schlafet	schliefet	hättet geschlafen	schlaft
geschlafen haben	schlafen	schliefen	hatten geschlafen	schlafen	schliefen	hätten geschlafen	schlafen Sie
44 **schwimmen**	schwimme	schwamm	war geschwommen	schwimme	schwömme	wäre geschwommen	
(to swim)	schwimmst	schwammst	warst geschwommen	schwimmest	schwömmest	wärest geschwommen	schwimme/schwimm
	schwimmt	schwamm	war geschwommen	schwimme	schwömme	wäre geschwommen	
schwimmend	schwimmen	schwammen	waren geschwommen	schwimmen	schwömmen	wären geschwommen	schwimmen wir
geschwommen	schwimmt	schwammt	wart geschwommen	schwimmet	schwömmet	wäret geschwommen	schwimmt
geschwommen sein	schwimmen	schwammen	waren geschwommen	schwimmen	schwömmen	wären geschwommen	schwimmen Sie
45 **schwören**	schwöre	schwor	hatte geschworen	schwöre	schwüre	hätte geschworen	
(to swear)	schwörst	schworst	hattest geschworen	schwörest	schwürest/schwürst	hättest geschworen	schwöre/schwör
	schwört	schwor	hatte geschworen	schwöre	schwüre	hätte geschworen	
schwörend	schwören	schworen	hatten geschworen	schwören	schwüren	hätten geschworen	schwören wir
geschworen	schwört	schwort	hattet geschworen	schwöret	schwüret	hättet geschworen	schwört
geschworen haben	schwören	schworen	hatten geschworen	schwören	schwüren	hätten geschworen	schwören Sie
46 **sitzen**	sitze	saß	hatte gesessen	sitze	säße	hätte gesessen	
(to sit)	sitzt	saßest	hattest gesessen	sitzest	säßest	hättest gesessen	sitze/sitz
	sitzt	saß	hatte gesessen	sitze	säße	hätte gesessen	
sitzend	sitzen	saßen	hatten gesessen	sitzen	säßen	hätten gesessen	sitzen wir
gesessen	sitzt	saßet	hattet gesessen	sitzet	säßet	hättet gesessen	sitzt
gesessen haben	sitzen	saßen	hatten gesessen	sitzen	säßen	hätten gesessen	sitzen Sie
47 **sprechen**	spreche	sprach	hatte gesprochen	spreche	spräche	hätte gesprochen	
(to speak)	sprichst	sprachst	hattest gesprochen	sprechest	sprächest	hättest gesprochen	sprich
	spricht	sprach	hatte gesprochen	spreche	spräche	hätte gesprochen	
sprechend	sprechen	sprachen	hatten gesprochen	sprechen	sprächen	hätten gesprochen	sprechen wir
gesprochen	sprecht	spracht	hattet gesprochen	sprechet	sprächet	hättet gesprochen	sprecht
gesprochen haben	sprechen	sprachen	hatten gesprochen	sprechen	sprächen	hätten gesprochen	sprechen Sie
48 **stehen**	stehe	stand	hatte gestanden	stehe	stünde/stände	hätte gestanden	
(to stand)	stehst	standest/standst	hattest gestanden	stehest	stündest/ständest	hättest gestanden	stehe/steh
	steht	stand	hatte gestanden	stehe	stünde/stände	hätte gestanden	
stehend	stehen	standen	hatten gestanden	stehen	stünden/ständen	hätten gestanden	stehen wir
gestanden	steht	standet	hattet gestanden	stehet	stündet/ständet	hättet gestanden	steht
gestanden haben	stehen	standen	hatten gestanden	stehen	stünden/ständen	hätten gestanden	stehen Sie

Infinitiv / Partizip I / Partizip II / Perfekt	INDIKATIV			KONJUNKTIV I	KONJUNKTIV II		IMPERATIV
	Präsens	Präteritum	Plusquamperfekt	Präsens	Präsens	Perfekt	
49 **stehlen**	stehle	stahl	hatte gestohlen	stehle	stähle/stöhle	hätte gestohlen	
(to steal)	stiehlst	stahlst	hattest gestohlen	stehlest	stählest/stöhlest	hättest gestohlen	stiehl
	stiehlt	stahl	hatte gestohlen	stehle	stähle/stöhle	hätte gestohlen	
stehlend	stehlen	stahlen	hatten gestohlen	stehlen	stählen/stöhlen	hätten gestohlen	stehlen wir
gestohlen	stehlt	stahlt	hattet gestohlen	stehlet	stählet/stöhlet	hättet gestohlen	stehlt
gestohlen haben	stehlen	stahlen	hatten gestohlen	stehlen	stählen/stöhlen	hätten gestohlen	stehlen Sie
50 **stoßen**	stoße	stieß	hatte gestoßen	stoße	stieße	hätte gestoßen	
(to bump)	stößt	stießest/stießt	hattest gestoßen	stoßest	stießest	hättest gestoßen	stoße/stoß
	stößt	stieß	hatte gestoßen	stoße	stieße	hätte gestoßen	
stoßend	stoßen	stießen	hatten gestoßen	stoßen	stießen	hätten gestoßen	stoßen wir
gestoßen	stoßt	stießt	hattet gestoßen	stoßet	stießet	hättet gestoßen	stoßt
gestoßen haben	stoßen	stießen	hatten gestoßen	stoßen	stießen	hätten gestoßen	stoßen Sie
51 **tragen**	trage	trug	hatte getragen	trage	trüge	hätte getragen	
(to carry)	trägst	trugst	hattest getragen	tragest	trügest	hättest getragen	trage/trag
	trägt	trug	hatte getragen	trage	trüge	hätte getragen	
tragend	tragen	trugen	hatten getragen	tragen	trügen	hätten getragen	tragen wir
getragen	tragt	trugt	hattet getragen	traget	trüget	hättet getragen	tragt
getragen haben	tragen	trugen	hatten getragen	tragen	trügen	hätten getragen	tragen Sie
52 **trinken**	trinke	trank	hatte getrunken	trinke	tränke	hätte getrunken	
(to drink)	trinkst	trankst	hattest getrunken	trinkest	tränkest	hättest getrunken	trinke/trink
	trinkt	trank	hatte getrunken	trinke	tränke	hätte getrunken	
trinkend	trinken	tranken	hatten getrunken	trinken	tränken	hätten getrunken	trinken wir
getrunken	trinkt	trankt	hattet getrunken	trinket	tränket	hättet getrunken	trinkt
getrunken haben	trinken	tranken	hatten getrunken	trinken	tränken	hätten getrunken	trinken Sie
53 **tun**	tue	tat	hatte getan	tue	täte	hätte getan	
(to do)	tust	tatest	hattest getan	tuest	tätest	hättest getan	tue/tu
	tut	tat	hatte getan	tue	täte	hätte getan	
tuend	tun	taten	hatten getan	tuen	täten	hätten getan	tun wir
getan	tut	tatet	hattet getan	tuet	tätet	hättet getan	tut
getan haben	tun	taten	hatten getan	tuen	täten	hätten getan	tun Sie
54 **waschen**	wasche	wusch	hatte gewaschen	wasche	wüsche	hätte gewaschen	
(to wash)	wäschst	wuschest/wuschst	hattest gewaschen	waschest	wüschest/wüschst	hättest gewaschen	wasche/wasch
	wäscht	wusch	hatte gewaschen	wasche	wüsche	hätte gewaschen	
waschend	waschen	wuschen	hatten gewaschen	waschen	wüschen	hätten gewaschen	waschen wir
gewaschen	wascht	wuscht	hattet gewaschen	waschet	wüschet/wüscht	hättet gewaschen	wascht
gewaschen haben	waschen	wuschen	hatten gewaschen	waschen	wüschen	hätten gewaschen	waschen Sie
55 **wissen**	weiß	wusste	hatte gewusst	wisse	wüsste	hätte gewusst	
(to know)	weißt	wusstest	hattest gewusst	wissest	wüsstest	hättest gewusst	wisse
	weiß	wusste	hatte gewusst	wisse	wüsste	hätte gewusst	
wissend	wissen	wussten	hatten gewusst	wissen	wüssten	hätten gewusst	wissen wir
gewusst	wisst	wusstet	hattet gewusst	wisset	wüsstet	hättet gewusst	wisst
gewusst haben	wissen	wussten	hatten gewusst	wissen	wüssten	hätten gewusst	wissen Sie

A26 Verb Tables

Irregular verbs

The following is a list of the principal parts of all strong and mixed verbs that are introduced as active vocabulary in **Mosaik**, as well as other sample verbs. For the complete conjugations of these verbs, consult the verb list on pages **A14–A15** and the verb charts on pages **A16–A25**. The verbs listed here are base forms. See **Strukturen Volume 2, 2B.2** and **3A.1** to review **Perfekt** and **Präteritum** forms of separable and inseparable prefix verbs.

Infinitiv		Präteritum	Partizip II
backen	to bake	backte	gebacken
beginnen	to begin	begann	begonnen
bieten	to bid, to offer	bot	geboten
binden	to tie, to bind	band	gebunden
bitten	to request	bat	gebeten
bleiben	to stay	blieb	(ist) geblieben
braten (brät)	to fry, to roast	briet	gebraten
brechen (bricht)	to break	brach	gebrochen
brennen	to burn	brannte	gebrannt
bringen	to bring	brachte	gebracht
denken	to think	dachte	gedacht
dürfen (darf)	to be allowed to	durfte	gedurft
empfehlen (empfiehlt)	to recommend	empfahl	empfohlen
essen (isst)	to eat	aß	gegessen
fahren (fährt)	to go, to drive	fuhr	(ist) gefahren
fallen (fällt)	to fall	fiel	(ist) gefallen
fangen (fängt)	to catch	fing	gefangen
finden	to find	fand	gefunden
fliegen	to fly	flog	(ist) geflogen
fließen	to flow, to pour	floss	(ist) geflossen
frieren	to freeze	fror	(hat/ist) gefroren
geben (gibt)	to give	gab	gegeben
gehen	to go, to walk	ging	(ist) gegangen
gelten (gilt)	to be valid	galt	gegolten
genießen	to enjoy	genoss	genossen
geschehen (geschieht)	to happen	geschah	(ist) geschehen
gewinnen	to win	gewann	gewonnen
gleichen	to resemble	glich	geglichen
graben (gräbt)	to dig	grub	gegraben
haben (hat)	to have	hatte	gehabt
halten (hält)	to hold, to keep	hielt	gehalten
hängen	to hang	hing	gehangen
heben	to raise, to lift	hob	gehoben
heißen	to be called, to mean	hieß	geheißen
helfen (hilft)	to help	half	geholfen
kennen	to know	kannte	gekannt
klingen	to sound, to ring	klang	geklungen
kommen	to come	kam	(ist) gekommen
können (kann)	to be able to, can	konnte	gekonnt
laden (lädt)	to load, to charge	lud	geladen
lassen (lässt)	to let, to allow	ließ	gelassen
laufen (läuft)	to run, to walk	lief	(ist) gelaufen

Infinitiv		Präteritum	Partizip II
leiden	to suffer	litt	gelitten
leihen	to lend	lieh	geliehen
lesen (liest)	to read	las	gelesen
liegen	to lie, to rest	lag	gelegen
lügen	to lie, to tell lies	log	gelogen
meiden	to avoid	mied	gemieden
messen (misst)	to measure	maß	gemessen
mögen (mag)	to like	mochte	gemocht
müssen (muss)	to have, to must	musste	gemusst
nehmen (nimmt)	to take	nahm	genommen
nennen	to name, to call	nannte	genannt
preisen	to praise	pries	gepriesen
raten (rät)	to guess	riet	geraten
reiben	to rub, to grate	rieb	gerieben
riechen	to smell	roch	gerochen
rufen	to call, to shout	rief	gerufen
schaffen	to create	schuf	geschaffen
scheiden	to divorce	schied	geschieden
scheinen	to shine, to appear	schien	geschienen
schieben	to push, to shove	schob	geschoben
schießen	to shoot	schoss	geschossen
schlafen (schläft)	to sleep	schlief	geschlafen
schlagen (schlägt)	to beat, to hit	schlug	geschlagen
schließen	to close	schloss	geschlossen
schlingen	to loop, to gulp	schlang	geschlungen
schneiden	to cut	schnitt	geschnitten
schreiben	to write	schrieb	geschrieben
schwimmen	to swim	schwamm	(ist) geschwommen
sehen (sieht)	to see	sah	gesehen
sein (ist)	to be	war	(ist) gewesen
senden	to send	sandte/sendete	gesandt/gesendet
singen	to sing	sang	gesungen
sinken	to sink	sank	(ist) gesunken
sitzen	to sit	saß	gesessen
sollen (soll)	to be supposed to	sollte	gesollt
sprechen (spricht)	to speak	sprach	gesprochen
stehen	to stand	stand	gestanden
stehlen (stiehlt)	to steal	stahl	gestohlen
steigen	to climb, to rise	stieg	(ist) gestiegen
sterben (stirbt)	to die	starb	(ist) gestorben
stoßen	to push, to thrust	stieß	(hat/ist) gestoßen
streichen	to paint, to cancel	strich	gestrichen
streiten	to argue	stritt	gestritten
tragen (trägt)	to carry	trug	getragen
treffen (trifft)	to hit, to meet	traf	getroffen
treten (tritt)	to kick, to step	trat	(hat/ist) getreten
trinken	to drink	trank	getrunken
tun	to do	tat	getan
vergessen (vergisst)	to forget	vergaß	vergessen

Infinitiv		Präteritum	Partizip II
verlieren	*to lose*	verlor	verloren
wachsen (wächst)	*to grow*	wuchs	(ist) gewachsen
waschen (wäscht)	*to wash*	wusch	gewaschen
weisen	*to indicate, to show*	wies	gewiesen
wenden	*to turn, to flip*	wandte/wendete	gewandt/gewendet
werben (wirbt)	*to advertise*	warb	geworben
werden (wird)	*to become*	wurde	(ist) geworden
werfen (wirft)	*to throw*	warf	geworfen
winden	*to wind*	wand	gewunden
wissen (weiß)	*to know*	wusste	gewusst
wollen (will)	*to want*	wollte	gewollt
ziehen	*to pull, to draw, to move*	zog	(hat/ist) gezogen

Glossary

This glossary includes all active vocabulary introduced in **Mosaik**, as well as some additional words and expressions. The singular and plural endings listed for adjectival nouns are those that occur after a definite article. The numbers following each entry are as follows:

(2) **1A** = (**Mosaik** Volume) **Chapter, Lesson**

The entry would be in **Mosaik 2**, Chapter 1, Lesson A.

Abbreviations used in this glossary

acc.	accusative	*gen.*	genitive	*poss.*	possessive
adj.	adjective	*inf.*	informal	*prep.*	preposition
adv.	adverb	*interr.*	interrogative	*pron.*	pronoun
conj.	conjunction	*m.*	masculine noun	*sing.*	singular
dat.	dative	*n.*	neuter noun	*v.*	verb
f.	feminine noun	*nom.*	nominative		
form.	formal	*pl.*	plural		

Deutsch-Englisch

A

abbiegen *v.* to turn (2) **4A**
  rechts/links abbiegen *v.* to turn right/left (2) **4A**
abbrechen *v.* to cancel (2) **3B**
Abend, -e *m.* evening (1) **2B**
  abends *adv.* in the evening (1) **2A**
Abendessen, - *n.* dinner (1) **4B**
aber *conj.* but (1) **1B**
abfahren *v.* to leave (2) **4A**
Abfall, ⁻e *m.* waste (3) **4B**
abfliegen *v.* to take off (2) **3B**
Abflug, ⁻e *m.* departure (2) **3B**
abheben *v.* to withdraw (money) (3) **3A**
Absatz, ⁻e *m.* paragraph (2) **1B**
abschicken *v.* to send (3) **3B**
Abschied, -e *m.* leave-taking; farewell (1) **1A**
Abschluss, ⁻e *m.* degree (1) **2A**
  einen Abschluss machen *v.* to graduate (2) **1A**
Abschlusszeugnis, -se *n.* diploma (transcript) (1) **2A**
abstauben *v.* to dust (2) **2B**
sich abtrocknen *v.* to dry oneself off (3) **1A**
acht eight (1) **2A**
Achtung! Attention!
adoptieren *v.* to adopt (1) **3A**
Adresse, -n *f.* address (3) **2A**
Allee, -n *f.* avenue (3) **2B**
allein *adv.* alone; by oneself (1) **4A**
Allergie, -n *f.* allergy (3) **1B**
allergisch (gegen) *adj.* allergic (to) (3) **1B**
alles *pron.* everything (2) **3B**
  Alles klar? Everything OK? (1) **1A**
  alles Gute all the best (3) **2A**
  Alles Gute zum Geburtstag! Happy birthday! (2) **1A**
Alltagsroutine, -n *f.* daily routine (3) **1A**
  im Alltag in everyday life
als *conj.* as; when (2) **4A**
  als ob as if (3) **2A**
also *conj.* therefore; so (3) **1B**
alt *adj.* old (1) **3A**
Altkleider *pl.* second-hand clothing (3) **4B**
Altpapier *n.* used paper (3) **4B**
Amerika *n.* America (3) **2B**
amerikanisch *adj.* American (3) **2B**
Amerikaner, - / Amerikanerin, -nen *m./f.* American (3) **2B**
Ampel, -n *f.* traffic light (3) **2B**
an *prep.* at; on; by; in; to (2) **1B**, (3) **2B**
Ananas, - *f.* pineapple (1) **4A**
anbieten *v.* to offer (3) **4B**

anfangen *v.* to begin (1) **4A**
Angebot, -e *n.* offer
  im Angebot on sale (2) **1B**
angeln gehen *v.* to go fishing (1) **2B**
angenehm *adj.* pleasant (1) **3B**
  Angenehm. Nice to meet you. (1) **1A**
angesagt *adj.* trendy (2) **1B**
Angestellte, -n *m./f.* employee (3) **3A**
Angst, ⁻e *f.* fear (2) **3A**
  Angst haben (vor) *v.* to be afraid (of) (2) **3A**
ankommen *v.* to arrive (1) **4A**
Ankunft, ⁻e *f.* arrival (2) **3B**
Anlass, ⁻e *m.* occasion (2) **1A**
  besondere Anlässe *m. pl.* special occasions (2) **1A**
anmachen *v.* to turn on (2) **4B**
Anruf, -e *m.* phone call (3) **3A**
  einen Anruf entgegennehmen *v.* to answer the phone (3) **3A**
anrufen *v.* to call (1) **4A**
  sich anrufen *v.* to call each other (3) **1A**
anschauen *v.* to watch, look at (2) **3A**
anspruchsvoll *adj.* demanding (3) **3B**
anstatt *prep.* instead of (2) **4B**
anstoßen *v.* to toast (2) **1A**
Antwort, -en *f.* answer
antworten (auf) *v.* to answer (1) **2A**
Anwendung *f.* application; usage
anziehen *v.* to put on (2) **1B**
  sich anziehen *v.* to get dressed (3) **1A**
Anzug, ⁻e *m.* suit (2) **1B**
Apfel, ⁻ *m.* apple (1) **1A**
Apotheke, -n *f.* pharmacy (3) **1B**
April *m.* April (1) **2A**, (2) **3A**
Arbeit, -en *f.* work (3) **3B**
  Arbeit finden *v.* to find a job (3) **3A**
arbeiten (an) *v.* to work (on) (1) **2A**, (2) **3A**
arbeitslos *adj.* unemployed (3) **2A**
Arbeitszimmer, - *n.* home office (2) **2A**
Architekt, -en / Architektin, -nen *m./f.* architect (1) **3B**
Architektur, -en *f.* architecture (1) **2A**
sich ärgern (über) *v.* to get angry (about) (3) **1A**
arm *adj.* poor; unfortunate (1) **3B**
Arm, -e *m.* arm (3) **1A**
Art, -en *f.* species; type (3) **4B**
Artischocke, -n *f.* artichoke (1) **4A**
Arzt, ⁻e / Ärztin, -nen *m./f.* doctor (3) **1B**
  zum Arzt gehen *v.* to go to the doctor (3) **1B**
Assistent, -en / Assistentin, -nen *m./f.* assistant (3) **3A**
Aubergine, -n *f.* eggplant (1) **4A**
auch *adv.* also (1) **1A**

auf *prep.* on, onto, to (2) **1B**
  Auf Wiedersehen. Good-bye. (1) **1A**
aufgehen *v.* to rise (sun) (3) **4A**
auflegen *v.* to hang up (3) **3A**
aufmachen *v.* to open (2) **4B**
aufnehmen *v.* to record (2) **4B**
aufräumen *v.* to clean up (2) **2B**
aufregend *adj.* exciting (3) **4A**
aufrichtig *adj.* sincere (1) **3B**
aufstehen *v.* to get up (1) **4A**
aufwachen *v.* to wake up (3) **1A**
Auge, -n *n.* eye (1) **3A**; (3) **1A**
Augenbraue, -n *f.* eyebrow (3) **1A**
August *m.* August (1) **2A**, (2) **3A**
aus *prep.* from (1) **4A**
Ausbildung, -en *f.* education (3) **3A**
Ausdruck, ⁻e *m.* expression
Ausfahrt, -en *f.* exit (2) **4A**
ausfüllen *v.* to fill out (3) **2A**
  ein Formular ausfüllen *v.* to fill out a form (3) **2A**
Ausgang ⁻e *m.* exit (2) **3B**
ausgefallen *adj.* offbeat (2) **1B**
ausgehen *v.* to go out (1) **4A**
Ausland *n.* abroad (2) **3B**
ausmachen *v.* to turn off (2) **4B**
sich ausruhen *v.* to rest (3) **1A**
ausschalten *v.* turn out, to turn off (3) **4B**
Aussehen *n.* look (style) (2) **1B**
außer *prep.* except (for) (1) **4B**
außerhalb *prep.* outside of (2) **4B**
Aussprache *f.* pronunciation
Aussterben *n.* extinction (3) **4B**
sich ausziehen *v.* to get undressed (3) **1A**
Auto, -s *n.* car (1) **1A**, (2) **4A**
Autobahn, -en *f.* highway (2) **4A**

B

Baby, -s *n.* baby (1) **3A**
Bäckerei, -en *f.* bakery (1) **4A**
Badeanzug, ⁻e *m.* bathing suit (2) **1B**
Bademantel, ⁻ *m.* bathrobe (3) **1A**
sich baden *v.* to bathe, take a bath (3) **1A**
Badewanne, -n *f.* bathtub (2) **2A**
Badezimmer, - *n.* bathroom (2) **2A**, (3) **1A**
Bahnsteig, -e *m.* track; platform (2) **4A**
bald *adv.* soon
  Bis bald. See you soon. (1) **1A**
Balkon, -e/-s *m.* balcony (2) **2A**
Ball, ⁻e *m.* ball (1) **2B**
Ballon, -e/-s *m.* balloon (2) **1A**
Banane, -n *f.* banana (1) **4A**

Bank, -̈e *f.* bench (3) **2B**
Bank, -en *f.* bank (3) **2A**
  auf der Bank *f.* at the bank (3) **2B**
Bankangestellte, -n *m./f.* bank employee (3) **3B**
bar *adj.* cash (3) **2A**
  bar bezahlen *v.* to pay in cash (3) **2A**
Bargeld *n.* cash (3) **2A**
Bart, -̈e *m.* beard (3) **1A**
Baseball *m.* baseball (1) **2B**
Basketball *m.* basketball (1) **2B**
Bauch, -̈e *m.* belly (3) **1A**
Bauchschmerzen *m. pl.* stomachache (3) **1B**
bauen *v.* to build (1) **2A**
Bauer, -n / Bäuerin, -nen *m./f.* farmer (3) **3B**
Bauernhof, -̈e *m.* farm (3) **4A**
Baum, -̈e *m.* tree (3) **4A**
Baumwolle *f.* cotton (2) **1B**
Baustelle, -n *f.* construction zone (2) **4A**
beantworten *v.* to answer (1) **4B**
bedeuten *v.* to mean (1) **2A**
bedeutend *adj.* important (3) **4A**
bedienen *v.* to operate, use (2) **4B**
sich beeilen *v.* to hurry (3) **1A**
Beförderung, -en *f.* promotion (3) **3B**
beginnen *v.* to begin (2) **2A**
Begrüßung, -en *f.* greeting (1) **1A**
behaupten *v.* to claim (3) **4B**
bei *prep.* at; near; with (1) **4A**
Beilage, -n *f.* side dish (1) **4B**
Bein, -e *n.* leg (3) **1A**
Beitrag -̈e *m.* contribution (3) **4B**
bekannt *adj.* well-known (3) **2A**
bekommen *v.* to get, to receive (2) **1A**
belegen *v.* to take (a class) (1) **2A**
benutzen *v.* to use (2) **4A**
Benutzername, -n *m.* screen name (2) **4B**
Benzin, -e *n.* gasoline (2) **4A**
Berg -e *m.* mountain (1) **2B**, (3) **4A**
berichten *v.* to report (3) **4B**
Beruf, -e *m.* profession; job (1) **3B**, (3) **3A**
Berufsausbildung, -en *f.* professional
  training (3) **3A**
bescheiden *adj.* modest (1) **3B**
beschreiben *v.* to describe (1) **2A**
Beschreibung, -en *f.* description (1) **3B**
Besen, - *m.* broom (2) **2B**
Besitzer, - / Besitzerin, -nen *m./f.* owner (1) **3B**
besonderes *adj.* special (3) **2A**
  nichts Besonderes *adj.* nothing special (3) **2A**
besorgt *adj.* worried (1) **3B**
Besorgung, -en *f.* errand (3) **2A**
  Besorgungen machen to run errands (3) **2A**
besprechen *v.* to discuss (2) **3A**
Besprechung, -en *f.* meeting (3) **3A**
besser *adj.* better (2) **4A**
Besserwisser, - / Besserwisserin, -nen *m./f.* know-
  it-all (1) **2A**
beste *adj.* best (2) **4A**
Besteck *n.* silverware (1) **4B**
bestehen *v.* to pass (a test) (1) **1B**
bestellen *v.* to order (1) **4A**
bestimmt *adv.* definitely (1) **4A**

besuchen *v.* to visit (1) **4A**
Bett, -en *n.* bed (2) **2A**
  das Bett machen *v.* to make the bed (2) **2B**
  ins Bett gehen *v.* to go bed (3) **1A**
Bettdecke, - n *f.* duvet (2) **2B**
bevor *conj.* before (2) **4A**
sich bewegen *v.* to move (around)
sich bewerben *v.* to apply (3) **3A**
Bewerber, - / die Bewerberin, -nen *m./f.*
  applicant (3) **3A**
Bewertung, -en *f.* rating (2) **3B**
bezahlen *v.* to pay (for) (1) **4A**
Bibliothek, -en *f.* library (1) **1B**
Bier, -e *n.* beer (1) **4B**
bieten *v.* to offer (3) **1B**
Bild, -er *n.* picture (2) **2A**
Bildschirm, -e *m.* screen (2) **4B**
Bioladen, -̈ *m.* health-food store (3) **1B**
Biologie *f.* biology (1) **2A**
biologisch *adj.* organic (3) **4B**
Birne, -n *f.* pear (1) **4A**
bis *prep.* until (1) **3B**
  Bis bald. See you soon. (1) **1A**
  Bis dann. See you later. (1) **1A**
  Bis gleich. See you soon. (1) **1A**
  Bis morgen. See you tomorrow. (1) **1A**
  Bis später. See you later. (1) **1A**
  bis zu *prep.* up to; until (3) **2B**
Bitte. Please.; You're welcome. (1) **1A**
Blatt, -̈er *n.* leaf (3) **4A**
blau *adj.* blue (1) **3A**
  blaue Fleck, -e *m.* bruise (3) **B1**
bleiben *v.* to stay (2) **1B**
  Bleiben Sie bitte am Apparat. *v.* Please
  hold. (3) **3A**
Bleistift, -e *m.* pencil (1) **1B**
Blitz, -e *m.* lightning (2) **3A**
blond *adj.* blond (1) **3A**
  blonde Haare *n. pl.* blond hair (1) **3A**
Blume, -n *f.* flower (1) **1A**
Blumengeschäft, -e *n.* flower shop (3) **2A**
Bluse, -n *f.* blouse (2) **1B**
Blutdruck *m.* blood pressure (3) **1B**
Boden, -̈ *m.* floor; ground (2) **2A**
Bohne, -n *f.* bean (1) **4A**
  grüne Bohne *f.* green bean (1) **4A**
Boot, -e *n.* boat (2) **4A**
Bordkarte, -n *f.* boarding pass (2) **3B**
braten *v.* to fry (1) **2B**
brauchen *v.* to need (1) **2A**
braun *adj.* brown (2) **1B**
braunhaarig *adj.* brown-haired, brunette (1) **3A**
brechen *v.* to break (1) **2B**
  sich (den Arm / das Bein) brechen *v.* to break
  (an arm / a leg) (3) **1B**
Bremse, -n *f.* brake (2) **4A**
brennen *v.* to burn (2) **1A**
Brief, -e *m.* letter (3) **2A**
  einen Brief abschicken *v.* to mail a letter (3) **2A**
Briefkasten, -̈ *m.* mailbox (3) **2A**
Briefmarke, -n *f.* stamp (3) **2A**
Briefträger, - / Briefträgerin, -nen *m./f.* mail
  carrier (3) **2A**

Briefumschlag, -̈e *m.* envelope (3) **2A**
Brille, -n *f.* glasses (2) **1B**
bringen *v.* to bring (1) **2A**
Brot, -e *n.* bread (1) **4A**
Brötchen, - *n.* roll (1) **4A**
Brücke, -n *f.* bridge (3) **2B**
Bruder, -̈ *m.* brother (1) **1A**
Brunnen, - *m.* fountain (3) **2B**
Buch, -̈er *n.* book (1) **1A**
buchen *v.* to make a (hotel) reservation (2) **3B**
Bücherregal, -e *n.* bookshelf (2) **2A**
Buchhalter, - / Buchhalterin, -nen *m./f.*
  accountant (3) **3B**
büffeln *v.* to cram (for a test) (1) **2A**
Bügelbrett, -er *n.* ironing board (2) **2B**
Bügeleisen, - *n.* iron (2) **2B**
bügeln *v.* to iron (2) **2B**
Bundespräsident, -en / Bundespräsidentin,
  -nen *m./f.* (federal) president (2) **4B**
bunt *adj.* colorful (3) **2A**
Bürgermeister, - / Bürgermeisterin, -nen *m./f.*
  mayor (3) **2B**
Bürgersteig, -e *m.* sidewalk (3) **2B**
Büro, -s *n.* office (3) **3B**
Büroklammer, -n *f.* paperclip (3) **3A**
Büromaterial *n.* office supplies (3) **3A**
Bürste, -n *f.* brush (3) **1A**
bürsten *v.* to brush
  sich die Haare bürsten *v.* to brush one's hair (3) **1A**
Bus, -se *m.* bus (2) **4A**
Busch, -̈e *m.* bush (3) **4A**
Bushaltestelle, -n *f.* bus stop (2) **4A**
Businessklasse *f.* business class (2) **3B**
Bußgeld, -er *n.* fine (monetary) (2) **4A**
Butter *f.* butter (1) **4A**

C

Café, -s *n.* café (1) **2A**
Camping *n.* camping (1) **2B**
CD, -s *f.* compact disc, CD (2) **4B**
Chef, -s / Chefin, -nen *m./f.* boss (3) **3B**
Chemie *f.* chemistry (1) **2A**
China *n.* China (3) **2B**
Chinese, -n / Chinesin, -nen *m./f.* Chinese
  (person) (3) **2B**
Chinesisch *n.* Chinese (language) (3) **2B**
Computer, - *m.* computer (1) **1B**
Cousin, -s / Cousine, -n *m./f.* cousin (1) **3A**

D

da there (1) **1A**
  Da ist/sind... There is/are... (1) **1A**
Dachboden, -̈ *m.* attic (2) **2A**
dafür *adv.* for it (2) **2A**
daher *adv.* from there (2) **2A**
dahin *adv.* there (2) **2A**
damit *conj.* so that (3) **2A**
danach *conj.* then, after that (3) **1B**
danken *v.* to thank (1) **2A**
  Danke. Thank you. (1) **1A**
dann *adv.* then (2) **3B**
daran *adv.* on it (2) **2A**

darauf *adv.* on it (2) **2A**
darin *adv.* in it (2) **2A**
das *n.* the; this/that (1) **1A**
dass *conj.* that (3) **2A**
Datei, - en *f.* file (2) **4B**
Datum (*pl.* Daten) *n.* date (2) **3A**
davon *adv.* of it (2) **2A**
davor *adv.* before it (2) **2A**
Decke, -n *f.* blanket (2) **2B**
decken *v.* to cover (2) **2B**
den Tisch decken *v.* to set the table (2) **2B**
denken *v.* to think (2) **1A**
denken an *v.* to think about (2) **3A**
denn *conj.* for; because (2) **2A**
der *m.* the (1) **1A**
deshalb *conj.* therefore; so (3) **1B**
deswegen *conj.* that's why; therefore (3) **1B**
deutsch *adj.* German (3) **2B**
Deutsch *n.* German (language) (3) **2B**
Deutsche *m./f.* German (man/woman) (3) **2B**
Deutschland *n.* Germany (1) **4A**
deutschsprachig *adj.* German-speaking
Dezember *m.* December (1) **2A**, (2) **3A**
Diät, -en *f.* diet (1) **4B**
auf Diät sein *v.* to be on a diet (1) **4B**
dick *adj.* fat (1) **3A**
die *f./pl.* the (1) **1A**
Dienstag, -e *m.* Tuesday (1) **2A**
dienstags *adv.* on Tuesdays (1) **2A**
dieser/diese/dieses *m./f./n.* this; these (2) **4B**
diesmal *adv.* this time (2) **3B**
Digitalkamera, -s *f.* digital camera (2) **4B**
Ding, -e *n.* thing
Diplom, -e *n.* diploma (degree) (1) **2A**
diskret *adj.* discreet (1) **3B**
doch *adv.* yes (contradicting a negative statement or question) (1) **2B**
Dokument, -e *n.* document (2) **4B**
Donner, - *m.* thunder (2) **3A**
Donnerstag, -e *n.* Thursday (1) **2A**
donnerstags *adv.* on Thursdays (1) **2A**
dort *adv.* there (1) **1A**
Dozent, -en / Dozentin, -nen *m./f.* college instructor (1) **2A**
draußen *prep.* outside; *adv.* out (2) **3A**
Es ist schön draußen. It's nice out. (2) **3A**
dreckig *adj.* filthy (2) **2B**
drei three (1) **2A**
dritte *adj.* third (1) **2A**
Drogerie, -n *f.* drugstore (3) **2A**
drüben *adv.* over there (1) **4A**
drücken *v.* to push (1) **3B**; to print (2) **4B**
Drucker, - *m.* printer (2) **4B**
du *pron.* (*sing. inf.*) you (1) **1A**
dumm *adj.* dumb (2) **4A**
dunkel *adj.* dark (1) **3A**
dunkelhaarig *adj.* dark-haired (1) **3A**
dünn *adj.* thin (1) **3A**
durch *prep.* through (1) **3B**
durchfallen *v.* to flunk; to fail (1) **1B**
durchmachen *v.* to experience (2) **4B**
dürfen *v.* to be allowed to; may (1) **3B**
(sich) duschen *v.* to take a shower (3) **1A**

Dutzend, -e *n.* dozen (1) **4A**
DVD, -s *f.* DVD (2) **4B**
DVD-Player, - *m.* DVD-player (2) **4B**

E

Ecke, -n *f.* corner (3) **2B**
egoistisch *adj.* selfish (1) **3B**
Ehe, -n *f.* marriage (2) **1A**
Ehefrau, -en *f.* wife (1) **3A**
Ehemann, ̈-er *m.* husband (1) **3A**
Ei, -er *n.* egg (1) **4A**
Eichhörnchen, - *n.* squirrel (3) **4A**
eifersüchtig *adj.* jealous (1) **3B**
ein/eine *m./f./n.* a (1) **1A**
Einbahnstraße, -n *f.* one-way street (2) **4A**
einfach *adj.* easy (1) **2A**
einfarbig *adj.* solid colored (2) **1B**
eingebildet *adj.* arrogant (1) **3B**
einkaufen *v.* to shop (1) **4A**
einkaufen gehen *v.* to go shopping (1) **4A**
Einkaufen *n.* shopping (2) **1B**
Einkaufszentrum, (*pl.* Einkaufszentren) *n.* mall; shopping center (3) **2B**
Einkommensgruppe, -n *f.* income bracket (2) **2B**
einladen *v.* to invite (2) **1A**
einmal *adv.* once (2) **3B**
eins one (1) **2A**
einschlafen *v.* to go to sleep (1) **4A**
einzahlen *v.* to deposit (money) (3) **2A**
Einzelkind, -er *n.* only child (1) **3A**
Eis *n.* ice cream (2) **1A**
Eisdiele, -n *f.* ice cream shop (1) **4A**
Eishockey *n.* ice hockey (1) **2B**
Eiswürfel, - *m.* ice cube (2) **1A**
elegant *adj.* elegant (2) **1B**
Elektriker, - / Elektrikerin, -nen *m./f.* electrician (3) **3B**
elf eleven (1) **2A**
Ell(en)bogen, - *m.* elbow (3) **1A**
Eltern *pl.* parents (1) **3A**
E-Mail, -s *f.* e-mail (2) **4B**
empfehlen *v.* to recommend (1) **2B**
Empfehlungsschreiben, - *n.* letter of recommendation (3) **3A**
endlich *adv.* finally (3) **1B**
Energie, -n *f.* energy (3) **4B**
energiesparend *adj.* energy-efficient (2) **2B**
eng *adj.* tight (2) **1B**
England *n.* England (3) **2B**
Engländer, - / Engländerin, -nen *m./f.* English (person) (3) **2B**
Englisch *n.* English (language) (3) **2B**
Enkelkind, -er *n.* grandchild (1) **3A**
Enkelsohn, ̈-e *m.* grandson (1) **3A**
Enkeltochter, ̈ *f.* granddaughter (1) **3A**
entdecken *v.* to discover (2) **2B**
entfernen *v.* to remove (2) **2B**
entlang *prep.* along, down (1) **3B**
entlassen *v.* to fire; to lay off (3) **3B**
sich entschließen *v.* to decide (1) **4B**
(sich) entschuldigen *v.* to apologize; to excuse
Entschuldigen Sie. Excuse me. (*form.*) (1)**1A**

Entschuldigung. Excuse me. (1) **1A**
sich entspannen *v.* to relax (3) **1A**
entwerten *v.* to validate (2) **4A**
eine Fahrkarte entwerten *v.* to validate a ticket (2) **4A**
entwickeln *v.* to develop (3) **4B**
er *pron.* he (1) **1A**
Erdbeben, - *n.* earthquake (3) **4A**
Erdbeere, -n *f.* strawberry (1) **4A**
Erde, -n *f.* earth (3) **4B**
Erderwärmung *f.* global warming (3) **4B**
Erdgeschoss, -e *n.* ground floor (2) **2A**
Erfahrung, -en *f.* experience (3) **3A**
erfinden *v.* to invent (2) **3A**
Erfolg, -e *m.* success (3) **3B**
erforschen *v.* to explore (3) **4A**
ergänzen *v.* complete
Ergebnis, -se *n.* result; score (1) **1B**
erhalten *v.* to preserve (3) **4B**
sich erinnern (an) *v.* to remember (3) **1A**
sich erkälten *v.* to catch a cold (3) **1A**
Erkältung, -en *f.* cold (3) **1B**
erkennen *v.* to recognize (2) **3A**
erklären *v.* to explain (1) **4A**
erneuerbare Energie, -n *f.* renewable energy (3) **4B**
ernst *adj.* serious (1) **3B**
erster/erste/erstes *adj.* first (1) **2A**
erwachsen *adj.* grown-up (3) **2A**
erzählen *v.* to tell (2) **3A**
erzählen von *v.* to talk about (2) **3A**
es *pron.* it (1) **1A**
Es geht. (I'm) so-so. (1) **1A**
Es gibt... There is/are... (1) **2B**
Essen, - *n.* food (1) **4A**
essen *v.* to eat (1) **2A**
essen gehen *v.* to eat out (1) **2B**
Esslöffel, - *m.* soup spoon (1) **4B**
Esszimmer, - *n.* dining room (2) **2A**
etwas *pron.* something (2) **3B**
etwas anderes something else (3) **2A**
euer (*pl. inf.*) *poss. adj.* your (1) **3A**

F

Fabrik, -en *f.* factory (3) **4B**
Fabrikarbeiter, - / Fabrikarbeiterin, -nen *m./f.* factory worker (3) **3B**
Fach, ̈-er *n.* subject (1) **2A**
fade *adj.* bland (1) **4B**
fahren *v.* to drive; to go (1) **2B**
Auto fahren *v.* to drive a car (2) **4A**
Fahrrad fahren *v.* to ride a bicycle (1) **2B**
geradeaus fahren *v.* to go straight ahead (2) **4A**
Fahrer, - / Fahrerin, -nen *m./f.* driver (2) **4A**
Fahrgemeinschaft, -en *f.* carpool (3) **4B**
Fahrkarte, -n *f.* ticket (2) **4A**
eine Fahrkarte entwerten *v.* to validate a ticket (2) **4A**
Fahrkartenschalter, - *m.* ticket office (2) **4A**
Fahrplan, ̈-e *m.* schedule (2) **4A**
Fahrrad, ̈-er *n.* bicycle (1) **2B**, (2) **4A**
Fahrstuhl, ̈-e *m.* elevator (2) **3B**
fallen *v.* to fall (1)**2B**

Familie, -n *f.* family (1) **3A**
Familienstand, ⁻e *m.* marital status (1) **3A**
Fan, -s *m.* fan (1) **2B**
fangen *v.* to catch (1) **2B**
fantastisch *adj.* fantastic (3) **2A**
Farbe, -n *f.* color (2) **1B**
färben *v.* to dye
  sich die Haare färben *v.* to dye one's hair (3) **1A**
fast *adv.* almost (1) **4A**
faul *adj.* lazy (1) **3B**
Februar *m.* February (1) **2A**, (2) **3A**
fegen *v.* to sweep (2) **2B**
feiern *v.* to celebrate (1) **2A**
Feiertag, -e *m.* holiday (2) **1A**
Feinkostgeschäft, -e *n.* delicatessen (1) **4A**
Feld, -er *n.* field (1) **4A**
Fenster, - *n.* window (1) **1A**
Ferien *pl.* vacation (2) **3A**
Fernbedienung, -en *f.* remote control (2) **4B**
fernsehen *v.* to watch television (2) **4B**
Fernsehen *n.* television (programming)
Fernseher, - *m.* television set (2) **4B**
fertig *adj.* ready; finished (3) **3B**
Fest, -e *n.* festival; celebration (1) **1A**
Festplatte, -n *f.* hard drive (2) **4B**
Feuerwehrmann, ⁻er / Feuerwehrfrau, -en (pl. Feuerwehrleute) *m./f.* firefighter (3) **3B**
Fieber, - *n.* fever (3) **1B**
  Fieber haben *v.* to have a fever (3) **1B**
finden *v.* to find (1) **2A**
Finger, - *m.* finger (3) **1A**
Firma (pl. die Firmen) *f.* firm; company (3) **3A**
Fisch, -e *m.* fish (1) **4A**, (3) **4A**
Fischgeschäft, -e *n.* fish store (1) **4A**
fit *adj.* in good shape (1) **2B**
Flasche, -n *f.* bottle (1) **4B**
Fleisch *n.* meat (1) **4A**
fleißig *adj.* hard-working (1) **3B**
fliegen *v.* to fly (2) **3B**
Flug, ⁻e *m.* flight (2) **3B**
Flughafen, ⁻ *m.* airport (2) **3B**
Flugticket, -s *n.* (plane) ticket (2) **3B**
Flugzeug, -e *n.* airplane (2) **3B**
Flur, -e *m.* hall (2) (1) **2A**
Fluss, ⁻e *m.* river (1) **3B**, (3) **4A**
folgen *v.* to follow (2) **1A**, (3) **2B**
Form, -en *f.* shape, form
  in guter/schlechter Form sein *v.* to be in/out of shape (3) **1B**
Formular, -e *n.* form (3) **2A**
  ein Formular ausfüllen *v.* to fill out a form (3) **2A**
Foto, -s *n.* photo, picture (1) **1B**
Frage, -n *f.* question (1) **1B**
fragen *v.* to ask (1) **2A**
  fragen nach *v.* to ask about (2) **3A**
  sich fragen *v.* to wonder, ask oneself (3) **1A**
Frankreich *n.* France (3) **2B**
Franzose, -n / Französin, -nen *m./f.* French (person) (3) **2B**
Französisch *n.* French (language) (3) **2B**
Frau, -en *f.* woman (1) **1A**; wife (1) **3A**
  Frau... Mrs./Ms.... (1) **1A**
Freitag, -e *m.* Friday (1) **2A**

freitags *adv.* on Fridays (1) **2A**
Freizeit, -en *f.* free time, leisure (1) **2B**
Freizeitaktivität, - en *f.* leisure activity (1) **2B**
Fremdsprache, -n *f.* foreign language (1) **2A**
sich freuen (über) *v.* to be happy (about) (3) **1A**
  Freut mich. Pleased to meet you. (1) **1A**
  sich freuen auf *v.* to look forward to (3) **1A**
Freund, -e / Freundin, -nen *m./f.* friend (1) **1A**
freundlich *adj.* friendly (1) **3B**
  Mit freundlichen Grüßen Yours sincerely (3) **3B**
Freundschaft, -en *f.* friendship (2) **1A**
Frischvermählte, -n *m./f.* newlywed (2) **1A**
Friseur, -e / Friseurin, -nen *m./f.* hairdresser (1) **3B**
froh *adj.* happy (1) **3B**
  Frohe Ostern! Happy Easter! (2) **1A**
  Frohe Weihnachten! Merry Christmas! (2) **1A**
früh *adj.* early; in the morning (1) **2B**
  morgen früh tomorrow morning (1) **2B**
Frühling, -e *m.* spring (1) **2B**, (2) **3A**
Frühstück, -e *n.* breakfast (1) **4B**
fühlen *v.* to feel (1) **2A**
  sich (wohl) fühlen *v.* to feel (well) (3) **1A**
füllen *v.* to fill
fünf five (1) **2A**
funktionieren *v.* to work, function (2) **4B**
für *prep.* for (1) **3B**
furchtbar *adj.* awful (2) **3A**
Fuß, ⁻e *m.* foot (3) **1A**
Fußball *m.* soccer (1) **2B**
Fußgänger, - / Fußgängerin, -nen *m./f.* pedestrian (3) **2B**

G

Gabel, -n *f.* fork (1) **4B**
Gang, ⁻e *m.* course (1) **4B**
  erster/zweiter Gang *m.* first/second course (1) **4B**
ganz *adj.* all, total (2) **3B**
ganztags *adj.* full-time (3) **3B**
Garage, -n *f.* garage (2) **1B**
Garnele, -n *f.* shrimp (1) **4A**
Gartenabfall, ⁻e *m.* yard waste (3) **4B**
Gärtner, - /Gärtnerin, -nen *m./f.* gardener (3) **3B**
Gast, ⁻e *m.* guest (2) **1A**
Gastfamilie, -n *f.* host family (1) **4B**
Gastgeber, - / Gastgeberin, -nen *m./f.* host/ hostess (2) **1A**
Gebäck, -e *n.* pastries; baked goods (2) **1A**
Gebäude, - *n.* building (3) **2A**
geben *v.* to give (1) **2B**
  Es gibt... There is/are... (1) **2B**
Geburt, -en *f.* birth (2) **1A**
Geburtstag, -e *m.* birthday (2) **1A**
  Wann hast du Geburtstag? When is your birthday? (2) **3A**
geduldig *adj.* patient (1) **3B**
Gefahr, -en *f.* danger (3) **4B**
gefährdet *adj.* endangered; threatened (3) **4B**
gefallen *v.* to please (2) **1A**
Gefrierschrank, ⁻e *m.* freezer (2) **2B**
gegen *prep.* against (1) **3B**
gegenüber (von) *prep.* across (from) (3) **2B**
Gehalt, ⁻er *n.* salary (3) **3A**

hohes/niedriges Gehalt, ⁻er *n.* high/low salary (3) **3A**
Gehaltserhöhung, -en *f.* raise (3) **3B**
gehen *v.* to go (1) **2A**
  Es geht. (I'm) so-so. (1) **1A**
  Geht es dir/Ihnen gut? *v.* Are you all right? (inf./form.) (1) **1A**
  Wie geht es Ihnen? (form.) How are you? (1) **1A**
  Wie geht's (dir)? (inf.) How are you? (1) **1A**
gehören *v.* to belong to (1) **4B**
Geländewagen, - *m.* SUV (2) **4B**
gelb *adj.* yellow (2) **1B**
Geld, -er *n.* money (3) **2A**
  Geld abheben/einzahlen *v.* to withdraw/deposit money (3) **2A**
Geldautomat, -en *m.* ATM (3) **2A**
Geldschein, -e *m.* bill (money) (3) **2A**
gemein *adj.* mean (1) **3B**
Gemüse, - *n.* vegetables (1) **4A**
genau *adv.* exactly
  genauso wie just as (2) **4A**
genießen *v.* to enjoy
geöffnet *adj.* open (3) **2A**
Gepäck *n.* luggage (2) **3B**
geradeaus *adv.* straight ahead (2) **4A**
gern *adv.* with pleasure (1) **2B**
  gern (+verb) to like to (+verb) (1) **2B**
  ich hätte gern... I would like... (1) **4A**
  Gern geschehen. My pleasure.; You're welcome. (1) **1A**
Geschäft, -e *n.* business (3) **3A**; store (1) **4A**
Geschäftsführer, - / Geschäftsführerin, -nen *m./f.* manager (3) **3A**
Geschäftsmann, ⁻er / Geschäftsfrau, -en (pl. Geschäftsleute) *m./f.* businessman/ businesswoman (1) **3B**
Geschenk, -e *n.* gift (2) **1A**
Geschichte, -n *f.* history (1) **2A**; story
geschieden *adj.* divorced (1) **3A**
Geschirr *n.* dishes (2) **2B**
  Geschirr spülen *v.* to do the dishes (2) **2B**
geschlossen *adj.* closed (3) **2A**
Geschmack, ⁻e *m.* flavor; taste (1) **4B**
Geschwister, - *n.* sibling (1) **3A**
Gesetz, -e *n.* law (3) **4B**
Gesicht, -er *n.* face (3) **1A**
gestern *adv.* yesterday (2) **1B**
gestreift *adj.* striped (2) **1B**
gesund *adj.* healthy (2) **4A**; (3) **1B**
  gesund werden *v.* to get better (3) **1B**
Gesundheit *f.* health (3) **1B**
geteilt durch divided by (1) **1B**
Getränk, -e *n.* beverage (1) **4B**
getrennt *adj.* separated (1) **3A**
gewaltfrei *adj.* nonviolent (3) **4B**
Gewerkschaft, -en *f.* labor union (3) **3B**
gewinnen *v.* to win (1) **2B**
Gewitter, - *n.* thunderstorm (2) **3A**
sich gewöhnen an *v.* to get used to (3) **1A**
gierig *adj.* greedy (1) **3B**
Giftmüll *m.* toxic waste (3) **4B**
Glas, ⁻er *n.* glass (1) **4B**
glatt *adj.* straight (1) **3A**
  glatte Haare *n. pl.* straight hair (1) **3A**

glauben *v.* to believe (2) **1A**
gleich *adj.* same
  ist gleich *v.* equals, is (1) **1B**
Glück *n.* happiness (2) **1A**
glücklich *adj.* happy (1) **3B**
Golf *n.* golf (1) **2B**
Grad *n.* degree (2) **3A**
  Es sind 18 Grad draußen. It's 18 degrees out. (2) **3A**
Gramm, -e *n.* gram (1) **4A**
Granit, -e *m.* granite (2) **2B**
Gras, ̈er *n.* grass (3) **4A**
gratulieren *v.* to congratulate (2) **1A**
grau *adj.* grey (2) **1B**
grausam *adj.* cruel
Grippe, -n *f.* flu (3) **1B**
groß *adj.* big; tall (1) **3A**
großartig *adj.* terrific (1) **3A**
Großeltern *pl.* grandparents (1) **1A**
Großmutter, ̈ *f.* grandmother (1) **3A**
Großvater, ̈ *m.* grandfather (1) **3A**
großzügig *adj.* generous (1) **3B**
grün *adj.* green (2) **1B**
  grüne Bohne (*pl.* die grünen Bohnen) *f.* green bean (1) **4A**
Gruß, ̈e *m.* greeting
  Mit freundlichen Grüßen Yours sincerely (1) **3B**
grüßen *v.* to greet (1) **2A**
günstig *adj.* cheap (2) **1B**
Gürtel, - *m.* belt (2) **1B**
gut *adj.* good; *adv.* well (1) **1A**
  gut aussehend *adj.* handsome (1) **3A**
  gut gekleidet *adj.* well-dressed (2) **1B**
  Gute Besserung! Get well! (2) **1A**
  Guten Appetit! Enjoy your meal! (4) **4B**
  Guten Abend! Good evening. (1) **1A**
  Guten Morgen! Good morning. (1) **1A**
  Gute Nacht! Good night. (1) **1A**
  Guten Tag! Hello. (1) **1A**

H

Haar, -e *n.* hair (1) **3A**, (3) **1A**
Haartrockner, - *m.* hair dryer (3) **1A**
haben *v.* to have (1) **1B**
Hagel *m.* hail (2) **3A**
Hähnchen, - *n.* chicken (1) **4A**
halb half; half an hour before (1) **2A**
Halbbruder, ̈ *m.* half brother (1) **3A**
Halbschwester, -n *f.* half sister (1) **3A**
halbtags *adj.* part-time (3) **3B**
Hallo! Hello. (1) **1A**
Hals, ̈e *m.* neck (3) **1A**
  Hals- und Beinbruch! Break a leg! (2) **1A**
Halskette, -n *f.* necklace (2) **1B**
Hand, ̈e *f.* hand (3) **1A**
handeln *v.* to act
  handeln von *v.* to be about; have to do with (2) **3A**
Handgelenk, -e *n.* wrist (3) **1B**
Handgepäck *n.* carry-on luggage (2) **3B**
Handschuh, -e *m.* glove (2) **1B**
Handtasche, -n *f.* purse (2) **1B**
Handtuch, ̈er *n.* towel (3) **1A**
Handy, -s *n.* cell phone (4) **4B**

hängen *v.* to hang (2) **1B**
Hase, -n *m.* hare (3) **4A**
hässlich *adj.* ugly (1) **3A**
Hauptspeise, -n *f.* main course (1) **4B**
Hauptstraße, -n *f.* main road (3) **2B**
Haus, ̈er *n.* house (2) **2A**
  nach Hause *adv.* home (2) **1B**
  zu Hause *adv.* at home (1) **4A**
Hausarbeit *f.* housework (2) **2B**
  Hausarbeit machen *v.* to do housework (2) **2B**
Hausaufgabe, -n *f.* homework (1) **1B**
Hausfrau, -en / Hausmann, ̈er *f./m.* homemaker (3) **3B**
hausgemacht *adj.* homemade (1) **4B**
Hausmeister, - / Hausmeisterin, -nen *m./f.* caretaker; custodian (3) **3B**
Hausschuh, -e *m.* slipper (3) **1A**
Haustier, -e *n.* pet (1) **3A**
Heft, -e *n.* notebook (1) **1B**
Hefter, - *m.* stapler (3) **3A**
heiraten *v.* to marry (1) **3A**
heiß *adj.* hot (2) **3A**
heißen *v.* to be named (1) **2A**
  Ich heiße... My name is... (1) **1A**
helfen *v.* to help (1) **2B**
  helfen bei *v.* to help with (2) **3A**
hell *adj.* light (1) **3A**; bright (2) **1B**
Hemd, -en *n.* shirt (2) **1B**
herauf *adv.* up; upwards (2) **2A**
heraus *adv.* out (2) **2A**
Herbst, -e *m.* fall, autumn (1) **2B**, (2) **3A**
Herd, -e *m.* stove (2) **2B**
Herr Mr. (1) **1A**
herunter *adv.* down; downwards (2) **2A**
heruntergehen *v.* to go down (3) **2B**
  die Treppe heruntergehen *v.* to go downstairs (3) **2B**
herunterladen *v.* to download (2) **4B**
Herz, -en *n.* heart
  Herzlichen Glückwunsch! Congratulations! (2) **1A**
heute *adv.* today (1) **2B**
  Heute ist der... Today is the... (1) **2A**
  Welcher Tag ist heute? What day is it today? (2) **3A**
  Der Wievielte ist heute? What is the date today? (1) **2A**
hier *adv.* here (1) **1A**
  Hier ist/sind... Here is/are... (1) **1B**
Himmel *m.* sky (3) **4A**
hin und zurück there and back (2) **3B**
sich hinlegen *v.* to lie down (3) **1A**
sich hinsetzen *v.* to sit down (3) **1A**
hinter *prep.* behind (2) **1B**
hinterlassen *v.* to leave (behind)
eine Nachricht hinterlassen *v.* to leave a message (3) **3A**
Hobby, -s *n.* hobby (1) **2B**
hoch *adj.* high (2) **4A**
hochgehen *v.* to go up, climb up (3) **2B**
  die Treppe hochgehen *v.* to go upstairs (3) **2B**
Hochwasser, - *n.* flood (3) **4B**
Hochzeit, -en *f.* wedding (2) **1A**
Hockey *n.* hockey (1) **2B**
Höflichkeit, -en *f.* courtesy; polite expression (1) **1A**
Holz, ̈er *n.* wood (2) **2B**

hören *v.* to hear; listen to (1) **2A**
Hörer, - *m.* receiver (3) **3A**
Hörsaal (*pl.* Hörsäle) *m.* lecture hall (1) **2A**
Hose, -n *f.* pants (2) **1B**
  kurze Hose *f.* shorts (2) **1B**
Hotel, -s *n.* hotel (2) **3B**
  Fünf-Sterne-Hotel *n* five-star hotel. (3) **3B**
Hotelgast, ̈e *m.* hotel guest (2) **3B**
hübsch *adj.* pretty (1) **3A**
Hund, -e *m.* dog (1) **3A**
Hundewetter *n.* terrible weather (2) **3A**
husten *v.* to cough (3) **1B**
Hut, ̈e *m.* hat (1) **1B**
Hybridauto, -s *n.* hybrid car (3) **4B**

I

ich *pron.* I (1) **1A**
Idee, -n *f.* idea (1) **1A**
Ihr (*form., sing/pl.*) *poss. adj.* your (1) **3A**
ihr (*inf., pl.*) *pron.* you (1) **1A**; *poss. adj.* her, their (1) **3A**
immer *adv.* always (1) **4A**
Immobilienmakler, - / Immobilienmaklerin, -nen *m./f.* real estate agent (3) **3B**
in *prep.* in (2) **1B**
Inder, - / Inderin, -nen *m./f.* Indian (person) (3) **2B**
Indien *n.* India (3) **2B**
indisch *adj.* Indian (3) **2B**
Informatik *f.* computer science (1) **2A**
sich informieren (über) *v.* to find out (about) (3) **1A**
Ingenieur, -e / Ingenieurin, -nen *m./f.* engineer (1) **3B**
Innenstadt, ̈e *f.* city center; downtown (3) **2B**
innerhalb *prep.* inside of, within (2) **4B**
Insel, -n *f.* island (3) **4A**
intellektuell *adj.* intellectual (1) **3B**
intelligent *adj.* intelligent (1) **3B**
interessant *adj.* interesting (1) **2A**
sich interessieren (für) *v.* to be interested (in) (3) **1A**
Internet *n.* Web (2) **4B**
  im Internet surfen *v.* to surf the Web (2) **4B**
Internetcafé, -s *n.* internet café (3) **2A**
Italien *n.* Italy (3) **2B**
Italiener, - / Italienerin, -nen *m./f.* Italian (person) (3) **2B**
Italienisch *n.* Italian (language) (3) **2B**

J

ja yes (1) **1A**
Jacke, -n *f.* jacket (2) **1B**
Jahr, -e *n.* year (2) **3A**
  Ein gutes neues Jahr! Happy New Year! (2) **1A**
  Ich bin... Jahre alt. I am... years old (1) **1B**
Jahrestag, -e *m.* anniversary (2) **1A**
Jahreszeit, -en *f.* season (2) **3A**
Januar *m.* January (1) **2A**, (2) **3A**
Japan *n.* Japan (3) **2B**
Japaner, - / Japanerin, -nen *m./f.* Japanese (person) (3) **2B**
Japanisch *n.* Japanese (language) (3) **2B**
Jeans *f.* jeans (2) **1B**
jeder/jede/jedes *adj.* any, every, each (2) **4B**

jemand *pron.* someone (2) **3B**
jetzt *adv.* now (1) **4A**
joggen *v.* to jog (1) **2B**
Joghurt, -s *m.* yogurt (1) **4A**
Journalist, -en / Journalistin, -nen *m./f.*
  journalist (1) **3B**
Jugendherberge, -n *f.* youth hostel (2) **3B**
jugendlich *adj.* young; youthful (3) **2A**
Juli *m.* July (1) **2A**, (2) **3A**
jung *adj.* young (1) **3A**
Junge, -n *m.* boy (1) **1A**
Juni *m.* June (1) **2A**, (2) **3A**
Juweliergeschäft, -e *n.* jewelry store (3) **2A**

K

Kaffee, -s *m.* coffee (1) **4B**
Kaffeemaschine, -n *f.* coffeemaker (2) **2B**
Kalender, - *m.* calendar (1) **1B**
kalt *adj.* cold (2) **3A**
sich (die Haare) kämmen *v.* to comb (one's hair)
  (3) **1A**
Kanada *n.* Canada (3) **2B**
Kanadier, - / Kanadierin, -nen *m./f.*
  Canadian (3) **2B**
Kandidat, -en *m.* candidate (3) **3A**
Kaninchen, - *n.* rabbit (3) **4A**
Karotte, -n *f.* carrot (1) **4A**
Karriere, -n *f.* career (3) **3B**
Karte, -n *f.* map (1) **1B**, *f.* card (1) **2B**; (2) **1A**
  eine Karte lesen *v.* to read a map (2) **3B**
  mit der Karte bezahlen *v.* to pay by (credit)
    card (3) **2A**
Kartoffel, -n *f.* potato (1) **4A**
Käse, - *m.* cheese (1) **4A**
Katze, -n *f.* cat (1) **3A**
kaufen *v.* to buy (1) **2A**
Kaufhaus, ⁻er *n.* department store (3) **2B**
Kaution, -en *f.* security deposit (2) **2A**
kein *adj.* no (1) **2B**
  Keine Zufahrt. Do not enter. (1) **3B**
Keks, -e *m.* cookie (2) **1A**
Keller, - *m.* cellar (2) **2A**
Kellner, - / Kellnerin, -nen *m./f.* waiter/
  waitress (1) **3B**, (1) **4B**
kennen *v.* to know, be familiar with (2) **1B**
  sich kennen *v.* to know each other (3) **1A**
  (sich) kennen lernen *v.* to meet (one another)
    (1) **1A**
Keramik, -en *f.* ceramic (2) **2B**
Kernenergie *f.* nuclear energy (2) **1B**
Kernkraftwerk, -e *n.* nuclear power plant (3) **4B**
Kind, -er *n.* child (1) **1A**
Kino, -s *n.* movie theater (3) **2A**
Kiosk, -e *m.* newspaper kiosk (3) **2A**
Kirche, -n *f.* church (3) **2B**
Kissen, - *n.* pillow (2) **2B**
Klasse, -n *f.* class (1) **1B**
  erste/zweite Klasse, -n first/second class (2) **4A**
**Klassenkamerad, -en / Klassenkameradin,
  -nen** *m./f.* (K-12) classmate (1) **1B**
Klassenzimmer, - *n.* classroom (1) **1B**
klassisch *adj.* classical (3) **2A**
Kleid, -er *n.* dress (2) **1B**

Kleidergröße, -n *f.* clothing size (2) **1B**
Kleidung *f. pl.* clothes (2) **1B**
klein *adj.* small; short (stature) (1) **3A**
Kleingeld *n.* change (money) (2) **2A**
Klempner, - / Klempnerin, -nen *m./f.* plumber (3) **3B**
klettern *v.* to climb (mountain) (1) **2B**
klingeln *v.* to ring (2) **4B**
Klippe, -n *f.* cliff (3) **4A**
Knie, - *n.* knee (3) **1A**
Knoblauch, -e *m.* garlic (1) **4A**
Koch, ⁻e / Köchin, -nen *m./f.* cook, chef (1) **4B**
kochen *v.* to cook (1) **2B**
Koffer, - *m.* suitcase (2) **3B**
Kofferraum, ⁻e *m.* trunk (2) **4A**
Kombi, -s *m.* station wagon (2) **4B**
Komma, -s *n.* comma (1) **1B**
kommen *v.* to come (1) **2A**
Kommilitone, -n / Kommilitonin, -nen *m./f.*
  (university) classmate (1) **1B**
Kommode, -n *f.* dresser (2) **2A**
kompliziert *adj.* complicated (3) **2A**
Konditorei, -en *f.* pastry shop (1) **4A**
können *v.* to be able, can (1) **3B**
Konto (pl. Konten) *n.* bank account (3) **2A**
Konzert, -e *n.* concert (2) **1B**
Kopf, ⁻e *m.* head (3) **1A**
Kopfhörer, - *m.* headphones (2) **4B**
Kopfschmerzen *m. pl.* headache (3) **1B**
Korea *n.* Korea (3) **2B**
der Koreaner, - / die Koreanerin, -nen *m./f.*
  Korean (person) (3) **2B**
Koreanisch *n.* Korean (language) (3) **2B**
Körper, - *m.* body (3) **1A**
korrigieren *v.* to correct (1) **2A**
Kosmetiksalon, -s *m.* beauty salon (3) **2A**
kosten *v.* to cost (1) **2A**
  Wie viel kostet das? *v.* How much is that? (1) **4A**
krank *adj.* sick (3) **1B**
  krank werden *v.* to get sick (3) **1B**
Krankenhaus, ⁻er *n.* hospital (3) **1B**
Krankenpfleger, - / Krankenschwester, -n *m./f.*
  nurse (3) **1B**
Krankenwagen, - *m.* ambulance (3) **1B**
Krawatte, -n *f.* tie (2) **1B**
Kreuzfahrt, -en *f.* cruise (2) **3B**
Kreuzung, -en *f.* intersection (3) **2B**
Küche, -n *f.* kitchen (2) **2A**
Kuchen, - *m.* cake; pie (1) **4A**
Kuh, ⁻e *f.* cow (3) **4A**
kühl *adj.* cool (2) **3A**
Kühlschrank, ⁻e *m.* refrigerator (2) **2B**
Kuli, -s *m.* (ball-point) pen (1) **1B**
Kunde, -n / Kundin, -nen *m./f.* customer (2) **1B**
kündigen *v.* to resign (3) **3B**
Kunst, ⁻e *f.* art (1) **2A**
Kunststoff, -e *m.* plastic (2) **2B**
kurz *adj.* short (1) **3A**
  kurze Haare *n. pl.* short hair (1) **3A**
  kurze Hose *f.* shorts (2) **1B**
kurzärmlig *adj.* short-sleeved (2) **1B**
Kurzfilm, -e *m.* short film
Kuss, ⁻e *m.* kiss (2) **1A**
küssen *v.* to kiss (2) **1A**
  sich küssen *v.* to kiss (each other) (3) **1A**
Küste, -n *f.* coast (3) **4A**

L

lächeln *v.* to smile (1) **3B**
lachen *v.* to laugh (1) **3B**
Ladegerät, -e *n.* battery charger (2) **4B**
laden *v.* to charge; load (2) **4B**
Lage, -n *f.* location (2) **3B**
Laken, - *n.* sheet (2) **2B**
Lampe, -n *f.* lamp (2) **2A**
Land, ⁻er *n.* country (2) **3B**
landen *v.* to land (2) **3B**
Landkarte, -n *f.* map (2) **3B**
Landschaft, -en *f.* landscape;
  countryside (3) **4A**
lang *adj.* long (1) **3A**
  lange Haare *n. pl.* long hair (1) **3A**
langärmlig *adj.* long-sleeved (2) **1B**
langsam *adj.* slow (1) **3B**
  Langsam fahren. Slow down. (1) **3B**
langweilig *adj.* boring (1) **2A**
Laptop, -s *m./n.* laptop (computer) (2) **4B**
lassen *v.* to let, allow (2) **2B**
laufen *v.* to run (1) **2B**
leben *v.* to live (1) **2A**
Lebenslauf, ⁻e *m.* résumé; CV (3) **3A**
Lebensmittelgeschäft, -e *n.* grocery store (1) **4A**
lecker *adj.* delicious (1) **4B**
Leder, - *n.* leather (2) **1B**
ledig *adj.* single (1) **3A**
legen *v.* to lay (2) **1B**; *v.* to put; lay (3) **1A**
Lehrbuch, ⁻er *n.* textbook (university) (1) **1B**
Lehrer, - / Lehrerin, -nen *m./f.* teacher (1) **1B**
leicht *adj.* light (1) **4B**; mild (3) **1B**
Leichtathletik *f.* track and field (1) **2B**
leider *adv.* unfortunately (1) **4A**
leiten *v.* to manage (3) **3B**
Lenkrad, ⁻er *n.* steering wheel (2) **4A**
lernen *v.* to study; to learn (1) **2A**
lesen *v.* to read (1) **2B**
letzter/letzte/letztes *adj.* last (1) **2B**
Leute *pl.* people (1) **3B**
Licht, -er *n.* light (3) **4B**
Liebe, -n *f.* love (2) **1A**
  Lieber/Liebe *m./f.* Dear (1) **3B**
lieben *v.* to love (1) **2A**
  sich lieben *v.* to love each other (3) **1A**
lieber *adj.* rather (2) **4A**
liebevoll *adj.* loving (1) **3B**
Liebling, -e *m.* darling
  Lieblings- favorite (1) **4B**
liegen *v.* to lie; to be located (2) **1B**
lila *adj.* purple (1) **1B**
Linie, -n *f.* line
Lippe, -n *f.* lip (3) **1A**
Lippenstift, -e *m.* lipstick (3) **1A**
Literatur, -en *f.* literature (1) **2A**
LKW, -s *m.* truck (2) **4A**
LKW-Fahrer, - / LKW-Fahrerin, -nen *m./f.* truck
  driver (3) **3B**
lockig *adj.* curly (1) **3A**
  lockige Haare *n. pl.* curly hair (1) **3A**
Los! Start!; Go! (1) **2B**
löschen *v.* to delete (2) **4B**
Lösung, -en *f.* solution (3) **4B**

eine Lösung vorschlagen *v.* to propose a solution (3) **4B**
Luft, ⁼e *f.* air (3) **4A**
lügen *v.* to lie, tell a lie
Lust, ⁼e *f.* desire
  Lust haben *v.* to feel like (2) **3B**
lustig *adj.* funny (1) **3B**

M

machen *v.* to do; make (1) **2A**
  Mach's gut! *v.* All the best! (1) **3B**
Mädchen, - *n.* girl (1) **1A**
Mahlzeit, -en *f.* meal (1) **4B**
Mai *m.* May (1) **2A**, (2) **3A**
Mal, -e *n.* time
  das erste/letzte Mal the first/last time (2) **3B**
  zum ersten/letzten Mal for the first/last time (2) **3B**
mal times (1) **1B**
Mama, -s *f.* mom (1) **3A**
man *pron.* one (2) **3B**
mancher/manche/manches *adj.* some (2) **4B**
manchmal *adv.* sometimes (2) **3B**
Mann, ⁼er *m.* man (1) **1A**; *m.* husband (1) **3A**
Mannschaft, -en *f.* team (1) **2B**
Mantel, ⁼ *m.* coat (2) **1B**
Markt, ⁼e *m.* market (1) **4A**
Marmelade, -n *f.* jam (1) **4A**
Marmor *m.* marble (2) **2B**
März *m.* March (1) **2A**, (3) **3A**
Material, -ien *n.* material (2) **1B**
Mathematik *f.* mathematics (1) **2A**
Maus, ⁼e *f.* mouse (2) **4B**
Mechaniker, - / Mechanikerin, -nen *m./f.* mechanic (2) **4A**
Medikament, -e *n.* medicine (3) **1B**
Medizin *f.* medicine (1) **2A**
Meer, -e *n.* sea; ocean (3) **4A**
Meeresfrüchte *f. pl.* seafood (1) **4A**
mehr *adj.* more (2) **4A**
mein *poss. adj.* my (1) **3A**
meinen *v.* to mean; to believe; to maintain (3) **4B**
Meisterschaft, -en *f.* championship (1) **2B**
Melone, -n *f.* melon (1) **4A**
Mensa (*pl.* Mensen) *f.* cafeteria (college/university) (1) **1B**
Mensch, -en *m.* person
Messer, - *n.* knife (1) **4B**
Metzgerei, -en *f.* butcher shop (1) **4A**
Mexikaner, - / Mexikanerin, -nen *m./f.* Mexican (person) (3) **2B**
mexikanisch *adj.* Mexican (3) **2B**
Mexiko *n.* Mexico (3) **2B**
Miete, -n *f.* rent (2) **2A**
mieten *v.* to rent (2) **2A**
Mikrofon, -e *n.* microphone (2) **4B**
Mikrowelle, -n *f.* microwave (2) **2B**
Milch *f.* milk (1) **4B**
Minderheit, -en *f.* minority (3) **4B**
Mineralwasser *n.* sparkling water (1) **4B**
minus minus (1) **1B**
mir *pron.* myself, me (2) **3A**

Mir geht's (sehr) gut. *v.* I am (very) well. (1) **1A**
Mir geht's nicht (so) gut. *v.* I am not (so) well. (1) **1A**
mit with (1) **4B**
Mitbewohner, - / Mitbewohnerin, -nen *m./f.* roommate (1) **2A**
mitbringen *v.* to bring along (1) **4A**
mitkommen *v.* to come along (1) **4A**
mitmachen *v.* to participate (2) **4B**
mitnehmen *v.* to bring with (3) **2B**
  jemanden mitnehmen *v.* to give someone a ride (3) **2B**
Mittag, -e *m.* noon (1) **2A**
Mittagessen *n.* lunch (1) **4B**
Mitternacht *f.* midnight (1) **2A**
Mittwoch, -e *m.* Wednesday (1) **2A**
  mittwochs *adv.* on Wednesdays (1) **2A**
Möbel, - *n.* furniture (2) **2A**
Möbelstück, -e *n.* piece of furniture (2) **2A**
möbliert *adj.* furnished (2) **2A**
modern *adj.* modern (3) **2A**
modisch *adj.* fashionable (2) **1B**
mögen *v.* to like (1) **4B**
  Ich möchte... I would like... (1) **4B**
Monat, -e *m.* month (1) **2A**, (2) **3A**
Mond, -e *m.* moon (3) **4A**
Montag, -e *m.* Monday (1) **2A**
  montags *adv.* on Mondays (1) **2A**
Morgen, - *m.* morning (1) **2B**
  morgens *adv.* in the morning (1) **2A**
morgen *adv.* tomorrow (1) **2B**
  morgen früh tomorrow morning (1) **2B**
Motor, -en *m.* engine (2) **4A**
Motorhaube, -n *f.* hood (of car) (2) **4A**
MP3-Player, - *m.* mp3 player (2) **4B**
müde *adj.* tired (1) **3B**
Müll *m.* trash (2) **2B**; *m.* waste (3) **4B**
  den Müll rausbringen *v.* to take out the trash (2) **2B**
Müllwagen, - *m.* garbage truck (3) **4B**
Mund, ⁼er *m.* mouth (3) **1A**
Münze, -n *f.* coin (3) **2A**
Musiker, - / Musikerin, -nen *m./f.* musician (1) **3B**
müssen *v.* to have to; must (1) **3B**
mutig *adj.* brave (1) **3B**
Mutter, ⁼ *f.* mother (1) **1A**
Mütze, -n *f.* cap (2) **1B**

N

nach *prep.* after; to; according to (1) **4B**; *prep.* past (time) (1) **2A**
  nach rechts/links to the right/left (2) **2A**
nachdem *conj.* after (3) **2A**
nachmachen *v.* to imitate (2) **4B**
Nachmittag, -e *m.* afternoon (1) **2B**
  nachmittags *adv.* in the afternoon (1) **2A**
Nachname, -n *m.* last name (1) **3A**
Nachricht, -en *f.* message (3) **3A**
  eine Nachricht hinterlassen *v.* to leave a message (3) **3A**
nächster/nächste/nächstes *adj.* next (1) **2B**
Nacht, ⁼e *f.* night (1) **2B**
Nachtisch, -e *m.* dessert (1) **4B**
Nachttisch, -e *m.* night table (2) **2A**

nah(e) *adj.* near; nearby (3) **2B**
Nähe *f.* vicinity (3) **2B**
  in der Nähe von *f.* close to (3) **2B**
naiv *adj.* naïve (1) **3B**
Nase, -n *f.* nose (3) **1A**
  verstopfte Nase *f.* stuffy nose (3) **1A**
nass *adj.* wet (3) **4A**
Natur, *f.* nature (3) **4A**
Naturkatastrophe, -n *f.* natural disaster (3) **4A**
Naturwissenschaft, -en *f.* science (1) **2A**
Nebel, - *m.* fog; mist (2) **3A**
neben *prep.* next to (1) **1B**
Nebenkosten *pl.* additional charges (2) **2A**
Neffe, -n *m.* nephew (2) **4B**
nehmen *v.* to take (1) **2B**
nein no (1) **1A**
nennen *v.* to call (2) **1A**
nervös *adj.* nervous (1) **3B**
nett *adj.* nice (1) **3B**
neugierig *adj.* curious (1) **3B**
neun nine (1) **2A**
nicht *adv.* not (1) **2B**
  nicht schlecht not bad (1) **1A**
nichts *pron.* nothing (2) **3B**
nie *adv.* never (1) **4A**
niedrig *adj.* low (3) **3A**
niemals *adv.* never (2) **3B**
niemand *pron.* no one (2) **3B**
niesen *v.* to sneeze (3) **1B**
noch *adv.* yet; still; in addition (1) **4A**
normalerweise *adv.* usually (3) **1B**
Notaufnahme, -n *f.* emergency room (3) **1B**
Note, -n *f.* grade (on an assignment) (1) **1B**
Notfall, ⁼e *m.* emergency (3) **3B**
Notiz, -en *f.* note (1) **1B**
November *m.* November (1) **2A**, (2) **3A**
Nummernschild, -er *n.* license plate (2) **4A**
nur *adv.* only (1) **4A**
nützlich *adj.* useful (1) **2A**
nutzlos *adj.* useless (1) **2A**

O

ob *conj.* whether; if (3) **2A**
Obst *n.* fruit (1) **4A**
obwohl *conj.* even though (2) **2A**; *conj.* although (3) **2A**
oder *conj.* or (1) **1B**
Ofen, ⁼ *m.* oven (2) **2B**
öffentlich *adj.* public (2) **4A**
  öffentliche Verkehrsmittel *n.* public transportation (2) **4A**
öffnen *v.* to open (1) **2A**
oft *adv.* often (1) **4A**
ohne *prep.* without (1) **3B**
Ohr, -en *n.* ear (3) **1A**
Ökologie *f.* ecology (3) **4B**
ökologisch *adj.* ecological (3) **4B**
Oktober *m.* October (1) **2A**, (2) **3A**
Öl, -e *n.* oil (1) **4A**
Olivenöl, -e *n.* olive oil (1) **4A**
Oma, -s *f.* grandma (1) **3A**
online sein *v.* to be online (2) **4B**

Opa, -s *m.* grandpa (1) **3A**
orange *adj.* orange (2) **1B**
Orange, -n *f.* orange (1) **4A**
ordentlich *adj.* neat, tidy (2) **2B**
Ort, -e *m.* place (1) **1B**
Österreich *n.* Austria (3) **2B**
Österreicher, - / Österreicherin, -nen *m./f.*
 Austrian (person) (3) **2B**

P

Paar, -e *n.* couple (1) **3A**
packen *v.* to pack (2) **3B**
Paket, -e *n.* package (3) **2A**
Papa, -s *m.* dad (1) **3A**
Papier, -e *n.* paper
 Blatt Papier (*pl.* Blätter Papier) *n.* sheet of paper
 (1) **1B**
Papierkorb, ¨e *m.* wastebasket (1) **1B**
Paprika, - *f.* pepper (1) **4A**
 grüne/rote Paprika *f.* green/red pepper (1) **4A**
Park, -s *m.* park (1) **1A**
parken *v.* to park (2) **4A**
 Parkverbot. No parking. (1) **3B**
Party, -s *f.* party (2) **1A**
 eine Party geben *v.* to throw a party (2) **1A**
Passagier, -e / Passagierin, -nen *m./f.*
 passenger (2) **3B**
passen *v.* to fit; to match (2) **1A**
passieren *v.* to happen (2) **1B**
Passkontrolle, -n *f.* passport control (2) **3B**
Passwort, ¨er *n.* password (2) **4B**
Pasta *f.* pasta (1) **4A**
Patient, -en / Patientin, -nen *m./f.* patient (3) **1B**
Pause, -n *f.* break, recess (1) **1B**
Pension, -en *f.* guesthouse (2) **3B**
Person, -en *f.* person (1) **1A**
Personalausweis, -e *m.* ID card (2) **3B**
Personalchef, -s / die Personalchefin, -nen *m./f.*
 human resources manager (3) **3A**
persönlich *adj.* personal (1) **3B**
Pfanne, -n *f.* pan (2) **2B**
Pfeffer, - *m.* pepper (1) **4B**
Pferd, -e *n.* horse (1) **2B**
Pfirsich, -e *m.* peach (1) **4A**
Pflanze, -n *f.* plant (2) **2A**
Pfund, -e *n.* pound (1) **4A**
Physik *f.* physics (1) **2A**
Picknick, -s, *n.* picnic (3) **4A**
 ein Picknick machen *v.* to have a picnic (3) **4A**
Pilz, -e *m.* mushroom (1) **4A**
Pinnwand, ¨e *f.* bulletin board (3) **3A**
Planet, -en *m.* planet (3) **4B**
 den Planeten retten *v.* to save the planet (3) **4B**
Platten, - *m.* flat tire (2) **4A**
 einen Platten haben *v.* to have a flat tire (2) **4A**
Platz, ¨e *m.* court (1) **1A**
plus plus (1) **1B**
Politiker, - / Politikerin, -nen *m./f.* politician (3) **3B**
Polizeiwache, -n *f.* police station (3) **2A**
Polizist, -en / Polizistin, -nen *m./f.* police
 officer (2) **4A**
Post *f.* post office; mail (3) **2A**
 zur Post gehen *v.* to go to the post office (3) **2A**

Poster, - *n.* poster (1) **2A**
Postkarte, -n *f.* postcard (3) **2A**
Praktikum (*pl.* die Praktika) *n.* internship (3) **3A**
prima *adj.* great (1) **1A**
probieren *v.* to try (1) **3B**
 Probieren Sie mal! Give it a try!
Problem, -e *n.* problem (1) **1A**
Professor, -en / Professorin, -nen *m./f.*
 professor (1) **1B**
Programm, -e *n.* program (2) **4B**
Prost! Cheers! (1) **4B**
Prozent, -e *n.* percent (1) **1B**
Prüfung, -en *f.* exam, test (1) **1B**
Psychologe, -n / Psychologin, -nen *m./f.*
 psychologist (3) **3B**
Psychologie *f.* psychology (1) **2A**
Pullover, - *m.* sweater (2) **1B**
Punkt, -e *m.* period (1) **1B**
pünktlich *adj.* on time (2) **3B**
putzen *v.* to clean (2) **2B**
 sich die Zähne putzen *v.* to brush one's teeth (3) **1A**

Q

Querverweis, -e *m.* cross-reference

R

Radiergummi, -s *m.* eraser (1) **1B**
Rasen, - *m.* lawn, grass (1) **3B**
 Betreten des Rasens verboten. Keep off the
 grass. (1) **3B**
sich rasieren *v.* to shave (3) **1A**
Rasierer, - *m.* razor (3) **1A**
Rasierschaum, ¨e *m.* shaving cream (3) **1A**
Rathaus, ¨er *n.* town hall (3) **2A**
rauchen *v.* to smoke
 Rauchen verboten. No smoking. (1) **3B**
rausbringen *v.* to bring out (2) **2B**
 den Müll rausbringen *v.* to take out the trash (2) **2B**
realistisch *adj.* realistic (3) **2A**
Rechnung, -en *f.* check (1) **4B**
Rechtsanwalt, ¨e / Rechtsanwältin, -nen *m./f.*
 lawyer (1) **3B**
Rechtschreibung *f.* spelling
recyceln *v.* to recycle (3) **4B**
reden *v.* to talk (2) **1A**
 reden über *v.* to talk about (2) **3A**
Referat, -e *n.* presentation (1) **2A**
Referenz, -en *f.* reference (3) **3A**
Regen *m.* rain (2) **3A**
Regenmantel, ¨ *m.* raincoat (2) **3A**
Regenschirm, -e *m.* umbrella (2) **3A**
Regierung, -en *f.* government (3) **4B**
regnen *v.* to rain (1) **2A**, (2) **3A**
reich *adj.* rich (1) **3B**
Reis *m.* rice (1) **4A**
Reise, -n *f.* trip (2) **3B**
Reisebüro, -s *n.* travel agency (2) **3B**
reisen *v.* to travel (1) **2A**
Reisende, -n *m./f.* traveler (2) **3B**
Reiseziel, -e *n.* destination (2) **3B**
reiten *v.* to ride (1) **2B**

rennen *v.* to run (2) **1A**
Rente, -n *f.* pension
 in Rente gehen *v.* to retire (2) **1A**
Rentner, - / Rentnerin, -nen *m./f.* retiree (3) **3B**
reparieren *v.* to repair (2) **4A**
Restaurant, -s *n.* restaurant (1) **4B**
retten *v.* to save (3) **4B**
Rezept, -e *n.* recipe (1) **4A**; prescription (3) **1B**
Richter, - / Richterin, -nen *m./f.* judge (3) **3B**
Richtung, -en *f.* direction (3) **2B**
 in Richtung *f.* toward (3) **2B**
Rindfleisch *n.* beef (1) **4A**
Rock, ¨e *m.* skirt (2) **1B**
rosa *adj.* pink (2) **1B**
rot *adj.* red (1) **3A**
rothaarig *adj.* red-haired (1) **3A**
Rücken, - *m.* back (3) **1A**
Rückenschmerzen *m. pl.* backache (3) **1B**
Rucksack, ¨e *m.* backpack (1) **1B**
ruhig *adj.* calm (1) **3B**
Russe, -n / Russin, -nen *m./f.* Russian
 (person) (3) **2B**
Russisch *n.* Russian (language) (3) **2B**
Russland *n.* Russia (3) **2B**

S

Sache, -n *f.* thing (1) **1B**
Saft, ¨e *m.* juice (1) **4B**
sagen *v.* to say (1) **2A**
Salat, -e *m.* lettuce; salad (1) **4A**
Salz, -e *n.* salt (1) **4B**
salzig *adj.* salty (1) **4B**
Samstag, -e *m.* Saturday (1) **2A**
 samstags *adv.* on Saturdays (1) **2A**
sauber *adj.* clean (2) **2B**
saurer Regen *m.* acid rain (3) **4B**
Saustall *n.* pigsty (2) **2B**
 Es ist ein Saustall! It's a pigsty! (2) **2B**
Schach *n.* chess (1) **2B**
Schaf, -e *n.* sheep (3) **4A**
Schaffner, - / Schaffnerin, -nen *m./f.* ticket
 collector (2) **4A**
Schal, -s *m.* scarf (2) **1B**
scharf *adj.* spicy (1) **4B**
schauen *v.* to look (2) **3A**
Scheibenwischer, - *m.* windshield wiper (2) **4A**
Scheinwerfer, - *m.* headlight (2) **4A**
scheitern *v.* to fail (3) **3B**
schenken *v.* to give (a gift) (2) **1A**
schicken *v.* to send (2) **4B**
Schiff, -e *n.* ship (2) **4A**
Schinken, - *m.* ham (1) **4A**
Schlafanzug, ¨e *m.* pajamas (3) **1A**
schlafen *v.* to sleep (1) **2B**
Schlafzimmer, - *n.* bedroom (2) **2A**
Schlange, -n *f.* line (3) **3B**; *f.* snake (3) **4A**
 Schlange stehen *v.* to stand in line (2) **3B**
schlank *adj.* slim (1) **3B**
schlecht *adj.* bad (1) **3B**
 schlecht gekleidet *adj.* badly dressed (2) **1B**
schließlich *adv.* finally (2) **3B**
Schlüssel, - *m.* key (2) **3B**

schmecken *v.* to taste (1) **4B**
Schmerz, -en *m.* pain (3) **1B**
sich schminken *v.* to put on makeup (3) **1A**
schmutzig *adj.* dirty (2) **2B**
Schnee *m.* snow (2) **3A**
schneien *v.* to snow (2) **3A**
schnell *adj.* fast (1) **3B**
schon *adv.* already, yet (1) **4A**
schön *adj.* pretty; beautiful (1) **3A**
  Schön dich/Sie kennen zu lernen. Nice to meet you. (1) **1A**
  Schönen Tag noch! Have a nice day! (1) **1A**
  Es ist schön draußen. It's nice out. (2) **3A**
Schrank, ̈e *m.* cabinet; closet (2) **2A**
schreiben *v.* to write (1) **2A**
  schreiben an *v.* to write to (2) **3A**
  sich schreiben *v.* to write one another (3) **1A**
Schreibtisch, -e *m.* desk (1) **1B**
Schreibwarengeschäft, -e *n.* paper-goods store (3) **2A**
Schublade, -n *f.* drawer (2) **2A**
schüchtern *adj.* shy (1) **3B**
Schuh, -e *m.* shoe (2) **1B**
Schulbuch, ̈er *n.* textbook (K–12) (1) **1B**
Schule, -n *f.* school (1) **1B**
Schüler, - / Schülerin, -nen (K–12) *m./f.* student (1) **1B**
Schulleiter, - / Schulleiterin, -nen *m./f.* principal (1) **1B**
Schulter, -n *f.* shoulder (3) **1A**
Schüssel, -n *f.* bowl (1) **4B**
schützen *v.* to protect (3) **4B**
schwach *adj.* weak (1) **3B**
Schwager, ̈ *m.* brother-in-law (1) **3A**
Schwägerin, -nen *f.* sister-in-law (1) **3A**
schwanger *adj.* pregnant (3) **1B**
schwänzen *v.* to cut class (1) **1B**
schwarz *adj.* black (2) **1B**
schwarzhaarig *adj.* black-haired (1) **3A**
Schweinefleisch *n.* pork (1) **4A**
Schweiz (die) *f.* Switzerland (2) **3A**
Schweizer, - / Schweizerin, -nen *m./f.* Swiss (person) (3) **2B**
schwer *adj.* rich, heavy (1) **4B**; *adj.* serious, difficult (3) **1B**
Schwester, -n *f.* sister (1) **1A**
Schwiegermutter, ̈ *f.* mother-in-law (1) **3A**
Schwiegervater, ̈ *m.* father-in-law (1) **3A**
schwierig *adj.* difficult (1) **2A**
Schwimmbad, ̈er *n.* swimming pool (1) **2B**
schwimmen *v.* to swim (1) **2B**
schwindlig *adj.* dizzy (3) **1B**
sechs six (1) **2A**
See, -n *m.* lake (3) **4A**
sehen *v.* to see (1) **2B**
sehr *adv.* very (1) **3A**
Seide, -n *f.* silk (2) **1B**
Seife, -n *f.* soap (3) **1A**
sein *v.* to be (1) **1A**
  (gleich) sein *v.* to equal (1) **1B**
sein *poss. adj.* his, its (1) **3A**
seit since; for (1) **4B**
Sekt, -e *m.* champagne (2) **1A**
selten *adv.* rarely (1) **4A**

Seminar, -e *n.* seminar (1) **2A**
Seminarraum, -räume *m.* seminar room (1) **2A**
Sender, - *m.* channel (2) **4B**
September *m.* September (1) **2A**, (2) **3A**
Serviette, -n *f.* napkin (1) **4B**
Sessel, - *m.* armchair (2) **2A**
setzen *v.* to put, place (2) **1B**; *v.* to put, set (3) **1A**
Shampoo, -s *n.* shampoo (3) **1A**
sicher *adv.* probably (3) **2A**
Sicherheitsgurt, -e *m.* seatbelt (2) **4A**
sie *pron.* she/they (1) **1A**
Sie *pron.* (*form., sing./pl.*) you (1) **1A**
sieben seven (1) **2A**
Silvester *n.* New Year's Eve (2) **1A**
singen *v.* to sing (1) **2B**
sitzen *v.* to sit (2) **1B**
Ski fahren *v.* to ski (1) **2B**
Smartphone, -s *n.* smartphone (2) **4B**
SMS, - *f.* text message (2) **4B**
Snack, -s *m.* snack (1) **4B**
so *adv.* so (1) **4A**
Socke, -n *f.* sock (2) **1B**
Sofa, -s *n.* sofa; couch (2) **2A**
  Sofa surfen *v.* to couch surf (2) **3B**
Sohn, ̈e *m.* son (1) **3A**
solcher/solche/solches *pron.* such (2) **4B**
sollen *v.* to be supposed to (1) **3B**
Sommer, - *m.* summer (1) **2B**, (2) **3A**
sondern *conj.* but rather; instead (2) **2A**
Sonne, -n *f.* sun (3) **4A**
Sonnenaufgang, ̈e *m.* sunrise (3) **4A**
Sonnenbrand, ̈e *m.* sunburn (3) **1B**
Sonnenbrille, -n *f.* sunglasses (2) **1B**
Sonnenenergie *f.* solar energy (3) **4B**
Sonnenuntergang, ̈e *m.* sunset (3) **4A**
sonnig *adj.* sunny (2) **3A**
Sonntag, -e *m.* Sunday (1) **2A**
  sonntags *adv.* on Sundays (1) **2A**
Spanien *n.* Spain (3) **3B**
Spanier, - / Spanierin, -nen *m./f.* Spanish (person) (3) **2B**
Spanisch *n.* Spanish (language) (3) **2B**
spannend *adj.* exciting (3) **2A**
Spaß *m.* fun (1) **2B**
  Spaß haben/machen *v.* to have fun/to be fun (1) **2B**
  (keinen) Spaß haben *v.* to (not) have fun (2) **1A**
spät *adj.* late
  Wie spät ist es? What time is it? (1) **2A**
spazieren gehen *v.* to go for a walk (1) **2B**
Spaziergang, ̈e *m.* walk
speichern *v.* to save (2) **4B**
Speisekarte, -n *f.* menu (1) **4B**
Spiegel, - *m.* mirror (2) **2A**
Spiel, -e *n.* match, game (1)c**2B**
spielen *v.* to play (1) **2B**
Spieler, - / Spielerin, -nen *m./f.* player (1) **2B**
Spielfeld, -er *n.* field (1) **2B**
Spielkonsole, -n *f.* game console (2) **4B**
Spitze! *adj.* great! (1) **1A**
Sport *m.* sports (1)
  Sport treiben *v.* to exercise (3) **1B**
Sportart, -en *f.* sport; type of sport (1) **2B**
Sporthalle, - n *f.* gym (1) **2A**

sportlich *adj.* athletic (1) **3A**
sprechen *v.* to speak (1) **2B**
  sprechen über *v.* to speak about (2) **3A**
Spritze, -n *f.* shot (3) **1B**
  eine Spritze geben *v.* to give a shot (3) **1B**
Spüle, -n *f.* (kitchen) sink (2) **2B**
spülen *v.* to rinse (2) **2B**
  Geschirr spülen *v.* to do the dishes (2) **2B**
  Spülmaschine, -n *f.* dishwasher (2) **2B**
Stadion (*pl.* **Stadien**) *n.* stadium (1) **2B**
Stadt, ̈e *f.* city (2) **1B**; *f.* town (3) **2B**
Stadtplan, ̈e *m.* city map (2) **3B**
Stahl *m.* steel (2) **2B**
stark *adj.* strong (1) **3B**
starten *v.* to start (2) **4B**
statt *conj.* instead of
Statue, -n *f.* statue (3) **2B**
staubsaugen *v.* to vacuum (2) **2B**
Staubsauger, - *m.* vacuum cleaner (2) **2B**
stehen *v.* to stand (2) **1B**
  Schlange stehen *v.* to stand in line (2) **3B**
stehlen *v.* to steal (1) **2B**
steif *adj.* stiff (3) **1B**
steigen *v.* to climb (2) **1B**
Stein, -e *m.* rock (3) **4A**
Stelle, -n *f.* place, position (3) **2A**; job (3) **3A**
  an deiner/Ihrer Stelle *f.* if I were you (3) **2A**
  eine Stelle suchen *v.* to look for a job (3) **3A**
stellen *v.* to put, place (2) **1B**
Stellenangebot, -e *n.* job opening (3) **3A**
sterben *v.* to die (2) **1B**
Stereoanlage, -n *f.* stereo system (2) **4B**
Stern -e *m.* star (3) **4A**
Stiefel, - *m.* boot (2) **1B**
Stiefmutter, ̈ *f.* stepmother (1) **3A**
Stiefsohn, ̈e *m.* stepson (1) **3A**
Stieftochter, ̈ *f.* stepdaughter (1) **3A**
Stiefvater, ̈ *m.* stepfather (1) **3A**
Stift, -e *m.* pen (1) **1B**
Stil, -e *m.* style (2) **1B**
still *adj.* still (1) **4B**
  stilles Wasser *n.* still water (1) **4B**
Stipendium, (*pl.* **Stipendien**) *n.* scholarship, grant (1) **2A**
Stock, ̈e *m.* floor (2) **2A**
  erster/zweiter Stock first/second floor (2) **2A**
stolz *adj.* proud (3) **3B**
Stoppschild, -er *n.* stop sign (2) **4A**
Strand, ̈e *m.* beach (1) **2B**
Straße, -n *f.* street (2) **4A**
sich streiten *v.* to argue (3) **1A**
Strom, ̈e *m.* stream (3) **4A**
Student, -en / Studentin, -nen *m./f.* (college/university) student (1) **1A**
Studentenwohnheim, -e *n.* dormitory (1) **2A**
studieren *v.* to study; major in (1) **2A**
Studium (*pl.* **Studien**) *n.* studies (1) **2A**
Stuhl, ̈e *m.* chair (1) **1A**
Stunde, -n *f.* lesson (1) **1B**; hour (1) **2A**
Stundenplan, ̈e *m.* schedule (1) **2A**
Sturm, ̈e *m.* storm (2) **3A**
suchen *v.* to look for (1) **2A**
  eine Stelle suchen *v.* to look for a job (3) **3A**

Supermarkt, ⸚e *m.* supermarket (1) **4A**
Suppe, -n *f.* soup (1) **4B**
surfen *v.* to surf (2) **4B**
  im Internet surfen *v.* to surf the Web (2) **4B**
süß *adj.* sweet, cute (1) **3B**, (1) **4B**
Süßigkeit, -en *f.* candy (2) **1A**
Sweatshirt, -s *n.* sweatshirt (2) **1B**
Symptom, -e *n.* symptom (3) **1B**

T

Tablet, -s *n.* tablet (2) **4B**
Tablette, -n *f.* pill (3) **1B**
Tafel, -n *f.* board, black board (1) **1B**
Tag, -e *m.* day (1) **1A**, (2) **3A**
  Welcher Tag ist heute? What day is it today? (2) **3A**
täglich *adv.* every day; daily (1) **4A**
Tal, ⸚er *n.* valley (3) **4A**
tanken *v.* to fill up (2) **4A**
Tankstelle, -n *f.* gas station (2) **4A**
Tante, -n *f.* aunt (1) **3A**
tanzen *v.* to dance (1) **2B**
Taschenrechner, - *m.* calculator (1) **1B**
Taschentuch, ⸚er *n.* tissue (3) **1B**
Tasse, -n *f.* cup (1) **4B**
Tastatur, -en *f.* keyboard (2) **4B**
Taxi, -s *n.* taxi (2) **4A**
Taxifahrer, - / Taxifahrerin, -nen *m./f.* taxi driver (3) **3B**
Technik *f.* technology (2) **4B**
  Technik bedienen *v.* to use technology (2) **4B**
Tee, -s *m.* tea (1) **4B**
Teelöffel, - *m.* teaspoon (1) **4B**
Telefon, -e *n.* telephone (2) **4B**
  am Telefon on the telephone (3) **3A**
Telefonnummer, -n *f.* telephone number (3) **3A**
Telefonzelle, -n *f.* phone booth (3) **2B**
Teller, - *m.* plate (1) **4B**
Tennis *n.* tennis (1) **2B**
Teppich, -e *m.* rug (2) **2A**
Termin, -e *m.* appointment (3) **3A**
  einen Termin vereinbaren *v.* to make an appointment (3) **3A**
teuer *adj.* expensive (2) **1B**
Thermometer, - *n.* thermometer (1) **1B**
Thunfisch, -e *m.* tuna (1) **4A**
Tier, -e *n.* animal (3) **4A**
Tierarzt, ⸚e / Tierärztin, -nen *m./f.* veterinarian (3) **3B**
Tisch, -e *m.* table, desk (1) **1B**
  den Tisch decken *v.* to set the table (2) **2B**
Tischdecke, -n *f.* tablecloth (1) **4B**
Toaster, - *m.* toaster (2) **2B**
Tochter, ⸚ *f.* daughter (1) **3A**
Toilette, -n *f.* toilet (2) **2A**
Tomate, -n *f.* tomato (1) **4A**
Topf, ⸚e *m.* pot (2) **2B**
Tor, -e *n.* goal (in soccer, etc.) (1) **2B**
Tornado, -s *m.* tornado (3) **4A**
Torte, -n *f.* cake (2) **1A**
Touristenklasse *f.* economy class (2) **3B**
tragen *v.* to carry; wear (1) **2B**
Trägerhemd, -en *n.* tank top (2) **1B**

trainieren *v.* to practice (sports) (1) **2B**
Traube, -n *f.* grape (1) **4A**
träumen *v.* to dream (2) **3A**
traurig *adj.* sad (1) **3B**
treffen *v.* to meet; to hit (1) **2B**
  sich treffen *v.* to meet (each other) (3) **1A**
treiben *v.* to float; to push
  Sport treiben *v.* to exercise (3) **1B**
Treibsand *m.* quicksand (3) **4A**
sich trennen *v.* to separate, split up (3) **1A**
Treppe, -n *f.* stairway (2) **2A**
trinken *v.* to drink (1) **3B**
Trinkgeld, -er *n.* tip (1) **4B**
trocken *adj.* dry (3) **4A**
trotz *prep.* despite, in spite of (2) **4B**
Tschüss. Bye. (1) **1A**
T-Shirt, -s *n.* T-shirt (2) **1B**
tun *v.* to do (3) **1B**
  Es tut mir leid. I'm sorry. (1) **1A**
  weh tun *v.* to hurt (3) **1B**
Tür, -en *f.* door (1) **1B**
  Türen schließen. Keep doors closed. (1) **3B**
Türkei (die) *f.* Turkey (3) **2B**
Türke, -n / die Türkin, -nen *m./f.* Turkish (person) (3) **2B**
Türkisch *n.* Turkish (language) (3) **2B**
Turnschuhe *m. pl.* sneakers (2) **1B**

U

U-Bahn, -en *f.* subway (2) **4A**
übel *adj.* nauseous (3) **1B**
über *prep.* over, above (2) **1B**
übernachten *v.* to spend the night (2) **3B**
überall *adv.* everywhere (1) **4A**
Überbevölkerung *f.* overpopulation (3) **4B**
überlegen *v.* to think over (1) **4A**
übermorgen *adv.* the day after tomorrow (1) **2B**
überqueren *v.* to cross (3) **2B**
überraschen *v.* to surprise (2) **1A**
Überraschung, -en *f.* surprise (2) **1A**
überzeugend *adj.* persuasive (3) **1B**
Übung, -en *f.* practice, exercise
Uhr, -en *f.* clock (1) **1B**
  um... Uhr at... o'clock (1) **2A**
  Wie viel Uhr ist es? *v.* What time is it? (1) **2A**
um *prep.* around; at (time) (1) **3B**
  um... zu in order to (2) **3B**
Umleitung, -en *f.* detour (2) **4A**
umtauschen *v.* to exchange (2) **2B**
Umwelt, -en *f.* environment (3) **4B**
umweltfreundlich *adj.* environmentally friendly (3) **4B**
Umweltschutz *m.* environmentalism (3) **4B**
umziehen *v.* to move (2) **2A**, (3) **1A**
  sich umziehen *v.* to change clothes (3) **1A**
unangenehm *adj.* unpleasant (3) **3B**
und *conj.* and (1) **1B**
Unfall, ⸚e *m.* accident (2) **4A**
  einen Unfall haben *v.* to have an accident (2) **4A**
Universität, -en *f.* university; college (1) **1B**
unmöbliert *adj.* unfurnished (2) **2A**
unser *poss. adj.* our (1) **3A**

unter *prep.* under, below (2) **1B**
untergehen *v.* to set (sun) (3) **4A**
sich unterhalten *v.* to chat, have a conversation (1) **1A**
Unterkunft, ⸚e *f.* accommodations (2) **3B**
Unterricht, -e *m.* class, instruction (1) **1B**
unterschreiben *v.* to sign (3) **2A**
Unterwäsche *f.* underwear (2) **1B**
Urgroßmutter, ⸚ *f.* great grandmother (1) **3A**
Urgroßvater, ⸚ *m.* great grandfather (1) **3A**
Urlaub, -e *m.* vacation (2) **3B**
  Urlaub machen *v.* to go on vacation (2) **3B**
  Urlaub nehmen *v.* to take time off (3) **3B**
USA (die) *pl.* USA (3) **2B**

V

Vase, -n *f.* vase (2) **2A**
Vater, ⸚ *m.* father (1) **3A**
Veranstaltung, -en *f.* class; course (1) **2A**
Verb, -en *n.* verb (3) **1A**
verbessern *v.* to improve (3) **4B**
verbringen *v.* to spend (1) **4A**
verdienen *v.* to earn (3) **3B**
Vereinigten Staaten (die) *pl.* United States (3) **2B**
Vergangenheit, -en *f.* past (3) **4A**
vergessen *v.* to forget (1) **2B**
verheiratet *adj.* married (1) **3A**
verkaufen *v.* to sell (1) **4A**
Verkäufer, - / Verkäuferin, -nen *m./f.* salesperson (2) **1B**
Verkehr *m.* traffic (2) **4A**
Verkehrsmittel *n.* transportation (2) **4A**
  öffentliche Verkehrsmittel *n. pl.* public transportation (2) **4A**
verkünden *v.* to announce (3) **4B**
sich verlaufen *v.* to get lost (3) **2B**
sich verletzen *v.* to hurt oneself (3) **1B**
Verletzung, -en *f.* injury (3) **1B**
sich verlieben (in) *v.* to fall in love (with) (3) **1A**
verlieren *v.* to lose (1) **2B**
verlobt *adj.* engaged (1) **3A**
Verlobte, -n *m./f.* fiancé(e) (1) **3A**
verschmutzen *v.* to pollute (3) **4B**
Verschmutzung *f.* pollution (3) **4B**
sich verspäten *v.* to be late (3) **1A**
Verspätung, -en *f.* delay (2) **3B**
Verständnis, -se *n.* comprehension
sich (das Handgelenk / den Fuß) verstauchen *v.* to sprain (one's wrist/ankle) (3) **1B**
verstehen *v.* to understand (1) **2A**
verstopfte Nase *f.* stuffy nose (3) **1B**
versuchen *v.* to try (2) **3B**
Vertrag, ⸚e *m.* contract (3) **3A**
verwandt *adj.* related (3) **2A**
Verwandte, -n *m.* relative (1) **3A**
viel *adv.* much, a lot (of) (1) **4A**
  Viel Glück! Good luck! (2) **1A**
  Vielen Dank. Thank you very much. (1) **1A**
vielleicht *adv.* maybe (1) **4A**
vier four (1) **2A**
Viertel, - *n.* quarter (2) **2A**; neighborhood (3) **2B**
  Viertel nach/vor quarter past/to (1) **2A**

Visum (*pl.* Visa) *n.* visa (2) **3B**
Vogel, ¨ *m.* bird (1) **3A**
voll *adj.* full (2) **3B**
  voll besetzt *adj.* fully occupied (2) **3B**
Volleyball *m.* volleyball (1) **2B**
von *prep.* from (1) **4B**
vor *prep.* in front of, before (2) **1B**; *prep.* to (1) **2A**
vorbei *adv.* over, past (2) **3A**
vorbereiten *v.* to prepare (1) **4A**
  sich vorbereiten (auf) *v.* to prepare oneself
    (for) (3) **1A**
  Vorbereitung, -en *f.* preparation
Vorhang, ¨ *m.* curtain (2) **2A**
Vorlesung, -en *f.* lecture (1) **2A**
vormachen *v.* to fool (2) **4B**
Vormittag, -e *m.* midmorning (1) **2B**
vormittags *adv.* before noon (1) **2A**
Vorspeise, -n *f.* appetizer (1) **4B**
vorstellen *v.* to introduce (3) **1A**
  sich vorstellen *v.* to introduce oneself (3) **1A**
  sich (etwas) vorstellen *v.* to imagine
    (something) (3) **1A**
Vorstellungsgespräch, -e *n.* job interview (3) **3A**
Vortrag, ¨ *m.* lecture (2) **2B**
Vulkan, -e *m.* volcano (3) **4A**

W

wachsen *v.* to grow (2) **1B**
während *prep.* during (2) **4B**
wahrscheinlich *adv.* probably (3) **2A**
Wald, ¨ *m.* forest (1) **2B**, (3) **4A**
Wand, ¨ *f.* wall (1) **1B**
wandern *v.* to hike (1) **1B**
wann *interr.* when (1) **2A**
  Wann hast du Geburtstag? When is your
    birthday? (1) **2B**
warm *adj.* warm (3) **2A**
warten *v.* to wait (for) (1) **2A**
  warten auf *v.* to wait for (2) **3A**
  in der Warteschleife sein *v.* to be on hold (3) **3B**
warum *interr.* why (1) **2A**
was *interr.* what (1) **2A**
  Was geht ab? What's up? (1) **1A**
  Was ist das? What is that? (1) **1B**
Wäsche *f.* laundry (2) **2B**
waschen *v.* to wash (1) **2B**
  sich waschen *v.* to wash (oneself) (3) **1A**
  Wäsche waschen *v.* to do laundry (2) **2B**
Wäschetrockner, - *m.* dryer (2) **2B**
Waschmaschine, -n *f.* washing machine (2) **2B**
Waschsalon, -s *m.* laundromat (3) **2A**
Wasser *n.* water (1) **4B**
Wasserfall, ¨ *m.* waterfall (3) **4A**
Wasserkrug, ¨ *m.* water pitcher (1) **4B**
Website, -s *f.* web site (2) **4B**
Weg, -e *m.* path (3) **4A**
wegen *prep.* because of (2) **4B**
wegräumen *v.* to put away (2) **2B**
wegwerfen *v.* to throw away (3) **4B**
weh tun *v.* to hurt (3) **1B**
Weihnachten, - *n.* Christmas (2) **1A**
weil *conj.* because (3) **2A**

Wein, -e *m.* wine (1) **4B**
weinen *v.* to cry (1) **3B**
weise *adj.* wise (1) **3B**
weiß *adj.* white (2) **1B**
weit *adj.* loose; big (2) **1B**; *adj.* far (3) **2B**
  weit von *adj.* far from (3) **2B**
  weiter geht's moving forward
welcher/welche/welches *interr.* which (1) **2A**
  Welcher Tag ist heute? What day is it today? (2) **3A**
Welt, -en *f.* world (3) **4B**
wem *interr.* whom (*dat.*) (1) **4B**
wen *interr.* whom (*acc.*) (1) **2A**
Wende, -n *f.* turning point (3) **4B**
wenig *adj.* little; not much (3) **2A**
wenn *conj.* when; whenever; if (3) **2A**
  wenn... dann if… then (3) **2A**
  wenn... nur if… only (3) **2A**
wer *interr.* who (1) **2A**
  Wer ist das? Who is it? (1) **1B**
  Wer spricht? Who's calling? (3) **3A**
werden *v.* to become (1) **2B**
werfen *v.* to throw (1) **2B**
Werkzeug, -e *n.* tool kit
wessen *interr.* whose (2) **4B**
Wetter *n.* weather (2) **3A**
  Wie ist das Wetter? What's the weather like? (2) **3A**
Wetterbericht, -e *m.* weather report (2) **3A**
wichtig *adj.* important (2) **3B**
wie *interr.* how (1) **2A**
  wie viel? *interr.* how much? (1) **1B**
  wie viele? *interr.* how many? (1) **1B**
  Wie alt bist du? How old are you? (1) **1B**
  Wie heißt du? *(inf.)* What's your name? (1) **1A**
wiederholen *v.* to repeat (1) **2A**
Wiederholung, -en *f.* repetition; revision
wiegen *v.* to weigh (2) **4B**
willkommen welcome (1) **1A**
  Herzlich willkommen! Welcome! (1) **1A**
Windenergie *f.* wind energy (3) **4B**
windig *adj.* windy (2) **3A**
Windschutzscheibe, -n *f.* windshield (2) **4A**
Winter, - *m.* winter (1) **2B**, (2) **3A**
wir *pron.* we (1) **1A**
wirklich *adv.* really (1) **4A**
Wirtschaft, -en *f.* business; economy (1) **2A**
wischen *v.* to wipe, mop (2) **2B**
wissen *v.* to know (information) (2) **1B**
Wissenschaftler, - / Wissenschaftlerin, -nen *m./f.*
  scientist (3) **3B**
Witwe, -n *f.* widow (1) **3A**
Witwer, - *m.* widower (1) **3A**
wo *interr.* where (1) **2A**
woanders *adv.* somewhere else (1) **4A**
Woche, -n *f.* week (1) **2A**
Wochenende, -n *n.* weekend (1) **2A**
woher *interr.* from where (1) **2A**; (2) **2A**
wohin *interr.* where to (1) **2A**
wohl *adv.* probably (3) **2A**
wohnen *v.* to live (somewhere) (1) **2A**
Wohnheim, -e *n.* dorm (2) **2A**
Wohnung, -en *f.* apartment (2) **2A**
Wohnzimmer, - *n.* living room (2) **2A**
Wolke, -n *f.* cloud (2) **3A**

wolkig *adj.* cloudy (2) **3A**
Wolle *f.* wool (2) **1B**
wollen *v.* to want (1) **3B**
Wörterbuch, ¨ **er** *n.* dictionary (1) **1B**
Wortschatz, ¨ **e** *m.* vocabulary
wünschen *v.* to wish (3) **1A**
  sich (etwas) wünschen *v.* to wish (for
    something) (3) **1A**
Würstchen, - *n.* (small) sausage (1) **4A**

Z

Zahn, ¨ *m.* tooth (3) **1A**
  sich die Zähne putzen *m.* to brush one's teeth (3) **1A**
Zahnarzt, ¨ **e** / **Zahnärztin, -nen** *m./f.* dentist (3) **1B**
Zahnbürste, -n *f.* toothbrush (3) **1A**
Zahnpasta (*pl.* Zahnpasten) *f.* toothpaste (3) **1A**
Zahnschmerzen *m. pl.* toothache (3) **1B**
Zapping *n.* channel surfing
Zebrastreifen, - *m.* crosswalk (3) **2B**
Zeh, -en *m.* toe (3) **1A**
zehn ten (1) **2A**
zeigen *v.* to show (1) **4B**
Zeit, -en *f.* time (1) **2A**
Zeitschrift, -en *f.* magazine (3) **2A**
Zeitung, -en *f.* newspaper (2) **3B**, (3) **2A**
Zelt, -e *n.* tent (2) **3B**
Zeltplatz, ¨ **e** *m.* camping area (2) **3B**
Zeugnis, -se *n.* report card, grade report (1) **1B**
ziehen *v.* to pull (1) **3B**
ziemlich *adv.* quite (1) **4A**
  ziemlich gut pretty well (1) **1A**
Zimmer, - *n.* room (2) **1A**
  Zimmer frei vacancy (2) **2A**
Zimmerservice *m.* room service (2) **3B**
Zoll, ¨ *m.* customs (3) **3B**
zu *adv.* too (1) **4A**; *prep.* to; for; at (1) **4B**
  bis zu *prep.* until (3) **2B**
  um... zu *prep.* (in order) to (2) **3B**
  Zum Wohl! Cheers! (1) **4B**
zubereiten *v.* to prepare (2) **3A**
zuerst *adv.* first (2) **3B**
Zug, ¨ *m.* train (2) **4A**
zumachen *v.* to close (2) **4B**
sich zurechtfinden *v.* to find one's way (3) **2B**
zurückkommen *v.* to come back (1) **4A**
zusammen *adv.* together (1) **3A**
zuschauen *v.* to watch (1) **4A**
Zutat, -en *m.* ingredient (1) **4A**
zuverlässig *adj.* reliable (3) **3B**
zwanzig twenty (1) **2A**
zwei two (1) **2A**
zweite *adj.* second (1) **2A**
Zwiebel, -n *f.* onion (1) **4A**
Zwilling, -e *m.* twin (1) **3A**
zwischen *prep.* between (2) **1B**
zwölf twelve (1) **2A**

Englisch-Deutsch

A

a ein/eine (1) **1A**
able: to be able to können *v.* (1) **3B**
about über *prep.* (2) **1B**
  to be about handeln von *v.* (2) **3A**
above über *prep.* (2) **1B**
abroad Ausland *n.* (2) **3B**
accident Unfall, ¨e *m.* (2) **4A**
  to have an accident einen Unfall haben *v.* (2) **4A**
accommodation Unterkunft, ¨e *f.* (2) **3B**
according to nach *prep.* (1) **4B**
accountant Buchhalter, - / Buchhalterin, -nen *m./f.* (3) **3B**
acid rain saurer Regen *m.* (3) **4B**
across (from) gegenüber (von) *prep.* (3) **2B**
address Adresse, -n *f.* (3) **2A**
adopt adoptieren *v.* (1) **3A**
afraid: to be afraid of Angst haben vor *v.* (2) **3A**
after nach *prep.* (1) **4B;** nachdem *conj.* (3) **2A**
afternoon Nachmittag, -e *m.* (1) **2B**
  in the afternoon nachmittags *adv.* (1) **2A**
against gegen *prep.* (1) **3B**
air Luft, ¨e *f.* (3) **4A**
airplane Flugzeug, -e *n.* (2) **3B**
airport Flughafen, ¨ *m.* (2) **3B**
all ganz *adj.* (2) **3B;** alle *pron.* (2) **3B**
allergic (to) allergisch (gegen) *adj.* (3) **1B**
allergy Allergie, -n *f.* (3) **1B**
allow lassen *v.* (1) **2B**
  to be allowed to dürfen *v.* (1) **3B**
almost fast *adv.* (1) **4A**
alone allein *adv.* (1) **4A**
along entlang *prep.* (1) **3B**
already schon (1) **4A**
alright: Are you alright? Alles klar? (1) **1A**
also auch *adv.* (1) **4A**
although obwohl *conj.* (3) **2A**
always immer *adv.* (1) **4A**
ambulance Krankenwagen, - *m.* (3) **1B**
America Amerika *n.* (3) **2B**
American amerikanisch *adj.* (3) **2B; (person)** Amerikaner, - / Amerikanerin, -nen *m./f.* (3) **2B**
  American football American Football *m.* (1) **2B**
and und *conj.* (1) **1B**
animal Tier, -e *n.* (3) **4A**
angry böse *adj.*
  to get angry (about) sich ärgern (über) *v.* (3) **1A**
anniversary Jahrestag, -e *m.* (2) **1A**
announce verkünden *v.* (3) **4B**
answer antworten *v.* (1) **2A;** beantworten *v.* (1) **4A;** Antwort, -en *f.*
  to answer the phone einen Anruf entgegennehmen *v.* (3) **3A**
anything: Anything else? Noch einen Wunsch? (1) **4B;** Sonst noch etwas? (1) **4A**
apartment Wohnung, -en *f.* (2) **2A**
appetizer Vorspeise, -n *f.* (1) **4B**
apple Apfel, ¨ *m.* (1) **1A**
applicant Bewerber, - / Bewerberin, -nen *m./f.* (3) **3A**
apply sich bewerben *v.* (3) *3A*

appointment Termin, -e *m.* (3) **3A**
April April *m.* (1) **2A**
architect Architekt, -en / Architektin, -nen *m./f.* (1) **3B**
architecture Architektur, -en *f.* (1) **2A**
argue sich streiten *v.* (3) **1A**
arm Arm, -e *m.* (3) **1A**
armchair Sessel, - *m.* (2) **2A**
around um *prep.* (1) **3B**
arrival Ankunft, ¨e *f.* (2) **3B**
arrive ankommen *v.* (1) **4A**
arrogant eingebildet *adj.* (1) **3B**
art Kunst, ¨e *f.* (1) **2A**
artichoke Artischocke, -n *f.* (1) **4A**
as als *conj.* (2) **4A**
  as if als ob (3) **2A**
ask fragen *v.* (1) **2A**
  to ask about fragen nach *v.* (2) **3A**
assistant Assistent, -en / Assistentin, -nen *m./f.* (3) **3A**
at um *prep.* (1) **3B;** bei *prep.* (1) **4A;** an *prep.* (2) **1B**
  at...o'clock um...Uhr (1) **2A**
athletic sportlich *adj.* (1) **2B**
ATM Geldautomat, -en *m.* (3) **2A**
Attention! Achtung!
attic Dachboden, ¨ *m.* (2) **2A**
August August *m.* (1) **2A**
aunt Tante, -n *f.* (1) **3A**
Austria Österreich *n.* (3) **2B**
Austrian österreichisch *adj.* (3) **2B; (person)** Österreicher, - / Österreicherin, -nen *m./f.* (3) **2B**
autumn Herbst, -e *m.* (1) **2B**
avenue Allee, -n *f.* (3) **2B**
awful furchtbar *adj.* (2) **3A**

B

baby Baby, -s *n.* (1) **3A**
back Rücken, - *m.* (3) **1A**
backache Rückenschmerzen *m. pl.* (3) **1B**
backpack Rucksack, ¨e *m.* (1) **1B**
bad schlecht *adj.* (1) **3B**
  badly dressed schlecht gekleidet *adj.* (2) **1B**
baked goods Gebäck *n.* (2) **1A**
bakery Bäckerei, -en *f.* (1) **4A**
balcony Balkon, - e *m.* (2) **2A**
ball Ball, ¨e *m.* (1) **2B**
balloon Ballon, -e *m.* (2) **1A**
ball-point pen Kuli, -s *m.* (1) **1B**
banana Banane, -n *f.* (1) **4A**
bank Bank, -en *f.* (3) **2A**
  at the bank auf der Bank *f.* (3) **2B**
bank account Konto (*pl.* Konten) *n.* (3) **2A**
bank employee Bankangestellte, -n *m./f.* (3) **3B**
baseball Baseball *m.* (1) **2B**
basketball Basketball *m.* (1) **2B**
bath: to take a bath sich baden *v.* (3) **1A**
bathing suit Badeanzug, ¨e *m.* (2) **1B**
bathrobe Bademantel, ¨ *m.* (3) **1A**
bathroom Badezimmer, - *n.* (3) **1A**
bathtub Badewanne, -n *f.* (2) **2A**
battery charger Ladegerät, -e *n.* (2) **4B**
be sein *v.* (1) **1A**
  Is/Are there... Ist/Sind hier...? *v.* (1) **1B;** Gibt es...? (1) **2B**

There is/are... Da ist/sind... *v.* (1) **1A;** Es gibt... (1) **2B**
beach Strand, ¨e *m.* (1) **2B**
bean Bohne, -n *f.* (1) **4A**
beard Bart, ¨e *m.* (3) **1A**
beautiful schön *adj.* (1) **3A**
beauty salon Kosmetiksalon, -s *m.* (3) **2A**
because denn *conj.* (2) **2A;** weil *conj.* (3) **2A**
  because of wegen *prep.* (2) **4B**
become werden *v.* (1) **2B**
bed Bett, -en *n.* (2) **2A**
  to go to bed ins Bett gehen *v.* (3) **1A**
  to make the bed das Bett machen *v.* (2) **2B**
bedroom Schlafzimmer, - *n.* (2) **2A**
beef Rindfleisch *n.* (1) **4A**
beer Bier, -e *n.* (1) **4B**
before vor *prep.* (2) **1B;** bevor *conj.* (2) **4A**
  before noon vormittags *adv.* (1) **2A**
begin anfangen *v.* (1) **4A;** beginnen *v.* (2) **4A**
behind hinter *prep.* (2) **1B**
believe glauben *v.* (2) **1A;** meinen *v.* (3) **4B**
belly Bauch, ¨e *m.* (3) **1A**
belong gehören *v.* (1) **4B**
below unter *prep.* (2) **1B**
belt Gürtel, - *m.* (2) **1B**
bench Bank, ¨e *f.* (3) **2B**
best beste/bester/bestes *adj.* (2) **4A**
All the best! Mach's gut! *v.* (1) **3B;** alles Gute (3) **2A**
better besser *adj.* (2) **4A**
  to get better gesund werden *v.* (3) **1B**
between zwischen *prep.* (2) **1B**
beverage Getränk, -e *n.* (1) **4B**
bicycle Fahrrad, ¨er *n.* (1) **2B**
big groß, weit *adj.* (1) **3A**
bill (money) Geldschein, -e *m.* (3) **2A**
biology Biologie *f.* (1) **2A**
bird Vogel, ¨ *m.* (1) **3A**
birth Geburt, -en *f.* (2) **1A**
birthday Geburtstag, -e *m.* (2) **1A**
  When is your birthday? Wann hast du Geburtstag? (1) **2B**
black schwarz *adj.* (2) **1B**
  black board Tafel, -n *f.* (1) **1B**
  black-haired schwarzhaarig *adj.* (1) **3A**
bland fade *adj.* (1) **4B**
blanket Decke, -n *f.* (2) **2B**
blond blond *adj.* (1) **3A**
  blond hair blonde Haare *n. pl.* (1) **3A**
blood pressure Blutdruck *m.* (3) **1B**
blouse Bluse, -n *f.* (2) **1B**
blue blau *adj.* (1) **3A**
board Tafel, -n *f.* (1) **1B**
boarding pass Bordkarte, -n *f.* (2) **3B**
boat Boot, -e *n.* (2) **4A**
body Körper, - *m.* (3) **1A**
book Buch, ¨er *n.* (1) **1A**
bookshelf Bücherregal, -e *n.* (2) **2A**
boot Stiefel, - *m.* (2) **1B**
boring langweilig *adj.* (1) **2A**
boss Chef, -s / Chefin, -nen *m./f.* (3) **3B**
bottle Flasche, -n *f.* (1) **4B**
bowl Schüssel, -n *f.* (1) **4B**
boy Junge, -n *m.* (1) **1A**

brakes Bremse, -n f. (2) **4A**
brave mutig adj. (1) **3B**
bread Brot, -e n. (1) **4A**
break brechen v. (1) **2B**
  to break (an arm / a leg) sich (den Arm/Bein) brechen v. (3) **1B**
  Break a leg! Hals- und Beinbruch! (2) **1A**
breakfast Frühstück, -e n. (1) **4B**
bridge Brücke, -n f. (3) **2B**
bright hell adj. (2) **1B**
bring bringen v. (1) **2A**
  to bring along mitbringen v. (1) **4A**
  to bring out rausbringen (2) **2B**
  to bring with mitnehmen v. (3) **2B**
broom Besen, - m. (2) **2B**
brother Bruder, ⸚ m. (1) **1A**
brother-in-law Schwager, ⸚ m. (1) **3A**
brown braun adj. (2) **1B**
  brown-haired braunhaarig adj. (1) **3A**
bruise blauer Fleck, -e m. (3) **1B**
brush Bürste, -n f. (3) **1A**
  to brush one's hair sich die Haare bürsten v. (3) **1A**
  to brush one's teeth sich die Zähne putzen v. (3) **1A**
build bauen v. (1) **2A**
building Gebäude, - n. (3) **2A**
bulletin board Pinnwand, ⸚e f. (3) **3A**
burn brennen v. (2) **1A**
bus Bus, -se m. (2) **4A**
bus stop Bushaltestelle, -n f. (2) **4A**
bush Busch, ⸚e m. (3) **4A**
business Wirtschaft, -en f. (1) **2A**; Geschäft, -e n. (3) **4A**
  business class Businessklasse f. (2) **3B**
  businessman / businesswoman Geschäftsmann, ⸚er / Geschäftsfrau, -en m./f. (pl. Geschäftsleute) (1) **3B**
but aber conj. (1) **1B**
  but rather sondern conj. (2) **2A**
butcher shop Metzgerei, -en f. (1) **4A**
butter Butter f. (1) **4A**
buy kaufen v. (1) **2A**
by an prep. (2) **1B**; bei; von (1) **4B**
Bye! Tschüss! (1) **1A**

C

cabinet Schrank, ⸚e m. (2) **2A**
café Café, -s m. (1) **2A**
cafeteria Cafeteria, (pl. Cafeterien) f.; **(college/university)** Mensa, Mensen f. (1) **1B**
cake Kuchen, - m. (1) **4A**; Torte, -n f. (2) **1A**
calculator Taschenrechner, - m. (1) **1B**
calendar Kalender, - m. (1) **1B**
call anrufen v. (1) **4A**; sich anrufen (3) **1A**; nennen v. (2) **1A**
  Who's calling? Wer spricht? (3) **3A**
calm ruhig adj. (1) **3B**
(to go) camping campen gehen n. (1) **2B**
camping area Zeltplatz, ⸚e m. (2) **3B**
can können v. (1) **3B**
Canada Kanada n. (3) **2B**
Canadian kanadisch adj. (3) **2B**; **(person)** Kanadier, - / Kanadierin, -nen m./f. (3) **2B**
cancel abbrechen, streichen v. (2) **3B**

candidate Kandidat, -en m. (3) **3A**
candy Süßigkeit, -en f. (2) **1A**
cap Mütze, -n f. (2) **1B**
car Auto, -s n. (1) **1A**
  to drive a car Auto fahren v. (2) **4A**
card Karte, -n f. (1) **2B**
career Karriere, -n f. (3) **3B**
caretaker Hausmeister, - / Hausmeisterin, -nen m./f. (3) **3B**
carpool Fahrgemeinschaft, -en f. (3) **4B**
carrot Karotte, -n f. (1) **4A**
carry tragen v. (1) **2B**
carry-on luggage Handgepäck n. (2) **3B**
cash bar adj. (3) **2A**; Bargeld n. (3) **2A**
  to pay in cash bar bezahlen v. (3) **2A**
cat Katze, -n f. (3) **3A**
catch fangen v. (1) **2B**
  to catch a cold sich erkälten v. (3) **1A**
celebrate feiern v. (2) **1A**
celebration Fest, -e n. (2) **1A**
cell phone Handy, -s n. (2) **4B**
cellar Keller, - m. (2) **2A**
ceramic Keramik, -en f. (2) **2B**
chair Stuhl, ⸚e m. (1) **1A**
champagne Sekt, -e m. (2) **1A**
championship Meisterschaft, -en f. (1) **2B**
change Kleingeld n. (3) **2A**
  to change clothes sich umziehen v. (3) **1A**
channel Sender, - m. (3) **4B**
  channel surfing Zapping n.
charge laden v. (2) **4B**
chat sich unterhalten v. (3) **1A**
cheap günstig adj. (2) **1B**
check Rechnung, -en f. (1) **4B**
Cheers! Prost! **4B**; Zum Wohl! (1) **4B**
cheese Käse, - m. (1) **4A**
chemistry Chemie f. (1) **2A**
chess Schach n. (1) **2B**
chicken Huhn, ⸚er n. (3) **4A**; **(food)** Hähnchen, - n. (1) **4A**
child Kind, -er n. (1) **1A**
China China n. (3) **2B**
Chinese (person) Chinese, -n / Chinesin, -nen m./f. (3) **2B**; **(language)** Chinesisch n. (3) **2B**
Christmas Weihnachten, - n. (2) **1A**
church Kirche, -n f. (3) **2B**
city Stadt, ⸚e f. (1) **1B**
  city center Innenstadt, ⸚e f. (3) **2B**
claim behaupten v. (3) **4B**
class Klasse, -n f. (1) **1B**; Unterricht m. (1) **1B**; Veranstaltung, -en f. (1) **2A**
  first/second class erste/zweite Klasse (2) **2A**
classical klassisch adj. (3) **2A**
classmate Kommilitone, -n / Kommilitonin, -nen; Klassenkamerad, -en / Klassenkameradin, -nen m./f. (1) **1B**
classroom Klassenzimmer, - n. (1) **1B**
clean sauber adj. (2) **2B**; putzen v. (2) **2B**
  to clean up aufräumen v. (2) **2B**
cliff Klippe, -n f. (3) **4A**
climb steigen v. (2) **1B**
  to climb (mountain) klettern v. (1) **2B**
  to climb (stairs) (die Treppe) hochgehen v. (3) **2B**
clock Uhr, -en f. (1) **1B**

at... o'clock um... Uhr (1) **2A**
close zumachen v. (2) **2B**; nah adj. (3) **2B**
  close to in der Nähe von prep. (3) **2B**
closed geschlossen adj. (3) **2A**
closet Schrank, ⸚e m. (2) **2A**
clothes Kleidung f. (2) **1B**
cloud Wolke, -n f. (2) **3A**
cloudy wolkig adj. (2) **3A**
coast Küste, -n f. (3) **4A**
coat Mantel, ⸚ m. (2) **1B**
coffee Kaffee, -s m. (1) **4B**
coffeemaker Kaffeemaschine, -n f. (3) **3B**
coin Münze, -n f. (3) **2A**
cold kalt adj. (2) **3A**; Erkältung, -en f. (3) **1B**
  to catch a cold sich erkälten v. (3) **1A**
college Universität, -en f. (1) **1B**
college instructor Dozent, -en / Dozentin, -nen m./f. (1) **2A**
color Farbe, -n f. (2) **1B**
  solid colored einfarbig adj. (2) **1B**
colorful bunt adj. (3) **2A**
comb Kamm, ⸚e m. (3) **1A**
  to comb (one's hair) sich (die Haare) kämmen v. (3) **1A**
come kommen v. (1) **2A**
  to come along mitkommen v. (1) **4A**
  to come back zurückkommen v. (1) **4A**
comma Komma, -s f. (1) **1B**
compact disc CD, -s f. (2) **4B**
company Firma (pl. die Firmen) f. (3) **3A**
complicated kompliziert adj. (3) **2A**
computer Computer, - m. (1) **1B**
computer science Informatik f. (1) **2A**
concert Konzert, -e n. (2) **1B**
congratulate gratulieren v. (2) **1A**
  Congratulations! Herzlichen Glückwunsch! (2) **1A**
construction zone Baustelle, -n f. (2) **4A**
contract Vertrag, ⸚e m. (3) **3A**
conversation: to have a conversation sich unterhalten v. (3) **1A**
cook kochen v. (1) **2B**; Koch, ⸚e / Köchin, -nen m./f. (1) **4B**
cookie Keks, -e m. (2) **1A**
cool kühl adj. (2) **3A**
corner Ecke, -n f. (3) **2B**
correct korrigieren v. (1) **2A**
cost kosten v. (1) **2A**
cotton Baumwolle f. (2) **1B**
couch Sofa, -s n. (2) **3B**
  to couch surf Sofa surfen v. (2) **3B**
cough husten v. (3) **1B**
country Land, ⸚er n. (2) **3B**
countryside Landschaft, -en f. (3) **4A**
couple Paar, -e n. (1) **3A**
courageous mutig adj.
course Veranstaltung, -en f. (1) **2B**; Gang, ⸚e m. (1) **4B**
  first/second course erster/zweiter Gang m. (1) **4B**
  main course Hauptspeise, -en f. (1) **4B**
court Platz, ⸚e m. (1) **1A**
cousin Cousin, -s / Cousine, -n m./f. (1) **3A**
cover decken v. (2) **2B**
cow Kuh, ⸚e f. (3) **4A**

cram (for a test) büffeln *v.* (1) **2A**
cross überqueren *v.* (3) **2B**
  to cross the street die Straße überqueren *v.* (3) **2B**
cross-reference Querverweis, -e *m.*
crosswalk Zebrastreifen, - *pl.* (3) **2B**
cruel grausam *adj.*; gemein *adj.* (1) **3B**
cruise Kreuzfahrt, -en *f.* (2) **3B**
cry weinen *v.* (1) **3B**
cup Tasse, -n *f.* (1) **4B**
curious neugierig *adj.* (1) **3B**
curly lockig *adj.* (1) **3A**
curtain Vorhang, ⁼e *m.* (2) **2A**
custodian Hausmeister, - / Hausmeisterin,
  -nen *m./f.* (3) **3B**
customer Kunde, -n /Kundin, -nen *m./f.* (2) **1B**
customs Zoll *m.* (2) **3B**
cut Schnitt, -e *m.* (2) **1B**
  to cut class schwänzen *v.* (1) **1B**
cute süß *adj.* (1) **3B**
CV Lebenslauf, ⁼e *m.* (3) **3A**

D

dad Papa, -s *m.* (1) **3A**
daily täglich *adv.* (1) **4A**
  daily routine Alltagsroutine *f.* (3) **1A**
dance tanzen *v.* (1) **2B**
danger Gefahr, -en *f.* (3) **4B**
dark dunkel *adj.* (1) **3A**
  dark-haired dunkelhaarig *adj.* (1) **3A**
darling Liebling, -e *m.*
date Datum (*pl.* Daten) *n.* (2) **3A**
  What is the date today? Der wievielte ist
  heute? (1) **2A**
daughter Tochter, ⁼ *f.* (1) **3A**
day Tag, -e *m.* (1) **1A**
  every day täglich *adv.* (1) **4A**
Dear Lieber/Liebe *m./f.* (1) **3B**
December Dezember *m.* (1) **2A**
decide sich entschließen *v.* (1) **4B**
definitely bestimmt *adv.* (1) **4A**
degree Abschluss, ⁼e *m.* (1) **2A**; Grad *n.* (2) **3A**
  It's 18 degrees out. Es sind 18 Grad
  draußen. (2) **3A**
delay Verspätung, -en *f.* (3) **3B**
delete löschen *v.* (2) **4B**
delicatessen Feinkostgeschäft, -e *n.* (1) **4A**
delicious lecker *adj.* (1) **4B**
demanding anspruchsvoll *adj.* (3) **3B**
dentist Zahnarzt, ⁼e / Zahnärztin, -nen *m./f.*
  (3) **1B**
department store Kaufhaus, ⁼er *n.* (3) **2B**
departure Abflug, ⁼e *m.* (2) **3B**
deposit (money) (Geld) einzahlen *v.* (3) **2A**
describe beschreiben *v.* (1) **2A**
description Beschreibung, -en *f.* (1) **3B**
desk Schreibtisch, -e *m.* (1) **1B**
despite trotz *prep.* (2) **4B**
dessert Nachtisch, -e, *m.* (1) **4B**
destination Reiseziel, -e *n.* (2) **3B**
detour Umleitung, -en *f.* (2) **4A**
develop entwickeln *v.* (3) **4B**
dictionary Wörterbuch, ⁼er *n.* (1) **1B**
die sterben *v.* (2) **1B**

diet Diät, -en *f.* (1) **4B**
  to be on a diet auf Diät sein *v.* (1) **4B**
difficult schwierig *adj.* (1) **2A**
digital camera Digitalkamera, -s *f.* (2) **4B**
dining room Esszimmer, - *n.* (2) **2A**
dinner Abendessen, - *n.* (1) **4B**
diploma Abschlusszeugnis, -se *n.* (1) **2A**; Diplom,
  -e *n.* (1) **2A**
direction Richtung, -en *f.* (3) **2B**
dirty schmutzig *adj.* (2) **2B**
discover entdecken *v.* (2) **2B**
discreet diskret *adj.* (1) **3B**
discuss besprechen *v.* (1) **4A**
dish Gericht, -e *n.* (1) **4B**
dishes Geschirr *n.* (2) **2B**
  to do the dishes Geschirr spülen (2) **2B**
dishwasher Spülmaschine, -n *f.* (2) **2B**
dislike nicht gern (+*verb*) (1) **3A**
divided by geteilt durch (1) **1B**
divorced geschieden *adj.* (1) **3A**
dizzy schwindlig *adj.* (3) **1B**
do machen *v.* (1) **2A**; tun *v.* (3) **1B**
  to do laundry Wäsche waschen *v.* (2) **2B**
  to do the dishes Geschirr spülen *v.* (2) **2B**
  to have to do with handeln von (2) **3A**
doctor Arzt, ⁼e / Ärztin, -nen *m./f.* (3) **1B**
  to go to the doctor zum Arzt gehen *v.* (3) **1B**
document Dokument, -e *n.* (2) **4B**
dog Hund, -e *m.* (1) **3A**
door Tür, -en *f.* (1) **1B**
dormitory (Studenten)wohnheim, -e *n.* (2) **2A**
down entlang *prep.* (1) **3B**; herunter *adv.* (2) **2A**
  to go down heruntergehen *v.* (3) **2B**
download herunterladen *v.* (2) **4B**
downtown Innenstadt, ⁼e *f.* (3) **2B**
dozen Dutzend, -e *n.* (1) **4A**
  a dozen eggs ein Dutzend Eier (1) **4A**
drawer Schublade, -n *f.* (2) **2A**
dream träumen *v.* (2) **3A**
dress Kleid, -er *n.* (2) **1B**
  to get dressed sich anziehen *v.* (3) **1A**
  to get undressed sich ausziehen *v.* (3) **1A**
dresser Kommode, -n *f.* (2) **2A**
drink trinken *v.* (1) **3B**
drive fahren *v.* (2) **4A**
  to drive a car Auto fahren *v.* (2) **4A**
driver Fahrer, - / Fahrerin, -nen *m./f.* (2) **4A**
drugstore Drogerie, -n *f.* (3) **2A**
dry trocken *adj.* (3) **4A**
  to dry oneself off sich abtrocknen *v.* (3) **1A**
dryer Wäschetrockner, - *m.* (2) **2B**
dumb dumm *adj.* (2) **4A**
during während *prep.* (2) **4B**
dust abstauben *v.* (2) **2B**
duvet Bettdecke, - n *f.* (2) **2B**
DVD DVD, -s *f.* (2) **4B**
DVD-player DVD-Player, - *m.* (2) **4B**
dye (one's hair) sich (die Haare) färben *v.* (3) **1A**

E

ear Ohr, -en *n.* (3) **1A**
early früh *adj.* (1) **2B**
earn verdienen *v.* (3) **3B**
earth Erde, -n *f.* (3) **4B**

earthquake Erdbeben, - *n.* (3) **4A**
easy einfach *adj.* (1) **2A**
eat essen *v.* (1) **2B**
  to eat out essen gehen *v.* (1) **2B**
ecological ökologisch *adj.* (3) **4B**
ecology Ökologie *f.* (3) **4B**
economy Wirtschaft, -en *f.* (1) **2A**
  economy class Touristenklasse *f.* (2) **3B**
education Ausbildung, -en *f.* (3) **3A**
egg Ei, -er *n.* (1) **4A**
eggplant Aubergine, -n *f.* (1) **4A**
eight acht (1) **2A**
elbow Ell(en)bogen, - *m.* (3) **1A**
electrician Elektriker, - / Elektrikerin,
  -nen *m./f.* (3) **3B**
elegant elegant *adj.* (2) **1B**
elevator Fahrstuhl, ⁼e *m.* (2) **3B**
eleven elf (1) **2A**
e-mail E-Mail, -s *f.* (2) **4B**
emergency Notfall, ⁼e *m.* (3) **3B**
emergency room Notaufnahme, -n *f.* (3) **1B**
employee Angestellte, -n *m./f.* (3) **3A**
endangered gefährdet *adj.* (3) **4B**
energy Energie, -n *f.* (3) **4B**
energy-efficient energiesparend *adj.* (2) **2B**
engaged verlobt *adj.* (1) **3A**
engine Motor, -en *m.* (2) **4A**
engineer Ingenieur, -e / Ingenieurin, -nen
  m./f. (1) **3B**
England England *n.* (3) **2B**
English (person) Engländer, - / Engländerin,
  -nen *m./f.* (3) **2B**; (**language**) Englisch *n.* (3) **2B**
enjoy genießen *v.*
  Enjoy your meal! Guten Appetit! (1) **4B**
envelope Briefumschlag, ⁼e *m.* (3) **2A**
environment Umwelt, -en *f.* (3) **4B**
  environmentally friendly umweltfreundlich
  adj. (2) **4B**
environmentalism Umweltschutz *m.* (3) **4B**
equal (gleich) sein *v.* (1) **1B**
eraser Radiergummi, -s *m.* (1) **1B**
errand Besorgung, -en *f.* (3) **2A**
  to run errands Besorgungen machen *v.* (3) **2A**
even though obwohl *conj.* (2) **2A**
evening Abend, -e *m.* (1) **2B**
  in the evening abends *adv.* (1) **2A**
every jeder/jede/jedes *adv.* (2) **4B**
everything alles *pron.* (2) **3B**
  Everything OK? Alles klar? (1) **1A**
everywhere überall *adv.* (1) **4A**
exam Prüfung, -en *f.* (1) **1B**
except (for) außer *prep.* (1) **4B**
exchange umtauschen *v.* (2) **2B**
exciting spannend *adj.* (3) **2A**; aufregend *adj.* (3) **4A**
Excuse me. Entschuldigung. (1) **1A**
exercise Sport treiben *v.* (3) **1B**
exit Ausgang, ⁼e *m.* (2) **1B**; Ausfahrt, -en *f.* (2) **4A**
expensive teuer *adj.* (2) **2B**
experience durchmachen *v.* (2) **4B**; Erfahrung,
  -en *f.* (3) **3A**
explain erklären *v.* (1) **4A**
explore erforschen *v.* (3) **4A**
expression Ausdruck, ⁼e *m.*

extinction Aussterben *n.* (3) **4B**
eye Auge, -n *n.* (1) **3A**
eyebrow Augenbraue, -n *f.* (3) **1A**

face Gesicht, -er *n.* (3) **1A**
factory Fabrik, -en *f.* (3) **4B**
factory worker Fabrikarbeiter, - / Fabrikarbeiterin, -nen *m./f.* (3) **3B**
fail durchfallen *v.* (1) **1B**; scheitern *v.* (3) **3B**
fall fallen *v.* (1) **2B**; (season) Herbst, -e *m.* (1) **2B**
to fall in love (with) sich verlieben (in) *v.* (3) **1A**
familiar bekannt *adj.*
to be familiar with kennen *v.* (2) **1B**
family Familie, -n *f.* (1) **3A**
fan Fan, -s *m.* (1) **2B**
fantastic fantastisch *adj.* (3) **2A**
far weit *adj.* (3) **2B**
far from weit von *adj.* (3) **2B**
farm Bauernhof, ⸚e *m.* (3) **4A**
farmer Bauer, -n / Bäuerin, -nen *m./f.* (3) **3B**
fashionable modisch *adj.* (2) **1B**
fast schnell *adj.* (1) **3B**
fat dick *adj.* (1) **3A**
father Vater, ⸚ *m.* (1) **3A**
father-in-law Schwiegervater, ⸚ *m.* (1) **3A**
favorite Lieblings- (1) **4B**
fear Angst, ⸚e *f.* (2) **3A**
February Februar *m.* (1) **2A**
feel fühlen *v.* (1) **2A**; sich fühlen *v.* (3) **1A**
to feel like Lust haben *v.* (2) **3B**
to feel well sich wohl fühlen *v.* (3) **1A**
fever Fieber, - *n.* (3) **1B**
to have a fever Fieber haben *v.* (3) **1B**
fiancé(e) Verlobte, -n *m./f.* (1) **3A**
field Spielfeld, -er *n.* (1) **2B**; Feld, -er *n.* (3) **4A**
file Datei, -en *f.* (2) **4B**
fill füllen *v.*
to fill out ausfüllen *v.* (3) **2A**
to fill up tanken *v.* (2) **4A**
filthy dreckig *adj.* (2) **2B**
finally schließlich *adv.* (2) **3B**
find finden *v.* (1) **2A**
to find one's way sich zurechtfinden *v.* (3) **2B**
to find out (about) sich informieren (über) *v.* (3) **1A**
fine (monetary) Bußgeld, -er *n.* (2) **4A**
I'm fine. Mir geht's gut. (1) **1A**
finger Finger, - *m.* (3) **1A**
fire entlassen *v.* (3) **3B**; Feuer, - *n.*
firefighter Feuerwehrmann, ⸚er / Feuerwehrfrau, -en (pl. Feuerwehrleute) *m./f.* (3) **3B**
firm Firma (pl. die Firmen) *f.* (3) **3A**
first erster/erste/erstes *adj.* (2) **2A**; zuerst *adv.* (2) **3B**
first course erster Gang *m.* (1) **4B**
first class erste Klasse *f.* (2) **4A**
fish Fisch, -e *m.* (1) **4A**
to go fishing angeln gehen *v.* (1) **2B**
fish store Fischgeschäft, -e *n.* (1) **4A**
fit passen *v.* (2) **1A**; fit *adj.* (1) **2B**
five fünf (1) **2A**
flat tire Platten, - *m.* (2) **4A**

to have a flat tire einen Platten haben *v.* (2) **4A**
flavor Geschmack, ⸚e *m.* (1) **4B**
flight Flug, ⸚e *m.* (2) **3B**
flood Hochwasser, - *n.* (3) **4B**
floor Stock, ⸚e *m.*; Boden, ⸚ *m.* (2) **2A**
first/second floor erster/zweiter Stock (2) **2A**
flower Blume, -n *f.* (1) **1A**
flower shop Blumengeschäft, -e *n.* (3) **2A**
flu Grippe, -n *f.* (3) **1B**
flunk durchfallen *v.* (1) **1B**
fly fliegen *v.* (2) **3B**
fog Nebel, - *m.* (2) **3A**
follow folgen *v.* (2) **1A**
food Essen, - *n.* (1) **4A**
foot Fuß, ⸚e *m.* (3) **1A**
football American Football *m.* (1) **2B**
for für *prep.* (1) **3B**; seit; zu *prep.* (1) **4B**
foreign language Fremdsprache, -n *f.* (1) **2A**
forest Wald, ⸚er *m.* (1) **2B**
forget vergessen *v.* (1) **2B**
fork Gabel, -n *f.* (1) **4B**
form Formular, -e *n.* (3) **2A**
to fill out a form ein Formular ausfüllen *v.* (3) **2A**
fountain Brunnen, - *m.* (3) **2B**
four vier (1) **2A**
France Frankreich *n.* (3) **2B**
French (person) Franzose, -n / Französin, -nen *m./f.* (3) **2B**; (language) Französisch *n.* (3) **2B**
free time Freizeit, -en *f.* (1) **2B**
freezer Gefrierschrank, ⸚e *m.* (2) **2B**
Friday Freitag, -e *m.* (1) **2A**
on Fridays freitags *adv.* (1) **2A**
friend Freund, -e / Freundin, -nen *m./f.* (1) **1A**
friendly freundlich *adj.* (1) **3B**
friendship Freundschaft, -en *f.* (2) **1A**
from aus *prep.* (1) **4A**; von *prep.* (1) **4B**
where from woher *interr.* (1) **2A**
front: in front of vor *prep.* (2) **1B**
fruit Obst *n.* (1) **4A**
fry braten *v.* (1) **2B**
full voll *adj.* (2) **3B**
full-time ganztags *adj.* (3) **3B**
fully occupied voll besetzt *adj.* (2) **3B**
fun Spaß *m.* (1) **2B**
to be fun Spaß machen *v.* (1) **2B**
to (not) have fun (keinen) Spaß haben *v.* (2) **1A**
function funktionieren *v.* (2) **4B**
funny lustig *adj.* (1) **3B**
furnished möbliert *adj.* (2) **2A**
furniture Möbel, - *n.* (2) **2A**
piece of furniture Möbelstück, ,-e *n.* (2) **2A**

game Spiel, -e *n.* (1) **2B**
game console Spielkonsole, -en *f.* (2) **4B**
garage Garage, -n *f.* (2) **1B**
garbage truck Müllwagen, - *m.* (3) **4B**
gardener Gärtner, - / Gärtnerin, -nen *m./f.* (3) **3B**
garlic Knoblauch *m.* (1) **4A**
gas Benzin, -e *n.* (2) **4A**
gas station Tankstelle, -n *f.* (2) **4A**

generous großzügig *adj.* (1) **3B**
German (person) Deutsche *m./f.* (3) **2B**; (language) Deutsch *n.* (3) **2B**
Germany Deutschland *n.* (1) **4A**
get bekommen *v.* (2) **1A**
to get up aufstehen *v.* (1) **4A**
to get sick/better krank/gesund werden *v.* (3) **1B**
gift Geschenk, -e *n.* (2) **1A**
girl Mädchen, - *n.* (1) **1A**
give geben *v.* (1) **2B**
to give (a gift) schenken *v.* (2) **1A**
glass Glas, ⸚er *n.* (1) **4B**
glasses Brille, -n *f.* (2) **1B**
global warming Erderwärmung *f.* (2) **4B**
glove Handschuh, -e *m.* (2) **1B**
go gehen *v.* (1) **2A**; fahren *v.* (1) **2B**
to go out ausgehen *v.* (1) **4A**
Go! Los! (1) **2B**
goal (in soccer) Tor, -e *n.* (1) **2B**
golf Golf *n.* (1) **2B**
good gut *adj.*; nett *adj.* (1) **1A**
Good evening. Guten Abend! (1) **1A**
Good morning. Guten Morgen! (1) **1A**
Good night. Gute Nacht! (1) **1A**
Good-bye. Auf Wiedersehen! (1) **1A**
Good luck! Viel Glück! (2) **1A**
government Regierung, -en *f.* (3) **4B**
grade Note, -n *f.* (1) **1B**
grade report Zeugnis, -se *n.* (1) **1B**
graduate Abschluss machen, ⸚e *v.* (2) **1A**
graduation Abschluss, ⸚e *m.* (1) **1B**
gram Gramm, -e *n.* (1) **4A**
100 grams of cheese 100 Gramm Käse (1) **4A**
granddaughter Enkeltochter, ⸚ *f.* (1) **3A**
grandson Enkelsohn, ⸚e *m.* (1) **3A**
grandchild Enkel, - *m.* (1) **3A**; Enkelkind, -er *n.* (1) **3A**
grandfather Großvater, ⸚ *m.* (1) **3A**
grandma Oma, -s *f.* (1) **3A**
grandmother Großmutter, ⸚ *f.* (1) **3A**
grandpa Opa, -s *m.* (1) **3A**
grandparents Großeltern *pl.* (1) **1A**
grape Traube, -n *f.* (1) **4A**
grass Gras, ⸚er *n.* (3) **4A**
gray grau *adj.* (2) **1B**
great toll *adj.* (1) **3B**; prima *adj.*; spitze *adj.* (1) **1A**
great grandfather Urgroßvater, ⸚ *m.* (1) **3A**
great grandmother Urgroßmutter, ⸚ *f.* (1) **3A**
greedy gierig *adj.* (1) **3B**
green grün *adj.* (2) **1B**
green bean grüne Bohne (pl. die grünen Bohnen) *f.* (1) **4A**
greet grüßen *v.* (1) **2A**
greeting Begrüßung, -en *f.* (1) **1A**; Gruß, ⸚e *m.* (1) **1A**
grocery store Lebensmittelgeschäft, -e *n.* (1) **4A**
ground floor Erdgeschoss, -e *n.* (2) **2A**
grow wachsen *v.* (2) **1B**
grown-up erwachsen *adj.* (3) **2A**
guest Gast, ⸚e *m.* (2) **1A**
hotel guest Hotelgast, ⸚e *m.* (2) **3B**
guesthouse Pension, -en *f.* (2) **3B**
gym Sporthalle, -n *f.* (1) **2A**

H

hail Hagel *m.* (2) **3A**
hair Haar, -e *n.* (1) **3A**
hair dryer Haartrockner, - *m.* (3) **1A**
hairdresser Friseur, -e / Friseurin, -nen *m./f.* (1) **3B**
half halb *adj.* (1) **2A**
half brother Halbbruder, ⁒ *m.* (1) **3A**
half sister Halbschwester, -n *f.* (1) **3A**
hall Flur, -e *m.* (2) **2A**
ham Schinken, - *m.* (1) **4A**
hand Hand, ⁒e *f.* (3) **1A**
handsome gut aussehend *adj.* (1) **3A**
hang hängen *v.* (2) **1B**
  to hang up auflegen *v.* (3) **3A**
happen passieren *v.* (2) **1B**
happiness Glück *n.* (2) **1A**
happy glücklich *adj.* (1) **3B** froh *adj.* (1) (1) **3B**
  Happy birthday! Alles Gute zum Geburtstag! (2) **1A**
  Happy Easter! Frohe Ostern! (2) **1A**
  Happy New Year! Ein gutes neues Jahr! (2) **1A**
  to be happy (about) sich freuen (über) *v.* (3) **1A**
hard schwer *adj.* (3) **1B**
hard drive Festplatte, -en *f.* (2) **4B**
hard-working fleißig *adj.* (1) **3B**
hare Hase, -n *m.* (3) **4A**
hat Hut, ⁒e *m.* (2) **1B**
have haben *v.* (1) **1B**
  Have a nice day! Schönen Tag noch! (1) **1A**
  to have to müssen *v.* (1) **3B**
he er *pron.* (1) **1A**
head Kopf, ⁒e *m.* (3) **1A**
headache Kopfschmerzen *m. pl.* (3) **1B**
headlight Scheinwerfer, -e *m.* (2) **4A**
headphones Kopfhörer, - *m.* (2) **4B**
health Gesundheit *f.* (3) **1B**
health-food store Bioladen, ⁒ *m.* (3) **1B**
healthy gesund *adj.* (2) **4A**
hear hören *v.* (1) **2A**
heat stroke Hitzschlag, ⁒e *m.* (3) **1B**
heavy schwer *adj.* (1) **4B**
hello Guten Tag!; Hallo! (1) **1A**
help helfen *v.* (1) **2B**
  to help with helfen bei *v.* (2) **3A**
her ihr *poss. adj.* (1) **3A**
here hier *adv.* (1) **1A**
  Here is/are... Hier ist/sind... (1) **1B**
high hoch *adj.* (2) **4A**
highway Autobahn, -en *f.* (4) **4A**
hike wandern *v.* (1) **2A**
his sein *poss. adj.* (1) **3A**
history Geschichte, -en *f.* (1) **2A**
hit treffen *v.* (1) **2B**
hobby Hobby, -s *n.* (1) **2B**
hockey Hockey *n.* (1) **2B**
hold: to be on hold in der Warteschleife sein *v.* (3) **3B**
  Please hold. Bleiben Sie bitte am Apparat! (3) **3A**
holiday Feiertag, -e *m.* (2) **1A**
home Haus, ⁒er *adv.* (2) **1B**
  at home zu Hause *adv.* (1) **4A**
home office Arbeitszimmer, - *n.* (2) **2A**
homemade hausgemacht *adj.* (1) **4B**
homemaker Hausfrau, -en / Hausmann, ⁒er *f./m.* (3) **3B**

homework Hausaufgabe, -n *f.* (1) **1B**
hood Motorhaube, -en *f.* (2) **4A**
horse Pferd, -e *n.* (1) **2B**
hospital Krankenhaus, ⁒er *n.* (3) **1B**
host / hostess Gastgeber, - / Gastgeberin, -nen *m./f.* (2) **1A**
host family Gastfamilie, -n *f.* (1) **4B**
hot heiß *adj.* (2) **3A**
hotel Hotel, -s *n.* (2) **3B**
  five-star hotel Fünf-Sterne-Hotel *n.* (2) **3B**
hour Stunde,-n *f.* (1) **2A**
house Haus, ⁒er *n.* (2) **2A**
housework Hausarbeit *f.* (2) **2B**
  to do housework Hausarbeit machen *v.* (2) **2B**
how wie *interr.* (1) **2A**
  How are you? (form.) Wie geht es Ihnen? (1) **1A**
  How are you? (inf.) Wie geht's (dir)? (1) **1A**
  how many wie viele *interr.* (1) **1B**
  how much wie viel *interr.* (1) **1B**
human resources manager Personalchef, -s / die Personalchefin, -nen *m./f.* (3) **3A**
humble bescheiden *adj.*
hurry sich beeilen *v.* (3) **1A**
hurt weh tun *v.* (3) **1B**
  to hurt oneself sich verletzen *v.* (3) **1B**
husband Ehemann, ⁒er *m.* (1) **3A**
hybrid car Hybridauto, -s *n.* (3) **4B**

I

I ich *pron.* (1) **1A**
ice cream Eis *n.* (2) **1A**
ice cream shop Eisdiele, -n *f.* (1) **4A**
ice cube Eiswürfel, - *m.* (2) **1A**
ice hockey Eishockey *n.* (1) **2B**
ID card Personalausweis, -e *m.* (2) **3B**
idea Idee, -n *f.* (1) **1A**
if wenn *conj.*; ob *conj.* (3) **2A**
  as if als ob (3) **2A**
  if I were you an deiner/Ihrer Stelle *f.* (3) **2A**
  if... only wenn... nur (3) **2A**
  if... then wenn... dann (3) **2A**
imagine sich (etwas) vorstellen *v.* (3) **1A**
imitate nachmachen *v.* (2) **4B**
important wichtig *adj.* (2) **3B**; bedeutend *adj.* (3) **4A**
improve verbessern *v.* (3) **4B**
in in *prep.* (2) **1B**
  in the afternoon nachmittags *adv.* (1) **2A**
  in the evening abends *adv.* (1) **2A**
  in the morning morgens *adv.* (1) **2A**
  in spite of trotz *prep.* (2) **4B**
India Indien *n.* (3) **2B**
Indian indisch *adj.* (3) **2B**; **(person)** Inder, - / Inderin, -nen *m./f.* (3) **2B**
ingredient Zutat, -en *f.* (1) **4A**
injury Verletzung, -en *f.* (3) **1B**
inside (of) innerhalb *prep.* (2) **4B**
instead sondern *conj.* (2) **2A**
  instead of statt *prep.*; anstatt *prep.* (2) **4B**
intellectual intellektuell *adj.* (1) **3B**
intelligent intelligent *adj.* (1) **3B**
interested: to be interested (in) sich interessieren (für) *v.* (3) **1A**
interesting interessant *adj.* (1) **2A**

internet café Internetcafé, -s *n.* (3) **2A**
internship Praktikum (*pl.* die Praktika) *n.* (3) **3A**
intersection Kreuzung, -en *f.* (3) **2B**
introduce: to introduce (oneself) (sich) vorstellen *v.* (3) **1A**
invent erfinden *v.* (2) **3A**
invite einladen *v.* (2) **1A**
iron Bügeleisen, - *n.* (2) **2B**; bügeln *v.* (2) **2B**
ironing board Bügelbrett, -er *n.* (2) **2B**
island Insel, -n *f.* (3) **4A**
it es *pron.* (1) **1A**
Italian (person) Italiener, - / Italienerin, -nen *m./f.* (3) **2B**; **(language)** Italienisch *n.* (3) **2B**
Italy Italien *n.* (3) **2B**
its sein *poss. adj.* (1) **3A**

J

jacket Jacke, -n *f.* (2) **1B**
jam Marmelade, -n *f.* (1) **4A**
January Januar *m.* (1) **2A**
Japan Japan *n.* (3) **2B**
Japanese (person) Japaner, - / Japanerin, -nen *m./f.* (3) **2B**; **(language)** Japanisch *n.* (3) **2B**
jealous eifersüchtig *adj.* (1) **3B**
jeans Jeans, - *f.* (2) **1B**
jewelry store Juweliergeschäft, -e *n.* (3) **2A**
job Beruf, -e *m.* (3) **3B**; Stelle, -n *f.* (3) **3A**
  to find a job Arbeit finden *v.* (3) **3A**
job interview Vorstellungsgespräch, -e *n.* (3) **3A**
job opening Stellenangebot, -e *n.* (3) **3A**
jog joggen *v.* (1) **2B**
journalist Journalist, -en / Journalistin, -nen *m./f.* (1) **3B**
judge Richter, - / Richterin, -nen *m./f.* (3) **3B**
juice Saft, ⁒e *m.* (1) **4B**
July Juli *m.* (1) **2A**
June Juni *m.* (1) **2A**
just as genauso wie (2) **4A**

K

key Schlüssel, - *m.* (2) **3B**
keyboard Tastatur, -en *f.* (2) **4B**
kind nett *adj.*
kiosk Kiosk, -e *m.* (3) **2A**
kiss Kuss, ⁒e *m.* (2) **1A**; küssen *v.* (2) **1A**
  to kiss (each other) sich küssen *v.* (3) **1A**
kitchen Küche, -n *f.* (2) **2A**
knee Knie, - *n.* (3) **1A**
knife Messer, - *n.* (1) **4B**
know kennen *v.* (2) **1B**; wissen *v.* (2) **1B**
  to know each other sich kennen *v.* (3) **1A**
know-it-all Besserwisser, - / Besserwisserin -nen *m./f.* (1) **2A**
Korea Korea *n.* (3) **2B**
Korean (person) Koreaner, - / Koreanerin, -nen *m./f.* (3) **2B**; **(language)** Koreanisch *n.* (3) **2B**

L

labor union Gewerkschaft, -en *f.* (3) **3B**
lake See, -n *m.* (3) **4A**
lamp Lampe, -n *f.* (2) **2A**

land landen *v.* (2) **3B**; Land, ¨er *n.* (2) **3B**
landscape Landschaft, -en *f.* (3) **4A**
laptop (computer) Laptop, -s *m./n.* (2) **4B**
last letzter/letzte/letztes *adj.* (1) **2B**
last name Nachname, -n *m.* (1) **3A**
late spät *adj.* (1) **2A**
  to be late sich verspäten *v.* (3) **1A**
laugh lachen *v.* (1) **2A**
laundromat Waschsalon, -s *m.* (3) **4A**
laundry Wäsche *f.* (2) **2B**
  to do laundry Wäsche waschen *v.* (2) **2B**
law Gesetz, -e *n.* (3) **4B**
lawyer Rechtsanwalt, ¨e / Rechtsanwältin,
  -nen *m./f.* (1) **3B**
lay legen *v.* (2) **1B**
lazy faul *adj.* (1) **3B**
leaf Blatt, ¨er *n.* (3) **4A**
learn lernen *v.* (1) **2A**
leather Leder, - *n.* (2) **1B**
leave abfahren *v.* (2) **4A**
lecture Vorlesung, -en *f.* (1) **2A**; Vortrag, ¨e *m.*
  (2) **2B**
lecture hall Hörsaal (*pl.* Hörsäle) *m.* (1) **2A**
leg Bein, -e *n.* (3) **1A**
leisure Freizeit *f.* (1) **2B**
lesson Stunde, -n *f.* (1) **1B**
let lassen *v.* (1) **2B**
letter Brief, -e *m.* (3) **2A**
  to mail a letter einen Brief abschicken *v.* (3) **2A**
  letter of recommendation
    Empfehlungsschreiben, - *n.* (3) **3A**
lettuce Salat, -e *m.* (1) **4A**
library Bibliothek, -en *f.* (1) **1B**
license plate Nummernschild, -er *n.* (2) **4A**
lie liegen *v.* (2) **1B**
  to lie down sich (hin)legen *v.* (3) **1A**
  to tell a lie lügen *v.*
light hell *adj.* (1) **3A**; leicht *adj.* (1) **4B**; Licht,
  -er *n.* (3) **4B**
lightning Blitz, -e *m.* (2) **3A**
like mögen *v.* **4B**; gern (+*verb*) *v.* (1) **2B**;
  gefallen *v.* (2) **1A**
  I would like... ich hätte gern... (1) **4A**; Ich
    möchte... (1) **4B**
line Schlange, -n *f.* (2) (1) **3B**; Linie, -n *f.*
  to stand in line Schlange stehen *v.* (2) **3B**
lip Lippe, -n *f.* (3) **1A**
lipstick Lippenstift, -e *m.* (3) **1A**
listen (to) hören *v.* (1) **2A**
literature Literatur, -en *f.* (1) **2A**
little klein *adj.* (1) **3A**; wenig *adj.* (3) **2A**
live wohnen *v.* (1) **2A**; leben *v.* (1) **2A**
living room Wohnzimmer, - *n.* (2) **2A**
load laden *v.* (2) **4B**
location Lage, -n *f.* (2) **3B**
long lang *adj.* (1) **3A**
  long-sleeved langärmlig *adj.* (2) **1B**
look schauen *v.* (2) **3A**
  to look at anschauen *v.* (2) **3A**
  to look for suchen *v.* (1) **2A**
  to look forward to sich freuen auf *v.* (3) **1A**
loose weit *adj.* (2) **1B**
lose verlieren *v.* (1) **2B**
  to get lost sich verlaufen *v.* (3) **2B**

love lieben *v.* (1) **2A**; Liebe *f.* (2) **1A**
  to fall in love (with) sich verlieben (in) *v.* (3) **1A**
  to love each other sich lieben *v.* (3) **1A**
loving liebevoll *adj.* (1) **3B**
low niedrig *adj.* (3) **3A**
luggage Gepäck *n.* (2) **3B**
lunch Mittagessen, - *n.* (1) **4B**

M

magazine Zeitschrift, -en *f.* (3) **2A**
mail Post *f.* (3) **2A**
  to mail a letter einen Brief abschicken *v.* (3) **2A**
mail carrier Briefträger, - / Briefträgerin,
  -nen *m.* (3) **2A**
mailbox Briefkasten, ¨ *m.* (3) **2A**
main course Hauptspeise, -n *f.* (1) **4B**
main road Hauptstraße, -n *f.* (3) **2B**
major: to major in studieren *v.* (1) **2A**
make machen *v.* (1) **2A**
makeup: to put on makeup sich schminken *v.* (3) **1A**
mall Einkaufszentrum (*pl.* Einkaufszentren) *n.* (3) **2B**
man Mann, ¨er *m.* (1) **1A**
manage leiten *v.* (3) **4B**
manager Geschäftsführer, - / die
  Geschäftsführerin, -nen *m./f.* (3) **3A**
map Karte, -n *f.* (1) **1B**; Landkarte, -n *f.* (2) **3B**
  city map Stadtplan, ¨e *m.* (2) **3B**
  to read a map eine Karte lesen *v.* (2) **3B**
marble Marmor *m.* (2) **2B**
March März *m.* (1) **2A**
marital status Familienstand, ¨e *m.* (1) **3A**
market Markt, ¨e *m.* (1) **4A**
marriage Ehe, -n *f.* (2) **1A**
married verheiratet *adj.* (1) **3A**
marry heiraten *v.* (1) **3A**
match Spiel, -e *n.* (1) **2B**; passen *v.* (2) **1A**
material Material, -ien *n.* (2) **1B**
mathematics Mathematik *f.* (1) **2A**
May Mai *m.* (1) **2A**
may dürfen *v.* (1) **3B**
maybe vielleicht *adv.* (1) **4A**
mayor Bürgermeister, - / Bürgermeisterin,
  -nen *m./f.* (3) **2B**
meal Mahlzeit, -en *f.* (1) **4B**
mean bedeuten *v.* (1) **2A**; meinen *v.*
  (3) **4B**; gemein *adj.* (1) **3B**
meat Fleisch *n.* (1) **4A**
mechanic Mechaniker, - / Mechanikerin,
  -nen *m./f.* (2) **4A**
medicine Medizin *f.* (1) **2A**; Medikament, -e *n.* (3) **1B**
meet (sich) treffen *v.* (1) **2B**; **(for the first time)**
  (sich) kennen lernen *v.* (3) **1A**
  Pleased to meet you. Schön dich/Sie kennen zu
    lernen! (1) **1A**
meeting Besprechung, -en *f.* (3) **3A**
melon Melone, -n *f.* (1) **4A**
menu Speisekarte, -n *f.* (1) **4B**
Merry Christmas! Frohe Weihnachten! (2) **1A**
message Nachricht, -en *f.* (3) **3A**
Mexico Mexiko *n.* (3) **2B**
Mexican mexikanisch *adj.* (3) **2B**; **(person)**
  Mexikaner, - / Mexikanerin, -nen *m./f.* (3) **2B**
microphone Mikrofon, -e *n.* (2) **4B**

microwave Mikrowelle, -n *f.* (2) **2B**
midmorning Vormittag, -e *m.* (1) **2B**
midnight Mitternacht *f.* (1) **2A**
mild leicht *adj.* (3) **1B**
milk Milch *f.* (1) **4B**
minority Minderheit, -en *f.* (3) **4B**
minus minus (1) **1B**
mirror Spiegel, - *m.* (2) **2A**
mist Nebel, - *m.* (2) **3A**
modern modern *adj.* (3) **2A**
modest bescheiden *adj.* (1) **3B**
mom Mama, -s *f.* (1) **3A**
Monday Montag, -e *m.* (1) **2A**
  on Mondays montags *adv.* (1) **2A**
money Geld, -er *n.* (3) **2A**
month Monat, -e *m.* (1) **2A**
moon Mond, -e *m.* (3) **4A**
mop wischen *v.* (2) **2B**
more mehr *adj.* (2) **4A**
morning Morgen, - *m.* (1) **2B**
  in the morning vormittags (1) **2A**
  tomorrow morning morgen früh (1) **2B**
mother Mutter, ¨ *f.* (1) **1A**
mother-in-law Schwiegermutter, ¨ *f.* (1) **3A**
mountain Berg, -e *m.* (1) **2B**; (3) **4A**
mouse Maus, ¨e *f.* (2) **4B**
mouth Mund, ¨er *m.* (3) **1A**
move umziehen *v.* (2) **2A**; sich bewegen *v.*
movie Film, -e *m.*
movie theater Kino, -s *n.* (3) **2A**
mp3 player MP3-Player, - *m.* (2) **4B**
Mr. Herr (1) **1A**
Mrs. Frau (1) **1A**
Ms. Frau (1) **1A**
much viel *adv.* (1) **4A**
mushroom Pilz, -e *m.* (1) **4A**
musician Musiker, - / Musikerin, -nen *m./f.* (1) **3B**
must müssen *v.* (1) **3B**
my mein *poss. adj.* (1) **3A**
myself mich *pron.*; mir *pron.* (3) **1A**

N

naïve naiv *adj.* (1) **3B**
name Name, -n *m.* (1) **1A**
  to be named heißen *v.* (1) **2A**
  What's your name? Wie heißen Sie? (form.) /
    Wie heißt du? (inf.) *v.* (1) **1A**
napkin Serviette, -n *f.* (1) **4B**
natural disaster Naturkatastrophe, -n *f.* (3) **4A**
nature Natur, -en *f.* (3) **4A**
nauseous übel *adj.* (3) **1B**
near bei *prep.* (1) **4B**; nah *adj.* (3) **2B**
neat ordentlich *adj.* (2) **2B**
neck Hals, ¨e *m.* (3) **1A**
necklace Halskette, -n *f.* (2) **1B**
need brauchen *v.* (1) **2A**
  to need to müssen *v.* (1) **3B**
neighborhood Viertel, - *n.* (3) **2B**
nephew Neffe, -n *m.* (2) **4B**
nervous nervös *adj.* (1) **3B**
never nie *adv.* **4A**; niemals *adv.* (2) **3 B**
New Year's Eve Silvester *n.* (2) **1A**

newlywed Frischvermählte, -n *m./f.* (2) **1A**
newspaper Zeitung, -en *f.* (2) **3B**
next nächster/nächste/nächstes *adj.* (1) **2B**
   next to neben *prep.* (2) **1B**
nice nett *adj.* (1) **3B**
   It's nice out. Es ist schön draußen. (2) **3A**
   Nice to meet you. Schön dich/Sie kennen zu lernen! (1) **1A**
   The weather is nice. Das Wetter ist gut. (2) **3A**
night Nacht, ⸚e *f.* (1) **2B**
   to spend the night übernachten *f.* (2) **3B**
night table Nachttisch, -e *m.* (2) **2A**
nine neun (1) **2A**
no nein (1) **1A**; kein *adj.* (1) **2B**
no one niemand *pron.* (2) **3B**
nonviolent gewaltfrei *adj.* (3) **4B**
noon Mittag, -e *m.* (1) **2A**
nose Nase, -n *f.* (3) **1A**
not nicht *adv.* (1) **2B**
   Do not enter. Keine Zufahrt. (1) **3B**
   not bad nicht schlecht (1) **1A**
   not much wenig *adj.* (3) **2A**
note Notiz, -en *f.* (1) **1B**
notebook Heft, -e *n.* (1) **1B**
nothing nichts *pron.* (2) **3B**
November November *m.* (1) **2A**
now jetzt *adv.* (1) **4A**
nuclear energy Kernenergie *f.* (3) **4B**
nuclear power plant Kernkraftwerk, -e *n.* (3) **4B**
nurse Krankenpfleger, - / Krankenschwester, -n *m./f.* (3) **1B**

O

ocean Meer, -e *n.* (3) **4A**
occasion Anlass, ⸚e *m.* (2) **1A**
   special occasions besondere Anlässe *m. pl.* (2) **1A**
October Oktober *m.* (1) **2A**
offer Angebot, -e *n.* (2) **1B**; bieten *v.* (3) **1B**; anbieten *v.* (3) **4B**
office Büro, -s *n.* (3) **3B**
office supplies Büromaterial, -ien *n.* (3) **3A**
often oft *adv.* (1) **4A**
oil Öl, -e *n.* (1) **4A**
old alt *adj.* (1) **3A**
   How old are you? Wie alt bist du? (1) **1B**
   I am... years old. Ich bin... Jahre alt. (1) **1B**
olive oil Olivenöl, -e *n.* (1) **4A**
on an *prep.*; auf *prep.* (2) **1B**
once einmal *adv.* (2) **3B**
one eins (1) **2A**; man *pron.* (2) **3B**
   by oneself allein *adv.* (1) **4A**
one-way street Einbahnstraße, -n *f.* (2) **4A**
onion Zwiebel, -n *f.* (1) **4A**
online: to be online online sein *v.* (2) **4B**
only nur *adv.* (1) **4A**
   only child Einzelkind, -er *n.* (1) **3A**
on-time pünktlich *adj.* (2) **3B**
onto auf *prep.* (2) **1B**
open öffnen *v.* (1) **2A**; aufmachen *v.* (2) **4B**; geöffnet *adj.* (3) **2A**
or oder *conj.* (1) **1B**
orange Orange, -n *f.* (1) **4A**; orange *adj.* (2) **1B**

order bestellen *v.* (1) **4A**
organic biologisch *adj.* (3) **4B**
our unser *poss. adj.* (1) **3A**
out draußen *adv.* (2) **3A**; heraus *adv.* (2) **2A**
   It's nice out. Es ist schön draußen. (2) **3A**
   to go out ausgehen *v.* (1) **4A**
   to bring out rausbringen (2) **2B**
outside draußen *prep.* (2) **3A**
   outside of außerhalb *prep.* (2) **4B**
oven Ofen, ⸚ *m.* (2) **2B**
over über *prep.* (2) **1B**; vorbei *adv.* (2) **3A**
   over there drüben *adv.* (1) **4A**
overpopulation Überbevölkerung *f.* (3) **4B**
owner Besitzer, - / Besitzerin, -nen *m./f.* (1) **3B**

P

pack packen *v.* (2) **3B**
package Paket, -e *n.* (3) **2A**
pain Schmerz, -en *m.* (3) **1B**
pajamas Schlafanzug, ⸚e *m.* (3) **1A**
pan Pfanne, -n *f.* (2) **2B**
pants Hose, -n *f.* (2) **1B**
paper Papier, -e *n.* (1) **1B**
   sheet of paper Blatt Papier (*pl.* Blätter) Papier *n.* (1) **1B**
paperclip Büroklammer, -n *f.* (3) **3A**
paper-goods store Schreibwarengeschäft, -e *n.* (3) **2A**
paragraph Absatz, ⸚e *m.* (2) **1B**
parents Eltern *pl.* (1) **3A**
park Park, -s *m.* (1) **1A**; parken *v.* (2) **4A**
   No parking. Parkverbot. (1) **3B**
participate mitmachen *v.* (2) **4B**
part-time halbtags *adj.* (3) **3B**
party Party, -s *f.* (2) **1A**
   to go to a party auf eine Party gehen *prep.* (3) **2B**
   to throw a party eine Party geben *v.* (2) **1A**
pass (a test) bestehen *v.* (1) **1B**
passenger Passagier, -e *m.* (2) **3B**
passport control Passkontrolle, -n *f.* (2) **3B**
password Passwort, ⸚er *n.* (2) **4B**
past Vergangenheit, -en *f.* (3) **4A**; nach *prep.* (1) **2A**
pasta Pasta *f.* (1) **4A**
pastries Gebäck *n.* (2) **1A**
pastry shop Konditorei, -en *f.* (1) **4A**
path Weg, -e *m.* (3) **4A**
patient geduldig *adj.* (1) **3B**; Patient, -en / Patientin, -nen *m./f.* (3) **1B**
pay (for) bezahlen *v.* (1) **4A**
   to pay by (credit) card mit der Karte bezahlen *v.* (3) **2A**
   to pay in cash bar bezahlen *v.* (3) **2A**
peach Pfirsich, -e *m.* (1) **4A**
pear Birne, -n *f.* (1) **4A**
pedestrian Fußgänger, - / Fußgängerin, -nen *m./f.* (3) **2B**
pen Kuli, -s *m.* (1) **1B**
pencil Bleistift, -e *m.* (1) **1B**
people Leute *pl.* (1) **3B**; Menschen *pl.*
pepper Paprika, - *f.* (1) **4A**; Pfeffer, - *m.* (1) **4B**
percent Prozent, -e *n.* (1) **1B**
period Punkt, -e *m.* (1) **1B**
person Person, -en *f.* (1) **1A**; Mensch, -en *m.*

personal persönlich *adj.* (1) **3B**
pet Haustier, -e *n.* (1) **3A**
pharmacy Apotheke, -n *f.* (3) **1B**
phone booth Telefonzelle, -n *f.* (3) **2B**
photo Foto, -s *n.* (1) **1B**
physics Physik *f.* (1) **2A**
picnic Picknick, -s *n.* (3) **4A**
   to have a picnic ein Picknick machen *v.* (3) **4A**
picture Foto, -s *n.* (1) **1B**; Bild, -er *n.* (2) **2A**
pie Kuchen, - *m.* (1) **4A**
pigsty Saustall, ⸚e *n.* (2) **2B**
   It's a pigsty! Es ist ein Saustall! (2) **2B**
pill Tablette, -n *f.* (3) **1B**
pillow Kissen, - *n.* (2) **1B**
pineapple Ananas, - *f.* (1) **4A**
pink rosa *adj.* (2) **1B**
place Ort, -e *m.* (1) **1B**; Lage, -n *f.* (2) **3B**; setzen *v.* (2) **2B**
   in your place an deiner/Ihrer Stelle *f.* (3) **2A**
plant Pflanze, -n *f.* (2) **2A**
plastic Kunststoff, -e *m.* (2) **2B**
plate Teller, - *m.* (1) **4B**
platform Bahnsteig, -e (2) **4A**
play spielen *v.* (1) **2A**
player Spieler, - / Spielerin, -nen *m./f.* (1) **2B**
pleasant angenehm *adj.* (1) **3B**
please bitte **1A**; gefallen *v.* (2) **1A**
   Pleased to meet you. Freut mich! (1) **1A**
plumber Klempner, - / Klempnerin, -nen *m./f.* (3) **3B**
plus plus (1) **1B**
police officer Polizist, -en / Polizistin, -nen *m./f.* (2) **4A**
police station Polizeiwache, -n *f.* (3) **2A**
politician Politiker, - / Politikerin, -nen *m./f.* (3) **3B**
pollute verschmutzen *v.* (3) **4B**
pollution Verschmutzung *f.* (3) **4B**
poor arm *adj.* (1) **3B**
pork Schweinefleisch *n.* (1) **4A**
position Stelle, -n *f.* (3) **3A**
post office Post, - *f.* (3) **2A**
   to go to the post office zur Post gehen *v.* (3) **2A**
postcard Postkarte, -n *f.* (3) **2A**
poster Poster, - *n.* (2) **2A**
pot Topf, ⸚e *m.* (2) **2B**
potato Kartoffel, -n *f.* (1) **4A**
pound Pfund, -e *n.* (1) **4A**
   a pound of potatoes ein Pfund Kartoffeln (1) **4A**
practice (sports) trainieren *v.* (1) **2B**; Übung, -en *f.*
pregnant schwanger *adj.* (3) **1B**
preparation Vorbereitung, -en *f.*
prepare vorbereiten *v.* (1) **4A**; zubereiten *v.* (2) **3A**
   to prepare oneself (for) sich vorbereiten (auf) *v.* (3) **1B**
prescription Rezept, -e *n.* (3) **1B**
presentation Referat, -e *n.* (1) **2A**
preserve erhalten *v.* (3) **4B**
president Präsident, - / Präsidentin, -nen *m./f.* (2) **4B**
   federal president Bundespräsident, - / Bundespräsidentin, -nen *m./f.* (2) **4B**
pretty hübsch *adj.* (1) **3A**
   pretty well ziemlich gut *adv.* (1) **1A**
principal Schulleiter, - *m.* / Schulleiterin, -nen *f.* (1) **1B**

print drucken *v.* (2) **4B**
printer Drucker, - *m.* (2) **4B**
probably wohl ; wahrscheinlich *adv.*(3) **2A**; sicher *adv.* (3) **2A**
problem Problem, -e *n.* (1) **1A**
profession Beruf, -e *m.* (1) **3B**
professional training Berufsausbildung, -en *f.* (3) **3A**
professor Professor, -en / Professorin, -nen *m./f.* (1) **1B**
program Programm, -e *n.* (2) **4B**
promotion Beförderung, -en *f.* (3) **3B**
pronunciation Aussprache *f.*
propose vorschlagen *v.* (3) **4B**
protect schützen *v.* (3) **4B**
proud stolz *adj.* (1) **3B**
psychologist Psychologe, -n / Psychologin, -nen *m./f.* (3) **3B**
psychology Psychologie *f.* (1) **2A**
public öffentlich *adj.* (2) **4A**
  public transportation öffentliche Verkehrsmittel *n. pl.* (2) **4A**
pull ziehen *v.* (1) **3B**
purple lila *adj.* (2) **1B**
purse Handtasche, -n *f.* (2) **1B**
push drücken *v.* (1) **3B**
put stellen *v.* (2) **1B**; legen *v.* (3) **1A**; setzen *v.* (3) **1A**
  to put away wegräumen *v.* (2) **2B**
  to put on anziehen *v.* (2) **1B**

Q

quarter Viertel, - *n.* (1) **2A**
  quarter past/to Viertel nach/vor (1) **2A**
question Frage, -n *f.* (1) **1B**
quicksand Treibsand *m.* (3) **4A**
quite ziemlich *adv.* (1) **4A**

R

rabbit Kaninchen, - *n.* (3) **4A**
rain Regen *m.* (2) **3A**; regnen *v.* (1) **2A**
raincoat Regenmantel, ¨ *m.* (2) **3A**
raise Gehaltserhöhung, -en *f.* (3) **3B**
rarely selten *adv.* (1) **4A**
rather lieber *adj.* (2) **4A**
rating Bewertung, -en *f.* (2) **3B**
razor Rasierer, - *m.* (3) **4A**
read lesen *v.* (1) **2B**
ready fertig *adj.* (3) **3B**
real estate agent Immobilienmakler, - / Immobilienmaklerin, -nen *m./f.* (3) **3B**
realistic realistisch *adj.* (3) **2A**
really wirklich *adv.* (1) **4A**
receive bekommen *v.* (2) **1A**
receiver Hörer, - *m.* (3) **3A**
recess Pause, -n *f.* (1) **1B**
recipe Rezept, -e *n.* (1) **4A**
recognize erkennen *v.* (2) **3A**
recommend empfehlen *v.* (1) **2B**
record aufnehmen *v.* (2) **4B**
recycle recyceln *v.* (3) **4B**
red rot *adj.* (1) **3A**
  red-haired rothaarig *adj.* (1) **3A**
reference Referenz, -en *f.* (3) **3A**

refrigerator Kühlschrank, ¨e *m.* (2) **2B**
related verwandt *adj.* (3) **2A**
relative Verwandte, -n *m.* (1) **3A**
relax sich entspannen *v.* (3) **1A**
reliable zuverlässig *adj.* (1) **3B**
remember sich erinnern (an) *v.* (3) **1A**
remote control Fernbedienung, -en *f.* (2) **4B**
remove entfernen *v.* (2) **2B**
renewable energy erneuerbare Energie, -en *f.* (3) **4B**
rent Miete, -n *f.* (2) **2A**; mieten *v.* (2) **2A**
repair reparieren *v.* (2) **4A**
repeat wiederholen *v.* (1) **2A**
repetition Wiederholung, -en *f.*
report berichten *v.* (3) **4B**
report card Zeugnis, -se *n.* (1) **1B**
reservation: to make a (hotel) reservation buchen *v.* (2) **3B**
resign kündigen *v.* (3) **3B**
rest sich ausruhen *v.* (3) **1A**
restaurant Restaurant, -s *n.* (1) **4B**
result Ergebnis, -se *n.* (1) **1B**
résumé Lebenslauf, ¨e *m.* (3) **3A**
retire in Rente gehen *v.* (2) **1A**
retiree Rentner, - / Rentnerin, -nen *m./f.* (3) **3B**
review Besprechung, -en *f.* (2) **4B**
rice Reis *m.* (1) **4A**
rich reich *adj.* (1) **3B**
ride fahren *v.* (1) **2B**; reiten *v.* (1) **2B**
  to give (someone) a ride (jemanden) mitnehmen *v.* (3) **2B**
  to ride a bicycle Fahrrad fahren *v.* (1) **2B**
ring klingeln *v.* (2) **4B**
rinse spülen *v.* (2) **2B**
rise (sun) aufgehen *v.* (3) **4A**
river Fluss, ¨e *m.* (1) **3B**
rock Stein, -e *m.* (3) **4A**
roll Brötchen, - *n.* (1) **4A**
room Zimmer, - *n.* (2) **1A**
room service Zimmerservice *m.* (2) **3B**
roommate Mitbewohner, - / Mitbewohnerin, -nen *m./f.* (1) **2A**
rug Teppich, -e *m.* (2) **2A**
run laufen *v.* (1) **2B**; rennen *v.* (2) **1A**
Russia Russland *n.* (3) **2B**
Russian (person) Russe, -n / Russin, -nen *m./f.* (3) **2B**; **(language)** Russisch *n.* (3) **2B**

S

sad traurig *adj.* (1) **3B**
salad Salat, -e *m.* (1) **4A**
salary Gehalt, ¨er *n.* (3) **3A**
  high/low salary hohes/niedriges Gehalt, ¨er *n.* (3) **3A**
sale Verkauf, ¨e *m.*
  on sale im Angebot (2) **1B**
salesperson Verkäufer, - / Verkäuferin, -nen *m./f.* (2) **1B**
salt Salz, -e *n.* (1) **4B**
salty salzig *adj.* (1) **4B**
same gleich *adj.*
Saturday Samstag, -e *m.* (1) **2A**
  on Saturdays samstags *adv.* (1) **2A**
sausage Würstchen, - *n.* (1) **4A**

save speichern *v.* (2) **4B**; retten *v.* (3) **4B**
  to save the planet den Planeten retten *v.* (3) **4B**
say sagen *v.* (1) **2A**
scarf Schal, -s *m.* (2) **1B**
schedule Stundenplan, ¨e *m.* (2) **2A**; Fahrplan, ¨e *m.* (2) **4A**
scholarship Stipendium (*pl.* Stipendien) *n.* (1) **2A**
school Schule, -n *f.* (1) **1B**
science Naturwissenschaft, -en *f.* (1) **2A**
scientist Wissenschaftler, - / Wissenschaftlerin, -nen *m./f.* (3) **3B**
score Ergebnis, -se *n.* (1) **1B**
screen Bildschirm, -e *m.* (2) **4B**
screen name Benutzername, -n *m.* (2) **4B**
sea Meer, -e *n.* (3) **4A**
seafood Meeresfrüchte *f. pl.* (1) **4A**
season Jahreszeit, -en *f.* (2) **3A**
seatbelt Sicherheitsgurt, -e *m.* (2) **4A**
second zweite *adj.* (1) **2A**
  second-hand clothing Altkleider *pl.* (3) **4B**
see sehen *v.* (1) **2B**
  See you later. Bis später! (1) **1A**
  See you soon. Bis gleich! / Bis bald. (1) **1A**
  See you tomorrow. Bis morgen! (1) **1A**
selfish egoistisch *adj.* (1) **3B**
sell verkaufen *v.* (1) **4A**
seminar Seminar, -e *n.* (1) **2A**
seminar room Seminarraum (*pl.* Seminarräume) *m.* (1) **2A**
send schicken *v.* (2) **4B**; abschicken *v.* (3) **3B**
separate (sich) trennen *v.* (3) **1A**
separated getrennt *adj.* (1) **3A**
September September *m.* (1) **2A**
serious ernst *adj.* (3) **3B**; schwer *adj.* (3) **1B**
set setzen *v.* (3) **1A**; **(sun)** untergehen *v.* (3) **4A**
  to set the table den Tisch decken *v.* (3) **4B**
seven sieben (1) **2A**
shampoo Shampoo, -s *n.* (3) **1A**
shape Form, -en *f.* (3) **1B**
  in good shape fit *adj.* (1) **2B**
  to be in/out of shape in guter/schlechter Form sein *v.* (3) **1B**
shave sich rasieren *v.* (3) **1A**
shaving cream Rasierschaum, ¨e *m.* (3) **1A**
she sie *pron.* (1) **1A**
sheep Schaf, -e *n.* (3) **4A**
sheet Laken, - *n.* (2) **2B**
  sheet of paper Blatt Papier (*pl.* Blätter) Papier *n.* (1) **1B**
ship Schiff, -e *n.* (2) **4A**
shirt Hemd, -en *n.* (2) **1B**
shoe Schuh, -e *m.* (2) **1B**
shop einkaufen *v.* (1) **4A**; Geschäft, -e *n.* (1) **4A**
  to go shopping einkaufen gehen *v.* (1) **4A**
shopping Einkaufen *n.* (2) **1B**
shopping center Einkaufszentrum, -(*pl.* Einkaufszentren) *n.* (3) **2B**
short kurz *adj.* (1) **3A**; **(stature)** klein *adj.* (1) **3A**
  short film Kurzfilm, -e *m.* (3) **2A**
  short-sleeved kurzärmlig *adj.* (2) **1B**
shorts kurze Hose, -n *f.* (2) **1B**
shot Spritze, -n *f.* (3) **1B**
  to give a shot eine Spritze geben *v.* (3) **1B**
shoulder Schulter, -n *f.* (3) **1A**

show zeigen *v.* (1) **4B**
shower: to take a shower (sich) duschen *v.* (3) **1A**
shrimp Garnele, -n *f.* (1) **4A**
shy schüchtern *adj.* (1) **3B**
sibling Geschwister, - *n.* (1) **3A**
sick krank *adj.* (3) **1B**
  to get sick krank werden *v.* (3) **1B**
side dish Beilage, -n *f.* (1) **4B**
sidewalk Bürgersteig, -e *m.* (3) **2B**
sign unterschreiben *v.* (3) **2A**; Schild, -er *n.*
silk Seide, -n *f.* (2) **1B**
silverware Besteck *n.* (1) **4B**
since seit (1) **4B**
sincere aufrichtig *adj.* (1) **3B**
  Yours sincerely Gruß, ¨e (1) **3B**
sing singen *v.* (1) **2B**
single ledig *adj.* (1) **3A**
sink Spüle, -n *f.* (2) **2B**
sister Schwester, -n *f.* (1) **1A**
sister-in-law Schwägerin, -nen *f.* (1) **3A**
sit sitzen *v.* (2) **1B**
  to sit down sich (hin)setzen *v.* (3) **1A**
six sechs (1) **2A**
size Kleidergröße, -n *f.* (2) **1B**
ski Ski fahren *v.* (1) **2B**
skirt Rock, ¨e *m.* (2) **1B**
sky Himmel *m.* (3) **4A**
sleep schlafen *v.* (1) **2B**
  to go to sleep einschlafen *v.* (1) **4A**
slim schlank *adj.* (1) **3A**
slipper Hausschuh, -e *m.* (3) **1A**
slow langsam *adj.* (1) **3B**
  Please speak more slowly. Sprechen Sie bitte langsamer! (1) **3B**
  Slow down. Langsam fahren. (1) **3B**
small klein *adj.* (1) **3A**
smartphone Smartphone, -s *n.* (2) **4B**
smile lächeln *v.* (2) **1A**
smoke rauchen *v.*
  No smoking. Rauchen verboten. (1) **3B**
snack Snack, -s *m.* (1) **4B**
snake Schlange, -n *f.* (3) **4A**
sneakers Turnschuhe *m. pl.* (2) **1B**
sneeze niesen *v.* (3) **1B**
snow Schnee *m.* (3) **3A**; schneien *v.* (2) **3A**
so so *adv.* (1) **4A**
  so far, so good so weit, so gut (1) **1A**
  so that damit *conj.* (3) **2A**
soap Seife, -n *f.* (3) **1A**
soccer Fußball *m.* (1) **2B**
sock Socke, -n *f.* (2) **1B**
sofa Sofa, -s *n.* (2) **2A**
soil verschmutzen *v.* (2) **2B**
solar energy Sonnenenergie *f.* (3) **4B**
solid colored einfarbig *adj.* (2) **1B**
solution Lösung, -en *f.* (3) **4B**
some mancher/manche/manches *pron.* (2) **4B**
someone jemand *pron.* (2) **3B**
something etwas *pron.* (2) **3B**
  something else etwas anderes *n.* (3) **2A**
sometimes manchmal *adv.* (2) **3B**
somewhere else woanders *adv.* (1) **4A**
son Sohn, ¨e *m.* (1) **3A**

soon bald (1) **1A**
  See you soon. Bis bald.; Bis gleich. (1) **1A**
sorry: I'm sorry. Es tut mir leid. (1) **1A**
so-so (I'm so-so) Es geht. (1) **1A**
soup Suppe, -n *f.* (1) **4B**
soup spoon Esslöffel, - *m.* (1) **4B**
Spain Spanien *n.* (3) **2B**
Spanish (person) Spanier, - / Spanierin, -nen *m./f.* (3) **2B**; **(language)** Spanisch *n.* (3) **2B**
sparkling water Mineralwasser *n.* (1) **4B**
speak sprechen *v.* (1) **2B**
  to speak about sprechen über; reden über *v.* (2) **3A**
special besonderes *adj.* (3) **2A**
  nothing special nichts Besonderes *adj.* (3) **2A**
species Art, -en *f.* (3) **4B**
spelling Rechtschreibung *f.*
spend verbringen *v.* (1) **4A**
spicy scharf *adj.* (1) **4B**
split up sich trennen *v.* (3) **1A**
spoon Löffel, - *m.* (1) **4B**
sport Sport *m.* (1) **2B**; Sportart, -en *f.* (1) **2B**
sprain (one's wrist/ankle) sich (das Handgelenk / den Fuß) verstauchen *v.* (3) **1B**
spring Frühling, -e *m.* (1) **2B**
squirrel Eichhörnchen, - *n.* (3) **4A**
stadium Stadion (*pl.* Stadien) *n.* (1) **2B**
stairs Treppe, -n *f.* (2) **2A**
  to go up/down stairs die Treppe hochgehen/ heruntergehen *v.* (3) **2B**
stamp Briefmarke, -n *f.* (3) **2A**
stand stehen *v.* (2) **1B**
  to stand in line Schlange stehen *v.* (2) **3B**
stapler Hefter, - *m.* (3) **3A**
star Stern, -e *m.* (3) **4A**
start starten *v.* (2) **4B**; anfangen *v.* (1) **4A**; beginnen *v.* (2) **2A**
station wagon Kombi, -s *m.* (2) **4B**
statue Statue, -n *f.* (3) **2B**
stay bleiben *v.* (2) **1B**
steal stehlen *v.* (1) **2B**
steering wheel Lenkrad, ¨er *n.* (2) **4A**
stepbrother Halbbruder, ¨ *m.* (1) **3A**
stepdaughter Stieftochter, ¨ *f.* (1) **3A**
stepfather Stiefvater, -s¨ *m.* (1) **3A**
stepmother Stiefmutter, ¨ *f.* (1) **3A**
stepsister Halbschwester, -n *f.* (1) **3A**
stepson Stiefsohn, ¨ *m.* (1) **3A**
stereo system Stereoanlage, -n *f.* (2) **4B**
still noch *adv.* (1) **4A**; still *adj.* (1) **4B**
  still water stilles Wasser *n.* (1) **4B**
stomachache Bauchschmerzen *m. pl.* (3) **1B**
stop sign Stoppschild, -er *n.* (2) **4A**
store Geschäft, -e *n.* (1) **4A**
storm Sturm, ¨e *m.* (2) **3A**
stove Herd, -e *m.* (2) **2B**
straight glatt *adj.* (1) **3A**
  straight hair glatte Haare *n. pl.* (1) **3A**
  straight ahead geradeaus *adv.* (2) **4A**
strawberry Erdbeere, -n *f.* (1) **4A**
stream Strom, ¨e *m.* (3) **4A**
street Straße, -n *f.* (2) **4A**
  to cross the street die Straße überqueren *v.* (3) **2B**
striped gestreift *adj.* (2) **1B**

strong stark *adj.* (1) **3B**
student Schüler, - / Schülerin, -nen *m./f.* (1) **1B**; **(college/university)** Student, -en / Studentin, -nen *m./f.* (1) **1A**
studies Studium (*pl.* Studien) *n.* (1) **2A**
study lernen *v.* (1) **2A**
stuffy nose verstopfte Nase *f.* (3) **1B**
style Stil, -e *m.* (2) **1B**
subject Fach, ¨er *n.* (1) **2A**
subway U-Bahn, -en *f.* (2) **4A**
success Erfolg, -e *m.* (3) **3B**
such solcher/solche/solches *pron.* (2) **4B**
suit Anzug, ¨e *m.* (2) **1B**
suitcase Koffer, - *m.* (2) **3B**
summer Sommer, - *m.* (1) **2B**
sun Sonne, -n *f.* (3) **4A**
sunburn Sonnenbrand, ¨e *m.* (3) **1B**
Sunday Sonntag, -e *m.* (1) **2A**
  on Sundays sonntags *adv.* (1) **2A**
sunglasses Sonnenbrille, -n *f.* (2) **1B**
sunny sonnig *adj.* (2) **3A**
sunrise Sonnenaufgang, ¨e *m.* (3) **4A**
sunset Sonnenuntergang, ¨e *m.* (3) **4A**
supermarket Supermarkt, ¨e *m.* (1) **4A**
supposed: to be supposed to sollen *v.* (1) **3B**
surf surfen *v.* (2) **4B**
  to surf the Web im Internet surfen *v.* (2) **4B**
surprise überraschen *v.* (2) **1A**; Überraschung, -en *f.* (2) **1A**
sweater Pullover, - *m.* (2) **1B**
sweatshirt Sweatshirt, -s *n.* (2) **1B**
sweep fegen *v.* (2) **2B**
sweet süß *adj.* (1) **3B**
swim schwimmen *v.* (1) **2B**
swimming pool Schwimmbad, ¨er *n.* (2) **2B**
Switzerland die Schweiz *f.* (2) **3A**
Swiss schweizerisch, Schweizer *adj.* (3) **2B**; **(person)** Schweizer, - / Schweizerin, -nen *m./f.* (3) **2B**
symptom Symptom, -e *n.* (3) **1B**

T

table Tisch, -e *m.* (1) **1B**
  to set the table den Tisch decken (2) **2B**
tablecloth Tischdecke, -n *f.* (1) **4B**
tablet Tablet, -s *n.* (2) **4B**
take nehmen *v.* (1) **2B**
  to take (a class) belegen *v.* (1) **2A**
  to take out the trash den Müll rausbringen (2) **2B**
  to take a shower (sich) duschen *v.* (3) **1A**
  to take off abfliegen *v.* (2) **3B**
talk reden *v.* (2) **1A**
  to talk about erzählen von; sprechen/reden über *v.* (2) **3A**
tall groß *adj.* (1) **3A**
tank top Trägerhemd, -en *n.* (2) **1B**
taste schmecken *v.* (1) **4B**; Geschmack, ¨e *m.* (1) **4B**
taxi Taxi, -s *n.* (2) **4A**
taxi driver Taxifahrer, - / Taxifahrerin, -nen *m./f.* (3) **3B**
tea Tee, -s *m.* (1) **4B**
teacher Lehrer, - / Lehrerin, -nen *m./f.* (1) **1B**
team Mannschaft, -en *f.* (1) **2B**

teaspoon Teelöffel, - *m.* (1) **4B**
technology Technik *f.* (2) **4B**
  to use technology Technik bedienen *v.* (2) **4B**
telephone Telefon, -e *n.* (2) **4B**
  on the telephone am Telefon (3) **3A**
telephone number Telefonnummer, -n *f.* (3) **3A**
television Fernsehen *n.*
  television (set) Fernseher -*m.* (2) **4B**
tell erzählen *v.* (2) **3A**
  to tell a story about erzählen von *v.* (2) **3A**
temperature Temperatur, -en *f.*
  What's the temperature? Wie warm/kalt ist es? (2) **3A**
tennis Tennis *n.* (1) **2B**
tent Zelt, -e *n.* (2) **3B**
ten zehn (1) **2A**
terrific großartig *adj.* (1) **3A**
test Prüfung, -en *f.* (1) **1B**
text message SMS, - *f.* (2) **4B**
textbook Lehrbuch, ⸚er *n.*; Schulbuch, ⸚er *n.* (1) **1B**
thank danken *v.* (1) **2A**
  Thank you. Danke! (1) **1A**
  Thank you very much. Vielen Dank! (1) **1A**
that das **1A**; dass *conj.* (3) **2A**
the das/der/die (1) **1A**
their ihr *poss. adj.* (1) **3A**
then dann *adv.* (2) **3B**
there da (1) **1A**
  Is/Are there...? Ist/Sind hier...? (1) **1B**; Gibt es...? (1) **2B**
  There is/are... Da ist/sind... (1) **1A**; Es gibt... (1) **2B**
  there and back hin und zurück (2) **3B**
  over there drüben *adv.* (1) **4A**
therefore also; deshalb *conj.* (3) **1B**
thermometer Thermometer, - *n.* (3) **1B**
these diese *pron.* (2) **4B**
  These are... Das sind... (1) **1A**
they sie *pron.* (1) **1A**
thick dick *adj.* (1) **3A**
thin dünn *adj.* (1) **3A**
thing Sache, -n *f.* (1) **1B**; Ding, -e *n.*
think denken *v.* (2) **1A**
  to think about denken an *v.* (2) **3A**
  to think over überlegen *v.* (1) **4A**
third dritter/dritte/drittes *adj.* (1) **2A**
this das **1A**; dieser/diese/dieses *pron.* (2) **4B**
  This is... Das ist... (1) **1A**
three drei (1) **2A**
through durch *prep.* (1) **3B**
throw werfen *v.* (1) **2B**
  to throw away wegwerfen *v.* (3) **4B**
thunder Donner, - *m.* (2) **3A**
thunderstorm Gewitter, - *n.* (2) **3A**
Thursday Donnerstag, -e *m.* (1) **2A**
  on Thursdays donnerstags *adv.* (1) **2A**
ticket Flugticket, -s *n.* (2) **3B**; Fahrkarte, -n *f.* (2) **4A**
ticket collector Schaffner, - / Schaffnerin, -nen *m./f.* (2) **4A**
ticket office Fahrkartenschalter, - *m.* (2) **4A**
tidy ordentlich *adj.* (2) **2B**
tie Krawatte, -n *f.* (2) **1B**
tight eng *adj.* (2) **1B**

time Zeit, -en *f.* (1) **2A**; Mal, -e *n.* (2) **3B**
  for the first/last time zum ersten/letzten Mal (2) **3B**
  the first/last time das erste/letzte Mal (2) **3B**
  this time diesmal *adv.* (2) **3B**
  What time is it? Wie spät ist es?; Wie viel Uhr ist es? (1) **2A**
times mal (1) **1B**
tip Trinkgeld, -er *n.* (1) **4B**
tired müde *adj.* (1) **3B**
tissue Taschentuch, ⸚er *n.* (3) **1B**
to vor *prep.* (1) **2A**; nach; zu *prep.* (1) **4B**; auf, an *prep.* (2) **1B**
  (in order) to um...zu (2) **3B**
  to the right/left nach rechts/links (2) **2A**
toast anstoßen *v.* (2) **1A**
toaster Toaster, - *m.* (2) **2B**
today heute *adv.* (1) **2B**
  Today is... Heute ist der... (1) **2A**
  What day is it today? Welcher Tag ist heute? (2) **3A**
toe Zeh, -en *m.* (3) **1A**
together zusammen *adv.* (1) **3A**
toilet Toilette, -n *f.* (2) **2A**
tomato Tomate, -n *f.* (1) **4A**
tomorrow morgen *adv.* (1) **2B**
  the day after tomorrow übermorgen *adv.* (1) **2B**
  tomorrow morning morgen früh (1) **2B**
too zu *adv.* (1) **4A**; auch *adv.* (1) **1A**
tool kit Werkzeug, -e *n.*
tooth Zahn, ⸚e *m.* (3) **1A**
toothache Zahnschmerzen *m. pl.* (3) **1B**
toothbrush Zahnbürste, -n *f.* (3) **1A**
toothpaste Zahnpasta (*pl.* Zahnpasten) *f.* (3) **1A**
tornado Tornado, -s *m.* (3) **4A**
toward in Richtung *f.* (3) **2B**
towel Handtuch, ⸚er *n.* (3) **1A**
town Stadt, ⸚e *f.* (3) **2B**
town hall Rathaus, ⸚er *n.* (3) **2A**
toxic waste Giftmüll *m.* (3) **4B**
track Bahnsteig, -e *m.* (2) **4A**
track and field Leichtathletik *f.* (1) **2B**
traffic Verkehr *m.* (2) **4A**
traffic light Ampel, -n *f.* (3) **2B**
train Zug, ⸚e *m.* (2) **4A**
transportation Verkehrsmittel, - *n.* (2) **4A**
  public transportation öffentliche Verkehrsmittel *n. pl.* (4) **4A**
trash Müll *m.* (2) **2B**
  to take out the trash den Müll rausbringen (2) **2B**
travel reisen *v.* (1) **2A**
travel agency Reisebüro, -s *n.* (2) **3B**
traveler Reisende, -n *m./f.* (2) **3B**
tree Baum, ⸚e *m.* (3) **4A**
trendy angesagt *adj.* (2) **1B**
trip Reise, -n *f.* (2) **3B**
truck LKW, -s *m.* (2) **4A**
truck driver LKW-Fahrer, - / LKW-Fahrerin, -nen *m./f.* (3) **3B**
trunk Kofferraum, ⸚e *m.* (2) **4A**
try probieren *v.* (1) **3B**; versuchen *v.* (2) **3B**
  Give it a try! Probieren Sie mal!
T-shirt T-Shirt, -s *n.* (2) **1B**
Tuesday Dienstag, -e *m.* (1) **2A**
  on Tuesdays dienstags *adv.* (1) **2A**

tuition fee Studiengebühr, -en *f.* (1) **2A**
tuna Thunfisch, -e *m.* (1) **4A**
Turkey die Türkei *f.* (3) **2B**
Turkish (person) Türke, -n / Türkin, -nen *m./f.* (3) **2B**; **Turkish (language)** Türkisch *n.* (3) **2B**
turn abbiegen *v.* (3) **2B**
  to turn right/left rechts/links abbiegen *v.* (2) **4A**
  to turn off ausmachen *v.* (2) **4B**; einschalten *v.* (3) **4B**
  to turn on anmachen *v.* (2) **4B**; auschalten *v.* (3) **4B**
turning point Wende, -n *f.* (3) **4B**
twelve zwölf (1) **2A**
twenty zwanzig (1) **2A**
twin Zwilling, -e *m.* (1) **3A**
two zwei (1) **2A**

ugly hässlich *adj.* (1) **3A**
umbrella Regenschirm, -e *m.* (2) **3A**
under unter *prep.* (2) **1B**
understand verstehen *v.* (1) **2A**
underwear Unterwäsche *f.* (2) **1B**
undressed: to get undressed sich ausziehen *v.* (3) **1A**
unemployed arbeitslos *adj.* (3) **2A**
unfortunate arm *adj.* (1) **3B**
unfortunately leider *adv.* (1) **4A**
unfurnished unmöbliert *adj.* (2) **2A**
university Universität, -en *f.* (1) **1B**
unpleasant unangenehm *adj.* (1) **3B**
until bis *prep.* (1) **3B**; bis zu *prep.* (3) **2B**
up herauf *adv.* (2) **2A**
  to get up aufstehen *v.* (1) **4A**
  to go up hochgehen *v.* (3) **2B**
USA die USA *pl.*; die Vereinigten Staaten *pl.* (3) **2B**
use benutzen *v.* (2) **4A**; bedienen *v.* (2) **4B**
  to get used to sich gewöhnen an *v.* (3) **1A**
useful nützlich *adj.* (1) **2A**
useless nutzlos *adj.* (1) **2A**

vacancy Zimmer frei *f.* (2) **2A**
vacation Ferien *pl.*; Urlaub, -e *m.* (2) **3B**
  to go on vacation Urlaub machen *v.* (2) **3B**
vacuum staubsaugen *v.* (2) **2B**
vacuum cleaner Staubsauger, - *m.* (2) **2B**
validate entwerten *v.* (2) **4A**
  to validate a ticket eine Fahrkarte entwerten *v.* (2) **4A**
valley Tal, ⸚er *n.* (3) **4A**
vase Vase, -n *f.* (2) **2A**
vegetables Gemüse *n.* (1) **4A**
verb Verb, -en *n.* (3) **1A**
very sehr *adv.* (1) **3A**
  very well sehr gut (1) **1A**
veterinarian Tierarzt, ⸚e / Tierärztin, -nen *m./f.* (3) **3B**
visa Visum (*pl.* Visa) *n.* (2) **3B**
visit besuchen *v.* (1) **4A**
vocabulary Wortschatz, ⸚e *m.*
volcano Vulkan, -e *m.* (3) **4A**
volleyball Volleyball *m.* (1) **2B**

W

wait warten *v.* (1) **2A**
  to wait for warten auf *v.* (2) **3A**
waiter / waitress Kellner, - / Kellnerin,
  -nen *m./f.* (1) **3B**
  Waiter! Herr Ober! (1) **4B**
wake up aufwachen *v.* (3) **1A**
walk Spaziergang, ⁻e *m.*
  to go for a walk spazieren gehen *v.* (1) **2B**
wall Wand, ⁻e *f.* (2) **1B**
want wollen *v.* (1) **3B**
warm warm *adj.* (3) **2A**
wash waschen *v.* (1) **2B**
  to wash (oneself) sich waschen *v.* (3) **1A**
washing machine Waschmaschine, -n *f.* (2) **2B**
waste Müll *m.* (3) **4B**; Abfall, ⁻e *m.* (3) **4B**
wastebasket Papierkorb, ⁻e *m.* (1) **1B**
watch zuschauen *v.* (1) **4A**; anschauen *v.* (2) **3A**
  to watch television fernsehen *v.* (2) **4B**
water Wasser *n.*
  sparkling water Mineralwasser *n.* (1) **4B**
  still water stilles Wasser *n.* (1) **4B**
water pitcher Wasserkrug, ⁻e *m.* (1) **4B**
waterfall Wasserfall, ⁻e *m.* (3) **4A**
we wir *pron.* (1) **1A**
weak schwach *adj.* (1) **3B**
wear tragen *v.* (1) **2B**
weather Wetter *n.* (2) **3A**
  What's the weather like? Wie ist das Wetter? (2) **3A**
weather report Wetterbericht, -e *m.* (2) **3A**
Web Internet *n.* (2) **4B**
  to surf the Web im Internet surfen *v.* (2) **4B**
Web site Website, -s *f.* (2) **4B**
wedding Hochzeit, -en *f.* (2) **1A**
Wednesday Mittwoch, -e *m.* (1) **2A**
  on Wednesdays mittwochs *adv.* (1) **2A**
week Woche, -n *f.* (1) **2A**
weekend Wochenende, -n *n.* (1) **2A**
weigh wiegen *v.* (2) **4B**
welcome (herzlich) willkommen (1) **1A**
  You're welcome. Gern geschehen! (1) **1A**
well gut *adv.*
  I am (very) well. Mir geht's (sehr) gut. (1) **1A**
  I am not (so) well. Mir geht's nicht (so) gut. (1) **1A**
  Get well! Gute Besserung! (2) **1A**
well-dressed gut gekleidet *adj.* (2) **1B**
well-known bekannt *adj.* (3) **2A**
wet nass *adj.* (3) **4A**
what was *interr.* (1) **2A**
  What is that? Was ist das? (1) **1B**
  What's up? Was geht ab? (1) **1A**
when wann *interr.* (1) **2A**
whenever wenn *conj.* (3) **2A**
where wo *interr.* (1) **2A**
  where from woher *interr.* (1) **2A**
  where to wohin *interr.* (1) **2A**
whether ob *conj.* (3) **2A**
which welcher/welche/welches *interr.* (1) **2A**
white weiß *adj.* (2) **1B**
who wer *interr.* (1) **2A**
  Who is it? Wer ist das? (1) **1B**
whom wen *acc. interr.* (1) **2A**; wem *dat. interr.* (1) **4B**

whose wessen *interr.* (2) **4B**
why warum *interr.* (1) **2A**
widow Witwe, -n *f.* (1) **3A**
widower Witwer, - *m.* (1) **3A**
wife Ehefrau, -en *f.* (1) **3A**
win gewinnen *v.* (1) **2B**
wind energy Windenergie *f.* (3) **4B**
window Fenster, - *n.* (1) **1A**
windshield Windschutzscheibe, -n *f.* (2) **4A**
windshield wiper Scheibenwischer, - *m.* (2) **4A**
windy windig *adj.* (2) **3A**
wine Wein, -e *m.* (1) **4B**
winter Winter, - *m.* (1) **2B**
wipe wischen *v.* (2) **2B**
wise weise *adj.* (1) **3B**
wish wünschen *v.* (3) **1A**
  to wish (for something) sich (etwas)
  wünschen, *v.* (3) **1A**
with mit (1) **4B**
withdraw (money) (Geld) abheben *v.* (3) **2A**
within innerhalb *prep.* (2) **4B**
without ohne *prep.* (1) **3B**
woman Frau, -en *f.* (1) **1A**
wonder sich fragen *v.* (3) **1A**
wood Holz *n.* (2) **2B**
wool Wolle *f.* (2) **1B**
work Arbeit, -en *f.* (3) **4B**; arbeiten *v.* (1) **2A**;
  funktionieren *v.* (2) **4B**
  at work auf der Arbeit (3) **3B**
  to work on arbeiten an *v.* (2) **3A**
world Welt, -en *f.* (3) **4B**
worried besorgt *adj.* (1) **3B**
write schreiben *v.* (1) **2A**
  to write to schreiben an *v.* (2) **3A**
  to write to one another sich schreiben *v.* (3) **1A**

Y

year Jahr, -e *n.* (2) **3A**
yellow gelb *adj.* (2) **1B**
yes ja **1A**; **(contradicting)** doch *adv.* (1) **2B**
yesterday gestern *adv.* (2) **1B**
yet noch *adv.* (1) **4A**
yogurt Joghurt, -s *m.* (1) **4A**
you du/ihr/Sie *pron.* (1) **1A**
young jung *adj.* (3) **3A**; jugendlich *adj.* (3) **2A**
your euer/Ihr *poss. adj.* (1) **3A**
youth hostel Jugendherberge, -n *f.* (2) **3B**

Index

Understanding the Index references

The numbers following each entry can be understood as follows:

(2A) **51** = (Chapter, Lesson) **page**

So, the entry above would be found in Chapter 2, Lesson A, page 51.

About the Authors

Christine Anton, a native of Germany, is Associate Professor of German and Director of the Language Resource Center at Berry College. She received her B.A. in English and German from the Universität Erlangen and her graduate degrees in Germanic Languages and Literatures from the University of North Carolina at Chapel Hill. She has published two books on German realism and German cultural memory of National Socialism, and a number of articles on 19th and 20th century German and Austrian literature, as well as on second language acquisition. Dr. Anton has received several awards for excellence in teaching and was honored by the American Association of Teachers of German with the Duden Award for her "outstanding efforts and achievement in the teaching of German." Dr. Anton previously taught at the State University of New York and the University of North Carolina, Chapel Hill.

Tobias Barske, a native of Bavaria, is an Associate Professor of German and Applied Linguistics at the University of Wisconsin-Stevens Point. He has a Ph.D. in German Applied Linguistics from the University of Illinois at Urbana-Champaign with emphases on language and social interaction as well as language pedagogy. He has also studied at the Universität Regensburg in Germany. Tobias has over 10 years of experience teaching undergraduate and graduate courses at the university level and has earned numerous awards for excellence in teaching.

Megan McKinstry has an M.A. in Germanics from the University of Washington. She is an Assistant Teaching Professor of German Studies and Co-Coordinator for Elementary German at the University of Missouri, where she received the University's "Purple Chalk" teaching award and an award for "Best Online Course." Ms. McKinstry has been teaching for over fifteen years.

Acknowledgments

On behalf of its authors and editors, Vista Higher Learning expresses its sincere appreciation to the teachers nationwide who reviewed materials from **Mosaik**. Their input and suggestions were vitally helpful in forming and shaping the program in its final, published form. Philippe Radelet from Benjamin Franklin High School, Baton Rouge, Louisiana provided a thorough accuracy check.

We also extend a special thank you to the contributing writers of **Mosaik** whose hard work was central to the publication.

Credits

Every effort has been made to trace the copyright holders of the works published herein. If proper copyright acknowledgment has not been made, please contact the publisher and we will correct the information in future printings.

Photography and Art Credits

All images © Vista Higher Learning unless otherwise noted. All Fotoroman photos provided by Xavier Roy.

Cover: Kevin Krautgartner/500PX.

Front Matter (SE): xiii: (l) Digital Vision/Getty Images; (r) Andres Rodriguez/Big Stock Photo; **xiv:** Johannes Simon/Getty Images; **xv:** (l) Konstantin Chagin/123RF; (r) Tyler Olson/Shutterstock; **xvi:** PH3/Patrick Hoffmann/WENN/Newscom.

Front Matter (TE): T11: Jean Glueck/Media Bakery; **T29:** Monkey Business Images/Bigstock; **T30:** Simmi Simons/iStockphoto; **T31:** Getty RF.

Überblick: 1: Xavier Roy; **7:** (tl) Rolf Fischer/iStockphoto; (tr) José Blanco; (bl) Clayton Hansen/iStockphoto; (br) Vanessa Bertozzi.
Chapter 1: 19: Xavier Roy; **22:** (top row: t) Brandon Blinkenberg/Shutterstock; (top row: ml) Tatiana Popova/Shutterstock; (top row: mml) Rafa Irusta/Shutterstock; (top row: mmr) Slon1971/Shutterstock; (top row: mr) Lusoimages/Shutterstock; (top row: bl) Sgame/Shutterstock; (top row: bml) HomeStudio/Shutterstock; (top row: bmr) Ljupco Smokovski/Shutterstock; (top row: br) George Dolgikh/Shutterstock; (bottom row) Ciro de Luca/Pacific Press/Newscom; **26:** Gerald Haenel/laif/Redux; **27:** (l) Dagmar Schwelle/Laif/Redux; (tr) Vario Images GmbH & Co.KG/Alamy; (br) S Lubenow/LOOK-foto/Getty Images; **33:** Altafulla/Big Stock Photo; **35:** Pixtal/AGE Fotostock; **37:** (l) Sven Hagolani/Corbis; (r) Gorilla/Big Stock Photo; **43:** (tl) Vasily Koval/Shutterstock; (tm) Gabriel Blaj/Fotolia; (tr) Dmitriy Shironosov/Shutterstock; (bl) Diana Lundin/iStockphoto; (bm) Blaj Gabriel/Shutterstock; (br) Moodboard Premium/Fotolia; **44:** Jason Stitt/Shutterstock; **48:** Nicole Winchell; **49:** (t) The Print Collector/Alamy; (b) Bloomberg/Getty Images; **54:** Aspireimages/Inmagine; **55:** (l) Tyler Olson/Shutterstock; (r) Wavebreak Media Ltd/123RF; **57:** Wavebreakmedia/Shutterstock; **58:** (tl) NickyBlade/iStockphoto; (tr) Martín Bernetti; (bl) Ray Levesque; (br) Dmitry Kutlayev/iStockphoto; **60:** (t) Rüdiger Niemann/Fotolia; (ml) Ernst Wrba/Media Bakery; (mr) INSADCO Photography/Alamy; (b) Carola Koserowsky/AGE Fotostock; **61:** (tl) Dainis Derics/Shutterstock; (tr) Corbis; (m) Sabine Schmidt/Shutterstock; (b) H Schulz/AGE Fotostock; **62:** Istvan Csak/Shutterstock; **64:** Stuart Pearce/AGE Fotostock; **65:** ImageBroker/SuperStock.
Chapter 2: 67: Xavier Roy; **69:** (tl) Katie Wade; (tm) Oscar Artavia Solano; (tr) Martín Bernetti; (bl) Vanessa Bertozzi; (bm) Vanessa Bertozzi; (bl) Torsten Lorenz/Fotolia; **74:** Fishman/Ullstein Bild/Getty Images; **75:** (l) Peter Bialobrzeski/Laif/Redux; (tr) George Clerk/iStockphoto; (br) Nicole Winchell; **78:** Sborisov/123RF; **79:** (tl) Martín Bernetti; (tr) Nicole Winchell; (bl) Gudrun Hommel; (bml) Nicole Winchell; (bmr) Martín Bernetti; (br) Anne Loubet; **83:** (tl) Gudrun Hommel; (tr) Katrina Brown/Shutterstock; (bl) José Blanco; (bm) Anne Loubet; (br) Dmitriy Shironosov/Shutterstock; **84:** Anne Loubet; **89:** (tl) Xavier Roy; (tm) Gudrun Hommel; (tr) Nicole Winchell; (bl) Raimund Linke/Media Bakery; (bm) Nicole Winchell; (br) Gudrun Hommel; **94:** AKG-Images/Newscom; **95:** (l) ZU_09/iStockphoto; (tr) Leo Mason/Corbis; (br) Clearlens/Shutterstock; **97:** (l) AllOver Images/Alamy; (r) Eyewave/iStockphoto; **98:** (tl) Ana Cabezas Martín; (tr) Yadid Levy/AGE Fotostock; (bl) HappyAlex/Big Stock Photo; (bml) Alexander Chaikin/Shutterstock; (bmr) Ruben Varela; (br) Nicole Winchell; **101:** Nicole Winchell; **102:** (left col: tl) Image Source/Corbis; (left col: tr) David R. Frazier Photolibrary, Inc/Alamy; (left col: ml) Markus Gann/Shutterstock; (left col: mr) Swisshippo/Big Stock Photo; (left col: bl) Volrab Vaclav/Big Stock Photo; (left col: br) Gudrun Hommel; (right col) Roslen Mack/Shutterstock; **103:** (l) Grafissimo/iStockphoto; (r) Pascal Pernix; **104:** (tl) Vario Images GmbH & Co.KG/Alamy; (tr) Jonathan Larsen/Diadem Images/Alamy; (m) FotoGrafas/iStockphoto; (b) Ingo Wagner/DPA/Picture-Alliance/Newscom; **105:** (tl) Heinz-Dieter Falkenstein Image Broker/Newscom; (tr) Joe.Gockel/Fotolia; (m) Kuttig-Travel/Alamy; (b) Alfredo Dagli Orti/The Art Archive at Art Resource, NY; **106:** (t) STR/Keystone/Corbis; (b) Ullstein Bild/Getty Images; **106-107:** Christophe Dessaigne/Trevillion Images; **108:** Media Bakery; **109:** Franz Marc Frei/AGE Fotostock.
Chapter 3: 111: Xavier Roy; **113:** (tl) Ragnarock/Shutterstock; (tm) Krzyzak/Alamy; (tr) Javier Larrea/AGE Fotostock; (bl) Dmitry Lavrenyuk/Fotolia; (bm) Rangizzz/Shutterstock; (br) Ewa Walicka/Shutterstock; **114:** (t) Anne Loubet; (ml) Andersen Ross/Blend Images; (mr) Martín Bernetti; (bl) Maurizio Gambarini/EPA/Newscom; (br) Janet Dracksdorf; **118:** Thomas Lohnes/DAPD/AP Images; **119:** (l) Moritz Hoffmann/AGE Fotostock; (tr) Sueddeutsche Zeitung Photo/Alamy; (br) StockLite/Shutterstock; **122:** (tl) LdF/iStockphoto; (tr) Paula Díez; (bl) Nikkytok/Big Stock Photo; (bml) Lynn Watson/Shutterstock; (bmr) Vasessa Bertozzi; (br) Volkoffa/123RF; **123:** Javier Larrea/AGE Fotostock; **126:** (t) Monkey Business Images/Shutterstock; (b) Andresr/Shutterstock; **127:** David Turnley/Corbis; **131:** (tl) Gudrun Hommel; (tm) Ana Cabezas Martín; (tr) Martín Bernetti; (bl) Nicole Winchell; (bm) Nicole Winchell; (br) Anne Loubet; **132:** (t) RazvanPhotography/

Big Stock Photo; (b) Nicole Winchell; **136:** Bundesarchiv, Bild 146-1980-091-21/Photo: O.Ang.; **137:** (l) Jochen Tack/AGE Fotostock; (tr) AKG-Images/Newscom; (br) Bettmann/Corbis, **142:** (t) Vario Images GmbH & Co.KG/Alamy; (b) Vanessa Bertozzi; **143:** (t) Paula Díez; (b) Fabián Montoya; **144:** (t) Hansok/iStockphoto; (ml) Imagebroker.net/SuperStock; (mr) Michael Weber/Image Broker/Alamy; (b) Sebastian Kahnert/DPA/Picture-Alliance/Newscom; **145:** (tl) Tom_u/123RF; (tr) Dennis Cox/Alamy; (m) Popperfoto/Getty Images; (b) Hirotaka Ihara/123RF; **146:** Isolde Ohlbaum/Laif/Redux; **148:** Paula Díez; **149:** Lucía Cóppola/iStockphoto.

Chapter 4: 151: Xavier Roy, **153:** (top row: tl) Hannes Schleicher/iStockphoto; (top row: tr) Gudrun Hommel; (top row: ml) John DeCarli; (top row: mr) Photographie.und.mehr/Big Stock Photo; (top row: bl) John DeCarli; (top row: br) Janet Dracksdorf; (bottom row: t) Vanessa Bertozzi; (bottom row: bl) Vanessa Bertozzi; (bottom row: bm) Dr. Wilfried Bahnmüller/Media Bakery; (bottom row: br) Giovanni Benintende/Shutterstock; **154:** (top row: t) Joshua Hodge Photography/iStockphoto; (top row: m) Lauren Krolick; (top row: b) Ali Burafi; (bottom row) Potapov Alexander/Shutterstock; **158:** Tbkmedia.de/Alamy; **159:** (l) Imagebroker/Alamy; (tr) Bettmann/Corbis; (br) Porojnicu Stelian/Shutterstock; **161:** Martín Bernetti; **162:** Nyul/Big Stock Photo; **166:** (t) Janet Dracksdorf; (ml) Brand X Pictures/Alamy; (mm) Janet Dracksdorf; (mr) Ali Burafi; (bl) Petrle/Fotolia; (bm) Janet Dracksdorf; (br) Corel/Corbis; **167:** Gudrun Hommel; **171:** (tl) Gudrun Hommel; (tm) Gudrun Hommel; (tr) S-Eyerkaufer/iStockphoto; (bl) Anne Loubet; (bm) Katie Wade; (br) Epsylon Lyrae/Shutterstock; **172:** (t) Gudrun Hommel; (b) Patrick Herrera/iStockphoto; **176:** Amin Akhtar/Laif/Redux; **177:** (l) Worldwide Picture Library/Alamy; (tr) Johannes Arlt/laif/Redux; (br) Gudrun Hommel; **180:** Jan Martin Will/Shutterstock; **181:** Sofia Andreevna/Shutterstock; **184:** (t) Nancy Camley; (ml) Travel Stock/Shutterstock; (mm) Vanessa Bertozzi; (mr) Nebojsa Markovic/Fotolia; (bl) Corbis RF; (bm) Newphotoservice/Shutterstock; (br) Index Open/Photolibrary; **185:** Gudrun Hommel; **186:** (t) Andreas Bauer/iStockphoto; (mt) Rolf Weschke/iStockphoto; (mb) LOOK Die Bildagentur der Fotografen GmbH/Alamy; (b) Arno Burgi/DPA/Corbis, **187:** (tl) Martin Geene/Vario Images GmbH & Co.KG/Alamy; (tr) Picture-Alliance/DPA/Newscom; (m) Stuart Forster Europe/Alamy; (b) ColouriserAL/Lebrecht Music & Arts; **188:** (tl) DPA Picture-Alliance GmbH; (bl) Bettmann/Corbis; (tr) Cyril Laubscher/Getty Images; **189:** Dirk Freder/iStockphoto; **190:** Florian Staudinger/Action Press/ZUMA Press; **191:** EdStock/iStockphoto.

Text Credits

106: Reproduced from: "Allein" by Hermann Hesse, Sämtliche Werke in 20 Bänden. Herausgegeben von Volker Michels. Band 10: Die Gedichte. © Suhrkamp Verlag Frankfurt am Main 2002. All rights with and controlled by Suhrkamp Verlag Berlin.

107: Reproduced from: "Todesfuge" by Paul Celan, Mohn und Gedächtnis © 1952, Deutsche Verlags-Anstalt, München, in der Verlagsgruppe Randome House GmbH.

146: "Der Erfinder", from: Peter Bichsel, Kindergeschichten. © Suhrkamp Verlag Frankfurt am Main 1997. All rights with and controlled by Suhrkamp Verlag Berlin.

188: Reproduced from: "Meine Nachtigall" by Rose Ausländer. Aus: Rose Ausländer. Gesammelte Werke in sieben Bänden. Band II, Die Sichel mäht die Zeit zu Heu. Gedichte 1957-1965. ©1985 S. Fischer Verlag GmbH, Frankfurt am Main.

Film Credits

85: Courtesy of Kurzfilm Agentur Hamburg.
127: Courtesy of Kurzfilm Agentur Hamburg.
167: Courtesy of Sarah Winkenstette, Director.

Television Credits

41: Courtesy of Central Krankenversicherung AG and Philipp und Keuntje GmbH.